Martin Miernicki

Collective Management of Copyrights between Competition, Regulation, and Monopolism

AF874982

Studien zum Unternehmens- und Wirtschaftsrecht Band 35
herausgegeben von Arthur Weilinger

Collective Management of Copyrights between Competition, Regulation, and Monopolism

A Comparison of European and U.S. Approaches to Collective Management Organizations

by

Dr. Martin Miernicki

Vienna 2017

Nomos facultas

Bibliografische Information Der Deutschen Nationalbibliothek

Die Deutsche Nationalbibliothek verzeichnet diese Publikation in der
Deutschen Nationalbibliografie; detaillierte bibliografische Daten sind im Internet über
http://dnb.d-nb.de abrufbar.

Alle Angaben in diesem Fachbuch erfolgen trotz sorgfältiger Bearbeitung ohne Gewähr, eine Haftung der Herausgeber, des Autors oder des Verlages ist ausgeschlossen. / Every effort has been made to ensure the accuracy of the texts printed in this book. The editors, the author, or the publisher accept no liability in the case of eventual errors.

© 2017 Facultas Verlags- und Buchhandels AG
facultas Universitätsverlag, A-1050 Wien
Alle Rechte, insbesondere das Recht der Vervielfältigung und der Verbreitung sowie der Übersetzung, sind vorbehalten. / This work is subject to copyright. All rights are reserved, specifically those of reprinting, broadcasting and translation.
Satz und Druck: Facultas Verlags- und Buchhandels AG
Printed in Austria
Österreich: ISBN 978-3-7089-1663-7 (facultas)
Deutschland: ISBN 978-3-8487-4805-1 (Nomos)

To my parents

Vorwort des Herausgebers

Das System des Schutzes der Verwertungsrechte des Urhebers und damit auch der Aufbau der Struktur und die Aufgaben der Verwertungsgesellschaften sind in Europa und in den Vereinigten Staaten von Amerika unterschiedlich. Während in Europa der Schwerpunkt der rechtspolitischen Betrachtung des Verwertungsrechts auf der Seite des Urhebers liegt, gewichtete das US-amerikanische Recht die Interessen der potentiellen Anwender bzw Nutzer stärker. Daraus ergibt sich, dass in der Alten Welt sich die Verwertungsgesellschaften in erster Linie als legitime Interessenvertreter der Urheber verstehen, während in den USA neben diesem Aspekt von den Verwertungsgesellschaften auch die berechtigten Interessen der Allgemeinheit an der Nutzung von besonderen Rechten, eben auch von klassischen Urheberrechten, betont wird.

Die vorliegende Arbeit basiert auf der von der Universität Wien approbierten Dissertation des Autors. Vor allem kann dadurch auch die unterschiedliche Struktur der Rechtsordnungen gezeigt werden, gleichwohl in Europa auch noch neben die europarechtlichen Vorgaben die nationalstaatlichen Normen treten.

Univ.-Ass. Dr. *Martin Miernicki* zeigt im vorliegenden Werk detailliert die unterschiedlichen Regulierungsansätze in Hinblick auf Verwertungsgesellschaften nach dem Recht der Vereinigten Staaten und dem Unionsrecht, wobei der Schwerpunkt der Untersuchung auf dem Kartellrecht liegt. Außerdem sind die umfassenden Ausführungen des Autors zur Rechtslage nach der EU-„Verwertungsgesellschaftenrichtlinie" 2014/26 – wozu es bislang wenig Grundlegendes in der Literatur gibt – besonders hervorzuheben.

Insgesamt leistet dieses Werk einen wichtigen Beitrag zur aktuellen fachlichen Diskussion und ist auch für die rechtspolitische Betrachtung von großer Bedeutung.

Wien, im November 2017 *Arthur Weilinger*

Preface and Acknowledgements

Intellectual property law and antitrust law have fascinated me already since the earlier stages of my legal studies. Against this background, it is not surprising that I decided to dedicate my doctoral thesis to the collective management of copyrights, as this topic involves questions at the intersection of both fields of law. Furthermore, the adoption of Directive 2014/26/EU gave an additional reason to conduct research on the topic. However, the collective management of copyrights is also a highly topical issue in the United States which is exemplified by the review of the "Consent Decrees" between 2014 and 2016 and recent "rate court" proceedings. Furthermore, the economic and technical environment for the collective management of copyrights has undergone profound changes in recent years; this implies the need for research on the corresponding legal framework, also *de lege ferenda*. A comparative approach was chosen in order to highlight that similar problems occur in the United States and the European Union. Those problems are, however, not always addressed in the same way. Accordingly, I hope that this work – an adapted version of my doctoral thesis which was accepted by the University of Vienna in October 2017 – promotes the exchange of ideas and that both jurisdictions can benefit from each other's experiences.

I would like to thank my supervisor *ao. Univ.-Prof. Mag. Dr. Siegfried Fina* who inspired and promoted my interest in technology law and IP law as well as the international and comparative dimension of these fields of law. He invested a great amount of time in supervising this dissertation and was always available for helpful guidance and comments. *O. Univ.-Prof Dr.Dr. Arthur Weilinger*, the head of the Institute of Business Law, greatly supported me in the thesis process and helped me in completing this research in time. I would like to thank him for his useful advice, his encouragement throughout this project, and for pomoting the publication of the thesis. Also, I would like to thank *Univ.-Prof. Dr. Friedrich Rüffler* for examining the thesis, as well as *Mrs. Elisabeth Kainberger, MA*, and *Mr. Peter Wittmann*, Facultas Verlags- und Buchhandels AG, for their help in the publication process.

Furthermore, I would like to thank my colleagues at the Institute of Business Law, *Mag. Luca Fuhrmann, Mag. Viktoria Ivanisevic, Mag. Bernhard Mazal, Mag. Viola Pondorfer, Mag. Georg Tuder, Mag. Monika Wallner, Mag. Alexander Wimmer*, as well as *Richard Franz, Gregor Grundei, Mag. Mirjam Holuschka*, and *Georg Kramer*, for the excellent collaboration and the friendly work environment. Especially, I would like to thank my former colleague *Mag. Dr. Clemens Bernsteiner, LL.M.*, for many interesting discussions on the present and other legal topics.

I also owe a great debt of gratitude to my friends and family; through their motivation, support, and friendship, they have contributed considerably to the completion of this project.

I would like to express special thanks to my parents for making my legal studies as well as this project possible. They have always been there for me and I could not have completed this work without their support and patience. This work is dedicated to them.

This research is connected to the Fellowship Program of the Stanford-Vienna Transatlantic Technology Law Forum (TTLF), a joint international initiative of Stanford Law School and the University of Vienna School of Law. I would also like to thank Stanford Law School as well as Professor Siegfried Fina and Professor Roland Vogl, the TTLF's Co-Directors, for giving me the opportunity to conduct a research visit at Stanford Law School in August 2016, without which this research would not have been possible. Finally, I would like to thank the International Office of the University of Vienna for providing funding for the research visit (short-term grant abroad – "KWA").

Vienna, November 2017 *Martin Miernicki*

Table of Contents

Abbreviations

AARC	Alliance of Artists and Recording Companies
AFBL	Adjustable fee blanket license
AG	Advocate General
AHRA	Audio Home Recording Act
Antitrust L. J.	Antitrust Law Journal
ARESA	Anglo-American Rights European Service Agency
ASCAP	American Society of Composers, Authors and Publishers
ASCAP Consent Decree / AFJ2	*United States v. American Society of Composers, Authors and Publishers*, 2001–2002 Trade Cas. (CCH) ¶ 73,474, 2001 U.S. Dist. LEXIS 23707 (S.D.N.Y. 2001).
ASCAP Distribution Rules	American Society of Composers, Authors and Publishers, *ASCAP's Survey and Distribution System: Rules and Policies* (2015), *available* at https://www.ascap.com/-/media/files/pdf/members/payment/drd.pdf (last visited May 23, 2017).
ASCAP Foreign Decree	*United States v. American Society of Composers, Authors and Publishers*, 1950 Trade Cas. (CCH) ¶ 62,594, 1950 U.S. Dist. LEXIS 1899 (S.D.N.Y. 1950).
ASCAP 1950 Decree	*United States v. American Society of Composers, Authors and Publishers*, 1950–1951 Trade Cas. (CCH) ¶ 62,595, 1950 U.S. Dist. LEXIS 4341 (S.D.N.Y. 1950).
ASCAP 1960 Order	*United States v. American Soc'y of Composers, Authors & Publishers*, 1960 Tr. Cas. (CCH), ¶ 69,612 (S.D.N.Y. 1960).
BEMIM	Bureau Européen des Médias de l'Industrie Musicale
BGH	Bundesgerichtshof (German Supreme Court)
BMI	Broadcast Music, Inc.
BMI Consent Decree	*United States v. Broadcast Music*, Inc., 1996-1 Trade Cas. (CCH) ¶71,378, 1994 U.S. Dist. LEXIS 21476 (S.D.N.Y. 1994).
B.U.L. Rev.	Boston University Law Review
Cal. L. Rev.	Cal. L. Rev.
CCC	Copyirght Clearance Center
CELAS	Centralised European Licensing and Administration Services
C.F.R.	Code of Federal Regulations
Charter of Fundamental Rights of the European Union	Charter of Fundamental Rights, 2012 O.J. (C326) 391–407
CISAC	Confédération Internationale des Sociétés d'Auteurs et Compositeurs
CMD / Collective Management Directive	Directive 2014/26 of the European Parliament and of The Council of 24 February 2014 on Collective Management of Copyright and Related Rights and Multi-territorial Licensing of Rights in Musical Works For Online Use in the Internal Market, 2014 O.J. (L84) 72–98.

CMO	Collective Management Organization
Columb J. L. & Arts	Columbia Journal of Law & the Arts
Compendium of ASCAP Rules	Compendium of ASCAP Rules and Regulations, and Policies Supplemental to the Articles of Association (2014), *available at* https://www.ascap.com/-/media/files/pdf/members/governing-documents/compendium- of-ascap-rules-regulations.pdf (last visited May 23, 2017).
Comp. L. & Econ.	Journal of Competition Law & Economics
Copyright Directive	Directive 2001/29/EC of The European Parliament and of The Council of 22 May 2001 on The Harmonisation of Certain Aspects of Copyright and Related Rights in The Information Society, 2001 O.J. (L167) 10–19.
CRB	Copyright Royalty Board
CREDIDAM	Centrul Român pentru Administrarea Drepturilor Artiștilor Interpreți
CRJ	Copyright Royalty Judges
DART	Digital Audio Recording Tape
Database Directive	Directive 96/9/EC of the European Parliament and of the Council of 11 March 1996 on the legal protection of databases, 1996 O.J. (L77) 20–28.
D.E.A.L.	Direct European Administration and Licensing
DG	Directorate General
DMCA	Digital Millenium Copyright Act
DOJ	Department of Justice
DRM	Digital Rights Management
ECJ	European Court of Justice / Court of Justice of the European Union
ECL	Extended Collective Licensing
EGC	(European) General Court / Court of First Instance
EEA	European Economic Area
E.I.P.R.	European Intellectual Property Review
EJI	Előadóművészi Jogvédő Iroda
Enforcement Directive	Directive 2004/48/EC of the European Parliament and of the Council of 29 April 2004 on the enforcement of intellectual property rights, 2004 O.J. (L157) 45–86.
EU	European Union
European J. Comm.	European Journal of Communication
EuZW	Europäische Zeitschrift für Wirtschaftsrechtt
Fordham Intell. Prop. Media & Ent. L. J.	Fordham Intellectual Property, Media & Entertainment Law Journal
GEMA	Gesellschaft für musikalische Aufführungs- und mechanische Vervielfältigungsrechte
Geo. Mason L. Rev.	George Mason Law Review
GPR	Zeitschrift für Gemeinschaftsprivatrecht
GRUR	Gewerblicher Rechtsschutz und Urheberrecht
GRUR Int	Gewerblicher Rechtsschutz und Urheberrecht, Internationaler Teil

GVL	Gesellschaft zur Verwertung von Leistungsschutzrechten
Harv. J. Sports & Entertainment L.	Harvard Journal of Sports and Entertainment Law
Hastings Comm. & Ent. L.J.	*Hastings Communications* and *Entertainment* Law Journal
HFA	Harry Fox Agency
Hous. L. Rev.	Houston Law Review
H.R.Rep.	House of Representatives Report
IFPI	International Federation of the Phonographic Industry
IIC	International Review of Intellectual Property and Competition Law
IJMBR	International Journal of Music Business Research
IME	Independent management entity
IMPEL	Independent Music Publishers European Licensing
Int. J. of Cultural Policy	International Journal of Cultural Policy
Iowa L. Rev.	Iowa Law Review
JCLE	Journal of Competition Law and Economics
JIPITEC	Journal of Intellectual Property, Information Technology and Electronic Commerce Law
J. Cop. Soc.	Journal of the Copyright Society U.S.A.
J. Intellec. Prop. Rights	Journal of Intellectual Property Rights
J. IP L. & Practice	Journal of Intellectual Property Law & Practice
L. & Contemp. Prob.	Law and Contemporary Problems
Masaryk U. J. L. & Tech.	Masaryk University Journal of Law and Technology
MCPS	Mechanical-Copyright Protection Society
MMR	MultiMedia und Recht
MPI	Max Planck Institute
MTL	Multi-territorial licensing
NBC Model	„Nordic and Baltic“ cooperation model
New Eng. L. Rev.	New England Law Review
No.	Number
ÖBl	Österreichische Blätter für gewerblichen Rechtsschutz und Urheberrecht
Orphan Works Directive	Directive 2012/28/EU of the European Parliament and of the Council of 25 October 2012 on certain permitted uses of orphan works, 2012 O.J. (L299) 5–12.
PEDL	Pan European Digital Licensing
PEL	Pan European Licensing Initiative of Latin American Repertoire
PPL	Per-program license
PPP index	Purchasing power parity index
PRS	Performing Rights Society
PRSfM	PRS for Music
RA	Representation Agreement

Rental & Lending Directive	Directive 2006/115/EC of the European Parliament and of the Council of 12 December 2006 on rental right and lending right and on certain rights related to copyright in the field of intellectual property, 2006 O.J. (L376) 28–35.
Resale Right Directive	Directive 2001/84/EC of the European Parliament and of the Council of 27 September 2001 on the resale right for the benefit of the author of an original work of art, 2011 O.J. (L272) 32–36.
RMLC	Radio Music License Committee
RRA	Reciprocal Representation Agreement
SABAM	Société Belge des Auteurs, Compositeurs et Éditeurs
SACEM	Société des Auteurs, Compositeurs et Éditeurs de Musique
Satellite & Cable Directive	Council Directive 93/83/EEC of 27 September 1993 on the coordination of certain rules concerning copyright and rights related to copyright applicable to satellite broadcasting and cable retransmission, 1993 O.J. (L248) 15–21.
SCAPR	Societies' Council for the Collective Management of Performers' Rights
Services Directive	Directive 2006/123/EC of the European Parliament and of the Council of 12 December 2006 on services in the internal market, 2006 O.J. (L376) 36–68.
SGAE	Sociedad General de Autores y Editores
SIAE	Società Italiana degli Autori ed Editori
SMEs	Small & medium-sized enterprises
SOCAN	Society of Composers, Authors and Music Publishers of Canada
Software Directive	Directive 2009/24/EC of the European Parliament and of the Council of 23 April 2009 on the legal protection of computer programs, 2009 O.J. (L111) 16–22.
STIM	Föreningen Svenska Tonsättares Internationella Musikbyrå
Studies in Cults., Orgs. and Socs.	Studies in Cultures, Organizations and Societies
SUISA	Société suisse pour les droits des auteurs d'œuvres musicales
Term Directive	Directive 2006/116/EC of the European Parliament and of the Council of 12 December 2006 on the term of protection of copyright and certain related rights, 2006 O.J. (L372) 12–18.
TEU	Consolidated Version of the Treaty on European Union, 2012 O.J. (C326) 13–46.
Texas Intell. Prop. L. J.	Texas Intellecutal Property Law Journal
Texas L. Rev.	Texas Law Review
TFEU	Treaty on The Functioning of the European Union, see Consolidated Version of the Treaty on The Functioning of the European Union, 2012 O.J. (C326) 47–390

TTTA license	Through-To-The-Audience License
TVMLC	Television Music License Committee
U. Pa. L. Rev.	University of Pennsylvania Law Review
U.S.	United States
U.S.C.	United States Code
VG Media	Gesellschaft zur Verwertung der Urheber- und Leistungsschutzrechte von Medienunternehmen
VG Wort	Verwertungsgesellschaft Wort
WIPO	World Intellectual Property Organization
Wm. Mitchell L. Rev.	William Mitchell Law Review
Yale L. J.	Yale Law Journal
ZUM	Zeitschrift für Urheber- und Medienrecht

I. Introduction

It has been said that "[c]opyright is founded on the concepts of the unique individual who creates something original and is entitled to reap a profit from those labors".[1] In following this idea, legal systems around the world decided to protect the authors of original creations by conferring exclusive rights upon them. These rights enable the "unique individuals" to exercise control over their works, which ensures their economic compensation and, to a more or lesser degree, protects their immaterial interests. By their very name, *exclusive* rights imply that the free discretion of enforcement and management of said rights is solely vested in the author,[2] enjoining others from certain acts like copying, distributing, or performing protected works. That being said, it becomes clear why authorship was declared "the functional and moral center of the [copyright] system".[3] Despite this framework of individuality,[4] the reality of copyright often does not correspond to this idea. Users nowadays obtain licenses for a vast number of works by concluding a single agreement with large organizations; such institutions represent thousands of right holders who themselves may not be involved at all in the licensing process. At the same time, lawmakers depart from the exclusive-rights approach by introducing rights to remuneration that do not provide for an equivalent legal position. It is therefore obvious that copyright law is not merely comprised of an individual side; the other side is of a collective nature and lies beyond the right holders' direct control, be it for legal or practical reasons. This collective side of copyright has several manifestations which on the one hand supplement, but on the other hand also limit the traditional individual approach to rights in original creations. Yet, copyrights and their management are subject to continuous changes. As will be seen, comparatively recent developments – like the major publishers' withdrawal of rights from collective licensing systems – suggest, to a certain

1 Mark Rose, *Authors and Owners: The Invention of Copyright* 2 (1993). *See also* Karl-Nikolaus Pfeifer, *Individualität im Zivilrecht* 55 (2001).

2 Under certain circumstances, the initial copyright owner can be different from the actual author; moreover, rights can be transferred. However, even where the right holder and the author are not the same person, this does not mean by itself that rights are managed or enforced individually or collectively.

3 Jane C. Ginsburg, *The Author's Place in the Future of Copyright*, 153 Proc. of the Am. Philos. Soc. 147, 148 (2009). Prof. Ginsburg looks the position of authors in relation to intermediaries and modern technologies. *See also* on German law Gernot Schulze, *§ 1 UrhG* in *Urheberrechtsgesetz: UrhG* ¶ 1–2 (Thomas Dreier & Gernot Schulze eds., 5th ed. 2015).

4 There are diverging opinions on what the system actually aims at by equipping individuals with exclusive rights. The two prevalent approaches discuss whether copyright law primarily exists for the benefit of the general public (utilitarian perspective) or serves the interest of the author (natural rights perspective), *see, e.g.,* for the theoretical foundations of copyright law Ulrich Loewenheim, *Einleitung* in *Urheberrecht* ¶ 8–19 (Ulrich Loewenheim et al. eds., 5th ed. 2017). *See also* Daniel Gervais, *Collective Management of Copyright: Theory and Practice in the Digital Age* in *Collective Management of Copyright and Related Rights* 1, 16–17 (Daniel Gervais ed., 3rd ed. 2016).

degree, a trend toward what could be called a "re-individualization" of copyright (management).[5]

1. Collective Rights Management – Rationales and Functions

The management of copyrights involves different tasks like concluding license agreements, collecting license fees, monitoring the use of protected content, and enforcing rights in case of infringement. These tasks are essential to copyright holders: A songwriter,[6] for instance, probably wants her music to be included in the program of several radio stations; she is most likely interested to know about the popularity and the usage of her creations in bars or discotheques, and she would complain and demand compensation if her songs were played in those venues without her authorization. However, it would be extremely onerous, if not impossible, to accomplish all of the above mentioned tasks successfully for an individual person. Similarly, users (i.e. prospective licensees)[7] face the same problem on the other side of the transaction channel, as it would be practically infeasible to locate and conclude license agreements with a myriad of copyright holders whose works are needed for the users' services. Thus, if copyright was solely managed individually, it would in many instances be virtually impossible to maintain a functional licensing system. Therefore, it is often useful for both right holders and users to turn to a collective management organization (CMO). These organizations grant licenses, monitor the use of works, enforce copyrights on behalf of the respective owners, and specialize on the collective representation of their members, thereby serving as solutions to the imperfections of the individual side of copyright.[8] There are unquestionably many advantages of this form of management. Yet, these benefits have limits; while in many fields collective management of copyrights is very common, in others it is not. In this vein, the "first principle"[9] of collective management has been postulated as follows:

5 *See also* Dinusha Mendis, *Directive 2014/26/EU on Collective Management of Copyright and Related Rights and Multi-Territorial Licensing of Rights in Musical Works for Online Use in the Internal Market* in *EU Regulation of E-Commerce* 290, 307–310 (Arno R. Lodder & Andrew D. Murray eds., 2017) (focusing on the CMD).

6 It should be noted, however, that there are different groups of right holders who do not necessarily share the same interests.

7 Users in this context are not consumers, but businesses which provide services or products associated with copyrighted content. Examples include innovating services like streaming just like traditional discotheques. *See* the concept of "users" in subsections and 3.2.1. and 3.2.6.f) below.

8 *See, e.g.,* Mihály Ficsor, *Collective Management of Copyright and Related Rights* 17 (WIPO Pub. No. 855, 2002), *available at* ftp://ftp.wipo.int/pub/library/ebooks/wipopublications/wipo_pub_855e.pdf (last visited May 23, 2017)*;* Gervais, *Theory and Practice, supra* at 8–12.

9 Mihály Ficsor, *Collective Rights Management from the Viewpoint of International Treaties, with Special Attention to the EU 'Acquis'* in *Collective Management of Copyright and Related Rights* 31, 55–56 n.69 (Daniel Gervais ed., 3rd ed. 2016).

> Collective management or other systems of joint management of copyright and related rights is justified where individual exercise of such rights – due to the number and other circumstances of uses – is impossible or, at least, highly impracticable. Such joint management of rights should be chosen, whenever possible, as an alternative to non-voluntary licensing.[10]

Hence, collective management can be seen as a solution to an array of legal and practical problems. These problems arise from the special subject-matter of copyright and the number and kind of recognized rights as well as technological developments.

First, copyright (and other IP) confers rights in intangible goods. Whereas a car can only be driven by one person at a time, songs can be sung, books can be read, and plays can be performed simultaneously in hundreds of places without interfering with one another. This is because the use of intellectual content is normally nonrivalrous and nonexclusive; in contrast to real property, immaterial goods are "ubiquitous" because access to them cannot be denied easily.[11] As a consequence, right holders will find it hard to enforce and monitor the use of their IP; individuals usually do not possess the capacity to consider all the uses of their works because these occur in considerable numbers, at different places, and at different times.[12]

Second, modern copyright is characterized by fragmentation.[13] Its most significant manifestation in the present context is that the legal position of right holders in modern copyright is characterized by several different exclusive rights. This provides more options for authors to benefit from their creations but, at the same time, makes rights management more complex. This process is paralleled by the historical development of copyright law: Back in the times when copyright legislation merely recognized the rights of reproduction and distribution, authors were able to enforce and monitor their rights personally;[14] any uses not falling within the scope of these rights did not conflict with applicable laws. However, over time, more rights (such as public performance rights[15]) were continuously conferred upon authors, thereby significantly expanding the scope of copyright law. This process continued throughout the

---

10 Ficsor, *Collective Management*, *supra* at 157.

11 *See, e.g.*, Guido Kucsko, *Einleitung* in *urheber.recht* LI (Guido Kucsko ed., 2008); Robert P. Merges et al., *Intellectual Property in The New Technological Age* 2 (5th ed. 2010); Marcel Bisges, *Ökonomische Analyse des Urheberrechts*, 58 ZUM 930, 933–934 (2014); Christopher S. Yoo, *Copyright and Public Good Economics: A Misunderstood Relation*, 155 U. Pa. L. Rev. 635 (2007).

12 Ficsor, *Collective Management*, *supra* at 17.

13 Fragmentation can be described as "the lack of cohesion, standardization and, to a certain extent, effective organization of both copyright law and collective management per se", *see* Daniel Gervais & Alana Maurushat, *Fragmented Copyright, Fragmented Management: Proposals to Defrag Copyright Management*, 2 Can. J. of L. & Tech. 15 (2003).

14 Jörg Reinbothe, *Vor §§ 1ff WahrnG* in *Urheberrecht* ¶ 1–2 (Ulrich Loewenheim et al. eds., 5th ed. 2017).

15 *Id.*

20th century; nowadays, copyright is often called a bundle of rights, formed by sub-rights like reproduction, public performance, communication to the public, translation, etc.[16] As a consequence, a single act of use of a work can affect several rights of various right holders who may be unknown, and to make things worse, each right can be held by more than one person. Therefore, even common processes easily become extremely confusing: For instance, a radio station that copies and saves music in a digital format in order to broadcast the content can require up to twenty licenses for every single song it wishes to add to its program, as rights can exist in the musical composition, the performance, and the sound recording.[17]

Third, advances in technology have been crucial to the development of copyright in general and especially to its collective management. As technologies like recording and television emerged and new devices triggering the mass proliferation of private copying of audio and video content were invented, copyright holders were increasingly faced with enforcement problems of their exclusive rights.[18] Levies – i.e. rights to remuneration – were introduced in many countries as an answer to private copying, for instance, in order to provide for the remuneration of right holders for copies made of their protected works.[19] In many cases, the revenues flowing from such levies are collected by a CMO.[20] Moreover, as mentioned before in connection with fragmentation, copyright law adapted to new forms of creations (*e.g.*, software) and dissemination (*e.g.*, the internet), thereby adding new rights to the copyright bun-

16 Gervais, *Theory and Practice*, *supra* at 12. In this context, *Prof. Shaffer Van Houweling* introduces the concept of copyright atomism in order to analyze the developments of modern copyright. Along with the fragmentation of the copyright bundle, she identifies proliferation (number of protected works) and distribution (number of copyright owners) as the three main factors that constitute atomism in the copyright realm, *see* Molly Shaffer Van Houweling, *Author Autonomy and Atomism in Copyright Law*, 96 Va. L. Rev. 549, 553 (2010).

17 Gervais, *Theory and Practice*, *supra* at 4, 14–15. There is a debate on whether copyright should be organized as a bundle of fragmented rights, *see, e.g.*, Note, *A Justification for Allowing Fragmentation in Copyright Law*, 124 Harv. L. Rev. 1751 (2011) (reviewing the applicable U.S. literature and emphasizing the advantages of fragmentation in copyright law).

18 Ferdinand Melchiar, *§ 45* in *Handbuch des Urheberrechts* ¶ 1–2 (Ulrich Loewenheim ed., 2nd ed. 2010).

19 For the historical development of copyright levies *see* P. Bernt Hugenholtz, *The Story of the Tape Recorder and the History of Copyright Levies* in *Copyright and the Challenge of the New* 179 (Brad Sherman & Leanne Wiseman eds., 2012).

20 In the United States, the Alliance of Artists and Recording Companies (AARC) was founded for the collection and distribution of private copying levies, *see* AARC, *What is the AARC?* http://wp.aarcroyalties.com/what-is-aarc/ (last visited April 14, 2017). SoundExchange collects royalties arising from the statutory license in relation to sound recordings, *see* section II.1.2.4. below. In Germany, for instance, existing institutions created an joint organization, the Zentralstelle für private Überspielungsrechte (ZPÜ) to collect private copying levies, *see* Reinhold Kreile, *Die Zusammenarbeit der Verwertungsgesellschaften* in *Recht und Praxis der GEMA* 783, 785–786 (Reinhold Kreile et al. eds., 2nd ed. 2008).

dle, since traditional rights did not fit the new types of uses.[21] It is thus apparent that technology is also an important reason for the fragmentation of the rights bundle.

The implications of the foregoing factors and the role of collective management become clear when put in the economic context.[22] The main benefit of collective management is seen by most authors in a reduction of transactions costs.[23] These comprise the costs of finding a trading partner and the respective relevant information (search costs), drafting and concluding agreements (contracting costs), monitoring compliance with negotiated agreements (monitoring costs), and enforcing said agreements in the event of noncompliance (enforcement costs); the latter two types also refer to users who have not obtained permissions, especially in the copyright realm.[24] In this connection,

21 Gervais, *Theory and Practice*, *supra* at 12–13. *See also* João Pedro Quintais, *On Peers and Copyright: Why the EU Should Consider Collective Management of P2P* 77–79 (2012) (stating that collective rights management is a viable answer to mass online uses such as P2P).

22 The economic foundations of collective management have been dicussed in several studies and need not be recounted here; a brief note on the most important aspects appears sufficient for the present purpose in order to put the intuitive advantages of collective management in a proper framework. For more details on the economics of collective management *see, e.g.*, Stanley M. Besen et al., *An Economic Analysis Of Copyright Collectives*, 78 Va. L. Rev. 383 (1992); Roya Ghafele & Benjamin Gibert, *Counting the Costs of Collective Rights Management of Music Copyright in Europe* (MPRA Paper No. 34646, 2011), *available at* https://mpra.ub.uni-muenchen.de/34646/1/MPRA_paper_34646.pdf (last visited May 23, 2017); Christian Handke & Ruth Towse, *Economics of Copyright Collecting Societies*, 38 Intern. Rev. of Int. Property & Competition L. 937 (2007); Gerd Hansen & Albrecht Schmidt-Bischoffshausen, *Ökonomische Funktionen von Verwertungsgesellschaften – Kollektive Wahrnehmung im Lichte von Transaktionskosten- und Informationsökonomik*, 56 GRUR Int 461 (2007); Ariel Katz, *Copyright Collectives: Good Solution, But For Which Problem?* (2009), *available at* https://papers.ssrn.com/sol3/papers.cfm?abstract_id=1416798 (last visited May 23, 2017); Mark A. Lemley, *Contracting Around Liability Rules*, 100 Cal. L. Rev. 463 (2012); Moritz Lichtenegger, *Verwertungsgesellschaften, Kartellverbot und Neue Medien* 214–277 (2014); Robert P. Merges, *Contracting into Liability Rules: Intellectual Property Rights and Collective Rights Organizations*, 84 Cal. L. Rev. 1293 (1996); Ruth Towse, *Economics of Copyright Collecting Societies and Digital Rights: Is There a Case for a Centralised Digital Copyright Exchange?*, 9 Rev. of Econ. Research on Copyright Issues 3 (2012); Richard Watt, *Copyright collectives: some basic economic theory* in *Handbook on the economics of copyright* 167–178 (Richard Watt ed. 2014); Zijian Zhang, *Rationale of Collective Management Organizations: An Economic Perspective*, 10 Masaryk U. J. L. & Tech. 73 (2016).

23 Christian Handke, *Collective administration* in *Handbook on the economics of copyright* 179 (Richard Watt ed. 2014). *See* for a critical opinion on this argument in connection with blanket licenses John Cirace, *CBS v. ASCAP: An Economic Analysis of a Political Problem*, 47 Fordham L. Rev. 277, 292–293 (1978). Some authors focus on an approach which centers risk allocation, *see, e.g.*, Lichtenegger, *Verwertungsgesellschaften*, *supra* at 222–225; Ana María Pérez Gómez Tétrel, *Efficient allocation of risk as an economic function of Collecting Societies* (2007), *available at* http://www.serci.org/2007/perezgomez.pdf (last visited May 23, 2017); Arthur Snow & Richard Watt, *Risk Sharing and the Distribution of Copyright Collective Income*, *available at* http://serci.org/2003/snowwatt.pdf (last visited April 14, 2017).

24 Handke, *Collective Administration*, *supra* at 183–184.

CMOs have generally been regarded as natural monopolies;[25] however, scholars have raised doubts about the efficiency of collective management[26] or question its design in light of the underlying normative foundations of copyright law.[27] It should be noted, however, that CMOs do not only fulfill economic functions. In many countries these organizations assume the role of "cultural agents", promoting creative production (*e.g.*, scholarships, events) and cultural diversity.[28]

2. Purpose and Structure of the Research

The environment for the collective management of copyrights has been subject to profound changes over the last several years. This development was triggered by public authorities, technological progress (especially in the digital field) and the emergence of new management models. Much research has been done in order to describe and explain these changes, however, mostly from a national (or regional) perspective. Less research has been done to compare the experiences made in other jurisdictions. The present research aims at filling this gap by providing a comprehensive comparison of the legal approaches taken by EU and U.S. law in relation to the collective management of copyrights.[29] The two jurisdictions are chosen because they have been at the forefront of the aforementioned developments; yet, they have established very different regulatory systems and legal practices. Highlighting these differences and putting them into perspective appears to be important not only for understanding the legal status quo but also for reflecting on the question whether or to what extent changes and reforms should be implemented. In this sense, the experiences made in the U.S. can be extremely valuable for the EU, and vice versa, provided, however, that due account is given to the differences in the respective underlying legal systems.

---

25 One speaks of a "natural monopoly" in situations "where a monopoly supplier is able to supply the market more efficiently than if there were competition […]", *see* Ruth Towse et al., *The Economics Of Copyright Law: A Stocktake of the Literature*, 5 Review of Economic Research on Copyright Issues 1, 4 (2008). *See also* Ivan L. Pitt, *Direct Licensing and the Music Industry* 115–123 (2015).

26 *See, e.g.,* Ariel Katz, *Commentary: Is Collective Administration of Copyrights Justified by the Economic Literature?* in *Competition Policy and Intellectual Property* 449 (Marcel Boyer et al. eds., 2009); Ariel Katz, *The Potential Demise Of Another Natural Monopoly: Rethinking The Collective Administration Of Performing Rights*, 1 JCLE 541 (2005). *Lichtenegger* argues that the availability of digital rights management (DRM) systems (at least partially) contradicts the natural monopolies approach, *see* Lichtenegger, *Verwertungsgesellschaften*, *supra* at 261–264; *see* however *id.* at 270–272 on the problem of consumer acceptance of DRM.

27 *See, e.g.,* Martin Kretschmer, *The Failure of Property Rules in Collective Administration: Rethinking Copyright Societies as Regulatory Instruments*, 24 E. I. P. R. 126 (2002).

28 *See* Gervais, *Theory and Practice*, *supra* at 7, 17–20.

29 Where collective management of copyrights is mentioned hereinafter, reference is also to related rights, except where otherwise indicated.

A comparative analysis usually consists of three major stages: First, the selection of what will be compared; second, the description of the respective legal systems; and third, the analysis.[30] Rather than presenting the U.S. and EU regulation overall in separate sections, the present research is grouped around concrete legal questions (*e.g.*, the applicability of antitrust laws to CMOs or the "partial withdrawals" of rights from a CMO's repertoire) and juxtaposes the answers given by the two jurisdictions. The starting point will be EU regulation (first the EU competition case law, then the sector-specific regulation), followed by the regulatory system in the United States. At the end of each chapter, the legal status quo will be commented on from a comparative perspective, which is meant to provide the basis for a better understanding of the European and U.S. legal system as well as for a more general reflection on the regulation of collective management.[31] In the last chapter, general characteristics and conclusions will be drawn to provide a comprehensive picture of the EU and the U.S. approaches to collective management. The aim of the present research is thus not only to describe and compare the legal status quo in the European Union and the United States but also to highlight whether or to what extent experiences made in one of the two jurisdictions can or should be taken into consideration and relied upon in the other.

Since the musical performance rights are paradigmatic for collective management of copyrights, especially in the United States, the research focuses on this field; reference to other types of rights will be made where necessary for the present purposes. However, many findings of this reseach do not only apply to musical performance rights but also to the collective management of copyrights in general.

Before turning to the actual analysis, three introductory sections on terminology, substantive copyright law, and historical developments aim at laying the foundations for the main part of the research.

3. Terminological Remarks

The different forms of rights management are fairly diverse and so are the terms generally used to refer to organizations that manage copyrights. In line

30 Gerhard Dannemann, *Comparative Law: Study of Similarities or Differences?* in *The Oxford Handbook of Comparative Law* 383, 406–419 (Mathias Reimann & Reinhard Zimmermann eds., 2006).

31 *See* in this context Klodi Shanto & Blerton Sinani, *Methods and Functions of Comparative Law*, 2 Acta Universitatis Danubius. Juridica 25, 31–33 (2013) on the notions of "micro-comparison" (comparing a specific legal institute like marriage) and "macro-comparison" (comparing the characteristics of two legal systems from a broader perspective) and *id.* at 34–37 on the functions of comparative law. *See* in this connection on the aims and functions of comparative law H. Patrick Glenn, *The aims of comparative law* in *Elgar Encyclopedia of Comparative law* 65 (Jan M. Smits ed., 2nd ed. 2012).

with what seems to be the most common and widespread use, *collective management organization* (CMO)[32] is understood as an umbrella term. The term refers to all kinds of organizational structures in which copyrights are not exercised individually but in the representation of a multitude of right holders and where the respective rights are owned by the members of these structures.[33] The following section gives a brief overview of related terms in order to facilitate the understanding of the ongoing debate.

3.1. Joint, Collective, and Centralized Management

From an international perspective, individual or direct management of copyright has been juxtaposed with the term *joint management*. The latter expression covers every non-individual form of copyright management, i.e. where the rights in a protected work are not managed by the copyright holder him or herself personally, but by an organization acting on his or her behalf.[34] Needless to say, such organizations take actions for a multitude of right owners; organizational structures that represent only a single right holder can be called agents or representatives,[35] depending on the arrangements in the specific case. Furthermore, joint management means that the managed rights are not held by the organization itself but by their members, in contrast to big enterprises that manage their own "catalogs" or "libraries".[36]

Joint management is a general term that can be subdivided into *collective management* and *centralized management*.[37] Collective management of copyright can be described as the tasks that are commonly associated with CMOs: These tasks encompass the enforcement and the monitoring of rights, the negotiation of licensing agreements, and the grant of licenses on the basis of a tariff system, as well as the collection and the distribution of the royalties.[38] On the contrary, centralized management or rights clearance has been defined as "a kind of agency-type activity" which is characterized by a reduction of the tasks performed by management organizations to a few elements like the col-

32 Josef Drexl et al., *Comments of the Max Planck Institute for Intellectual Property and Competition Law on the Proposal for A Directive of The European Parliament and of The Council on Collective Management Of Copyright and Related Rights and Multi-Territorial Licensing of Rights in Musical Works for Online Uses in The Internal Market Com (2012) 372* 3 n.2 (Max Planck Institute for Intellectual Property and Competition Law Research Paper No. 13-04, 2013), *available at* https://papers.ssrn.com/sol3/papers.cfm?abstract_id=2208971 (last visited May 23, 2017). *See* for more details on the classification of CMOs Gervais, *Theory and Practice*, *supra* at 8.

33 *See* the definition of the CMD section II.1.1.4. below.

34 Ficsor, *Collective Management*, *supra* at 16.

35 Schulze, *§ 1 UrhG*, *supra* at ¶ 1.

36 Ficsor, *Collective Management*, *supra* at 16.

37 *Id.* at 22–24.

38 *Id.* at 17.

lection and distribution of royalties.[39] In some cases, the only remaining joint element is the offer of a single licensing source along with individualized licensing conditions.[40] Hence, centralized management differs from collective management, inasmuch as copyright owners retain greater control over their works, while, at the same time, taking advantage of the economic benefits inherent to centralization. In this light, it is clear that both models can help reduce transaction costs and that collective management as described above is necessarily centralized. However, "traditional" collective management is seen as a task that does not only fulfill economic functions: It features a greater degree of cohesion among the members, since its aim can be described as the "advancement of the Creators' moral interests and the defence of the material interests of Creators and publishers";[41] this requires a real community of authors that share common goals and interests.[42] Furthermore, organizations engaged in collective management can in some respects be seen as performing cultural and social functions that go beyond actual rights management and the representation of their members, thereby causing beneficial effects for the general public.[43]

3.2. Collecting Societies and Copyright Collectives

There are several terms referring to organizations that offer copyright management services. Often used in this context – apart from the term "collective management organization" – are *collecting society* and *copyright collective.*[44] In the United States, copyright collectives are understood as organizations that offer licenses under conditions which are set by the collective with no or little competition within the repertoire.[45] Thus, the business model of a copyright

[39] *Id.* at 22. In the same context, but in a slightly different manner, the term centralized licensing has been used in contrast to collective licensing. It can be defined as "the aggregation of collective management societies into an umbrella society for the sole purpose of providing a central point of information", *see* Gervais & Maurushat, *Fragmented Copyright, supra* at 25. It therefore incorporates the idea of centralized rights clearing, but within a structure that associates multiple CMOs. Organizations which base their operations on this model can also be called *one-stop shops, see* Ficsor, *Collective Management, supra* at 98.

[40] Ficsor, *Collective Management, supra* at 22.

[41] CISAC Statutes Art 8(b), June 6, 2014, AG10-1275R6, http://www.cisac.org/What-We-Do/Governance/Statutes [hereinafter CISAC Statute]. CISAC (Confédération Internationale des Sociétés d'Auteurs et Compositeurs) is an international umbrella organization for CMOs composed of more than 230 member societies and was founded in 1926, *see* CISAC, *Who We Are,* http://www.cisac.org/Who-We-Are (last visited April 14, 2017).

[42] Ficsor, *Collective Management, supra* at 20.

[43] *Id.* at 20–21. *See also* Melchiar, *§ 45, supra* at ¶ 5.

[44] Less common are *authors societies, copyright societies, collective rights management organizations, intellectual property rights exchange institutions* etc.

[45] Glynn Lunney, *Copyright Collectives and Collecting Societies: The United States Experience* in *Collective Management of Copyright and Related Rights* 319, 319–320 (Daniel Gervais ed., 3rd ed. 2016).

collective can be regarded as a form of "traditional" collective management. On other hand, collecting societies operate on the basis of licensing terms set by the individual right holder and they merely enforce and collect the licensing fees.[46] Therefore, collecting societies fit best within the realm of centralized management.[47] On the other side of the Atlantic Ocean, the terminology differs. In the European literature (in English), the two terms do not seem as clearly distinguished, if not altogether used synonymously; however, generally, the expression *copyright collective* is rarely used. European publications often prefer the term *collecting societies*, and the usage of this notion indicates a broad concept of this type of organization. They appear to be understood as a rather heterogeneous group of organizations which share the common task of collective rights management in general.[48]

3.3. PROs and RROs

In the United States, one frequently refers to *Performing Rights Societies* or *Performance Rights Organizations* (PROs) when discussing the collective copyright management of musical works. Basically, these are CMOs that specialize in a certain field of rights as their activity generally encompasses the licensing of "the public performance of nondramatic musical works on behalf of copyright owners of such works".[49] It is worthwhile to note that this defini-

46 *Id.*

47 Yet, the terminology is not uniform throughout the U.S. literature, *see, e.g.,* C. Scott Hemphill, *Competition and the Collective Management of Copyright* 34 Colum. J. of L. & Arts 645 (2011) (describing the CCC – a collecting society under the terminology explained by *Prof. Lunney* – as a "copyright collective"). *See also* II Paul Goldstein, *Goldstein On Copyright* § 7.9 (3rd ed. 2014, updated 06/2016) (using the term "collecting society" to refer to ASCAP and BMI).

48 *See, e.g.,* Ruth Towse & Christian Handke, *Regulating Copyright Collecting Societies: Current Policy in Europe* 1 (2007), http://www.serci.org/2007/towsehandke.pdf (last visited May 23, 2017); KEA European Affairs, *The Collective Management of Rights in Europe: The Quest for Efficiency* 14 (2006), *available at* http://www.europarl.europa.eu/meetdocs/2004_2009/documents/dv/study-collective-management-rights-/study-collective-management-rights-en.pdf (last visited May 23, 2017); BOP Consulting et al., *Collecting Societies Codes of Conduct* 8–9 (2012), *available at* https://www.gov.uk/government/uploads/system/uploads/attachment_data/file/310172/ipresearch-collecting-071212.pdf (last visited May 23, 2017). Note in this context that the final version article 3(a) of the CMD changed the proposal's definition from "collecting society" to "collective management organisation". *See* for the proposal European Commission, *Proposal for a Directive of The European Parliament and of The Council on collective management of copyright and related rights and multi-territorial licensing of rights in musical works for online uses in the internal market* (COM(2012) 372 final), *available at* http://ec.europa.eu/internal_market/copyright/docs/management/com-2012-3722_en.pdf (last visited May 23, 2017). In this connection, it is noteworthy that the Satellite & Cable Directive's (*see* section 4. below) art. 1(4) contains a definition of the term "collecting society" ("any organization which manages or administers copyright or rights related to copyright as its sole purpose or as one of its main purposes").

49 17 U.S.C. § 101.

tion is based on the type of right (public performance) and the nature of the work (nondramatic musical work) and not on the licensing practices or the existence of a uniform tariff system. However, neither of the most important American PROs[50] follows individualized licensing models as a principle.[51] A different organizational type, which is also defined by the managed rights, is the *Reproduction Rights Organization* (RRO). Its task is the management of a distinct set of rights, in particular the rights to photocopying and to other forms of reproductions.[52]

4. Introduction to EU and U.S. Copyright Law

This section provides a succinct overview of the copyright regimes in the United States and the European Union. In line with the focus of this research, the emphasis is put on U.S. federal law and European Union law; besides the constitutional background and a general overview, rights relevant to the public performance of music are especially mentioned.

4.1. Constitutional Background

The design of the constitutional foundation in the United States and the European Union (the EU treaties) feature fundamental differences. EU *primary law*[53] influences national copyright laws in numerous ways. First of all, general provisions of the EU treaties,[54] like the free movements of goods[55] and services,[56] competition law,[57] and the principle of non-discrimination,[58] govern the national law-making in the field of copyright. Legal acts adopted by

50 These are ASCAP, BMI and SESAC. They are explicitly recognized by the U.S. Copyright Act, *see* 17. U.S.C. § 101.

51 Lunney, *The United States Experience*, *supra* at 320.

52 World Intellectual Property Organization & International Federation of Reproduction Rights Organisations, *Collective Management in Reprography* 5 (WIPO Pub. No. 924, 2005), *available at* http://www.wipo.int/edocs/pubdocs/en/copyright/924/wipo_pub_924.pdf (last visited May 23, 2017).

53 *See* for a succinct overview of the sources of EU law European Parliament, *Sources and Scope of European Union Law* (2017), http://www.europarl.europa.eu/ftu/pdf/en/FTU_1.2.1.pdf (last visited May 23, 2017). *See* for more details Matthias Ruffert, *Art. 1 AEUV* in *EUV/AEUV* ¶ 8–15 (Christian Calliess & Matthias Ruffert eds., 5th ed. 2016).

54 The most important sources of EU primary law are the Treaty on European Union, *see* Consolidated Version of the Treaty on European Union, 2012 O.J. (C326) 13–46 [hereinafter: TEU]; and The Treaty on The Functioning of the European Union, *see* Consolidated Version of the Treaty on The Functioning of the European Union, 2012 O.J. (C326) 47–390 (hereinafter: TFEU).

55 TFEU art. 28–44.

56 *Id.* at art. 56–62.

57 *Id.* at art. 101–106.

58 *Id.* at art. 18.

the EU on the basis of the treaties are referred to as *secondary law*.[59] Important parts of EU secondary law are regulations and directives. These legal acts are distinct on a decisive point: A regulation is directly applicable in the member states, whereas a directive is only binding with regard to the result that is to be achieved, but the exact way of implementation is in the member states' discretion.[60] Because of this feature, directives are a means of approximating the standards applicable in the member states, a process that is called *harmonization* of national laws; this process is prevalent in European copyright law.[61] Directives harmonize the respective fields either vertically or horizontally: The first case refers to situations where the directive in question only applies to a specific subject matter, whereas in the second case, the directive is of a scope that permits a more general application.[62] With respect to the EU's competence in the field of copyright law-making, the TFEU contains two provisions of special relevance:

> In the context of the establishment and functioning of the internal market, the European Parliament and the Council, acting in accordance with the ordinary legislative procedure, shall establish measures for the creation of European intellectual property rights to provide uniform protection of intellectual property rights throughout the Union and for the setting up of centralised Union-wide authorisation, coordination and supervision arrangements.[63]
>
> [T]he European Parliament and the Council shall [...] adopt the measures for the approximation of the provisions laid down by law, regulation or administrative action in Member States which have as their object the establishment and functioning of the internal market.[64]

Surprising as it may seem, many copyright-related directives are based, *inter alia*, on the latter provision and not on the IP-specific provision.[65] This may be due to that article 118 TFEU had not come into existence before the adoption of the Treaty of Lisbon;[66] however, it reveals how EU law looks at copyrights. It is a conspicuous difference between U.S. and EU copyright leg-

---

59 *See* for more details Werner Schroeder, *Art. 288 AEUV* in *EUV/AEUV* ¶ 23–24 (Rudolf Streinz ed., 2nd ed. 2012).

60 TFEU art. 288.

61 Silke von Lewinski, *Introduction* in *European Copyright Law* 3, 14 (Michel M. Walter & Silke von Lewinski eds., 2010).

62 Silke von Lewinski & Michel M. Walter, *Status of Harmonization and Outlook* in *European Copyright Law* 1463, 1464–1465 (Michel M. Walter & Silke von Lewinski eds., 2010).

63 TFEU art. 118. The scope of the provision is not entirely clear; however, the prevailing opinion argues that the article provides a basis for copyright legislation, *see, e.g.,* Reinhold Beiser & Nikolaus Zorn, *Art 118 AEUV* in *Kommentar zu EUV und AEUV* ¶ 4 (Heinz Mayer & Karl Stöger eds., updated 05/2010 at rdb.at); Ana Ramalho, *Conceptualising the European Union's Competence in Copyright – What Can the EU Do?*, 45 IIC 178, 184–185 (2014); Christian Wichard, *Art. 118 AEUV* in *EUV/AEUV* ¶ 2 (Christian Calliess & Matthias Ruffert eds., 5th ed. 2016).

64 TFEU art. 114(1).

65 Ramalho, *Competence in Copyright, supra* at 179.

66 Treaty of Lisbon Amending the Treaty on European Union and the Treaty Establishing the European Community, 2007 O.J. (C 306) 1–271. *See* Beiser & Zorn, *Art 118 AEUV*, *supra* at ¶ 1.

islation that most directives are based on general competences which center the four freedoms and the Internal Market established in the EU Treaties – constituting a business law approach – whereas U.S. acts rely on the Intellectual Property Clause of the U.S. Constitution. The legal situation is somewhat comparable to the introduction of the Lanham Act,[67] a trademark statute that was first based on this provision, then repealed by the Supreme Court and subsequently redesigned on the basis of the Commerce Clause.[68] The consequence implied by the TFEU is that EU law provides for nothing more than a general framework of copyright law set up by directives introducing the standards for national copyright laws.

The U.S. Constitution contains the broad basis for federal copyright legislation, which is referred to as the *Intellectual Property Clause* or *Exclusive Rights Clause:*[69]

> Congress shall have the power [...] to promote the progress of science and useful arts, by securing for limited times to authors and inventors the exclusive right to their respective writings and discoveries [...][70]

Although state legislation can apply to copyright-related questions in certain cases, Congress is empowered to enact a comprehensive copyright regime.[71] State law may apply to copyrights when not preempted by the federal statute.[72]

4.2. Overview of Copyright-Related Legislation

As indicated before, there are several European directives relevant to copyright:[73]

- Council Directive 93/83/EEC of 27 September 1993 on the coordination of certain rules concerning copyright and rights related to copyright applicable to satellite broadcasting and cable retransmission, 1993 O.J. (L248) 15–21 (hereinafter: Satellite & Cable Directive).
- Directive 96/9/EC of the European Parliament and of the Council of 11 March 1996 on the legal protection of databases, 1996 O.J. (L77) 20–28. (hereinafter: Database Directive).

---

67 15 U.S.C. §§ 1051–1141n.

68 U.S. const. art. I, § 8, cl. 3.; Merges et al., *Intellectual Property, supra* at 734.

69 *See, e.g.,* Yochai Benkler, *Through The Looking Glass: Alice and The Constitutional Foundation of The Public Domain*, 66 L. & Contemp. Prob. 173, 175 n.10 (2003).

70 U.S. Const. art. I, § 8, cl. 8.

71 Limitations on the powers of Congress exist, however. *See, e.g., Goldstein v. California*, 412 U.S. 546, 561 (1973) (stating that the constitutional term "writings" refers to "any *physical rendering* of the fruits of creative intellectual or aesthetic labor", emphasis added). *See* for further details I Goldstein on Copyright, *supra* at § 2.0.

72 17 U.S.C. § 301(b). *See* for more details III Goldstein on Copyright, *supra* at § 17.

73 Please note that the directives may have been amended or corrected since their adoption and that some of the mentioned instruments codify preexisting directives.

- Directive 2001/29/EC of The European Parliament and of The Council of 22 May 2001 on The Harmonisation of Certain Aspects of Copyright and Related Rights in The Information Society, 2001 O.J. (L167) 10–19 (hereinafter: Copyright Directive).
- Directive 2001/84/EC of the European Parliament and of the Council of 27 September 2001 on the resale right for the benefit of the author of an original work of art, 2011 O.J. (L272) 32–36 (hereinafter: Resale Right Directive).
- Directive 2004/48/EC of the European Parliament and of the Council of 29 April 2004 on the enforcement of intellectual property rights, 2004 O.J. (L157) 45–86 (hereinafter: Enforcement Directive).
- Directive 2006/115/EC of the European Parliament and of the Council of 12 December 2006 on rental right and lending right and on certain rights related to copyright in the field of intellectual property, 2006 O.J. (L376) 28–35 (hereinafter: Rental & Lending Directive).
- Directive 2006/116/EC of the European Parliament and of the Council of 12 December 2006 on the term of protection of copyright and certain related rights, 2006 O.J. (L372) 12–18 (hereinafter: Term Directive).
- Directive 2009/24/EC of the European Parliament and of the Council of 23 April 2009 on the legal protection of computer programs, 2009 O.J. (L111) 16–22 (hereinafter: Software Directive).
- Directive 2012/28/EU of the European Parliament and of the Council of 25 October 2012 on certain permitted uses of orphan works, 2012 O.J. (L299) 5–12 (hereinafter: Orphan Works Directive).

In the present context, Directive 2014/26 of the European Parliament and of The Council of 24 February 2014 on Collective Management of Copyright and Related Rights and Multi-Territorial Licensing of Rights in Musical Works for Online Use in the Internal Market, 2014 O.J. (L84) 72–98. (hereinafter: Collective Management Directive or CMD) is cleary the most relevant.

The central source of copyright law in the United States is the federal Copyright Act of 1976[74] which replaced the federal Copyright Act of 1909 and became effective in 1978.[75]

4.3. Communication to the Public and Performance Rights

Performance rights are highly relevant to collective copyright management, especially with regard to musical works.[76] This is illustrated by that important

74 An Act for the General Revision of the Copyright Law, Title 17 of the United States Code, and for other purposes, Pub. L. No. 94-553, 90 Stat. 2541 (1976), as amended (hereinafter: U.S. Copyright Act).

75 17. U.S.C. § 301.

76 Al Kohn & Bob Kohn, *Kohn On Music Licensing* 1247 (4th ed. 2010) ("Of all the forms of using music [...] clearly the most common use is its *performance*").

U.S. CMOs like ASCAP or BMI (and also comparable English or Irish societies) are commonly referred to as performing rights organizations. Performance rights are recognized, to a lesser or greater extent, in both the EU and the U.S.

Article 3(1) of the Copyright Directive confers upon authors the exclusive right to prohibit or authorize the communication to the public[77] of their protectable works, by wire or wireless means. This right is understood in a broad sense, covering all communication where the public is "not present at the place where the communication originates".[78] Conversely, direct acts of communication – without any transmission to a remote place – have not been harmonized yet; hence, member states may enact their own rules in this respect.[79] The communication right under the Copyright Directive includes the right of making protected content available to the public. This "sub-right" refers to interactive uses[80] and aims at clarifying and harmonizing the legal qualification of uses in the online environment (*e.g.*, interactive on-demand transmissions).[81] Hence, the performance right applies to all forms of communications that involve a distance element (i.e. the public is gathered at a different place than

77 As this notion is not defined by the directive, the case law of the ECJ is especially important. The notion includes two cumulative criteria, first, an "act of communication", *see Staatlich genehmigte Gesellschaft der Autoren, Komponisten und Musikverleger registrierte Genossenschaft mbH v. Zürs.net Betriebs GmbH*, C-138/16, ¶ 23 (ECJ 2017) ("any transmission of the protected works, irrespective of the technical means or process used, and every transmission or retransmission of a work which uses a specific technical means must, as a rule, be individually authorised by the author of the work in question", citing prior case law), and second, the "public", *see Reha Training Gesellschaft für Sport- und Unfallrehabilitation mbH v. Gesellschaft für musikalische Aufführungs- und mechanische Vervielfältigungsrechte*, C-117/15, ¶ 41 (ECJ 2016) ("the term 'public' refers to an indeterminate number of potential recipients and implies, moreover, a fairly large number of persons", citing prior case law). *See also Ochranný svaz autorský pro práva k dílům hudebním o.s. v. Léčebné lázně Mariánské Lázně*, C-351/12, ¶ 33, 41 (ECJ 2014) (deeming a transmission of a signal to the individual rooms of a spa a communication to the public).

78 Copyright Directive recital 23. The recital reads in full: "This Directive should harmonise further the author's right of communication to the public. This right should be understood in a broad sense covering all communication to the public not present at the place where the communication originates. This right should cover any such transmission or retransmission of a work to the public by wire or wireless means, including broadcasting. This right should not cover any other acts". Further communication rights are set forth especially in article 2 of the Satellite & Cable Directive (broadcasting by satellite) and article 5(d) of the Database Directive (communication to the public of databases). As a general rule, the Copyright Directive leaves these directives unaffected, *see* Copyright Directive recital 20.

79 Von Lewinski & Walter, *Status of Harmonization*, *supra* at 1480; Copyright Directive recital 23. An exception can be found in the Database Directive's article 5(d) which expressly mentions public display and performance.

80 In the sense that "members of the public may access [the protected works] from a place and at a time individually chosen by them", *see* Copyright Directive art. 3(1).

81 *Id.* recital 25.

where the communication originates), like online transmissions, but also broadcasting (communication to the public in the broad sense).[82]

The U.S. right to public performance applies to "literary, musical, dramatic, and choreographic works, pantomimes, and motion pictures and other audiovisual works".[83] To "perform" a work, within the meaning of the U.S. Copyright Act, means to "recite, render, play, dance, or act it, either directly or by means of any device or process or, in the case of a motion picture or other audiovisual work, to show its images in any sequence or to make the sounds accompanying it audible."[84] This rather broad concept covers acts like (publicly)[85] singing a song, transmissions by broadcasters or retransmissions by cable television systems.[86] The U.S. Copyright Act does not, unlike the Copyright Directive, contain an explicit "making available right".[87] However, the different rights granted by section 106 can apply to the various circumstances in which copyright owners may want to control the access of their works online.[88] For example, offering a work for downloading can constitute an act of distribution;[89] and unauthorized "streaming" of music can violate the public performance right.[90]

---

82 Silke von Lewinski & Michel M. Walter, *Information Society Directive* in *European Copyright Law* 921, 981–982 (Michel M. Walter & Silke von Lewinski eds., 2010); von Lewinski & Walter, *Status of Harmonization*, *supra* at 1479–1480.

83 17 U.S.C. § 106(4).

84 17 U.S.C. § 101.

85 *See* for a definition what constitutes performing (or displaying) a work "publicly" 17 U.S.C. § 101. In general, the performance right bears a close relation to the right to public display. The U.S. display right applies to the same work categories, adding pictorial, sculptural and graphic works to its scope, *see* 17 U.S.C. § 106(5). However, showing a sequence of images falls within the scope of the performance right, *see* II Goldstein on Copyright, *supra* at § 7.10.

86 H.R. Rep No. 94-1476, at 63 (1976). *See also* II Goldstein on Copyright, *supra* at § 7.7.1.

87 *See* for the current state of U.S. law and recommendations in this respect United States Copyright Office, *The Making Available Right In The United States* (2016), *available at* https://www.copyright.gov/docs/making_available/making-available-right.pdf (last visited May 23, 2017).

88 *Id.* at 74. There remain, however, some inconsistencies in the application and interpretation of this section, *see id.* at 75–76.

89 II Goldstein on Copyright, *supra* at § 7.5.1. (noting a tendency to expand "the concept of public distribution to encompass a right to make copyrighted works available to the public, regardless of the transfer of copies or phonorecords"). *See* for more details Peter S. Menell, *In Search of Copyright's Lost Ark: Interpreting The Right to Distribute in The Internet Age*, 59 J. Cop. Soc. USA 1 (2011).

90 *See, e.g., Am. Broad. Cos. v. Aereo, Inc.*, 573 U.S. ___ (2014); Rebecca Giblin & Jane C. Ginsburg, *We (Still) Need to Talk About Aereo: New Controversies and Unresolved Questions After the Supreme Court's Decision*, 38 Colum. J. K. & Arts 109 (2015); U.S. Copyright Office, *Making Available Right*, *supra*, at 37–47. *See* for the definition of the term „transmit" 17 U.S.C. § 101.

4.4. Performers' Rights

The Copyright Directive confers upon performers the exclusive making available right with respect to the fixation of their performances;[91] consequently, they additionally possess the right to fixation of their performances.[92] It should, however, be noted that the right to communication to the public in the broad sense – as described above and set forth by the Copyright Directive – is as such not applicable to performers, but stipulated in a limited form in article 8 of the Rental & Lending Directives.[93] Under this rule, performers have the exclusive right to authorize or prohibit the broadcasting or communication of their performances to the public, unless "the performance is itself already a broadcast performance or is made from a fixation".[94]

While EU law often protects performers under the label "related rights",[95] U.S. law draws no conceptual difference to traditional copyrights in works of authorship and introduces "sound recordings"[96] as a separate work category.[97] While the performance right[98] applies to most work categories, sound recordings do not fall within the scope of this right.[99] Instead, the exclusive right to

---

[91] Copyright Directive art. 3(2)(a). The perfomers' exclusive right to reproduction of fixations of their performances is contained in the Coypright Directive's article 2(b). It should be noted that phonogram producers possess comparable rights, *see* Copyright Directive art. 2(c), 3(b).

[92] Rental & Lending Rights Directive art. 7(1).

[93] Von Lewinski & Walter, *Status of Harmonization, supra* at 1488. *See also* Satellite & Cable Directive art. 4.

[94] Rental & Lending Rights Directive art. 8(1). Article 8(2) of the same directive provides for a right to remuneration in this context, *see* section II.3.2.5. below.

[95] *See, e.g.,* title of the chapter II of the Rental & Lending Directive. Related rights (also neighboring rights, *droits voisins*) are conceptually based on labors and endeavors which are related to copyright but do not possess the necessary requirements, in particular originality, to fulfill the requirements of copyright protection or aim at providing and supply consumers with protected works, *see, e.g.,* Michel M. Walter, *Österreichisches Urheberrecht* 644 (2008). *See also* Gervais, *Theory and Practice, supra* at 3 n.1. The European directives acknowledge that performers carry out "creative and artistic" activities, *see, e.g.,* Copyright Directive recitals 10, 11; Rental & Lending Rights Directive recital 5; Directive 2011/77/EU of the European Parliament and of the Council of 27 September 2011 amending Directive 2006/116/EC on the term of protection of copyright and certain related rights recital 4, 2011 O.J. (L265) 15.

[96] These are "works that result from the fixation of a series of musical, spoken, or other sounds, but not including the sounds accompanying a motion picture or other audiovisual work, regardless of the nature of the material objects, such as disks, tapes, or other phonorecords, in which they are embodied", *see* 17 U.S.C. § 101. For example, an artist's recorded rendition of a song qualifies for a sound recording; however, the sound recording is distinct from the underlying song or the phonorecords, in which the performance is fixed, *see* I Goldstein on Copyright, *supra* at § 2.13.

[97] 17 U.S.C. §102(a)(7).

[98] 17 U.S.C. § 106(4).

[99] *Id.* at § 114(a). *Goldstein* speaks of the "second-class status that copyright jurisprudence has historically assigned to performers' rights", *see* II Goldstein on Copyright, *supra* at § 7.7.

perform sound recordings publicly refers to performances "by means of a digital audio transmission".[100] Hence, important uses – such as analog broadcasts and performances and non-transmitted performances (*e.g.*, by CD player in an establishment) – are not covered by this right.[101] New legislation referred to as the *Performance Right Act*, aiming at an expansion of the performance right in sound recordings, has been proposed, but not enacted for the time being.[102]

5. Emergence of Collective Management Organizations

The following section provides a brief overview of the first emergence of CMOs in Europe and the United States. Afterward, their historical similarities will be summarized. The regulatory developments at the EU level will be addressed in connection with the Collective Management Directive (*see* section II.1.1.4. below).

5.1. Emergence of Collective Management in France

The history of collective management can be traced back to 18th century France. At that time, French authors were in a weak position with regard to revenues for the use of their works, often being pressured to abandon their rights; in fact, actors were more powerful than the creators of the underlying language they performed within the *Comédie Française*.[103] Determined to change this situation and to ensure compensation for authors and writers, playwright *Pierre Augustin Caron de Beaumarchais* met with twenty fellow writers and established the first organization engaged in collective management in 1777, whose purpose was the collection of royalties in the entire country; this organization later became known as the Society of Dramatists and Dramatic Composers (*Société des Auteurs et Compositeurs Dramatiques – SACD*).[104] However, it was not until the frequently referenced events of the year 1847 that "fully-fledged" copyright collectives[105] emerged. In this year, the

See for the background and development of performance rights in sound recordings Lunney, *The United States Experience*, *supra* at 343–347.

100 17 U.S.C. § 106(6). *See* for the definition "digital audio tranismission" *id.* at § 114(j)(5) and § 101.

101 II Goldstein on Copyright, *supra* at § 7.7. *See* for an overview of the most important statutory licenses section II.3.2.5. below.

102 Mary La France, *From Whether to How: The Challenge of Implementing a Full Public Performance Right in Sound Recordings*, 2 Harv. J. Sports & Entertainment L. 221 (2011). *See also* Gary McIntyre, *The Performance Right Act: Radio Broadcasting Faces Major Challenge in Long Battle Against Music Licensing*, 17 J. Radio & Audio Media 135, 137 (2010).

103 Nathalie Piaskowski, *Collective Management in France* in *Collective Management of Copyright and Related Rights* 169, 171 (Daniel Gervais ed., 2nd ed. 2010).

104 *Id.*

105 Ficsor, *Collective Management, supra* at 19.

composer *Ernest Bourget* spent an evening at the café *Les Ambassadeurs* in Paris. He refused to settle the bill that charged an extra amount for the music pieces played in the café, which included his own compositions,[106] addressing the following to the restaurant staff: "You consume my music, I consume your beverages; property against property".[107] A couple of lawsuits arose from this dispute, in which the courts ultimately confirmed Bourget's performance rights based on a statute of 1791; this success eventually led to the foundation of SACEM (Société des Auteurs, Compositeurs et Éditeurs de Musique) in 1850–51.[108] Subsequently, further CMOs were founded in France.[109]

5.2. Emergence of Collective Management in Germany

More than fifty years after the founding of SACEM,[110] collective management emerged in Germany. In 1901, the new copyright act (LUG)[111] introduced a reformed version of the performance rights, which were available for authors to gain profit from their works. Interestingly, this act caused composers and publishers to abandon the plans to create a German CMO at first because important demands, like the extension of the term of protection to fifty years, had not been satisfied by the newly enacted legislation.[112] Their opinion changed when the Austrian Society of Authors, Composers and Music Publishers (*Gesellschaft der Autoren, Komponisten und Musikverleger – AKM*) revealed plans to extend its actions to Germany, precisely because a CMO had not come to existence in this country.[113] As a consequence, the Institute for Musical Performing Rights (*Anstalt für musikalisches Aufführungsrecht* – AFMA) and the Cooperative of German Composers (*Genossenschaft deutscher Tonsetzer – GDT*) were founded in 1903.[114] The famous composer *Richard Strauss* contributed significantly to this development.[115] In the following years, further CMOs in this field emerged, among them the Cooperative for the Administration of Musical Performance Rights (*Genossenschaft zur Verwertung musika-*

106 Piaskowski, *Collective Management in France, supra* at 171.

107 Martin Kretschmer, *Intellectual Property in Music: A Historical Analysis of Rhetorical and Institutional Practices*, 6 Studies in Cults., Orgs. and Socs. 197, 211 (2000).

108 *Id.*

109 Piaskowski, *Collective Management in France, supra* at 172.

110 *See* on the representation of German authors by French CMOs Jörg Reinbothe, *Collective Rights Management in Germany* in *Collective Management of Copyright and Related Rights* 205, 206–207 (Daniel Gervais ed., 3rd ed. 2016).

111 Gesetz betreffend das Urheberrecht an Werken der Literatur und Tonkunst (LUG) (Act on literary and musical works) of 19th of June 1901; published in [1901] RGBl 227–239.

112 Manuela Maria Schmidt et al., *Geschichte der musikalischen Verwertungsgesellschaften* in *Recht und Praxis der GEMA* 5, 12 (Reinhold Kreile et al. eds., 2nd ed. 2008).

113 *Id.*

114 *Id.* at 12–13.

115 Melchiar, *§ 45, supra* at ¶ 10; Reinbothe, *Management in Germany, supra* at 207; Lichtenegger, *Verwertungsgesellschaften, supra* at 37.

lischer Aufführungsrechte – GEMA) in 1915, and competition arose between these organizations.[116] Multiple CMOs in the same field were, however, considered to be unfavorable and confusing, especially for users.[117] For this reason, the existing organizations joined together and formed the Music Protection Association (*Musikschutzverband*) in 1930, thereby establishing a defacto monopoly.[118] German legislation followed the idea of a monopoly for collective management of copyright in 1933. Consequently, when GEMA and GDT merged, the resulting Authorized Society for the Adminstration of Copyright in Music (*Staatlich genehmigte Gesellschaft zur Verwertung musikalischer Urheberrechte – STAGMA*) was equipped with a legal monopoly under German copyright law.[119] Besides, the statutory action introduced further regulation and is generally referred to as STAGMA-act (*STAGMA-Gesetz*).[120] After 1945, the monopoly was abolished by the Allied Control Council and STAGMA was renamed into GEMA which is still active today.[121]

As reflected by the foregoing, the first German CMOs were all engaged in the field of music.[122] In 1926, a judgment by the German *Reichsgericht* confirmed that an unauthorized radio broadcast of a protected work infringed the author's exclusive rights.[123] A direct consequence of this ruling was the foundation of the Society for Broadcasting Rights (*Gesellschaft für Senderechte mbG*) which was the first CMO in Germany managing copyrights in literary works.[124] However, for the next decades, collective management in this field was rather unsuccessful, as a couple of subsequently established organizations went bankrupt.[125] In 1958, the *VG Wort* was founded. The organization could ultimately overcome its initial financial troubles, a development that was mainly due to a ruling of the German Supreme Court of 1962.[126] In this judgment, the court held that the public communication of literary works by means of television devices constituted copyright infringement.[127]

---

116 Reinbothe, *Vor §§ 1ff WahrnG*, *supra* at ¶ 2.

117 Melchiar, *§ 45*, *supra* at ¶ 11.

118 *Id.*

119 Reinbothe, *Vor §§ 1ff WahrnG*, *supra* at ¶ 4.

120 Schmidt et al., *Verwertungsgesellschaften*, *supra* at 19–20.

121 Reinbothe, *Vor §§ 1ff WahrnG*, *supra* at ¶ 4. *See* for the subsequent development Reinbothe, *Management in Germany*, *supra* at 209–211.

122 Martin Vogel, *Wahrnehmungsrecht und Verwertungsgesellschaften in der Bundesrepublik Deutschland – Eine Bestandsaufnahme im Hinblick auf die Harmonisierung des Urheberrechts in der Europäischen Gemeinschaft*, 95 GRUR 512, 513 (1993).

123 *Der Tor und der Tod*, German Imperial Court (Reichsgericht), 12.05.1926, Case I 287/25, Rgz 113, 413.

124 Thomas Gergen, *Die Verwertungsgesellschaft VG Wort – Genese und neue Herausforderungen*, 1 J. European History L. 14, 16 (2010).

125 Melchiar, *§ 45*, *supra* at ¶ 12–13.

126 *Id.*

127 *Fernsehwiedergabe von Sprachwerken,* German Supreme Court, 18 December 1962, Case I ZR 54/61, 65 GRUR 213 (1963).

5.3. Emergence of Collective Management in the United States

The oldest CMO in the United States is the American Society of Composers, Authors and Publishers (ASCAP). Its history began in 1913, when the composer *Victor Herbert* and his attorney, *Nathan Burkan*, met with several other composers and music publishers in New York to debate copyrights in the performance of protected works.[128] This meeting paved the way for the subsequent foundation of ASCAP in February 1914.[129] The first major success of the young organization was achieved before the U.S. Supreme Court three years later. Performance rights had been recognized under federal law since 1897; under the Copyright Act of 1909, the exclusive right only extended to public performances "for profit", an expression of which the exact meaning was unclear and thus fairly quickly led to legal disputes.[130] These cases centered on the question whether the public performance of musical works in restaurants for entertainment purposes constituted copyright infringement even though there was no separate charge for the music itself or a door charge to enter the restaurants.[131] The question was eventually answered by the Supreme Court's frequently cited ruling in *Herbert v. Shanley Co.*[132] The court held the restaurant's conduct to be inconsistent with the performance right stating that "if music did not pay, it would be given up. If it pays, it pays out of the public's pocket. Whether it pays or not, the purpose of employing it is profit and that is enough".[133] Thus, the live performance at the restaurant was "for profit" and therefore copyright infringement. The successful litigation for ASCAP continued in 1923 when performances via radio broadcast were held to be "for profit", even in absence of a charge for the program.[134] This development was extremely favorable for the organization. The revenues collected by ASCAP grew significantly over the course of the following years, leading to a market position that resembled a monopoly in the 1930s.[135] In 1931, the organization raised its fees by 300% followed by further increases throughout the decade.[136] This licensing policy resulted in a boycott of ASCAP's repertoire by radio broadcasters and further in the foundation of Broadcast Music, Inc. (BMI) in 1939, a CMO which since then has been competing with ASCAP.[137] Soon af-

---

128 Maria A. Pallante, *Comments on ASCAP's Birthday: ASCAP at 100*, 61 J. Copyright Soc'y 545, 547 (2014).

129 *Id.* at 548.

130 Lunney, *The United States Experience*, *supra* at 325.

131 *Id.*

132 *Herbert v. Shanley Co.*, 242 U.S. 591 (1917).

133 *Id.* at 595.

134 *M. Witmark & Sons v. L. Bamberger & Co*, 291 F. 776 (D.N.J. 1923); Pallante, *Comments*, *supra* at 548.

135 Michael A. Einhorn, *Intellectual Property and Antitrust: Music Performing Rights in Broadcasting*, 24 Colum.-VLA J. L. & Arts 349, 354–355 (2001).

136 McIntyre, *Performance Right Act*, *supra* at 139 (2010).

137 *Id.* at 139–141.

terward, both organizations were faced with antitrust challenges which could be settled by negotiating consent decrees.[138] The Society of European Stage Authors and Composers (nowadays only SESAC), had already come into existence in 1930 but had never been subject to a consent decree, because of its being relatively small.[139] The three CMOs mentioned so far were all founded to enforce and manage performance rights in musical works.[140] An example for a CMO engaged in different fields is the Copyright Clearance Center (CCC) which was established in 1978; its activities encompass the licensing of reproductive uses like photocopying.[141]

5.4. Common Developments

In reviewing the historical developments outlined above, it becomes clear that the first emergence of collective management in France, Germany and the United States was closely related to the introduction of performance rights.[142] This fits in with the theoretical framework of fragmentation as identified above. Yet, even though legislative action was a necessary prerequisite, it was not the only condition for the establishment of CMOs. It took the efforts of multiple persons committed to the intellectual creation and the improvement of the authors' status in their respective countries. These groups were spearheaded by well-known characters like *Ernest Bourget, Richard Strauss*, and *Victor Herbert*. However, the old stories revolving around the conception of CMOs run the risk of being nostalgically idealized.[143] In any event, one cannot deny the role that the courts played in this process. In the case of ASCAP, SACEM, and VG Wort, the judgments mentioned contributed largely to the establishment and/or to the further development of the organizations. The resemblance of some of the mentioned cases is conspicuous, especially in the example of Herbert and Bourget. Interestingly, the respective exclusive rights had already been enacted in the three national examples; however, they had yet to be enforced by litigation, and the courts were willing to interpret the laws in the copyright holders' favor. This was an important supplement to the legislative actions taken before.

138 *See* section II.1.2.2. below.

139 Einhorn, *Music Performing Rights*, *supra* at 354–355.

140 Lunney, *The United States Experience*, *supra* at 320.

141 *Id.* at 348.

142 *See also* Fedor Seifert et al., *Die Lizensierung* in *Recht und Praxis der GEMA* 749, 751 (Reinhold Kreile et al. eds., 2nd ed. 2008). *Lichtenegger* argues that the lack of a common European understanding of CMOs can be traced back to the foundation of CMOs against the background of legal and societal developments of that time in the different European nationalities, *see* Lichtenegger, *Verwertungsgesellschaften*, *supra* at 39–41.

143 *See* for the case of ASCAP Bennie L. De Whitt, *The American Society of Composers, Authors and Publishers 1914–1938* 10–12 (1977); McIntyre, *Performance Right Act*, *supra* at 137 (2010). *See* for inaccuracies in respect of the anecdotic tales on the emergence of CMOs in France, Lichtenegger, *Verwertungsgesellschaften*, *supra* at 36.

II. The Regulation of Collective Management Organizations

Collective management of copyrights in the United States and the European Union has never operated in a sphere free from legal obligation and responsibilities. However, some time elapsed before CMOs were first faced with the legal boundaries which accompany their activities, raising the awareness that such organizations can be harmful for the functioning of licensing markets and the interests of copyright holders if left fully unsupervised. Antitrust law doctrines have since served as the preeminent rules[144] governing the activities of CMO on both sides of the Atlantic, and they were thereby also applied as tools of regulation.[145] However, the manner and degree of their application, as well as the aims pursued, vary significantly in the United States and the EU. While the laws ensuring the proper functioning of the markets have been the only source of regulation for a long time, further obligations arise from other general principles as well as from specific legislation. The following section provides an overview of the regulatory frameworks in both jurisdictions; and afterward, the restrictions and obligations put on CMOs will be discussed in detail regarding their relations with right holders, users and other CMOs. Laws on merger control, although relevant for CMOs,[146] are not the focus of this thesis and will hence not be discussed.

---

[144] Ernst-Joachim Mestmäcker & Heike Schweitzer, *Europäisches Wettbewerbsrecht* 872 (2014) (stating that collective management is representative for the relation between antitrust and copyright law). While in the EU, one usually speaks of "competition law", the term "antitrust law" is more frequently used in the U.S. context. Hereinafter, the terms will be used synonymously.

[145] Scholars have distinguished the differences between legislative regulation and competition law, thereby creating the notion of "regulatory competition law". Its main characteristics are an administrative-technocratic enforcement (rather than an adversarial procedure) which is implemented *ex ante*, prescriptive competition law doctrines (in contrast to proscriptive measures), remedies which stipulate positive obligations and the tendency to optimizing the results instead of just prohibiting anti-competitive behavior, *see* Niamh Dunne, *Commitment Decisions in EU Competition Law*, 10 J. Comp. L. & Eco. 399, 411–432 (2014) (arguing that the use of commitment decision by the European Commission possesses regulatory features).

[146] Josef Drexl, Max Planck Institute for Intellectual Property and Competition Law, Munich, *Copyright, Competition and Development* 206–209 (2013), *available at* http://www.ip.mpg.de/fileadmin/ipmpg/content/forschung_aktuell/02_copyright_competition/report_copyright-competition-development_december-2013.pdf (last visited May 23, 2017). In this connection Council Regulation (EC) No 139/2004 of 20 January 2004 on the control of concentrations between undertakings (the EC Merger Regulation) 2004 O.J. (L24) 1–22 (hereinafter: Merger Regulation) is especially relevant. *See, e.g.,* for commitments imposed on PRSfM, GEMA and STIM in a proceeding under the Merger Regulation *PRSfM/STIM/GEMA/JV*, Commission Decision of 16.06.2015, case COMP/M.6800, art. 2 and Annex 1, *available at* http://ec.europa.eu/competition/mergers/cases/decisions/m6800_20150616_20600_4523168_EN.pdf (last visited May 22, 2017).

1. Regulatory Frameworks

1.1. EU Regulation

1.1.1. Primary Law

European CMOs frequently have had to deal with accusations made by the Commission under the competition rules set forth in the articles 101 and 102 of the TFEU.[147] While European law provides for an instrument similar[148] to the U.S. consent decrees – commitment decisions[149] –, this tool has not been of comparable importance in the context of collective management, even though it is frequently applied in other sectors.[150] Before the Competition Regulation was enacted, there was no comparable mechanism under EU law. However, settlements between the Commission and the defendant did occur[151] and the ECJ accepted the practice of the Commission to issue so-called "comfort letters" instead of formally closing a proceeding.[152] In the context of collective management, the Commission reached a settlement with GEMA, an important German CMO, for instance, one that caused the society to drop an appeal against one of the authority's decisions.[153] In the decision on the Cannes

---

147 The Commission is the authority competent to enforce EU competition law, *see* Council Regulation (EC) No 1/2003 of 16 December 2002 on the implementation of the rules on competition laid down in Articles 81 and 82 of the Treaty art. 4, 2003 O.J. (L1) 1–25 [hereinafter: Competition Regulation]. *See also* TEU art. 17, TFEU art. 337. The Berne Convention for The Protection of Literary and Artistic Works, Sept. 9, 1886, as revised at Paris on July 24, 1971 and amended in 1979, Treaty Doc. No. 99–27 (1986), does not foreclose the the application of European competition law to CMOs, *see* Christoph Wünschmann, *Die kollektive Verwertung von Urheber- und Leistungsschutzrechten nach europäischem Wettbewerbsrecht* 52, 54 (2000).

148 *See, e.g.,* Daniel P. Ducore, *Settlement of Competition Conduct Violations At The United States Antitrust Agencies And At The European Commission – Some Observations* in *Annual Proceedings of the Fordham Corporate Law Institute* 227 (Barry E. Hawk ed., 2006); Giovanna Massarotto, *The Detterrent and Enunciating Effects Of Consent Decrees*, 11 Comp. L. & Econ. 493 (2015); Wouter P.J. Wils, *The Use of Settlements in Public Antitrust Enforcement: Objectives and Principles* 7 (2008), *available at* https://papers.ssrn.com/sol3/papers.cfm?abstract_id=1135627 (last visited May 23, 2017).

149 Competition Regulation art. 9.

150 Heike Schweitzer, *Commitment Decisions in the EU and in the Member States: Functions and risks of a new instrument of competition law enforcement within a federal enforcement regime* 2 (2012), *available at* https://papers.ssrn.com/sol3/papers.cfm?abstract_id=2101630 (last visited May 23, 2017).

151 Dunne, *Commitment Decisions, supra* at 402; Wouter P.J. Wils, *Settlements of EU Antitrust Investigations: Commitment Decisions under Article 9 of Regulation No 1/2003* 4–6, 23 (2006), *available at* https://papers.ssrn.com/sol3/Papers.cfm?abstract_id=900801 (last visited May 23, 2017).

152 *See, e.g., Marty v. Lauder*, case 37/79 (ECJ 1980).

153 Anke Schierholz, *Collective Rights Management in Europe – Practice and Legal Framework* in *European Copyright Law* 1145, 1158–1159 (Michel M. Walter & Silke von Lewinski eds., 2010). *See* on the GEMA cases especially section 3.1.below. Another example is

Extension Agreement, the Commission accepted commitments offered by the parties.[154] In many other cases, however, EU authorities have relied on "traditional" antitrust proceedings, which typically end in the finding of an antitrust violation. Starting in 1971, an evolving body of case law, consisting of decisions of the European Commission, the General Court (formerly Court of First Instance), and the ECJ, has formed the legal framework of collective management, which however has not clarified all questions in detail. Furthermore, CMOs[155] and their regulation on the national level must comply with the freedoms guaranteed in the TFEU, like the free movement of goods and the freedom to provide services.[156]

1.1.2. The Services Directive[157]

The question whether and to what extent Directive 2006/123/EC[158] on services in the Internal Market applies to CMOs has been a source of controversy.

the CISAC case, where CISAC offered commitments, but the case did eventually result in a settlement, *see* Schierholz, *Collective Rights* Management, *supra* at 1181.

154 *Cannes Extension Agreement*, Commission Decision of 04.10. 2006, COMP/C2/38.681, ¶ 49–50, *available at* http://ec.europa.eu/competition/antitrust/cases/dec_docs/38681/38681_216_1.pdf (last visited May 22, 2017). *See also Notice published pursuant to Article 27(4) of Council Regulation (EC) No 1/2003 in Cases COMP/C2/39152 — BUMA and COMP/C2/39151 SABAM (Santiago Agreement — COMP/C2/38126)* ¶ 6, 2005 O.J. (C200) 11–12, ¶ 8–12.

155 *See* for the direct applicability of the freedoms to CMOs Lichtenegger, *Verwertungsgesellschaften, supra* at 94–96.

156 *See, e.g.,* G. *Basset v. Societé Des Auteurs, Compositeurs Et Èditeurs De Musique*, case 402/85, ¶ 17 (ECJ 1987) (freedom of goods); *OSA*, C-351/12 at ¶ 78 (freedom to provide services). *See also* Josef Drexl, *Collective Management of Copyrights and the EU Principle of Free Movement of Services after the* OSA *Judgment – In Favour of a More Balance Approach* in *Varieties of European Economic Law and Regulation* 459 (Kai Purnhagen & Peter Rott eds., 2014). *See* on the applicability of article 18 of the TFEU to CMOs section 3.1.1. below. *See* on the freedom to provide services section 1.1.5.

157 A further directive sometimes discussed in connection with CMOs is Directive 2000/31/EC of the European Parliament and of the Council of 8 June 2000 on certain legal aspects of information society services, in particular electronic commerce, in the Internal Market, 2000 O.J. (L178) 1–16. *See* for details Lichtenegger, *Verwertungsgesellschaften, supra* at 137–139 (rejecting the applicability in principle). In turn, CMD art. 42 confirms the applicability of Directive 95/46/EC of the European Parliament and of the Council of 24 October 1995 on the protection of individuals with regard to the processing of personal data and on the free movement of such data, 1995 O.J. (L281) 31–50. As of 2018, this directive will be replaced by Regulation (EU) 2016/679 of the European Parliament and of the Council of 27 April 2016 on the protection of natural persons with regard to the processing of personal data and on the free movement of such data, and repealing Directive 95/46/EC (General Data Protection Regulation) art. 94(2), 2016 O.J. (L119) 1–88.

158 Directive 2006/123/EC of the European Parliament and of the Council of 12 December 2006 on services in the internal market, 2006 O.J. (L376) 36–68 [hereinafter: Services Directive]. According to its article 1, the directive aims at "facilitating the exercise of the freedom of establishment for service providers and the free movement of services, while maintaining a high quality of services".

If this was the case, the validity of national models of regulation of collective management,[159] which have been implemented to a greater or lesser degree by EU member states, could be challenged regarding their being consistent with the freedom of establishment and the free movement of services specified in chapters III and IV of the said directive. Regarding the first, member states may only make the access to or the exercise of a service activity subject to authorization schemes, where such schemes are justified by overriding reasons of the public interest, where they are non-discriminatory, and where their objective cannot be achieved by less restrictive measures.[160] While the public interest covers the protection of intellectual property,[161] it is uncertain whether national regulation laws comply with the other two requirements.[162] Regarding the free movement of services, the directive urges national governments to provide only for "requirements"[163] in respect of the access to or the exercise of service activities in case they are non-discriminatory, necessary and proportional.[164] Because the notion "necessity" covers only reasons of public policy, public security, public health or the protection of the environment and since CMOs are often justified by their economic benefits as they ensure efficient copyright management, it is more than questionable whether national regulation schemes dealing with collective management would comply with this clause.[165]

The discussion also centered on the interpretation of the derogation clauses contained in the Services Directive, especially because "copyrights and neighboring rights" are expressly exempted from the application of article 16.[166] The European Commission was undoubtedly of the opinion that the foregoing article applied to CMOs, a view that the authority reiterated on several occasions.[167] Most importantly, the Commission's opinion was included in the pro-

---

159 *See, e.g.,* Robert Heine & Sonja Eisenberg, *Verwertungsgesellschaften im Binnenmarkt – Die Kollektive Wahrnehmung von Urheberrechten nach der Dienstleistungsrichtlinie*, 58 GRUR Int. 277 (2009).

160 Services Directive art. 9.

161 Services Directive recital 40.

162 Thomas Riis, *Collecting Societies, Competition and the Services Directive*, 6 J. Intellectual Property L. & Pract. 482, 490 (2011).

163 According to article 4(7) of the Services Directive, the term "requirement" encompasses "any obligation, prohibition, condition or limit provided for in the laws, regulations or administrative provisions of the Member States or in consequence of case-law, administrative practice, the rules of professional bodies, or the collective rules of professional associations or other professional organisations, adopted in the exercise of their legal autonomy". The evaluation of national requirements should be carried out according to the freedom of establishment and does not concern European competition law, *see id.* recital 69.

164 Services Directive art. 16(1).

165 Riis, *Collecting Societies*, *supra* at 490; Heine & Eisenberg, *Verwertungsgesellschaften*, *supra at* 282.

166 Services Directive art. 17(11).

167 Commission of the European Communities, *Handbook on Implementation of the Services Directive* 42 (2007), *available at* http://bookshop.europa.eu/en/handbook-on-implementation-

posal for the Collective Management Directive.[168] However, the recital was not incorporated into the final version of the directive. While this fact by itself does not allow a conclusive inference of the non-applicability of article 16, scholars have convincingly noted that from an article that regulates services, only services can be exempted and that the exemption regarding copyright thus covers the associated collective management services;[169] moreover the application of the said directive could lead to a regulatory vacuum due to its effects on national regulation schemes.[170] Eventually, the ECJ considered the question in its *OSA* decision.[171] First of all, the court confirmed that CMOs provide services within the meaning of the directive (and TFEU art. 56).[172] In upholding the opinion of the Advocate General,[173] the judges ruled that the exception contained in article 17 applied to collective management services; thus, it is now clarified that article 16 does not apply to CMOs.[174] The court went on to consider the case in the light of EU primary law (art. 56 TFEU). This is not

---

of-the-services-directive-pbKM7807096/ (last visited May 23, 2017); European Commission, *Commission Staff Working Document Impact Assessment Accompanying The Document Proposal for a Directive of The European Parliament and of The Council on Collective Management of Copyright and Related Rights and Multi-Territorial Licensing of Rights in Musical Works for Online Uses in the Internal Market* 11 n. 43 (2012) http://eur-lex.europa.eu/legal-content/EN/TXT/?uri=CELEX:52012SC0204 (last visited May 23, 2017). Some commentators joined the Commission in arguing in favor of the applicability, *see, e.g.*, Robert Heine, *Wahrnehmung von Online-Musikrechten durch Verwertungsgesellschaften im Binnenmarkt* 252–253 (2008); Heine & Eisenberg, *Verwertungsgesellschaften*, *supra at* 280 (both arguing that proposed amendments which would have expressly excluded CMOs from the directive's scope were not incorporated into the final directive). *See also* Johan Axhamn & Lucie Guibault, *Cross-border extended collective licensing: a solution to online dissemination of Europe's cultural heritage?* 55–56 (2011), *available at* https://www.ivir.nl/publicaties/download/292 (last visited May 23, 2017).

168 Propsal 2012 at recital 3. The provision reads: "When established in the Union, collecting societies – as service providers – must comply with the national requirements pursuant to Directive 2006/123/EC of the European Parliament and of the Council of 12 December 2006 on services in the internal market which seeks to create a legal framework for ensuring the freedom of establishment and the free movement of services between the Member States. This implies that collecting societies should be free to provide their services across borders, to represent rightholders resident or established in other Member States or grant licences to users resident or established in other Member States". *See also* annex 2 of the proposal.

169 Riis, *Collecting Societies*, *supra* at 491. Other scholars are of different opinion, *see, e.g.*, Lucie Guibault, *Collective Rights Management Directive* in *EU copyright law* 696, 720 (Irinia A. Stamatoudi & Paul Torremans eds., 2014) ("Although the final text of the [Collective Management] Directive no longer explicitly refers to the Directive 2006/123/EC […], it is reasonable to think that services offered in the Member States should be in accordance with the principles of that Directive […]"). *See also* Drexl, *Free Movement of Services*, *supra at* 460.

170 Drexl et al., *Comments of the MPI*, *supra* at 17.

171 *OSA*, C-351/12.

172 *Id.* at ¶ 57–63. The term "service" is defined in article 4(1) of the Services Directive.

173 *Ochranný svaz autorský pro práva k dílům hudebním o.s. v. Léčebné lázně Mariánské Lázně a.s.*, C-351/12 (ECJ 2014), Opinion of AG Sharpston, ¶ 61–64.

174 *OSA*, C-351/12 at ¶ 64–66.

surprising because, already prior to the *OSA*, scholars had highlighted that in this respect, the inapplicability of the Service Directive left the broad scope of the EU treaties without prejudice.[175] However, the court did not expressly address the question whether the other parts of the Services Directive (*e.g.*, article 9) applied to CMOs. It can be inferred from this opinion that the ECJ implicitly accepted the AG's view that CMOs do not provide non-economic services of general interest and are thus not exempted from the scope of the entire directive according to article 2(2)(a), because, even though many CMOs follow a non-profit principle, they still have to cover staff and administrative costs and hence require remuneration.[176] If the ECJ had not agreed with this opinion, the court would not have had to deal with a specific derogation clause such as article 17(11). According to this reading of the decision, CMOs are not exempted from the Services Directive by article 2(2)(a).[177] It has been argued that CMOs can be exempted from scope of the directive by virtue of article 1(2) which excludes the liberalization of "services of general economic interest" because these organizations act on a non-profit basis, often follow cultural and social purposes, and provide licensing solutions on a repertoire scale for users.[178] This line of argumentation is, on the one hand, supported by OSA in that it was implicitly confirmed that CMOs provide economic services (even though acting on a not-for-profit basis related to cultural and social functions might point in another direction). On the other hand, again, if the ECJ had deemed CMOs excluded from the directive, there would have been no need for interpreting the special derogation clauses. Furthermore, article 1(2), must be construed in light of TFEU art. 106(2);[179] yet the ECJ has repeatedly refused to apply this provision to CMOs.[180] It also seems debatable whether the services offered by CMOs, regardless of their unquestioned importance for the creative sector, are comparable to the examples enumerated in article 17 which employs the same expression as article 1(2).[181] This list is not of an exhaustive nature, but nevertheless – also for the purposes of the latter provision – might give an insight into the importance of the services covered by this expression. Last, if one makes a decisive criterion of whether a CMO operates on a non-profit basis, CMOs that aim at achieving profits, either as "collective management organizations" or "independent management entities"[182] within the mean-

175 *See, e.g.*, Drexl et al., *Comments of the MPI*, *supra* at 18.

176 *OSA*, C-351/12, Opinion of AG Sharpston at ¶ 59.

177 However, admittedly, the question referred was limited to the Services Directive's article 16.

178 Anita Huss-Eckerhult, *Collective Management Organisations (CMOs) at the Intersection Between EU Competition Law and the Freedom to Provide Services*, 7 Int. In-House Counsel J. 1, 6 (2014).

179 Christian Calliess & Stefan Korte, *Dienstleistungsrecht in der EU* 294 (2011).

180 *See* section 2.1.6. below.

181 According to article 17(1), services of general economic interest encompass, *inter alia*, the electricity sector, the gas sector and water distribution.

182 CMD art. 3(a), (b). *See* for these terms subsection 1.1.4.e) below.

ing of the Collective Management Directive, would possibly fall within the scope of the Services Directive. As a consequence, national regulation of such CMOs would be under stricter scrutiny from a European law perspective (with the effect that national schemes would have to be adapted and most likely liberalized). It has to be questioned whether this result is fully coherent, especially in the case a for-profit CMO is owned by its members; in this respect, the Collective Management Directive, at least, does not differentiate between CMOs.

1.1.3. General Copyright-Related Directives

Several EU directives that deal with copyrights make references to collective management. The Copyright Directive, for instance, stipulates in its recitals that CMOs should achieve a higher level of "rationalization and transparency with regard to compliance with competition";[183] it is, however, silent on what measures are to be taken by the member states in order to achieve this aim. While provisions of this kind do not carry substantial normative content on their own, they show that collective management is presupposed by EU law and that the existence of CMOs is regarded as an integral element of the copyright system.[184] Further directives expressly clarify that it is up to the member states whether specific legislation should be enacted regarding collective management[185] or emphasize that collective management services should at least be available for right holders.[186] In this respect, the Satellite and Cable Directive is of a distinct (and exceptional)[187] nature, as it sets forth rules that are binding and precise for the administration of the cable retransmission right. Under this regime, member states are obliged to introduce mandatory collective management schemes; this means that only CMOs can grant or refuse to license said right.[188] The directive also contains a definition of the term "collecting society".[189] The Enforcement Directive grants "intellectual property collective rights-management bodies" (i.e. CMOs) the right to apply for enforce-

---

183 Copyright Directive recital 17. Recital 26 of the same directive states that collective licensing arrangements in respect of the making available in on-demand services "are to be encouraged".

184 Schierholz, *Collective Rights Management*, *supra* at 1165.

185 Satellite and Cable Directive art. 3(2), 13; Rental and Lending Rights Directive art. 5(4); Orphan Works Directive recitals 4, 24; Resale Right Directive recitals 28, 30, art. 6(2). *See also* Copyright Directive recital 18. *See also* Schierholz, *Collective Rights Management*, *supra* at 1165–1166 (stating that the resale directive includes a "strong, implicit recommendation for collective rights management").

186 Rental and Lending Rights Directive recital 12, art. 5(3).

187 Ficsor, *International Treaties*, *supra* at 54 (arguing that mandatory collective management is exceptionally permitted under EU law in accordance with international copyright law).

188 Satellite and Cable Directive art. 9. Collective management is not mandatory for the own broadcast of a broadcasting organization, *see id.* at art. 10. *See also* Term Directive art. 3(2d), as amended.

189 Satellite and Cable Directive art. 1(4). *See* section I.3. above.

ment measures, procedures, and remedies, which the directive sets forth in its chapter 2.[190] These encompass, *inter alia*, a right of information, injunctions, and the availability of damages.[191]

It is obvious that the mentioned directives are far from creating a comprehensive legal framework since they either contain very general provisions or are very limited in scope. In light of the fragmentary legislation summarized above and its insufficient supplement through competition case law, it is not surprising that efforts were made with the aim of introducing more detailed rules throughout the EU, which eventually led to the adoption of the Collective Management Directive in 2014.[192]

1.1.4. Sector-Specific Regulation: Collective Management Directive

For a long time, the slowly evolving case law of the European Courts and the European Commission in exercise of the competition rules contained in EU primary law and the sparse references made by some directives were the prevailing sources for the regulation of CMOs.[193] This situation changed with the adoption of the Collective Management Directive in 2014. The directive is the outcome of legislative efforts on the EU level during a period of almost twenty years.

a) Background and Development

First references to collective management can be found in the Green Paper on Copyright and Related Rights in the Information Society published by the European Commission in 1995.[194] Two years later and in response, the European Parliament stated that the "the practice of centralized administration should be encouraged and the role of collecting societies should be safeguarded [...]".[195] In 2003, a report of the European Parliament[196] was published, which became known by the name of its rapporteur, the *Echerer* Report.[197]

190 Enforcement Directive recital 18, art. 4(c).

191 *Id.* at art. 8, 11, 13.

192 *See* for development and the drafting history of the directive section 1.1.4.a) below.

193 Guibault, *Collective Management Directive*, *supra* at 698.

194 Commission of the European Communities, *Green Paper of 27 July 1995 on Copyright and Related Rights in the Information Society* 26–28 COM(1995) 382 final, *available at* http://eur-lex.europa.eu/legal-content/EN/TXT/PDF/?uri=CELEX:51995DC0382&from=EN (last visited May 23, 2017).

195 Minutes of the Sitting of Thursday 23 October 1997 169, 1997 O.J. (C339) 86–404.

196 Raina A. Mercedes Echerer, Committee on Legal Affairs and the Internal Market, European Parliament, *Report on a Community Framework for Collecting Societies for Authors Rights* (2002/2274(INI)) (2003), *available at* http://www.europarl.europa.eu/sides/getDoc.do?pubRef=-//EP//NONSGML+REPORT+A5-2003-0478+0+DOC+PDF+V0//EN (last visited May 23, 2017).

197 Schierholz, *Collective Rights Management, supra* at 1167–1168.

The report must be put in the context of the discussion of DRM systems because the parliament saw the danger that, by industry lobbying, CMOs might be weakened by the introduction of these systems to the detriment of authors and right holders.[198] Thus, the document acknowledged that CMOs played an important role in fostering creativity as well as cultural and linguistic diversity.[199] It also recognized the importance of CMOs as intermediaries and emphasized the importance of a balance between artists and users.[200] However, the state of legislation was considered to be unsatisfactory, which is why the report called for action on the EU level.[201] The Commission[202] reacted with a communication in 2004.[203] In contrast to the *Echerer Report*, it is of rather technical and legal nature offering an analysis of and the authority's opinion on several important issues like DRM systems, individual rights management, and the functions of CMOs as well as associated implications of competition law.[204] It should be noted that the Commission carefully considered the issue of Union-wide licensing.[205] It made positive remarks regarding the traditional system of reciprocal representation, stating that CMOs did "already provide for a one-stop-shop [...]. This constitute[d] a significant advantage for right-holders and users alike and should not be jeopardised. [C]entralised licensing arrangements [...] could be fostered by eliminating further any disparities in Member States' laws [...]".[206] However, the Commission highlighted the necessity to provide for harmonized rules and conditions on collective rights management.[207] It was emphasized that the control of CMOs by competition law was, even though it constituted an effective instrument, not sufficient in order to achieve the most efficient outcomes; this control should be complemented by a framework of good governance.[208] Therefore, the authority enumerated four main aspects that were deemed necessary to be made subject to

198 *Id.* at 1167.

199 Echerer, *Report*, *supra* at 8.

200 *Id.* at 8–9.

201 The explanatory statement of the report enumerated and elaborated several points in which actions were most urgent, like the organizational form of CMOs, supervision, their internal structure, reciprocal agreements and transparency, *see* Echerer, *Report*, *supra* at 17–19.

202 The Commission possesses the right of legislative initiative, *see* TFEU art. 17(2).

203 Commission of the European Communities, *Communication from the Commission to the Council, the European Parliament and the European Economic and Social Committee The Management of Copyright and Related Rights in the Internal Market* COM(2004) 261 final, *available at* http://eur-lex.europa.eu/legal-content/EN/TXT/PDF/?uri=CELEX:52004DC0261&from=ENpoint (last visited May 23, 2017).

204 Lucie Guibault & Stef van Gompel, Collective Management in the European Union in *Collective Management of Copyright and Related Rights* 135, 151–153 (Daniel Gervais ed., 2nd ed. 2010).

205 Communication 2004 at 8–9.

206 *Id.* at 9. The Echerer Report had dealt with this issue more briefly, *see* Echerer, *Report*, *supra* at. 11, 16, 18, 21.

207 Communication 2004 at 5.

208 *Id.* at 17–19.

legislative action at the EU level. The establishment of CMOs should follow similar rules in all member states because they fulfill economic, cultural and social functions; the management of copyright in respect to users should be transparent, subject to review procedure, and licensing agreements should be based on appropriate conditions; the relation of CMOs to right holders should be governed by the principles of transparency, good governance, non-discrimination, and accountability in light of the acquisition of rights, membership rules, etc.; finally, external control of CMOs should be available in all member states and harmonized in order to avoid distortions of the Internal Market.[209] A consequence of the Commission's actions was a code of conduct to which many CMOs have committed themselves, holding up the principles of good governance, non-discrimination, transparency, and accountability.[210]

The developments accelerated after 2004. In the year following, the Commission published three interrelated documents[211] which had a significant impact on the European licensing market. The remarks made by the Commission are mainly based on the impact of online technology on the licensing market in which music was considered to be "at the forefront of online development".[212] The Commission stressed that, with regard to cross-border collective management services, a dynamic and fully efficient market had not yet developed[213] and argued that this was due to that commercial users faced difficulties in obtaining cross-border grants of licenses and that the distribution of royalties across national borders did not work in an optimal manner.[214] The Commission reflected on three possible options: first, not taking any action; second, eliminating territorial restrictions and discriminatory provisions in the reciprocal representation agreements concluded between CMOs; and third, giving right-holders the choice to authorize CMOs of their choice to manage their online rights for the entire EU.[215] Option three was regarded as the best

---

209 *Id.* at 18–19.

210 Schierholz, *Collective Rights Management, supra* at 1172.

211 Commission of the European Communities, *Commission Staff Working Document Study on a Community Initiative on the Cross-border Collective Management of Copyright* (2005), *available at* http://ec.europa.eu/internal_market/copyright/docs/management/study-collective mgmt_en.pdf (last visited May 23, 2017); Commission of the European Communities, *Staff Working Document Impact Assessment Reforming Cross-Border Collective Management of Copyright and Related Rights for Legitimate Online Music Services* SEC(2005) 1254, *available at* http://ec.europa.eu/internal_market/copyright/docs/management/sec_2005_1254_en.pdf (last visited May 23, 2017); Commission Recommendation of 18 May 2005 on collective cross border management of copyright and related rights for legitimate online music services, 2005 O.J. (L276) 54–57. Recommendation 2005 contains a wrong date, *see* Corrigendum to Commission Recommendation 2005/737/EC of 18 May 2005 on collective cross-border management of copyright and related rights for legitimate online music service, 2005 O.J. (L284) 10.

212 Impact assessment 2005 at 5.

213 Study 2005 at 6–7.

214 *Id.* at 9–14.

215 *Id.* at 33–36.

the solution, whereas option one was rejected because users would not be able to choose the CMO which grants the licenses.[216] Regarding the second option, the Commission argued that, while EU action could improve the existing system of reciprocal agreements to a certain extent, it would not ensure that CMOs actively compete for the business of right holders or that varied repertoires would be offered.[217] In contrast, option three was most effective in the Commission's view, because it would, in departing from the traditional reciprocal agreements and thereby abolishing the intermediary organization, create a competitive environment for the cross-border licensing market in which right holders could benefit from faster and less costly administration as well as more innovative services.[218] Building on this basis and only a week after the publication of the Impact Assessment 2005, the Commission issued the Recommendation 2005. This document basically sums up what had already been contained in rulings of the ECJ and the Commission (non-discrimination against members, etc.), other publications of the latter authority, codes of conduct of various umbrella organizations of CMOs (distribution, accountability, etc.) as well as what had been self-evident and already practiced.[219] As indicated by the title, the Commission decided to take action first in the online music sector, because realizing option three in relation to offline uses was considered to be achievable only in the long-term;[220] thus, this recommendation arguably represents the first step toward a comprehensive alteration of collective management in Europe as such. In expanding the implications of option three in the previous documents, the Commission strived to eliminate the system of reciprocal representation agreements.[221] The core reasoning was that right holders should be put in a position that will allow them to define the territory for which they mandate CMOs as well as permitting them to directly grant licenses in a chosen territory without intermediary organizations, and this would ultimately lead to Union-wide competition between CMOs.[222] The Recommendation 2005 was heavily criticized in the legal literature.[223] First of all, commen-

216 *Id.* at 34.

217 *Id.* at 34–35.

218 *Id.* at 35, 54.

219 Schierholz, *Collective Rights Management, supra* at 1179–1180.

220 Study 2005 at 54–55; Recommendation 2005 at point 1(f) and point 2.

221 Recommendation 2005 point 5(d) reads: "where a right-holder has transferred the management of an online right to another collective rights manager, without prejudice to other forms of cooperation among rights managers, all collective rights managers concerned should ensure that those online rights are withdrawn from any existing reciprocal representation agreement concluded amongst them."

222 Schierholz, *Collective Rights Management, supra* at 1180.

223 *See, e.g., id.* at 1184–1185; Josef Drexl, *Auf dem Weg zu einer neuen europäischen Marktordnung der kollektiven Wahrnehmung von Online Rechten der Musik? – Kritische Würdigung der Kommissionsempfehlung vom 18. Oktober 2005* in *Wahrnehmungsrecht in Polen, Deutschland und Europa* 193 (Karl Riesenhuber ed., 2006); Lucie Guibault & Stef van Gompel, Collective Management in the European Union in *Collective Management of Copyright and Related Rights* 139, 165–166 (Daniel Gervais ed., 3rd ed. 2016); Christoph B. Gra-

tators expressed concerns that the cultural diversity in Europe could be threatened. Unlike in the case of mainstream music, management of less popular repertoires could become more expensive due to a lower demand which could result in lower remuneration for right holders or, even worse, the access to such contents could altogether become harder so that it could not be used at all.[224] In this context, users might face higher search costs under the model of the Commission.[225] Moreover, the Commission uniformly spoke of right holders, not distinguishing between creative artists like composers and those that acquired the copyrights from them (like music publishers).[226] In general, the document did not follow the principles set out by the Communication 2004 in two ways: On the one hand, by choosing a non-binding recommendation, a true legislative framework was not created; on the other hand, it failed to propose comprehensive solutions, as it only applied to the online environment.[227]

In the aftermath of the Recommendation 2005, it was time for the European Parliament to react. Two resolutions[228] expressed fierce criticism against the Commission's actions by producing an entire list of perceived shortcomings. The Parliament accused the Commission of having circumvented the democratic process by failing to undertake an adequate consultation process and by not formally involving the Parliament.[229] Indeed, starting a short three-week consultation process in the middle of the holiday season could not be regarded as adequate.[230] The Parliament went on to state that the Commission had created legal uncertainty due to a lack of clear wording and that collective management required a flexible framework created by a directive, not mere soft-law.[231] Moreover, the existing system of reciprocal representation agree-

---

ber, *Collective Rights Management, Competition Policy and Cultural Diversity: EU Lawmaking at a Crossroads,* 4 W.I.P.O.J. 35 (2012); Pavel Tuma, *Pitfalls and Challenges of the EC Directive of Collective Management of Copyright and Related Rights*, 2006 E.I.P.R. 220.

224 Schierholz, *Collective Rights Management, supra* at 1184–1185; Tuma, *Pitfalls and Challenges*, *supra* at 228.

225 Josef Drexl, *Collecting Societies and Competition Law* 11–12 (2007), http://www.ip.mpg.de/shared/data/pdf/drexl_-_crmos_and_competition.pdf (last visited April 16, 2015).

226 Graber, *Collective Rights Management, supra* at 39–40.

227 Guibault & van Gompel, *Collective Management 2010, supra* at 156.

228 European Parliament resolution of 13 March 2007 on the Commission Recommendation of 18 October 2005 on collective cross-border management of copyright and related rights for legitimate online music services (2005/737/EC), doc. no. P6_TA(2007)0064, *available at* http://www.europarl.europa.eu/sides/getDoc.do?pubRef=-//EP//TEXT+TA+P6-TA-2007-0064+0+DOC+XML+V0//EN (last visited May 23, 2017); European Parliament resolution of 25 September 2008 on collective cross-border management of copyright and related rights for legitimate online music services, doc. no. P6_TA(2008)0462, *available at* http://www.europarl.europa.eu/sides/getDoc.do?pubRef=-//EP//TEXT+TA+P6-TA-2008-0462+0+DOC+XML+V0//EN (last visited May 23, 2017).

229 Resolution 2007 at points A-C, F.

230 Schierholz, *Collective Rights Management, supra* at 1178.

231 Resolution 2007 at point C.

ments should be preserved.[232] Despite all critical comments, the Commission confirmed its competition-oriented strategy in the *CISAC*[233] case.[234] Again, the authority faced harsh criticism.[235] In 2013, the General Court reversed important parts of the Commission's decision.[236]

The Commission responded to the criticism by publishing the Proposal 2012 which was accompanied by the Impact Assessment 2012. The draft directive contained general rules on transparency, membership and rights of right holders, the internal structure of CMOs and their relations to users as well as collection and distribution of royalties (title II).[237] Moreover, title III[238] introduced a model system for multi-territorial licensing – the "European licensing passport".[239] It should be noted that the proposal did not prohibit reciprocal agreements as such.[240] Legal writings generally welcomed the Commission's initiative to introduce binding rules on collective management but suggested several changes and raised a number of concerns. Among these were that the Commission, again, did not adequately take the non-economic functions of CMOs into account and that it did not distinguish between the different groups of right holders.[241] In general, many provisions – especially those contained in title II – were considered to be too vague, and it was argued that more detailed substantive criteria would be required.[242] Since the draft directive proposed minimum standards, it was feared that CMOs in member states providing for a higher degree of control might face disadvantages in the Internal

232 *Id.* at point N, O.

233 *CISAC Agreement,* Commission Decision of 16.07.2008, Case COMP/C2/38.698, *available at* http://ec.europa.eu/competition/antitrust/cases/dec_docs/38698/38698_4567_1.pdf (last visited May 22, 2017).

234 Adriane Porcin, *The Quest for Pan-European Copyright Licensing Solutions: A Series of Unfortunate Events*, 2009 Concurrences 57, 60.

235 *See, e.g.,* Resolution 2008.

236 *International Confederation of Societies of Authors and Composers v. Commission,* Case T-442/08 (EGC 2013). *See* section 3.3.5. for more details.

237 Proposal 2012 at art. 4–20.

238 *Id.* at art. 21–33.

239 Impact Assessment 2012 at 42–44.

240 Proposal 2012 at art. 13.

241 Graber, *Collective Rights Management*, *supra* at 41–42. This does not only concern the distinction between "creative" and derivative right holders, but also right holders who are not members of the CMO in question, yet nevertheless represented by the organization. Such a situation can arise if right holders conclude a service agreement (especially if they do not fulfill membership requirements), claim remuneration ex-post (especially in connection with mandatory collective licensing) or in extended collective licensing systems, *see* Drexl et al., *Comments of the MPI, supra* at 15–16.

242 Drexl et al., *Comments of the MPI, supra* at 35–36 (also favoring a centralized European authorization system); João Pedro Quintais, *Proposal for a Directive on Collective Rights Management and (Some) Multi-Territorial Licensing* (Amsterdam Law School Legal Studies Research Paper No. 2013-69, 2013), *available at* http://papers.ssrn.com/sol3/papers.cfm?abstract_id=2351186 (last visited May 23, 2017).

Market.[243] Scholars also urged for an express obligation to contract, in relation to right holders as well as in relation to users;[244] the sparse rules with respect to the latter group were considered to be inadequate.[245] As regards the proposed MTL model, the scope was considered to be too narrow because it merely applied to "works" and not related rights.[246] Furthermore, it was questioned whether the competition between CMOs under the new licensing model was a desirable option in the first place.[247]

b) The Role of the Commission

In reviewing the events until 2014, it is apparent that achieving EU-wide regulation was quite a cumbersome path. It was characterized by an antagonistic relationship between the Commission and the Parliament.[248] Through its initiatives (Communication 2004, Recommendation 2005, *CISAC* decision, and Proposal 2012), the Commission limited the actors from other EU bodies and commentators in legal writings to CMOs to only being able to comment on the conceived way of action. It is notable that the authority was not willing to modify even slightly any key point of its proposals, even though the vast majority of the comments was almost unilaterally critical about the actions taken or proposed, especially after 2004. Obviously, the Commission viewed collective management through the economic lens, entirely putting its focus on the (possible) benefits of competition. However, it would be simplistic to merely speak of "the Commission". The authority has never existed as uniformly structured, and this requires a differentiated analysis along the time axis and in light of its organizational design. In regard to the first aspect, it must be highlighted that a new Commission replaced its predecessor in 2005. While the old Commission showed a certain understanding for the complexity of the topic, favoring harmonization at the EU level and reinforcing the protection of creators, the new Commission did not reflect much about cultural diversity but aimed at abandoning the system of reciprocal representation agreements

243 Ruprecht Podszun, *Verwertungsgesellschaften vor der Neuordnung: Der Vorschlag der Kommission zu einer Richtlinie über die kollektive Wahrnehmung von Urheberrechten und verwandten Schutzrechten*, 2013 GPR 97, 99–100, 102.

244 Drexl et al., *Comments of the MPI, supra* at 7–8.

245 Podszun, *Neuordnung*, *supra*, at 100.

246 Quintais, *Proposal for a Directive*, *supra* at 19; Drexl et al., *Comments of the MPI, supra* at 26–27.

247 Nuno Sousa e Silva, *The proposed Directive on multi-territorial licensing for online music – Is competition a good idea?* 24–25 (2013), *available at* http://papers.ssrn.com/sol3/papers.cfm?abstract_id=2375886 (last visited May 23, 2017). *See also* Adolf Dietz, *The European Commission's Proposal for a Directive on Collecting Societies and Cultural Diversity – a Missed Opportunity*, IJMBR, April 2014, at 7 (focusing on the cultural functions of CMOs).

248 Riis, *Collecting Societies*, *supra* at 483. *See also* Adolf Dietz, *Marketing and Enforcing Intellectual Property in Europe European Parliament Versus Commission: How to Deal with Collecting Societies?*, 35 IIC 809 (2004) (addressing the divergences and similarities in the opinion of the institutions).

and at creating competition between CMOs; moreover, it strongly promoted cross-border licensing of online music services.[249] It has been observed that the Commission as of 2005 essentially had in mind the business interests of major music publishers, and not those of individual "creative" authors.[250] Regarding its organizational design, it has to be noted that different Directorates General (DGs)[251] were involved in the developments which ultimately led to the final Collective Management Directive.[252] DG Internal Market and Services (DG MARKT) was mainly concerned with drafting the legislative initiatives and related formal documents;[253] DG Competition (DG COMP) was competent to enforce the European competition rules; and DG Information Society and Media (DG INFSO)[254] contributed from the internet perspective by issuing a Communication on creative content in the online environment.[255] The collaboration between these DGs was not always in harmony. DG MARKT and DG COMP had different conceptions about what efficiency meant to them.[256] Moreover, whereas DG MARKT took the view that the system of RRAs should be abandoned as such and favored a system without an intermediary society, DG COMP merely highlighted that such agreements must not be discriminatory or result in a territorial portioning of the market.[257] However, in the *CISAC* decision, DG COMP contributed further to an abolishment of the system, largely in line with Recommendation 2005. With regard to DG INFSO and DG MARKT, the approaches taken by the two DGs were regarded to be "divergent and incompatible", the first only thinking of internet service providers, and the second only of major music publishers.[258] The example of the Commission's treatment of CMOs discloses structural weaknesses of its insti-

---

249 Schierholz, *Collective Rights Management, supra* at 1177–1178, 1184.

250 *Id.* at 1184–1185.

251 The European Commission is structured into several DGs agencies and other departments, *see* European Commission, *Departments and executive agencies*, http://ec.europa.eu/about/ds_en.htm (last visited April 16, 2017).

252 Hellenic Foundation for European and Foreign Policy, *Collecting Societies And Cultural Diversity In The Music Sector* 21 (2009), *available at* http://www.europarl.europa.eu/RegData/etudes/etudes/join/2009/419110/IPOL-CULT_ET(2009)419110_EN.pdf (last visited May 23, 2017); Lichtenegger, *Verwertungsgesellschaften, supra* at 140.

253 *See* for an overview European Commission, *Management of Copyright and Related Rights*, http://ec.europa.eu/internal_market/copyright/management/index_en.htm (last visited April 16, 2017).

254 The DG is now called Directorate General for Communication Networks, Contents and Technology (DG Connect), *see* European Commission, *DG Connect*, http://ec.europa.eu/dgs/connect/ (last visited April 16, 2017).

255 Commission of the European Communities, *Communication from the Commission to the European Parliament, the Council, the European Economic and Social Committee and the Committee of the Regions on Creative Content Online in the Single Market* COM(2007) 836 final (2008), *available at* http://eur-lex.europa.eu/LexUriServ/LexUriServ.do?uri=COM:2007:0836:FIN:EN:PDF (last visited May 23, 2017).

256 KEA European Affairs, *Collective Management, supra* at 19 (2006).

257 *Id.* at 56–57.

258 Schierholz, *Collective Rights Management, supra* at 1184.

tutional design, as there seems to be a need for better coordination between the different DGs; especially for an office that is capable of maintaining an overview of the full complexity of the topic, since collective management involves intellectual property legislation, competition law, Internal Market matters, cultural issues, and the implications of digital technologies. However, the numerous changes made to the Proposal 2012 in relation to the final directive indicate a change of attitude, at least in the last stage of the drafting. The problem is possibly connected to the fact the Commission at that time might have been too large since every member state sends a commissioner to Brussels.[259]

c) The Emergence of New Licensing Models After 2005

The licensing market and management practices in Europe did not await the adoption of a binding directive on collective management. Major changes can be observed after 2005 as direct consequences of the initiatives taken by the Commission of which the most important were the Recommendation 2005 and the decision in *CISAC*.[260] At the outset, it should be noted that the Recommendation 2005 did not achieve what it aimed for, that is, introducing competition between CMOs at the level of right holders and facilitating multi-territorial licensing.[261] This was acknowledged by the Commission in the Impact Assessment 2012, inasmuch as it admitted that the practice lacked sufficient compliance with the Commission's instruments.[262] However, not only did it not achieve its aims, it additionally created an environment of severe legal uncertainty, which was reinforced by the CISAC decision.[263] Most importantly, the system of RRAs was altered. This system was targeted by the Commission because it was considered to be inefficient and in need of an unnecessary intermediary organization; moreover, the possibility to monitor and directly license copyrights using new technologies would render them obsolete.[264] In order to abandon this system, the Recommendation 2005 called for the right holders' ability to choose without restrictions the kind of rights and the territorial scope of the management service they wish to entrust to CMOs with as well as to withdraw rights from one CMO and transfer them to another.[265] Thereby, the Commission essentially accepted a trade-off: The inducement of competition and facilitated access to multi-territorial licenses was promoted in return for the risk of repertoire fragmentation, as CMOs do not necessarily manage all rights of a right holder.[266] This risk has partly become true: As of 2005, major

259 The TFEU actually provides for a rotation system, *see* art. 244 TFEU.

260 Guibault & van Gompel, *Collective Management 2010, supra* at 138.

261 Guibault, *Collective Management Directive*, *supra* at 763.

262 Impact assessment 2012 at 106–109.

263 Guibault & van Gompel, *Collective Management 2010, supra* at 160.

264 Schierholz, *Collective Rights Management, supra* at 1186.

265 Recommendation 2005 at point 5.

266 Reto M. Hilty & Sylvie Nérisson, *Collective Copyright Management and Digitization: The European Experience* 8–11 (Max Planck Institute for Intellectual Property & Competition

music publishers withdrew their (mechanical) online rights in the popular Anglo-American repertoire from CMOs and started licensing them directly by establishing new licensing platforms or by relying on agents.[267] This trend is still in active development but can be characterized by four main features: First of all, the offer involves multi-territorial licenses, so that only one license is necessary for the territory of at least two member states. Second, these licenses do not provide access to the world repertoire; rather, the access is confined to the rights of a limited group of right holders (or actually only one). Third, such licenses typically refer to online rights and not to the traditional exploitation offline. Last, most initiatives involve a (usually large) CMO that serves the purposes of one major music publisher.[268] In the context of the new licensing models, one often speaks of "hybrid entities". Such entities typically occupy a position between collective and individual management because they, on the one hand, manage a multitude of works but, on the other hand, represent only one right holder (publisher).[269]

CELAS (Centralised European Licensing and Administration Services) is often mentioned as a paradigmatic example for this development.[270] The organization was established in 2007 as a joint venture owned by the British CMO PRS for Music (PRSfM) and its German sister society GEMA.[271] It originally managed the EMI repertoire; however the EMI group was dissolved in 2011 and the publishing branch was sold to Sony Corporation of America (and Mubadala Development Company, an Abu Dhabi public joint stock company) while the recorded music branch was acquired by Universal International Music by way of a subsidiary.[272] The Commission approved both mergers in

Law Research Paper No. 13-09, 2013), *available at* http://papers.ssrn.com/sol3/papers.cfm?abstract_id=2247870 (last visited May 23, 2017).

267 Impact Assessment 2012 at 12–13.

268 Andreas Wiebe et al., *Rights Clearance for Online Music* 38–39 (2014). *See also* Schierholz, *Collective Rights Management, supra* at 1186.

269 Emanuela Arezzo, *Competition and Intellectual Property Protection in the Market for the Provision of Multi-Territorial Licensing of Online Rights in Musical Works – Lights and Shadows of the New European Directive 2014/26/EU*, 46 IIC 534, 545 (2015); Reto M. Hilty & Sylvie Nérisson, *Collective copyright management* in *Handbook on the Digital Creative Economy* 222, 227–229 (Ruth Towse & Christian Handke eds., 2013).

270 *See, e.g.,* Michael Karbaum et al., *Rechtsbeziehungen der GEMA zu ausländischen Verwertungsgesellschaften* in *Recht und Praxis der GEMA* 792, 812–816 (Reinhold Kreile et al. eds, 2nd ed. 2008).

271 Hellenic Foundation for European and Foreign Policy, *Cultural Diversity, supra* at 29–30.

272 *Sony/Mubadala Development/EMI Music Publishing*, Commission Decision of 19.04.2012, case COMP/M.6459, ¶ 1–4, *available at* http://ec.europa.eu/competition/mergers/cases/decisions/m6459_4326_2.pdf (last visited May 22, 2017); *Universal Music Group/EMI Music*, Commission Decision of 21.09.2012, case COMP/M.6458, ¶ 1–4, *available at* http://ec.europa.eu/competition/mergers/cases/decisions/m6458_20120921_20600_3188150_EN.pdf (last visited May 22, 2017). *See also* Sebastian Felix Schwemer, *The licensing of online music streaming services in Europe* in *Handbook on the Economics of Copyright* 141, 153 n. 22 (Richard Watt ed. 2014).

2012.[273] GEMA was put in a two-sided relationship with Sony due to the merger. On the one hand, it managed Sony/ATV's repertoire through its subsidiary PAECOL,[274] and, on the other hand, CELAS licensed rights owned by Sony/ATV because the company had acquired EMI's rights.[275] As a direct consequence, a new joint venture called SOLAR Music Rights Management between GEMA, PRSfM and Sony was announced in order to "cover the exploitation of the combined Anglo-American catalogues of Sony/ATV and EMI Music Publishing. […] This consolidated offering ensures that licensees have easy access to both repertoires."[276] It is planned to offer a single license on a pan European basis along with copyright administration services for online and mobile uses.[277] This indicates that the tasks formerly carried out by CELAS and PAECOL will be transferred to SOLAR. Indeed, the joint venture is conceived to replace the pre-existing structures.[278] Further examples of new licensing models and initiatives are ARESA (Anglo-American Rights European Service Agency),[279] ZETA,[280] D.E.A.L (Direct European Administration and Licensing),[281] PEDL (Pan European Digital Licensing),[282] PEL (Pan European Li-

---

[273] *Sony/Mubadala Development/EMI Music Publishing,* case COMP/M.6459; *Universal Music Group/EMI Music*, case COMP/M.6458. Another relatively recent change in the music sector concerned the merger between SONY and BMG which was approved by the Commission in 2007, *see Sony/BMG*, Commission Decision of 03.10.2007, case COMP/M.3333, *available at* http://ec.europa.eu/competition/mergers/cases/decisions/m3333_20071003_590_en.pdf (last visited May 22, 2017).

[274] PAECOL (Pan-European Central Online Licensing) is a 100% exclusive subsidiary of GEMA and was founded in 2008 for the management of Sony/ATV's mechanical rights in the online environment, *see* Hellenic Foundation for European and Foreign Policy, *Cultural Diversity*, *supra* at 31.

[275] Even though it was not formally a party of the merger, Sony/ATV was identified to also administer the EMI Music Publishing catalogue, *see Sony/Mubadala Development/EMI Music Publishing,* case COMP/M.6459 at ¶ 5.

[276] PRS for Music, *Sony/ATV, PRS for Music and GEMA launch joint venture*, http://www.prsformusic.com/aboutus/press/latestpressreleases/pages/sony-atv-prs-for-music-gema-launch-joint-venture.aspx (last visited April 16, 2017). The original CELAS homepage (www.celas.eu) was subsequently deactivated and has not been renewed as of April 2017.

[277] *Id.*

[278] *Id.* According to its website, SOLAR manages "the combined Anglo-American catalogues of Sony/ATV and EMI Music Publishing for online and mobile licensing across the EU and other regions", *see* SOLAR, *SOLAR MUSIC*, http://www.solar-music.com/ (last visited April 17, 2017). *See also* GEMA, *Subsidiary Companies*, https://www.gema.de/en/about-gema/organisation/ subsidiary-companies/ (last visited April 17, 2017).

[279] ARESA is wholly owned by GEMA and represents the mechanical rights in the Anglo-American repertoire of BMG Rights Management, *see* ARESA, *Info*, http://aresa-music.com/homepage_en.html (last visited April 17, 2017).

[280] ZETA is a collaboration between GEMA, PRSfM and STIM (Swedish CMO) for the combined licensing of their and other repertoires, *see PRSfM/STIM/GEMA/JV*, case COMP/M.6800 at ¶ 4–20.

[281] D.E.A.L. was created in 2008 by Universal Music Publishing and SACEM for the management of Universal's mechanical rights in respect of its Anglo-American repertoire, *see* Giuseppe Mazziotti, *New Licensing Models for Online Music Services in the European Un-*

censing Initiative of Latin American Repertoire),[283] IMPEL (Independent Music Publishers European Licensing),[284] ARMONIA,[285] and MERLIN.[286]

Despite that a lot of information is not publicly available[287] and that the current status of some initiatives is not fully disclosed, the underlying consequence of Recommendation 2005 and *CISAC* is clear: CMOs are no longer national one-stop shops for online rights in musical works;[288] commentators go as far as speaking of an "erosion process" of the system of reciprocal representation agreements.[289] However, apart from the Anglo-American reper-

---

ion: From Collective to Customized Management, 34 Colum. J. of Law & the Arts 757, 772 (2011); Christoph Schütt, *Fortschritt bei der europaweiten Lizenzierung von Online-Musikrechten*, MMR May 2008, at XVIII. The conclusion of new license deals has recently been announced, *see, e.g.,* SACEM, *SACEM, Universal Music Publishing International and SoundCloud Strike New European Deal*, https://societe.sacem.fr/en/press-resources/per-publication/Press-releases/a-new-deal-license-sacem-universal-music-publishing-international-and-soundcloud-strike-new-european-deal (last visited April 16, 2017).

282 PEDL was initially launched by Warner/Chappell in 2006 in order to set up a new licensing model directing itself to interested national European CMOs which were invited to act as non-exclusive agents for the grant of pan-European licenses with regard to the mechanical rights in Warner's Anglo-American repertoire for digital exploitation, *see* Hellenic Foundation for European and Foreign Policy, *Cultural Diversity*, *supra* at 32–33. The first CMOs joined in 2008, *see* Johann Heyde, *Die grenzüberschreitende Lizenzierung von Online-Musikrechten in Europa* 142 (2011).

283 PEL was set up as a collaboration between SGAE on the one hand and Sony/ATV, Peer Music and Central and South American CMOs on the other hand, *see* Hellenic Foundation for European and Foreign Policy, *Cultural Diversity*, *supra* at 31–32. *See also* Impact Assessment 2012 at 107 n. 238.

284 IMPEL (Independent Music Publishers European Licensing) is an initiative which is open for independent publishers who entrust the British CMO MCPS (Mechanical Copyright Protection Society) with the management multi-territorial licensing of their mechanical rights in their Anglo-American repertoire, *see* PRS for Music, *IMPEL*, http://www.prsformusic.com/impel/pages/default.aspx (last visited April 16, 2017).

285 ARMONIA is a platform for the aggregation of the repertoires of multiple European CMOs for the multi-territorial licensing of online rights the roots of which go back to 2007. It was founded by SACEM, SGAE and (later also) SIAE (Italian CMO) and current consists of nine national CMOs, *see* ARMONIA, *Armonia in Numbers*, http://armoniaonline.com/ (last visited April 16, 2017); Hellenic Foundation for European and Foreign Policy, *Cultural Diversity*, *supra* at 33–34; Mazziotti, *New Licensing Models*, *supra* at 774–775.

286 MERLIN is a platform established in 2007 which offers multi-territorial (or, according to its website, global) licenses by bundling the rights held by independent record labels, *see* MERLIN, *What we do*, http://www.merlinnetwork.org/what-we-do (last visited April 16, 2017). *See also* KEA, *Music licensing and transaction costs in Europe* 32 (2012), *available at* http://www.keanet.eu/docs/music%20licensing%20and%20transaction%20costs%20-%20full.pdf (last visited May 23, 2017).

287 This is illustrated by the numerous blanked portions in *PRSfM/STIM/GEMA/JV*, Commission Decision of 16.06.2015, case COMP/M.6800.

288 Heyde, *Lizenzierung*, *supra* at 151.

289 Tilo Gerlach, *Vor §§ 1 ff UrhWG* in *Praxiskommentar zum Urheberrecht: UrhR* ¶ 31 (Artur-Axel Wandtke & Winfried Bullinger eds., 4th ed. 2014).

toire, the subsistence of RRAs has to be assumed, although uncertainty exists regarding their contents.[290]

d) The Union's competence to regulate collective management

The CMD is based on rules which aim for attaining the freedom of establishment and the free movement of services in the Internal Market.[291] According to the directive, the TFEU's article 50(1) confers the power to harmonize safeguards and protection of members of CMOs, right holders, and third parties.[292] Article 53(1) permits the Union to regulate the access to collective management and its supervisory framework as well as the governance of CMOs.[293] Since these organizations offer services, article 62 supplements the legal basis with regard to the freedom to provide services.[294]

In the past, it was sometimes questioned whether the EU treaties provided a sufficient basis to regulate collective management, stressing that there is no general competence of the Union to regulate collective management or the cultural sector.[295] It was, therefore, suggested that regulation at the EU level should exclusively encompass Internal Market matters that aim for the elimination of trade barriers.[296] The problem is that it is often hard to tell which provisions refer to the Internal Market and which to cultural matters. For example, the final directive sets forth that right holders should be able to freely choose which CMO to mandate, the types of rights that ought to be managed, etc.[297] On the one hand, if one considers the cross-border licensing market, binding a right holder with all her rights to a national CMO would constitute a restriction of the freedom to provide services for other member states' CMOs, thus belonging to the field of the Internal Market. One the other hand,

290 Hilty & Nérisson, *Digitization*, *supra* at 10–11.

291 TFEU art. 50(1), 53(1), 62. The legal bases (for the adoption of a directive, for instance) are indicated in the preamble of the instrument, *see* the preamble of the CMD. *See, e.g.,* on the requirements for the legal bases *Commission v. Council of the European Union*, C-94/03 (ECJ 2006); Stefan Kadelbach, *EUV Artikel 5* in *Europäisches Unionsrecht* ¶ 20 (Hans von der Groeben et al. eds., 7th ed. 2015).

292 CMD recital 7. The Proposal 2012 referred to article 50(2)(g) instead, *see* Proposal 2012 at recital 6.

293 CMD recital 8.

294 *Id.* Article 62 of the TFEU declares article 51–52 TFEU applicable to services.

295 *See, e.g.,* Karl Riesenhuber & Alexander v. Vogel, *Europäisches Wahrnehmungsrecht Zur Mitteilung der Kommission über die Wahrnehmung von Urheberrechten und verwandten Schutzrechten im Binnenmarkt*, 15 EuZW 519, 521 (2004); Tuma, *Pitfalls and Challenges* at 223.

296 Tuma, *Pitfalls and Challenges* at 223. According to article 6 of the TFEU, the Union has the competence "to carry out actions to support, coordinate or supplement the actions of the Member States" in the field of culture (*inter alia*). According to article 167, "the Union shall contribute to the flowering of the cultures of the Member States, while respecting their national and regional diversity and at the same time bringing the common cultural heritage to the fore."

297 CMD art. 5.

this can affect member states which provide for mandatory collective management schemes and other arrangements under their respective cultural policies.[298] Should the interests of the Internal Market or member states' sovereignty to regulate cultural matters prevail? It was precisely this point, among others, which was criticized again with regard to the Proposal 2012.[299] However, if one suggests that the Union should refrain from interfering with national mandatory collective management schemes and related arrangements because these topics belong to cultural policy, one must also consider the reverse situation: Is the Union competent to provide for mandatory collective management in the Satellite & Cable Directive? May it oblige member states to provide for fair compensation of authors in article 5 of the Copyright Directive? It is submitted that there exists doubt on whether competition between CMOs in the EU is a desirable option; however, the mere fact that the option chosen by European law makers is not regarded as ideal does not mean that the Union has exceeded its authorities. The final version of the Collective Management might at least meet some of the concerns regarding the Union's competence. First of all, the directive expressly states that it does not interfere with national copyright management rules, like individual management, extended collective licensing, mandatory collective management and legal presumptions of representation, and transfer of rights to CMOs.[300] Moreover, since there is an obligation for CMOs to represent right holders also smaller and less popular repertoires should be not be facing disadvantages at this stage of the management process, at least.[301] With regard to smaller CMOs, title III of the directive appears to be in their favor, although some questions remain.[302]

In summary and facing the final version of the directive, it seems that European lawmakers did not go beyond the powers conferred on the Union by the cited articles of the TFEU. Moreover, challenges arising from the principles of subsidiarity and proportionality were overcome during the negotiations between Proposal 2012 and the adoption of the directive, which led to the introduction of considerable flexibilities for the member states.[303] The other side is, of course, that national laws regulating the collective management of copy-

---

298 Graber, *Collective Rights Management*, *supra* at 41.

299 *Id.* 41–42.

300 CMD recital 12.

301 CMD Article 5(2); Drexl et al., *Comments of the MPI*, *supra* at 7.

302 Graber, *Collective Rights Management*, *supra* at 42 (referring to the interpretation of the expression "same category").

303 Mihály Ficsor, *Collective Management and Multi-territorial Licensing: Key Issues of the Transposition of Directive 2014/26/EU* in *New Developments in EU and International Copyright Law* 211, 213–218 (Irini A. Stamatoudi ed., 2016); Stef van Gompel, *Directive 2014/26/EU* in *Concise European Copyright Law* 541, 543 (Thomas Dreier & P. Bernt Hugenholtz eds., 2nd ed., 2016); Guibault, *Collective Management Directive*, *supra* at 701–702. *See also* CMD recital 55; Proposal 2012 at 7–8.

right will continue to differ also after the transposition of the CMD (*see* subsection 1.1.5. below).

e) Scope of the Collective Management Directive

The Collective Management Directive, adopted on 2/4/2014, is the result of 19 years of discussion, a time span, in which the landscape of collective management in Europe altered significantly responding to technological developments and the initiatives of the Commission. While the final version maintains the overall structure of the Proposal 2012, numerous changes that stakeholders had urged for were incorporated in the directive. For this reason, scholars were more favorable to the Collective Management Directive than to previous work of the Commission, stating that it constituted a "serious effort to a balanced and effective framework around the collective management of copyright and related rights".[304] The following pages give an overview of the scope and the most important principles governing the Collective Management Directive.

The three main goals of the Collective Management Directive are to establish a harmonized framework which ensures that members of CMOs can exercise control over the activities of such organizations, that CMOs follow basic principles of transparency throughout the Union, and that users can rely on a functional system of the multi-territorial licensing of online rights in musical works.[305] The CMD is structured into five titles which differ in their scope and level of detail. The construction of the terms "collective management organization" and "independent management entity" (IME) is crucial to the applicability of the different titles. Collective management organizations are defined as

> [...] any organisation which is authorised by law or by way of assignment, licence or any other contractual arrangement to manage copyright or rights related to copyright on behalf of more than one rightholder, for the collective benefit of those rightholders, as its sole or main purpose, and which fulfils one or both of the following criteria:
> i) it is owned or controlled by its members
> ii) it is organised on a not-for-profit basis;[306]

The definition incorporates the basic elements of the traditional understanding of CMOs identified above, emphasizing their roles as trustees ("on behalf")[307] and the collective solidarity ("collective benefit") among a multitude

[304] Guibault, *Collective Management Directive*, *supra* at 702; Guibault & van Gompel, *Collective Management*, *supra* at 142–143. *See* for a more critical view Ficsor, *Key Issues*, *supra* at 248–249.

[305] CMD recital 55, art 1.

[306] CMD art. 3(a).

[307] This should not be understood literally, as CMOs usually manage and enforce rights in their own name, *see* 2 Michel Walter, *Urheber- und Verwertungsgesellschaftenrecht '15* 227 (2015).

of right holders.[308] It is crucial that the organization is owned or controlled by its members (not: the right holders) or, alternatively, that it does not aim at obtaining profits – also those organizations which do not have members due to their specific legal form (like foundations, for instance) but offer collective management services, may, therefore, qualify as CMOs.[309] Furthermore, the provisions of the directive also apply in cases of circumvention.[310] Therefore, corporate sub-structures created by CMOs in order to avoid legal obligations fall within the scope of the directive, provided that these units are directly or indirectly controlled by the CMOs and that they carry out collective management activities.[311] However, there are organizations that are not owned or controlled by their members and that are organized on a for-profit basis but offer copyright management services just like CMOs. These organizations are called independent management entities[312] (hereinafter: IMEs) within the meaning of the directive. Although they generally fall within the scope of the directive, only a couple of articles are deemed applicable which mainly relate to transparency duties.[313] For this reason, the inclusion of IMEs in the directive cannot be primarily considered as a measure against circumvention of legal obligations because such situations are covered by the very definition of CMOs in connection with article 2(3) of the CMD.[314] These rules ensure the full applicability of the "relevant provisions" of the directive and not merely the limited obligations put on IMEs. Recital 16 stresses that audiovisual producers, record producers and broadcasters are not to be regarded as IMEs because they act in their own interest. Hence, it follows *e contrario* that IMEs do not act in their own interests.[315]

The directive specifies a certain group of CMOs that grants "multi-territorial licenses for online rights in musical works"[316] (hereinafter: MTL-CMOs).

---

308 Drexl et al., *Comments of the MPI*, *supra* at 19–20 (criticizing the unsatisfactory solution of the proposal). *Ficsor* criticizes especially the "more than one rightholder" requirement, *see* Ficsor, *International Treaties*, *supra* at 42–44; Ficsor, *Key Issues*, *supra* at 234–235.

309 CMD recital 14.

310 *Id.*

311 Article 2(3) of the CMD reads: "The relevant provisions of this Directive apply to entities directly or indirectly owned or controlled, wholly or in part, by a collective management organisation, provided that such entities carry out an activity which, if carried out by the collective management organisation, would be subject to the provisions of this Directive." *See also* Drexl et al., *Comments of the MPI*, *supra* at 19–20.

312 Except for the highlighted point, the definition is identical to CMOs, *see* CMD art. 3(b).

313 CMD art. 2(4), recital 15. *Walter* has rightly criticized the limited scope of the directive in this respect; member states may, however, enact stricter rules, *see* 2 Walter, *Verwertungsgesellschaftenrecht*, *supra* at 228.

314 Of course, it also addresses some cases of potential circumvention, *see* Guibault, *Collective Management Directive*, *supra* at 711–712.

315 Robert Staats, *Umsetzung der EU-Richtlinie für Verwertungsgesellschaften in deutsches Recht*, 58 ZUM 470, 471 n. 10 (2014).

316 CMD art. 23. Recital 40 suggests that the expression "musical works" also covers lyrics, *see* 2 Walter, *Verwertungsgesellschaftenrecht*, *supra* at 231.

These organizations license the rights of reproduction and communication to the public that exist in musical works in the territories of more than one member state, insofar as these rights are necessary for the provision of an online service.[317] More precisely, the directive refers to the right of making available to the public and not to the broad right of communication to the public, since it requires interactive services on the internet.[318] It should be highlighted that only proper copyrights fall within the scope of the definition of MTL-CMOs. Related rights are excluded, even though the expression "online rights in musical works" refers to articles 2 and 3 of the Copyright Directive, which also mention the rights of performers, phonogram producers, and broadcasting organizations.[319] This is due to that the Collective Management Directive only speaks of the "rights of an author in a musical work provided for under Articles 2 and 3 of Directive 2001/29/EC". In a different provision, the term "authors' rights" is used.[320] Holders of related rights are not authors, neither in the general meaning of the term nor in the sense of the Copyright Directive, which is why related rights must be excluded from the scope of the definition (and thereby title III).[321] As a final remark, it should be noted that only CMOs and IMEs established in the territory of the EU are subject to the Collective Management Directive[322] (hereinafter: EU CMOs/EU MTL-CMOs/EU IMEs).

The following table provides an overview of the different titles of the CMD and their respective scope[323] and contents:

317 CMD art. 3(m), (n); Copyright Directive art. 2, 3.

318 Guibault, *Collective Management Directive*, *supra* at 713.

319 CMD art. 3(n).

320 *Id.* at art. 2(2). *See also id.* at recital 12.

321 *See also* Impact Assessment 2012 p. 6 ("[...] specific problems have been identified regarding the collective management of the rights of authors' in musical works (i.e. composers of music and authors of lyrics) for online uses."). *See* apparently for a different opinion Guibault, *Collective Management Directive*, *supra* at 713 (stating that authors, performers and phonogram producers hold online rights in musical works). *See also* Drexl et al., *Comments of the MPI*, *supra* at 26–27 (criticizing the exclusion in the proposal, as well as the limitation to online services); CMD recital 27. Also note the terminological difference in U.S. copyright law where sound recordings are considered as "works of authorship", *see* 17 U.S.C. § 102 (a)(7) and section I.4.4. above.

322 CMD recital 20, art. 2.

323 *Id.*, at art. 2.

	Subject-Matter	Applicability to CMOs	Applicability to IMEs
Title I	General provisions, scope, definitions	All EU CMOs	-
Title II	Rights of members (right holders), internal structure, reciprocal representation agreements, relation to users, transparency	All EU CMOS	All EU IMEs, but only art. 16(1), 18, 20, 21(1)(a),(b),(c),(e),(f),(g)
Title III	Multi-territorial licensing	EU MTL-CMOs	-
Title IV	Enforcement measures	All EU CMOs; art. 34(2), 38 only EU MTL-CMOs	All EU IMEs, but only art. 36
Title V	Final provisions[324]; privacy	All EU CMOs	All EU IMEs, but only art. 42

Table 1: Scope of the Collective Management Directive

f) Main features of the Collective Management Directive

The substantive provisions of the Collective Management Directive can be grouped around the following principles:

- Focus on right holders

The directive clearly centers the relationship between CMOs and right holders. This is not only the case for right holders that are members of CMOs but also for right holders that are not members but are nevertheless represented by the organization. To this effect, the rules on the protection and rights of right holders are more extensive than in respect to any other group of stakeholders that entertain relations to CMOs. This underlying principle becomes clear when reading article 4 of the Collective Management Directive:

> member states shall ensure that collective management organisations act in the best interest of rightholders whose rights they represent and that they do not impose on them any obligations which are not objectively necessary for the protection of their rights and interests or for the effective management of their rights.[325]

The directive aims at maximizing the freedom of right holders by introducing a set of rights[326] and ensures their role in the decision-making and management process by prescribing rules on membership, collection and distribution of revenues and representation in the organizational structure. In contrast, the provisions that govern the relationship of CMOs and users are comparatively sparse, stipulating general principles rather than detailed rules.

324 The transposition date was April 10, 2016, *see* CMD art. 43.

325 *Id.* at art. 4; Podszun, *Neuordnung*, *supra* at 99.

326 *See, e.g.*, CMD recital 19, art. 5.

- Equal treatment of right holders

In two respects, the Collective Management Directive prohibits CMOs to differentiate between right holders: First, the principle of non-discrimination between right holders, as known from European case law applicable to collective management and flowing from article 18 TFEU, is incorporated in the directive.[327] Therefore, a CMO must not discriminate against right holders on the basis of their nationality and has to base its decisions on objective criteria.[328] This principle not only applies to right holders who are members of the CMO in question[329] but also to those right holders whose rights are managed in representation for other CMOs, be it under a respective agreement or under the MTL obligation.[330] The directive also contains safeguards for right holders who are represented by an organization but are not its members.[331] Second, the directive does not, in principle, distinguish between different categories of right holders.[332] This uniform concept flows from the previous work by the Commission, especially the Recommendation 2005, which sets forth that all right holders must be treated equally.[333] This point was criticized in the Proposal 2012 due to that "creative" right holders are normally in a weaker position than publishers and that the latter group might enjoy unjustified advantages; moreover, article 12 of the proposal seemed to lead to legal uncertainty.[334] The final version of the Collective Management Directive modified its approach in several ways. The directive now allows for the option that CMOs have a dual board of administration which can be composed of different categories of members.[335] Additionally, the last sentence of article 13(1)[336] was deleted, as suggested by the MPI. This does not automatically alter the uniform definition in article 3, which was left untouched in this respect. However, the rules that prescribe a "fair and balanced" representation of different categories of members in the decision-making process and with regard to supervisory functions,[337] should properly address the concerns of weaker right

327 Guibault, *Collective Management Directive*, *supra* at 720–721; Guibault & van Gompel, *Collective Management*, *supra* at 149. The principle of non-discrimination is also prescribed with regard to users, *see* CMD art. 16(2). The wording of article 5(2) suggests that this principle applies not only to EU citizens, *see* 2 Walter, *Verwertungsgesellschaftenrecht*, *supra* at 235.

328 CMD recital 18, art. 5(1).

329 *Id.* at recital 20, art 6(2); *see also* recital 28.

330 *Id.* at recital 11, 30, art. 14, 29, 30(3).

331 *Id.* art. 7. *See also* Drexl et al., *Comments of the MPI*, *supra* at 15–16.

332 CMD art. 3(c) reads: "'rightholder' means any person or entity, other than a collective management organisation, that holds a copyright or related right or, under an agreement for the exploitation of rights or by law, is entitled to a share of the rights revenue".

333 CMD recital 6.

334 Drexl et al., *Comments of the MPI*, *supra* at 13–15.

335 CMD art. 3(g); Guibault, *Collective Management Directive*, *supra* at 712.

336 The initially proposed article 12(1) reads: "The collecting society shall carry out such distribution and payments accurately, ensuring equal treatment of all categories of rightholders."

337 CMD recital 22, art. 6(3), 8(11) 9((2); *see also* recital 29 and art. 8(10).

holders.[338] In light of the foregoing, the Collective Management Directive takes an interesting two-fold direction: As a general principle, it maintains its uniform concept of right holders. At the same time, it acknowledges the need to distinguish between different groups of members by incorporating several provisions that call for "fair and balanced" representation. These provisions are of great significance because internal bodies composed of right holders have the power to make important decisions related to the functioning of the organization as in the case of the general assembly, for instance.[339]

- Transparency

A harmonized framework for transparency had been on the collective management agenda long before the adoption of the final directive.[340] Accordingly, transparent conduct by CMOs within the management process is one of the main aims of the directive; obligations to provide information can be found regarding all fields that fall within its scope.[341] This principle is fundamental to the underlying reasoning of the Commission (to introduce competition between CMOs) because the broad catalog of the rights of right holders would be incomplete and ineffective without being supplemented by an adequate supply of information. Only in this way right holders are able to compare the services offered by different organizations and choose the most suitable and efficient one for their respective needs.[342] Also, in situations where there is no competitive environment, transparency ensures accurate processing of the revenue stream. Access to information is furthermore crucial to users and other CMOs;[343] however, in line with its general orientation, the provisions concerning right holders are most extensive. The main rules are contained in chapter 5 of title II (articles 18–22). The obligations of CMOs to provide information are built on the different categories of recipients.[344] In addition to the typical groups (right holders, users, other CMOs), the general public is introduced as a fourth category. Under this regime, CMOs are obliged to publish general in-

338 Drexl et al., *Comments of the MPI*, *supra* at 14.

339 CMD art. 8(5) reserves the general assembly important competences, like the determination of the general policy of distribution.

340 Communication 2004 at 7, 10, 16; Echerer, *Report*, *supra* at 10–11; European Commission, *Communication from the Commission to the Parliament, the Council, the European Economic and Social Committee and the Committee of the Regions A Single Market for Intellectual Property Rights Boosting Creativity and Innovation to Provide Economic Growth, High Quality Jobs and First Class Products and Services in Europe* 10–11 (2011), *available at* http://ec.europa.eu/internal_market/copyright/docs/ipr_strategy/COM_2011_287_en.pdf (last visited May 23, 2017); Impact Assessment 2012 at 7–8, 17–19, 116–118; Recommendation 2005 recitals 10, 13 and points 6, 7.

341 *See, e.g.*, CMD recitals 9, 20, 28, 34, 36, 41, 45.

342 *Id.* at recital 36.

343 *Id.* at recital 34.

344 Guibault, *Collective Management Directive*, *supra* at 761; Guibault & van Gompel, *Collective Management*, *supra* at 156.

formation like the statute, membership and standard licensing terms or the general distribution policy.[345] Furthermore, CMOs must publish a transparency report for each financial year, which contains an extensive set of information on collection and distribution of royalties.[346] A point that should be emphasized is that the directive takes account of the practical difficulties that arise in a market like the EU where the right holders represented by one CMO or the users that request license grants can be spread all over the continent. For this reason, CMOs have to allow for the option to communicate with them by electronic means.[347] Right holders may even exercise their membership rights by using these technologies,[348] and important pieces of information must be made accessible in this way.[349] While these rules mitigate the obstacles for the practice of collective management by a single organization in the entire Union in light of the geographical distance, it can be questioned whether the proper functioning regarding the language barrier is ensured. The rules on transparency do not stipulate which languages CMOs must use to provide information. This might prevent right holders or users from other member states to contract with a CMO from another member state (and a different language) or to fully exercise their rights. However, if it is assumed that CMOs enter into competition with each other, it seems likely that they would voluntarily make translations availables (at least in some languages) in order to attract users and right holders from other linguistic backgrounds.[350] In any event, an English translation of the basic documents seems to be the minimum requirement to foster a dynamic cross-border licensing market.

- Sectorial approach to multi-territorial licensing

The Collective Management Directive introduces a new licensing system in title III (articles 23–32), which is meant to promote granting multi-territorial licenses in the European Union. It can also be understood as a countermeasure to clarify the legal uncertainty that arose in the wake of the Recommendation 2005.[351] First of all, it sets forth the requirements that a CMO must fulfill in order to grant multi-territorial licenses. These are mainly related to the capacity to process great amounts of data as well transparency duties.[352] Most importantly, the directive introduces an obligation to represent other CMOs that do not offer MTL services. This obligation is put on CMOs that meet the foregoing criteria, already represent one or more CMOs for MTL purposes, and

345 CMD art. 21.

346 *Id.* at art. 22 and the annex of the directive.

347 *Id.* at art. 6(4), art. 16(4).

348 *Id.* at recital 23.

349 *Id.* at art. 19, 20, 25, 27.

350 *See* for a similar estimation van Gompel, *Directive*, *supra* at 601.

351 Guibault, *Collective Management Directive*, *supra* at 763–764.

352 CMD art. 24–28.

manage the same categories of online rights in musical works.[353] Alternatively, if a CMO does not offer MTL services, right holders can withdraw their online rights from it and entrust another organization with this task or license their rights individually.[354]

As explained above in connection with the definition of MTL-CMOs, the new provisions bear a triple restriction: First, as regards the category of protected works, only musical works fall within the scope of title III; second, as regards the type of rights, this only applies to "online" rights; and third, as regards the category of right holders, only authors' rights (but not related rights) are covered.[355] It is for this reason that the adopted system takes a sectorial approach to multi-territorial licensing.[356] Its scope covers services which are typically offered in the online environment, such as downloading and streaming music, including movies and games, if music is an important element.[357] It does not apply to cable or satellite transmission because these do not require online technologies;[358] furthermore, license grants to radio and television broadcasters that want to make their programs and associated material available online are exempted from the scope of title III.[359] It has been questioned whether the limitation to musical works is justified because, in the future, a need for an MTL system for e-books and pictures could arise.[360] The Commission stated that it had observed a higher degree of fragmentation and a more costly rights clearance process than in the case of other work categories, and that online music services providers more than others were in need of multi-territorial licensing solutions for the entire aggregated EU repertoire.[361] Yet, the provisions are likely to have an impact on other sectors, too (*e.g.,* cross-border licensing of music in print).[362]

- Minimum standards

As is the case with many other directives, the Collective Management Directive – with regard to title II[363] – prescribes minimum standards. This means

---

353 *Id.* at art. 30.

354 *Id.* at art. 31.

355 van Gompel, *Directive, supra* at 567, 569–570, 602 (also highlighting that compositions and lyrics are covered).

356 Drexl et al., *Comments of the MPI, supra* at 27. *See also* Mendis, *Directive 2014/26/EU, supra* at 311 (referring to the "twin aims" of the CMD).

357 Quintais, *Proposal for a Directive, supra* at 12; *see also* CMD recital 37.

358 Quintais, *Proposal for a Directive, supra* at 12.

359 CMD art. 32. *See* for the rationale of this provision van Gompel, *Directive, supra* at 614–615. *See also* Guibault & van Gompel, *Collective Management, supra* at 173; Ficsor, *Key Issues, supra* at 246–247. Recital 40 furthermore excludes sheet music from the scope of the directive.

360 Drexl et al., *Comments of the MPI, supra* at 27.

361 Impact assessment 2012 at 6, 23–24; *see also* CMD recital 40.

362 Huss-Eckerhult, *Collective Management Organisations, supra* at 2.

363 van Gompel, *Directive, supra* at 542–543; Christian Handig, *Das neue VerwertungsgesellschaftenG 2016 Eine kurze Übersicht über die wesentlichen Änderungen*, 65 ÖBl 164 (2016).

that the member states have to transpose into national law at least the level of regulation and protection contained in the directive, but they are also free to provide for more stringent standards or to add additional requirements.[364] As a consequence, substantial differences in the regulation of CMOs will subsist in the different member states, even after the transposition of the directive into national law (*see* immediately).[365]

1.1.5. Implications for the National Regulation of EU Member States

National regulative frameworks have existed long before collective management came into the focus of EU policy. However, the degree of regulation differs significantly.[366] These differences were also a major justification for action at the EU level because they were considered to be an obstacle to the efficient functioning of collective management in the Internal Market.[367] The Collective Management Directive harmonizes this status quo, so that the differences will be decreased in the future. However, they will not disappear due to the directive's minimum standard principle. Moreover, important fields are excluded from the scope of the directive. Member states maintain their freedom to regulate CMOs that are established outside the EU (non-EU CMOs) but operate in their territory.[368] They are also not limited in their power to provide for extended collective licensing or mandatory collective management schemes and legal presumptions of representation and transfer of rights to CMOs.[369] Finally, the directive does not affect rights to fair compensation for exceptions and limitations to copyright that are consistent with EU law.[370] In order to ensure compliance with the directive, member states must designate competent authorities that monitor the CMOs established in their territory and exchange information with other national competent authorities.[371] In this connection, it is noteworthy that, according to the ECJ, article 2(a) and 3(1) of the Copyright Directive preclude national legislation from giving an approved

---

364 *See, e.g.*, CMD recitals 9, 23, 27, 29, art. 24(2).

365 Depending on the legal form of CMOs, directives within the realm of corporate law can apply, *see* Lichtenegger, *Verwertungsgesellschaften*, *supra* at 125 n. 551.

366 *See, e.g.*, Impact Assessment 2012 at 120–142; Tuma, *Pitfalls and Challenges*, *supra* at 221–222. *See also* Adolf Dietz, *Legal Regulation of Collective Management of Copyright (Collecting Societies Law) in Western and Eastern Europe*, 49 J. Copyright Soc'y 897 (2001–2002) (discussing the national regulation of CMOs in several European countries).

367 CMD recital 5.

368 *Id.* at recital 10.

369 *Id.* at recital 12.

370 *Id.* at recital 13. The definition of the term CMO also indicates, that they may be mandated by law, *see* van Gompel, *Directive*, *supra* at 568.

371 CMD art. 36–37. *Ficsor* convincingly argues that article 37(2) should be interpreted as applying only to the cross-border licensing of online rights in musical works, *see* Ficsor, *International Treaties*, *supra* at 73; Ficsor, *Key Issues*, *supra* at 232–233. *See* however *e.g.* Staats, *Umsetzung*, *supra* at 472; 2 Walter, *Verwertungsgesellschaftenrecht*, *supra* at 297.

CMO the right to authorize the reproduction and digital performance of "out-of-print books", even if the author can, in principle, oppose or put an end to that practice.[372]

However, national regulation of CMOs does not only have to comply with European directives but also with primary law like the competition rules of articles 101 and 102 TFEU and the freedoms guaranteed in this treaty. In its OSA judgment, the ECJ had to consider the question of whether national laws that establish a monopoly for a CMO for a certain category of works in the territory of a member state violated article 56 (freedom to provide services) or the Union's competition rules. As regards the freedom to provide services, the court deemed article 56 applicable and found a restriction of the freedom granted therein. However, the protection of intellectual property rights constituted an "overriding reason in public interest" and the measure was regarded as suitable for this purpose; thus, the restriction could be justified.[373] In analyzing the question whether that measure was necessary, the court took into account that copyright protection is based on the principle of territoriality and that reciprocal agreements were established as a solution to that problem.[374] It held that because there was no method capable of ensuring the same level of protection other than territory-based copyright supervision and because a different view would lead to significant monitoring problems, the measure was necessary and thus consistent with article 56 TFEU.[375] Regarding European competition law, the ECJ confirmed that establishing a dominant position by conferring exclusive rights upon an organization like a CMO was not inconsistent with article 102 TFEU unless an actual abuse could be established of that position induced by the rights conferred.[376] Since this was not the case, the court held the national (Czech) rule to be consistent also with EU competition law.[377] Thus, under such circumstances, national laws that mandate a single organization to carry out the task of collective management are not in breach

372 *Soulier v. Premier Ministre*, C-301/15, ¶ 52 (ECJ 2016). The AG also mentioned CMD art. 5(2) and 5(7) – without, however, referencing recital 12 – in support of his opinion, *see Soulier v. Premier Ministre*, C-301/15 (ECJ 2016), Opinion of AG Wathelet, ¶ 58–60.

373 OSA, C-351/12 at ¶ 68–72.

374 *Id.* at ¶ 73–75.

375 *Id.* at ¶ 76–79. The fact that the decision referred to the situation prior to the enactment of the CMD does not change this result, *see* Clemens Appl, *Es kann nur eine geben! – Monopol und Wettbewerb von Verwertungsgesellschaften*, 16 ipComptence 28, 36–37 (2016); Staats, *Umsetzung*, *supra* at 473. *See* however *e.g.* Lichtenegger, Verwertungsgesellschaften, *supra* at 90–94; Karl-Nikolaus Pfeifer, *Umsetzung der EU-Richtlinie für Verwertungsgesellschaften in deutsches Recht*, 58 ZUM 453, 458 (2014).

376 *OSA*, C-351/12 at ¶ 83–84.

377 However, the ECJ did not address the question whether the fees charged were "appreciably" higher than in other member states and that an abuse of a dominant position, potentially attributable to national legislation, had occurred. If the fees were found to be abusive and if this could be attributed to national laws, the member state would be in breach of the TFEU's articles 102, 106(1).

of EU competition law.[378] This is also in line with the directive – except, of course, its title III on MTL of online rights in musical works.[379]

In conclusion, all the foregoing indicates, apart from the harmonized basis introduced by the Collective Management Directive, that significant differences in national regulation will subsist in the future.[380]

1.2. U.S. Regulation

1.2.1. Antitrust Law

In the United States, the Sherman Act[381] constitutes the core of the antitrust law and provides a basis for both criminal sanctions and civil remedies.[382] Among the latter, the majority of cases are settled by so-called consent decrees[383] (or consent judgments), which have also been applied to U.S. CMOs.

---

378 Huss-Eckerhult, *Collective Management Organisations supra* at 8–10. Arguably, member states might be even obliged to do so under international law, *see* Ficsor, *International Treaties, supra* at 47–49; Ficsor, *Key Issues, supra* at 236–238.

379 *Id.* at 233 (stating that it may be justified to prescribe notification obligations). *See also* Appl, *Monopol und Wettbewerb, supra* at 34–35, 37; Handig, *VerwertungsgesellschaftenG, supra* at 166. Recital 50 of the CMD states that the directive "should remain neutral as regards the prior authorisation and supervision regimes in the Member States […] in so far as those regimes are compatible with Union law and do not create an obstacle to the full application of this Directive." Recital 51 states that member states should set forth specific provisions on the monitoring of CMOs in order to ensure compliance with the rules on MTL.

380 *See also* Ficsor, *International Treaties, supra* at 72; Ficsor, *Key Issues, supra* at 211.

381 15 U.S.C. §§ 1–7. Other important, yet, for the present purposes, not equally relevant antitrust statutes are the Clayton Act (prohibiting certain practices of price discrimination, mergers, etc.), codified at 15 U.S.C. §§ 12–27, and the Federal Trade Commission Act (establishing the Federal Trade Commission and prohibiting, for instance, unfair methods of competition), codified at 15 U.S.C. §§ 41–58. *See* for more details on the Sherman Act section 2.2. below.

382 *See* for a discussion of the remedies for antitrust violations II Phillip E. Areeda & Herbert Hovenkamp, *Antitrust Law: An Analysis of Antitrust Principles and Their Application* ¶ 303 (4th ed. 2013, updated 04/2016).

383 Douglas H. Ginsburg & Joshua D. Wright, *Antitrust Settlements: The Culture of Consent* ¶ 1, 11 (George Mason University Law and Economics Research Paper Series 13–18, 2013), *available at* https://papers.ssrn.com/sol3/papers.cfm?abstract_id=2225894 (last visited May 23, 2017). *See also* Farell Malone & J. Gregory Sidak, *Should Antitrust Consent Decrees Regulate Post-Merger Pricing*, 3 Comp. L. & Econ. 471 (2007) (focusing on the merger context); Massarotto, *Deterrent and Enunciating Effects, supra*; Ann O'Brien, *Antitrust Division U.S. Department of Justice, Cartel Settlements in the U.S. and EU: Similarities, Differences & Remaining Questions* (2008), *available at* https://www.justice.gov/atr/file/519681/download (last visited May 23, 2017) (comparing U.S and EU practices); F. Joseph Warin et al., *To Plead or Not to Plead? Reviewing a Decade of Criminal Antitrust Trials*, July 2006 theantitrustsource, *available at* http://www.americanbar.org/content/dam/aba/publishing/antitrust_source/Jul06_FullSource7_21.authcheckdam.pdf (last visited May 23, 2017) (focusing on criminal antitrust enforcement). In this connection, it has been reported that the criminal antitrust fines have increased significantly in the course of the past decades, *see* Andrew I. Gavil et al., *Antitrust Law in Perspective: Cases, Concepts and Problems in Competition Policy* (2nd ed. 2008).

Yet, even though the general scope of the Sherman Act in principle applies to all CMOs operating in the country, only the two most important performing rights organizations – ASCAP and BMI – have been made subject to consent decrees.[384] These decrees stem from lawsuits initiated by the Department of Justice's (DOJ) Antitrust Division as the federal authority responsible for the enforcement violations of the Sherman Act.[385] Its role for the regulation of CMOs is therefore comparable to the European Commission. While the Federal Trade Commission (FTC) is also entrusted with the enforcement of antitrust violations[386] which may, in fact, overlap with the DOJ's jurisdiction, it has not been of special relevance in the context of the collective management of copyrights.

Apart from antitrust regulation, CMOs are in principle free to engage in their market activities, as specific rules have not been enacted at this point. This is particularly the case for those CMOs that do not act within the scope of a consent decree. However, consent decrees are not the only way to ensure the application of the antitrust laws. While compliance with these decrees has often immunized ASCAP and BMI from further antitrust claims,[387] SESAC, which remains unregulated by a consent decree, has recently[388] faced private claims based on antitrust law.[389] In *Meredith v. SESAC*, it was alleged that it had violated antitrust laws by changing its fee policy and licensing terms in a way that effectively rendered alternatives to the blanket license worthless.[390] Similar accusations were made in *Radio Music License Committee v. SESAC*.[391] Both cases were settled[392] with substantial concessions on SESAC's

384 *See* for ASCAP *United States v. American Society of Composers, Authors and Publishers*, 2001–2002 Trade Cas. (CCH) ¶ 73,474, 2001 U.S. Dist. LEXIS 23707 (S.D.N.Y. 2001) [hereinafter: ASCAP Consent Decree]; for BMI *United States v. Broadcast Music, Inc.*, 1996-1 Trade Cas. (CCH) ¶ 71,378, 1994 U.S. Dist. LEXIS 21476 (S.D.N.Y. 1994) [hereinafter: BMI Consent Decree]. The ASCAP Consent Decree is also often referred to as "Second Amended Final Judgement" or simply "AJF2".

385 15 U.S.C. § 4, 28 C.F.R. § 0.40–0.41.

386 The FCT enforces "unfair methods of competition" and "unfair or deceptive acts or practices", *see* 15 U.S.C. § 45(a).

387 *See, e.g., Buffalo Broadcasting Co. v. American Society of Composers, Authors and Publishers*, 744 F. 2d 917 at 927 (2nd Cir. 1984); *Meredith Corp. v. SESAC, LLC*, 1 F. Supp. 3d 180 at 185, 195 (S.D.N.Y. 2014). *See however M. Witmark & Sons v. Jensen*, 80 F. Supp. 843 at 849 (D. Minn. 1948) ("[I]t may be noted that the consent decree of 1941 permitting individual copyright owners to issue individual licenses for performance rights does not preclude a finding that Ascap is in violation of the anti-trust laws in other respects."). *See* for details on the rate-setting process section 3.2.4. below.

388 SESAC was faced with private antitrust litigation before, *see Affiliated Music Enterprises, Inc. v. Sesac, Inc.*, 160 F. Supp. 865 (S.D.N.Y.1958), aff'd, 268 F.2d 13 (2d Cir. 1959).

389 Lunney, *The United States Experience*, *supra* at 351–353. (Treble) damages are available under § 4 of the Clayton Act, *see* 15 U.S.C. § 15. This section is also applicable to the Sherman Act due to the definition of "Antitrust laws", *see* 15 U.S.C. § 12(a). *See also* 15 U.S.C. § 26.

390 *Meredith*, 1 F. Supp. 3d 180.

391 *Radio Music License Comm., Inc. v. SESAC, Inc.*, 29 F. Supp. 3d 487 (E.D. Pa. 2014).

side. This shows that even in the absence of regulation set up by consent decrees, private antitrust enforcement plays an important role in the regulation of CMOs.

1.2.2. Regulation by Consent Decrees: Background and Development

A consent decree is a settlement negotiated between the antitrust agency and the defendant which is filed with a court and incorporated into a judicial order and immunizes the defendant from the government's antitrust claims based on conduct covered by the decree.[393] For such a decree – which constitutes the result of a bargain of the involved parties – to be approved, the court must examine whether the proposed decree lies in the public interest.[394] For this purpose, the DOJ is required to follow a certain procedure set forth in the so-called Tunney Act.[395] Consent decrees neither immunize the defendant against claims brought by third parties[396] nor impose obligations on parties who did not consent to the decree.[397] However, they do give an indication that compliance with their terms implies lawfulness under the antitrust doctrines.[398]

---

392 *Meredith Corp. v. SESAC, LLC*, 87 F. Supp. 3d 650 (S.D.N.Y. 2015); Radio Music License Committee, *SESAC*, http://www.radiomlc.org/pages/6282116.php (last visited April 17, 2017). *See* for the settlement agreement between SESAC and the RMLC Radio Music License Committee, *Settlement Agreement*, http://imgsrv.radiomlc.org/image/rmlc/UserFiles/File/Final%20SESAC%20RMLC%20Settlement%20Agreement.pdf (last visited April 17, 2017).

393 II Areeda & Hovenkamp, *Antitrust Principles*, *supra* at ¶ 327a. *See* for more details Richard A. Epstein, *Antitrust Consent Decrees in Theory and Practice* (2007).

394 15 U.S.C. § 16(e), (f); II Areeda & Hovenkamp, *Antitrust Principles*, *supra* at ¶ 327a. *See also* II Areeda & Hovenkamp, *Antitrust Principles*, *supra* at ¶ §327e (stating that such approval is often "perfunctory"). *See* in this connection *United States v. Gillette Co.*, 406 F. Supp. 713 at 716 (D. Mass. 1975) ("It is not the court's duty to determine whether this is the best possible settlement that could have been obtained if, say, the government had bargained a little harder.") The purpose of the Tunney Act is sometimes expressed so as to prevent courts to "rubber stamp" decrees proposed by the DOJ, *see, e.g.*, *United States v. Microsoft Corp.*, 56 F. 3d 1448 at 1458 (D.C. Cir. 1995).

395 *See* for details on the procedure 15 U.S.C. § 16(b)-(h). *See also* II Areeda & Hovenkamp, *Antitrust Principles*, *supra* at ¶ 327d3; Gavil et al., *Antitrust Law*, *supra* at 1124–1128.

396 *Sam Fox Publ'g Co., Inc. v. United States*, 366 U.S. 683 at 690 (1961).

397 *Firefighters v. City of Cleveland*, 478 U.S. 501 at 529 (1986). Arguably, via their membership contracts, the members of ASCAP and BMI acquiesce in the terms of the Consent Decrees, *see* United States Copyright Office, *Views of the United States Copyright Office Concerning PRO Licensing of Jointly Owned Works* 27 (2016), *available at* https://www.copyright.gov/policy/pro-licensing.pdf (last visited May 23, 2017).

398 *Broadcast Music, Inc. v. Columbia Broadcasting System, Inc.*, 441 U.S. 1 at 13 (1979) ("[I]t cannot be ignored that the Federal Executive and Judiciary have carefully scrutinized ASCAP and the challenged conduct, have imposed restrictions on various of ASCAP's practices, and, by the terms of the decree, stand ready to provide further consideration, supervision, and perhaps invalidation of asserted anticompetitive practices."). *See* for the principles of the interpretation of consent decrees *e.g. United States v. American Society of Composers, Authors and Publishers (Application of Turner Broadcasting System, Inc.)*, 782 F. Supp. 778 at 787–789 (S.D.N.Y. 1991), *aff'd per curiam*, 956 F. 2d 21 (2nd Cir. 1992); *United States v. Amer-*

In the context of collective management, regarding ASCAP and BMI, the consent decrees determine questions relating to licensing, tariffs and membership. As ASCAP was the first CMO that emerged in the U.S., it was also the first to face antitrust challenges. Facing practically no competitive pressure, the organization held a market share of 80% of all musical works performed on the radio in 1934, the year of the first antitrust suit initiated by the Department of Justice.[399] After several years passed, the authority decided to employ a prescriptive policy of "regulated competition"[400] and enacted the first ASCAP consent decree in 1941.[401] The underlying logics of this policy are still valid today: CMOs are free to act on the market, as long as their practices do not conflict with competition law, the boundaries of which are more specifically defined by the consent decree. In parallel, the same strategy was applied to the then comparatively recent CMO BMI; this corresponding consent decree also entered into force in 1941.[402] Since then, the consent decrees have been repeatedly revised and adapted.[403] The current version of the ASCAP Consent Decree dates from 2001 and is also referred to as "Second Amended Final Judgement" (AFJ2); the current BMI Consent Decree is even seven years older, dating from 1994.[404] The DOJ announced a public consultation in 2014 for the purpose of adapting the judgments to changes that have occurred since their last revision.[405] In August 2016, the DOJ issued a closing statement in which it explained that it did not intend to change the consent decrees current-

---

ican Society of Composers, Authors and Publishers (Application of Muzak, LLC), 309 F. Supp. 2d 566 at 570–577 (S.D.N.Y. 2004); *United States v. Broadcast Music, Inc. (Application of AEI Music Network, Inc.)*, 275 F. 3d 168 at 174–175 (2nd Cir. 2001).

399 Einhorn, *Music Performing Rights*, *supra* at 354–355. *See also* Kohn & Kohn, *Music Licensing*, *supra* at 1249–1250; Bernard Korman, *U.S. Position On Collective Administration Of Copyright And Antitrust-Law*, 43 J. Copyright Soc'y 158, 161–167 (1995–1996); Lunney, *The United States Experience*, *supra* at 328–329; section I.5.3. above.

400 The term is used by *Merges* in the context of consent decrees, *see* Robert P. Merges, *The Continuing Vitality of Music Performance Rights Organizations* 26 (UC Berkeley Public Law Research Paper No. 1266870, 2008), *available at* https://papers.ssrn.com/sol3/papers.cfm?abstract_id=1266870 (last visited May 23, 2017). *See also* Ginsburg & Wright, *Culture of Consent*, *supra* at ¶ 2–3.

401 *United States v. American Society of Composers, Authors and Publishers*, 1941 Trade Cas. (CCH), ¶ 56,104, 1941 U.S. Dist Lexis 3944 (S.D.N.Y. 1941).

402 *United States v. Broadcast Music Industry*, 1940–1943 Trade Cas. (CCH), ¶ 56, 096 (E.D. Wis. 1941).

403 *See* on the modification and termination of consent decrees II Areeda & Hovenkamp, *Antitrust Principles*, *supra* at ¶ 327b. *See also* United States Copyright Office, *Copyright And The Music Marketplace* 146 (2nd ed. 2016), *available at* https://www.copyright.gov/policy/musiclicensingstudy/copyright-and-the-music-marketplace.pdf (last visited May 23, 2017) (noting that the longevity of the ASCAP and BMI Consent Decrees is exceptional compared to other sectors).

404 Hereinafter, the current versions of the ASCAP and BMI Consent Decrees will collectively be referred to as the "Consent Decrees".

405 Department of Justice, *Consent Decree Review – ASCAP and BMI 2014*, https://www.justice.gov/atr/ascap-bmi-decree-review (last visited April 17, 2017).

ly in place because "the industry has developed in the context of, and in reliance on, these decrees [...]".[406] However, the authority has urged for a legislative solution that comprehensively addresses the issues of the collective management of the performance right.[407]

1.2.3. Main Features of the ASCAP and BMI Consent Decrees

Just like in connection with the CMD, the provisions of the consent decrees can be grouped around the following core characteristics:

- Focus on users

The most detailed and extensive rules of the ASCAP and BMI Consent Decrees refer to the relationship of the two CMOs and their licensees, setting forth different types of licenses that must be offered and defining basic rules which govern the conclusion and terms of licensing agreements.[408] Perhaps most conspicuous is the introduction of a judicial rate-setting process in cases where the CMOs and users cannot agree on the royalties due from the use of protected content.[409] It should be noted that the decrees are not identical; they are, however, generally considered to be very similar, especially in connection with users.[410]

- Non-discrimination of users

Both the ASCAP and BMI Consent Decrees specify that "similarly situated" users must be treated equally under ordinary circumstances.[411] Moreover, they cannot refuse to grant to any music user a license for the use of their rep-

406 Department of Justice, *Statement of the Department of Justice on the Closing of the Antitrust Division's Review of the ASCAP and BMI Consent Decrees* 22 (2016), *available at* https://www.justice.gov/atr/file/882101/download (last visited May 23, 2017).

407 *Id.* However, the DOJ underlined that it interpreted the Consent Decrees so as to not allow fractional licenses, *see id.* at 3, 11–13, accordingly CMOs are obliged to offer "full work licenses". Fractional licenses are those which only cover the rights of only one of multiple owners, *id.* at 8. The DOJ's opinion was met with heavy criticism, *see* BMI, *BMI & ASCAP Join Forces to Fight the Department of Justice's Interpretation of Their Consent Decrees*, http://www.bmi.com/news/entry/bmi_ascap_join_forces_to_fight_the_department_of_justices_interpretation_of (pursuing a judicial solution) (last visited April 17, 2017); ASCAP, *Message from ASCAP President Paul Williams on Strategy to Fight DOJ Consent Decree Interpretation*, http://www.ascap.com/playback/2016/07/action/doj-strategy.aspx (pursuing a legislative solution) (last visited April 17, 2017). *See* section 3.2.1.c) below for more details.

408 *See* for a definition of "user" ASCAP Consent Decree § II(G). *See also* section 3.2.1.c) below.

409 ASCAP Consent Decree § IX; BMI Consent Decree § XIV.

410 *See, e.g., ASCAP (Application of Muzak)*, 309 F. Supp. 2d 566 at 580–581.

411 *See, e.g.,* ASCAP Consent Decree § IV(C); BMI Consent Decree § VIII(A). Equal treatment of right holders is ensured *e.g.* in connection with the access to membership which may not be denied upon the fulfillment of certain criteria.

ertoire.[412] At the same time, however, the decrees distinguish different categories of users.[413]

- Non-exclusivity

As will be seen, it has been crucial to the application of antitrust law to U.S. CMOs in the music sector that the rights grant made by the members of these organization is non-exclusive. This applies especially to the paradigmatic blanket licenses.[414] This means that individual right holders, be they publishers or songwriters, retain the right to directly license their works when they decide to join ASCAP or BMI, in parallel to the CMOs' ability to license the work collectively.[415]

- Transparency

In various contexts, the consent decrees oblige ASCAP and BMI to comply with basic transparency rules. This applies to both users and right holders. For instance, ASCAP must make available online a public electronic list which contains information concering the repertoire and members;[416] furthermore, the organization must provide users with information on request.[417] Transparency duties also apply in relation to right holders.[418]

- Sectorial approach to musical rights

The consent decrees are clearly designed for managing (non-dramatic) performance rights in musical works.[419] This does not necessarily mean that other categories of rights may not be managed at all but reflects the long-standing practice under which ASCAP and BMI have operated.

1.2.4. CMOs and Statutory Licenses

Not all CMOs operating in the United States are the result of the private collective efforts of individuals to ensure their remuneration for the use of their works. Especially in connection with the introduction of statutory licenses – which often would be too burdensome to administrate by individuals, just like exclusive rights – the question has arisen which organization should be responsible for the management of the expected revenue stream. A strategy has

---

412 ASCAP Consent Decree § VI; BMI Consent Decree § XIV.

413 *See* for more details section 3.2.1.c) below.

414 *See* section 3.2.2. below.

415 ASCAP Consent Decree § IV(B); BMI Consent Decree § IV(A). *See also* in this connection ASCAP Consent Decree § II(E), (J) and (K) which define the respective license types as a non-exclusive licenses and *id.* § IV(A) which prohibits ASCAP to manage rights other than performance rights on a non-exclusive basis.

416 ASCAP Consent Decree § II(N), (O), X(B).

417 *Id.* at § X(A).

418 *Id.* at § XI(B)(1); BMI Consent Decree § VIII(a).

419 *See, e.g.,* ASCAP Consent Decrees § IV(A). *See also id.* at § II(U).

been to rely on newly created organizations rather than on existing ones.[420] A well-known example is SoundExchange. This CMO[421] deals with the management of royalties arising from statutory licenses for the uses of sound recordings.[422] Even though SoundExchange does not operate under a consent decree, its actions are subject to a twofold limitation. First, the normative material expressly sets forth the guidelines which designated organizations must comply with.[423] Second, SoundExchange's authorization to manage the royalty flow is not carved in stone. It is therefore reasonable for the organization to comply with the regulatory requirements as fully as possible.

1.3. Comments on the Regulatory Frameworks and their Development

The most conspicuous difference between the regulatory approaches to CMOs in the EU and the U.S. is the specific legislation provided for by the European Collective Management Directive, whereas the United States has not (yet) pursued a comparable strategy. However, the directive has existed only comparatively recently.[424] Already before its enactment, competition law was applied to CMOs, and remains applicable to these organizations[425] very much like in the United States. However, divergences can also be found in antitrust practice. U.S. antitrust enforcement has followed a regulatory approach by providing for consent decrees in respect to the oldest and most important U.S. CMOs, whereas European commitment decisions have not gained comparable importance in relation to CMOs in the EU, although settlements occurred in several instances. When pursuing such a strategy, antitrust authorities have entered into what could be called a dialogue with the respective CMOs. Additionally, in both jurisdictions, the antitrust law set up a framework for the practices of CMOs, also in respect to the U.S. CMO which remain unregulated by consent decrees. However, as is demonstrated by the U.S. experience in

420 Lemley, *Contracting Around Liability Rules*, *supra* at 478 (referring to SoundExchange). Another example is the Alliance of Artists and Recording Companies (AARC) which was founded to manage the royalties arising from the Audio Home Recording Act (AHRA) (17 U.S.C. §§ 1001–1008), *see* for more information Alliance of Artists and Recording Companies, *AARC Summary & Methodology*, https://aarcroyalties.files.wordpress.com/2013/01/aarc-summary-and-methodology.pdf (last visited April 18, 2017).

421 Even though SoundExchange does not technically issue license when it operates under a statutory license, it represents right holders within the collection and distribution process as well as in proceedings before the copyright royalty judges.

422 17 U.S.C. §§ 112, 114. *See* SoundExchange, *licensing 101*, https://www.soundexchange.com/service-provider/licensing-101/ (last visited April 18, 2017).

423 *See, e.g.,* CFR § 382.13(f) on the distribution obligation, etc and CFR § 370.5(c) which provides for reporting obligations.

424 The "soft law" approach followed by the Recommendation 2005 was abandoned due to its failure, *see* CMD recital 6.

425 *See* for more details on the relationship between the Collective Management Directive and European competition law section 2.1.1. below.

relation to SESAC, private enforcement appears to significantly assist the antitrust compliance in the field of collective management.[426]

A more subtle aspect concerns the authorities involved in the regulation of CMOs. In many EU member states, agencies or departments specialized in copyright and cultural affairs supervise the CMOs,[427] while in the United States, an antitrust authority – the DOJ's antitrust division – along with the rate courts, has primarily been overseeing the CMO's operations.[428] On the European level, the different DGs of the Commission were involved in the development. Whether CMOs are regulated by cultural or antitrust authorities can make a difference, as these often pursue different policies and objectives.[429] The assumption that such authorities do not always collaborate coherently is corroborated by the legislative history of the Collective Management. In this connection, the U.S. experience of CMOs is no exception. Consider, for instance, the diametrically divergent positions taken by the U.S. Copyright Office and the DOJ with respect to the licensing of jointly owned works under the ASCAP and BMI Consent Decrees.[430] It is thus necessary to develop a thorough understanding of CMOs, both from the competition and copyright perspective.[431] This applies to both the EU and the United States.

2. Applicability of Antitrust Laws to CMOs

There are several reasons why the activities of CMOs can be in conflict with competition laws. First of all, CMOs tend to create monopolies – a conduct which is under close scrutiny in the United States as well as in the European Union, as there is the danger that monopolists abuse their powers in the market.[432] In many European countries, a sector-specific legislation applies to

426 This does not mean, however, that the decisions of European authorities do not affect the conduct of third parties. Already in *Greenwich*, for instance, the AG noted that two CMOs changed their rules voluntarily in light of a Commission decision, *see Greenwich Film Production v. Societé Des Auteurs, Compositeurs Et Èditeurs De Musique (SACEM)*, Case 22/79 (ECJ 1979), Opinion of AG Warner at 3293.

427 Impact Assessment 2012 at 120–142 (summarizing national regulation of CMOs).

428 A copyright-focused authority influences CMOs insofar as rates for statutory licenses are set by the Copyright Royalty Board (CRB), *see* section 3.2.5. below.

429 Korman, *U.S. Position*, *supra* at 160.

430 *See* for more details section 3.2.1.c) below.

431 Drexl, *Competition and Development*, *supra* at 210, 270. In this regard, the CMD sets up an expert group, *see* CMD art. 41. This addition has been regarded as a useful feature of the directive, *see* Guibault & van Gompel, *Collective Management*, *supra* at 157–158.

432 *See, e.g.,* Rafael Allendesalazar & Roberto Vallina, *Collecting Societies: The Usual Suspects* in *European Competition Law Annual 2005: The Interaction between Competition Law and Intellectual Property Law* 371 (Claus Dieter Ehlermann & Isabela Atanasiu eds., 2007); Yee Wah Chin, *Copyright collective management in the twenty-first century from a competition law Perspective* in *The Evolution and Equilibrium of Copyright in the Digital Age* 269 (Susy Frankel & Daniel Gervais, eds., 2014).

CMOs *in addition* to competition law; in some, they also enjoy a legal monopoly. Furthermore, agreements between different CMOs can be regarded as agreements between competitors.[433] This is especially the case for European CMOs since they have often exclusively operated in the territory of the country of their establishment. This system has been preserved by a network of reciprocal representation agreements, which was scrutinized under EU competition law since it aims at overcoming national borders in order to create a single market.[434] The following section explains the scope of the U.S. antitrust law (Sherman Act) and EU competition law (TFEU), as far as it is relevant for the collective management of copyrights; it does not, however, envisage a comprehensive comparison between the two regimes in every detail.

2.1. Treaty on the Functioning of the European Union

Several conditions must be met in order to determine the applicability of the EU competition rules contained in article 101 and 102 TFEU. Both articles only apply to "undertakings"; article 101 focuses on "agreements between undertakings, decisions by associations of undertakings and concerted practices". Article 102 only covers the "abusive"[435] practices by undertakings that occupy a "dominant" market position. Both articles incorporate the requirement of a cross-border element. The applicable case law has frequently confirmed that CMOs can fulfill these requirements.

2.1.1. Preliminary Question: The Relationship of EU Competition Law and the Collective Management Directive

The provisions on competition have ceased to be the only major source of the regulation of CMOs since the Collective Management Directive has been introduced. Therefore, one might wonder whether the case law which has been compiled since the 1970s is still applicable, especially in those cases, where the new directive contains explicit rules. Some provisions of the Collective Management Directive address this problem. It is explicitly stated that the directive is "without prejudice to the application of rules on competition [...]"[436] and that it does not preclude the conclusion of representation agreements between CMOs, provided that these agreements are "in compliance with the rules of competition [...]".[437] It is furthermore clarified that the exception contained

433 *Id.*

434 *See, e.g.*, Allendesalazar & Vallina, *The Usual Suspects*, *supra* at 371; David Wood, *Collective Management and EU Competition Law* 3 (2001), *available at* http://ec.europa.eu/competition/speeches/text/sp2001_025_en.pdf (last visited May 23, 2017).

435 Whether a CMO abuses its dominant position is one of the major issues of the Commission's and the ECJ's case law. Section 3 takes a closer look at this question.

436 CMD recital 56; *see also* recital 32.

437 *Id.* at recital 11.

in title III for the online communication to the public of radio and television programs must not be construed to an effect which would be contrary to articles 101 and 102 TFEU.[438] Moreover, these articles are part of EU primary law which, as a general principle, cannot be altered by directives that are part of the secondary law; the secondary law must be interpreted in accordance with primary law.[439] This leads to the conclusion that the case law based on EU competition law remains (in principle) applicable to CMOs.[440] These cases can also be used to interpret the Collective Management Directive because large parts of the directive are based on those cases, especially with regard to the provisions governance and transparency (mainly title II).[441] Finally, the directive is not fully comprehensive, and the ECJ's case law can serve to supplement its rules. This applies first and foremost to the CMOs' relationship with users, as the directive only contains sparse provisions in this respect. It remains to be seen (and this is not unlikely) whether the Collective Management Directive or its transposition into national law has an impact on the Commission's enforcement of competition law.[442]

2.1.2. Undertakings

As to the construction of the term "undertaking", it is useful to remember that a functional definition is applied to interpret the notion.[443] Therefore, an undertaking is "every entity engaged in an economic activity, regardless of the

438 *Id.* at recital 48, art. 32.

439 Matthias Ruffert, *Art. 288 AEUV* in *EUV/AEUV* ¶ 8–9 (Christian Calliess & Matthias Ruffert eds., 5th ed. 2016) (also highlighting that secondary law can be used to further specify and give effect to the principles established by primary law); Peter Vcelouch, *Art 288 AEUV* in *Kommentar zu EUV und AEUV* ¶ 9 (Heinz Mayer & Karl Stöger eds., updated 12/2010 at rdb.at). *See also* Drexl, *Collecting Societies, supra* at 2; Lichtenegger, *Verwertungsgesellschaften, supra* at 326–328 (referring to the presumption of legality of secondary law). TFEU art. 103 provides a legal basis to adopt regulations or directive in accordance with art 101 and 102; however, the CMD was based on different provisions, *see* section 1.1.4.d) above.

440 Guibault & van Gompel, *Collective Management, supra* at 146; Huss-Eckerhult, *Collective Management* Organisations, *supra* at 2; Mestmäcker & Schweitzer, *Wettbewerbsrecht, supra* at 888.

441 Proposal 2012 at 8; Guibault, *Collective Management Directive, supra* at 715; van Gompel, *Directive, supra* at 542.

442 *See also* Guibault & van Gompel, *Collective Management, supra* at 140; Ernst Joachim Mestmäcker, *Collecting Societies* in *European Competition Law Annual 2005: The Interaction between Competition Law and Intellectual Property Law* 343, 352–353 (Claus Dieter Ehlermann & Isabela Atanasiu eds., 2007) (in connection with German regulation).

443 Jan Busche, *Art. 102 AEUV* in 3 *Kölner Kommentar zum Kartellrecht* ¶ 8 (Jan Busche & Andreas Röhling eds., 2016); Jens Thomas Füller, *Art. 101 AEUV* in 3 *Kölner Kommentar zum Kartellrecht* ¶ 10–12 (Jan Busche & Andreas Röhling eds., 2016); Daniela Hengst, *Art. 101 AEUV* in 2 *Kartellrecht* ¶ 5 (Hermann-Josef Bunte ed., 12th ed. 2014); Peter Lewisch, *Art 102 AEUV* in *Kommentar zu EUV und AEUV* ¶ 3 (Heinz Mayer & Karl Stöger eds., updated 08/2013 at rdb.at); Hanno Wollmann, *Art 101 AEUV* in *Kommentar zu EUV und AEUV* ¶ 31 (Heinz Mayer & Karl Stöger eds., updated 12/2011 at rdb.at).

legal status of the entity and the way in which it is financed […]".[444] Economic activities are also those which do not aim at obtaining profits.[445] The Commission applied these basic competition doctrines to CMOs and confirmed that they "participate in the commercial exchange of services and are therefore engaged in the exercise of economic activities"; thus, CMOs qualified as "undertakings" within the meaning of EU competition rules.[446] Some decisions came to the same result without, however, deeming it necessary to make express mention to this effect,[447] while the ECJ expressly confirmed this principle in *OSA*.[448] Additionally, the Commission clarified that CMOs organized on a non-profit basis fall within the scope of the competition rules.[449] It should be noted that also individual (natural) persons,[450] like artists or athletes, for instance, can be undertakings within the meaning of the EU competition rules.[451]

2.1.3. Article 101 TFEU

Article 101 applies to agreements and concerted practices between two undertakings or decisions by associations formed by such entities. The assessment under this article consists of two basic steps: First, one must ask whether an agreement which is capable of affecting trade between member states has actual or potential restrictive effects on competition or an anti-competitive object; second, one must determine, under the conditions set forth by article 101(3),[452] whether the agreement in question has pro-competitive effects

444 *See, e.g., K. Höfner v. Macrotron GmbH*, C-41/90, ¶ 21 (ECJ 1991); *Confederación Española de Empresarios de Estaciones de Servicio v. Compañía Española de Petróleos SA*, C-217/05, ¶ 39 (ECJ 2006).

445 *Heintz van Landewyck SARL v. Commission*, joined cases 209 to 215 and 218/78, ¶ 88 (ECJ 1980).

446 *GEMA I*, Commission Decision of 02.06.1971, Case IV/26 760, 1971 O.J. (L134) 15–29, ¶ II(A); *IFPI Simulcasting*, Commission Decision of 08.10.2002, Case COMP/C2/38.014, 2003 O.J. (L107) 58–84, ¶ 59; Mestmäcker & Schweitzer, *Wettbewerbsrecht*, *supra* at 876.

447 *See, e.g., Belgische Radio en Televisie v. Société Belge des Auteurs, Compositeurs et Éditeurs*, case 127-73, ¶ 5–8 (ECJ 1974); *Musik-Vertrieb Membran GmbH v. GEMA*, joined cases 55/80 and 57/80, ¶ 18 (ECJ 1981). *See also Phil Collins v. Imtrat Handelsgesellschaft mbH*, joined cases C-92/92 and C-326/92, ¶ 22 (ECJ 1993).

448 *OSA*, C-351/12 at ¶ 80. *See also Autortiesību un komunicēšanās konsultāciju aģentūra / Latvijas Autoru apvienība v. Konkurences padome*, C-177/16, ¶ 32–33 (ECJ 2017).

449 *GVL*, Commission Decision of 29.10.1981, Case IV/29.839, 1981 O.J. (L370) 49–59, ¶ 43–44.

450 Rainer Bechtold et al., *EU Kartellrecht* 18 (2014); Hengst, *Art. 101 AEUV*, *supra* at ¶ 14.

451 *RAI/UNITEL*, Commission Decision of 26 May 1978, Case 78/516/EEC, 1978 O.J. (L157) 39–41, ¶ IV(1.)(a); Helmut Schröter, *Vorbemerkungen zu den Artikeln 101 bis 105 AEUV* in *Europäisches Wettbewerbsrecht* ¶ 69, 75 (Helmut Schröter et al. eds., 2nd ed. 2014); Wollmann, *Art 101 AEUV*, *surpa* at ¶ 28. *See also* Drexl, *Competition and Development*, *supra* at 207 n. 719 (noting that individual artists are not undertakings to the extent they act as employees).

452 Article 101(3) reads:
The provisions of paragraph 1 may, however, be declared inapplicable in the case of:

outweighing the anti-competitive effects.[453] In the context of collective management, article 101 has primarily been applied to the different forms of (horizontal) cooperation among CMOs from different countries, in most instances under the conclusions of RRAs.[454] These agreements will be primarily examined under article 101 to the extent that the involved CMOs are or become actual or potential competitors with respect to the services they offer.[455]

However, not only agreements between CMOs can be subject to competition law. Also, the terms contained in the statutes of CMOs under which they acquire rights from right holders could be interpreted as agreements which aim at fixing trading conditions, thus conflicting with the competition rules.[456] The agreements in question are concluded between a CMO and individual right holders; however, one could also speak of agreements between individual right holders, especially when establishing the CMOs. In principle, one could also think of decisions by associations of undertakings.[457] As mentioned before, individual right holders qualify as undertakings: In the case of businesses like music publishers, this is rather obvious. In the case of individual authors, the

- any agreement or category of agreements between undertakings,
- any decision or category of decisions by associations of undertakings,
- any concerted practice or category of concerted practices,

which contributes to improving the production or distribution of goods or to promoting technical or economic progress, while allowing consumers a fair share of the resulting benefit, and which does not:

(a) impose on the undertakings concerned restrictions which are not indispensable to the attainment of these objectives;

(b) afford such undertakings the possibility of eliminating competition in respect of a substantial part of the products in question.

453 European Commission, *Communication from the Commission – Guidelines on the applicability of Article 101 of the Treaty on the Functioning of the European Union to horizontal co-operation agreements* ¶ 20, 2011 O.J. (C11) 1–72.

454 *See, e.g., IFPI Simulcasting*, COMP/C2/38.014 at ¶ 60; *Ministère public v. Jean-Louis Tournier*, case 395/87, ¶ 16–20 (ECJ 1989). *See also* CMD recital 11; *CISAC Agreement,* COMP/C2/38.698 at ¶ 14–17, 223.

455 Guibault & van Gompel, *Collective Management, supra* at 159. Co-operation is of a "horizontal nature" if an agreement is entered into between actual or potential competitors, *see* European Commission Guidelines on Horizontal Co-Operation, *supra* at ¶ 1. The Commission has held that CMOs can be both actual and potential competitors, *see CISAC Agreement,* COMP/C2/38.698 at ¶ 111, 113. The criteria for determining the relevant market are largely identical for an analysis under article 102, *see* Lewisch, *Art 102 AEUV, supra* at ¶ 26; Wolfgang Weiß, *Art. 102 AEUV* in *EUV/AEUV* ¶ 6 (Christian Calliess & Matthias Ruffert eds., 5th ed. 2016). *See also* Commission of the European Communities, *Commission Notice on the definition of relevant market for the purposes of Community competition law*, 1997 O.J. (C372) 5–13. *See* however *Raiffeisen Zentralbank Österreich AG v. Commission*, joined cases T-259/02 to T-264/02 and T-271/02, ¶ 172 (EGC 2006), *appeal dismissed*, joined cases C-125/07 P, C-133/07 P, C-135/07 P and C-137/07 P (ECJ 2009) ("[I]t must be borne in mind, first, that the definition of the relevant market differs according to whether Article 81 EC or Article 82 EC is to be applied.").

456 Schierholz, *Collective Rights Management, supra* at 1158.

457 Füller, *Art. 101 AEUV, supra* at ¶ 104; Sousa e Silva, *The Proposed Directive, supra* at 9.

rulings of the ECJ clearly indicate that natural persons fall within the meaning of this term if they independently engage in economic activities like transferring their rights to a CMO;[458] right holders like songwriters or performing artists fulfill this criterion when carrying out such a transfer.[459] Even though article 101 would thus be applicable to a CMOs' bylaws, statutes etc., neither the Commission nor the ECJ has profoundly touched upon this issue. The Commission handed down a decision which could be understood as meaning that amendments to a CMO's statute which do not go beyond the "nature and purpose of a CMO" are not in conflict with EU competition law,[460] even though the traditional model of collective management eliminates competition between individual members to large extent.[461] The ECJ took a similar approach in *BRT v. SABAM*.[462] Therefore, commentators have concluded that the European authorities have accepted the activities essential to collective management as being compatible with article 101.[463] Reciprocal representation agreements have therefore been and are likely to continue to be the most important field of application of article 101 in the collective management context.

Agreements, decisions and concerted practices can be exempted from article 101 by virtue of its subsection 3. Formerly, a permission issued by the Commission was required; such permission has only been granted once for collective management purposes in the context of simulcasting.[464] The current Competition Regulation does not necessarily make the effects of article 101(3) con-

458 *Belgium v. Jean Claude Becu*. C-22/98, ¶ 26–27 (ECJ 1999); Hengst, *Art. 101 AEUV*, *supra* at ¶ 14; Mestmäcker & Schweitzer, *Wettbewerbsrecht*, *supra* at 876–877. *See also Deutsche Grammophon GmbH v. Metro-SB-Grossmärkte GmbH*, case 78/70, ¶ 17–18 (ECJ 1971); Wollmann, *Art 101 AEUV*, *supra* at ¶ 28; Wünschmann, *Kollektive Verwertung*, *supra* at 60–61.

459 Mestmäcker & Schweitzer, *Wettbewerbsrecht*, *supra* at 876.

460 *GEMA III*, Commission Decision of 04.12.1981, Case IV/29-971, 1982 O.J. (L84) 12–20, ¶ 54. The Commission stated however, that it would not deal with this matter in this case. The Commission furthermore dealt with article 101 and CMOs in the course of preparing the decisions in GEMA I and II, *see* Mestmäcker & Schweitzer, *Wettbewerbsrecht*, *supra* at 877–878. Furthermore, and account was given in a case relating to MTV/VPL, *see* section 2.3.3. below.

461 Riis, *Collecting Societies*, *supra* at 484.

462 *BRT*, 127-73 at ¶ 10 ("For an association effectively to protect its rights and interests it must enjoy a position based on the assignment in its favour, by the associated authors, of their rights to the extent required for the association to carry out its activity on the necessary scale").

463 Berend-Jan Drijber, *European competition law aspects of copyright collecting societies* in *Collective Administration of Copyrights in Europe* 67, 75 (Herman Cohen Jehoram et al. eds., 1995); Mestmäcker & Schweitzer, *Wettbewerbsrecht*, *supra* at 878; Schierholz, *Collective Rights Management*, *supra* at 1158. *See also* Mestmäcker, *Collecting Societies*, *supra* at 344 ("[T]here is consent that collecting societies are a valid form of rights management"); Richard Whish, *Competition Law* 803 (7th ed. 2012) ("[T]here is nothing intrinsically objectionable about the establishment of collecting societies [...]"). The exact legal reasons for this view will be discussed in section 2.3.3. below.

464 Schierholz, *Collective Rights Management*, *supra* at 1157–1158.

tingent upon a formal intervention by the Commission.[465] Therefore, CMOs have to assess and prove in a given case that their reciprocal agreements do not violate EU competition law.[466] A conclusive answer to the question what kind of reciprocal agreements could be exempted from article 101 can thus not be given; it can, however, be assumed that the interpretation of the clause will continue to be restrictive.[467]

2.1.4. Article 102 TFEU

In order to fall within the scope of article 102 CMOs, must possess a dominant position. According to the ECJ, such a position relates to "a position of economic strength enjoyed by an undertaking which enables it to prevent effective competition being maintained on the relevant market by giving it the power to behave to an appreciable extent independently of its competitors, customers, and ultimately of its consumers".[468] Yet, it has been emphasized that CMOs occupy a special position within the application practice of article 102.[469] CMOs usually possess a degree of dominance that goes beyond the powers of "regular" undertakings, and this implies an elevated level of responsibility;[470] furthermore, their specific objective lies in the protection of the interest of their members, a feature which is not common to market-driven companies. As a consequence, the general case law is not applicable to CMOs without specific consideration as to their nature; moreover, "safe harbors" established by the general case law are of limited scope due to their market power.[471] However, the mere existence of a dominant position is not sufficient; it is furthermore necessary to establish an abuse of such position.[472]

An undertaking can only occupy a dominant position in respect of a certain relevant market. Products (services) usually belong to the same market if they are regarded as substitutable or interchangeable by the consumer.[473] In

465 Competition Regulation art. 1(2), 10.

466 *Id.* at art. 2.

467 Schierholz, *Collective Rights Management*, *supra* at 1158.

468 *United Brands Co. v. Commission*, case 27/76, ¶ 65 (ECJ 1978).

469 *See, e.g., Ministère public v. Jean-Louis Tournier,* case 395/87 (ECJ 1989), Opinion of AG Jacobs, ¶ 43.

470 *Id.*

471 Allendesalazar & Vallina, *The Usual Suspects*, *supra* at 373–374.

472 *See, e.g., Nederlandsche Banden-Industie Michelin v. Commission*, case 322/81, ¶ 57 (ECJ 1983). *See also OSA*, C-351/12 at ¶ 83 ("As regards the interpretation of Article 102 TFEU in such a context, it is settled case-law that the mere creation of a dominant position through the grant of exclusive rights within the meaning of Article 106(1) TFEU is not in itself incompatible with Article 102 TFEU. A Member State will be in breach of the prohibitions laid down by those two provisions only if the undertaking in question, merely by exercising the exclusive rights conferred upon it, is led to abuse its dominant position or where such rights are liable to create a situation in which that undertaking is led to commit such abuses [...]").

473 *See, e.g., United Brands*, 27/76 at ¶ 12; European Commission Guidelines on the Definition of Relevant Market ¶ 15, *see* ¶ 20 for supply substitution ("This means that suppliers are able

the case of CMOs, one must consider that their main task is to engage in two interrelated, yet very distinct activities. On the one hand, they offer licensing options for users, and on the other hand, they offer management services for right holders. Competition law must be applied in both cases.[474] Since European CMOs have for the most part enjoyed legal or de facto monopolies, they occupy a dominant market position within the meaning of article 102 in both markets: First, they are often the only legitimate source for protected works (user side), and second, they are often the only provider of collective management services for a particular category of works or rights (right holder side).[475] The ECJ and the Commission have repeatedly confirmed this view.[476] The case law shows that the relevant (product) market regarding the management and licensing of copyrights is related, on the one hand, to the respective categories of rights, and, on the other hand, to the types of works.[477] The geo-

to switch production to the relevant products and market them in the short term without incurring significant additional costs or risks in response to small and permanent changes in relative prices.", footnotes omitted).

474 Huss-Eckerhult, *Collective Management Organisations*, *supra* at 7. *See also* Drexl, *Competition and Development*, *supra* at 231; Mestmäcker & Schweitzer, *Wettbewerbsrecht*, *supra* at 876.

475 Kretschmer, *The Failure of Property Rules*, *supra* at 126; P. Sean Morris, *The Reform of Article 82 and the Operation of Competition Principles upon the Normal Trading Functions of Copyright Collecting Societies*, 4 J. IP L. & Practice 566, 568 (2009).

476 Mestmäcker, *Collecting Societies*, *supra* at 343 ("Market power in relevant markets is usually a forgone conclusion").

477 *GVL*, IV/29.839 at ¶ 45. This reasoning was confirmed by the ECJ, *see Gesellschaft zur Verwertung von Leistungsschutzrechten mbH v. Commission*, case 7/82, ¶ 44–45 (ECJ 1983). In this case, the service market for the management of secondary rights of performers and manufactures was considered as the relevant market. The court rejected a market definition based on "the management of the royalties due to performing artists as a result of the secondary exploitation of their performances", *see id.* at ¶ 43. *See also Gesellschaft zur Verwertung von Leistungsschutzrechten mbH v. Commission*, case 7/82 (ECJ 1983), Further Opinion of AG Reischl, 525–526 (rejecting a market definition extending to "transactions between artists and the users of their works"). In the *Daft Punk-decision*, the Commission stated: "Le marché du produit concerné est celui de la prestation des services de gestion des droits d'auteur de musique.", *see Daft Punk*, Commission Decision of 06.08.2002, Case COMP/C2/37.219, 8, *available at* http://ec.europa.eu/competition/antitrust/cases/dec_docs/37219/37219_11_3.pdf (last visited May 22, 2017) (the decision is only available in French). It hence based its market definition on the management services of artistic works of a certain category (repertoire), *see* Jorg Sladiĉ, *Introduction to Copyright and Collective Management in Competition Law*, 5 LeXonomica 37, 47 (2013). In its decision on the Cannes Extension Agreement, the Commission distinguished the market for mono- and multi-territorial licenses, *see Cannes Extension Agreement*, COMP/C2/38.681 at ¶ 19. In *IFPI Simulcasting*, the relevant market referred to multi-territorial administration and licensing services in respect of simulcasting rights, *see IFPI Simulcasting*, COMP/C2/38.014 at ¶ 32. *See also Kanal 5 Ltd v. STIM*, C-52/07, ¶ 20 (ECJ 2008) ("Swedish market for making available music protected by copyright for television broadcast"); *Basset*, 402/85 at ¶ 9 ("[…] a national copyright management society, which enjoys a *de facto* monopoly for the protection of its repertoire"); *Tournier*, 395/87 at ¶ 6 ("the management of its members' rights"); note however that the referring court did not ask the ECJ to determine the relevant markets in these three

graphical market has traditionally been confined to the territory of a member state;[478] however, it should be noted that the relevant market can be subject to change over time, especially in light of technological development.[479] As already mentioned above, efforts to create MTL systems aim at overcoming the national scope of copyright management, especially for online uses.

2.1.5. Cross-Border Element

Traditionally, European CMOs have been national in scope – they have operated only within the borders of one member state. The different organizations have been linked to one another through reciprocal representation agreements in order to cover the repertoire of the entire Union (and beyond). However, the EU competition rules require that a conduct has an effect on more than one member state: Article 101 and article 102 only prohibit practices which "affect trade between member states". The former article further requires the "prevention, restriction or distortion of competition within the Internal Market or in a substantial part of it"; the latter speaks of a dominant position "within the Internal Market". Even though CMOs have operated within a national scope of activities, European authorities have frequently confirmed that the conduct of (national) CMOs can affect trade between member states. This can especially be the case if a measure leads to an unjustified partitioning of the Internal Market; copyrights fall within the scope of this principle.[480] In the context of collective management, CMOs will especially fulfill this condition if they impede the free movement of services. The ECJ held that the refusal of a CMO to accept nationals from other member states as (full) members constituted such a conduct because this prevented these right holders from fully

---

cases. *See* in general on markets and IP rights Clemens Appl, *Technische Standardisierung und Geistiges Eigentum* 412–416 (2012).

478 *See, e.g., GVL*, IV/29.839 at ¶ 45; *Kanal 5*, C-52/07 at ¶ 20. *See also* Ralf Capito, *Article 82 EC* in *European Media Law* 151, 159 (Oliver Castendyk et al., eds. 2008) (noting that the market definition in the media sector is often confined to one country of one single language area); Krzysztof Kuik & Anthony Dawes, *Media* in *The EU Law of Competition* 1709, 1760 (Jonathan Faull & Ali Nikpay eds., 3rd ed. 2014) (in the context of mergers). *See also* section 2.1.5. immediately.

479 Antonio Capobianco, *Licensing of Music Rights: Media Convergence, Technological Developments and EC Competition Law*, 26 E.I.P.R. 113, 120 (2004) (also stating that the market might be different according to respective users). In *CISAC*, the Commission delineated three relevant product markets for public performance rights: i) The provision of copyright administration services to right holders, (ii) the provision of copyright administration services to other collecting societies, (iii) the licensing of public performance rights for satellite, cable and internet transmissions to commercial users. The latter market possessed specific features due to technical options of remote monitoring and copyright exploitation and was thus different from previous cases decided by the ECJ *see CISAC Agreement*, COMP/C2/38.698 at ¶ 48–64 (also discussing the relevant geographical markets). *See also CISAC v. Commission*, Case T-442/08, ¶ 16–19 (2013); *IFPI Simulcasting*, COMP/C2/38.014 at ¶ 32.

480 *Deutsche Grammophon*, 78/70 at ¶ 12–13; *Membran*, 55/80 and 57/80 at ¶ 12–13.

exploiting their rights within the Internal Market.[481] The same reasoning applies if a contract only covers performances that take place in countries that are not part of the Union.[482] Conversely, the fact that a CMO merely operates on the territory of one member state does not preclude the application of the competition rules.[483] Furthermore, trade between member states can be affected, even if a CMO, by implementing unfavorable conditions, encourages right holders from their home state – who are not willing to accept its conditions – to turn to a CMO in another member state. This is because rights are typically managed under reciprocal representation agreements which could diminish the right holders' income due to additional administrative fees etc.[484] It is not necessary to show that the measure actually affects the trade between member states; it must only be capable ("may affect") to do so.[485]

As regards the assessment whether a CMO holds a dominant position "within the internal market", European authorities have consistently held this condition to be fulfilled when such an organization possesses a quasi-(de facto, legal) monopoly, even if it merely operated on the territory of a single member state. For this purpose, a dominant position in Belgium,[486] the Czech Republic,[487] France,[488] Germany,[489] Latvia,[490] and Sweden,[491] respectively, has been regarded as sufficient to trigger applying the EU competition law. A CMO possessing a dominant position in one member state can hence in principle be considered to have a dominant position within the Internal Market.

The conclusion that can be drawn from the foregoing is that neither the Commission nor the ECJ has ever had serious doubts that the activities of

---

481 *GVL*, 7/82 at ¶ 34–39. The AG expressed certain doubts whether, in the circumstances of the particular case, the restrictions imposed by CMOs were actually capable of affecting trade to a *significant* extent. This reasoning was mainly based on the fact that only few (133) artists from other member states joined the CMO after the ban was lifted, *see GVL v. Commission*, 7/82 (ECJ 1983), Further Opinion of AG Reischl at 529–530. The ECJ did not address these concerns; obviously, it deemed this condition fulfilled or not relevant in the context of collective management. *See also GEMA I*, IV/26 760 at ¶ II(D).

482 *Greenwich Film Production*, 22/79 at ¶ 11–13.

483 *GVL*, IV/29.839 at ¶ 63; *Autortiesību un komunicēšanās konsultāciju aģentūra / Latvijas Autoru apvienība*, C-177/16 at ¶ 28–29 (stressing that the CMO in question also managed rights of foreign right holders). *See also Autortiesību un komunicēšanās konsultāciju aģentūra – Latvijas Autoru apvienība v. Konkurences padome*, C-177/16 (ECJ 2017), Opinion of AG Wahl ¶ 27–29.

484 *Daft Punk*, COMP/C2/37.219 at 9–10.

485 *Greenwich*, 22/79 at ¶ 12.

486 *BRT*, 127/73 at ¶ 5.

487 *OSA*, C-351/12 at ¶ 86.

488 *Cf. Tournier*, 395/87 at ¶ 35, 38, 43; *Daft Punk*, COMP/C2/37.219 at 8–9.

489 *GEMA I*, IV/26 760 at ¶ II(B); *GVL*, 7/82 at ¶ 44–45.

490 *Autortiesību un komunicēšanās konsultāciju aģentūra / Latvijas Autoru apvienība*, C-177/16 at ¶ 34.

491 *Kanal 5*, C-52/07 at ¶ 22.

CMOs affect trade between member states or that they occupy a dominant position within the Internal Market.[492] The latter consideration could, however, pose problems if viewed in connection with a possible competition between CMOs on the markets vis-à-vis right holders and users. If such a system developed and, say, four or five CMOs were competing within the EU, it must be asked whether these CMOs still hold a dominant position within the Internal Market; in such a situation, the case law based on article 102 (prohibiting discriminatory practice etc.) would not apply to these organizations anymore.[493]

2.1.6. Article 106 TFEU

CMOs have tried to avoid the obligations under EU competition law by asserting their exclusion from these rules by virtue of article 106(2) TFEU as "undertakings entrusted with the operation of services of general economic interest". European authorities have consistently rejected this argument. According to the ECJ, CMOs, by managing intellectual property rights, serve private interests rather than general interests.[494] In *GVL*, the judges were also unwilling to acknowledge that CMOs are "entrusted" with a task by a member state.[495] In this decision, the ECJ stated that the national (German) copyright act did not mandate "specific undertakings" with the task of collective management but described in a general manner the rules that governed the activities of CMOs.[496] Nevertheless, member states act in the public interest[497] when they protect copyright holders to the extent permitted (or required) by EU law; organizations subject to these laws serve private interests if they offer rights management services "even though intellectual property rights protect-

[492] It is noticeable that in the aftermath of the *Lucazeau* and *Tournier* cases, the Commission refused to deal with complaints about SACEM brought by BEMIM – an association representing users – due to the lack of Community interest; thus it was the task of national courts rule on the CMO's conduct. The Court of First Instance confirmed the Commission's decision in this respect, *see BEMIM v. Commission*, T-114/92, ¶ 93–94 (1995). *See* for an analysis and the background of the case Paul L.C. Torremans & Irini A. Stamatoudi, *Collecting Societies: sorry, the Community is no longer interested!* 22 E.L. Rev. 352 (1997).

[493] Schierholz, Collective Rights Management, *supra* at 1188 (stating that it can be doubted whether the Commission was aware of this possible consequence arising from its initiatives).

[494] BRT, 127/73 at ¶ 23. *See also IFPI-Simulcasting*, COMP/C2/38.014 at ¶ 59; *GVL*, IV/29.839 at ¶ 68.

[495] *GVL*, 7/82 at 29–32. *See also GEMA I*, IV/26 760 at ¶ III(1).

[496] *GVL*, 7/82 at 31. It has not been entirely clarified whether the article would apply to a specific CMO which is exclusively mandated by the law of member state to carry out management tasks, like the case of SIAE in Italy, *see* Drexl, *Competition and Development, supra* at 63 n. 115. *See also* Lichtenegger, *Verwertungsgesellschaften, supra* at 343–348; Maria Riccio & Giorgio Giannone Codiglione, *Copyright Collecting Societies, Monopolistic Positions and Competition in the EU Single Market*, 7 Masaryk U. J. L. & Tech. 287 (2013); Wünschmann, *Kollektive Verwertung, supra* at 73.

[497] In connection with the fundamental freedoms *see, e.g., Football Association Premier League, Ltd v. QC Leisure*, joined cases C-403/08 and C-429/08, ¶ 93–94 (ECJ 2011). *See also* Services Directive recital 40.

ed by law" are at issue.[498] Additionally, it should be noted that the fact that CMOs often also fulfill social and cultural functions[499] has no bearing on the assessment under article 106(2); this is because this provision only refers to *economic interests*.[500] Conversely, the ECJ emphasized that article 106(1) applied to CMOs when a member state provides for a legal monopoly.[501] Yet, the article does not say more than deeming the competition rules applicable to the national legislation: The provision is directed toward member states and not to undertakings.[502] In summary, CMOs cannot escape the obligations provided for by the articles 101 and 102 under article 106. In any event, it should be remembered that, even if one is of the opinion that article 106(2) applies to CMOs, the application of EU competition law would only be restricted inasmuch as it would "obstruct the performance, in law or in fact, of the particular tasks assigned to them".

2.2. Sherman Act

The U.S. Sherman Act, on a fundamental level, applies to "persons" who engage in prohibited practices which lead to a "restraint of commerce or trade among the several States" either by i) coordinating their conduct with competitors or by ii) abusing a monopoly (and conspiring to monopolize).[503] Furthermore, the Clayton Act subjects the acquisition of assets or capital to merger control.[504] While CMOs can in principle violate all three of these "pillars" of modern Antitrust law,[505] the former two are of special interest for the present purposes. CMOs have often been confronted with alleged violations of section 1 or both section 1 and 2 of the Sherman Act;[506] in rarer circumstances, courts have found CMOs to be in breach of antitrust law solely on the basis of section 2.[507]

2.2.1. Persons

Violations of the Sherman Act can be committed by a "person". Section 1 states that "[e]very person who shall make any contract or engage in any com-

498 *OSA*, C-351/12 at ¶ 81 (emphasis added).

499 *See, e.g.*, CMD art. 12(4).

500 *GEMA I*, IV/26.760 at ¶ III(2).

501 *OSA*, C-351/12 at ¶ 82.

502 Lewisch, *Art 102 AEUV*, *supra* at ¶ 11–12.

503 15 U.S.C. §§ 1–2.

504 15 U.S.C. § 18.

505 Chin, *Copyright Collective Management*, *supra* at 269–270.

506 *See, e.g., BMI v. CBS*, 441 U.S. 1 at 6; *Meredith*, 1 F. Supp. 3d 180 at 186. *See also Columbia Broadcasting System, Inc. v. American Society of Composers, Authors and Publishers*, 620 F. 2d 930 at 932 (2nd Cir. 1980); *K-91, Inc. v. Gershwin Publishing Corp.*, 372 F. 2d 1 at 2 (9th Cir. 1967); *Buffalo Broadcasting*, 744 F. 2d 917 at 919; *Witmark & Sons*, 80 F. Supp. 843 at 849 at 849–850.

507 *See, e.g., Radio Music License Comm.*, 29 F. Supp. 3d 487 at 498–499.

bination or conspiracy hereby declared to be illegal shall be deemed guilty [...]"; similarly, section 2 provides that "[e]very person who shall monopolize, or attempt to monopolize, or combine or conspire with any other person or persons, to monopolize [...] shall be deemed guilty [...]." The term is defined by the statute and includes "corporations and associations existing under or authorized by the laws of either the United States, the laws of any of the Territories, the laws of any State, or the laws of any foreign country".[508] The statute thus provides a broad understanding of this notion. It follows that CMOs can be subject to the provisions of the Sherman Act in many organizational forms; however, also individual right holders can be regarded to fall within the reach of the act's language.[509] Nevertheless, courts have not expressly dealt with the interpretation of this notion in the context of collective management,[510] obviously presupposing that CMOs and their members[511] fall within the scope of the Sherman Act.

2.2.2. Section 1 Sherman Act

Section 1 of the Sherman declares illegal "[e]very contract, combination in the form of trust or otherwise, or conspiracy, in restraint of trade or commerce among the several States, or with foreign nations [...]".[512] This language applies only to multilateral and not to unilateral conduct[513] which is, in turn, covered by section 2 of the act. However, concerted actions are likely to raise more concern than independent actions, as such conduct "inherently is fraught with anticompetitive risk".[514] The history of antitrust cases involving U.S. CMOs shows, as the Court noted in *Meredith v. SESAC*, that the requirement of multilateral action is often deemed fulfilled without larger discussion.[515] The par-

---

508 15 U.S.C. § 7; *see also* 15 U.S.C. § 12(a).

509 *Standard Oil Co. of New Jersey v. United States*, 221 U.S. 1 at 61 (1911).

510 In other contexts, they did, *see, e.g., United States Postal Serv. v. Flamingo Indus. (USA) Ltd.*, 540 U.S. 736 (2004) (holding that the U.S. postal service is not a person within the meaning of the statute).

511 *See, e.g., Meredith*, 1F. Supp. 3d 180 at 209: ("A juror could find that these persons affiliated with SESAC with each expecting and agreeing that the rights to the works of all SESAC affiliates would be jointly offered in a blanket license.")

512 15 U.S.C. § 1.

513 *Monsanto Co. v. Spray-Rite Serv. Corp.*, 465 U.S. 752 at 781 (1984). It must be established that there was "conscious commitment to a common scheme designed to achieve an unlawful objective", *see id.* at 771 (citing prior case law).

514 *Copperweld Corp. v. Independence Tube Corp.*, 467 U.S. 752 at 768–769 (1984).

515 *Meredith*, 1 F. Supp. 3d 180 at 207. From the case law of the Supreme Court: "[ASCAP and BMI] plainly involve concerted action in a large and active line of commerce, and it is not surprising that [...] [neither] ASCAP nor BMI is a stranger to antitrust litigation", *see BMI v. CBS*, 441 U.S. 1 at 10. In some cases, however, this element is of importance, *see, e.g., Broadcast Music, Inc. v. Moor-Law, Inc.*, 527 F. Supp. 758 at 774 (D. Del. 1981), *aff'd without opinion*, 691 F. 2d 490 (3rd Cir. 1982) (no proof of conspiracy); *Radio Music License Comm.*, 29 F. Supp. 3d 487 at 497 (rejecting the existence of a "hub-and-spoke conspiracy").

ties concerting their actions are individual copyright holders who, via the respective CMOs, pool their exclusive rights for the purposes of their collective administration.[516] As ASCAP's history reveals, such pooling can imply great market power and raise serious antitrust issues, such as price fixing allegations. In fact, in the earlier days of collective management in the United States, it was questioned whether copyright holders were permitted to join together in the first place. In the 1930s, the DOJ strived to prohibit, based on the Sherman Act, ASCAP's activities altogether for being an unlawful combination but later decided to negotiate a consent decree instead.[517] The hostile approach against collective management is perhaps best illustrated by a frequently cited portion of the ruling in *Alden-Rochelle*:

> Almost every part of the Ascap structure, almost all of Ascap's activities in licensing motion picture theatres, involve a violation of the anti-trust laws. Although each member of Ascap is granted by the copyright law a monopoly in the copyright work, it is unlawful for the owners of a number of copyrighted works to combine their copyrights by any agreement or arrangement, even if it is for the purpose of thereby better preserving their property rights.[518]

However, in the following decades, courts did not interpret the Sherman Act as outlawing CMOs as such, also in view of their regulation by the consent decrees.[519] In fact, § 1 does not ban every restraint of trade but only those which are unreasonable or undue.[520] This means that as long as the CMOs' practices are justifiable under antitrust doctrines, no violation of the laws will be found. Under long-standing U.S. antitrust doctrines, unreasonable restraint can be established under the so-called per-se rule or under the rule of reason. The per se rule applies to agreements or practices which are so "plainly anticompetitive, and so often lack any redeeming virtue, that they are conclusive-

516 *See, e.g., Witmark & Sons*, 80 F. Supp. 843 at 850 ("It cannot be denied, therefore, that plaintiffs and their associates, acting in concert through Ascap, fix prices and completely control competition and thereby restrained trade in violation of Section 1 of the Sherman Anti-Trust Act […]"). *See also Alden-Rochelle, Inc. v. American Soc. of Composers, Authors and Publishers*, 80 F. Supp. 888 at 894–95 (S.D.N.Y. 1948). The persons acting in concert can also be described as right holders acting along with the CMOs, *see, e.g., Radio Music License Comm.*, 29 F. Supp. 3d 487 at 496 ("The relevant inquiry, therefore, is whether SESAC entered into an agreement with its affiliates, either express or tacit, the object of which was to fix the price of SESAC's blanket license").

517 *BMI v. CBS*, 441 U.S. 1 at 10–11; Lunney, *The United States Experience*, *supra* at 328–329.

518 *Alden-Rochelle*, 80 F. Supp. 888 at 893. *See also CBS v. ASCAP*, 620 F. 2d 930 at 935–936.

519 *See, e.g., K-91*, 372 F. 2d 1 at 4 ("ASCAP is certainly a combination, but not every combination is a combination in restraint of trade or a monopoly […], so long as ASCAP complies with the decree, it is not the price fixing authority."). *See also CBS v. ASCAP*, 620 F. 2d 930 at 938.

520 *Standard Oil*, 221 U.S. 1 at 60; VII Phillip E. Areeda & Herbert Hovenkamp, *Antitrust Law: An Analysis of Antitrust Principles and Their Application* ¶ 1500 (3rd ed. 2006, updated 04/2016).

ly presumed illegal without any further examination [...]."[521] A classic example of such agreements is price fixing.[522]

Cases which are resolved under the per se doctrine are generally examined under the rule of reason. In this regime, a certain agreement is tested in light of its effects on competition. This includes an analysis of the pro- and anti-competitive effects of the agreement in question which in turn implies the consideration of a number of factors.[523] An agreement complies with the antitrust rules if the pro-competitive factors prevail.[524] This requires "an inquiry into market power and market structure designed to assess the combination's actual effect".[525] CMOs have repeatedly dealt with claims deeming their conduct a per se infringement.[526] This also applies, perhaps most prominently, to the practice of blanket licensing, in relation to which the Supreme Court ordered to apply the rule of reason.[527]

2.2.3. Section 2 Sherman Act

Section 2 declares illegal to "monopolize, or attempt to monopolize, or combine or conspire with any other person or persons, to monopolize any part of the trade or commerce among the several States, or with foreign nations [...]". The two elements contained in this section are "(1) the possession of monopoly power in the relevant market and (2) the will acquisition or mainte-

---

521 *BMI v. CBS*, 441 U.S. 1 at 8 (internal quotations marks and citations omitted). *See also State Oil Company v. Kahn*, 522 U.S. 3 at 10 (1997).

522 *See, e.g., United States v. Socony-Vacuum Oil Co.*, 310 U.S. 150 at 223 (1940); *Northern Pacific Railway Co. v. United States*, 356 U.S. 1 at 5–6 (1958).

523 "The true test of legality is whether the restraint imposed is such as merely regulates and perhaps thereby promotes competition or whether it is such as may suppress or even destroy competition. To determine that question the court must ordinarily consider the facts peculiar to the business to which the restraint is applied; its condition before and after the restraint was imposed; the nature of the restraint and its effect, actual or probable. The history of the restraint, the evil believed to exist, the reason for adopting the particular remedy, the purpose or end sought to be attained, are all relevant facts.", *see Board of Trade of Chicago v. United States*, 246 U.S. 231 at 238 (1918); *Nat'l Soc'y of Prof'l Engineers v. United States*, 436 U.S. 679 at 691 (1978). *See also Arizona v. Maricopa Cnty. Medical Soc'y*, 457 U.S. 332 at 343 n. 13 (1982); Areeda & Hovenkamp, *Antitrust Principles 2006*, *supra* at ¶ 1511c (developing a scheme incorporating both rule of reason and the per se rule).

524 *See, e.g., Nat'l Soc'y of Prof'l Engineers*, 436 U.S. 679.

525 *Copperweld Corp.*, 467 U.S. 752 at 768. *See* for the courts' approach in determining the relevant market for the collective management of copyrights in context of § 2 of the Sherman act section 2.2.3 below – courts have relied on case law based on section 2 of the Sherman act to construe also the market for § 1, *see, e.g., Meredith*, 1 F. Supp. 3d 180 at 217–218 (citing prior case law). The Supreme Court highlighted, however, that "Monopoly power under § 2 requires, of course, something greater than market power under § 1", *Eastman Kodak Co. v. Image Tech. Serv.*, 504 U.S. 451 at 481 (1992).

526 *See, e.g., Witmark & Sons*, 80 F. Supp. 843 at 849–850.

527 *See* for more details section 3.2.2. below.

nance of that power as distinguished from growth or development as a consequence of a superior product, business acumen, or history accident".[528] The first element can be subdivided into monopoly power and the relevant market. The relevant (product)[529] market is defined by the products which are reasonably interchangeable with one another from a consumer's perspective ("cross-elasticity of demand").[530] Clearly, this definition, albeit its importance, can vary from case to case; as regards CMOs, courts have only rarely, at least expressly, dealt with these issues and have employed different definitions for purposes of their antitrust analyses.[531] A monopoly within this market will be found if the defendant has the power to control prices or to unreasonably restrict competition.[532] Courts have consistently held, where relevant, that CMOs fulfill this requirement,[533] despite the fact that CMOs in the United States have for the longest time, unlike their European counterparts, been in competition with one another. This analysis, of course, is greatly intertwined with the market definition. Next, as regards the second element, the found monopoly must have been acquired by unlawful means[534] or, although acquired lawfully,

---

528 *United States v. Grinnell Corp.*, 384 U.S. 563 at 571 (1966); *Eastman Kodak*, 504 U.S. 451 at 481.

529 For the geographic market *see, e.g., Tampa Elec. Co. v. Nashiville Coal Co.*, 365 U.S. 320 (1961). *See also Broadcast Music, Inc. v. Hearst/ABV Viacom Ent. Services*, 746 F. Supp. 320 at 327 (S.D.N.Y. 1990) ("The relevant geographic market is a national one, as BMI offers licenses to cable services across the country.")

530 *Eastman Kodak*, 504 U.S. 451 at 469–470; *United States v. E.I. du Pont de Nemours & Co.*, 351 U.S. 377 at 400 (1956).

531 *See, e.g., Meredith*, 1 F. Supp. 3d 180 at 218–219 ("market for television-performance rights to works within SESAC's repertory"); *Hearst/ABV Viacom*, 746 F. Supp. 320 at 327 ("Here, the relevant product market is apparent: copyrighted musical compositions in BMI's repertoire"); *CBS v. ASCAP*, 620 F. 2d 930 at 934 ("[T]he relevant market is the licensing of performing rights to the television networks"); *Alden-Rochelle*, 80 F. Supp. 888 at 894 ("monopoly of the music that is used in the production of motion pictures […]"); *Witmark & Sons*, 80 F. Supp. 843 at 847 ("control of performance rights for motion pictures […]"). As the *Radio Music Licensing Committee* court saw direct evidence of monopoly power, it did not deal with the relevant market, *see Radio Music License Comm.*, 29 F. Supp. 3d 487 at 500. *See also BMI v. CBS*, 441 U.S. 1 at 24 ("[T]he blanket license has provided an acceptable mechanism for at least a large part of the market for the performing rights to copyrighted musical compositions […]"); *see also id.* at 29–30 (J.P. Stevens, dissenting).

532 *Du Pont de Nemours*, 351 U.S. 377 at 389.

533 *See, e.g., Pandora Media, Inc. v. American Society of Composers, Authors and Publishers*, 785 F. 3d 73 at 75–76 (2nd Cir. 2015); *Radio Music License Comm.*, 29 F. Supp. 3d 487 at 499–500; *Broadcast Music, Inc. v. DMX Inc.*, 683 F. 3d 32 at 45, 48 (2nd Cir. 2012); *American Society of Composers, Authors and Publishers v. Showtime/Movie Channel, Inc.*, 912 F. 2d 563 at 569–570 (2nd Cir. 1990); *Hearst/ABV Viacom*, 746 F. Supp. 320 at 327; *Moor-Law*, 527 F. Supp. 758 at 774 *Alden-Rochelle*, 80 F. Supp. 888 at 893; *Witmark & Sons*, 80 F. Supp. 843 at 846. The court in *BMI v. CBS* did not assess § 2 of the Sherman Act, *see BMI v. CBS*, 441 U.S. 1 at 24 n. 43. *See also CBS v. ASCAP*, 620 F. 2d 930 at 933.

534 *Grinnell*, 384 U.S. 563 at 571; *Eastman Kodak*, 504 U.S. 451 at 481.

abused.[535] For this purpose, courts will generally examine whether there are lawful justifications[536] for the conduct in question,[537] a variant of a rule of reason analysis.[538]

2.2.4. Interstate Commerce

The Sherman Act, as a part of federal law, only applies to restraints to "trade or commerce among the several States".[539] The requirement is generally interpreted broadly.[540] As far as can be seen, this requirement has not been problematic in connection with U.S. CMOs; this is not surprising since their activities are not restricted to the territory of a particular U.S. state.

2.3. Comments on the Applicability of Antitrust Laws to CMOs

2.3.1. General Remarks

The foregoing observations highlight that U.S. and EU antitrust law have taken different approaches to CMOs, especially when it comes to the prohibition of cartels (*see* the following section); however, they concur as far as as antitrust laws can be used as a tool to regulate CMOs;[541] and acknowledge that collective management of copyrights constitutes a field which occupies a special field of antitrust practice. An AG once stated:

> At first sight, we are confronted with an absolute exclusivity *de facto,* a total compartmentalization of the common market within national frontiers, and a complete absence of competition, all of which would, *in any other sector*, be manifestly incompatible with Article 85(1).[542]

From the U.S. perspective, *Prof. Lunney* similarly notes that ASCAP's practices would have been objected to by the DOJ much faster, "had it been

---

535 *United States v. Griffith*, 334 U.S. 100 at 107 (1948); *Eastman Kodak*, 504 U.S. 451 at 482–483.

536 *Eastman Kodak*, 504 U.S. 451 at 483.

537 Prime examples of prohibited anticompetitive conduct are exclusionary and predatory practices, *see, e.g., Aspen Skiing Co. v. Aspen Highlands Skiing Corp.*, 472 U.S. 585 at 602 (1985) (focusing on the defendant's intent).

538 *See* for the similarities and differences in the analysis under § 1 and § 2 of the Sherman Act VII Areeda & Hovenkamp, *Antitrust Principles 2006*, *supra* at ¶ 1512.

539 15 U.S.C. §§ 1–2. Clearly, this expression refers to U.S. states; trade "with foreign nations" is, however, also covered by the provisions.

540 *See* for a discussion IB Areeda & Hovenkamp, *Antitrust Principles*, *supra* at ¶ 265–267.

541 Also from an international perspective, CMOs as such are exempted from antitrust law only in exceptional cases, Drexl, *Competition and Development*, *supra* at 33–34.

542 *Tournier,* 395/87, Opinion of AG Jacobs at ¶ 33 (emphasis added). *See also* Irini A. Stamatoudi, *The European Court's Love-Hate Relationship with Collecting Societies*, 6 E.I.P.R. 289, 292 (1997) (referring to a "sui generis" competition regime).

any other industry".[543] A difference lies, however, in the question why the application of antitrust law is exceptional: While both sources refer to copyright, the AG must also take into consideration the aim of the EU Internal Market[544] as well as the fact that copyright legislation differs significantly across EU member states.

2.3.2. What are the Relevant Markets and What is their Nature?

Defining the market is a task that must take into consideration the particularities of the respective sector; in the media sector, determining the relevant market can be especially challenging.[545] In the context of collective management of copyrights, the competent authorities have not in all cases discussed the relevant market as a preliminary question for their antitrust analysis. Those that have done so delineated the relevant markets primarily according to i) the types of rights and ii) the categories of works.[546] Thus, for the present purposes, the relevant market will comprise public performance rights in musical works or performances (sound recordings); the court may, of course, however, adapt that definition to the specific needs of the individual case. Such analysis can be relatively general;[547] they can also, however, practically pre-determine the finding of a substantial market power. The latter will be the case especially if the relevant market is narrowed down to the performance rights in the works contained in the repertoire of a specific CMO. This is more customary in the EU when a specific CMO is the only legitimate licensing source holding a national monopoly in a particular member state because in this case, the repertoire represented by this organization will contain large parts of the repertoires of its foreign sister organizations. Competition is conceivable under such circumstances if right holders manage their rights directly[548] or the country is covered by an MTL system.[549] However, in light of this European experience, it is somewhat surprising, at first glance at least, how U.S. authorities have approached SESAC. SESAC has been reported to be considerably smaller than its larger competitors ASCAP and BMI, holding a market share of up to

543 Lunney, *The United States Experience*, *supra* at 328.

544 *See, e.g.*, Christian Kersting & Daisy Karoline Walzel, *Art. 101 AEUV* in 3 *Kölner Kommentar zum Kartellrecht* ¶ 522–523 (Jan Busche & Andreas Röhling eds., 2016).

545 Capito, *Article 82*, *supra* at 158–159.

546 This is in line with the (merger related) case law on music publishing services, *see* Kuik & Dawes, *Media*, *supra* at 1760.

547 *See, e.g.*, *CBS v. ASCAP*, 620 F. 2d 930 at 934 where the decision was based on the market for the licensing of performing rights to TV networks (special group of licensees) or the Commission's decision in *CISAC*, where the authority focused especially on performance rights for satellite, cable retransmission and internet use, *see CISAC Agreement*, COMP/C2/38.698 at ¶ 153, art. 4(2) (special types of performances).

548 Unless there is a provision which provides for mandatory collective management.

549 *See* section 3.3. below. *See also Cannes Extension Agreement*, COMP/C2/38.681 at ¶ 24–26.

10% in the performance rights market.[550] Under EU antitrust practice, it is unlikely that a dominant position will be found below a market share of 25%.[551] However, if the market definition does not refer to musical performance rights in general but only to those pertaining to SESAC's repertoire, then it will be relatively straightforward to establish substantial market power. Thus, from this perspective, the question of the CMOs' market power revolves not so much on the market share thresholds applied but rather on the market definition itself.

It should be noted that CMOs occupy a special position in this context. This is because the concept of substitutability cannot be applied to copyrighted content as easily as to other products.[552] Given that copyrightable works require some form of originality – or individuality – it is not always possible to substitute one work for another.[553] Thus, if there is but one licensing source for a work or a certain group of works, it is reasonable to adjust the market definition accordingly, implicitly acknowledging the peculiarities of the licensing market for copyrighted works. Substitutability can also be absent for

---

550 U.S. Copyright Office, *Music Marketplace*, *supra* at 20.

551 Lewisch, *Art 102 AEUV*, *supra* at ¶ 64; however, this fact as such does not preclude the application of competition law, *see* Busche, *Art. 102 AEUV*, *supra* at ¶ 53–55.

552 *See, e.g.*, *Belgische Radio en Televisie v. Société Belge des Auteurs, Compositeurs et Éditeurs*, case 127-73 (ECJ 1974), Opinion of AG Mayras at 324 ("The question which usually arises in respect of markets in industrial products, namely whether substitute products exist, is not relevant in the case of copyrights held by composers or music publishers."); Resolution 2007 point H ("music is not a commodity"); Ficsor, *Key Issues*, *supra* at 217 (highlighting the double nature in the context of international law and the TFEU); Drexl, *Competition and Development*, *supra* at 127. *See also Meredith*, 1 F. Supp. 3d 180 at 219 (refusing to include ASCAP's and BMI's repertoires in the definition of the relevant market); U.S. Copyright Office, *Music Marketplace*, *supra* at 149. The characteristics of copyrighted content should however not be confused with the product characteristics of music distribution services, *e.g.* traditional radio as opposed to online services, *see* Peter DiCola, *Copyright Equality: Free Speech, Efficiency, and Regulatory Parity in Distribution*, 93 B.U.L. Rev. 1837, 1867–1877 (2013).

553 This is reflected by the fact that users have generally acquired licenses from ASCAP, BMI and SESAC, *see, e.g.*, *Meredith*, 1 F. Supp. 3d 180 at 189; Lunney, *The United States Experience*, *supra* at 324. However, admittedly, this could also be due to the problem of split copyrights, *see* DOJ, *Antitrust Division's Review*, *supra* at 9; U.S. Copyright Office, *Jointly Owned Works*, *supra* at 17–18. *See also BMI v. CBS*, 441 U.S. 1 at 33 (J.P. Stevens, dissenting) (stating that a highly competitive market for copyrights is possible); Drexl, *Competition and Development*, *supra* at 75 (stating that a product does not need to be identical to be substitutable in terms of competition law). *Cirace* gives a placative example, *see* Cirace, *Economic Analysis*, *supra* at 282 n. 35 ("[E]conomists do not hesitate to discuss the demand for automobiles, even though Volkswagens and Cadillacs are no more than substantially interchangeable."). *Drexl*, presupposing competition between copyrighted works according to consumer preference and popularity, develops the concept of "creative competition" to promote "competition between a larger number of works and culturally more diverse works at the price of restraining competition between collecting societies." In this model, CMOs must accept right holders, *see* Drexl, *Collecting Societies*, *supra* at 22.

certain categories of rights.[554] However, such a comparatively narrow market definition does not necessarily lead to the finding of a dominant position,[555] especially if alternative licensing systems open up other avenues for obtaining permission to use the works represented by the organization. This could be the case if the CMO's members license their works directly to users (based on a non-exclusive rights grant),[556] or possibly if an MTL system covers the territory in which the organization is active.[557] Hence, market definitions narrower than those which might be found in other antitrust contexts and which facilitate the finding of a dominant position held by CMOs will be justified to the extent that the peculiarities of the product – works (performances) protected by copyright – justify such special treatment. A further (and perhaps more prominent) argument can be made: CMOs provide, by aggregating rights, a new product which is different from what individual right holders or other CMOs can offer.[558]

Yet, it is questionable whether this approach is justified with respect to all markets in which CMOs are active. The right holder market,[559] though interrelated,[560] appears to be very different from the user market. Management services typically compromise tasks like the collection and distribution of royalties as well as monitoring and enforcing their members' rights. Such tasks are

---

554 Kuik & Dawes, *Media*, *supra* at 1760 (referring to the merger context).

555 In general, it must be pointed out that the ownership of an intellectual property right as such does not confer a dominant position, *see Radio Telefis Eireann v. Commission*, joined cases C-241/91 P and C-242/91 P, ¶ 46 (ECJ 1995); *Deutsche Grammophon*, 78/70 at ¶ 16; IIB Areeda & Hovenkamp, *Antitrust Principles*, *supra* at ¶ 518c2; Capito, *Article 82*, *supra* at 165; I Herbert Hovenkamp et al., *IP and Antitrust An Analysis of Antitrust Principles Applied to Intellectual Property Law* § 22.3c1 (2nd ed. 2010, 2015 Supplement). This is different, however, if an organization compiles large repertoires of works, *see* Drexl, *Competition and Development*, *supra* at 81–82. Naturally, this raises the question at what point a CMOs falls out of the scope of the competition rules, if its repertoire shrinks (due to competitive pressure, for instance).

556 *See, e.g., Radio Music License Comm.*, 29 F. Supp. 3d 487 at 501 (holding that direct licensing can lead to competition between right holders and CMOs). *See* on the non-exclusivity of the rights grant section 3.1.3. below. *See also Cannes Extension Agreement*, COMP/C2/38.681 at ¶ 24–26.

557 One could of course argue that the market for mono- and multi-territorial licenses is not identical, *see, e.g., CISAC Agreement,* COMP/C2/38.698 at ¶ 55–56.

558 *BMI v. CBS*, 441 U.S. 1 at 23–24. *See also* Drexl, *Competition and Development*, *supra* at 214, 267; Guibault & van Gompel, *Collective Management*, *supra* at 160–161; I Hovenkamp et al., *IP and Antitrust*, *supra* at § 22.3a1.; Mestmäcker & Schweitzer, *Wettbewerbsrecht*, *supra* at 874–875. The Commission employed this rationale in the *IFPI Simulcasting*, *see IFPI Simulcasting*, COMP/C2/38.014 at ¶ 62, 87–88, 113.

559 One could call the relevant market in this connection the market for the management of copyrights, Capito, *Article 82*, *supra* at 158–159. Another market would be management services for other collecting societies, *see CISAC Agreement,* COMP/C2/38.698 at ¶ 52–53.

560 Drexl, *Collecting Societies*, *supra* at 5.

not "original" to a particular organization;[561] in fact, it is what all CMOs around the world do. Thus, it is necessary to account for i) the management services (product) and ii) substitutability when analyzing the relevant markets since competition is more likely to occur.[562] The ASCAP Consent Decree acknowledges this difference insofar as many provisions on the protection of right holders were removed over time.[563] It should be noted, however, that national regulation can make such services "original" to certain organizations, especially of a legal monopoly is provided for.

2.3.3. CMOs as Unlawful Combinations

Already a while ago, it has been observed that "[t]he most fundamental and in many respects, the most revealing issue is the extent to which performing rights organisations infringe the prohibition of concerted restrictions of competition […]".[564] At first glance, it seems that CMOs fulfill all the requirements of a horizontal price-fixing agreement, especially when offering blanket licenses; however, both U.S. law and EU law have acknowledged that a moderate approach is in order, taking into consideration both pro- and anti-competitive effects of the CMOs' conduct.[565]

The question of interest in this context is how the establishment of a CMO, its bylaws and decisions based thereon[566] should be assessed under article 101 TFEU and § 1 of the Sherman Act on the one hand and article 102 and § 2 of the Sherman Act on the other. Under U.S. law, both articles have been deemed applicable to CMOs without serious doubts, practically from the first day that CMOs faced antitrust challenges. CMOs are regarded as unlawful combinations because there is the danger that right holders unlawfully expand the monopoly conferred upon them by copyright law[567] by joining together and bundling their rights. U.S. antitrust practice is generally suspicious of such bundling. In *Paramount*, for instance, the Supreme Court held it to be illegal to force licensees to buy package licenses containing several protected works

---

561 *See also* Drexl, *Competition and Development*, *supra* at 81 ("In a two-sided market, [CMOs] may compete for right-holders, but they do not compete for users. For users, such as radio stations, the repertoires of the different CMOs do not constitute viable substitutes.")

562 *See also IFPI Simulcasting*, COMP/C2/38.014 at ¶ 35–38.

563 *See* section 3.1.1. for more details.

564 Ernst-Joachim Mestmäcker, *Performing Rights Organizations in the Common Market: Comparative Observations* in *Ernst-Joachim Mestmäcker – Beiträge zum Urheberrecht* 227, 228 (Karl Riesenhuber ed., 2006).

565 Drexl, *Competition and Development*, *supra* at 212–216.

566 The CMOs' bylaws and management contracts should be assessed within a uniform analysis, *see* Lichtenegger, *Verwertungsgesellschaften*, *supra* at 369–370; Mestmäcker & Schweitzer, *Wettbewerbsrecht*, *supra* at 877; Wünschmann, *Kollektive Verwertung supra* at 90.

567 This principle was developed in the context of patent law, *see, e.g., Motion Picture Patents Co. v. Universal Film Co.*, 243 U.S. 502 at 518 (1917); *Mercoid Corp. v. Mid-Continent Investment Co.*, 320 U.S. 661 at 664–665 (1944).

(so called "block booking").[568] Due to this dual nature of CMOs, U.S. antitrust law practice has not clearly distinguished between § 1 and § 2 of the Sherman Act with regard to the collective management of copyrights. This is in line with the foregoing because especially the earlier CMO-related cases involved situations in which, due to the large market power of CMOs, it would most likely not have mattered whether this conduct is carried out by a single or several persons.[569] In contrast, neither the Commission nor the ECJ has given conclusive guidance as to whether CMOs can be regarded as unlawful combinations or decisions of individual right holders,[570] even though bundling (or tying) of IP rights in license agreements can in principle violate article 101 TFEU.[571] From a dogmatic point of view (at least) four lines of explanations for this application practice are conceivable:

First, it is conceivable that article 101 is not applicable to the collective management of copyrights. Yet, this explanation is not convincing. At the outset, it should be highlighted that the TFEU's articles 351 (on the obligation arising from agreements concluded with third countries before 1958) and 345 (on the member states' systems of property ownership) do not as such prevent the application of the competition rules to CMOs;[572] intellectual property is not excluded from the scope of the competition rules.[573] In this connection, however, it is conceivable to deem article 101 inapplicable, referring to the ECJ's case law in which the court recognized the specific subject-matter of IP rights.[574] For copyrights, this entails both moral and economic rights.[575] Thus,

568 *United States v. Paramount Pictures*, 334 U.S. 131 at 156–157 (1948) ("Block-booking prevents competitors from bidding for single features on their individual merits. [...] That enlargement of the monopoly of the copyright was condemned below in reliance on the principle which forbids the owner of a patent to condition its use on the purchase or use of patented or unpatented materials"). *See also CBS v. ASCAP*, 620 F. 2d 930 at 935–936.

569 Ernst-Joachim Mestmäcker, *Sind urheberrechtliche Verwrtungsgesellschaften Kartelle?* in *Ernst-Joachim Mestmäcker – Beiträge zum Urheberrecht* 1, 15–17 (Karl Riesenhuber ed., 2006) (referring to *Alden-Rochelle*). Please note that reference is here only to the scope and applicability of the articles in principle; it is of course possible that the differences in the antitrust analysis under both sections leads to different results, also in connection with standards of proof regarding the existence of an agreement, for instance.

570 Jens Gaster, *Artikel 101 AEUV* in *Europäisches Wettbewerbsrecht* ¶ 1071 (Helmut Schröter et al. eds., 2nd ed. 2014).

571 *See in general* Füller, *Art. 101 AEUV, supra* at ¶ 308–310; Stefan Gering, *Vereinbarungen betreffend gewerbliche Schutzrechte und F&E in Europäisches Kartellrecht* 234, 259–260 (Thorsten Mäger ed., 2nd ed. 2011). *See also* European Commission, Communication from the Commission, *Guidelines on the application of Article 101 of the Treaty on the Functioning of the European Union to technology transfer agreements* ¶ 221–225, 2014 O.J. (C89) 3–50.

572 Lichtenegger, *Verwertungsgesellschaften, supra* at 312–316.

573 This is also highlighted by the Commissions, *see* European Commission Guidelines on TT-Agreements at ¶ 7. *See also* Gaster, *Artikel 101 AEUV, supra* at ¶ 1002–1024; Dorothea Senn, *Competition Law Aspects of Digital and Collective Rights Management* in *Digital Rights Management: The End of Collecting Societies?* 123, 126 (Christoph Beat Graber et al. eds., 2005).

574 *Deutsche Grammophon*, 78/70 at ¶ 10–11. *See also Sirena S.R.L. v. EDA S.R.L.*, case 40/70, ¶ 5 (ECJ 1971).

provided that copyrights are commercially exploited, in a way that must be regarded as the "normal exploitation of copyright, no infringement of the competition rules will be found".[576] This justification does not apply to the abusive exercise of rights for maintaining or creating artificial barriers within the market.[577] Even when CMOs do not create such barriers, it has rightly been argued that the notion of the specific subject-matter of copyright does not automatically foreclose the application of the competition rules to CMOs. This is because this notion does not lead to the inapplicability of these rules per se but must be considered precisely when applying competition law.[578] Yet, also when assessing collective management under EU competition law, the specific subject-matter of copyright cannot be invoked by CMOs because, on the one hand, the joining-together of a multitude of right holders leads to options for exploitation that often go far beyond the options available to individual right holders and hence cannot be regarded as "normal exploitation".[579] On the other hand – especially in situations where individual right holders could practically not exploit their works without collective management – it must be taken into consideration that the specific subject-matter of copyright does not only affect article 101 but also article 102 of the TFEU. The latter article has served as a fundamental basis for the regulation of CMOs; if it ceased to apply, even clearly abusive conduct would be excluded from competition law control.[580] Last, one could argue that the agreements relating to collective management are not the type of cooperation referred to by this provision "by virtue of their nature and purpose".[581] The ECJ developed this case law in the context of collective bargaining agreements between employers and employees which aim at improving employment and working conditions.[582] The exact dogmatic grounds for this exclusion have not been entirely clarified.[583] However, it appears that collective management of exclusive IP rights is not covered by this rationale; the same concerns with regard to article 102 as just mentioned in connection with the specific subject-matter of copyright apply. CMOs are frequently compared to labor unions in this connection; although there are similarities,[584] they have no implications for the application of competition law. This

575 *Phil Collins*, C-92/92 and C-326/92 at ¶ 20; Gaster, *Artikel 101 AEUV*, *supra* at ¶ 1059 (stating that the scope with regard to moral rights remains controversial).

576 *Football Association Premier League,* C-403/08 and C-429/08 at ¶ 106–107; *EMI Electrola GmbH v. Patricia Im- und Export Verwaltungsgesellschaft mbH*, case 341/87, ¶ 7 (ECJ 1989); *Basset*, 402/85 at ¶ 16; Mestmäcker & Schweitzer, *Wettbewerbsrecht*, *supra* at 793.

577 *EMI Electrola*, 341/87 at ¶ 8.

578 Lichtenegger, *Verwertungsgesellschaften*, *supra* at 320–321.

579 Wünschmann, *Kollektive Verwertung*, *supra* at 58–59.

580 Lichtenegger, *Verwertungsgesellschaften*, *supra* at 409–410. *See* in this connection *GEMA I*, IV/26 760 at ¶ 22.

581 *H. van der Woude v. Stichting Beatrixoord*, C-222/98, ¶ 22 (ECJ 2000).

582 *Id. See also* Schröter, *Vorbemerkungen*, *supra* at ¶ 78.

583 Füller, *Art. 101 AEUV*, *supra* at ¶ 60.

584 Daniel Gervais, *Keynote: The Landscape of Collective Management Systems* 34 Colum. J. of L. & Arts 591, 598 (2011); Peter Lerche, *Verwertungsgesellschaften als Unternehmen "sui*

is because the special treatment of unions rests on the argument that they are no undertakings.[585] Yet, as mentioned above, the ECJ has repeatedly confirmed that CMOs constitute undertakings for the purposes of the competition rules.

Second, one could allege that a CMO constitutes a single undertaking rather than a combination of several right holders; article 101 would hence be inapplicable because it requires the involvement of at least two undertakings. In this light, the practice of applying competition law to CMOs reflects the boundaries between article 101 and article 102 TFEU.[586] However, this explanation is contradicted by that individual right holders constitute undertakings within the meaning of these provisions and there is no reason why forming an organization of these right holders should rule out article 101 to assess the relations of the single right holders between one another, and between right holders and CMOs.[587]

Third, one might assert that CMOs – in principle – fall within the scope of article 101 but that they do not prevent, restrict, or distort competition in the Internal Market. Two sublines of argumentations shall be mentioned in the present context: i) right holders are not competitors;[588] ii) a rule of reason under article 101(1) applies. Neither of these explanations, however, is fully convincing. On the one hand, there is nothing in the case law of the ECJ which indicates that – even though content needs to possess some form of individuality to be protected – the authors of copyrighted works cannot compete with one another.[589] On the other hand, it is admittedly controversial whether there is a rule of reason doctrine under EU law (on the level of article 101(1)).[590] If one accepts the existence of such doctrine, one could indeed approach CMOs weighing their pro- and anticompetitive effects and conclude that they do not

generis" in *Recht und Praxis der GEMA* 25, 27 (Reinhold Kreile et al. eds., 2nd ed. 2008). A related arguments concerns the exemption of CMOs due to the principle of solidarity, *see* Sladiĉ, *Collective Management*, *supra* at 43. *See also Kattner Stahlbau GmbH v. Maschinenbau- und Metall- Berufsgenossenschaft*, C-350/07, ¶ 33, 44–59 (ECJ 2009).

585 Wünschmann, *Kollektive Verwertung*, *supra* at 61–66. *See also* Volker Emmerich & Daniel Zimmer, *Artikel 101 Abs. 1 AEUV* in 1 *Wettbewerbsrecht* ¶ 25–26 (Ulrich Immenga & Ernst-Joachim Mestmäcker eds., 5. ed 2012); Füller, *Art. 101 AEUV*, *supra* at ¶ 59–60; Schröter, *Vorbemerkungen*, *supra* at ¶ 78.

586 Sousa e Silva, *The Proposed Directive*, *supra* at 9.

587 Article 101 and 102 can be applied in the same case if the respective requirements are fulfilled, *see Compagnie Maritime Belge Transports v. Commission*, joined cases C-395/96 P and C-396/96 P, ¶ 33 (ECJ 2000). *See also* Lewisch, *Art 102 AEUV*, *supra* at ¶ 16.

588 In order to find a prevention, restriction or distortion of competition, the involved undertakings must usually be (actual or potential) competitors, *see, e.g.,* European Commission Guidelines on Horizontal Co-Operation at ¶ 29–30. Füller, *Art. 101 AEUV*, *supra* at ¶ 175–185.

589 *See also* Lichtenegger, *Verwertungsgesellschaften*, *supra* at 372–373. In this connection, it is conspicuous that this rationale is obviously not pronounced – by both U.S. and EU authorities – when it comes to defining the relevant market for CMOs. Presumably, this is difference can be justified by the large aggregation of rights ordinarily effected by CMOs.

590 *See, e.g.,* Füller, *Art. 101 AEUV*, *supra* at ¶ 236.

violate article 101(1).[591] Yet, the structure of article 101 indicates that weighing the effects of a measure on competition should rather be dealt within under article 101(3).[592]

Perhaps the most coherent way from a dogmatic perspective is to assess CMOs under article 101(3).[593] As *Wünschmann* convincingly shows, CMOs ordinarily fulfill all the requirements set up by this provision.[594] By aggregating exclusive rights, CMOs provide a new product which individual copyright owners would not be able to offer. Furthermore, and at least equally important, the argument is heavily based on article 167 TFEU. According to this provision, the Union must take cultural aims into account;[595] this includes the application of competition law[596] also in the context of collective management of copyrights.[597] The Commission emphasizes that cultural aims must be accounted for under article 101(3) and not under article 101(1).[598] This is also

591 Drijber, *Competition law aspects*, *supra* at 68, 75; Schierholz, *Collective Rights Management*, *supra* at 1158. This also appears to be the position of the Commission in *GEMA III*. *See also* John Temple Lang, *Media, Multimedia and European Community Antitrust Law* 45, *available at* http://ec.europa.eu/competition/speeches/text/sp1997_070_en.pdf (last visited April 19, 2017); Lichtenegger, *Verwertungsgesellschaften*, *supra* at 397–410; Stamatoudi, *Love-Hate Relationship*, *supra* at 292 n. 23. The Commission might be understood to go in this direction in *IFPI*, when it considers whether certain clauses in RRAs are "objectively necessary" for ensuring an appropriate level of remuneration for right holders in order to determine whether there is a restriction of competition, *see IFPI Simulcasting*, COMP/C2/38.014 at ¶ 70.

592 Füller, *Art. 101 AEUV*, *supra* at ¶ 236; Wünschmann, *Kollektive Verwertung*, *supra* at 93–102. *Lichtenegger* highlights that Commission Regulation (EU) No 316/2014 of 21 March 2014 on the application of Article 101(3) of the Treaty on the Functioning of the European Union to categories of technology transfer agreements, 2014 O.J. (L93) 17–23 is not applicable to CMOs, *see* Lichtenegger, *Verwertungsgesellschaften*, *supra* at 411–414.

593 Admittedly, however, it appears that a "rule of reason" analysis under article 101(1) would most likely lead to similar results.

594 Wünschmann, *Kollektive Verwertung*, *supra* at 102–110 (assessing the single requirements); with the same result for the offline environment Lichtenegger, *Verwertungsgesellschaften*, *supra* at 414–442 (highlighting that the justification does not apply to CMOs per se, but depends on the individual case). In respect of the online environment, *Lichtenegger* takes not only into account whether individual management is practically feasible but also whether it is necessary in order to stimulate creative production, *see* Lichtenegger, *Verwertungsgesellschaften*, *supra* at 463–464.

595 Matthias Niedobitek, *Art. 167 AEUV* in *EUV/AEUV* ¶ 35 (Rudolf Streinz ed., 2nd ed. 2012).

596 Hermann-Josef Blanke, *Art. 167 AEUV* in *EUV/AEUV* ¶ 15 (Christian Calliess & Matthias Ruffert eds., 5th ed. 2016); Jens Budischowsky, *Art 167* in *Kommentar zu EUV und AEUV* ¶ 8 (Heinz Mayer & Karl Stöger eds., updated 05/2010 at rdb.at).

597 Wünschmann, *Kollektive Verwertung*, *supra* at 38–42; Jürgen Schwarze, *Die Verwaltung von Urheberrechten im Lichte des europäischen Wettbewerbsrechts* in *Recht und Praxis der GEMA* 47, 60–61 (Reinhold Kreile et al. eds., 2nd ed. 2008). *See also* Lichtenegger, *Verwertungsgesellschaften*, *supra* at 352–355, 418–419, 421, 423 (also summarizing counterarguments).

598 *See* Commission of the European Communities, *Communication from the Commission — Notice — Guidelines on the application of Article 81(3) of the Treaty* ¶ 42, 2004 O.J. (C101) 97–118; Johnathan Faull et al., *Article 101* in *The EU Law of Competition* 183, 186–187 (Jonathan Faull & Ali Nikpay eds., 3rd ed. 2014).

in line with the Commission's assessment in an (unpublished) case relating to MTV and VPL, a British CMO. In a Statement of Objections, the authority alleged that the combination of large record companies in a CMO could violate article 101(1) and that a justification was only possible under article 101(3).[599]

In conclusion, article 101 cannot only be applied to contracts that a CMO concludes with members, users, and other CMOs but also to a CMO's bylaws and decisions based thereon; however, the exception according to article 101(3) might apply.[600] Whether this provision applies depends on the interpretation of the single requirements in the individual case. That affords courts enough leeway to flexibly respond to the CMOs' practice as well as to changed circumstance (*e.g.*, a development of new technologies).[601] As the experience in the *MTV/VPL* case shows, the assessment under art 101(3) will certainly be stricter if a number of large right holders decide to license their works exclusively through a CMOs and refuse to negotiate direct licenses. Indeed, a CMO with five or six members has little to do with the traditional understanding of such organizations,[602] although the Collective Management Directive would in principle also cover this extreme case. A stricter approach is also in line with the ECJ's understanding of CMOs as actors safeguarding the right holders' adequate bargaining position vis-à-vis large users. It is clear that distinguishing large from small right holders is a difficult task;[603] however, so is the related question of market dominance and its abuse. Nevertheless, it should be noted that the presence of large right holders in CMOs can be necessary for the management mechanism as a whole to function as well as for the benefit of smaller right holders.[604] In this case, it seems appropriate to justify a combination of large right holders in the organization to the extent necessary for the functioning of said system; however it is critical that internal rules of the CMOs provide for a balanced internal structure for the different categories of right holders.

All the foregoing relates first and foremost to the "typical" European model of collective management where CMOs require right holders to consent to an

599 Hamish Porter, *European Union Competition Policy: Should the Role of Collecting Societies Be Legitimsed*, 12 E.I.P.R. 672, 675–676 (1996); Wünschmann, *Kollektive Verwertung*, *supra* at 88. The case was ultimately settled, so that the Commission did not take a decision, *see* Jeff Clark-Meads, *MTV Europe, VPL Resolve Years-Ling Licensing Dispute*, Billboard, May 16, 1998, at 1, 16.

600 Wünschmann, *Kollektive Verwertung*, *supra* at 78.

601 *See* for a detailed account on the competition law implications of the online environment Lichtenegger, *Verwertungsgesellschaften*, *supra* at 452–472.

602 Ficsor, *International Treaties*, *supra* at 42.

603 Drijber, *Competition law aspects*, *supra* at 68.

604 Wünschmann, *Kollektive Verwertung*, *supra* at 110–114. *See also* Drijber, *Competition law aspects*, *supra* at 68; Lang, *Antitrust Law*, *supra* at 46.

exclusive rights grant.[605] One could reasonably question – very similar to the U.S. doctrine under which the ability of right holders to license their works directly is fundamental – whether there is a restriction of competition in the first place if users can always choose to negotiate with right holders directly. Non-exclusivity in this regard would certainly be favorable to CMOs when applying EU competition law, just like in the U.S. example.

One last observation can be drawn in this connection: It appears that the application of the types of conduct typically prohibited – the formation of cartels and the abuse of a dominant position – move towards convergence in the context of collective management. *Mestmäcker* has observed that the weighing of the involved interests necessary in CMO cases is almost identical under section 1 of the Sherman Act and article 102 TFEU[606] and that in earlier cases decided by U.S. courts, it would not have mattered had the courts applied section 1 or 2 of the Sherman Act. This stems from the fact that ASCAP possessed monopoly power; its practices would thus have most likely been unlawful regardless of the number of persons participating in the conduct.[607] This should be similar under article 101 and 102 TFEU. For a violation of article 101, it is in principle not necessary to show that the involved undertakings possess great market power;[608] however, the Commission considers this element when assessing the effect on trade.[609] Yet, as already mentioned before, the right holder side and the user side differ conceptually as to the market power of CMOs due to the differences of the services offered. In this connection, non-applicability of article 101 to CMOs does not mean that EU competition law leaves a CMO unregulated, as article 102 continues to serve as an additional layer of regulation. At least with regard to users, a dominant position in the CMO's repertoire will be easily found if the market is defined accordingly. Moreover, if the ECJ finds legitimate aims within the meaning of article 102, this will most likely also apply to article 101.

2.3.4. New Licensing Models and Competition Law

CMOs and new licensing models may not only be subject to the Collective Management Directive but furthermore, be controlled through competition law. However, different requirements apply: Whereas the CMD applies to all CMOs – or to those offering online MTL services – article 101 and 102 TFEU only apply in more specific situations. In this connection, it is noteworthy that GEMA, PRS, and STIM conceded that article 102 TFEU will apply to their

605 Wünschmann, *Kollektive Verwertung*, *supra* at 91, 108–109. *See also* Drijber, *Competition law aspects*, *supra* at 68.

606 Mestmäcker, *Comparative Observations*, *supra* at 230.

607 Mestmäcker, *Verwertungsgesellschaften*, *supra* at 15–17.

608 *Compagnie Maritime*, C-395/96 P and C-396/96 P at ¶ 34.

609 European Commission Guidelines on Horizontal Co-Operation at ¶ 5.

joint venture,[610] thereby implying that it will occupy a dominant position. Indeed, it can be considered with respect to the many new licensing models whether they possess such a characteristic. This also applies to the CMOs involved, as the Commission has emphasized in connection with PRSfM's matching performance rights.[611] This is an interesting account because traditionally, CMOs have been considered as occupying a dominant position due to their *de facto* or *de jure* monopolies in their respective countries of establishment. However, on the online MTL market, the situation might be entirely different.[612] Moreover, the new licensing platforms stem from agreements between CMOs. Article 101 will, therefore, ensure that such arrangements will not have unjustified anti-competitive effects; merger control additionally applies and is fully functional as demonstrated by the Commission in several decisions and the many commitments imposed on the parties in connection with the ZETA/DELTA joint venture. In this context, the commitments put on PRSfM in connection with matching performing rights is of special interest[613] because it might practically amount to an obligation similar to the rules set forth in the directive's article 16. Furthermore, the authority stated that the aggregation of repertoires above a certain limit would immediately trigger close scrutiny under article 101.[614]

3. The Regulation of the Different Relations of CMOs: Right Holders, Users, Sister Organizations

3.1. CMOs and Right Holders

3.1.1. General Remarks

European competition law in the field of collective management has to a great extent been applied as a means to protect authors from excessive claims of CMOs; a fact which might be surprising in light of their purpose to protect the interests of right holders.[615] However, in turn, it cannot be denied that certain measures must be taken in order to ensure efficient and effective copyright management; precisely these measures are necessary to protect right hold-

610 *PRSfM/STIM/GEMA/JV*, COMP/M.6800 at ¶ 237.

611 *Id.* at ¶ 382.

612 The Commission – in the merger context – considers the market for online music licensing market as an independent market, leaving however open whether it must be further subdivided according to geographical criteria (mono- or multi-territorial licensing), *see PRSfM/STIM/GEMA/JV*, COMP/M.6800 at ¶ 118.

613 *Id.* at Annex I, Section B. Furthermore, the language used by the Commission in ¶ 367 of the decision resembles like an actual obligation to contract.

614 *Id.* at ¶ 248, 303.

615 *See, e.g.,* CISAC Statute art. 6; CMD art. 4.

ers, a consideration which has caused competent authorities to allow for certain restrictions put on right holders in assignment contracts and membership terms. This consideration is narrow in scope and subject to a balance of interest. The ECJ developed a general standard in order to determine whether a CMO imposes unfair conditions on right holders. The court stated:

> [A]ccount must be taken of all the relevant interests, for the purpose of ensuring a balance between the requirement of maximum freedom for authors, composers, and publishers to dispose of their works and that of the effective management of their rights by an undertaking which in practice they avoid joining.
>
> Consequently, it is desirable to examine whether the practices in dispute exceed the limit absolutely necessary for the attainment [of the object of effective protection and efficient management of copyrights], with due regard also to the interest which the individual author may have that his freedom to dispose of his work is not limited more than need be.[616]

In spelling out the foregoing, the court established a general framework for the relationship between CMOs and right holders. The balancing of interests between individual right holders and the organization representing the collective is expressly recognized; this principle governs all relations between the two counterparts and determines whether a rule, restriction, or procedure applied to right holders is consistent with EU competition law. Hence, the question is not so much whether CMOs may impose restrictions on right holders, but to what extent they are permitted to do so. Two basic standards for this assessment can be inferred from the cited portions: i) the aim of effective protection cannot be achieved without the measure taken[617] and ii) the freedom of the individual right holder in respect to his or her works is not unnecessarily restricted by this measure. The court applies an "indispensability test" and an "equity test" to CMOs;[618] both tests must be passed in order to fulfill the requirements of the EU competition rules. As *Wood* points out, the indispensability test is not a proper proportionality test because it is not sufficient to show that the benefits of a measure taken by CMOs outweigh the restrictions imposed on a right holder; the measure must be as least restrictive as possible.[619] This can require a complex economic analysis of each individual case.[620] The Collective Management Directive codifies the ruling of the ECJ inasmuch as it recognizes the balancing of interest in article 4 and provides for a wording that can be read as an indispensability test ("not objectively necessary") and an equity test ("in the best interests of right holders").[621]

---

616 *BRT*, 127/73 at ¶ 9, 11.

617 The ruling in *BRT v. SABAM* concerned the interpretation of article 102. The indispensability test has also been applied in connection with article 101, *see Tournier*, 395/87 at ¶ 31.

618 Guibault & van Gompel, *Collective Management 2010*, *supra* at 140.

619 Wood, *Collective Management*, *supra* at 5.

620 *Id.*

621 *See also* CMD recital 18 (stating that the freedom to exercise copyright should not be "unduly affected"). *See also* recital 22. One might argue, however, that the "not objectively necessary" criterion refers to a proportionality test rather than to a strict indispensability test.

The prohibition of non-discrimination based on nationality is a fundamental principle of EU law. The ECJ confirmed in its *Phil Collins* ruling that this principle also applies to copyright law.[622] CMOs are precluded from discriminating against nationals from other member states by article 102 TFEU since this would be inconsistent with the aims of article 18 TFEU; accordingly, the Commission held that such conduct must immediately be regarded as a violation of EU competition law.[623] Whether article 18 can be directly applied to CMOs (or private entities in general) has not yet been fully clarified by the ECJ.[624] The court confirmed the applicability in special cases.[625]

The U.S. case law on the relationship of CMOs and right holders is rather sparse compared that of the European Union; legally binding rules on the relationship between CMOs and right holders can, however, be found in the consent decrees that govern the operations of ASCAP and BMI. While these rules address some important questions, the regulatory framework is much less detailed as compared to the European Union. This is not to say that U.S. authorities are unaware of this matter;[626] in fact, detailed provisions on ASCAP's internal structure were included in prior versions of its consent decree (the ASCAP 1960 Order).[627] However, many of those rules were removed in the current version of the decree,[628] presumably because the powers of competition between ASCAP and BMI (and SESAC) were deemed sufficient to protect the interests of right holders.[629]

In what follows, the applicable rules regarding the members of CMOs and other right holders under both EU and U.S. law will be analyzed, the latter with a focus on the BMI and ASCAP Consent Decrees. In order to contemplate whether the forces of competition adequately protect right holders, the ASCAP

---

622 *Phill Collins*, C-92/92 and C-326/92 at ¶ 27.

623 *GVL*, IV/29.839 ¶ 46. The ECJ did not explicitly confirm this point in its subsequent decision; for an analysis whether article 102 contains a prohibition of discrimination based on nationality and whether the *GVL*-case is in line with the ruling in *Phil Collins*, *see* Stamatoudi, *Love-Hate Relationship*, *supra* at 291–292.

624 1 Walter Frenz, *Handbuch Europarecht* 1233–1234 (2d ed. 2012); Lichtenegger, *Verwertungsgesellschaften*, *supra* at 78–79.

625 *See, e.g.*, *B.N.O. Walrave v. Association Union Cycliste Internationale*, case 36/74 (ECJ 1974).

626 *See, e.g.*, *Sam Fox Publ'g*, 366 U.S. 683 at 685–686 (highlighting the overrepresentation of large publishers in ASCAP's Board of Directors).

627 Lunney, *The United States Experience*, *supra* at 334–335.

628 *Id.* at 336. *See* for the decree *United States v. American Soc'y of Composers, Authors & Publishers*, 1960 Tr. Cas. (CCH), ¶ 69,612 (S.D.N.Y. 1960).

629 Department of Justice, *Memorandum of the United States in Support of the Joint Motion to Enter Second Amended Final Judgment, United States v. ASCAP,* No. 41–1395 at 42 *(S.D.N.Y. 2000)*, *available at* https://www.justice.gov/atr/case-document/file/485996/download (last visited May 23, 2017) ("Competition from BMI and SESAC is likely to be far more effective in disciplining ASCAP's distribution practices than regulation by the Department or the Court"); Einhorn, *Music Performing Rights*, *supra* at 364–365.

Articles of Association [hereinafter: ASCAP Statute], as well as applicable membership contracts of ASCAP and BMI, will be included where appropriate in order to supplement this analysis.

3.1.2. Access to Collective Management Services

It is not necessary to emphasize that collective management services are of fundamental importance for right holders to benefit from the use of their works. Accordingly, right holders should have access to these services under fair conditions.[630] European competition law has been applied in connection with this issue in a number of cases, in which the question of the treatment of right holders (persons who hold copyrights or related rights) was to a great extent equivalent to the question of the treatment of members of CMOs (right holders who were accepted to join the organization). In the Commission's *GEMA I* decision, for instance, the German CMO GEMA distinguished the assignment contract (Berechtigungsvertrag) in which members had to authorize the organization to manage their rights and the membership application (Aufnahmeantrag); the conclusion of the assignment contract was a requirement for a successful membership application.[631] Thus, restrictions contained in the assignment contract could at the same time pose obstacles to the accession as a member. For this reason, it was not necessary for the Commission to distinguish between the rights of right holders in general and those rights which could only be exercised by formal members of the CMO. On the contrary, the Collective Management Directive clearly delineates "rightholders" from "members". It states that

> 'rightholder' means any person or entity, other than a collective management organisation, that holds a copyright or related right or, under an agreement for the exploitation of rights or by law, is entitled to a share of the rights revenue; […]
>
> 'member' means a rightholder or an entity representing rightholders, including other collective management organisations and associations of rightholders, fulfilling the membership requirements of the collective management organisation and admitted by it;[632]

When interpreting the directive and comparing it to the competition case law on which it is based in large parts, it is crucial to note that where the term "right holder" is used, a membership is not required for the purpose of the particular provision; conversely, some rights require the acquisition of membership. The directive follows the principle that the rights that protect the freedom to exercise copyrights are granted to all right holders[633] while the rights

[630] Drexl, *Competition and Development*, *supra* at 235 (calling collective management services an "essential facility").

[631] *GEMA I*, IV/26.760 at ¶ I(A)(1)(c), I(A)(1)(g).

[632] CMD art. 3(c), (d).

[633] Arezzo, *Lights and Shadows*, *supra* at 540 (noting that the rights are independent of a particular category of rights or works).

relating to the governance structure and the internal functioning of CMO are reserved for the right holders who fulfill the membership requirements.[634]

Compared to the case law (and the Proposal 2012),[635] the Collective Management Directive contains an important addition in this context. It provides for an obligation of CMOs to conclude management contracts with (all) right holders; it may only refuse to manage rights on two grounds: i) the CMO has objectively justified reasons for the refusal or ii) the management request falls outside of the CMO's scope of activities.[636] Discriminatory practices based on nationality certainly do not qualify as "objectively justified reasons", as indicated by language of article 5 and the cases law on the competition rules;[637] the meaning of the notion "scope of activities" can be construed in light of the general practice of collective management and the wording of recital 20[638] by referring to the types of works (*e.g.*, musical, literary), the rights or categories of rights (*e.g.*, related rights, "mechanical" rights etc.), or other subject-matter. Indeed, it would not make much sense forcing a CMO specialized on literary works to manage performance rights in musical creations. The case law does not explicitly highlight this fact, but it can be assumed that the Commission and the ECJ did implicitly presuppose this rationale. The obligation to represent right holders is independent of the membership requirements set up by a CMO because article 5 uniformly refers to "right holders"; thus, all right holders should have access to collective management services if they choose this option.[639]

Both ASCAP and BMI are obliged to offer their management services to right holders, i.e. writers and publishers, within the meaning of the consent decrees. The requirements – and at the same time the definitions of these groups of right holders – are generally that a writer has commercially published at least one of his or her musical works and that a publisher is actively engaged in the music publishing business, which especially entails the assumption of

634 Due to the development of the *acquis* and in order to highlight the interrelation of the competition case law and the statute, the rules of the directive will be presented along with the substantive questions the case law dealt with. Since, as stated above, the case law refers in its largest parts to "members", also rights of right holders in general will mentioned in this context; however, attention will be drawn to the distinction wherever necessary. Several provisions of the CMD distinguish between right holders and members, *see, e.g.*, art. 7–8.

635 Proposal 2012 at art. 5(2).

636 CMD art. 5(2).

637 *See also id.* at recital 18.

638 The recital refers to *membership requirements*, but employs the same expression.

639 Examples for situations where right holders are represented by a CMO but do not join these organizations as their members can be found, for instance, where national laws provide for statutory remuneration schemes or extended collective licensing systems, *see* Drexl et al., *Comments of the MPI*, *supra*, at 15–16. In light of competition and international copyright law, it can be argued that CMOs must also represent nationals from non-EU countries, *see* Drexl, *Competition and Development*, *supra* at 237–238. *See also* 2 Walter, *Verwertungsgesellschaftenrecht*, *supra* at 235 (on the CMD art. 5).

the financial risk associated with such business.[640] The obligation to accept right holders as members can also be put in the context of the case law on blanket licensing.[641] Accordingly, the consent decrees prohibit discrimination among right holders in that ASCAP and BMI must not refuse a membership application whenever the requirements are fulfilled.[642] In this respect, it becomes clear that the consent decrees only bind the mentioned CMOs because SESAC is capable of openly stating that it is very selective in accepting new members.[643] However, a writer can usually not become a member of more than one U.S.[644] CMO.[645] On the other hand, large publishers can belong to both ASCAP and BMI, often establishing separate subsidiaries for this purpose.[646]

3.1.3. Acquisition of Membership

Three main aspects can be highlighted in this context: the nationality requirement, the global assignment requirement and questions relating to individual management.

a) Nationality Requirement

Among the first issues scrutinized by the European Commission were the terms and contracts used by CMOs in order to determine the group of right holders who were eligible for the acquisition of membership. Up to the seventies, many CMOs required that right holders, as a precondition for full mem-

640 ASCAP Consent Decree § XI(A); BMI Consent Decree § V(A); Kohn & Kohn, *Music Licensing*, *supra* at 1258–1259; Articles of Association of the American Society of Composers, Authors and Publishers, art. III(2)(3) (2002), *available at* https://www.ascap.com/~/media/files/pdf/members/governing-documents/articles-of-association.pdf (last visited May 23, 2017).

641 Absent a duty to represent, the blanket license could have a potential foreclosure effect, *see* I Hovenkamp et al., *IP and Antitrust*, *supra* at § 22.4a1.

642 Grounds for refusal are explicitly included in BMI's decree, *see* BMI Consent Decree § V(A).

643 SESAC, *How To Affiliate With SESAC*, https://www.sesac.com/writerspublishers/affiliate.aspx (last visited April 19, 2017) ("In order to keep this PRO advantage, SESAC requires potential affiliates or their representatives to have a pre-existing relationship with a member of the Creative Services Department. At this time, SESAC is not taking unsolicited affiliation applications."); U.S. Copyright Office, *Music Marketplace*, *supra* at 20. *See also Radio Music License Comm.*, 29 F. Supp. 3d 487 at 498 ("[S]ESAC offers its affiliates higher profits and greater exclusivity than they could achieve through alternative forms of licensing.") (footnotes omitted).

644 Compendium of ASCAP Rules and Regulations, and Policies Supplemental to the Articles of Association § 1.3. (2014), *available at* https://www.ascap.com/-/media/files/pdf/members/governing-documents/compendium-of-ascap-rules-regulations.pdf (last visited May 23, 2017) (last visited May 23, 2017). Affiliation with a foreign society is generally permitted, *see id.* at § 1.3.1.

645 Kohn & Kohn, *Music Licensing*, *supra* at 1259.

646 *Id. See also* U.S. Copyright Office, *Jointly Owned Works*, *supra* at 15 (citing ASCAP and BMI membership agreements). *See also* ASCAP Consent Decree § IV(B); BMI Consent Decree § VI(A).

bership, held the citizenship of the country in which the organization was based or have their place of residency in that country. Such conduct was found to constitute an abuse of a dominant position in *GEMA I* because nationals from other members states could only obtain a position equivalent to German nationals by moving to Germany and were hence effectively precluded from the benefits of (full) membership. This deterred citizens from other member states from joining the organization, a consequence which was deemed incompatible with the aims of the Internal Market.[647] It follows from this finding that if one talks about the membership terms in this context, one talks about full membership: A limited form of membership for nationals of other member states would not be sufficient to avoid a violation of article 102 because this would still discourage these persons from joining these organizations. The rights available have to confer an equal position with no disadvantages whatsoever attached to the nationality of the right holders. Even if GEMA had dropped the requirement of nationality, and merely demanded a place of residence in Germany, the Commission would have most likely reached the same result because such a construction is one of the paradigmatic examples of disguised discrimination which is prohibited by EU law.[648] Other forms of indirect discrimination were also considered to be in breach of the competition rules, especially GEMA's practice of not taking into account the income generated in other CMOs within the Union in connection with a certain annual average income as a precondition for membership.[649] The same applies to companies like music publishers that naturally have no nationality like natural persons: The full membership must be available also in cases where the head office is located in another member state or where personal or economic relations exist to publishers from other member states.[650]

The proceeding against GVL[651] centered on a similar situation. Prior to 1980, GVL concluded management contracts exclusively with artists of German nationality or those who were German residents.[652] Even though an amendment of the organization's statute – which was held to be in accordance with article 102 – had already been approved at its general meeting,[653] the Commission instituted a proceeding against the CMO.[654] In light of the obvi-

647 *GEMA I*, IV/26.760 at ¶ II.C(1)(a). The decision is not available in English (the authentic language of the text is German). The obligation to make notice of a change of nationality was also in breach of art. 102, *see id.* at II(C)(1)(e).

648 *See* on the issue in general Michael Enzinger, *Art 49 AEUV* in *Kommentar zu EUV und AEUV* ¶ 23 (Heinz Mayer & Karl Stöger eds., updated 01/2016 at rdb.at).

649 *GEMA I*, IV/26.760 at ¶ II(C)(1)(c).

650 *Id.* at ¶ II(C)(1)(b).

651 GVL is a German CMO that manages related rights.

652 *GVL*, IV/29.839 at ¶ 33.

653 *Id.* at ¶ 34. 71–73.

654 This fact led to the preliminary procedural question whether the Commission was competent to prosecute the competition rules despite the fact that GVL had already terminated its abusive conduct. The AG argued that the Commission lacked the competence to adopt a de-

ous discriminatory effects of the membership rules, GVL asserted that its conduct was justifiable because copyright laws in the different member states were (at that time) to a great extent divergent with regard to the rights of performers and manufacturers and that a connection to Germany was henc objectively necessary; moreover, since German artists could not demand royalties for their performances in other member states, it was equitable to require such a connection.[655] The arguments were rejected by the Commission and, on appeal, by the ECJ. The court ruled that, due to the exclusion of essential management services, artists from other member states could be deprived of the royalties they were entitled to under the applicable copyright regimes.[656] Hence, such rules constituted a violation of article 102 TFEU. In its decision, the Commission furthermore made clear that a justification cannot merely rest on the divergence of national laws.[657] In view of the current state of European copyright law, this argument must nowadays also be rejected on the grounds that important related rights (including the performing rights of artists) have been harmonized by means of directives.[658] However, even though the CMD gives right holders the option of mandating multiple CMOs for their rights,[659] it has been noted that the case law does not prohibit CMOs from preventing cases of dual membership (where more than one CMO is mandated to manage the same rights within the same territories) by employing corresponding provisions in reciprocal representation agreements. This would lead to great inefficiencies within the management process.[660]

The *GEMA I* and *GVL* decisions clarify that there is no justification for CMOs to discriminate against right holders from other member states. The Collective Management Directive specifies that CMOs must accept as members all right holders[661] who fulfill the membership requirements set forth in the statute or membership terms. These requirements must be based on "objective, transparent and non-discriminatory criteria".[662] This relates especially to direct or indirect discrimination on the basis of nationality, place of resi-

---

cision, mainly because article 105(1) of the TFEU instructs the Commission to bring an infringement of the competition rules "to an end", *see Gesellschaft zur Verwertung von Leistungsschutzrechten mbH v. Commission*, case 7/82 (ECJ 1983), Opinion of AG Reischl. The ECJ was of a different opinion and confirmed the Commission's competence because the court found a "legitimate interest" to hand down a decision in this particular case, *see GVL*, 7/82 at ¶ 16–28.

655 *GVL*, IV/29.839 at ¶ 37–41, 56–62.

656 *GVL*, 7/82 at ¶ 54–57.

657 *GVL*, IV/29.839 at ¶ 74.

658 *See, e.g.,* Rental & Lending Rights Directive chapter II.

659 van Gompel, *Directive*, *supra* at 572.

660 Schierholz, *Collective Rights Management*, *supra* at 1160. Under the CMD, efficiency concerns could serve as an objective reason to reject a management request.

661 This also includes "entities representing rightholders".

662 CMD art. 6(2). Such criteria can relate to a minimum yearly income, for instance, *see* Impact Assessment 2012 at 64.

dence, or place of establishment.[663] Furthermore, a rejection of a membership application must be accompanied by the reasons for this decision.[664] This can especially be the case when a membership request refers to categories of rights or types of works which are not managed by the CMO.[665]

As far as can be seen, U.S. PROs have traditionally not distinguished between right holders from different parts of the United States; in fact, the consent decrees apply to all writers and publishers covered by the respective definitions and requirements. However, their application is generally confined to the territory of the United States (and its territories and possessions).[666]

b) (Global) Assignment Requirement

The mere fact that a right holder grants a license to a CMO is not a violation of EU competition law since collective management would otherwise not be possible; however, this may change when the scope of the license is too broad.[667] Similar to the nationality requirement, CMOs often required right holders to assign the rights in their works in four comprehensive aspects: First, as to the categories or rights, all rights for all uses had to be assigned (the rights aspect); second, as to the date of creation, the assignment referred to the rights in all works created in the past and the future (the time aspect); third, as to the territorial scope, the agreement applied to the entire world (the geographical aspect); and finally, right holders were bound for considerable time (duration). The Commission considered this conduct as a clear abuse of a dominant position because it unduly restricted the freedom of right holders in exercising their copyrights.[668] This was especially the case in respect of the rights aspect and the geographical aspect. With regard to the first, the Commission enumerated seven categories between which right holders should at least be able to choose whether they are assigned to one CMO or split up between several organizations.[669] Regarding the latter, the Commission highlighted the right holders' freedom to determine the territorial scope of the

663 CMD recital 18.

664 *Id.* at art. 6(2).

665 *Id.* at recital 20.

666 ASCAP Consent Decree § III; BMI Consent Decree § III.

667 Morris, *Trading Functions*, *supra* at 570 (stating that this might cause CMO to charge excessive fees to users and other CMOs).

668 *GEMA I*, IV/26.760 at ¶ II(C)(2)(a).

669 The categories became known as the "GEMA-categories". These were 1) the general performing right, 2) the broadcasting right, including rights of transmission, 3) the right of cinematographic representation, 4) the right for mechanical reproduction and diffusion, including transmission rights, 5) the right of cinematographic production, 6) the right to produce, reproduce, diffuse and transmit on bases for optical sound and 7) the right of exploitation resulting from technical development or a change in the law in the future, *see id.* at ¶ II(C)(2)(a). For the purposes of the translation of the authentic German text, reference was made to Wood, *Collective Management*, *supra* at 6.

mandate given to CMOs.[670] The time aspect was not objected to as such; this decision should, however, be read in conjunction with the requirement that members should be able to terminate the mandate within a year.[671] The ECJ confirmed the principles of the Commission's ruling in *BRT v. SABAM*, without however explicitly reviewing the single GEMA-categories. The court stated that "a compulsory assignment of all copyrights, both present and future, no distinction being drawn between the different generally accepted types of exploitation, may appear an unfair condition [...]",[672] thus leading to a violation of the competition rules for being an abuse of a dominant position. In this context, the court developed the proportionality and indispensability test (*see* above). As an expression of these requirements, the ECJ acknowledged that CMOs were in need of a sufficient basis of assigned copyrights in order to effectively fulfill their functions;[673] whether this balance was properly struck was, however, the task of the national court.[674] The court's reference to "generally accepted types of exploitation" could be understood as upholding the general reasoning of the Commission with regard to the rights categories, especially in the *GEMA II* decision (*see* subsection 3.1.4.a).

The Collective Management Directive stipulates that right holders shall be able to freely choose which CMO to entrust with the management of their rights.[675] In order to provide them with a great degree of flexibility, right holders can also determine the categories of rights (rights aspect) and the territorial scope of the assignment agreement.[676] This, of course, raises the question of what is meant by these expressions. With regard to the "categories of rights", the most straightforward solution would simply be to rely on the "old" GEMA-categories. However, it is clear that these categories, which were articulated in 1971, need to be adapted to the legal and technological changes that have occurred since then.[677] Indeed, the Commission considered redrafting the rights categories in the Communication 2004[678] but decided not to pursue

670 *GEMA I*, IV/26.760 at ¶ II(C)(2)(a).

671 *Id.*

672 *BRT*, 127/73 at ¶ 12. The use of the word "may" can be explained by the ECJ's concerns to interfere with intellectual property issues. In this way, the responsibility was shifted to national judges, *see* Stamatoudi, *Love-Hate Relationship*, *supra* at 293.

673 *BRT*, 127/73 at ¶ 10.

674 *Id.* at ¶ 13–14.

675 CMD art. 5(2); consent must be given for each category specifically, *see id.* art 5(7).

676 A novelty compared to the GEMA-categories is the right holders' freedom to determine the types of works which shall be covered by the mandate.

677 Wood, *Collective Management*, *supra* at 8. *See also* Thomas Vinje & Ossi Niiranen, *The Application of Competition Law to Collecting Societies in a Borderless Digital Environment in Competition Law Annual 2005: The Interaction between Competition Law and Intellectual Property Law* 399, 405–406 (Claus-Dieter Ehlermann & Isabela Atanasiu eds., 2007). However, the category on yet-to-be-developed uses affords some flexibilities.

678 Communication 2004 at 16.

this idea and to maintain them in the Study 2005.[679] However, it can be said that the Commission eventually departed from the GEMA-categories in the course of the legislative work on the Collective Management Directive. In the Impact Assessment 2012, the Commission stated that CMOs "should allow authors and publishers to exercise their choice in relation to categories of rights which are separable from an economic perspective, taking into account national legislation on copyright [...]".[680] Here, the Commission alludes to the "utilization categories" developed in the *GEMA II* decision.[681] Although the utilization categories were developed in the context of the duration of assignment agreements, it seems that the Commission wishes to make them the general rule, thereby abandoning the GEMA-categories. Attention should be given to the fact that there is no exhaustive catalog of the utilization categories. The question is now whether the final version of the Collective Management Directive reflects the reasoning of the Commission. Recital 19 stipulates that "the rights, categories of rights [...] managed by the collective management organization should be determined by the general assembly of members [...], if they are not already determined in its statute or prescribed by law".[682] Thus, in principle, it is up to every single CMO to define and tailor the rights categories for which the organization offers management services, provided that no obligation arises from the national law. It is necessary to take these decisions carefully so that right holders are not deprived of their freedom, for instance, in case the categories are worded very broadly because a right holder may want to split up two "smaller" rights categories between two CMOs. However, the directive provides some indication how this is to be executed. First of all, recital 19 mentions in its first paragraph that right holders should be free to entrust CMOs with the rights of communication to the public and reproduction rights, or "categories of rights related to exploitation", like broadcasting or theatrical exhibition.[683] Second, the second paragraph of recital 19 calls for a careful consideration of the balance of interests between the freedom of right holders and the interest of effective collective management with a view on the particular category of rights and the respective creative sector. This consideration seems to stem from the cases decided by the ECJ, especial-

679 Manuela Maria Schmidt, *Die kollektive Verwertung der Online-Musikrechte im Europäischen Binnenmarkt*, 49 ZUM 783, 784 (2005).

680 Impact Assessment 2012 at 65.

681 *GEMA II*, Commission Decision of 06.07.1972, IV/26.760, 1972 O.J. (L166) 22–23, ¶ II(3). *See* for more details subsection 3.1.4.a) below.

682 The general assembly also has the power to amend the statute, *see* CMD art. 8(3).

683 It seems that both the *GEMA I* and the *GEMA II* decision have influenced this provision. Like in *GEMA I*, recital 19 mentions categories of rights (reproduction, communication to the public) and exploitation related categories like in *GEMA II*. It is however not clear from the wording of the directive whether CMOs must make available all categories enumerated in the two decisions; it would have been possible to include a minimum catalogue in the directive. In any event, the question can be addressed by the national transposition.

ly *BRT v. SABAM*. In this context, it should be noted that CMOs will continue to be subject to control under the competition rules, in spite of that the role of members in the decision-making process is ensured or that the CMD provides for relatively detailed rules. In this respect, the "old" categories, bearing in mind technological and legal developments, can still serve as benchmarks for abusive conduct or assist in the interpretation of the directive. In this system of the directive, member states will additionally monitor the compliance of CMOs with EU law.[684] A final remark regarding the independence of CMOs to determine the rights categories shall be made. Problems could arise if a right holder wants to transfer her rights to another CMO (*e.g.*, for reasons of more efficient management or lower administration fees) and corresponding categories do not exist in this organization, or the categories overlap only in parts. While it is expected that such situations will not occur on a regular basis, guidance at the EU level would be desirable in order to avoid such divergences; moreover, this would assist in determining the "scope of activities" within which a CMO is obliged to conclude management agreements (*see* subsection 3.1.2.). This could be achieved by an adequate application of the balance of interest requirement developed by the case law and provided for in recital 19. It is however submitted that under the regimes set forth in the *GEMA* cases, divergences were possible too.

The directive furthermore sets forth the general assembly's ability to determine the categories of *works* managed and mentions literary, musical, and photographic works while the balance of interests test also applies in this respect.[685] As regards the geographical aspect of assignment agreements, European CMOs are of course free to provide their services throughout the Union as they benefit from the guarantees of the EU treaties. Reciprocal representation agreements with clauses stating otherwise must be compatible with the competition rules.[686]

It is obvious that the Collective Management Directive confers a great amount of freedom upon right holders. Concerns were expressed whether the rights contained in article 5 could be abused; therefore, the Committee of Legal Affairs of the European Parliament suggested introducing appropriate safeguards in the directive. These concerns were obviously not included in the final version of the text.[687]

684 CMD art. 36.

685 *Id.* at recital 19.

686 *Id.* at recital 11.

687 Marielle Gallo, Committee on Legal Affairs, European Parliament, *Report on the Proposal for a Directive of the European Parliament and of the Council on Collective Management of Copyright and Related Rights and Multi-Territorial Licensing of Rights in Musical Works for Online Uses in the Internal Market Proposed Amendment*, 2012/0180(COD), 55 (2013), *available at* http://www.europarl.europa.eu/sides/getDoc.do?pubRef=-//EP//TEXT+REPORT+A7-2013-0281+0+DOC+XML+V0//EN (last visited May 23, 2017). *See also* Guibault,

The U.S. Consent Decrees put several restrictions on ASCAP and BMI when concluding membership contracts. ASCAP may only license rights of public performance in musical compositions (on a non-exclusive basis),[688] which excludes above all, mechanical rights and puts special constraints on the licensing of "synchronization" rights. Mechanical rights refer to the making and distribution of phonorecords, a task which is primarily carried out by the Harry Fox Agency.[689] Synchronization rights cover the recording (i.e. reproduction) of music on film (or other visual content like television).[690] In this context, theater owners ("motion picture theater exhibitors" within the language of the decree) are excluded from the licensing activities concerning the performance rights for music synchronized with motion pictures.[691] The rules on the synchronization rights stem from rather early litigation involving theater owners on the one side and ASCAP on the other. According to the then prevailing practice, when theater owners acquired movies from producers, the theater owners had to hold an additional ASCAP license for the corresponding performance rights in the music used in said movies; the producers only licensed the synchronization rights from the right holders directly, who in turn were prohibited by their contracts with ASCAP from licensing the performance rights to them.[692] In two cases, courts condemned this practice and held ASCAP to be in breach of sections 1 and 2 of the Sherman Act.[693] At least partially responding to these judgments, the DOJ negotiated amendments to the ASCAP Consent Decree (the ASCAP 1950 Decree)[694] which included, among further additions, first and foremost the mentioned provisions as well as the through-to-the-audience license not only for radio stations[695] but also for television

Collective Management Directive, *supra* at 723. *See however* Tobias Holzmüller, *Umsetzung der EU-Richtlinie für Verwertungsgesellschaften in deutsches Recht*, 58 ZUM 468 (2014) (stating that the rights contained in article 5(2) are not likely to lead to changes in (German) practice).

688 ASCAP Decree § IV(A). An exception is provided for in the same section for home recording devices and media in accordance with the applicable statutes.

689 U.S. Copyright Office, *Music Marketplace*, *supra* at 21, 28–32; II Goldstein on Copyright, *supra* at § 7.2.1.1.a.; 2 Melville B. Nimmer & David Nimmer, *Nimmer on Copyright* § 8.19[A] (Matthew Bender, Rev. ed. 2015). *See also* Pitt, *Direct Licensing*, *supra* at 51–53 (referring to the problems HFA faced due to the emergence of digital technology).

690 *Buffalo Broadcasting*, 744 F. 2d 917 at 920; *CBS v. ASCAP*, 620 F. 2d 930 at 934; *Alden-Rochelle*, 80 F. Supp. 888 at 892. Apart from the reproduction right, it can also affect the right to prepare derivative works (17 U.S.C. § 106(2)), *see, e.g., Agee v. Paramount Commc'ns, Inc.*, 59 F.3d 317 at 321 (2d Cir. 1995); U.S. Copyright Office, *Music Marketplace*, *supra* at 25 n. 65.

691 ASCAP Consent Decree § IV(E). *See also* § (IV)(G).

692 *Alden-Rochelle*, 80 F. Supp. 888 at 892–893; Lunney, *The United States Experience*, *supra* at 330.

693 *Alden-Rochelle*, 80 F. Supp. 888 at 894–985; *Witmark & Sons*, 80 F. Supp. 843 at 849–850.

694 *United States v. American Society of Composers, Authors and Publishers*, 1950–1951 Trade Cas. (CCH) ¶ 62,595, 1950 U.S. Dist. LEXIS 4341 (S.D.N.Y. 1950).

695 Before the cases involving theater owners, ASCAP had struggled with the radio industry, *see* Korman, *U.S. Position*, *supra* at 161–163.

networks and producers.[696] In contrast to ASCAP's decree, the BMI Consent Decree does not expressly prevent BMI from licensing certain types of rights[697] so that it may arguably license mechanical and synchronization rights. However, BMI has only done so to a very limited extent.[698] The decrees do not prevent the covered organizations from requiring right holders to assign all their performance rights upon becoming a member. Accordingly, the ASCAP and BMI membership agreements generally apply to all (non-dramatic) performance rights for musical works written or for which control was gained during or prior to the term of the agreements.[699]

c) *Individual/Direct Management*

Although the *GEMA* and *GVL* cases give valuable insights into the interpretation of article 102 TFEU, it should be noted that they do not expressly deal with the question of individual management. In *GEMA I*, the Commission ruled that right holders should be able to choose between *different* CMOs; in *BRT v. SACEM*, the ECJ made general remarks in connection with the global assignment of rights. Almost thirty years after the ECJ's ruling, the question arose whether a CMO may refuse to accept as members those right holders who wish to manage certain rights categories individually, while at the same time entrusting the CMO with the remaining rights. The Commission addressed the issue in the *Daft Punk* decision. The members of the music group "Daft Punk" wanted to individually manage their rights to the reproduction of

---

[696] Lunney, *The United States Experience*, *supra* at 331. *See also* on licensing practices 2 Nimmer on Copyright, *supra* at § 8.19[A].

[697] However, it can be inferred that the decree presupposes that BMI licenses rights in musical works, *see, e.g.,* BMI Consent Decree § II(C), IV, V, VI, IX.

[698] BMI requested to clarify the consent decree with regard to this point, *see* Broadcast Music, Inc., *Public Comments of Broadcast Music, Inc.* 16–17, n. 28 (2014), *available at* https://www.justice.gov/sites/default/files/atr/legacy/2014/08/13/307859.pdf (last visited May 23, 2017) (also stating that BMI licenses "sync" rights to a limited extent and DART royalties according to 17 U.S.C. § 1001). *See also* U.S. Copyright Office, *Music Marketplace*, *supra* at 150.

[699] American Society of Composers, Authors and Publishers, *ASCAP Writer Agreements* § 1, *available at* https://www.ascap.com/-/media/files/pdf/join/ascap-writer-agreement.pdf (last visited April 19, 2017) (hereinafter: ASCAP Writer Agreement); American Society of Composers, Authors and Publishers, *ASCAP Publisher Agreements* § 1, *available at* https://www.ascap.com/-/media/files/pdf/join/ascap-publisher-agreement.pdf (last visited April 19, 2017) (hereinafter: ASCAP Publisher Agreement); Broadcast Music, Inc., *BMI Standard Writer Agreement* § 1(b), 4–5, *available at* https://www.bmi.com/forms/affiliation/bmi_writer_agreement_W800.pdf (last visited April 19, 2017) (hereinafter: BMI Writer Agreement); Broadcast Music, Inc., *BMI Standard Publisher Agreement* § 2–4, *available at* https://www.bmi.com/forms/affiliation/bmi_publisher_kit.pdf (last visited April 19, 2017) (hereinafter: BMI Publisher Agreement). The BMI contracts contain special rules for performance rights in certain "dramatic or dramatico-musical" works. *See also* ASCAP Statute at art. III(5), (6); 2 Nimmer on Copyright, *supra* at § 8.19[A] (referring to *Kubik v. American Composer Alliance*, Inc., 54 N.Y.S.2d 764 (N.Y. Sup. Ct. 1945) on the global assignment requirement).

their works regarding recorded images and sounds as well as their rights resulting from technical development, especially regarding the Internet, DVD, CD-ROM, etc.[700] SACEM, the French CMO involved in the case, rejected the request based on its statute which obliged members to entrust their rights to another CMO, in case they did not wish to assign them to SACEM.[701] Thereby, it provided for a collective management-related "all-or-nothing" clause which practically amounted to a form of mandatory collective management, albeit split up between several CMOs. SACEM argued that this restriction was objectively necessary on the grounds of two main arguments: On the one hand, collective management ensured sufficient bargaining power to achieve acceptable licensing terms in agreements with users. On the other hand, it was deemed incompatible with the solidarity principle inherent to CMOs to permit right holders to reserve for themselves the most profitable rights ("l'écrémage" or "cherry-picking") while leaving the organization the rights which were cumbersome to manage; this would result in higher costs for collective management and, consequently, in drawbacks for all members.[702] At the first glance, these arguments appear to be in line with the guidelines set forth by former decisions because SACEM permitted right holders to choose another CMO for certain categories and due to that the ECJ acknowledged their protection as a legitimate aim of collective management.[703] However, the Commission was of the view that the test developed by the ECJ in the seventies had to be adapted because it had been developed in the analog era and did not take technological developments into consideration.[704] Therefore, an abuse in SACEM's conduct was found because, unlike a couple of decades before, individual management of copyrights was economically feasible by the use of digital technology. Moreover, it was argued that individual management safeguarded the moral rights since authors were in a superior position to control the use of their works. Finally, the Commission ascertained that only very few CMOs imposed such restrictions and accordingly, there was no need for them, also in connection with the problem of "*l'écrémage*".[705]

Important questions relating to SACEM's line of argumentation remain unanswered by the Commission's reasoning. First, the fact that individual management is possible nowadays cannot by itself substantiate the conclusion that authors will be protected against unreasonable claims made by economically potent users.[706] Second, the Commission did not properly address the concerns

---

700 *Daft punk*, COMP/C2/37.219 at 2.

701 *Id.*

702 *Id.* at 4.

703 *Tournier*, 395/87 at ¶ 31; *BRT*, 127/73 at ¶ 9.

704 Wood, *Collective Management*, *supra* at 7. In the 1970s, the Commission had accepted the practice, *see* Drexl, *Free Movement of Services*, *supra* at 477.

705 *Daft punk*, COMP/C2/37.219 at 11–12.

706 Allendesalazar & Vallina, *The Usual Suspects*, *supra* at 390–391.

regarding the solidarity principle that existed between the members of CMOs or why individual management reinforces the authors' moral rights; however, it was indeed hard for CMOs to prove that a restriction as to individual management fulfills the indispensability requirement, given the fact that (in that time) the great majority of CMOs did not provide for such condition.[707] Facing these accusations, SACEM amended its statute whereby it could satisfy the Commission's demands. The organization agreed to permit individual management of certain categories of rights in accordance with a case-by-case assessment of every corresponding application.[708] Such an application would only be rejected in exceptional cases and on the basis of objective criteria.[709] Accordingly, the Commission accepted refusals of applications in situations where i) the request was not motivated, ii) the quantitative evolution of individual management contradicts the grant of an application, or iii) technological problems could arise.[710] To a certain extent, the two criteria created legal uncertainties: The decision did not specify the number of requests for individual rights management necessary to justify a refusal of an application; moreover, it is uncertain exactly which technological problems, especially in the future, could have this effect.[711]

The Collective Management Directive acknowledges the right to individually manage copyrights while at the same time mandating CMOs for the management of other rights inasmuch right holders can freely choose which rights should be transferred to such organizations.[712] The last sentence of recital 19 specifies that nothing in the directive should "prejudice the possibility for rightholders to manage their right individually, including for non-commercial uses". To this effect, right holders have the right to grant licenses for non-commercial uses.[713] However, further references to individual management can also be found in connection with the withdrawal of rights:[714] The directive prohibits making the assignment of rights to another CMO a precondition for the withdrawal of rights from the CMO in question.[715] It can be assumed that the

707 *Id.* at 391–392.

708 *Daft Punk*, COMP/C2/37.219 at 6.

709 *Id.* at 12. The decisions must also comply with the competition rules and jurisprudence of the ECJ (especially the indispensability and equity test), *see id.* at 13.

710 Allendesalazar & Vallina, *The Usual Suspects*, *supra* at 392.

711 *Id.* at 392–393.

712 *See also* CMD recital 2. According to recital 12, the directive leaves national rules with respect to individual management unaffected.

713 CMD art. 5(3). *See* on the background and the interpretation of the provision Axel Metzger & Tobias Heinemann, *The Right of the Author to Grant Licenses for Non-Commercial Use*, 6 JIPITEC 11 (2015); 2 Walter, *Verwertungsgesellschaftenrecht*, *supra* at 236. *See also* Gerhard Pfennig, *Umsetzung der EU-Richtlinie für Verwertungsgesellschaften in deutsches Recht,* 58 ZUM 484, 486 (2014) (stating that this provision might put pressure on authors to license their rights under this provision).

714 *See* CMD recital 19.

715 *Id.* at art. 5(6).

drafters of the directive had the factual situation that led to the *Daft Punk* decision in mind. According to the wording, however, a CMO could require right holders to accept this condition at the time of the (first) conclusion of the assignment contract; the right holder could then "opt out" and withdraw the rights according to the applicable term of the agreement, even though he or she wanted to manage those rights individually in the first place. Since this additional transaction does not make sense economically and since it is inconsistent with the directive's aim to maximize the freedom of right holders with regard to the management of their rights, the provision should be interpreted to an effect that already at the time of the (first) conclusion of the assignment agreement, CMOs must not require right holders to transfer their rights to another CMO if they are not entrusted to themselves.[716] This of course leaves open the question how the concerns related to individual management as to the functioning of collective management as such can be properly addressed. On the one hand, it could be part of the decision-making process (defining the rights categories) to monitor the concerns raised by SACEM in *Daft Punk*. On the other hand, article 5(6) does not, at least explicitly, preclude the solution found in *Daft Punk*, to make each application for individual management subject to a case-by-case decision. This does not solve the problems mentioned above regarding the criteria for this assessment. However, since every other possible solution that could be developed in the future will imply the need to balance the involved interests, the directive does not preclude the implementation of new solutions to this problem in the future. An example could be a reasonable and objective policy regarding management fees.[717] Last, the freedom to opt for individual management can also be restricted where member states (or EU law) provide for mandatory collective management schemes.[718]

The issue of individual management has been approached differently in the United States. The right of ASCAP's and BMI's members to negotiate and grant licenses directly to users is a fundamental principle of the Consent Decrees and the antitrust case law and must be viewed in connection with the practices of blanket licensing. Effectively, it means that the rights grant by right holders to the CMOs is non-exclusive.[719] This right to direct licensing exists in parallel with the CMOs' authorization to grant licenses to the respective repertoires, so that a user can – in theory – choose between a "right holder license" and a "administrator license". Even though not by the constraints of a

716 In this context, the Impact Assessment 2012 specifies that CMO may not refuse a *membership* request, on the mere ground that a right holder wants to manage its right individually, *see* Impact Assessment 2012 at 64.

717 Allendesalazar & Vallina, *The Usual Suspects*, *supra* at 394 (stating that objectively adjusted management fees could be regarded as a less restrictive way in order to avoid financial risks of cherry-picking).

718 CMD recital 19.

719 2 Nimmer on Copyright, *supra* at § 8.19[A]; ASCAP Consent Decree § IV(B). *See also* Compendium of ASCAP Rules at § 2.7; BMI Consent Decree § IV(A).

consent decree, but as a result of private antitrust enforcement, SESAC entered into an agreement with local television stations, which stipulates that SESAC may not interfere with its affiliates' rights to issue direct licenses.[720]

3.1.4. Modification and Termination of Membership Agreements and Assignment Contracts

a) Withdrawal and Termination

Just as in the beginning of the management relationship between right holders and CMOs, the question of to what extent changes to this relationship were permissible attracted the attention of the Commission under European competition law. The main practice which the authority objected to was the tendency of membership agreements and assignment contracts to unduly bind right holders to a CMO. In this process, two interrelated main issues can be observed: On the one hand, the freedom of right holders to withdraw certain (categories of) rights from a CMO and, on the other hand, the duration of said contractual arrangements. The Commission stated in *GEMA I* that it was an abuse of a dominant position to impede the transfer of rights to other CMOs.[721] Therefore, it ruled that members should be able to withdraw each of the rights mentioned in the GEMA-categories from the mandate given to the CMO no longer than within a year after giving notice to that effect.[722] GEMA, although it accepted the decision, expressed some concerns and argued that this time would be too short from an economic perspective and that it would not ensure the protection of right holders against strong user groups.[723] Accordingly, it applied to amend the former decision by extending the period to three years. In the ensuing decision, the Commission highlighted that a balance had to be struck between the duration of the membership agreement and the restrictions put on right holders therein.[724] It explained that the seven categories were enumerated with a view to a maximum duration of one year;[725] a longer duration would therefore not be precluded as such by the decision, provided however that GEMA conferred upon right holders a greater degree of freedom than within the framework of the seven GEMA-categories. For this purpose, the Commission provided a non-exhaustive list of twelve "utilization categories".[726]

---

720 *Meredith*, 87 F. Supp. 3d 650 at 657–658. *See also* Todd Brabec, *The Performance Right – A World in Transition*, 42 Wm. Mitchell L. Rev. 16, 28 (2016).

721 *GEMA I*, IV/26.760 at ¶ II(C)(2)(c).

722 *Id.* at ¶ II(C)(2)(a). GEMA had originally provided for a six year term without an option of cancellation, *see id.* at I(A)(1)(c).

723 *GEMA II*, IV/26.760 at ¶ I.

724 *Id.* at ¶ II(2).

725 *Id.* at ¶ II(1).

726 The categories were defined as 1) the general performance right, 2) the broadcasting right, 3) the public performance right of broadcasting works, 4) the television rights, 5) the public performance right of televised works, 6) the right of cinematographic exhibition, 7) the right

These categories are similar to the original categories but more narrowly defined.[727]

The CMD confers upon right holders the right to terminate completely the relationship to a particular CMO or to withdraw from the mandate any rights, categories of rights or types of works for the territories of their choice.[728] The standard under the directive is now that a notice of termination or withdrawal must be effective within a maximum period of six months; however, a CMO can decide that any notice takes effect only at the end of a financial year.[729] In the decision-making process and in light of the balancing of interests at stake, CMOs must keep in mind that it should be easy for right holders to withdraw their rights.[730] Special safeguards ensure that right holders benefit from the revenues due between the notice and the effective date of the termination and withdrawal.[731]

In the United Sates, the aim to stimulate direct licensing has not been very effective, as users have only rarely made use of this option, preferring blanket licenses over licenses acquired from single right holders.[732] Avoiding the co-existence of direct licenses and CMO-issued licenses in the sense that a CMO manages some rights and the right holder (exclusively) reserves the management of certain rights in the CMOs' repertory for herself, has been intensely discussed in connection with the withdrawal of rights. As of 2010, music publishers expressed the wish to withdraw from ASCAP their "New Media rights" which they thought could be more effectively administered by themselves.[733]

of mechanical reproduction and diffusion, 8) the public performance right of mechanically produced works, 9) the cinematographic production right, 10) the right to produce, reproduce, and diffuse on video tape, 11) the public performance right of works reproduced on video tape, 12) the exploitation rights resulting from technical developments or future changes in the law, *see GEMA II* at II(3). For the purposes of the translation of the authentic German text, reference was made to Wood, *Collective Management*, *supra* at 6.

727 Allendesalazar & Vallina, *The Usual Suspects*, *supra* at 387 n. 44. Different to *GEMA I*, the examples for usages types were only included in the grounds of decision but not in its normative part. This part speaks of usage "types" in general, with no reference to single categories or types. However, this should not imply material differences between the two decisions.

728 *Pfeifer* notes that the wording of the directive is not confined to exclusive rights, but covers also rights to remuneration, *see* Pfeifer, *Umsetzung*, *supra* at 459.

729 CMD art. 5(4). According to recital 19, contractual arrangements are not precluded, *see* 2 Walter, *Verwertungsgesellschaftenrecht*, *supra* at 237.

730 CMD recital 19.

731 *Id.* at art. 5(4).

732 Lunney, *The United States Experience*, *supra* at 347–348; Kohn & Kohn, *Music Licensing*, *supra* at 1264–1266 (distinguishing source and direct licenses).

733 *In Re Pandora Media, Inc.*, Nos.12-cv-8035, 41-cv1395, 2013 U.S. Dist. LEXIS 133133, at *6 (S.D.N.Y. Sept. 17, 2013). The main reasons for this step were that i) fees for online music did not reflect the market value; ii) fees for musical compositions were much lower than for sound recordings, *see Broadcast Music, Inc. V. Pandora Media*, Inc., 140 F. Supp. 3d 267 at 275, 284 (S.D.N.Y. 2015). It should be noted that these withdrawals concerned performance

When Pandora, a music streaming service, brought suit in order to establish that ASCAP – by permitting publishers to withdraw digital rights – was in breach of the consent decree, the court ruled that the decree forced ASCAP to license nothing less than all performance rights existing in the works contained in its repertory.[734] In an analogous case, the same was found to apply to BMI and its respective decree.[735] Although the rulings differ in detail,[736] the baseline is clearly construed: The Consent Decrees establish an all-in or all-out policy.[737] It is hence not possible for right holders to benefit from the CMOs' services regarding certain (performance) rights while licensing other rights in the same work directly and in an *exclusive* manner. In this sense, the prohibition of exclusive licensing, regarding the same works is two-fold: Neither ASCAP or BMI nor their members may issue exclusive licenses to the works contained in the CMOs' repertoire.[738] As a consequence, the only option for publishers would be to withdraw their works entirely in order to prevent the digital rights from being covered by the licenses issued by ASCAP or BMI.[739]

ASCAP and BMI – eager to keep publishers satisfied in order to avoid their complete withdrawal from the CMOs' repertoires[740] – lobbied for an amendment of the Consent Decrees, officially asking the DOJ for corresponding modifications.[741] While the DOJ considered this request in a review, it eventually refused to renegotiate the decrees.[742] Accordingly, for the time being, a partial

rights, while the withdrawals in Europe in the wake of the Recommendation 2005 generally concerned mechanical rights, *see* section 3.1.7.d) below.

734 *In Re Pandora Media, Inc.*, 2013 U.S. Dist. LEXIS 133133 at *13–22. The 2nd Circuit ultimately confirmed this reasoning on appeal, *see Pandora v. ASCAP 2015*, 785 F. 3d 73 at 77–78. *See* for the CMD's definition of the term "repertoire" art. 3(l).

735 *Broadcast Music, Inc. v. Pandora Media, Inc.*, Nos. 13-cv-4037, 64-cv-3787, 2013 U.S. Dist. LEXIS 178414, at *12–15 (S.D.N.Y. Dec. 19, 2013).

736 The BMI rate court held that "[w]hen portions of [the right to license the performance right] are withdrawn, the affected compositions are no longer eligible membership in BMI's repertory, and it cannot include them in a blanket license or license them at all", *see BMI v. Pandora 2013*, U.S. Dist. LEXIS 178414 at *13. Taking the reverse approach, the court in the *ASCAP* case held that "musical compositions remain "in the ASCAP repertory" so long as ASCAP retains *any* licensing rights for them", *see In Re Pandora Media, Inc.*, 2013 U.S. Dist. LEXIS 133133 at *20 (emphasis added).

737 Lunney, *The United States Experience*, *supra* at 360.

738 *See also* Compendium of ASCAP Rules § 2.7.2.(b).

739 It has been suggested that withdrawing entirely does (currently) not make sense due to the relatively low new media royalties in comparison to traditional media, *see* Brabec, *Performance Right*, *supra* at 25.

740 *Pandora v. ASCAP 2015*, 785 F. 3d 73 at 76 (referring to EMI); U.S. Copyright Office, *Music Marketplace*, *supra* at 151–152.

741 American Society of Composers, Authors and Publishers, *Public Comments of the American Society of Composers, Authors and Publishers Regarding Review of the ASCAP and BMI Consent Decrees* 18–22 (2014), *available at* https://www.justice.gov/sites/default/files/atr/legacy/2014/08/14/307803.pdf (last visited May 23, 2017); BMI, *Public Comments 2014*, *supra* at 11–16.

742 DOJ, *Antitrust Division's Review*, *supra* at 4, 16–17.

withdrawal of rights must be assumed to be incompatible with the Consent Decrees absent of modifications or legislative action.

The ASCAP Consent Decree stipulates that members have the right to withdraw from membership at the end of any calendar year upon a three months' advance notice in writing.[743] This provision (and the other subsections of § XI(B) of the ASCAP Consent Decree in general) is only effective if an order in a case relating to BMI contains a "substantially identical provision".[744] However, such provision has not become effective as regards BMI.[745] The BMI Consent Decree specifies that BMI may not require right holders to enter into management contracts for a period in excess of five years.[746] Nevertheless, ASCAP members may withdraw from membership annually.[747]

b) Coordination of Membership Agreement and Rights Grant

It is a general idea of European case law that, if rights are transferred to CMOs, right holders should be in a position to assert their interest in these organizations, especially by the way of membership rights. However, some statutes of CMO set forth that the end of the membership relation did not affect the validity of the assignment agreement – a right holder would thus "lose" his or her rights while the organization is still in the position to benefit from the assignment. In essence, this technique serves to bind members to a certain CMO. The resulting misbalance led European authorities to hold this practice as inconsistent with article 102 TFEU. In general, the Commission called for a coordination of membership and rights assignment so that both arrangements would terminate at the same date.[748] A six-year term stipulated in the assignment contract, regardless of the subsistence of the membership relation, was considered to be an unlawful abuse; this was especially the case if the assignment covered all future works of the author because he or she would be deprived of the option to assign new works to a different CMO.[749] The ECJ confirmed this ruling and explicitly stated that it could amount to an unfair restriction, "if such assignment is required for an extended period after the member's withdrawal".[750]

In view of the Collective Management Directive, the issue should be understood as the coordination of the rights assignment and rights in a more general

743 ASCAP Consent Decree § XI(B)(3).

744 *Id.* at XI(C). *See also* AFJ2 Memo at 42–43.

745 *See also In Re Pandora Media, Inc.*, 2013 U.S. Dist. LEXIS 133133 at *26–27.

746 BMI Consent Decree § V(B).

747 Compendium of ASCAP Rules § 1.11.1. *See also* Einhorn, *Music Performing Rights*, *supra* at 365. *See also* II Goldstein on Copyright, *supra* at § 7.9. See, however, Pitt, *Direct Licensing*, *supra* at 75–77 (stating that the process of resigning from a CMO is often very burdensome).

748 *GEMA II*, IV/26.760 at ¶ II(2).

749 *GEMA I*, IV/26.760 at ¶ II(C)(2)(c).

750 *BRT*, 127/73 at ¶ 12.

sense, rather than proper membership. As stated above, the case law has dealt with situations in which important rights were linked to the capacities of members and where the assignment contract was used as a vehicle to bind right holders. Conversely, the most important rights under the CMD in this respect are independent of the fulfillment of membership requirements, since article 5 uniformly speaks of right holders. This relates especially to the ability to withdraw (categories of) rights as well as to terminate the mandate. Therefore, at least as regards the problems scrutinized by the case law, a coordination of membership and assignment is not necessary since right holders are given all tools to freely organize the scope of their assignment, so that it does not seem possible to unduly bind a right holder to a CMO by the way of the assignment agreement. In any event, it can be expected that within the framework of the new directive, CMOs will require an assignment agreement as a precondition for membership; should the assignment be terminated, this will most likely be the case for the membership too. Problems could arise if the notice of termination of the mandate immediately puts an end to the membership while the end of the assignment has not taken effect. For these months, the right holder would be deprived of membership rights which primarily relate to the decision-making process but were not at issue in the competition decision. It is, however, doubtful whether such criteria would qualify as "objective, transparent and non-discriminatory", as required by the directive in relation to membership rules since it would place at disadvantage right holders who lawfully exercise their rights guaranteed by the Collective Management Directive. Yet, it should be noted that the issue is more complicated with regard to license agreements that were concluded with users prior to the right holder's withdrawal and which are still in effect. The CMD leaves the parties free to contractually resolve this problem as long as this does not create an "obstacle to the full application of this Directive".[751]

Under ASCAP's policy, any resignation from membership does not affect so-called "Licenses-In-Effect" which especially include license agreements concluded with users throughout the term of the agreement and determination resulting from rate court proceedings.[752] However, the resigning member continues to receive payments.[753] The BMI Consent Decree stipulates that upon the termination of a membership contract, BMI "shall continue to pay for per-

751 CMD recital 19. It is unclear how this provision is to be interpreted; however, it seems appropriate to weigh the involved interests, *see also* van Gompel, *Directive*, *supra* at 574. The CMD's article 5(5) deems certain rights applicable in relation to acts of exploitation which occurred before the termination or withdrawal took effect.

752 Compendium of ASCAP Rules § 1.11.3.

753 *Id.* at § 1.11.5. However, § 1.111.6. specifies that ASCAP may deny payments if it exercises this option in respect of all resigning members alike. *See also In Re Pandora Media, Inc.*, 2013 U.S. Dist. LEXIS 133133 at * 21; ASCAP Consent Decree § XI(B)(3); Brabec, *Performance Right*, *supra* at 24.

formances [...] for so long as such performing rights are not otherwise licensed".[754]

3.1.5. Governance Structure

The European case law is relatively sparse on the internal structure and governance rules of CMOs. First of all, obligations derive from the general principle of non-discrimination. A reference to this principle can be found in *GEMA I* where a restriction of membership rights due to nationality was considered to be an abuse of a dominant position. Moreover, the Commission ruled that all members, regardless of nationality, must be eligible for the participation in the administrative council of the CMO.[755] Further governance standards were developed in the course of the preparatory work for the Collective Management Directive. For this reason, it contains very detailed rules on the internal functioning, governance standards, and transparency obligations. The core document of a CMO in this respect is the *statute* under the regime of the directive, which can be understood as the "constitution" of the organization.[756] It contains the basic structure and policies of a CMO.

Prior versions of the ASCAP Consent Decree contained detailed rules on the election of the board of directors and the representation of right holders and especially dealt with balancing the interests of the different categories of right holders, i.e. writers and publishers.[757] These rules are not part of the current ASCAP Consent Decree which dates from 2001.[758] Nevertheless, the *Sam Fox Publishing* case indicates that the relationship between CMOs and right holders is – to some extent at least – regulated by antitrust law, especially in cases of certain groups of right holders being extremely underrepresented in the decision-making process.[759] The BMI Consent Decree does not contain substantial institutional provisions.

a) General Policies

The most important institutional provisions of the Collective Management Directive relate to the general assembly which is to be established in every

754 BMI Consent Decree § IV(C). *See also* BMI Writer Agreement § 8, 10–11; BMI Publisher Agreement § 7, 9–10.

755 *GEMA I*, IV/26.760 at ¶ II(C)(1)(d).

756 It is defined as "the memorandum and articles of association, the statute, the rules or documents of constitution of a collective management organization", *see* CMD art. 3(e).

757 *See, e.g.*, ASCAP 1960 Order § IV referring to § XIII of the ASCAP 1950 Decree.

758 Lunney, *The United States Experience*, *supra* at 336.

759 In this case, ASCAP was asserted to violate § 1 of the Sherman Act by massively underrepresenting writers and small publishers because a few large publishers were able to control the Board of Directors and the distribution of the royalty stream, *see Sam Fox Publ'g*, 366 U.S. 683 at 685–686. When the case finally reached the Supreme Court, it did not deal with this matter due to procedural questions, *see id.* at 690–693.

CMO. It is composed of the *members* of the organization.[760] The assembly is competent to make fundamental decisions that govern the management activities of the CMO.[761] Therefore, it may adopt amendments to the statute or the membership terms.[762] It also directly controls the activities of the overall administration by appointing and dismissing the directors (the members of the board of administration) and the auditor as well as by approving the annual transparency report.[763] Furthermore, the general assembly determines the general policy on the distribution of collected revenues and deductions, the use of non-distributable amounts, the general investment and risk management policy, etc.[764] Under certain circumstances, the competencies can be delegated to the body exercising the supervisory function or to an assembly of delegates.[765] Following the minimum protection principle, member states may decide to add further fields to the scope of activities of the general assembly.[766]

ASCAP's Articles of Association stipulate that the Board of Directors [the Board] – which is equipped with important powers like the collection and distribution of the royalties[767] – is equally composed of writer and publisher members.[768] A general meeting is held at last once a year, where the Board reports "on the status of the society".[769]

b) Membership Rights[770]

The general idea of the CMD is that members should be able to participate in the decision-making process of a CMO; this is ensured by a set of membership rights.[771] Accordingly, all members have the right to participate and to

760 CMD art. 8(9).

761 *Id.* at recital 23

762 *Id.* at art. 8(3).

763 *Id.* at art. 8(4), (8). The general assembly also reviews the performance of the directors and determines their remuneration and other benefits granted by the CMO. Where there is a dual board, the powers in relation to the directors (the members of the management board) can be delegated to the supervisory board. Member states may provide for alternative systems for auditors.

764 CMD art. 8(5).

765 *Id.* at art. 8(6), (11). Where a CMO has members that represent right holders, member states can decide to transfer all or some of the competencies to an assembly of right holders, *see* art. 8(13).

766 *Id.* at art. 8(5).

767 ASCAP Statute art. V, XVII.

768 *Id.* at art. IV(1). It further distinguishes „symphonic and concert" members from other members. *See also id.* at art. XXIII.

769 *Id.* at art. XVIII.

770 CMD recital 23 and art. 8(12) provide for a rule with regard to organizations which do not have members and declare the body entrusted with the supervisory function competent to exercise the powers of the general assembly. *See also id.* at art. 8(11), (13).

771 *Id.* at recital 22, 23, art, 6(3). The detailed definition of the rights will depend on the national transposition of these provisions. Since the term "participation" alone leaves wide room

vote in the general assembly.[772] Members can decide to exercise their voting rights by relying on a proxy whereby this must not lead to a conflict of interest; the authorization is valid for a single general assembly.[773] Membership rights can be exercised by electronic means.[774] As stated above, these rules should assist the flexibility of right holders to entrust CMOs from other member states with the management of their rights.[775]

When the Collective Management Directive refers to membership rights, this means the rights of a full member. It expressly states that *all* members[776] should participate and vote in the general assembly; the definition of the term "members" does not include any exception or room for modification. However, this does not mean that a classification between different groups of members is forbidden as such. In two respects, the directive allows for the modification of the principle of equal treatment of members or for restrictions which are put on the exercise of the respective rights. First, individual restrictions[777] are expressly permitted. For this purpose, member states may restrict or allow CMOs to restrict the exercise of membership rights in the decision-making process on the grounds of i) the duration of membership and ii) the revenues generated or distributed to a member.[778] Second, the directive acknowledges, to a certain extent, that collective restrictions[779] may be necessary to ensure a proper and fair functioning of the CMOs. In this respect, the directive takes into account that many CMOs represent different "categories" of members.

for implementation, several membership rights can be expected to be conferred upon members, also depending on the corporate structure of the CMO.

772 *Id.* at art. 8(9).

773 *Id.* at art. 8(10). This rule was introduced to prevent publishers or producers from requiring original ("creative") right holders to appoint them permanently as proxies, *see* van Gompel, *Directive*, *supra* at 581–582. *See also* Holzmüller, *Umsetzung*, *supra* at 469–470 (highlighting that the rules on representation might put the balance between the different groups of right holders at risk). Member states can provide for appropriate restrictions in this respect, *see* CMD recital 23.

774 *Id.* at art. 6(4), recital 23.

775 *See also* in this context the rules on the participation in the general meeting by electronic means contained in article 8 of the Directive 2007/36/EC of the European Parliament and of the Council of 11 July 2007 on the exercise of certain rights of shareholders in listed companies, 2007 O.J. (L184) 17–24.

776 Member states may also provide right holders who are not members of the organization with the right to participate in the decision-making process, *see id.* at recital 21, art 7(2).

777 Individual restrictions are understood here as restrictions which are put on a particular right holder because he or she does not fulfill certain criteria. It is possible to lift these restrictions. The focus is put on the relation between the individual member and the organization.

778 CMD art. 8(9).

779 Collective restrictions are understood here as being defined on the basis of general personal characteristics by which several persons are grouped into a category. It is practically not possible to lift these restrictions (except by abandoning the current business and joining the other group). The focus is put on the relation between a group of members and the organization or other groups of members.

Typically, the different groups have diverging interests, like those of music producers and performers;[780] however, since a CMO must act in best "collective" interests of all right holders that they represent,[781] this aim would be hard to achieve without a certain degree of flexibility. As one can imagine, both individual and collective restrictions of membership rights are only permitted to a limited extent. According to the wording of the CMD, individual restrictions are exclusively allowed on the basis of the two criteria mentioned before (duration of membership, income) and additionally, such criteria must be "fair and proportionate".[782] There are no explicit criteria for collective restrictions, so that members states (and CMOs, depending on implementation) are given certain leeway. However, all rules leading to a different treatment of member categories must be "fair and balanced".[783] It should be noted that the two tests are not identical: In the former case, there is a fairness and proportionality test and, in the latter, a fairness and balance test. One must assume that this is a deliberate terminological distinction; moreover, the distinction also appears in other language versions of the directive.[784] It appears that the two tests are based on distinct underlying considerations: Basing rights for the duration of membership or the generated income can be seen as a reward for the loyalty of a member toward a CMO, or as an acknowledgment of his or her importance for the organization. In contrast, distinguishing the categories of members serves to give certain groups which typically have asymmetric economic leverage an equal say in the decision-making process. Restrictions are only allowed inasmuch as they are necessary to maintain a balance between these groups; in this is way, they do not actually aim at curtailing rights but rather at ensuring the rights, as there should be an equal opportunity to participate for members of every category, with no advantage of one group over the other. One example could be found in connection with the generated income: It can be assumed that it will be easier for music publishers to achieve a certain threshold than for composers; a higher threshold with respect to the member category of publishers could, therefore, be justified.[785]

Article XX of the ASCAP Statute is titled "membership rights" but rather deals with the questions relating to the ending of membership due to expulsion, death, etc. The most fundamental membership rights comprise the right to elect the Board of Directors[786] as well as to participate in the enactment procedure

---

780 CMD recital 22. *See also* art 8(10).

781 *Id.* at recital 22.

782 *Id.* at recital 23, art. 8(9).

783 *Id.* at recital 22, art. 6(3), 8(11)(b), 9(2).

784 *See, e.g.*, German, French, Italian and Spanish version of the directive.

785 Furthermore, one must remember that the Commission condemned the practice to prescribe as a condition for the full exercise of membership rights a certain average income throughout five consecutive years and, at the same time, not taking into account the revenues generated before in a CMO from another member states, *see GEMA I*, IV/26.760 at ¶ II(C)(1)(c).

786 ASCAP Statute art. IV(4).

of the articles of association; members have the right to propose amendments, which is subject to approval by the Board of Directors.[787] The directors of the Board are elected by the membership.[788] The weighted voting rights vary according to the performance credits received in the latest available fiscal year; in absence of any credits, there is no right to vote.[789] Amendments to the statute are subject to approval by all voting members (weighted like for the purposes of electing the Board), whereas writers and publishers make up half of the votes, respectively.[790] The obligation to report to the members at each General Meeting implies the right of the members to participate in this meeting. Furthermore, members are in principle entitled to receiving royalties,[791] including the right to protest to the Board of Review.[792]

c) Administration and Supervision

Under the Collective Management Directive, the administrative tasks of a CMO can be carried out by a unitary board (administrative board) or by a dual board (management board and supervisory board), depending on the applicable national laws or the statute of the CMO.[793] The members of the board(s) ("directors") are elected by the general assembly, but managers can also be hired on the basis of a contract.[794] Every person entrusted with the management of the business must act in a "sound, prudent and appropriate manner" which includes accounting procedures and internal control mechanisms.[795] This group of people must also make an annual individual statement which is submitted to the general assembly, disclosing financial flows from the organization and conflicts of interest; member states are obliged to enact appropriate safeguards to avoid these conflicts.[796]

In order to ensure that CMOs are managed in accordance with the general guidelines made by the general assembly, CMOs must possess a supervisory function.[797] This function can be carried out by a separate body, like the supervisory board in a dual system, or by members of the administrative board who are not involved in the business management in a unitary system.[798] The competent body has the task to monitor the persons who manage the business

787 *Id.* at art. XXI.

788 *See* for the details of the election procedure *id.* at art IV(4).

789 *Id.* at art. IV(4)(i). *See also* ASCAP Writer Agreement § 7; ASCAP Publisher Agreement § 7.

790 ASCAP Statute art. XXI.

791 *Id.* at art. XVII.

792 *Id.* at art. XIV(4). An appeal is possible.

793 CMD art. 3(g).

794 *Id.* at recital 25.

795 *Id.* at art. 10(1).

796 *Id.* at art 10(2).

797 *Id.* at art. 9(1).

798 *Id.* at recital 24. However, the provision does not require that each CMO have a separate supervisory body, *see* van Gompel, *Directive*, *supra* at 583.

of the CMO; furthermore, the general assembly can delegate further duties to the supervisory body.[799] The directive acknowledges that these tasks are essential for the interests of different groups of members, which is why it calls for participation of members in this process as well as "fair and balanced" representation of different categories of members.[800] Just like the managers, supervisors must make an annual individual statement to the general assembly.[801]

In the case of ASCAP, the most important administrative tasks are carried out by the Board.[802] Besides other functions like the treasurer and the secretary,[803] the statute provides for standing committees among which, most notably, is the Board of Review which fulfills important supervisory tasks concerning the royalty distribution. It is elected by the membership and equally composed of writers and publishers who must not serve on the Board of Directors.[804] The Board of Review also has the final decision in the matter of expulsion of members.[805]

d) Transparency and Reporting Obligation

Given the size of ASCAP, BMI, and many European CMOs and the complexity of the royalty distribution process, transparency is vital in order to keep right holders informed about the organization's actions; in fact, this is also the requirement for a competitive market for collective management services.

The obligation to provide right holders with information under the Collective Management Directive is three-fold: First, CMOs must "inform" right holders about their rights that ensure their freedom to choose a CMO throughout the Union and that prevent CMOs from binding them.[806] Second, there are pieces of information which a CMO must "make available" to right holders (at least once a year). These include, *inter alia*, the rights revenues attributed to a right holder, the amounts paid to him or her per rights category or type of use, and the deductions made for management fees and other purposes.[807] Last, some information must be available "on request" of right holders, like the works a CMO manages and represents and the territorial scope of its activities.[808] The different wording of the three types can be read as gradually

---

799 CMD art. 9(4). For instance, the assembly can delegate the power to appoint and dismiss the members of the administrative board if the CMO has implemented a dual board system, *see id.* at art. 8(4).

800 *Id.* at recital 24, art. 9(2).

801 *Id.* at art. 9(3), recital 25.

802 *See* for details of powers of the Board ASCAP Statute art. V.

803 *Id.* at art IX, X.

804 *Id.* at art. XIV(5).

805 *Id.* at art 5(9).

806 CMD art. 5(8).

807 *Id.* at art. 18.

808 *Id.* at art. 20. Further transparency obligations can be found in connection with the MTL system (art. 25–26).

classifying the intensity of the transparency obligations.[809] While in the first case, CMOs should ensure that right holders actually take note of the rights and perhaps, to a certain extent, also understand their scope,[810] it must only make the information accessible in the second case; in the third case, it must only do so on a corresponding request. This reading of the directive is reinforced by the purpose of the provisions: The rights set forth in article 5 are fundamental to the protection of right holders as evidenced by the competition case law and assist their freedom to enjoy their copyrights; thus, it seems reasonable to provide for an elevated standard of information. The second type of transparency obligation primarily serves "to enhance the trust of right holders […] in the management of rights" by CMOs;[811] by this information, right holders are provided with an image of the accuracy, efficiency, and quality of the management services offered by CMOs. The third type of transparency obligations has the purpose of providing an overview of the scope of activity of a particular CMO. Moreover, only "duly justified" requests must be answered, and it must only be done so by electronic means; member states can decide whether fees can be charged.[812] Finally, it should be highlighted that the scope of the transparency obligations with regard to certain groups of right holders differs: The third type of information must be available to "any right holder" (and users/certain CMOs).[813] In the case of the second type, only right holders who have a claim to revenues or other payments must be provided with information; the first type relates to right holders in the course of establishing of the representation relationship.

The ASCAP Consent Decree stipulates that the general methods of calculation of the revenues shall be "fully and clearly disclosed to all members" and provides for a rather broad frame stating that "upon written request of any

809 Similar techniques and wordings are used in other fields of EU law, *e.g.* Directive 2014/92/EU of the European Parliament and of the Council of 23 July 2014 on the comparability of fees related to payment accounts, payment account switching and access to payment accounts with basic features art. 8, 14, 2014 O.J. (L257) 214–246 ("the payment service provider informs the consumer" as opposed to "make available to consumers"). *See* for more details on this directive Georg Tuder, *§ 8* in *VZKG* ¶ 15–21 (Arthur Weilinger ed., 2016).

810 Article 5(8) of the directive implies that the consent required to lawfully manage a right holder's copyrights requires for its validity that CMOs inform them about their rights. Whether the assignment contract is deemed void or can be nullified if a CMO fails to comply with this rule, is ultimately a question of national private law doctrines. Article 12(1) seems to point in a similar direction.

811 CMD recital 34.

812 *Id.* at recital 35, art. 20. It follows *e contrario* that fees are not permissible in respect of the other types of information.

813 Under article 20, right holders, users, and other CMOs represented under a representation agreement can file requests for information. *Van Gompel* notes that the obligation applies only to right holders and users "within the specific field of operation of the CMO" and that the obligation also applies to prospective users, *see* van Gompel, *Directive*, *supra* at 598–599.

member, ASCAP shall disclose information sufficient for that member to determine exactly how that member's payment was calculated by ASCAP".[814] In contrast, the BMI Consent Decree provides for an express obligation to make available, at "reasonable intervals", to all members information on the calculation of the payment rates.[815] However, the Compendium of ASCAP Rules states that an annual statement on the distribution of the royalties is issued to the members.[816] This report, in turn, is relevant for the exercise of membership rights because any protests against the distribution must be filed within nine months of the receipt of said report.[817]

e) Dispute Resolution

It is clear that disputes can arise between CMOs and right holders, especially when it comes to the distribution of the revenues collected. The Commission held it to be an abuse of a dominant position to contractually exclude any recourse to the courts. Even if a member state implemented a special supervision over CMOs, a consideration of an individual claim would not necessarily be guaranteed in this way.[818]

The Collective Management Directive supplements this *acquis* by requiring CMOs to implement complaints procedures to resolve disputes regarding, for instance, the authorization to manage rights, the termination and withdrawal of rights, membership terms, and the distribution of collected revenues.[819] CMOs are obliged to respond to complaints in writing and to give reasons for rejections.[820] These rules also apply to right holders who are not members of the CMO.[821] This is a reasonable solution since they can be in need of such procedures just like members. It goes without saying that only members can complain about questions related to membership rights under these procedures.

---

814 ASCAP Consent Decree § XI(B)(1). *See, e.g.*, in reference to the ASCAP 1960 Order *United States v. American Society of Composers*, Authors and Publishers, 129 F. Supp. 2d 327 at 331–332 (S.D.N.Y. 2001) (holding that ASCAP was obliged to provide access to documents but not to perform onerous tasks in order to compile information). *See also* Compendium of ASCAP Rules § 1.5.2. *See*, however, Pitt, *Direct Licensing*, *supra* at 69–70 (criticizing complex and intransparent royalty computation and survey methodologies employed by U.S. CMOs).

815 BMI Consent Decree § VII(A). *See also* BMI Writer Agreement § 7; BMI Publisher Agreement § 6.

816 Compendium of ASCAP Rules § 1.16. The statements reflect all credited performances for the respective period which is twelve months, *see id.* at § 1.16.1.

817 ASCAP Statute art. XIV(4). However, according to Compendium of ASCAP Rules § 1.16.2., claims must be made within nine months from the end of that period.

818 *GEMA I*, IV/26.760 at ¶ II(C)(2)(b). *See* now recital 49 of the CMD discussing alternative dispute resolution "without prejudice to the right of access to a tribunal".

819 CMD art. 33(1).

820 *Id.* at art. 33(2).

821 *Id.* at recital 49, art. 7.

Additionally, member states have the option to enact alternative dispute resolution procedures.[822]

The BMI Consent Decree provides that all contracts which BMI concludes with right holders contain a clause requiring the parties to submit to the arbitration in New York under the rules of the American Arbitration Association "all disputes of any kind".[823] While the ASCAP Consent Decree does not contain a comparable rule, the ASCAP Statute gives right holders (and ASCAP itself) the option to appeal decisions of the Board of Review regarding the royalty distribution, referring the matter to a panel in New York under the rules of the American Arbitration Association.[824]

3.1.6. Financial Flows between Right Holders and CMOs

Payments, monetary obligations, and further financial flows can be observed between right holders and CMOs in two principle ways. These can help right holders collect license fees for the use of their works and maintain the facilities necessary for the collective management.

a) Collection, Use, and Distribution of the Income

Since a great number of right holders contribute to the overall income of CMOs, it is a delicate task to find a fair formula according to which a distribution among these right holders takes place. The sum that can ultimately be distributed depends on the implemented collection policy and the use of the collected revenues.

European competition law was concerned with the clarification of questions of details in connection with distribution policies. It flows from the principle of non-discrimination that right holders from other member states should not be put at a disadvantage in the distribution process, as scrutinized in the Commission's ruling in *GEMA I*. In this case, GEMA maintained that it treated all right holders equally, regardless of nationality, according to its general distribution scheme. However, the Commission ruled that this was not enough

822 *Id.* at art. 34 (1). There is, however an obligation to provide for alternative dispute resolution for the purposes of title III on MTL, *see id.* at art. 34(2).

823 BMI Consent Decree § VII(C). This provision also applies to disputes with users with the exception of rate court proceedings under § XIV of the decree. *See also* BMI Writer Agreement § 21; BMI Publisher Agreement § 20; Kohn & Kohn, *Music Licensing*, *supra* at 1282. *See* for disputes regarding the acquisition of membership BMI Consent Decree § V(A).

824 ASCAP Statute art. XIV(4), (6). *See also United States v. ASCAP*, 129 F. Supp. 2d 327 at 334; *United States v. American Society of Composers, Authors and Publishers*, 832 F. Supp. 82 at 84 (S.D.N.Y. 1993), *aff'd* 32 F. 3d 727 (2nd Cir. 1994); ASCAP Writer Agreement § 8; ASCAP Publisher Agreement § 8.

to justify the discrimination which it had found in relation to the acquisition of membership because members could influence the distribution policy.[825] Furthermore, GEMA had implemented a special scheme for the allocation of non-distributable sums (*Wertungsverfahren*) which included amounts where the person directly entitled could not be ascertained at reasonable costs[826] like interest yields, administrative fees, liquidated damages, deductions for social and cultural purposes, and profits from the collection of copyright levies.[827] In order to be eligible for the extra payments, members had to fulfill several requirements (like full membership for at least three years)[828] which excluded other right holders from participating in the distribution. The Commission held this practice to be inconsistent with the competition rules because it was abusive to offer a loyalty bonus for only some members while these funds were supplied by the entirety of all members.[829] It should be highlighted that the discrimination based on nationality[830] was only one ground for the Commission to prohibit this practice; the other was that members who had fulfilled the requirements at that time were facing unjustified advantages. GEMA argued that the extra payments were an objective compensation because members who generated a higher income caused proportionally lower administration costs compared to "low-income" members, the costs being equally assumed by all members; the Commission, however, rejected this argument by rightly pointing out that implemented procedure did not reflect this thought through the requirements stipulated.[831] The legal assessment was similar regarding the CMO's insurance funds (*Sozialkasse*). Since GEMA required a duration of full membership of twenty years as a precondition, it was considered as a means of binding members to the organization; a waiting period of five years was regarded as the maximum permissible under article 102 TFEU.[832]

The Commission again dealt with questions relating to distribution in the *GVL* decision. GVL implemented a distribution scheme according to which artists and manufacturers respectively received a share of fifty percent of GVL's overall income. The amounts due to individual artists flowing from the secondary exploitation managed by the CMO were (on a diminishing scale) cal-

825 *GEMA I*, IV/26.760 at ¶ II(C)(1)(a).

826 *Id.* at ¶ II(C)(2)(b).

827 *Id.* at ¶ I(A)(2)(a), (b).

828 *Id.* at ¶ I(A)(3)(b). Additional payments were made after a duration of twenty years of full membership, *see id.* at ¶ I(A)(3)(h).

829 *Id.* at ¶ II(C)(2)(b). In turn, the Commission's decision can be interpreted as allowing taking into account this factor in principle if justified in the individual case.

830 Nationals of other member states could hardly acquire full membership under the original rules, *see* section 3.1.3.a) above.

831 *GEMA I*, IV/26.760 at ¶ II(C)(2)(b).

832 *Id.* at ¶ II(C)(2(c). The Commission did not object to the threshold of income a person entitled to social payments was not allowed to exceed. Of course, GEMA's practice also constituted a discrimination based on nationality, *see id.* at ¶ 2(C)(2)(a).

culated on the basis of the royalties earned from the primary exploitation[833] of the performances for the territory of Germany within one financial year. Since not all of GVL's members had income from primary exploitation, only about half of them were considered in the distribution procedure.[834] GVL itself submitted that a calculation on the basis of the actual use of the performances (frequency and length of broadcasts etc.), i.e. a "follow the dollar approach",[835] would come closer to the requirement of "equitable remuneration" (*angemessene Vergütung*) required by German law but argued that it would be too burdensome and often impossible to ascertain the data required for that purpose.[836] The Commission accepted this reasoning and did not find any abuse.[837] This, however, implies that a re-evaluation of the policy might be necessary if, especially with the development of the proper technological means, a more accurate calculation is feasible. The question was not scrutinized by the ECJ on appeal because the question was not covered in GVL's submission of the case.[838]

The Collective Management Directive contains comparatively detailed rules on the management of the rights revenue in its chapter 2 but at the same time, relies on general expressions to delineate the framework for national transposition. This should leave member states a certain leeway in the course of implementation. The standard for the collection and use of the rights revenues is that CMOs must act in a "diligent" way.[839] Subsequently, the directive gives several guidelines for what is meant by this expression. CMOs must keep the rights revenue and the income arising from investments separate from any owned assets, management fees, or other activities in its accounts.[840] In principle, rights revenues may only be used for direct distribution to right holders; where this is not the case, all different uses must serve the interests of the right holders. For this reason, the permitted uses for investments and deductions of management fees must be based on the guidelines defined by the general assembly. Investments may only be made if the security, quality, liquidity, profitability, and proper diversification of the portfolio are guaranteed.[841] The directive generally permits deductions[842] from the rights revenue; however, un-

---

833 The rights of primary exploitation under German law reserved for artists the rights to use their performances in public, record them on visual and audio media, reproduce and broadcast them; the right of secondary exploitation covered rights to remuneration where a lawfully made recording was broadcast or otherwise performed publicly, *see GVL*, IV/29.839 ¶ 3–4.

834 *Id.* at ¶ 30–32.

835 Gervais, *Theory and Practice*, *supra* at 11–12.

836 *GVL*, IV/29.839 at ¶ 41.

837 *Id.* at ¶ 72–73.

838 *GVL*, 7/82 at ¶ 6.

839 CMD art. 11(2). *See also id.* at recital 26.

840 *Id.* at art. 11(3).

841 *Id.* at art 11(4), (5). Member states may provide for further restrictions, *see id.* at recital 27.

842 The term „deduction" is not defined in the directive and must most likely be understood in relation to the term „management fees", *see* Guibault, *Collective Management Directive*, *supra* at 741; Guibault & van Gompel, *Collective Management*, *supra* at 153.

der the general standard, these must be "reasonable in relation to the services provided by the CMO" and must be based on objective criteria.[843] Deductions for social, cultural, and educational purposes must be based on "fair criteria" in relation to the access to and the extent of the services offered.[844]

The standard for the distribution of amounts due to right holders is expressed by the obligation of CMOs to "regularly, diligently and accurately" distribute these amounts in accordance with the guidelines of the general assembly. This process should be carried out rapidly, so that right holders receive their share "as soon as possible".[845] The maximum time span given to CMOs to make the corresponding payments is *nine months* from the end of the financial year in which the amounts were collected; only objective reasons beyond the control of the organization, like delays on the part of users or members or the identification of rights, can justify an extension of this period.[846] A special problem in the context of distribution arises when a right holder who is entitled to payments cannot be identified or located. In such cases all necessary measures have to be taken in order to identify and locate the right holder in question; this includes the obligation to make relevant information available to the other right holders represented by the CMO and to the CMOs with which it has concluded representation agreements no later than three months following the nine-month period.[847] The second step is to make the information available to the public within a year after the expiry of the aforementioned period if the efforts taken prove unsuccessful.[848] In case all measures fail to succeed in identifying the right holder in question, the amounts are considered as non-distributable after three years from the end of the financial year of collection and can be used in accordance with the decisions taken by the general assembly; however, the right holder may retain the right to claim the amounts, since the directive leaves the national rules on the statute of limitation of claims unaffected.[849]

Distribution issues can arise in connection with the treatment of different categories of right holders.[850] In the Commission's GVL decision already men-

[843] CMD art. 12(2).

[844] *Id.* at art. 12(3), (4). In order to ensure that deductions do not conflict with the protection of right holders, the general assembly is competent to determine the general policies; deductions provided for by national law are (in principle) not affected by the directive, *see id.* at recital 28.

[845] *Id.* at art. 13(1).

[846] *Id.* at recital 29, art. 13(1).

[847] *Id.* at art. 13(3). Furthermore, CMOs must verify the records referred to in art. 6(5) and other "readily available records"; this includes, for instance, the European database on orphan works, *see* van Gompel, *Directive*, *supra* at 590. The requirements of the CMD are, however, less strict than the "reasonable search" prescribed by the Orphan Works Directive, *see* 2 Walter, *Verwertungsgesellschaftenrecht*, *supra* at 257.

[848] CMD art. 13(3).

[849] *Id.* at art. 13(4), (5). Member states may specify the use of those amounts, *see id.* at art. 13(6).

[850] *See* in this context *id.* at recital 28.

tioned, a distribution scheme was implemented that allocated to artists and manufacturers an equal share of the income.[851] The Commission did not allude to this point in its legal assessment; thus, it can be concluded that this practice was considered to be compatible with article 102 TFEU. It is now for the general assembly (in which the different member categories are represented) to determine the general policy for distribution. However, from a competition law perspective, it seems that such decision must be made in accordance with the principle of non-discrimination and based on objective criteria.

The ASCAP Consent Decree sets forth the general principles regarding the organization's royalty management. The distribution is carried out according to the performances of its members' works, whereas directly licensed works diminish the claim of the respective member.[852] The basis for this task are objective surveys;[853] ultimately, the goal of the distribution policy is to reflect "the value to ASCAP of performances in the various media".[854] Within this regime, ASCAP's internal rules specify the distribution of the income. The general approach to distribution can perhaps best be described by a strict, however formalistic, balance of interests between writers and publishers. The royalties are distributed following a strict principle of equal treatment: One-half is distributed among publishers, the other half among writers.[855] The details of the procedure are determined by the writer and publisher members of the Board for their respective peer groups.[856] ASCAP has published the policies regarding its survey and distribution system.[857] The organization is furthermore bound

---

851 *GVL*, IV/29.839 at ¶ 30.

852 ASCAP Consent Decree § XI(B)(1); Compendium of ASCAP Rules § 3.4.3.

853 Such surveys shall be based on a census or scientific and randomly selected surveys, reflecting the number and identification of performances. The design for this determination must be made and "periodically reviewed by an independent and qualified person", *see* ASCAP Consent Decree § XI(B)(2). *See also* ASCAP Statute art. XVII(1)(e). These methods are very complex and rely on statistical methods, *see* Kohn & Kohn, *Music Licensing*, *supra* at 1280–1282 (stating that most data are drawn from broadcast sources). Often, estimations are relied upon, *see* U.S. Copyright Office, *Music Marketplace*, *supra* at 130–131.

854 ASCAP Consent Decree § XI(B)(1). Special awards are permitted for works of "unique prestige value, or which make a significant contribution to the ASCAP repertory".

855 ASCAP Statute art. XVII(1)(c). *See also* Kohn & Kohn, *Music Licensing*, *supra* at 1261–1262 (noting that the distribution for foreign works may vary from society to society). *See also L. Spier Inc., v. Bourne Comp.*, 953 F.2d 774 at ¶ 4 (2nd Cir. 1992) (mentioning the 50/50 songwriter-publisher split); *Alden-Rochelle*, 80 F. Supp. 888 at 891 (mentioning several different groups of right holders). It has been noted that this rule was originally introduced to encourage publishers to join ASCAP, *see Broadcast Music, Inc. v. Taylor*, 10 Misc. 2d 9, 55 N.Y.S. 2d 94 (N.Y. Sup. Ct. 1945). *See* in this connection on the distribution via international sub-publishing *Universal/BMG Music Publishing*, Commission Decision of 22 May 2007, case COMP/M.4404, ¶ 165–166, *available at* http://ec.europa.eu/competition/mergers/cases/decisions/m4404_20070522_20600_en.pdf (last visited May 22, 2017).

856 ASCAP Statute art. XVII(1)(d).

857 American Society of Composers, Authors and Publishers, *ASCAP's Survey and Distribution System: Rules and Policies* (2015), *available at* https://www.ascap.com/-/media/files/pdf/

on a contractual basis, as the membership agreements stipulate that ASCAP shall use its "best endeavors to promote the objects for which it was organized, and to hold and apply all royalties, profits [...] to the uses and purposes as provided in its Articles of Association."[858] The objects of the organization include the collection and the distribution of royalties paid by users promoting "by all lawful means the interests of composers, authors and publishers of music works".[859] Moreover, ASCAP's membership agreement specifies that all adoptions to the royalty distribution regime are subject to a "fair, just and equitable" distribution standard.[860] Distributable revenues are computed for calendar quarters and are distributed quarterly.[861] Unclaimed royalties remain in the organization's general fund for three years.[862] Three months prior to the expiration of this period, ASCAP must notify the persons entitled to the royalties; after that period royalties remaining unclaimed become ASCAP's property.[863]

The BMI Consent Decree, in turn, implies that royalty payments are to be made to right holders, rather than expressly setting forth such obligation. On the one hand, it stipulates that BMI has no duty to make payments with respect to performances directly licensed by members.[864] On the other hand, it requires BMI to disclose the calculation methods regarding its royalty payments.[865] In this light, it appears that the decree presupposes the organization's important function as royalty distributor to right holders.[866] However, the decree does not provide for an (even generalized) standard of distribution which would be comparable to the ASCAP Consent Decree. However, even though BMI is owned by radio and television stations, i.e. users, the royalties are not paid to the shareholders but to the right holders.[867] BMI's membership agree-

members/payment/drd.pdf (last visited May 23, 2017). The distribution system is based on the "follow-the-dollar" principle, i.e. that attributable license fees paid by users should reflect the rates paid to members, with the addition that the value of the respective performances is taken into account according to a weighting formula and that primary consideration is given to the actual performance of the compositions, *see* ASCAP Distribution Rules § 1.2–1.3.

858 ASCAP Writer Agreement § 3; ASCAP Publisher Agreement § 3. The equal payment principles regarding writers and publishers is furthermore contained in ASCAP Writer Agreement § 7 and ASCAP Publisher Agreement § 7.

859 ASCAP Statute art. I(1)(f), (g).

860 ASCAP Writer Agreement § 8; ASCAP Publisher Agreement § 8.

861 ASCAP Distribution Rules § 3.1.1., 3.2.; Compendium of ASCAP Rules § 1.2.

862 ASCAP Statute art. XVII(3).

863 *Id.* These rules apply, unless applicable U.S. (state) law provides otherwise.

864 BMI Consent Decree § IV(A).

865 *Id.* at § VII(A). *See also id.* at § V(C) which states that BMI is obliged to continue making payments to authors who have resigned from the organization, for so long as the rights are not otherwise licensed.

866 In this connection, the decree also hints at the equal treatment of right holders, *see* BMI Consent Decree § V (C); *see also* BMI Writer Agreement § 6; BMI Publisher Agreement § 5.

867 Kohn & Kohn, *Music Licensing*, *supra* at 1257.

ments provide for a right to claim royalties; this right, however, is subject to the current "standard practices upon the basis of the then current performance rates".[868] The rate is, in principle, based on estimates of the number of performances.[869] The royalties are – in absence of special agreements among right holders – normally equally divided among publishers and writers,[870] and are in most cases distributed quarterly.[871] In case a song is co-written by several right holders pertaining to different CMOs (ASCAP and BMI in most cases), the CMOs collect and distribute only the share of their respective members.[872]

b) Management Fees

The CMD does not contain many rules on the management fees that CMOs may charge right holders under their representation and membership contracts in order to cover the expenses for their services.[873] Article 12(3) specifies that the fees should not "exceed the justified and documented costs incurred by collective management organizations in managing copyright [...]".[874] In interpreting this provision, it should be kept in mind that the management costs are not equal for every single right holder. This issue was observed in connection with the Commission's *Daft Punk* decision. After it agreed to permit individual management of certain categories of rights, SACEM modified its statute so that it could charge different fees if a right holder did not assign all rights to the organization.[875] From the competition law perspective, it should be noted that the Commission held in *GEMA I* that the grant of loyalty bonuses to some members constituted an abuse if all members contributed to these funds. The practice is comparable to SACEM's conduct after Daft Punk: While in both cases, all members maintain their position in general, some members are put in a worse position by the obligation to pay additional fees; conversely, in the *GEMA*-case, some members are put in a better position by being granted additional payments. Thus, the juxtaposed conducts can be viewed as types of discrimination between right holders. It is true that the case law condemned loyalty rebates to be "almost a per se violation" of article 102;[876] however, if one has a look at the decision in *GEMA I*, it seems that the Commission did not altogether deny the possibility that GEMA's conduct could be justified by the argument that administration costs may be lower for the man-

868 BMI Writer Agreement § 6; BMI Publisher Agreement § 5.

869 *Id.*

870 BMI, *BMI Royalty Policy Manual*, http://www.bmi.com/creators/royalty_ print (last visited April 20, 2017).

871 *Id.*

872 U.S. Copyright Office, *Jointly Owned Works*, *supra* at 15–17; Compendium of ASCAP Rules § 3.4.1.

873 *See* for the definition of the term "management fees" CMD art. 3(i).

874 *See also id.* at recital 28.

875 Allendesalazar & Vallina, *The Usual Suspects*, *supra* at 393–394.

876 *Id.*

agement of the rights of some members. It merely said that GEMA's existing statute did not serve this purpose, i.e. that the implemented procedures were not suited to achieve this aim.[877] For this reason, the question is rather whether the different treatment of right holders can be justified than whether it may take place at all. With regard to SACEM's conduct, it seems that a supplementary fee in cases where not all rights are assigned can be objectively justified because the CMO incurs higher administrative costs if a member opts for individual management. In any event, the fee increase must be proportional in relation to the additional costs incurred by the individual management.[878] In light of the Collective Management Directive, the wording of article 12(3) implies that different fees may be charged to right holders as long as a CMO can prove that the difference is paralleled by a corresponding (*shall not exceed*) divergence of management costs (*documented* costs) and that this divergence cannot be avoided by implementing more efficient management procedures (*justified costs*). It can, however, be pretty hard to establish these facts in practice.[879]

The ASCAP Consent Decree specifies that ASCAP shall distribute the royalties "less its costs".[880] The decree does not give an express standard for the calculation of the management fees.[881] The ASCAP Statute specifies that all expenses of operation are deducted from the collected sum prior to distribution.[882] The Board may authorize the imposition of fees under three conditions: i) the fees must reflect and offset the expenses commonly incurred, ii) such expenses must benefit the membership as a whole and, iii) generally, all members are obliged to pay such fees.[883]

Neither the BMI Consent Decree nor the BMI membership agreements expressly regulate – with minor exceptions[884] – the deduction for the organization's management expense. These fees are generally deducted from the income prior to distribution.[885] Further charges apply in particular cases.[886]

---

877 *GEMA I*, IV/26.760 at ¶ II(C)(2)(b).

878 Allendesalazar & Vallina, *The Usual Suspects*, *supra* at 394.

879 *Id.*

880 ASCAP Consent Decree § XI(B).

881 *Cf. id.* at Art VII(B) (referring to "reasonable costs of administering the license"), in the context of users, however.

882 ASCAP Statute art. XVII(1)(a). The Board of Directors can also decide that a maximum of 10% of the distributable amount shall be added to the Reserve Fund, *see id.* at art XVII(b).

883 Compendium of ASCAP Rules § 1.15.

884 *See, e.g.,* BMI writer agreement § 6(a)(iii); BMI Publisher Agreement §5(2).

885 "All fees, less BMI's operating expenses, are paid to our affiliated songwriters, composers, and music publishers in the form of royalties", *see* BMI, *Licensing FAQ*, http://www.bmi.com/licensing (under "What happens to the fees that businesses pay and how much profit does BMI make?") (last visited April 20, 2017). *See also Moor-Law*, 527 F. Supp. 758 at 762.

886 *See, e.g.,* BMI, *Royalty Policy Manual*, *supra* (*e.g.*, "Legal Process Administration Charges").

3.1.7. Comments on the Relationship between CMOs and Right Holders

a) General Remarks

In the EU, article 102 of the TFEU has been applied to regulate the relationship between CMOs and right holders. Under this article, European authorities have developed a flexible system. Only where a CMO discriminates against nationals of other member states, it is not necessary to evaluate whether the practice in question fulfills a balance-of-interest test; such conduct can be considered as failing this test virtually per-se, therefore amounting to a violation of EU competition. In less serious cases, the ECJ has developed the indispensability and equity test, under which a measure by a CMO that restricts the freedom of right holders to exploit their works can be justified if it is objectively necessary. The four most important parameters considered in this connection with the rights grant to CMOs are i) the scope of the rights grant, ii) the duration, iii) the geographical scope and iv) whether rights are covered in future works. If one factor is deemed to be excessive, it can be counterbalanced by making another less restrictive. This was the approach taken by the Commission in *GEMA II* by offering GEMA two options to draft their member contracts.[887] Similarly, the Commission did not categorically prohibit the exclusion of individual management in *Daft Punk* but also tried to strike a balance. However, such a multi-factor analysis has not only been conducted in connection with the rights grant as such: An excellent example of the aim to balance the involved interests is the Commission's decision in *GEMA III*. In this case, GEMA asked the Commission to approve an amendment to its statutes which prohibited its members from joining together with licensees to avoid that users unduly privilege the works of those members when using GEMA's repertoire.[888] GEMA's concern was that in absence of such a ban, members could manipulate their royalty share which is based on the relative use of their works; or users could rely on their market power to force right holders to pay some of their revenues to them.[889] The Commission referred to the principles established by the ECJ in *BRT v. SABAM*, carefully weighed the right holders' freedom of exploitation against the necessary requirements for collective management in the light of this background and eventually approved the amendment.[890] The CMD also incorporates a flexible system in relation to right holders.[891]

While the relation between right holders and CMOs marked the starting point (and, until today, essentially the main focus) of the European regulation of CMOs, the binding rules of the U.S. law are comparatively sparse in rela-

887 Vinje & Niiranen, *Digital Environment*, *supra* at 405–406.

888 *GEMA III*, IV/29–971 at ¶ 20.

889 *Id.* at ¶ 21–28.

890 *Id.* at ¶ 36 (also mentioning the indispensability and equity test); *see also id.* at ¶ 37–53.

891 *See, e.g.*, CMD art. 3 ("objectively necessary"), art. 6(3) ("fair and balanced").

tion to right holders. An analysis of the ASCAP and BMI Consent Decrees, supplemented by the membership contracts and the ASCAP Statute has, however, shown that there exist rules and safeguards which refer to problems comparable to the issues addressed by EU competition law as well as by the Collective Management Directive. Yet, no generally applicable rules exist in the United States to date, and the rules of the directive set up a framework far more comprehensive than the safeguards for right holders under U.S. law. Still, it must be pointed out that, while the CMD sets up comprehensive rules, these are often rather unclear and leave member states and courts considerable leeway in application and transposition; it seems that, in the short run at least, the rather diverging approach to the national regulation of CMOs will subsist. Despite all this, the CMD is a good start toward a level playing field for CMOs in the EU in respect of the right holders; nevertheless, the U.S. experience shows that the forces of competition between the CMOs on the market for management services should not be underestimated. The existence of actual competition between U.S. CMOs is reflected by the fact that many of them offer advances to attract new members.[892] CMOs can furthermore compete on criteria like membership terms, royalty calculation and distribution, claim adjustment procedures, or educational opportunities.[893] However, lower fees alone do not necessarily translate into better collective management services, the question here being whether the lower fees are made possible by increasing the efficiency of the organization, by lowering the distributed amounts (or allocating them to other right holders), or rather by a less accurate monitoring and enforcement policy overall. Furthermore, there remains the question of how the rules set forth by the mentioned documents are applied in practice. In Europe, one would additionally ask to what extent competition in this respect would serve niche repertoires and economically less potent right holders to ensure cultural diversity.[894] Yet, even if one concludes that there is a higher level of protection of right holders in the EU, it does not necessarily mean that such a level of protection is desirable, at least in all respects.

b) Obligation to Represent

Both U.S. and EU law have acknowledged that an obligation to represent, i.e. to offer management services to every right holder who needs them, is an essential regulatory tool in relation to organizations which aggregate large copyrighted repertoires.[895] While the Collective Management Directive puts a

[892] Kohn & Kohn, *Music Licensing*, *supra* at 1260. *See* also *Meredith*, 1 F. Supp. 3d 180 at 191 (noting that SESAC recruited from ASCAP and BMI "high profile" composers and publishers).

[893] U.S. Copyright Office, *Jointly Owned Works*, *supra* at 26, n. 135 (also noting that while BMI and ASCAP distribute royalties quarterly, SESAC does so monthly).

[894] *See* section III.2.2. below.

[895] *See* for reasons why CMOs may want to reject members Drexl, *Competition and Development*, *supra* at 234–235.

general obligation on all CMOs, there is no comparable legislation in the United States: ASCAP and BMI are obliged to represent right holders due to their respective consent decrees. Hence, SESAC is not required to offer its service to every right holder. However, it is not impossible that SESAC would be assessed in a similar manner under the CMD since the definition of "CMO" covers only organizations which are owned or controlled by their members or are organized on a not-for-profit basis. Since SESAC is a for-profit organization, it is doubtful whether article 5(2) of the CRM-Directive would apply in the first place.[896] Moreover, even though the definition of the term "right holder" under the CMD is comparatively broad, there should not arise substantial problems in practice, as ASCAP and BMI are usually described as fairly open to new right holders.[897] In this connection, it is noteworthy that the ASCAP Consent Decree establishes an obligation to admit right holders to membership, whereas article 5 of the CMD applies to right holders in general.[898]

c) Exclusivity of the Rights Grant

As will be seen in the next chapter, under U.S. law, it is a basic requirement for the collective management of copyrights as traditionally practiced that the rights grant from right holders to the CMO is of a non-exclusive nature. In contrast, EU competition practice has not focused on this issue to a comparable extent; the *GEMA* cases focused on a combination of different licensing conditions deemed unfair. In fact, it has been noted that neither the Commission nor the ECJ has expressly commented on this issue; and that exclusivity is paradigmatic for the collective management of copyrights in the EU.[899] However, some statements of the Commission might give an indication. In *GEMA III*, the Commission stated the right holders'

> forgoing of an individual contractual relationship with the users should in fact restore the balance between beneficiaries and users, thereby fulfilling the objective need to preclude, as far as possible, agreements between beneficiaries on an individual basis, which could affect GEMA's charges.[900]

This indicates that the Commission is – in principle – willing to accept exclusive management contracts in order to ensure the right holders' collective

[896] The answer to this question depends on the internal organization of SESAC.

[897] Kohn & Kohn, *Music Licensing*, *supra* at 1258.

[898] ASCAP Consent Decree § XI(A) ("membership, non-participating or otherwise").

[899] Drexl, *Competition and Development*, *supra* at 174, 244–245. *See also* Metzger & Heinemann, *Non-Commercial Use*, *supra* at 15 (stating that the Dutch CMO Buma/Stemra was, in 2007, the "first European collecting society experimenting whether collective rights management and individual licensing can be combined [...]"). *See*, however, Quintais, *On Peers and Copyright*, *supra* at 42 (stating that voluntary collective licensing – where right holders are free to directly conclude licensing contracts with users despite having joined a CMO – is a typical rights management model in the EU).

[900] *GEMA III*, IV/29-971 at ¶ 41 (non-authentic English version of the text). GEMA required exclusive rights grants from right holders, *id.* at ¶ 2, 46.

bargaining position. In any event, had the Commission considered such conduct as a violation of the EU competition rules, it would have had numerous opportunities to express this view.[901] *Drijber* derives from the ECJ's ruling in *BRT v. SABAM* that an exclusive assignment of rights will be permitted, as long as it is proportionate to the task carried out by the CMO.[902] The CMD, at any rate, does not contain an express prohibition of exclusive rights grants.[903] However, in the present context, article 5(3) – which affords right holders the right to issue non-commercial licenses – deserves special mention. On the one hand, this provision must be read as permitting right holders to grant such license for the use of content covered by the management contract with the CMO because otherwise, given the broad right to withdrawals, the provision would be unnecessary.[904] On the other hand, it indicates *e contrario* that the directive allows CMOs to acquire exclusive licenses for commercial uses; the possibility to directly issue non-commercial licenses is the exception rather than the rule. This is because this provision would be plainly unnecessary if CMOs were prohibited from requiring exclusive rights grants from right holders in the first place.

It can, of course, be debated whether the exclusivity of the rights grants is indispensable in order to adequately maintain the CMOs' bargaining power.[905] It seems that collective management in the United States is still working, even though the Consent Decrees prescribe the strict non-exclusivity of mandates. A related but different problem in this context is the so-called "cherry-picking" which is addressed in the next subsection.

d) The (Partial) Withdrawal Issue

The "partial" withdrawal issue is debated both in the EU and the U.S. and refers to the question whether a CMO represents, or must represent, a right holder on an "all-or-nothing" basis. This should not be confused with the exclusivity of the rights grant: The question here is whether a right holder has the power to decide to deny a CMO the ability to license certain (categories

---

901 The Commission referred to this as "parallel direct licensing", *see* Impact Assessment 2012 at 44–45 and noted during the drafting of the CMD that U.S. CMOs may not demand exclusive mandates, *see id.* at 143–144. Whether EU law prohibits an exclusive rights grant is closely related to the question whether the joining together of right holders violates art. 101 TFEU, *see* Drijber, *Competition law aspects*, *supra* at 69 and section 2.3.3. above.

902 Drijber, *Competition law aspects*, *supra* at 69 (referring to article 101). *See also* Kevin Coates et al., *Intellectual Property* in *The EU Law of Competition* 1443, 1498 (Jonathan Faull & Ali Nikpay eds., 3rd ed. 2014); Lichtenegger, *Verwertungsgesellschaften*, *supra* at 105.

903 In respect of MTL representation agreements, however, the directive expressly provides for non-exclusivity, *see* CMD recital 44, art. 29(1). *See also* CMD art. 31.

904 Metzger & Heinemann, *Non-Commercial Use*, *supra* at 19. *See also* Holzmüller, *Umsetzung*, *supra* at 469 (criticizing that the provision departs from the exclusivity principle); van Gompel, *Directive*, *supra* at 573.

905 Drexl, *Competition and Development*, *supra* at 245.

of) rights, while other rights *in the same works* are managed by the CMO. This question might be conceived as the flipside of the question whether CMOs constitute unlawful combinations which asks when right holders *must* withdraw from CMOs in order avoid antitrust scrutiny. The directive is extremely liberal toward right holders and allows them to withdraw any (categories of)[906] rights or types of works.[907] In stark contrast, the rate courts have denied U.S. right holders the option to partially withdraw categories of rights for the purpose of direct management.

While in the U.S. the withdrawals concerned "New Media Transmissions",[908] in the EU, "option 3" publishers are referred to as publishers who have withdrawn their online mechanical rights from the CMOs' repertoires in the wake of the Recommendation 2005; often they license their rights in cooperation with one or more CMOs of their choice which act as services providers.[909] Different models exist in this respect. While under the PEDL initiative, Warner Chappel grants non-exclusive licenses to competing CMOs, separate organizations have been founded for this purpose. These organizations are called "hybrid entities".[910] The withdrawal mainly concerns the Anglo-American repertoire,[911] a development the reason for which – besides legal reasons set out immediately below – is straightforward: Works belonging to this repertoire are among the most profitable and popular throughout the entire EU and the involved publishers are among the most important actors on the market.[912]

It seems to be established that the main reason for the different treatment of mechanical and performance rights is attributable to the different traditions of collective management practiced in the United States and the EU: While in the former jurisdiction, CMOs typically managed only performing rights, their European counterparts were also entrusted with the management of mechanical rights; for this reason, the mechanical rights in *Anglo-American* works were

906 Yet, it remains to be seen how such categories will be defined.

907 Furthermore, it remains to be seen how the withdrawal will take place in practice under the respective CMOs' policies; the *Daft Punk* case indicates that certain restrictions can be justified.

908 *See, e.g., PRSfM/STIM/GEMA/JV*, COMP/M.6800 at ¶ 27 n. 24; *Sony/Mubadala Development/EMI Music Publishing*, COMP/M.6459 at ¶ 80 n. 31.

909 *PRSfM/STIM/GEMA/JV*, COMP/M.6800 at ¶ 27–28. Option 3 publishers include the "majors" (Sony/ATV, Universal, Warner/Chappel, BMG). However, also small and medium-sized businesses can act as option 3 publishers, *see id.* at ¶ 201. *See also* PRS for Music, *Definition of Terms*, https://www.prsformusic.com/creators/memberresources/licensing_the_future/licensingthefutureforwriters/definitionsofterms/Pages/definitionsofterms.aspx (last visited April 21, 2017) (offering a definition of "option 3").

910 *See also* section 1.1.4.c) above.

911 Note that withdrawals do not only concern Anglo-American works as is illustrated by SGAE's management of Sony's Latin-American repertoire.

912 *See, e.g.,* Hellenic Foundation for European and Foreign Policy, *Cultural Diversity*, *supra* at 98–106 (focusing on UK repertoire); Mazziotti, *New Licensing Models*, *supra* at 777.

readily available for publishers.[913] However, since both performance and mechanical rights must be cleared, some hybrids license the performance rights indirectly. Entities like CELAS need the national CMOs' authorization to represent these rights for this task. In respect of U.S. repertoire, licensing hubs, hybrids, and European CMOs license the performing rights of ASCAP, BMI, etc., on a multi-territorial basis to the extent that they "match" the option 3 publishers' mechanical rights.[914] The status quo is, however, not entirely clear. With respect to the Anglo repertoire, PRSfM occupies a leading role, since it controls the performing rights matching the publishers' mechanical rights.[915]

Option 3 publishers would have an option other than those mentioned above: They could simply license their rights directly to commercial users, without the intervention of CMOs or hybrid entities. The problem here is that such right holders would have to build up their own licensing infrastructure. It is estimated that this task would take major publishers about one or two years, with projected costs ranging from one to three million Euros.[916]

The developments mentioned above imply fundamental changes to the system of reciprocal representation which governed the relation between CMOs for the longest time. On the one hand – independent from the Collective Management Directive's impact – representation agreements without reciprocal element have been concluded in the online environment. On the other hand, the repertoire that CMOs are able to license under RRAs is dramatically decreasing and can be referred to as the "residual world repertoire".[917]

Whether partial withdrawals of rights are a desirable development is critically debated in the literature. The state of the licensing market in the EU has been described – due to such withdrawals – as rather chaotic, not user-friendly, and potentially inefficient.[918] The CMD, however, assumes that it is a viable tool to induce competition between CMOs to the benefit of right holders.[919]

---

913 *Sony/Mubadala Development/EMI Music Publishing*, COMP/M.6459 at ¶ 77–79; Impact Assessment 2012 at 12–14; Heyde, *Lizenzierung*, *supra* at 210–212; KEA, *Music Licensing*, *supra* at 29; Lichtenegger, *Verwertungsgesellschaften*, *supra* at 47–48; Mazziotti, *New Licensing Models*, *supra* at 778–779 (noting that the appointment of sub-publishers assisted the withdrawal of mechanical rights).

914 *PRSfM/STIM/GEMA/JV*, COMP/M.6800 at ¶ 246 n. 162. As for hybrids, one can say that European CMOs "contribute" the U.S. American repertoire to the publishers' mechanical rights represented by way of representation agreements, *see id.* at ¶ 27 n. 24, 247 n. 163.

915 *Id.* at ¶ 207.

916 *Id.* at ¶ 141.

917 *See* for the impact on representation agreement section 3.3.8. below.

918 Hilty & Nérisson, *Collective copyright Management*, *supra* at 229; Drexl, *Competition and Development*, *supra* at 221–222, 268–269 (also stating that the Commission did not aim at creating the most efficient system for users but for right holders).

919 CMD recital 19. *See also* Bruce H. Kobayashi, *Opening Pandoras Black Box: A Coasian 1937 View of Performance Rights Organizations in 2014*, 22 Geo. Mason L. Rev. 925, 941 (2014) (stating that, from the perspective of U.S. publishers, the withdrawals are in line with

The question is of course who these right holders are. Perhaps the biggest concern is that partial withdrawals practically only benefit large and/or economically potent right holders – first and foremost publishers.[920] Withdrawals of a crucial part of the repertoire can lead to prohibitive management costs which could put songwriters and other small right holders at disadvantage.[921] The Commission's *Daft Punk* decision can be seen in this context, as it involved the question whether right holders have the right to "cherry-pick" the most valuable rights for direct licensing. This right potentially conflicts with the solidarity principle inherent in traditional CMOs. It is conspicuous that, at first glance, the rate courts reinforced this principle when forbidding partial withdrawals. It is hard to reconcile to the attempts of large publishers with the solidarity function. Indeed, it seems that the option of broad withdrawals employed by the CMD has little to do with the traditional idea of collective management. It is also questionable whether only the withdrawing right holders' situation or rather, efficiency overall and its effects on smaller right holders and users ("repertoire fragmentation") should be assessed. It is furthermore a crucial question what "partial" means in the context of withdrawals: While withdrawals for some categories of rights could be detrimental, others might lead to adequate results.[922]

Additionally, one could ask, should withdrawals decrease the market share of CMOs significantly, whether strict control of CMOs would still be warranted since large right holders are not subject to comparable supervision.[923]

---

economic theory). *Einhorn* states that partial withdrawals should be allowed in principle but that i) there should be restrictions on the possibility of publishers to re-entering the CMOs' repertoire in order to negotiate favorable terms ii) smaller publishers should be allowed to license their works through agents other than ASCAP or BMI, *see* Michael A. Einhorn, *The ASCAP And BMI Consent Decrees: Is Partial Withdrawal Wise?*, 62 J. Copyright Soc'y 199, 206 (2014). *See also* Pitt, *Direct Licensing*, *supra* at 265 (stating that partial withdrawals would exacerbate existing problems in music licensing).

920 U.S. Copyright Office, *Music Marketplace*, *supra* at 152–153; Pitt, *Direct Licensing*, *supra* at 266–267. The European Parliament actually intended to include a provision that would have permitted CMOs to establish rules in order to prevent right holders from "misusing" the withdrawal rights; however, a corresponding provision was not included in the directive, *see* Gallo, *Report*, *supra* at 13–14, 36–37. *See* in the context of the right to grant non-commercial licenses Metzger & Heinemann, *Non-Commercial Use*, *supra* at 14.

921 U.S. Copyright Office, *Music Marketplace*, *supra* at 153; Guibault, *Collective Management Directive*, *supra* at 723; Guibault & van Gompel, *Collective Management*, *supra* at 151.

922 *Einhorn* advocates a withdrawal category of "New Media" services, encompassing digital performance rights and performances rights in sound recordings, reproduction rights, synchronization rights, or cloud services, *see* Einhorn, *Partial Withdrawal*, *supra* at 209. *See also* U.S. Copyright Office, *Music Marketplace*, *supra* at 159–160 (advocating equal treatment of copyright owners in musical works and sound recordings and a "limited" right to withdraw digital rights).

923 U.S. Copyright Office, *Music Marketplace*, *supra* at 153. *See also* section e) and section III. 1.3.

e) Of Right Holders, Publishers, and Composers

Equal treatment of right holders is nowadays a general principle of the collective management of copyrights. In fact, the CMD's broad definition of right holders[924] was introduced in order to cover all different categories that belong to this group.[925] However, in many cases, it is more appropriate to speak of the equal treatment of *categories of* right holders. This is reasonable, as the interests of writers and publishers, for instance, can diverge significantly.[926] The Consent Decrees acknowledge this difference as far as as they do not provide a uniform definition, but they distinguish writers and publishers; moreover, a similar distinction is inherent to the ASCAP Statute. One could, of course, ask whether such a distinction is sufficient: As the concentration of rights in the hands of large publishers continues, it might be adequate to distinguish between large publishers and small publishers along with the author – publisher dichotomy.[927] Furthermore, right holders are not only distinguished by their types of business but also according to their rights. Thus, the focus should be put on the holders of copyrights (composers) and related rights/sound recordings.[928] There are even cases where the boundaries between users and right holders cannot be clearly drawn.[929] In any event, the directive appears to give member states enough leeway to make objective distinctions. In this connection, it should be noted that safeguards for authors or performances vis-à-vis larger right holders also apply in the realm of statutory licensing. In inter-

924 CMD art. 3(c).

925 Guibault & van Gompel, *Collective Management*, *supra* at 144; van Gompel, *Directive*, *supra* at 569. The language used in the Consent Decrees employ not as comprehensive – but still broad – definitions, *see* ASCAP Consent Decree § XI(A), BMI Consent Decree § V.

926 *See, e.g.*, *GEMA III*, IV/29-971 at ¶ 4, 38. *See also* Pitt, *Direct Licensing*, *supra* at 61–64 (referring to different stakeholders in the music licensing process) and 84–88 (stating that the interests of CMOs and right holders are not always compatible).

927 It is noteworthy that a similar debate on the protection of SMEs exists in connection with the laws on consumer protection, *see, e.g.*, Jules Stuyck, *Do We Need 'Consumer Protection' for Small Businesses at EU Level?* in *Varieties of European Economic Law and Regulation* 359 (Kai Purnhagen & Peter Rott eds., 2014).

928 *See, e.g.*, Lydia Pallas Loren, *The Dual Narratives In The Landscape Of Music Copyright*, 52 Hous. L. Rev. 537, 566 (2014); Lunney, *The United States Experience*, *supra* at 343–344 (stating that musical work copyright owners opposed the introduction of sound recording right). This might require an overall perspective as these right holders are often not organized in one single CMO. *See* for the so-called "rate disparity" section 3.2.6.d) below. Yet another group would be right holders represented by the CMO under a representation agreement, *see* CMD art. 14.

929 Already in *Alden-Rochelle* the court noted that motion picture producers had acquired publishers who in turn were members of ASCAP, *see Alden-Rochelle*, 80 F. Supp. 888 at 892–893. *See also Showtime/Movie Channel*, 912 F. 2d 563 at 567 n. 7; *GEMA I*, IV/26 760 at ¶ II(C)(2)(b) (prohibiting the rejection of full membership due to economic relation with users but allowing less restrictive means); Mestmäcker & Schweitzer, *Wettbewerbsrecht*, *supra* at 885. It is notable that BMI was founded by users (radio broadcasters) and not right holders, *see* Korman, *U.S. Position*, *supra* at 167–168.

preting the "fair compensation" requirement of the Copyright Directive's article 5, which relates to the statutory license for acts of reproduction, the ECJ ruled that the amounts flowing from such licenses must be paid to authors, and not to publishers.[930] In the U.S., for instance, artists featured on sound recordings are entitled to a fixed amount of royalties under section 114.[931] This provision is a "forced division of statutory license fees among those who make creative contributions to a sound recording".[932]

3.2. CMOs and Users

3.2.1. General Remarks

Just like in connection with right holders, competition law has served to assess the relationship which CMOs entertain with licensees. This relationship centers around the conditions under which users obtain authorization to utilize the protected content and which are stipulated in licensing terms that govern the agreements concluded between these parties. Within this relation, several aspects can lead to disputes. The relevant case law deals with questions arising from the access to the repertoire, the general methods of calculation, and the actual level fees that a user is required to pay. Before turning to questions of detail, general principles of European and U.S. case law will be presented in connection with the rules of the Collective Management Directive.

a) Principles of European Case Law

Both articles 101 and 102 have been applied to the relationship between CMOs and users. However, as there is no exhaustive list of possible abusive conducts that fall under article 102, the case law only covers a small part of practices which are potentially in breach of EU competition law.[933] The ECJ has refrained from expressly spelling out a general test under this article in relation to users. In contrast, the ECJ set forth the general principles of applying of article 101 to the relationships between CMOs and users in its *Tournier* ruling:

---

930 *Hewlett-Packard Belgium SPRL v. Reprobel SCRL*, C-572/13, ¶ 46–49 (ECJ 2015); *see also Soulier*, C-301/15 at ¶ 48. It is not fully clarified whether this also relates the CMOs' internal distribution policies, *see* Handig, *VerwertungsgesellschaftenG*, *supra* at 167; Karl Riesenhuber, *Wachsende Bedeutung zentralisierter Rechtewahrnehmung und die Rolle der Verwertungsgesellschaften*, 60 ZUM 216, 221 (2016). The BGH has applied this principle to a German CMO, *Verlegeranteil*, German Supreme Court, 21 April 2016, Case I ZR 198/13, 19 MMR 471, 473–474 (2016).

931 17 U.S.C. § 114(g)(2). *See* for more details on U.S. statutory licenses section 3.2.5. below.

932 II Goldstein on Copyright, *supra* at § 7.8.6.2. *See also* 17 U.S.C. § 1006(b) on the statutory distribution scheme.

933 Vinje & Niiranen, *Digital Environment*, *supra* at 407.

> Copyright-management societies pursue a legitimate aim when they endeavour to safeguard the rights and interests of their members vis-à-vis the users of recorded music. The contracts concluded with users for that purpose cannot be regarded as restrictive of competition for the purposes of Article 85 unless the contested practice exceeds the limits of what is necessary for the attainment of that aim.[934]

In regard to the competition case law which governs the relationship between CMOs and right holders, it seems clear that the test set forth by the ECJ in relation to users derives from its decision in *BRT v. SABAM*. In his opinion, the AG had favored an adaptation of the test with respect to users,[935] so that one can speak of an "adapted *BRT v. SABAM* test". Thus, also the relationships that CMOs entertain with users are subject to a balancing of the involved interests, this time between the interest of users in obtaining a license for running their business at reasonable conditions and the "legitimate aim" of protecting the interests of right holders against a powerful group of prospective licensees. Furthermore, the court did not employ a uniform concept of "users", as it assessed the "general nature of the contracts entered into by the societies with a certain *category of users* [...]".[936] The assessment can hence vary from case to case; for instance, it could make a difference whether a CMO concludes agreements with TV channels, radio stations, or discotheques. Four interrelated issues must be looked at more closely in this context: i) the compatibility of the general test of the relationship between users and CMOs as set out in *Tournier* with the test developed in *BRT v. SABAM*; ii) the relationship between the opinion of the AG in *Tournier* and the opinion of the court; iii) the compatibility of the general test with other (parts of) rulings of the ECJ; and iv) the application of the general test to the practice of blanket licensing.

As stated above, the ruling is very similar to the wording of the *BRT* case. However, there are important differences which must be taken into consideration when comparing the decisions. First of all, this relates to the core elements of *BRT v. SABAM* – the indispensability test and the equity test. In *Tournier*, the court simply referred to the question whether a measure was "necessary" for the protection of right holders; in *BRT*, it stated that a measure must be "absolutely necessary" for attaining of the aim of effective and efficient copyright management. Does this mean that the court spelled out a proper proportionality test rather than a strict indispensability test? If one assumes that the court followed the AG's reasoning, it seems more plausible not to attribute undue importance to the omission of the word "absolutely" because AG *Jacobs* was of the opinion that it may be enough to simply adopt the *BRT* ruling

---

934 *Tournier*, 395/87 at ¶ 31. It should also be emphasized that there is a general part of this section of the ECJ's ruling (the first and second sentences of ¶ 31) which immediately precedes a special part that only refers to the practice of blanket licensing (third sentence of ¶ 31). Thus, the ruling on blanket licensing is an application of the general test set forth before.

935 *Tournier*, 395/87, Opinion of AG Jacobs at ¶ 46.

936 *Tournier*, 395/87 at ¶ 30 (emphasis added).

for the purpose of this question.[937] In contrast, however, it can be advanced that right holders require a high level of protection; in this light, the ECJ developed the strict indispensability test. One should also keep in mind the conceptual differences between the two cases. Even though both tests involve a balancing of interests, they serve different purposes: In *BRT*, the court ordered to achieve a balance between the freedom of the individual right holders and the interests of the collective, i.e. effective collective management; however, this is a concept that also individual authors benefit from. In contrast, the underlying concept of the *Tournier* case was market power in dysfunctional markets: The balance had to be achieved between the interests of right holders in general and the users' wish to obtain licenses according on acceptable terms. The protection of right holders would hence merit a strict examination of the demands of powerful users of protected works. Moreover, the decision does not (expressly, at least) reference the equity test. This also points in the direction that the level of protection in respect of the users is not as high as the level in respect of right holders.

The most obvious divergence between the rulings, however, is that the court had applied article 102 in *BRT v. SABAM* but refers to article 101 in *Tournier*. Two observations deserve special mention from this perspective. First, the AG examined the global license in light of article 102, since he considered the practice of blanket licenses to be predominantly attributable to SACEM, a CMO which constituted one single undertaking.[938] In contrast, the ECJ expressly stated that the question at issue was the compatibility of the contracts concluded between CMOs and users with article 101.[939] Second, in spite of the foregoing difference, the court obviously incorporated the AG's substantive reasoning in its decision. Although the ECJ distinguished the *Tournier* case from *BRT*, it applied a test based on the AG's approach right in the next paragraph of its judgment. Whereas the AG advocated that, based on the *BRT* case, the global license must not "exceed what is necessary for effective copyright management",[940] the ECJ ruled that such a license must not exceed what is necessary to "safeguard the rights and interests of their members *vis-à-vis* the users"[941] – two ideas that can be considered to be largely consistent (especially the ECJ's application of this test to blanket licenses can be read as referring "effective management"), insofar as the need to protect right holders is expressly acknowledged. In this connection, it should be noted that the application of article 101 to the relationship between CMOs and users is rather exceptional, as the article is normally used in respect of reciprocal representation

937 *Tournier,* 395/87, Opinion of AG Jacobs at ¶ 50.

938 *Id.* at ¶ 20. Initially, the AG interpreted the question of the referring court as encompassing article 101, too, *see id.* at ¶ 18.

939 *Tournier*, 395/87 at ¶ 30.

940 *Tournier,* 395/87, Opinion of AG Jacobs at ¶ 50.

941 *Tournier*, C-395/87 at ¶ 31.

agreements concluded between national CMOs. Yet, this does not mean that article 101 is not applicable to the relationship between CMOs and users. Both CMOs and (commercial) users are "undertakings" within the meaning of the provision and the licensing contracts, even though they might be unfavorable for users, can be qualified as "agreements". These contracts possess characteristics of vertical agreements since CMOs and users (like discotheque owners for instance) are not competitors but rather operate at different market levels.[942] The case law shows that agreements of this type fall within the scope of article 101.[943] However, the reason why the ECJ applies article 101 might simply be that, as stated above, it read the question of the referring court as focusing on article 101 and therefore did not give its opinion on the interpretation of article 102. In any event, the Commission does not rule out a parallel application of article 101 and 102 to vertical agreements.[944] Moreover, it seems that the adapted *BRT v. SABAM* test under article 101 is highly similar if not identical to the test that must be applied when assessing the same practice under article 102.[945] When reading the judgment in conjunction with the opinion of the AG, one has the impression that it would not have mattered whether the national court had asked the ECJ for the interpretation of article 101 or article 102. After all, it is easy for CMOs to fulfill the criteria of both articles when contracting commercial users, so that the differences in the scope of the articles do not seem to pose specific problems.[946]

b) The Collective Management Directive

The Collective Management Directive contains only two articles on the relationship between CMOs and users, and these rules are of a very general nature but at least indicate the directive's line of approach. Users and CMOs should act in good faith when negotiating licensing agreements and provide one another with sufficient information for this purpose.[947] Whilst this is a no-

942 *See, e.g.,* Bechtold et al., *EU Kartellrecht, supra* at 27; Thorsten Mäger, *Einführung und Grundlagen* in *Europäisches Kartellrecht* 39, 65 (Thorsten Mäger ed., 2nd ed. 2011). While CMOs usually offer licenses for commercial uses, users offer their services to consumers. *See also Bayer AG v. Commission,* T-41/96, ¶ 70–72 (EGC 2000), *appeal dismissed,* joined cases C-2/02 P and C-3/01 P (ECJ 2004) (referring to measures "apparently adopted unilaterally" in connection with cooperation between manufacturers and their dealers). *See also* Senn, *Competition Law Aspects, supra* at 137–138 (arguing that content providers might use DRM systems to escape the application of the competition rules).

943 *See, e.g., Société Technique Minière v. Maschinenbau Ulm GmbH,* case 56/65, Rep. of Cases English 1966, 235 at 248–249 (ECJ 1966) (stating that TFEU art. 101 does not distinguish between horizontal and vertical agreements).

944 European Commission, *Commission Notice Guidelines on Vertical Restraints* ¶ 1, 2010 O.J. (C130) 1–46.

945 Wünschmann, *Kollektive Verwertung, supra* at 150 (stating that the ECJ assesses under both article 101 and 102 whether restrictions are necessary for the functioning of CMOs).

946 *See already* section 2.3.3. above.

947 CMD art. 16(1).

ble principle, it does not mean that the results of the negotiations will satisfy all parties, especially if a CMO occupies a strong bargaining position.[948] Moreover, it is not clear how the directive deals with the information asymmetry and what obligations are linked thereto. Do CMOs and users have to disclose trade secrets, and to what extent should privacy standards be taken into account?[949] In the Proposal 2012, the obligation to disclose applicable tariffs and standard licensing contracts concerned the requests of users (and right holders/other CMOs);[950] it was argued that CMOs were required to supply this kind of information only in respect of the category that the requesting users belonged to because otherwise, the bargaining power of these organizations would have been diminished.[951] The final version of the directive transfers this obligation to article 21, which deals with the disclosure of information to the general public, without any clarification as to its scope. Does this mean that all tariffs must be available to the public at all times? The newly introduced notion of "standard" applicable tariffs suggests that CMOs do not have to publish every individually negotiated tariff; rather, the notion refers to collectively negotiated agreements as well as a "model" contracts.[952] Moreover, the CMD stipulates that CMOs must inform the users concerned of the criteria used for the setting of tariffs.[953] It will be up to the member states in the course of transposition to further clarify these points.

In this connection, the CMD sets forth the important addition that licensing terms should be based on "objective and non-discriminatory" criteria.[954] Discrimination between users is conceivable between users of the same category[955] or between different categories of users.[956] The requirement of "non-discriminatory criteria" can be interpreted as obliging CMOs to offer equivalent licensing terms to users in equivalent positions. This reading is reinforced by the second sentence of article 16(2), which states that CMOs are, as a precedent for future licensing negotiations, not required to use licensing terms which were agreed upon with a user who provides a new type of online services that

948 Guibault, *Collective Management Directive*, *supra* at 750.

949 *See* CMD art. 42.

950 Proposal 2012 at art. 18.

951 Drexl et al., *Comments of the MPI*, *supra* at 25.

952 2 Walter, *Verwertungsgesellschaftenrecht*, *supra* at 271.

953 CMD art.16(2). *Cf. also* ASCAP Consent Decree § IX(C) which contains a similar provision.

954 CMD art. 16(2).

955 *See, e.g.*, for the category "TV stations" *Kanal 5*, C-52/07 at ¶ 48 (2008). In this case, the ECJ gave its opinion on the different treatment of public and private TV stations, although one might argue that public and private TV stations do not belong to the same user category in the first place.

956 *See, e.g.*, for the categories "discotheques" and "TV stations" *Tournier*, 395/87 at ¶ 44; *Lucazeau v. SACEM*, joined cases 110/88, 241/88 and 242/88, ¶ 31 (ECJ 1989). In these cases, discotheque owners asserted that they were treated unfairly compared to other users. The *Tournier* and *Lucazeau* cases contain facts that compare very well should be read in conjunction. The opinion of the AG refers to both cases and the ECJ's rulings are in large parts identical.

has been available to the public in the Union for less than three years.[957] This provision must be understood as an exception from the general principle and was introduced in order to foster innovative online services by permitting flexibility in the licensing process.[958] With this in mind, it follows by *argumentum e contrario* that in situations where this exception is not applicable, licensing terms used in the past may serve as benchmarks for future negotiations. This does not mean that CMOs must offer the same terms to all users who seek access to their repertoire; however, the terms should be based on objective considerations that justify differences in the treatment. It seems to be a general principle that users should not be placed at a competitive disadvantage when offering equivalent services.[959]

Scholars advocated introducing an obligation to contract users just like right holders because CMOs were considered to hold a natural monopoly on both of these services markets.[960] The Collective Management Directive stipulates that CMOs

> shall reply without undue delay to requests from users, indicating, inter alia, the information needed in order for the collective management organisation to offer a licence. Upon receipt of all relevant information, the collective management organisation shall, without undue delay, either offer a licence or provide the user with a reasoned statement explaining why it does not intend to license a particular service.[961]

It is unclear from this language whether the directive introduces such an obligation. Moreover, the relevant recitals fail to give conclusive guidance on this question. Two considerations assist the interpretation of the provision. On the one hand, a comparison of the text of the final directive with the Proposal 2012; and on the other hand, the language used in respect of the other obligations to contract contained in the directive. As for the Proposal 2012, there is no reference whatsoever to the acceptance or refusal of licensing requests. In comparison, the Collective Management Directive provides for a clearer and more stringent standard which could be understood as an obligation to contract. In regard to the obligation to contract with right holders, it must be observed, however, that the CMD leaves no doubt that CMOs are required to contract unless objective reasons justify a refusal. It states that CMOs "shall be obliged to manage such rights";[962] in respect of the obligation to represent other CMOs under the new MTL regime, it sets forth that the requested CMO "is required to agree to such a request".[963] It can be inferred from these two provisions that, where an actual obligation to contract is provided for, the di-

957 CMD art. 16(2).

958 *Id.* at recital 32.

959 *Kanal 5,* C-52/07 at ¶ 48.

960 Drexl et al., *Comments of the MPI, supra* at 8.

961 CMD art. 16(3).

962 *Id.* at art. 5(2).

963 *Id.* at art. 30(1).

rective uses clear and unambiguous language. A CMO must only provide users with a "reasoned statement" when it does not wish to grant a license; this standard is not comparable to the obligations put on CMOs with respect to right holders and the MTL regime.[964] It, therefore, appears to be more appropriate to deal with refusals to grant user licenses by relying on the tools available under general competition law since, given the circumstances of the individual case, such a conduct may constitute an abuse of a dominant position. Furthermore, even though there is no exact obligation to contract, the requirement of a reasoned statement should prevent CMOs from rejecting licensing requests on arbitrary and discriminatory grounds. In this connection, the requirement that licensing terms be based on "objective and non-discriminatory criteria" will prevent CMOs from favoring certain users over others. In any event, there is nothing in the directive which curtails the member states' freedom to provide for an obligation to contract users. This follows from the CMD's recital 9 (minimum protection principle) which should not only be applied for the protection of right holders but also in relation to users.

The focus that the Collective Management Directive puts on right holders can again be observed in this connection, since even in the two short articles on the relationship between CMOs and users, there is a reference to the protection of right holders. However, quite surprisingly, the directive is not as clear as the case law when it comes to the question of to what extent the interest of right holders must be protected. This may be for the reason that this provision has primarily in mind the determination of tariffs as an important but only partial aspect of the relationship between CMOs and users rather than the relations between these groups from a general perspective. There is neither an explicit reference to blanket licensing nor to other conditions in the licensing agreements. The case law and the adapted *BRT v. SABAM* test developed in *Tournier* can, therefore, be used as a general guideline. At any rate, the language of the CMD seems to be in line with the case law because it sets forth that licensing negotiations should be based on the premise that right holders shall receive appropriate remuneration.[965] This will safeguard their interests, as required by the ECJ. Conversely, non-objective and discriminatory criteria would not be regarded as "necessary" for the protection of the right holders' interest under the standard of the CMD or the competition-based case law.

c) Principles of U.S. Law

The U.S. case law dealing with the relations between CMOs and users is impressive and under dynamic development. Litigation has occurred both un-

---

[964] To the same effect Pfeifer, *Umsetzung*, *supra* at 461; van Gompel, *Directive*, *supra* at 594. *See* however Guibault & van Gompel, *Collective Management*, *supra* at 155 (stating that the directive "went a long way in the direction of an obligation to license").

[965] CMD art. 16(2).

der the rules of the Consent Decrees as well as under the Sherman Act's general regime. The focus is put especially on the types of license that a CMO is required to offer as well as the corresponding fees. A general principle is the equal treatment of users. Both the ASCAP and the BMI Consent Decrees stipulate that the organizations may not discriminate in rates or terms between licensees "similarly situated".[966] This, in turn, implies that users may be treated differently, whenever they are not similarly situated, be it due to "applicable business factors"[967] or due to that users do not operate in the same industry, cause different administrative costs, do not compete against one another, etc.[968]

Both ASCAP and BMI, in principle, face the obligation to license their repertoires to interested users under their respective decrees.[969] In fact, however, users may perform the works contained in the organizations' repertoires once they file an application for a license, as there is no requirement of immediate payment.[970] Furthermore, the obligation to issue performance licenses to users implies that the license grants are non-exclusive.[971] The ASCAP Consent Decree broadly defines a "music user" as

> any person that (1) owns or operates an establishment or enterprise where copyrighted musical compositions are performed publicly, or (2) is otherwise directly engaged in giving public performances of copyrighted musical compositions [...].[972]

This concept does not translate into uniform obligations because the Consent Decrees – just like in respect of right holders – distinguish between different categories of users. In ASCAP's case, these special categories most importantly include "background/foreground music services", "broadcasters", and "on-line music users".[973] The BMI Consent Decree, besides regular music us-

966 ASCAP Consent Decree § IV(C), VIII(A), IX(F), (G); BMI Consent Decree § VIII(A), XIV(C). *See also* BMI Consent Decree at § X(B). *See* on this issue *BMI v. Pandora 2015*, 140 F. Supp. 3d 267 at 288–289; *In Re Pandora*, 6 F. Supp. 3d 317 at 369–372 (S.D.N.Y. 2014).

967 BMI Consent Decree § VIII(A).

968 ASCAP Consent Decree § II(R).

969 ASCAP Decree § VI, IX; BMI Consent Decree § XIV; U.S. Copyright Office, *Music Marketplace*, *supra* at 91–92.

970 ASCAP Consent Decree § IX(E), (F); BMI Consent Decree § XIV(A), (B); U.S. Copyright Office, *Music Marketplace*, *supra* at 94, 157; ASCAP, *Public Comments 2014*, *supra* at 15; BMI, *Public Comments 2014*, *supra* at 19. The situation that a user does not have to pay for certain performances might also occur in connection with the calculation methods which applies to the license, *see, e.g.*, *American Society of Composers, Authors and Publishers v. MOBITV, Inc.*, 681 F.3d 76 at 87–88 (2nd Cir. 2012).

971 *See* for the express language of ASCAP's decree ASCAP Consent Decree § II(E), (J), (K), IV(A), VI.

972 ASCAP Consent Decree § II(G); the BMI Consent Decree does not contain comparable definitions.

973 *See* for the respective definitions ASCAP Consent Decree § II(D), (F) and (H). *See also* *ASCAP (Application of Muzak)*, 309 F. Supp. 2d 566 at 568 (qualifying *Muzak* as a background/foreground music provider). A further category is "motion picture exhibitors", *see*

ers, distinguishes between ("unlicensed") broadcasters and networks. Qualifying for one of the mentioned groups can lead to different obligations put on the CMOs.[974]

U.S. CMOs have for a long time offered blanket licenses as a means to grant users access to their repertoires and are required to do so upon a user's request.[975] A blanket license is characterized by two basic features. First, it includes the entire repertoire of the licensing CMO. Second, a user obtains the right to perform – in exchange for a single fee – all the works as often as desired for the term of the license.[976] Thus, the license fee does not directly depend on the extent that the user actually makes use of, i.e. performs, the licensed works.[977] The practice of blanket licensing has long been observed critically from the antitrust perspective and has therefore been subject to extensive litigation (*see* subsection 3.2.2. immediately). The ASCAP Consent Decree specifies three further types of licenses.[978] Under a per-program license (PPL), a broadcaster obtains access to ASCAP's entire repertoire, while the license fee depends on the broadcaster's programs which contain ASCAP's music.[979] The license extends to ambient and incidental uses.[980] The analogous

ASCAP Consent Decree § IV(G). *See also Meredith*, 1 F. Supp. 3d 180 at 190 (stating that TV stations are eligible for per-program licenses); AJF 2 Memo at 21–22, n. 20.

974 *See, e.g.*, ASCAP Consent Decree § V on the obligation to issue a through-to-the-audience license or § VII on further types of licenses (*see* immediately). *See also* BMI Consent Decree § VIII(B), IX(A), (C). Furthermore, calculation methods can differ, as different benchmarks might be in order. *See also United States v. American Society of Composers, Authors and Publishers (Application of Shenandoah Valley Broadcasting, Inc.)*, 331 F. 2d 117 at 123 (2nd Cir. 1964) (distinguishing different types of music users and their rights under the decree in force at that time).

975 *See* in respect of the BMI Consent Decree *BMI (Application of AEI Music Network)*, 275 F. 3d 168 at 175–176.

976 *BMI v. CBS*, 441 U.S. 1 at 5. *See also ASCAP (Application of Muzak)*, 309 F. Supp. 2d 566 at 579 n. 19; *United States v. American Society of Composers, Authors and Publishers (In re Capital Cities/ABC, Inc.)*, 157 F.R.D. 173 at 204–205 (S.D.N.Y. 1994) (highlighting that no reporting or recording keeping is necessary on the users' part).

977 ASCAP Consent Decree § II(E). However, courts have not employed a strict reading of the blanket license by ruling that users may apply for a blanket license with a different calculation of fees, *BMI v. DMX Inc.*, 683 F. 3d 32 at 43–44. *See also BMI (Application of AEI Music Network)*, 275 F. 3d 168 at 171, 175–177; *ASCAP (Application of Muzak)*, 309 F. Supp. 2d 566 at 581. This emphasis on the first aspect of the license types (entire repertoire of the organization) points to a convergence of the different license types – also if not specifically mentioned in the decree – which are primarily distinguishable by the calculation of the respective fees. *See* for more details section 3.2.6.e) below.

978 The BMI Consent Decree does not contain comparable definitions, but *see* BMI Consent Decree § VIII(B). *See also Meredith*, 1 F. Supp. 3d 180 at 190–191.

979 ASCAP Consent Decree § II(J), *see* § II(M) for a definition of the term "program". *See also ASCAP (Application of Turner Broadcasting System)*, 782 F. Supp. 778 at 817 (holding – in relation to the previous version of the decree – that a cable program supplier was entitled to obtain such a license).

980 ASCAP Consent Decree § VII(A)(1). This provision is sometimes called a "miniblanket" license, *see, e.g.*, Lunney, *The United States Experience*, *supra* at 342. It should not be con-

license type for background music services and online music users is the per-segment license.[981] Finally, a "through-to-the-audience" license (TTTA license) authorizes the simultaneous or "delayed" performances of ASCAP's repertoire which are contained in content transmitted by a user to another with whom the licensee has an economic relationship relating to that content.[982] Comparing the per-program license and the per-segment license with the blanket license, it becomes apparent that the three types of licenses refer to the same selection of works, i.e. the entire CMO's repertoire; however, they differ as far as the license fee calculation is concerned.[983] Since the amount of use is a relevant factor for both the per-program and the per-segment license, record keeping is necessary[984] except where ambient and incidental uses are concerned.[985] The BMI Consent Decree obliges the organization, with regard to unlicensed broadcasters, to license the performance rights to its repertoire on a "per program" or "per programming period" basis (per-program license).[986] In respect of the networks, it provides for a single license (and consequently a single license fee) for the simultaneous broadcast by all the network's stations.[987]

The CMOs' repertoire that the mentioned license types refer to are defined as all works for which the organizations have acquired the right to license the right of public performance.[988] Thus, the repertoire definition is based on works or, more specifically, musical compositions, rather than on types of rights in these compositions.[989] Accordingly, the courts in the *Pandora* cases ruled that the right holders' withdrawal of certain rights category (in this case: "new

fused with a license – also called miniblanket license – that covers only certain parts of the repertoire, *see Moor-Law*, 527 F. Supp. 758 at 767.

981 ASCAP Consent Decree § II(K); Lunney, *The United States Experience*, *supra* at 341–342. A "segment" refers to the users' performances of the licensed works and not to the publishers' catalogs, *see ASCAP (Application of Muzak)*, 309 F. Supp. 2d 566 at 573–574.

982 ASCAP Consent Decree § II(S). ASCAP has to issue this license to broadcasters, online users, background/foreground music services, and "operators of any yet-to-be-developed technology", *see id.* at § V. *See* for the scope of the provision, in its previous wording, however, *ASCAP (Application of Turner Broadcasting System)*, 782 F. Supp. 778 at 808 (holding that the decree applies to cable program suppliers).

983 *See also Buffalo Broadcasting*, 744 F. 2d 917 at 926 n. 7; Korman, *U.S. Position*, *supra* at 162.

984 *ASCAP (In re Capital Cities/ABC)*, 157 F.R.D. 173 at 205; ASCAP Consent Decree § VII(A)(2); Kohn & Kohn, *Music Licensing*, *supra* at 1266–1267.

985 ASCAP Consent Decree § VII(A)(1), (2).

986 BMI Consent Decree § VIII(B); *BMI (Application of AEI Music Network)*, 275 F. 3d 168 at 172. *See* for the definition of the term "programming period" BMI Consent Decree § II(B).

987 *Id.* at § IX(A). This type of license corresponds to ASCAP's though-to-the-audience license, *see* U.S. Copyright Office, *Music Marketplace*, *supra* at 36. *See also Nat'l Cable Television Ass'n v. Broadcast Music.*, Inc., 772 F. Supp. 614 at 650 (D.D.C. 1991) (holding that provision applies to cable television). Different types of licenses are also offered by SESAC, *see, e.g., Meredith*, 1 F. Supp. 3d 180 at 191–194 (referring to negotiations about SESAC's per-program license).

988 ASCAP Consent Decree § II(C); BMI Consent Decree § II(C).

989 *See* on types of rights ASCAP and BMI may license immediately below.

media rights") was not compatible with the controlling repertoire definition.[990] A similar question concerns the licensing of works in which the copyrights are split among several right holders. Traditionally, CMOs have only licensed the rights of their members; hence, in cases where not all co-owners of the copyrights in a work are members of the CMO issuing the license, the user obtains a so-called fractional license, i.e. a license that only covers the rights represented by this particular organization.[991] In order to lawfully perform the work publicly, he or she must obtain further licenses, either from a CMO or the right holder directly. This is one of the reasons why users have usually obtained licenses from all U.S. CMOs.[992] However, in the course of the 2014–2016 review of the Consent Decrees, the DOJ took the position that both the ASCAP and the BMI Consent Decrees required "full work" or "100 percent licensing". This means that the decrees oblige the organizations to grant licenses which fully authorize the user to perform the work even if they do not represent all the copyright co-owners; moreover, they may only include the works they can license on this basis.[993] This is possible in principle, since under U.S. copyright law – unlike under many other jurisdictions – a joint work[994] can be licensed by only one co-owner, in absence of contractual arrangements stating otherwise.[995] Accordingly, the DOJ is of the opinion that ASCAP's and BMI's repertoire refers to all works which the CMOs are able to license on a full-work basis. The opposite reading of the Consent Decrees was employed by the Copyright Office which, based on the doctrine of divisibility of copyrights,[996] argued that ASCAP or BMI were not prohibited from offering fractional licenses.[997] This interpretation– at least in relation to the BMI Consent Decree – was later confirmed by Judge Stanton who ruled upon the CMO's request that the "Consent Decree neither bars fractional licensing nor requires full-work licensing."[998]

ASCAP and BMI usually do not grant licenses to specific works in their repertoires.[999] However, such a license can be obtained in cases where both a

---

990 *See* for more details section 3.1.4.a) above.

991 U.S. Copyright Office, *Jointly Owned Works*, *supra* at 15–17.

992 *Id.* at 17–18; DOJ, *Antitrust Division's Review*, *supra* at 9.

993 DOJ, *Antitrust Division's Review*, *supra* at 8, 11–13.

994 17 U.S.C. § 201(a).

995 I Goldstein on Copyright, *supra* at § 4.2.2.

996 17 U.S.C § 201(d). This provision states that the ownership of a copyright can be subdivided and transferred "in whole and in part".

997 U.S. Copyright Office, *Jointly Owned Works*, *supra* at 13–15.

998 *United States v. Broadcast Music, Inc.*, No. 64 Civ. 3787 (LLS) (S.D.N.Y. Sept. 16, 2016). The DOJ subsequently appealed the decision, *see* Ed Christman, *Department of Justice Appeals Consent Decree Ruling, BMI Hits Back*, Billboard May 18, 2017, *available at* http://www.billboard.com/articles/business/7800937/department-justice-appeals-consent-decree-bmi-comment (last visited Oct. 11, 2017).

999 *BMI v. CBS*, 441 U.S. 1 at 28 (J.P. Stevens, dissenting) ("Neither ASCAP nor BMI has ever offered to license anything less than its entire portfolio [...]"); *Moor-Law*, 527 F. Supp.

prospective user and a right holder send a corresponding request to ASCAP (or where the right holder does not reply in time).[1000] This makes sense since a right holder can always decide to license her rights directly. In this connection, one could ask whether a CMO must offer access to certain parts or categories of works within its repertoire. In *Shenandoah*, television stations asserted that ASCAP was obliged to issue a license that excluded programs obtained from a television network and programs consisting of material made by independent producers.[1001] The court rejected a literal reading of the ASCAP Consent Decree[1002] and dismissed this claim, stating that such a reading would ignore "both context and good sense".[1003] This principle was later acknowledged by the Supreme Court.[1004] In a similar case, a district court denied a motion for summary judgment which alleged that BMI was required to issue licenses for certain categories of musical works of its repertoire (*e.g.,* "country and western music").[1005] This does not, however, mean that the license types mentioned by the Consent Decrees are exhaustive.[1006]

---

758 at 767–769 (holding that BMI is not required to offer "mini-blanket" licenses); U.S. Copyright Office, *Music Marketplace*, *supra* at 36.

1000 ASCAP Consent Decree § VI. *See also BMI v. CBS*, 441 U.S. 1 at 11. *See* on BMI's "per piece" license BMI Consent Decree § IX(C) and *BMI (Application of AEI Music Network)*, 275 F. 3d 168 at 172, 177–178 (also interpreting the notion "with the consent of the copyright proprietor").

1001 *ASCAP (Application of Shenandoah)*, 331 F. 2d 117 at 121.

1002 The decree reads, in relevant part: "ASCAP shall, upon receipt of a written request for a license for the right of public performance of any, some or all of the works in the ASCAP repertory, advise the music user in writing of the fee that it deems reasonable for the license requested […]", *see* ASCAP Consent Decree § XI(A). The court gave its opinion on an older version of the decree but it remained essentially unchanged in this respect. BMI's decree is substantially similar, *see* BMI Consent Decree § XIV(A).

1003 *ASCAP (Application of Shenandoah)*, 331 F. 2d 117 at 121. *See also ASCAP (Application of Muzak)*, 309 F. Supp. 2d 566 at 576–577 (summarizing the case law and stating that this did not apply to claims for reasonable fees).

1004 *BMI v. CBS*, 441 U.S. 1 at 12 ("The courts have twice construed the decree not to require ASCAP to issue licenses for selected portions of its repertory").

1005 *Moor-Law*, 527 F. Supp. 758 at 767–769. *See also* I Hovenkamp et al., *IP and Antitrust*, *supra* at § 22.4a.2 (stating that no rivals are being foreclosed).

1006 *BMI v. DMX Inc.*, 683 F. 3d 32 at 43–44; ASCAP Consent Decree § VII(C). Courts have been, however, skeptical to prescribe conditions for an "incidental use fee" which would have applied to advertisements, promotions, etc. with no reporting obligations. Such a license would neither be a blanket license nor a PPL, *see ASCAP (In re Capital Cities/ABC)*, 157 F.R.D. 173 at 203–205. *See also United States v. American Society of Composers, Authors and Publishers (Application of AOL, RealNetworks and Yahoo, Inc.)*, 559 F. Supp. 2d 332 at 490 (S.D.N.Y. 2008), *aff'd in part, vacated and remanded in part*, 627 F. 3d 64 (2nd Cir. 2010). *See* however *United States v. American Society of Composers, Authors and Publishers (Application of Salem Media of California, Inc.)*, 981 F. Supp. 199 at 220 (S.D.N.Y. 1994) ("Thus, we conclude that an incidental use fee that is predicated on the share of distribution credits allocated by ASCAP to incidental music is appropriate").

3.2.2. Blanket Licenses

In licensing agreements, it is crucial to define the scope of the license by determining (apart from the types of uses, the duration, etc.) what works or categories of works shall be covered by the contract. The traditional practice employed by CMOs has been to offer one license for all the works that were represented by the organization, regardless of whether a user merely sought access to certain group of works or parts of the repertoire. This conduct was objected to by discotheque owners in the *Tournier* case which involved the French CMO SACEM. The main argument put forward on the side of the users was that they were forced to pay for something they did not want because the global license provided for by SACEM also covered works which were not very popular with the target group of the discotheques. Therefore, SACEM ought to offer a licensing option that covered the works which were relevant for their business, namely the works of Anglo-American origin, which were represented under reciprocal representation agreements.[1007] SACEM, on the other hand, argued that such an offer would lead to practical difficulties and inefficiencies which might even increase the costs for users.[1008]

It generally seems reasonable to think about a licensing option tailored to the needs of discotheque owners, given the fact that a quarter of SACEM's collected revenues was raised by this group of users at that time.[1009] In some respects, however, the underlying reasoning of their demands is somewhat unclear because the use of foreign works would have led to the same of amount of remuneration as domestic works in light of the national treatment principle and under SACEM's applicable tariffs.[1010] Moreover, the exact scope of the license desired by discotheque owners was ambiguous because it was not specified whether such a "limited" license should only cover the foreign works or certain new and not (yet) clearly defined categories like, for instance, popular dance music.[1011] In any event, the core argument can be understood as follows: Since not the entire repertoire of musical works was used, the license fee should consequently be lower than the fee charged for a blanket license.[1012] The ECJ resolved the issue by setting forth a general guideline to assist the national court in its decision. The judges ruled that agreements between CMOs and users which provided for a blanket license were not as such restrictive of competition; however, they could be unlawful in situations where the requirements of the adapted *BRT v. SABAM* test were not fulfilled, i.e. where the agreements went beyond what was necessary to protect the interests of right

1007 *Tournier,* 395/87, Opinion of AG Jacobs at ¶ 44.

1008 *Id.* at ¶ 45.

1009 *Id.* at ¶ 70.

1010 Schierholz, *Collective Rights Management*, *supra* at 1161 n.70.

1011 *Tournier,* 395/87, Opinion of AG Jacobs at ¶ 44. The ECJ read the question of the referring court as relating to the licensing of foreign works, *see Tournier*, 395/87 at ¶ 27.

1012 *Tournier,* 395/87, Opinion of AG Jacobs at ¶ 44.

holders.[1013] This could especially be the case where a license agreement of a limited scope could fully safeguard the interests of right holders, without however increasing the costs of management and monitoring; this assessment could vary from member state to member state.[1014] At first glance, the court appears to include three principles in its decision: First, it did not actually weigh the interests of users and right holders but rather stated that the right holders' interests must be "entirely" safeguarded. Second, the court stated that an increase of the costs incurred by a CMO is in itself contrary to the interests of right holders, and not only the increase of management fees (although, admittedly, this might be a direct consequence thereof). Third, the efficiency of the methods employed by a CMO in the management and monitoring process is not a crucial consideration for assessing whether an organization must license sub-parts of its repertoire, as the ECJ merely prohibited higher costs than in the existent situation.[1015] However, the decision might not be as hostile to users as it seems. As regards the first point, one could argue that the blanket license also serves the users' interest because they are then more flexible in the use of SACEM's repertoire and do not have pay higher license fees due to increased management costs. This idea is connected to the second point: Actually, SACEM could have prevented right holders from paying higher management fees by simply raising the license fees for the users who sought a license for a subset of its repertoire. With respect to the last point, elsewhere in the judgment, the court indicated that it was aware of the high level of SACEM's administrative costs and rejected one of the CMO's arguments for this reason.[1016] One should, therefore, interpret the judgment as referring to an increase of the *justified* administrative costs. This interpretation is supported by the AG's opinion in *Tournier*, in which he stated that royalty rates must be compared to "necessary costs of the effective management of copyright".[1017] Moreover, in the *Kanal 5* case, the ECJ held a calculation method to be consistent with EU competition law, unless there was another method which was better suited to identify the use and audience and did not "disproportionately" lead to an increase in the management costs.[1018] While this point was made in relation to calculation methods and the level of royalty rates – two issues which are conceptually different from the scope of the blanket license – it is noteworthy that the ECJ adopted a wording in *Kanal 5*, which was obviously derived from its ruling in *Tournier*; from this perspective, it is reasonable to ask whether the ECJ would clarify its opinion on blanket licenses in light of the *Kanal 5*, if faced with the question again. The ECJ in *Tournier* ultimately left the decision

---

1013 *Tournier*, 395/87 at ¶ 31.

1014 *Id.* at ¶ 31–32.

1015 Meaning that the court did not assess whether SACEM managed the rights efficiently at that time.

1016 *Tournier*, 395/87 at ¶ 42.

1017 *Tournier*, 395/87, Opinion of AG Jacobs at ¶ 74.

1018 *Kanal 5*, C-52/07 at ¶ 41.

for national courts to rule on the issue, according to the principles established in this case.[1019] The AG gave several factors, also referencing U.S. case law, which could assist courts in applying the test, like the convenience of applying a global license, the flexibility it confers upon users, the categorization and monitoring costs associated with with establishing a new category tailored to discotheques, whether access is simply sought to the foreign parts of the repertoire, and the relative bargaining power of the involved parties.[1020] Ultimately, it must be considered whether there are viable alternatives to a blanket license; within this assessment, the interest in the effective collective management of copyrights must be acknowledged.[1021]

Blanket licensing was discussed in the United States already long before the ECJ's *Tournier* ruling. In different contexts, courts had touched upon the issue whether this practice violated U.S. Antitrust laws[1022] before the Supreme Court gave its opinion on this matter in *BMI v. CBS*.[1023] To fully understand the court's appraisal, it is necessary to recall the concept of blanket license the judges had in mind: A license which permits a licensee to perform all works in the organizations' respective repertoires, for which the license fee does not depend on the amount of use made of by the licensee.[1024] CBS, a major U.S. television network, complained that ASCAP and BMI were unlawful monopolies which, by blanket licensing, engaged in illegal price fixing, tying arrangements, concerted refusal to deal as well as misuse of copyrights.[1025] The fundamental question before that court was whether this constituted a per se infringement of the Sherman Act.[1026] The court not only analyzed the anticompetitive effects of this licenses type, but also the benefits deriving from it. It held that blanket licensing was not a "naked" restraint of trade, but served to efficiently overcome the practical problems associated with the licensing, monitoring, and enforcement of copyrights.[1027] Therefore, to the extent that the blanket license streamlines and accelerates the licensing process and introduces flexibilities for users, ASCAP did not act as a joint agency for copyright holders, but as a separate seller for a new product.[1028] Due to the beneficial effects of this license type taken together with the fact that licensees could always

1019 *Tournier*, C-395/87 at ¶ 32.

1020 *Tournier*, 395/87, Opinion of AG Jacobs at ¶ 49. *See also Kanal 5 Ltd v. STIM*, C-52/07 (ECJ 2008), Opinion of AG Trstenjak, ¶ 55.

1021 *Tournier*, 395/87, Opinion of AG Jacobs at ¶ 50.

1022 *See, e.g., K-91*, 372 F. 2d 1 at 4–8 (in connection with the antitrust laws of the State of Washington); *Witmark & Sons*, 80 F. Supp. 843 at 845–846 (in connection with direct licensing).

1023 *BMI v. CBS*, 441 U.S. 1.

1024 *Id.* at 5. Since then, courts have developed a rather flexible approach to the calculation of fees under a blanket license, *see* section 3.2.6.e) below.

1025 *BMI v. CBS*, 441 U.S. 1 at 6.

1026 *Id.* at 4, 18.

1027 *Id.* at 20–21.

1028 *Id.* at 22–23.

negotiate with right holder directly, the Supreme Court did not prohibit blanket licensing under the per se rule.[1029] Concluding, the Supreme Court held that blanket licensing must be examined under the rule of reason, thereby reversing the Court of Appeal's judgment which had considered blanket licensing as price fixing in the "literal sense".[1030]

While the court highlighted the positive effects of the blanket license in more detail, another less pronounced but nonetheless important consideration influenced the court's analysis: The regulation of ASCAP and BMI by consent decrees.[1031] In this connection, CBS's arguments were from the beginning undermined by the fact that it had actually always had the choice to obtain direct licenses from ASCAP's and BMI's members.[1032] This reinforced the court's analysis that the blanket license is a viable solution to an actual problem which could be efficiently solved by blanket licensing.

However, the Supreme Court did not provide a conclusive answer on the compatibility of blanket licenses with antitrust laws; the question remained whether blanket licenses were permitted under the rule of reason. It was the tasks of other courts to shed further light on this issue,[1033] and the courts reached favorable conclusions for the CMOs. On remand, the Second Circuit held that blanket licensing did not constitute a restraint of competition.[1034] It based its findings on the fact that licensees could – realistically and not only potentially[1035] – negotiate with individual right holders; if they choose not to do so, "then it is customer preference for the blanket license, and not the license itself, that causes the lack of price competition among songs".[1036] That said, it was not necessary to weigh the pro- and anti-competitive effects of

1029 *Id.* at 24–25.

1030 *Id.* at 8, 24–26. However, the Court of Appeals – in *Columbia Broadcasting System, Inc. v. American Society of Composers, Authors and Publishers*, 562 F. 2d 130 (2nd Cir. 1977) – did not plainly reject blanket licensing and made some restrictions, *see BMI v. CBS*, 441 U.S. 1 at 17 n. 27. *See also* I Hovenkamp et al., *IP and Antitrust*, *supra* at § 22.3a1.

1031 *See, e.g., BMI v. CBS*, 441 U.S. 1 at 13 ("In these circumstances, we have a unique indicator that the challenged practice may have redeeming competitive virtues and that the search for those values is not almost sure to be in vain"). At that time, however, the argument as regards the rate court only applied to ASCAP since BMI's rate court was not established until the new BMI Consent Decree in 1994.

1032 *See, e.g., id.* at 12, 23–24. In this regard, Justice Stevens agreed with the majority of the court, *see id.* at 28–29 (J.P. Stevens, dissenting). *See also* Chin, *Copyright Collective Management*, *supra* at 271; I Hovenkamp et al., *IP and Antitrust*, *supra* at § 22.3a1; Korman, *U.S. Position*, *supra* at 174.

1033 In a dissenting opinion, Justice Stevens explained that, even though concurring with the other judges insofar as blanket licensing did not constitute a per se violation of the Sherman Act, blanket licensing was not permissible under the rule of reason doctrine, *see BMI v. CBS*, 441 U.S. 1 at 25–26 (J.P. Stevens, dissenting).

1034 *CBS v. ASCAP*, 620 F. 2d 930 at 834, 939. The court was careful to state that its judgement only applied to blanket licenses in relation to the television networks, *see id.* at 934, n. 6.

1035 *Id.* at 936–939.

1036 *Id.* at 935.

this type of license.[1037] A cornerstone in this connection was the actual (and not merely potential) feasibility of direct licensing. The Second Circuit held that individual licenses were an actual alternative because i) the problems associated with the increased complexity on the licensee's side were – though costly – not insurmountable, ii) right holders were not found to be reluctant in granting licenses, and iii) hold-ups by individual right holders were not expected.[1038] This rationale was later further generalized and applied to local TV stations in *Buffalo Broadcasting v. ASCAP*[1039] where the Second Circuit held that in fact, there existed several realistic alternatives to blanket licensing. In addition to direct licensing, licensees could, in principle, also opt for per-program licenses or negotiate to acquire the required performance rights via "source licensing" from the content producers.[1040]

These principles have not only been applied to ASCAP and BMI. In *Meredith v. SESAC*, groups of local TV stations complained that SESAC's and its affiliates' practices created a situation where no practical alternative to SESAC's blanket license existed.[1041] Indeed, the court found that, while direct licenses were permitted under SESAC's standard membership agreements, some members entered into a supplementary agreement which imposed large monetary penalties if the right holders decided to directly license their works.[1042] In line with the prior judgments, it held that a blanket license itself did not constitute a per se violation of the antitrust laws;[1043] this also applied to the supplementary agreements because they were "not pure horizontal agreements among competitors to fix prices" but had "a significant vertical dimension".[1044] However, the supplemental agreements could reasonably be found to be a concerted action resulting in a restraint of trade since they effectively removed any alternative from SESAC's blanket license.[1045] This was deemed to harm com-

1037 *Id.* at 934.

1038 *Id.* at 937–938.

1039 *Buffalo Broadcasting*, 744 F. 2d 917. *See also Schumann v. Albuquerque Corp.*, 664 F. Supp. 473 at 477–478 (D.N.M.1987) (referring to radio stations); *Hearst/ABV Viacom*, 746 F. Supp. 320 at 325–326 (referring to a cable television program service); *Nat'l Cable Television Ass'n*, 772 F. Supp. 614 at 636 (referring to cable system operators); *United States v. American Society of Composers, Authors and Publishers (Application of Capital Cities/ABC, Inc.)*, 831 F. Supp. 137 at 141, 144, 153–155 (S.D.N.Y. 1993) (referring to TV networks); *ASCAP (In re Capital Cities/ABC)*, 157 F.R.D. 173 at 202 (referring to local TV stations).

1040 *Buffalo Broadcasting*, 744 F. 2d 917 at 926–932. Producers could acquire performance rights either by operation of law ("composer-for-hire music") or contract with the copyright owners, *see id.* at 929–930.

1041 *Meredith*, 1 F. Supp. 3d 180 at 186.

1042 *Id.* at 193.

1043 *Id.* at 204 (also rejecting claims that the absence of a consent decree required a different ruling).

1044 *Id.* at 205–206.

1045 *Id.* at 212–217 (also rejecting SESAC's per-program license or source licensing as viable alternatives to the blanket license).

petition because the anti-competitive factors clearly outweighed their pro-competitive counterparts.[1046] In a similar case[1047] brought by the Radio Music License Committee (RMLC),[1048] the court held that SESAC was not in breach of section 1 of the Sherman Act because no concerted action could be established.[1049] However, it found that SESAC practically forced users to buy its blanket license and thereby abused its monopoly power under section 2 of the Sherman Act.[1050]

One of the main reasons why U.S. CMOs have faced antitrust challenges in respect of their blanket licenses is that such licenses do not permit price competition between the works (and, therefore, right holders) in their repertoires.[1051] In other words, this type of licenses was alleged to constitute a form of price fixing among competitors, and this allegation was also the main focus of the analysis *BMI v. CBS*.[1052] However, blanket licensing can also be looked at from the perspective of illegal tying ("block booking")[1053] which Justice Stevens investigated in more detail in his dissenting opinion.[1054] Thus, blanket licensing requires justification under antitrust law. The line of judgments shows that, under U.S. doctrine, the permissibility of blanket licensing rests on two fundamental pillars: On the one hand, the increased efficiency of the licensing process and, on the other hand, the lack of negative effects on competition.[1055] The efficiency argument – which is based on the significant decrease of transaction costs – was the cornerstone of the Supreme Court's ruling that blanket licensing should not be regarded as a per se violation of the Sherman Act.[1056] The blanket license was essentially regarded as a new product, different from

1046 *Id.* at 217–221. SESAC's conduct was also analyzed under § 2 of the Sherman Act, *see id.* at 221–224. The lawsuit was later settled, *see Meredith*, 87 F. Supp. 3d 650.

1047 *Radio Music License Comm.*, 29 F. Supp. 3d 487.

1048 The RMLC is a non-profit organization which negotiates performance licenses on behalf of radio stations, *see Radio Music License Comm.*, 29 F. Supp. 3d 487 at 491. *See also* Radio Music License Committee, *Our Mission*, http://www.radiomlc.org/ (last visited April 23, 2017).

1049 *Radio Music License Comm.*, 29 F. Supp. 3d 487 at 498–499 (also noting that SESAC's members are generally not precluded from direct licensing).

1050 *Id.* at 501–502.

1051 *See, e.g., BMI v. CBS*, 441 U.S. 1 at 23–24; *id.* at 32 (J.P. Stevens, dissenting); *CBS v. ASCAP*, 620 F. 2d 930 at 935; *Moor-Law*, 527 F. Supp. 758 at 765; Lunney, *The United States Experience*, *supra* at 320.

1052 I Hovenkamp et al., *IP and Antitrust*, *supra* at § 22.3a1.

1053 *Id.*; IX Areeda & Hovenkamp, *Antitrust Principles 2006*, *supra* at ¶ 1717f3.

1054 *BMI v. CBS*, 441 U.S. 1 at 30–33 (J.P. Stevens, dissenting). This issue was later discussed again in *Moor-Law*, 527 F. Supp. 758 at 765–766. Further antitrust problems include prohibited refusal to deal, *see, e.g., Radio Music License Comm.*, 29 F. Supp. 3d 487 at 495–496.

1055 It must however not be forgotten that these elements which focus on the per se rule and the rule of reason – albeit their pronounced attention in the litigation history – are only parts of the complete analysis, a fact that the recent SESAC litigation has rightfully pointed attention to.

1056 XIII Areeda & Hovenkamp, *Antitrust Principles 2006*, *supra* at ¶ 2104b1.

anything that could be obtained by individual licensing.[1057] This rationale is not only relevant for the question of whether there is a per se violation, but also for weighing the pro- and anticompetitive factors in the course of the rule of reason analysis. In this vein, courts have upheld the blanket license under this rule due to its positive effects.[1058] One must not, however, confuse this finding with the preliminary question of whether there is a restraint of competition in the first place. For this appraisal, courts have looked at the available alternatives to blanket licensing rather than toward increases in efficiency. This is demonstrated by *ASCAP v. CBS* where a restraint of competition was expressly *not* found. Also, the Supreme Court based its opinion on the finding that the alternative of direct licensing existed.[1059] This finding, however, must be made per each individual case and can vary in different sectors of the industry. Alternative licensing sources will only rule out the existence of a restraint of competition if their practical and realistic feasibility is established and courts have indeed rejected the alternatives as unfeasible.[1060]

It is therefore that the efficiency of blanket licensing and feasibility of its alternatives apply to different aspects of the antitrust analysis of blanket licenses. Yet, the two concepts are not always clearly demarcated. For instance, one could suggest that a licensing method is so inefficient compared to the blanket license that it ceases to be a realistic alternative.[1061] In this connection, the Supreme Court considered the fact that users had a "real choice" to negotiate with right holders directly, but nevertheless preferred buying blanket licenses as an indication of the blanket license's positive effects toward ruling out a per se violation.[1062]

1057 *BMI v. CBS*, 441 U.S. 1 at 22–23. Therefore, tying is not likely to be found, *see* I Hovenkamp et al., *IP and Antitrust*, *supra* at § 22.3a1.

1058 *See, e.g.*, *Moor-Law*, 527 F. Supp. 758 at 763, 769 (rejecting claims that a "mini-blanket" license achieved efficiencies comparable to a blanket license); *Nat'l Cable Television Ass'n,* 772 F. Supp. 614 at 646. *See also Buffalo Broadcasting*, 744 F. 2d 917 at 932–933; I Hovenkamp et al., *IP and Antitrust*, *supra* at § 22.3a1.

1059 *BMI v. CBS*, 441 U.S. 1 at 12, 23–24. *See also* Chin, *Copyright Collective Management*, *supra* at 271 (stating that the availabiltiy of alternatives to blanket licenses was a "crucial factor" for the court).

1060 *See, e.g.*, *Moor-Law*, 527 F. Supp. 758 at 763; *Hearst/ABV Viacom*, 746 F. Supp. 320 at 327 (not ruling out the option that CMO's members agreed not to license directly); *Nat'l Cable Television Ass'n,* 772 F. Supp. 614 at 636 (holding that only source licensing is feasible but not direct licensing); *Meredith*, 1 F. Supp. 3d 180 at 212–217.

1061 For the Supreme Court, it was important that direct licensing was feasible based on the district court's record, *see BMI v. CBS*, 441 U.S. 1 at 24. The district court found that a licensing infrastructure could be set up in about a year, *see id.* at 35 (J.P. Stevens, dissenting). *See also* I Hovenkamp et al., *IP and Antitrust*, supra at § 22.3a1.

1062 *BMI v. CBS*, 441 U.S. 1 at 23–24. In *Meredith*, the court held that there was no per se violation, even though the supplemental agreement rendered direct licensing practically unfeasible, thereby shifting this question to the rule of reason analysis, *see Meredith*, 1 F. Supp. 3d 180 at 205–206. *See also BMI v. CBS*, 441 U.S. 1 at 29–30 (J.P. Stevens, dissenting).

It is sometimes questioned whether the rationales of the nearly 40-year-old judgment still apply today, especially in light of the technological development.[1063] Even if it is established that CMOs as suppliers of blanket licenses have lost, at least to certain extent or in some markets, their fundamental importance in the licensing process of performance rights, the question is, of course, what legal consequence is attached to this finding. Should blanket licenses be regarded as per se violations under these circumstances? One should remember that under ordinary circumstances, blanket licensing is different from other forms of anticompetitive conduct. First of all, it is not an ordinary horizontal agreement outlawed by the per se rule.[1064] Moreover, right holders as licensors can, by the joining the CMO, add their works to the scope of the license so that no foreclosure concerns subsist.[1065] Even though a blanket license technically "fixes" prices, this does not necessarily lead to an antitrust violation.[1066] In the cases where direct licensing is feasible, one should ask whether there is anticompetitive output reduction whatsoever.[1067] Also the tying aspect of blanket licenses must be viewed at from this perspective, as there will be no coercion on users if the blanket license is not the exclusive source of licenses.[1068] It may very well be the case (and this fact is often emphasized in CMO-critical treatises) that direct licensing by right holders has been greatly facilitated by technologies, making the needs for CMOs less obvious. However, if one argues that it was crucial for the Supreme Court that direct licensing was possible as an alternative,[1069] does not the advent of such technology make a case against a per se violation? After all, if direct licensing is perfectly feasible over the Internet (thereby avoiding the CMOs' administration machineries), why do users still buy the blanket licenses, if collective licensing is not needed anymore? In other words: Is it not the buyer's preference in the market

1063 *See, e.g.*, Chin, *Copyright Collective Management*, *supra*; Harry First, *Online Music Joint Ventures: Taken for a Song* 22 (NYU Law School, Public Law and Legal Theory Research Paper No. 78, 2004), *available at* https://papers.ssrn.com/sol3/papers.cfm?abstract_id=508685 (last visited May 23, 2017) (stating that "the efficiency which justified the refusal to offer individual licenses likely not longer holds"); Pitt, *Direct Licensing*, *supra* at 133. Admittedly, the Supreme Court stated that "of course changes brought about by new technology or new marketing techniques might also undercut the justification for the practice", *see BMI v. CBS*, 441 U.S. 1 at 21 n. 34.

1064 *BMI v. CBS*, 441 U.S. 1 at 23–24; *Meredith*, 1 F. Supp. 3d 180 at 205–206 (emphasizing vertical components).

1065 I Hovenkamp et al., *IP and Antitrust*, *supra* at § 22.4a1. This argument is less pronounced in SESAC's case, as this CMO is under no obligation to represent right holders. The introduction of such an obligation should however be considered, *see* section III.3.2. below.

1066 IX Areeda & Hovenkamp, *Antitrust Principles 2006*, *supra* at ¶ 1907c.

1067 *Id.*; II Hovenkamp et al., *IP and Antitrust*, *supra* at § 33.6a. *See also Nat'l Cable Television Ass'n*, 772 F. Supp. 614 at 644 (also holding that a blanket license might have output increasing effects).

1068 I Hovenkamp et al., *IP and Antitrust*, *supra* at § 23.3a1. *See also* X Areeda & Hovenkamp, *Antitrust Principles 2006*, *supra* at ¶ 1717f3.

1069 Chin, *Copyright Collective Management*, *supra* at 271.

to buy the package at a flat fee instead of its components for multiple individual fees?[1070] In fact, all requirements for such dealing are available, and the Consent Decrees ensure that CMOs do not constrain the member's freedom of directly licensing their works.[1071] In an overall assessment, it therefore seems that a CMO issuing blanket licenses does not act so "plainly anticompetitive" that the application of the per se rule would be in order. If one, however, acknowledges that blanket licensing is not a per se violation, the finding that feasible alternatives to blanket licenses exist will also immunize it under the rule of reason, since no restraint of trade will be found in these situations. It may thus be that CMOs do not always require special treatment under antitrust laws in order to avoid violations.

3.2.3. Refusal to Issue Cross-Border Licenses[1072]

National monopolies of European CMOs on the licensing of copyrights can be threatened inasmuch as users who seek access to foreign repertoire can obtain a license directly from a CMO which operates in another country; then, the foreign CMO can license its repertoire for territory in which the users operate. In the *Tournier* and *Lucazeau* cases, users complained that CMOs denied the issuance of cross-border licenses to their repertoires and asserted that this was a consequence of a concerted practice. Such a practice would perpetuate national monopolies and would thus be incompatible with the aims of the Internal Market and European competition law.[1073] Provisions to this end had been removed from the reciprocal representation agreements on the request of the Commission prior to the proceeding, but CMOs kept refusing to license their repertoire to users from other member states.[1074] The problem for the court was that there was no proof of the existence of an actual concerted prac-

---

1070 XI Areeda & Hovenkamp, *Antitrust Principles 2006*, *supra* at ¶ 1907c. It should however be noted that even consumer preference might not necessarily justify illegal conduct, *see CBS v. ASCAP*, 620 F. 2d 930 at 935. However, as stated above, this might also be an indication of efficiency.

1071 Also in the *Meredith*, where new technologies were available and where no consent decree governed SESAC's operations, the court refused to condemn the blanket license under the per se rule, *see Meredith*, 1 F. Supp. 3d 180 at 196. It is of course possible that a blanket license in a concrete form is "so plainly anticompetitive" to justify the application of the per se rule but it appears that blanket licenses are usually not devoid of "any redeeming value"; they rather offer benefits which might have been mitigated by new technologies, but have not disappeared. A 2015 study of the U.S. Copyright Office revealed that the benefits of blanket licensing were (still) widely acknowledged and it was furthermore recommended to license mechanical rights under a blanket license, *see* U.S. Copyright Office, *Music Marketplace*, *supra* at 170.

1072 As this section concerns problems relating to the EU Internal Market, the U.S. case law has not dealt with comparable issues and is therefore not referred to in this section.

1073 *Tournier*, 395/87 at ¶ 22; *Lucazeau,* 110/88, at ¶ 16.

1074 *Tournier*, 395/87 at ¶ 20–21; *Lucazeau,* 110/88, at ¶ 14–15.

tice between the CMOs in question. Since the case originated in a reference for a preliminary ruling, it ordered the national court to ascertain whether such a practice could actually be found.[1075] Instead, the court presented guidelines in case such a practice could be discovered and ruled that wherever the object of agreements or concerted practices between CMOs cause the refusal to grant licenses to users from other member states, such agreements or practices must be considered as conflicting with article 101.[1076] However, a concerted practice could not be presumed if a CMO was able to substantiate other reasons for the refusal of a license.[1077] Indeed, SACEM argued that denying such license requests was the only economically viable option because otherwise, it would be forced to establish a management infrastructure within the territories of the other member states.[1078] Moreover, it should be borne in mind that such a cross-border license would only cover SACEM's French repertoire and not the works managed in accordance with reciprocal agreements.[1079]

While the refusal to license could in principle also be regarded as an abuse of a dominant position, the ECJ considered the case under article 101 just like in connection with blanket licenses. However, the situation before the court was different from the circumstances under which it gave its opinion on these global licenses. The refusal to license concerned the relationship between CMOs to a greater extent; and users were affected as a direct consequence of this relation.[1080] In contrast, the ECJ examined blanket licenses under article 101 in light of contracts concluded directly between the CMOs and the users. For this reason, it is not possible to apply the adapted *BRT v. SABAM* test set forth above to the present question (and neither did the ECJ). Guidance should rather be sought from the cases that deal with the relationships between different CMOs. What can be said is that CMOs will not conflict with EU law if the refusal to issue cross-border licenses can be explained by reasons other than the existence of a concerted practice.[1081] Applying this concept to the Collective Management Directive, a CMO would not be in breach of the principle of "objective and non-discriminatory" licensing terms[1082] when refusing a licensing request if a justification of this sort can be established.[1083]

1075 *Tournier*, 395/87 at ¶ 25; *Lucazeau,* 110/88, at ¶ 19.

1076 *Tournier*, 395/87 at ¶ 26; *Lucazeau,* 110/88, at ¶ 20.

1077 *Tournier*, 395/87 at ¶ 24; *Lucazeau,* 110/88, at ¶ 18.

1078 *Tournier,* 395/87, Opinion of AG Jacobs at ¶ 32.

1079 *Id.* at ¶ 38.

1080 *Tournier,* 395/87, Opinion of AG Jacobs at ¶ 38.

1081 Schierholz, *Collective Rights Management*, *supra* at 1162. This argument was also important in the CISAC litigation, *see* section 3.3.5. below.

1082 CMD art. 16.

1083 The efficiency-driven argument is comparable to the avoidance of double membership, *see* Schierholz, *Collective Rights Management*, supra at 1160.

3.2.4. License Fees and Royalties

The amount that a user is required to pay for using the repertoire represented by a CMO is the result of a process which involves two intertwined main considerations: First, a CMO defines a general method according to which the license fees are calculated (*e.g.*, by a proportion of the income of the user); second, it determines the particular rates which apply to the users in question (*e.g.*, 10% of the amount determined in the first step).[1084] These sub-processes have raised concerns from the competition law perspective in the EU. Also in the United States, the CMOs' fee policy can be subject to an assessment under sections 1 and 2 of the Sherman Act. In practice, however, the special rules of the Consent Decrees are more relevant where ASCAP and BMI are concerned. The decrees provide for i) license types which are (partly) defined by the fee calculation (*e.g.*, per-program licenses),[1085] ii) special rules on the calculation of fees,[1086] and iii) a specific procedure for the negotiations with users as well as judicial rate-setting ("rate court" proceedings). This proceeding can be outlined as follows:[1087] ASCAP is required to quote a reasonable fee for the type of license sought upon receiving a music user's written request. If the parties cannot agree on a fee within sixty days, the user can petition the court to determine a reasonable fee which applies retroactively to the date of the written request for a license.[1088] In the ensuing proceeding before the rate court, the burden of proof is on ASCAP to show that the license fee sought is reasonable.[1089] The BMI Consent Decree contains substantially similar provisions.[1090] It is important to note that due to the principle of non-discrimination among licensees, the rate court's determination can have industry-wide importance.[1091] However, even though this proceeding (in ASCAP's case) has been available

1084 One could define as a third factor certain deductions from standard rates which CMOs frequently grant users, *see, e.g., Tournier*, 395/87, Opinion of AG Jacobs at ¶ 57 (also highlighting that this might raise discrimination issues).

1085 *See* section 3.2.1.c) above.

1086 *See, e.g.*, ASCAP Consent Decree § IV(H); BMI Consent Decree § (X).

1087 ASACP Consent Decree § IX(A).

1088 ASCAP can do so within 90 days. *See* for more details on the reasonableness standard immediately. The court has the authority to set an interim fee upon the application of one of the parties, *see* ASCAP Consent Decree § IX(F). This option is, however, not commonly used, *see* U.S. Copyright Office, *Music Marketplace*, *supra* at 158.

1089 ASCAP Consent Decree § IX(B), (D). A modification applies to per-segment licenses.

1090 BMI Consent Decree § XIV. *See also BMI v. DMX Inc.*, 683 F. 3d 32 at 44–45.

1091 *United States v. Broadcast Music., Inc.*, 426 F. 3d 91 at 98 (2nd Cir. 2005) ("We are conscious that rate court decisions have effects that reach beyond the litigants involved in the proceedings"); ASCAP Consent Decree § IX(G); BMI Consent Decree § XIV(C). *See* however *ASCAP (Application of Salem Media of California)*, 981 F. Supp. 199 at 217 ("[...] the task in this rate proceeding is to determine whether ASCAP's proposed per-program fee rates provide a genuine choice for the applicant stations, not whether those fee rates make the per-program license available to a significant segment of the entire radio industry"). *See also* U.S. Copyright Office, *Jointly Owned Works*, *supra* at 26 n. 139 (highlighting that the licensing rates of ASCAP and BMI vary from year to year).

for decades, it has recently been used more frequently.[1092] Furthermore, not only the license types specially mentioned in the decree are subject to rate court determinations.[1093] SESAC is not subject to a consent decree, but has recently agreed to binding arbitration with Television Music Licensing Committee (TVMLC) in licensing fee disputes.[1094]

a) General Remarks

License fees are usually the result of the negotiations between licensor and licensee but can be modified or prohibited by competition law. Bearing in mind that CMOs possess a dominant position and a corresponding bargaining power that goes beyond regular undertakings,[1095] license fees can be looked at from the perspective of excessive pricing practices that can amount to an abuse of a dominant position. The seminal case for the question of whether a price is excessive under article 102 TFEU is *United Brands v. Commission.*[1096] In this ruling, the ECJ clarified that it considered a price to be excessive if it bore no reasonable relation to the economic value of the product supplied; a possible method of determining whether this relation is reasonable is identifying the undertaking's profit margin by comparing the selling price of the product and the costs of its production.[1097] If this analysis discloses an excessive price, one must ask whether a price is unfair in itself or in comparison to competing products.[1098] The question whether this reasoning applied to the collective management of copyrights has not been answered uniformly. The AG in *Tournier* mentioned that the ruling could not simply be relied on in the copyright context because i) the judgment concerned products rather than services, ii) it was impossible to quantify the costs of production of a work stemming from artistic creation, and iii) there was no basis to compare the

1092 Daniel A. Crane, *Bargaining In The Shadow Of Rate-Setting Courts*, 76 Antitrust L. J. 307, 310–311 (2009) (also noting that the proceedings constitute only a small fraction of the CMOs' licensing transactions); Brontë Lawson Turk, *"It's Been a Hard Day's Night" for Songwriters: Why the ASCAP and BMI Consent Decrees Must Undergo Reform*, 26 Fordham Intell. Prop. Media & Ent. L. J. 493, 512 (2016). *See also Showtime/Movie Channel*, 912 F. 2d 563 at 565 (noting the this was the first a appeal to challenge a rate court's ruling); *United States v. Broadcast Music, Inc. (Application of Music Choice, Inc.)*, 316 F. 3d 189 at 194 (2nd Cir. 2003) (noting that this was the first time to review a rate under the BMI Consent Decree).

1093 *BMI (Application of AEI Music Network)*, 275 F. 3d 168 at 176–177.

1094 *Meredith*, 87 F. Supp. 3d 650 at 657–658; Brabec, *Performance Right*, *supra* at 19.

1095 *Tournier*, 395/87, Opinion of AG Jacobs at ¶ 43.

1096 *United Brands*, 27/76. *See* for a discussion of the case Miguel de la Mano et al., *Article 102* in *The EU Law of Competition* 329, 514–515, 517–522 (Jonathan Faull & Ali Nikpay eds., 3rd ed. 2014).

1097 *United Brands*, 27/76 at ¶ 250–251.

1098 *Id.* at ¶ 252. *See* for a concise summary of the most important decisions of the court *Autortiesību un komunicēšanās konsultāciju aģentūra / Latvijas Autoru apvienība*, C-177/16, Opinion of AG Wahl at ¶ 15–23.

royalties charged by SACEM because there were no competitors in the market for copyright management.[1099] While these arguments cannot be denied, there are good reasons to examine the relation between the license fee and the economic value of using the licensed rights. On the one hand, the ECJ in *United Brands* stated that the comparison to the production costs was only one possible way of determining whether the price is unfair;[1100] on the other hand, the economic value has traditionally been used to determine an equitable remuneration for a particular work.[1101] Moreover, the arguments mentioned by the AG might be coherent for musical works, but for CMOs which manage neighboring rights, the analysis might be different. In the case of sound recording manufacturers, for instance, where products rather than artistic endeavors are at issue, it will be possible determine the costs of production more accurately, and depending on the individual circumstances, there might even be competitors in the market. However, the AG stated also in reference to the *SABAM* ruling that it was necessary to base the analysis whether a fee is excessive on objective grounds which consist in the comparison between the level of the royalty and the costs of *effective* copyright management, keeping in mind the aim to provide reasonable remuneration to the right holders;[1102] thus, the AG advocated an adapted *United Brands* approach because the costs of production were replaced by the costs of effective management. This solution is principally in line with *United Brands* because, as stated before, the ECJ deemed the reference to production costs only one possible method of comparison. The ECJ seemed to sympathize with this reasoning in the *Tournier/Lucazeau* cases by rejecting one of SACEM's core arguments in the case,[1103] as the court referred to the costs of a "hypothetical efficient firm"[1104] but did not make further references to this line of argumentation in the *Tournier* case. Later, the ECJ referred to *United Brands* in *Kanal 5 v. STIM* when it assessed calculation methods that were applied by a Swedish CMO. The court did pronounce the management costs aspect but confirmed expressly that it had to be ascertained whether the royalties are reasonable in relation to the economic value of the service provided by the CMO in question, i.e. making the represented repertoire available to users.[1105] It also alluded, well in accordance with the adapted

1099 *Tournier,* 395/87, Opinion of AG Jacobs at ¶ 53 (citing the national court).

1100 *United Brands*, 27/76 at ¶ 253.

1101 Allendesalazar & Vallina, *The Usual Suspects*, *supra* at 383 (referring to EU case law). *See also Kanal 5,* C-52/07, Opinion of AG Trstenjak at ¶ 61.

1102 *Tournier,* 395/87, Opinion of AG Jacobs at ¶ 57, 69.

1103 *Lucazeau,* 110/88, at ¶ 29; *Tournier*, 395/87 at ¶ 42.

1104 Massimo Motta & Alexandre de Streel, *Excessive Pricing in Competition Law: Never Say Never?* in *The Pros and Cons of High Prices* 14, 34 (Konkurrensverket, Swedish Competition Authority ed., 2007), *available at* http://www.kkv.se/globalassets/english/research/the-pros-and-cons-of-high-prices-14mb.pdf (last visited May 23, 2017). However, it must be admitted that the core notions of "effective" and "efficient" copyright management are slightly different.

1105 *Kanal 5,* C-52/07 at ¶ 29. *See also Autortiesību un komunicēšanās konsultāciju aģentūra / Latvijas Autoru apvienība*, C-177/16 at ¶ 35.

BRT v. SABAM test, to the balance which had to be struck between right holders and users.[1106] All these principles seem to have influenced the Collective Management Directive which introduces the following guidelines:

> Rightholders shall receive appropriate remuneration for the use of their rights. Tariffs for exclusive right and rights to remuneration shall be reasonable in relation to, inter alia, the economic value of the use of the rights in trade, taking into account the nature and scope of the use of the work and other subject-matter, as well as in relation to the economic value of the service provided by the collective management organisation.[1107]

Several observations can be made when taking a look at the language of the directive. First of all, the most important points highlighted by the case law can be recognized: The provision stipulates that the tariffs shall bear a reasonable relation to the economic value of the use of the rights in trade as well as to the economic value of the service provided by the CMO. Furthermore, it draws the attention to right holders and makes their appropriate remuneration a criterion for the assessment of license fees. This can be understood as a reference to the adapted *BRT v. SABAM* test which provides for the balancing of interests between right holders and users. Put differently, a licensing scheme does not conflict with European competition law or the Collective Management Directive as long as it strives to secure appropriate remuneration for the right holders. Further observations can be made in relation to the scope of the provision. The reasonable relation test applies to exclusive rights and rights to remuneration alike. For statutory remuneration rights, determining their value in trade might, however, be hard because in most instances, there is no corresponding commercial market.[1108] Therefore, the application of the directive's standard must leave enough leeway to take full account of the conceptual differences between rights to equitable remuneration, fair compensation, and exclusive rights.[1109] Of course, the test provided for by this provision is not applicable where, based on other sources of EU law, the issue is subject to national regulation.[1110] It should finally be observed that the directive does not provide for an exhaustive list of factors governing the tariffs determined by CMOs ("*inter alia*"). This should, on the one hand, reinforce the required flexibility; on the other hand, it flows from the wording of the provision that the economic value of the work in trade and the economic value of the CMOs' service are necessarily part of the comparison. It is noteworthy that the test can be applied to calculation methods as well as to the level

---

1106 *Id.* at ¶ 31, 33, 35. Again, the court drew no clear line between the application of article 101 and 102 TFEU.

1107 CMD art. 16(2).

1108 Drexl et al., *Comments of the MPI*, *supra* at 25.

1109 Quintais, *Proposal for a Directive*, *supra* at 19. *See also Kanal 5,* C-52/07, Opinion of AG Trstenjak at ¶ 47; Guibault, *Collective Management Directive*, *supra* at 750.

1110 Quintais, *Proposal for a Directive*, *supra* at 11 (referring to the Rental & Lending Rights Directive art. 3(6), 5, 6, 8(2), 11 and the Copyright Directive art. 5(2)(b).)

of fees; the exact criteria for this appraisal will be set forth in the following two subsections.

The underlying U.S. standard for the fee calculation is paraphrased as a "reasonable fee".[1111] Thus, whenever a licensee is of the opinion that ASCAP or BMI demand a fee which is not reasonable, he or she may institute a rate court proceeding. Under ordinary circumstances, the availability of this proceeding will shield the organizations from antitrust violations.[1112] In other words, licensees will have to ask the rate court to set a reasonable fee instead of suing ASCAP or BMI for antitrust violations. Courts have construed the reasonableness standard uniformly for both ASCAP's and BMI's decrees[1113] as referring to the license fee which reflects the fair market value under (hypothetical)[1114] competitive conditions, i.e. "the price that a willing buyer and a willing seller would agree to in an arm's length transaction".[1115] In order to determine this price for the purposes of a specific case, courts have, in absence of an actual competitive market, relied on appropriate benchmarks.[1116] For this purpose, prior licensing agreements can be relied upon, provided that they are comparable to the dispute in question. Comparability must be established in relation to i) the involved negotiating parties, ii) the rights at issue, iii) the economic circumstances affecting the negotiations as well as iv) the degree of competition in the market in which the agreement that shall serve as a benchmark was concluded.[1117] The latter point is vital because it accounts for the typically great market power of CMOs: If a CMO uses its power to impose high license fees, this agreement will not constitute a useful benchmark because it is precisely the purpose of the Consent Decrees to protect users against the CMOs' market power.[1118]

1111 ASCAP Consent Decree § IX(A); BMI Consent Decree § XIV(A).

1112 *ASCAP (Application of Capital Cities/ABC, Inc.)*, 831 F. Supp. 137 at 154 (citing *Buffalo Broadcasting*, 744 F. 2d 917).

1113 *See, e.g., United States v. BMI*, 426 F. 3d 91 at 95 (applying a standard from a case centering ASCAP to BMI). *See also BMI (Application of Music Choice, Inc.)*, 316 F. 3d 189 at 194 ("We see no reason why our approach to this case should differ from any of the numerous occasions on which we have reviewed rate court decisions pursuant to the ASCAP consent decree").

1114 *See* on this point *In Re Pandora*, 6 F. Supp. 3d 317 at 353–354.

1115 *BMI v. DMX Inc.*, 683 F. 3d 32 at 45; *United States v. BMI*, 426 F. 3d 91 at 95; *Showtime/Movie Channel*, 912 F. 2d 563 at 569.

1116 *See* for a critical opinion on this method Crane, *Rate-Setting Courts*, *supra* at 315–316. It can be observed that most of the litigation revolves around the question what constitutes the appropriate benchmark rather than questioning whether this is the right approach in the first place; however, it is difficult to find viable alternative within the current framework.

1117 *BMI v. Pandora 2015*, 140 F. Supp. 3d 267 at 270–271; *BMI v. DMX Inc.*, 683 F. 3d 32 at 45; *United States v. BMI*, 426 F. 3d 91 at 95.

1118 *ASCAP (Application of Muzak)*, 309 F. Supp. 2d 566 at 578; *Showtime/Movie Channel*, 912 F. 2d 563 at 570.

While some benchmarks are applicable in the long run, they may also change rather rapidly. This is reflected by the *Pandora* cases, where the BMI rate court found that the benchmark relied on by the ASCAP rate court no longer applied due to a "far more extensive" record, although not even two years had passed since the former judgment.[1119] Finding appropriate benchmarks will be an especially difficult task if no comparable historic agreements exist due to the technological development[1120] or if the established benchmarks stem from different contexts.[1121] Courts will generally not adopt a fee structure which is likely to lead to further disputes between CMOs and users.[1122] In any event, a license rate must be both substantively reasonable (factual findings) and procedurally reasonable (legal conclusions).[1123] Moreover, the Consent Decrees and statutory law sometimes provide guidelines on whether certain benchmarks can be relied upon.[1124]

The reasonable fee standard has been applied to blanket licenses as well as to other license types. The fee aspect of the blanket license should, however, be distinguished from the underlying question of whether a blanket license (covering the entire repertoire for a fee independent from actual use) is permissible as such, since this question is, for the time being, (still) governed by *BMI v. CBS*.[1125] Conversely, other judgments control when determining the reasonable fees that amount to the application of the blanket license to an individual licensee. This aspect can, in turn, be subdivided into the calculation methods and the final rate which is applied; even though these elements are conceptually different, they are clearly and strongly intertwined.[1126]

1119 *BMI v. Pandora 2015*, 140 F. Supp. 3d 267 at 290, referring to the rate court's decision in the *Pandora* litigation in respect of ASCAP which was affirmed a couple of days before its own ruling, *see Pandora v. ASCAP 2015*, 785 F. 3d 73. *See also* Lunney, *The United States Experience*, *supra* at 361.

1120 *ASCAP (Application of AOL)*, 559 F. Supp. 2d 332 at 400 ("In this novel proceeding, there are no perfect comparables. [...] This unprecedented capability to make millions of songs available to the entire nation all at once far outstrips the music distribution capabilities of all other, passive media such as radio or television").

1121 *See, e.g., ASCAP (Application of Salem Media of California)*, 981 F. Supp. 199 at 215–216 (refusing to apply a benchmark developed for the television industry to the radio industry).

1122 *See, e.g., ASCAP (Application of AOL)*, 559 F. Supp. 2d 332 at 490.

1123 *Pandora v. ASCAP 2015*, 785 F. 3d 73 at 78; *United States v. BMI*, 426 F. 3d 91 at 96.

1124 *See, e.g.,* 17 U.S.C. § 114(i) (licensee fees for the public performance of sound recordings may not be taken into account); ASCAP Consent Decree § IX(C) (no benchmark for fee negotiations during the first five years ASCAP licenses music in that industry). U.S. law furthermore provides for special rules for the determination of reasonable fees for "individual proprietors" *see* 17 U.S.C. § 513. *See* for more details 2 Nimmer on Copyright, *supra* at § 8.19[C][2]. *See also* CMD art. 16(2).

1125 *See* section 3.2.2. above.

1126 *Cf. also BMI (Application of AEI Music Network)*, 275 F. 3d 168 at 176–177 (distinguishing calculation of fee under blanket license from the definition of the license type); *ASCAP (In re Capital Cities/ABC)*, 157 F.R.D. 173 at 198 ("We reject ASCAP's attempt to have us look only to fee-setting methodology while ignoring the actual dollar figure that results

The ASCAP Consent Decree furthermore provides that ASCAP shall "avoid any discrimination among the various types of licenses offered to any group of similarly situated music users [...] that would deprive those music users of a genuine choice [...]" between those licenses.[1127] This provision ensures that the licenses offered by ASCAP remain economically reasonable options so that the organization cannot compel users into accepting a particular type of license by overpricing another.[1128] Thus, it primarily relates to the calculation of the license fees. This makes sense especially in connection with per-program and per-segment license, as they differ from the blanket license solely with respect to their rate construction.[1129] The BMI Consent Decree does not contain a comparable rule so that the application of these principles to BMI is not entirely clear. However, the Second Circuit has held that as regards the fee calculation, the ASCAP and BMI decrees are nearly identical.[1130] Moreover, as mentioned before, a rate policy which renders infeasible license types other than the blanket license will trigger scrutiny under the Sherman Act.[1131]

b) Calculation Methods

Calculation methods define the general formulas and parameters which are used to determine the licensee fee. The first question which arose in this respect under EU law was of a very fundamental nature and centered around the question of whether a CMO was permitted to claim license fees based on rights which were provided for in one member state, but not in others. In *Basset v. SACEM,*[1132] the ECJ dealt with this question in light of the free movement of goods and the prohibition of the abuse of a dominant position. French law provided for a "supplementary mechanical reproduction fee" which was payable in addition to a general performance fee if the works were used in public; in most other member states, the right to claim such a supplementary fee was not available at that time.[1133] SACEM charged this fee with respect to sound re-

therefrom. Section IX of the Consent Decree imposes upon us the duty to set a reasonable fee, and any approach that completely ignores the actual fee burden resulting from a particular formula fails properly to consider the reasonableness of the fee itself").

1127 ASCAP Consent Decree § VIII(A).

1128 *ASCAP (Application of Muzak)*, 309 F. Supp. 2d 566 at 580. *See also ASCAP (Application of Salem Media of California)*, 981 F. Supp. 199 at 217–218 (finding that ASCAP's proposed fees are in line with the genuine choice provision).

1129 A special rule for per-program and per-segment licenses is contained in § VIII (B), *see* immediately below.

1130 *ASCAP (Application of Muzak)*, 309 F. Supp. 2d 566 at 580–581.

1131 *See, e.g., Meredith*, 1 F. Supp. 3d 180 at 214–216 (citing an expert's statement that SESAC changed its calculation formula for its per-program license in order to make this license type commercially infeasible).

1132 *Basset*, 402/85.

1133 *G. Basset v. Societé Des Auteurs, Compositeurs Et Èditeurs De Musique*, case 402/85 (ECJ 1987), Opinion of AG Lenz, ¶ 3–4. The rationale behind this construction was that the right to reproduction was licensed to manufacturers of sound recordings only in respect of the cordings that were lawfully marketed in another member state in which there was no such fee, and for this reason, the national court worried about possible conflicts with EU law. However, the ECJ did not find an infringement of the free movement of goods. The court considered it to be a normal exploitation of copyright for a CMO to avail itself of the possibilities offered by the national law; thus, such a practice could not be regarded as a measure having an equivalent effect.[1134] As regards article 102, the answer is in fact rather straightforward. The AG pointed out that SACEM treated nationals of other member states and French citizens equally, that no effect on trade could be observed, and that the exercise of the right to claim a supplementary fee did not concern SACEM's dominant position since every right holder was entitled to such remuneration under French law.[1135] Accordingly, the ECJ ruled that SACEM's conduct did not conflict with the aims of article 102.[1136]

The *Basset* case shows that CMOs may rely on the possibilities provided for by national law; however, this does not mean that abusive conduct is impossible within these limits. Although the *GEMA I* case is mainly known in connection with right holders, it also offers some insights on the relationship between CMOs and users. Two practices which affected users[1137] in connection with the calculation method of fees were objected to by the Commission. On the one hand, GEMA applied the full fee to sound recordings, even if not all musical works embodied in these sound recordings were covered by its repertoire;[1138] on the other hand, it put at a disadvantage parallel imports from other member states.[1139] The Commission stated that, in calculating license fees, a CMO must distinguish between products (like sound recordings) where the content is entirely comprised by a CMO's repertoire and where the licensed content only represents a part of the product; otherwise, a CMO would expand copyright to non-protected material, which amounted to an abuse of a dominant position.[1140] It was furthermore held to constitute an abuse to discriminate against parallel imports (in this case: discrimination between manufacturers

---

private use of these recordings; if a user wanted to play the music embodied in the sound recording in public, he or she was required to pay for i) the performance and ii) the reproduction for public uses which had not been covered by the fee charged to the manufacturer, *see Basset,* 402/85 at ¶ 8.

1134 *Basset,* 402/85 at ¶ 16.

1135 *Basset,* 402/85, Opinion of AG Lenz at ¶ 36–39.

1136 *Basset,* 402/85 at ¶ 21.

1137 Users in this context must be understood in a broader sense, also encompassing importers and manufacturers of sound recordings, since these groups also require a license for their activities and thus make use of protected works.

1138 *GEMA I,* IV/26 760 at ¶ I(B)(1)(a). If the length of the sound recording was covered by GEMA's repertoire only by less than a third, it applied a third of the full fee, *see id.* at ¶ I(B)(1)(b).

1139 *Id.* at ¶ I(B)(2).

1140 *Id.* at ¶ II(C)(4).

and importers) within the Internal Market by the calculation methods.[1141] It is important to highlight the differences between the *Tournier* case and the situation in *GEMA I*: While in both cases, CMOs offered something that could be called a global license, GEMA applied it in respect of a product, whereas SACEM used in respect of its repertoire. Consequently, SACEM did not expand copyright to non-protected works. Moreover, it should be noted that GEMA's practices were objected to as such; expanding copyright beyond its limits and discrimination in respect of the cross-border trade within the Internal Market thus constitutes an infringement of article 102.

In order to show that fees are compatible with EU law, it is important, as stated above, to establish a reasonable relation between the licensee fee and the economic value of using the licensed rights and the services provided. It is, therefore, necessary to examine how license schemes implemented by CMOs can satisfy these requirements. In *Coditel*, the ECJ ruled that it was legitimate to use the "actual or probable number" of performances as a basis for the calculation of license fees.[1142] It is apparent that such a method brings the license fee close to the importance of the licensed works to the user, which in turn is linked to its economic value. However, for different reasons, CMOs have not always relied on this exact method of calculation. In *Tournier*, the schemes implemented by SACEM linked the royalty rates to the gross turnover of the users (discotheques) by applying a certain percentage to all incomes generated by the establishment – including entry charges, sales of drinks, etc.[1143] It is plausible to consider whether this question is lawful because it focuses on the user's ability to pay rather than on the actual use of the licensed works.[1144] The AG proposed simply applying the general test developed in the context of blanket licenses for this purpose.[1145] The ECJ accepted this approach and ruled that such a license scheme would only constitute an abuse of a dominant position if other calculation methods were capable of fully safeguarding the right holders' interest without thereby increasing the management costs.[1146] The

1141 *Id.* at ¶ II(C)(5). While the Commission permitted GEMA to charge the differences between the license fee in Germany and other member states, this practice was later declared incompatible with the principle of (Union-wide) exhaustion, *see* Drexl, *Competition and Development*, *supra* at 254.

1142 *Coditel v. Ciné Vog Films*, case 62/79, ¶ 13 (ECJ 1980). It should however be noted that the decision concerned the freedom to provide services and did not specifically involve CMOs. *See also Tournier,* 395/87, Opinion of AG Jacobs at ¶ 12; *Kanal 5,* C-52/07, Opinion of AG Trstenjak at ¶ 28. In *GEMA III*, the Commission noted that GEMA applied a flat fee to performance and broadcasting rights (depending on the exact kind of use and its duration) and a fee based on the number of sold copies to mechanical rights, *see GEMA III*, IV/29-971 at ¶ 9–10.

1143 *Tournier,* 395/87, Opinion of AG Jacobs at ¶ 11.

1144 *Id.* at ¶ 55.

1145 *Id.* at ¶ 56.

1146 *Tournier*, 395/87 at ¶ 45. In the *Basset* case, the ECJ similarly upheld the licensing method, *see Basset,* 402/85 at ¶ 15–16. *See also Kanal 5,* C-52/07 at ¶ 32.

Tournier case does not go beyond these brief references to the methods for the calculation of license fees. However, this issue later became the central question in the *Kanal 5* case. STIM, a Swedish CMO for the management of musical rights, applied three different types of tariffs to television channels. i) Under the *principal tariff*, a variable percentage (based on the amount of time that music was broadcast within a year) of the channels' income arising from advertising or subscription revenues determined the payable amount. The amount of time of the music broadcasts was calculated retroactively by reports submitted by the users and certain deductions applied. ii) Under the *minimum tariff*, applicable to smaller channels with a low turnover, the license fee was calculated on the basis of the amount of time music was broadcast within a year as well as the actual number of viewers per day. iii) A *special tariff* applied to SVT, a publicly financed broadcasting company operating in Sweden, which took into account notional advertising revenues and the amount of time music was broadcast within a year; this amount, however, was calculated in advance.[1147] Kanal 5 and TV 4, private television broadcasters, were required to pay their fees according to the principle tariff and entered into a proceeding against STIM, which was considered by the ECJ by way of a reference for a preliminary ruling. Kanal 5 asserted that the principle tariff constituted an abuse of STIM's dominant position and that the different treatment of a public TV channel like SVT amounted to a discriminatory practice.[1148] In determining whether STIM's calculation models fulfilled the requirements of the reasonable relation test, *AG Trstenjak*, in a general manner, considered calculation schemes which incorporated a fixed proportion of a TV station's gross income and concluded that these would not be compatible with article 102 because they would result in "substantial disparities" between the economic value of the benefit conferred by CMOs and the license fee.[1149] Conversely, a variable royalty rate designed as a percentage of the turnover was regarded as lawful, provided that it took the extent of using the CMO's repertoire sufficiently into account.[1150] In applying these thoughts, the AG's opinion can be interpreted, in principle and with reservations, as deeming STIM's principal tariff to be in line with the EU competition rules because it relied on a variable percentage to calculate the fees; however, should there be a disproportion between the fee and the benefits of the license, abusive conduct could be found, provided that there was an alternative calculation method that more accurately quantified the use of the protected works, without thereby leading to inefficiencies.[1151] The ECJ

1147 *Kanal 5,* C-52/07, Opinion of AG Trstenjak at ¶ 9.

1148 *Id.* at ¶ 14–16.

1149 *Id.* at ¶ 54.

1150 *Id.* at ¶ 67, 64. Whether this was the case was a matter of fact and therefore a question for the national court, *see id.* at ¶ 72–76.

1151 *Id.* at ¶ 101, 116. For a conclusive answer, an array of further questions had to be answered for which national courts were competent in proceedings relating to preliminary rulings. First of all, the AG stated that whether STIM's tariff system took sufficient account of the use of did not deal expressly with the underlying in-depth analysis of the AG. The court upheld its ruling in *Basset* and *Tournier* and stated that a license fee that was calculated as a percentage of a user's gross turnover was to be considered as a normal exploitation of copyright and thus did not constitute an abusive behavior as such;[1152] thus, STIM's calculation method was reasonable in principle in relation to the economic value of the services provided.[1153] This would only be different if there was another method which could more accurately identify and quantify the use and the number of viewers and which could safeguard the interests of right holders without thereby disproportionally increasing the costs of management.[1154]

Several points of the ruling deserve special mention. At the first glance, the court did not attach great importance to the differences between the different categories of users. In turn, the AG had doubts whether the *Basset* judgment, in which the ECJ did not regard a calculation method based on a fixed percentage as an abuse, was fully applicable to the case. She considered TV stations to be in a position different to that of discotheques because the latter group was assumed to make far more extensive use of the licensed music than the former, thus being dependent from the CMO's repertoire to a greater extent.[1155] This concern is supported by the *Tournier* case, since there, the ECJ developed the adapted *BRT v. SABAM* test in light of a non-uniform concept of users (*see* above). The ECJ, on the one hand, expressly deemed the "discotheque cases"[1156] – *Basset*, *Tournier* (and *Lucazeau*) – applicable to the circumstances in *Kanal 5*. On the other hand, however, the court was careful to tailor its judgment precisely to television channels, whereas the language of the discotheque cases was of a more general nature.[1157] More importantly, in its assessment of whether the implemented methods bore a reasonable relation to the value of the service provided, it is obvious that it was not irrelevant for the court that STIM calculated the fees according to the actual amount of time during which the music was used.[1158] Thus, the *Kanal 5* ruling is different from the judgment

the licensed work was a question of fact, *see id.* at ¶ 72. The main factors for this analysis were considered to be i) possible variations of advertising and subscription revenues according to program and broadcast time (¶ 81–86) and ii) the direct and indirect consideration of the actual or potential viewing figures (¶ 87–94). Furthermore, it could be assessed whether an increase of the TV station's revenue was due to the use of protected works or other reasons; this would however not lead to an abuse by itself (¶ 95–100, 103).

1152 *Kanal 5,* C-52/07 at ¶ 32–34.

1153 *Id.* at ¶ 37.

1154 *Id.* at ¶ 40.

1155 *Kanal 5,* C-52/07, Opinion of AG Trstenjak at ¶ 28, 52. The underlying rationale of this line of argumentation is that for this reason, the use of the licensed music would also be reflected appropriately by a fixed rate, *see id.* at ¶ 53; *see* however *id.* at ¶ 100. *See also id.* at ¶ 64 (deeming the approach taken in *Basset* applicable).

1156 *Id.* at ¶ 28.

1157 *Tournier*, 395/87 at ¶ 45; *Basset,* 402/85 at ¶ 16–18.

1158 *Kanal 5,* C-52/07 at ¶ 39.

in *Basset* if the latter is construed as permitting the application of a fixed rate to discotheques[1159] since the opinion in *Kanal 5* is based on STIM's variable royalty rate. The logical consequence of this reading of the decisions, in order to preserve the consistency in the case law, is that the assessment of whether a calculation method applied by a CMOs constitutes an abuse of a dominant position varies from category to category of users, namely between discotheques and television channels; for the former, a fixed rate would be lawful, for latter (only) a variable rate.[1160] It must, however, be kept in mind that the ECJ proactively included a safety valve since the "emergence" of new calculation methods can render traditional ones abusive.

It should be noted that the ECJ, as stated above, expressly referred to the protection of the right holders' interest but did not include such language into the normative part of the decision; however, it alluded to the management and monitoring costs[1161] as already known from the *Tournier* case.[1162] In this respect, the court included an important modification to its approach taken in that ruling, which is presumably attributable to the AG's opinion. The AG pointed out that efficiency gains may justify the application of a calculation method, even if there existed another method for more accurately determining the amount of use of protected works, but which was more complex to implement.[1163] Yet, such efficiency gains had to be put in relation to the inherent loss of accuracy of the less costly method, so that the latter could even amount to an abuse of a dominant position if the use of the licensed works could only be determined with great uncertainties. Thus, a calculation method, under appropriate circumstances, could very well constitute the only lawful alternative, even though it would be more expensive than a more generalized method.[1164] It seems that the ECJ included this thought by the expression "disproportionate increase" of costs in its decision to meet the arguments raised by the AG. Since this word does not appear in the *Tournier* ruling, one can say that the

1159 *Kanal 5,* C-52/07, Opinion of AG Trstenjak at ¶ 51.

1160 The ECJ ruled that the royalty schemes applied to a television channel must be "proportionate overall to the quantity of musical works protected by copyright actually or likely to be broadcast" if the royalty is based on the revenue of this channel, *see Kanal 5,* C-52/07 at ¶ 41. It is submitted that, in a business like discotheques, where extensive use of licensed music is made, a fixed rate might be considered as "proportionate" from the outset (without prejudice to the level of the fee), so that the difference between fixed and variable royalty rates and the *Basset* and *Kanal 5* rulings is diminished. A similar allegation could be made when referring to music channels which mainly broadcast music (videos).

1161 It ruled that in order for the calculation method to be lawful, there must not exist another method which "enables the use of those works and the audience to be identified more precisely without however resulting in a disproportionate increase in the costs incurred for management of contracts and the supervision of the use of those works", *see Kanal 5,* C-52/07 at ¶ 41.

1162 *Tournier*, 395/87 at ¶ 45.

1163 *Kanal 5,* C-52/07, Opinion of AG Trstenjak at ¶ 76.

1164 *Id.* at ¶ 77.

court adapted (or, at least clarified) the test spelled out in that case. Hence, after *Kanal 5*, efficiency gains must be dealt with by a proportionality test and not a mere ban on the increase of the administrative costs.[1165]

A core issue of the reasonable relation test concerns the questions of what exactly the license schemes should be compared to. In her opinion in *Kanal 5*, AG Trstenjak referred to the "benefit" provided by a CMO for this purpose. This benefit, on an abstract level, consists of the granting of a license to use the repertoire represented by a CMO.[1166] In other words, the transactions costs are lowered significantly (for users and right holders alike) by the services of a CMO.[1167] The case law, as well as the Collective Management Directive, stipulates that a tariff applied by a CMO must be reasonable in relation to the economic value i) of the use of the rights in trade and ii) of the services provided by CMOs.[1168] These are two different concepts. The AG's understanding of the benefit provided by CMOs must refer the second point because it does not refer to the use of the licensed rights but to the services that facilitate the access to them. However, the other factor must also be accounted for. It is true that users like television channels benefit from the services of CMOs by getting access to entire repertoire and not just individual works; however, this alone is not the reason why they use protected works in the first place. Copyrighted works like songs are used as a means to generate a greater income for the channels by attracting a greater audience, be it through subscriptions or advertising revenues.[1169] In principle, TV stations could also achieve this result by negotiating individual licenses with the respective right holders. This is where the value of the service that is specific to the field of collective management comes into play. Conversely, the value of the use of protected works in trade is not specific to collective management and could also be ascertained in the cases where rights are individually licensed. The ECJ does not draw a clear distinction between these aspects of the economic value concept:

> Furthermore, those royalties, which represent the consideration paid for the use of musical works protected by copyright for the purposes of television broadcast, must, in particular, be analysed with respect to the value of that use in trade.
>
> In that connection, in so far as such royalties are calculated on the basis of the revenue of the television broadcasting societies, they are, in principle, reasonable in relation to the economic value of the service provided by STIM.[1170]

Thus, because a royalty scheme must be analyzed in light of the value of the use of the licensed works in trade, STIM's licensing model is reasonable in relation to the value of the services provided because it is calculated on the

[1165] The difference between calculation methods and the level of royalties does not, in my view, contradict this principle.

[1166] *Kanal 5,* C-52/07, Opinion of AG Trstenjak at ¶ 40.

[1167] *Id.* at ¶ 41–42.

[1168] *Kanal 5,* C-52/07 at ¶ 29, 36; CMD art. 16(2).

[1169] *Kanal 5,* C-52/07, Opinion of AG Trstenjak at ¶ 44.

[1170] *Kanal 5,* C-52/07 at ¶ 36–37.

basis of the revenues of the TV stations. Such reasoning is not fully coherent because the revenues in music-based businesses primarily reflect the economic value of the protected content. A proper understanding of the judgment might be the following: The economic value of the use of the works in trade is primarily reflected by the "nature and scope"[1171] of the use that is made of them;[1172] in *Kanal 5*, the ECJ deemed a calculation method compatible with this principle because it took into account the number of works "actually broadcast" by applying a variable percentage rate to the channel's revenue base.[1173] In turn, the economic value of the service provided by a CMO corresponds to the efficiency gains and costs savings achieved by collective licensing the rights in question.[1174] At least, under the Collective Management Directive, it is necessary to conduct an analysis in respect of both aspects of the economic value concept; furthermore, additional factors may be referred to for this purpose.[1175]

In the United States, on account of the structure of the Consent Decrees and the principles set forth in *Shenandoah*,[1176] courts have predominantly ruled on the fees due for blanket licenses,[1177] per-program, and per-segment licenses. The fee charged for a blanket license has traditionally been derived from a per-

1171 CMD art. 16(2).

1172 *Coditel*, 62/79 at ¶ 12; *Tournier*, 395/87 at ¶ 12; *Kanal 5*, C-52/07 at ¶ 38. *See also*, possibly to this effect, *Kanal 5*, C-52/07, Opinion of AG Trstenjak at ¶ 110. *See also Stichting ter Exploitatie van Naburige Rechten v. Nederlandse Omroep Stichtig*, C-245/00, ¶ 37 (ECJ 2003) (referring to the value of the use in trade in the context of "equitable remuneration", *see* section 3.2.5. below); *IFPI Simulcasting*, COMP/C2/38.014 at ¶ 114. Factors for this analysis could include, for instance, the audience reached or language versions applied, *see* van Gompel, *Directive*, *supra* at 594.

1173 *Kanal 5*, C-52/07 at ¶ 39.

1174 *Kanal 5*, C-52/07, Opinion of AG Trstenjak at ¶ 40–42. It is noteworthy that this precise circumstance might simultaneously lead to higher license fees for users because, as a collective, the bargaining power will be greater, as especially reflected by the U.S. case law dealing with CMOs. However, this should not affect the analysis: Responding to this dominant position, CMOs must not abuse this position under competition rules and are subject to the special regulation of the CMD, which orders them to conduct licensing negotiations in good faith. The collective can therefore be seen to establish a balance, rather than destroying it, because the interests of right holders can better be safeguarded in this way. In the U.S. *DMX* litigation, DMX argued that its fee proposal comprised "a fee for the rights to perform the works in BMI's repertoire, and a fee to compensate BMI for the value it provides by assembling its repertoire and the benefits its blanket coverage gives to DMX", *see Broadcast Music, Inc. v. DMX, Inc.*, 726 F. Supp. 2d 355 at 357 (S.D.N.Y. 2010), *aff'd*, 683 F. 3d 32 (2nd Cir. 2012). The district court followed DMX's approach, *see id.* at 367. The Second Circuit affirmed, *see BMI v. DMX Inc.*, 683 F. 3d 32 at 48–49. *See* on this case Turk, *Hard Day's Night*, *supra* at 517–518. *See also ASCAP (Application of Capital Cities/ABC, Inc.)*, 831 F. Supp. 137 at 162.

1175 CMD art. 16(2) ("*inter alia*"). For example, reference can be made to recitals 9–12 of the Copyright Directive, *see* 2 Walter, *Verwertungsgesellschaftenrecht*, *supra* at 264.

1176 *ASCAP (Application of Shenandoah)*, 331 F. 2d 117. *See* section 3.2.1.c) above.

1177 Even though the BMI Consent Decree does not specifically mention blanket licenses, they fall within the scope of its § XIV, *see BMI (Application of AEI Music Network)*, 275 F. 3d 168 at 175–177.

centage of the licensee's total revenues or expressed as a flat dollar amount.[1178] Courts have also dealt with different calculation approaches, like, for instance, a fee based on the user's total entertainment expense[1179] or the number of his or her establishments which use the music belonging to a CMO's repertoire.[1180] In this connection, the relation between the accuracy of the methods and the related administration costs can be taken into account.[1181]

The principle that no further adjustments apply to the blanket license fee was challenged in *United States v. BMI*.[1182] There, users complained that the fee for BMI's blanket license did not take into account works directly licensed by its members, a right guaranteed by the Consent Decrees.[1183] The Second Circuit agreed and held that the fee reductions ("carve-outs") for works licensed directly (or under the "per piece" license)[1184] did not constitute a new type of license, but are merely a blanket license with a modified fee calculation.[1185] Accordingly, BMI was bound by its consent decree to quote a reasonable fee for a blanket license with a corresponding fee structure.[1186] The principles set forth in this case are also applicable to the ASCAP Consent Decree[1187] and have been proven relevant for SESAC, too.[1188] A blanket license

1178 *BMI v. CBS*, 441 U.S. 1 at 5. *See also Buffalo Broadcasting*, 744 F. 2d 917 at 922; Korman, *U.S. Position, supra* at 162. *See also BMI v. Pandora 2015*, 140 F. Supp. 3d 267 at 294, where the fee was expressed as a percentage of the licensee's revenues. *See* for the advantages of this method *ASCAP (Application of AOL)*, 559 F. Supp. 2d 332 at 397–398; *ASCAP (Application of Capital Cities/ABC, Inc.)*, 831 F. Supp. 137 at 158. A flat fee as such is generally permissible, *see BMI v. CBS*, 441 U.S. 1 at 8 n. 13.

1179 *Moor-Law*, 527 F. Supp. 758 at 772–773 (rejecting copyright misuse claims due to the convenience of the method).

1180 *BMI (Application of AEI Music Network)*, 275 F. 3d 168 at 172, 176 (holding that the rate court proceedings applies also to licenses with a different fee structure). *See also BMI v. DMX Inc.*, 683 F. 3d 32.

1181 *See also United States v. American Society of Composers, Authors and Publishers (Application RealNetworks and Yahoo, Inc.)*, 627 F. 3d 64 at 78 n. 13 (2nd Cir. 2010) ("One reason a district court may use a less precise metric is because it is impracticable to use a more precise one, for example if relevant statistics are unobtainable or unreliable", referring to prior case law).

1182 *BMI (Application of AEI Music Network)*, 275 F. 3d 168.

1183 *Id.* at 173.

1184 BMI Consent Decree § XI(C).

1185 *BMI (Application of AEI Music Network)*, 275 F. 3d 168 at 176–177. However, carve-out provisions existed already before, *see, e.g., Buffalo Broadcasting*, 744 F. 2d 917 at 922, 930 n. 10.

1186 *BMI (Application of AEI Music Network)*, 275 F. 3d 168 at 177.

1187 *ASCAP (Application of Muzak)*, 309 F. Supp. 2d 566 at 578–581. *See also* Lunney, *The United States Experience, supra* at 343 (criticizing the court's clarification that the ruling would only apply to future license agreements). The deductions on the users' side are mirrored by § XI(B)(1) of the ASCAP Consent Decree, stating that "works licensed by the member directly" are not taken into account in the distribution process.

1188 *Radio Music License Comm.*, 29 F. Supp. 3d 487 at 493, 498–499, 501–502 (rejecting claims under section 1 of the Sherman Act but upholding claims under section 2 (partly) for "discouraging direct licensing by refusing to offer carve-out rights").

combined with "carve out" provisions is nowadays also known as an "adjustable fee blanket license" (AFBL).[1189] The underlying rationale is perhaps that a calculation method should not result in a user becoming obliged to make double payments for the same works and discouraging of direct licensing.[1190] In situations where the fee is based on a percentage of the licensee's gross revenues, one should generally take into account the value of the licensed right which is reflected by the licensee's actual music use.[1191] For this reason, in *Capital Cities*, the court ordered to adjust the licensee fee to reflect changes in average revenue and average music use.[1192] This logic was later applied to internet companies by the Second Circuit.[1193]

Different benchmarks have been used in order to calculate "reasonable" license fees for blanket licenses. Already before a "rate court" was installed for BMI, a court refused to consider an agreement as a benchmark because it was concluded "in a materially different market".[1194] More recently, in *BMI v. DMX*,[1195] the rate court set a license fee for an AFBL which relied on direct licensing agreements as benchmarks and included a floor fee independent of the actual use of the works in BMI's repertoire which were also directly licensed; the maximum fee ("blanket fee") is reduced according to the works

---

1189 *BMI v. DMX Inc.*, 683 F. 3d 32 at 39–40 (citing the district court). *See also Meredith*, 1 F. Supp. 3d 180 at 191 n. 8.

1190 *Cf. BMI v. DMX Inc.*, 683 F. 3d 32 at 46, 48–49. *See also* Lunney, *The United States Experience*, *supra* at 343 n. 148. *See also* in connection with the TTTA license *MOBITV*, 681 F.3d 76 at 88 ("If an upstream content provider has already acquired a TTTA license from ASCAP, it would be unfair to require Mobi to make a second payment for the same content").

1191 *ASCAP (Application RealNetworks and Yahoo, Inc.)*, 627 F. 3d 64 at 76; *ASCAP (Application of Capital Cities/ABC, Inc.)*, 831 F. Supp. 137 at 156–158. It should be noted, however, that *Capital Cities* was decided in relation to TV networks; the analysis might differ for users which depend on music to a greater extent, *see id.* at 158 n. 54. The court furthermore declined to rely on net profits rather than on gross revenues to construe the rate, *see id.* at 159 and rejected to make yearly changes according to audience reached or binding the fee to the consumer price index, *see id.* at 161–162. *See also ASCAP (In re Capital Cities/ABC)*, 157 F.R.D. 173 at 197–198 (reaffirming this view but allowing for modifications in the methodology, so long as the final license fee is reasonable).

1192 *ASCAP (Application of Capital Cities/ABC, Inc.)*, 831 F. Supp. 137 at 164–166. *See also ASCAP (In re Capital Cities/ABC)*, 157 F.R.D. 173 at 204–206. If the determination of the use is too burdensome, this might however alter the analysis, *see ASCAP (Application of Salem Media of California)*, 981 F. Supp. 199 at 219 ("Given the impracticality of ASCAP's current proposal, the court deems it appropriate to set an incidental use fee that is based on a fixed percentage of the applicant stations' adjusted gross revenues", ruling in the context of a PPL).

1193 *ASCAP (Application RealNetworks and Yahoo, Inc.)*, 627 F. 3d 64 at 76–80 (upholding the district court's rationale in lowering the revenue base to reflect amounts not attributable to the performance of music but rejecting the particular way of implementation).

1194 *Moor-Law*, 527 F. Supp. 758 at 771 (referring to hotel-motel owners as opposed to a radio station).

1195 *BMI v. DMX Inc.*, 683 F. 3d 32.

directly licensed.[1196] In *BMI v. Pandora*, the fee calculation followed similar principles and included a floor fee as well as the deductions.[1197] In both cases, the courts allowed BMI to take into account an administrative fee meant to compensate the organization for the increased administrative expenses of an AFBL over a traditional blanket license.[1198]

The ASCAP Consent Decree stipulates that any calculation of fees for the per-program and per-segment license shall approximate the fee for a blanket license.[1199] Thus, this provision reinforces the general principle that a user should have a "genuine choice" between the different types of licenses.[1200] ASCAP may express the license fee for a per-program license and for any per-segment license issued to an online user as a flat dollar amount or as a percentage of the music user's revenue attributable to each program (or segment) that contains ASCAP music not otherwise licensed.[1201] A comparable (but not identical) provision applies to BMI in relation to unlicensed broadcasters.[1202]

With respect to ASCAP's TTTA license, the ASCAP Consent Decree specifies that the license fee "shall take into account the value of all performances made pursuant to the license".[1203] Depending on the circumstances, the license fee can be derived especially from a percentage of the respective service's or

---

1196 *Id.* at 42–43, 47–49. The Second Circuit called the floor fee a recognition the CMOs' important services, both in relation to users and right holders, *see id.* at 48. *See also* Turk, *Hard Day's Night*, *supra* at 517.

1197 *BMI v. Pandora 2015*, 140 F. Supp. 3d 267 at 292–294 (also discussing discounts for publisher withdrawals and advertising costs).

1198 *Id.* at 293–294; *BMI v. DMX 2010*, 726 F. Supp. 2d 355 at 363. *See also* ASCAP Consent Decree § VII(B).

1199 ASCAP Consent Decree § VIII(B). The provision reads: "For a representative music user, the total license fee for a per-program or per-segment license shall, at the time the license fee is established, approximate the fee for a blanket license; for the purpose of making that approximation, it shall be assumed for the purposes of this Section VIII(B) that all of the music user's programs or segments that contain performances of ASCAP music are subject to an ASCAP fee." *See* on the background of this provision Lunney, *The United States Experience*, *supra* at 340–342. *See also* (prior to the AFJ2) *ASCAP (In re Capital Cities/ABC)*, 157 F.R.D. 173 at 202–203.

1200 AFJ2 Memo at 29–30. In *Meredith*, 1 F. Supp. 3d 180 at 190, the record showed that ASCAP's and BMI's per-program licenses were in principle genuine alternatives to blanket licenses. In *Capital Cities*, the court ruled differently in respect of ASCAP's licenses, *see ASCAP (In re Capital Cities/ABC)*, 157 F.R.D. 173 at 202–203.

1201 ASCAP Consent Decree § VII(D). *See* on the similar provision from the former version of the decree *ASCAP (In re Capital Cities/ABC)*, 157 F.R.D. 173 at 206–207. The per-program license refers to broadcasters, *see* ASCAP Consent Decree § II(J). ASCAP Consent Decree § IV(H), however, enjoins ASCAP from charging a percentage-of-total-revenue fee unless so requested, *see* AFJ2 Memo at 20.

1202 BMI Consent Decree § VIII(B).

1203 ASCAP Consent Decree § V.

product's retail price[1204] or from the wholesale revenues.[1205] In the recent *Pandora* litigation, the debated rates applied to the licensee's revenues.[1206]

c) Level of License Fees

It is a principle of the EU *Basset* case that a CMO may avail itself of the possibilities provided for by national law; however, an excessive level of the royalties charged could still amount to an imposition of unfair conditions, constituting an abuse of a dominant position, which is prohibited by article 102.[1207] The level of license fees is of course intertwined with the calculation methods applied by a CMO, but for two reasons, it is necessary to draw a distinction. First, the case law acknowledges this difference.[1208] Second, one must take into consideration the conceptual differences between the two parts of the tariff system. The mere fact that a calculation method (*e.g.*, based on the gross turnover of a user) is compatible with European competition law or the Collective Management Directive does not automatically mean that the level of fee is lawful (and *vice versa*). Moreover, one cannot always without special consideration apply the criteria used for the assessment of the level of a royalty to a calculation method.[1209]

There are several ways to examine whether a particular royalty rate is excessive. Following the ECJ's ruling in *United Brands*, the license fee would have to be compared to the production costs of the work.[1210] Since, as stated above, this is not possible, several proposals have been made in order to assess the level of license fees. Moreover, tests of different nature of been proposed.[1211] The following tests –which are conceptually comparable to the U.S. rate courts' "benchmark" approach to "reasonable" fees – were influenced by

---

1204 *United States v. BMI*, 426 F. 3d 91 at 97; *BMI (Application of Music Choice, Inc.)*, 316 F. 3d 189 at 195.

1205 *MOBITV,* 681 F.3d 76 at 85–88 (also distinguishing the case from the *Music Choice* litigation, *see* previous note). The wholesale revenue had two elements: First, the sum the cable television networks received from Mobi, the ASCAP licensee (which effectively equals Mobi's costs) and second, the sum that Mobi received from wireless carriers which distributed the content to end users, *see id.* at 83.

1206 *In Re Pandora*, 6 F. Supp. 3d 317 at 320. *See* for a critical view U.S. Copyright Office, *Music Marketplace*, *supra* at 153–155.

1207 *Basset,* 402/85 at ¶ 18–19. *See also Tournier,* 395/87, Opinion of AG Jacobs at ¶ 52.

1208 *See, e.g., Basset,* 402/85, Opinion of AG Lenz at ¶ 37; *Tournier,* 395/87, Opinion of AG Jacobs at ¶ 52.

1209 *Kanal 5,* C-52/07, Opinion of AG Trstenjak at ¶ 63.

1210 *United Brands,* 27/76 at ¶ 252.

1211 In the following, reference will only be made to the most important considerations presented in the *Tournier/Lucazeau* cases. A variety of other methods is conceivable, of course, but full consideration of all of these would go beyond the limits of this work. *See* for a discussion Lang, *Antitrust Law*, *supra* at 51–58. *See also Autortiesību un komunicēšanās konsultāciju aģentūra / Latvijas Autoru apvienība*, C-177/16, Opinion of AG Wahl at ¶ 19 (citing the case law of the ECJ).

a number of actors, like the parties of the *Tournier* case, national courts, the Commission, and the AG's opinion on the case:

Comparison with the royalty fees charged in other member states: The royalty rates in one member state are compared to the rates applied by different CMOs in one or more other member states. While this method gives some useful indications, it is hard to establish an objective basis for the comparison, especially due to the divergence of national copyright legislation and different calculation methods implemented by CMOs throughout the Union.[1212] An example of how hard this can be is contained in the *Tournier* case. In the course of the preparatory works for the proceeding, the Commission had prepared a study which suggested that SACEM's royalties were similar to those in Italy, but many times higher than in most other member states. However, the Commission's results were not fully accepted on the following main grounds: The study took no account of i) the divergences of national copyright laws, ii) the different calculation methods applied by CMOs (a circumstance which was admitted by the Commission itself), or iii) applicable rebates and/or additional fees, and that they contained iv) a major methodological error.[1213] Finally, the divergence of rates in other member states cannot be dealt with from the perspective of discrimination since a national CMO is not responsible for the tariffs in another member state.[1214]

Comparison with the royalty fees charged in relation to other categories of users: Users are grouped into categories (like discotheques, TV channels or radio stations), and the differences between the applicable rates are compared. One should also have regard to applicable rebates (in the *Tournier* case, most discotheque owners paid less than the actual fee) and whether there was an objective justification for a different treatment.[1215] It was also proposed to link the royalty rate to user categories grouped according to the importance of the licensed works for their respective business. However, the AG rejected this argument because he deemed the concept of importance inapplicable in the case of discotheques; these establishments were pincipally dependent on the CMOs' licenses since without the access to musical works they would have to stop their business.[1216] In this context, abusive conduct was found in *GEMA I*. GEMA applied higher rates (flowing from the German private copying levy) to the importers of recording devices than to German manufacturers of such devices. The Commission held this practice to be discriminatory and that it constituted an abuse of a dominant position.[1217]

1212 *Tournier,* 395/87, Opinion of AG Jacobs at ¶ 60.

1213 *Id.* at ¶ 61–62.

1214 *Id.* at ¶ 56.

1215 *Id.* at ¶ 57.

1216 *Id.* at ¶ 65. *See also* – however, in a different context – *Autortiesību un komunicēšanās konsultāciju aģentūra / Latvijas Autoru apvienība*, C-177/16 at ¶ 47–50.

1217 *GEMA I*, IV/26 760 at ¶ II(C)(6).

Comparison with the amounts distributed to right holders: The license fee charged and subsequently collected from a certain category of users is compared to the portion of this amount which is ultimately distributed to right holders.[1218] As a precondition for this appraisal, it is necessary i) to establish the amount of revenues flowing from a certain category of users and ii) to define the group of persons who benefit from the distribution of these revenues. With respect to the second point, the AG underlined that it would be misleading to solely refer to composers because especially in the case of musical works, there were usually numerous other persons (like publishers for instance) who were also entitled to remuneration.[1219] It can be said that this method strives to take into consideration the efficiency of collective management services offered by a CMO since, provided a stable flow of royalty rates, the amount available for distribution will be indirectly proportional to the management costs.[1220] This thought can be placed in context with the AG's adapted *United Brands* approach (*see* shortly below).

Comparison with the total costs incurred by the user: The costs of the access to a CMO's repertoire (the license fee) are compared to the overall expenses necessary for running the user's business (including labor, rental, and supply costs, etc.).[1221] SACEM argued that its royalty fee should be regarded as a reasonable proportion of these expenses. The AG rejected this argument because, for discotheques, even excessive prices would be reasonable to pay, given their strong dependence on SACEM's repertoire and the lack of any alternative providers.[1222] Moreover, as argued by the Commission, by this reasoning alone, SACEM could not justify differences in the treatment of user categories because this only indicated the internal coherence of the rates but not their lawfulness from an external perspective, given the possibility that they could all be excessive.[1223]

Comparison to the necessary costs of effective collective management: The cost structure of a particular CMO is analyzed in view of the overall income flowing from one user category and the management costs necessary for this task (consisting mainly of the costs of licensing, costs of collection, distribution, and monitoring costs). After having established what would constitute the justified costs for an efficient ("necessary") and effective administration scheme for the CMO in question, these costs are compared to the royalty rate

[1218] *Tournier,* 395/87, Opinion of AG Jacobs at ¶ 58.

[1219] *Id.* at ¶ 59.

[1220] The ECJ relied on this thought in a more recent decision, *see Autortiesību un komunicēšanās konsultāciju aģentūra / Latvijas Autoru apvienība*, C-177/16 at ¶ 58 (*see* below).

[1221] In *Tournier*, SACEM stated that it charged about 8,25% (less deductions) of the discotheque's gross turnover, amounting to roughly about 10% of their incurred costs, *Tournier,* 395/87, Opinion of AG Jacobs at ¶ 62, 66.

[1222] *Id.* at ¶ 66.

[1223] *Id.* at ¶ 67.

applicable to the respective user category, keeping in mind the need to ensure the reasonable remuneration of right holders.[1224] Since this test was developed on the basis of the ECJ's ruling in *United Brands*, this method can be referred to as an adapted *United Brands* approach.[1225] In essence, this method is a special variation of method three (*see* above) because it involves the amount due to right holders but from an overall perspective.[1226]

Comparison of the royalty rates applied to users of the same category: In case the royalty rates vary within a user category, the different rates can be compared in order to assess whether a CMO engages in abusive conduct. A reference under these circumstances is to article 102(c), as such practices may be regarded as the application of dissimilar conditions to equivalent transactions.[1227]

The AG favored methods two (other user categories) and five (necessary costs of effective management) and included method one (fees in other member states) as indicative of an abuse.[1228] Faced with all these options, the ECJ chose the first method in order to establish whether the level of a royalty fee constituted an abuse of a dominant position. The court ruled:

> *[…] Article 86 of the Treaty must be interpreted as meaning that a national copyright-management society holding a dominant position in a substantial part of the common market imposes unfair trading conditions where the royalties which it charges to discothèques are appreciably higher than those charged in other Member States, the rates being compared on a consistent basis. That would not be the case if the copyright-management society in question were able to justify such a difference by reference to objective and relevant dissimilarities between copyright management in the Member State concerned and copyright management in the other Member States.*[1229]

The ECJ emphasized, in line with the AG's opinion, that the comparison of the level of fees in different member states had to be conducted on a "consistent basis". Moreover, it stated that a CMO could justify possible differences in the applicable rates. The main criteria for whether such difference exists are whether the fees are "appreciably higher" than those in "other member states". Each of these elements raises specific questions.

First of all, it is not clear what the ECJ meant when it referred to the expression in "other member states". Should the fees be compared to all other member states or only some of them? What if the fees are (significantly) higher

1224 *Id.* at ¶ 69–72. The AG's opinion can be understood as casting doubts whether *SACEM* implemented an efficient management model.

1225 *Id.* at ¶ 68–69.

1226 *Id.* at ¶ 59.

1227 *Id.* at ¶ 57.

1228 *Id.* at ¶ 74.

1229 *Tournier*, 395/87 at ¶ 46; *Lucazeau,* 110/88 at ¶ 33. *See also* Steven Anderman & Hedvig Schmidt, *EU Competition Law and Intellectual Property Rights* 156–159 (2nd ed. 2011) (noting that the comparison by members states is an approach different to *United Brands* and calling the ECJ decisions a "harsh treatment" of CMOs).

than in one group of member states, but still lower than in another group?[1230] Furthermore, the notion "appreciably higher" leaves open considerable room for interpretation. The court did not specify whether the fees must be many times higher or whether smaller differences were sufficient to trigger the application of article 102;[1231] however, it seems that the rulings in *Tournier* and *Lucazeau* are only applicable in extreme cases in which the royalty rates are in fact many times higher than in other member states.[1232] Finally, it must be analyzed under what circumstances CMOs can rely on objective dissimilarities in order to justify the difference in the fee policy.[1233] Two important observations were made in this context: On the one hand, the dissimilarities must be "objective and relevant"; this means that the differences must be independent of the will of the CMO in question and that they must be proportional to the fees charged.[1234] On the other hand, the ECJ was rather strict in interpreting possible justifications, as it dismissed SACEM's argument that higher fees could be justified by French copyright legislation which, unlike most other member states, provided for a supplementary mechanical reproduction fee.[1235] However, the AG and the legal literature argued that the existence of an additional way of remunerating right holders must necessarily increase their incomes. Hence, such divergences in national copyright legislation should be, at least, regarded as an objective dissimilarity.[1236] For this question, it is necessary to refer to the purpose of the particular right provided for. As explained by the AG in the *Basset* case, manufacturers of sound recordings were charged the initial reproduction fee, but only in respect of private uses, and users who used the work publicly were charged the supplementary fee.[1237] Therefore, the public performance was not covered in the initial reproduction fee.[1238] In sum, both private and public uses were hence considered by the fee policy.[1239] If the fee had been charged to manufacturers for private *and* public uses in absence of a special supplementary fee, one could assume that the overall level of royalties would remain the same. As a consequence, given this assumption, the fees charged in respect of users like discotheques would have been lower. In this light, it is worth considering whether a special right provided for by national legislation leads to an overall increase in the royalty payments, or whether it simply splits up the obligation to pay a roughly stable amount of royalties

1230 Allendesalazar & Vallina, *The Usual Suspects*, *supra* at 376–378.

1231 *Id.* at 378–379.

1232 *Id.* at 379–380.

1233 The judgement can be interpreted as putting the burden of proof on CMOs, *see* Drijber, *Competition law aspects*, *supra* at 72–73.

1234 Allendesalazar & Vallina, *The Usual Suspects*, *supra* at 380.

1235 *Tournier*, 395/87 at ¶ 40; *Lucazeau,* 110/88 at ¶ 27.

1236 Allendesalazar & Vallina, *The Usual Suspects*, *supra* at 380–381; *Tournier,* 395/87, Opinion of AG Jacobs at ¶ 60.

1237 *Basset,* 402/85, Opinion of AG Lenz at ¶ 3–4.

1238 *Basset,* 402/85 at ¶ 8.

1239 It should however be noted that these fees concerned the right to reproduction.

among different (groups of) users. In the latter case, one should take into consideration that a particular group of users is likely to face higher fees than in member states where a corresponding right does not exist. It must also be kept in mind that the ECJ's understanding of the supplementary mechanical reproduction fee as "constituting part of the payment for an author's right over the public performance" caused the court to uphold the construction chosen by French legislation in relation to the free movements of goods.[1240] Thus, one must consider whether this conclusion would also be possible with a different conception of this fee. Last, it is noteworthy that the ECJ in Tournier rejected the argument that the different calculation methods and collection traditions could justify differences in the level of fees because SACEM implemented comparatively high monitoring procedures. The court stated that it could be "precisely the lack of competition" that caused high management costs and, consequently, a high level of fees.[1241]

The ECJ did not as such reject method two set forth above (comparison with the fees charged in relation to other user categories); it merely stated that the parties had not suggested a consistent basis for this purpose.[1242] Besides this reference, the judges did not allude to further methods of comparison. *Allendesalazar & Vallina* draw attention to the fact that the key element in the appraisal whether a royalty is unfair is the comparison of rates on a *consistent basis*. The ECJ merely favored the comparison with the rates charged in other member states because this was the only criterion where there was sufficient data available.[1243] Therefore, other criteria are consistent with the *Tournier* ruling as long as the rates in question are compared on a consistent basis.[1244] This is fully compatible with the Collective Management Directive. The standards for the tariffs are not exhaustive, so that there is no reason why other criteria could not be applied, provided objective and consistent foundations. In fact, the directive brings the necessary analysis closer to the adapted *United Brands* approach developed by the AG in *Tournier* because it relies directly on the question whether a price bears a reasonable relation to the economic value of the product (or service), simply adapting the former judgment to the needs of copyright.[1245] In turn, the "appreciably higher test" in principle gives an indica-

1240 *Basset,* 402/85 at ¶15–16.

1241 *Tournier*, 395/87 at ¶ 41–42; *Lucazeau,* 110/88 at ¶ 29–30. *See also Autortiesību un komunicēšanās konsultāciju aģentūra / Latvijas Autoru apvienība*, C-177/16 at ¶ 58.

1242 *Tournier*, 395/87 at ¶ 44; *Lucazeau,* 110/88 at ¶ 31. *See* for a critical account Wünschmann, *Kollektive Verwertung*, *supra* at 159–161.

1243 Allendesalazar & Vallina, *The Usual Suspects*, *supra* at 376.

1244 *Id.* The criteria for such analysis include whether the content and services offered are similar, whether the prices compared are from a similar time period, and whether the licensing agreement contain similar terms and conditions, *see* Kuik & Dawes, *Media*, *supra* at 1749.

1245 *Tournier,* 395/87, Opinion of AG Jacobs at ¶ 68–69. However, the level of administrative expenses is also a part of the comparison in the ECJ's judgment in *Tournier*, *see* Mestmäcker, *Collecting Societies*, *supra* at 359.

tion of whether a royalty rate is reasonable in relation to the rates charged in other member states. In this connection, the court did not reference the reasonable relation test developed in *United Brands*. Conversely, in *Kanal 5,* the ECJ largely relied on that judgment but in relation to calculation methods and not the level of fees; the "appreciably higher test" cannot be applied in these methods because it is purely relative. Of course, one can indirectly infer conclusions: If the rates are high in the majority of the member states, it is likely that the economic value of the use of the works in question is high too. In any event, whatever view is taken, divergences in the level of fees charged in different member states can influence the analysis due to the broad wording of the directive. It should not be forgotten, however, that it is one of the rationales of the *Kanal 5* case that CMOs can adapt royalties to the laws in the territory of operation.[1246] More recently, the ECJ stated in *OSA* that fees – compared on a consistent basis – that are appreciably higher than in other members are "indicative" of an abuse of a dominant position; such abuse could be found especially if the fee level was excessive in relation to the economic value of the service provided.[1247]

In 2016, a new case relating to the assessment of the CMOs' fee policy under article 102 TFEU was referred to the court. In his opinion, the AG favored – in principle – a combination of different methods in order to determine whether there exists an excess between the price actually charged and the (hypothetical) competitive price.[1248] As regards the collective management of copyrights, the AG considered the comparison between the rates charged in several member states as an appropriate method, provided, however, that i) the analysis is based on objective, appropriate and verifiable criteria and that ii) no other alternative methods (which could have been used in combination with the geographical comparison) are available.[1249] Moreover, he deemed the purchasing power parity index ("PPP index") a potentially useful instrument in carrying out the comparison.[1250] The AG went on to state that excessive prices conflicting with article 102 TFEU are only those which are significantly and persistently above the benchmark price.[1251] Finally, the AG confirmed that CMOs can, by reference to objective dissimilarities, justify high prices charged[1252] and that competition authorities may base fines imposed on CMOs on the total turnover of such organizations (which also includes the remunera-

1246 Morris, *Trading Functions, supra* at 570 (in connection with the system of reciprocal representation).

1247 *OSA*, C-351/12 at ¶ 87–88.

1248 *Autortiesību un komunicēšanās konsultāciju aģentūra / Latvijas Autoru apvienība*, C-177/16, Opinion of AG Wahl at ¶ 43–45.

1249 *Id.* at ¶ 56–81.

1250 *Id.* at ¶ 95.

1251 *Id.* at ¶ 100–113. The AG expressly mentioned the "appreciably higher" test, *see id.* at ¶ 107.

1252 *Id.* at ¶ 114–140.

tion paid to right holders).[1253] In its decision, the ECJ mainly confirmed the AG's opinion and reaffirmed its approach taken in *Tournier* and *Lucazeau*, stating that appreciably higher fees than in other member states could be indicative of an abuse of a dominant position if the analysis is carried out on a consistent basis.[1254] Furthermore, the court stressed that there is no minimum threshold above which a rate must be regarded as "appreciably higher".[1255] Interestingly, the court permitted to compare the level of fees and the amounts distributed to right holders in order to justify price differences, thereby taking into account the efficiency of the organization in question.[1256]

In the United States, the level of license fees or the exact rate (*e.g.*, applied to a revenue base) due in an individual case depends on methods of comparison, primarily on the benchmarks which the parties can convince the court to adopt, and therefore requires a case-by-case analysis. This is, however, a delicate task. Indeed, it has been observed that courts often confine themselves to pick a license fee "somewhere between a low fee proposed by the licensee and a high license fee proposed by [the CMO]".[1257] Thus, one must be careful when drawing general conclusions in this connection. It is, however, safe to say that, just like in connection with calculation methods, the license rates are subject to the reasonableness standard and review by the rate court.[1258] Once a rate has been set for the first period of the license term, it is likely that it will be reasonable for the entire license period.[1259] This is also due to the rationale

---

1253 *Id.* at ¶ 141–144. *See* on this point, however, *Autortiesību un komunicēšanās konsultāciju aģentūra / Latvijas Autoru apvienība*, C-177/16 at ¶ 62–71.

1254 *Autortiesību un komunicēšanās konsultāciju aģentūra / Latvijas Autoru apvienība*, C-177/16 at ¶ 38, 44, 53. The court added that a comparison is not insufficient merely because it takes a limited number of member states into account; the selection depends on the circumstances of each individual case. Moreover, it ordered to take the PPP index into account *see id.* at ¶ 40–43, 46. In the case at hand, fees were between 50% and 100% higher than in other member states, whereas higher fees were charged in Romania in certain situations, *see id.* at ¶ 54.

1255 *Id.* at ¶ 55.

1256 *Autortiesību un komunicēšanās konsultāciju aģentūra / Latvijas Autoru apvienība*, C-177/16 at ¶ 58–60. This rationale had already been mentioned by the AG in *Tournier*, *see* above.

1257 Lunney, *The United States Experience*, *supra* at 340 (referring to ASCAP). It has been noted that rate courts have recently been more inclined to adopting the rate proposed by users, *see* Turk, *Hard Day's Night*, *supra* 518, 521 (referring to the decisions in *DMX*, *Pandora* and *MOBITV*). *See also* Brabec, *Performance Right*, *supra* at 20 n. 22 (referring to *AOL*).

1258 The court in *MOBITV* briefly sums up the interplay between calculations methods and the level of fee, *see MOBITV,* 681 F.3d 76 at 88 ("Although the size of the fee is clearly relevant to its reasonableness, there is no requirement that the District Court explicitly engage in a testing of the fee resulting from its formula").

1259 *In Re Pandora*, 6 F. Supp. 3d 317 at 355. *See also id.* at 356–357 ("Absent some unusual circumstances, the value of music to a user is assumed to remain constant through the term of a license. And an escalating rate is not necessary for the licensor to share in the success of the licensee: with a single rate as a percentage of revenue a joint interest is created between the parties in the growth of the licensee's business. Adoption of a single rate facilitates business planning, encourages reliance on historical data, and discourages resort to contestthat right holders should not have a right to higher royalties merely because of the licensee's success which might stem from an innovative business model, for instance.[1260] Even though benchmarks are evaluated for individual cases, longstanding practices may, however, have considerable influence: As regards TTTA licenses, a general three-tiered rate structure applying to the cable television network's revenue was negotiated between the users and ASCAP.[1261] The rates were based on the "music intensity" and distinguished whether the programmed network was "music intensive" (0,9%), "general entertainment" (0,375%) or "news and sports" (0,1375%).[1262] This system was accepted as a benchmark later by the Second Circuit.[1263] It is thus crucial, in situations where a user offers different types of services, that the royalty rates are tailored to the "varying nature and scope of [the licensee's] music use".[1264] This might very well result in applying different rates to the same user, so long as this is feasible.[1265] With regard to the types of licenses, the percentage rates applied to PPLs have traditionally been higher than those charged for blanket licenses, since the latter refers to the user's total revenues.[1266]

From a user's perspective, a rate will only be unacceptable to the extent that it is perceived too high. This may also raise antitrust concerns; however, under U.S. antitrust doctrine, "an excessive price alone does not establish a violation of the antitrust laws".[1267] On the other hand, a user does not necessarily need to show that excessive fees have actually been imposed or what a reasonable

ed projections.") On appeal, the Second Circuit affirmed but highlighted that "the district court expressly observed that its holding did not depend on the existence of such a presumption", *see Pandora v. ASCAP 2015*, 785 F. 3d 73 at 78.

1260 *In Re Pandora*, 6 F. Supp. 3d 317 at 368–369.

1261 *In Re Application of MOBITV*, 712 F. Supp. 2d 206 at 222 (S.D.N.Y. 2010), *aff'd*, 681 F. 3d 76 (2nd Cir. 2012).

1262 *Id.* The court accepted this benchmark, *see id.* at 246.

1263 *MOBITV*, 681 F.3d 76. In this case, the court focused mainly on the revenue base, and not the exact rates. *See also* Turk, *Hard Day's Night, supra* at 514–516. *See also In Re Pandora*, 6 F. Supp. 3d 317 at 355 ("[…] the historical division between interactive and non-interactive internet music services requires that Pandora be licensed well below the 3.0% rate at which ASCAP licenses interactive music services."). A court can of course refuse to adopt historical benchmarks, *see, e.g., ASCAP (Application of AOL)*, 559 F. Supp. 2d 332 at 401; *ASCAP (In re Capital Cities/ABC)*, 157 F.R.D. 173 at 198–199.

1264 *ASCAP (Application RealNetworks and Yahoo, Inc.)*, 627 F. 3d 64 at 81 (faulting the district court for applying a uniform rate). *See* for an almost identical wording CMD art. 16(2).

1265 *Id.* at 83–84 (referring to the different uses made of the music by Yahoo). The court stated, however, that there were other ways to set a reasonable fee, *see id.* at 84.

1266 Korman, *U.S. Position, supra* at 162. *See also Buffalo Broadcasting*, 744 F. 2d 917 at 923 (referring to a 1954 settlement according to which the rate for a PPL was set to 9% of the local stations' total revenues, while the rate for the blanket licenses was fixed at 2,05%). *See also id.* at 926 ("[I]t is inevitable that the rate for a local station's blanket license will be less than the rate for a program license […]"); *ASCAP (In re Capital Cities/ABC)*, 157 F.R.D. 173 at 199.

1267 *See, e.g., Nat'l Cable Television Ass'n*, 772 F. Supp. 614 at 643.

fee would be if the conduct on the CMO's side suggests a threat of unlawful excessive pricing. In *Alden-Rochelle*, the court granted an injunction because ASCAP notified theatre owners that license fees would be raised by a factor of 15, even though a lower fee was later offered.[1268] It should be noted that the latter two cases were brought to court before the rate court mechanism was installed because it is, as mentioned earlier, precisely the availability of this remedy which will usually rule out an antitrust law-based claim that license fees are "too high".[1269] This does not apply to SESAC, for which no rate court has been installed. In this connection, it is worthwhile that a fee structure for alternatives to blanket license that results in a very high level of fees may render these alternatives licensing sources infeasible and thus make the blanket license itself subject to closer antitrust scrutiny.[1270]

3.2.5. Excursus: Statutory Licensing of Musical Rights

Statutory licenses are contained in several European directives. The most prominent examples can be found in the Copyright Directive,[1271] the Rental & Lending Rights Directive,[1272] and the Orphan Works Directive.[1273] Under EU law, member states retain considerable freedom as to the implementation of statutory licenses under these directives, as many provisions – like those of the Copyright Directive – are mere authorization clauses stating that member states may implement statutory licenses;[1274] however, if they decide to do so, they have to provide for "fair compensation" within the meaning of the Copyright Directive.[1275] Moreover, as a general principle, exceptions to exclusive rights

1268 *Alden-Rochelle*, 80 F. Supp. 888 at 895 ("At the trial, plaintiffs did not attempt to prove that the 1934 rates, which cover the period of this suit, were excessive. Nor did plaintiffs attempt to prove what a proper rate would be."), 898–899 (holding ASCAP's conduct to be an "indication of the power that [it] has unlawfully acquired by its own arrangements with its members and by their arrangements with the motion picture producers"). The court did not, however, award damages, *see id.* at 899–900. *See also Buffalo Broadcasting*, 744 F. 2d 917 at 927 ("[T]he relative cheapness of the blanket rate does not necessarily mean that it is not a restraint […]").

1269 *Buffalo Broadcasting*, 744 F. 2d 917 at 927.

1270 *Meredith*, 1 F. Supp. 3d 180 at 214–217.

1271 *See, e.g.,* Copyright Directive art. 5(2)(a), (b) and (e).

1272 Rental & Lending Rights Directive art. 6, 8(2).

1273 Orphan Works Directive art. 6(5).

1274 *See, e.g.,* Copyright Directive art. 5(2) which states that "Member States *may* provide for exceptions or limitations to the reproduction right provided for in Article 2 in the following cases […]" (emphasis added). Member states may however not go beyond the limits set forth by article 5 because the (admittedly extensive) list of exceptions and limitations is exhaustive, *see* Copyright Directive recital 32.

1275 *Copydan Båndkopi v. Nokia Danmark A/S*, C-463/12, ¶ 19 (ECJ 2015); *Amazon.com Int'l Sales, Inc. v. Austro-Mechana Gesellschaft zur Wahrnehmung mechanisch-musikalischer Urheberrechte Gesellschaft mbH*, C-521/11, ¶ 19 (ECJ 2013); *Stichting de Thuiskopie v. Opus Supplies Deutschland GmbH*, C-462/09, ¶ 22 (ECJ 2011); *Padawan SL v. Sociedad General de Autores y Editores de España*, C-467/08, ¶ 30 (ECJ 2010). *See also Padawan SL* must be interpreted in a narrow fashion,[1276] even though some decisions indicate the court's willingness to follow a more flexible approach.[1277] The statutory rights in EU law refer to both actual authors' and performers' rights.

In the United States, besides the licensing of performance rights in musical compositions, the second important set of rights users must usually clear are the rights which exist in sound recordings.[1278] These rights may be licensed directly;[1279] however, the U.S. Copyright Act includes a complicated set of statutory licenses.[1280] Statutory licenses are also relevant for musical compositions.[1281]

It is not the purpose of the following section to discuss the statutory licensing systems under EU and U.S. law in detail, but rather to give an over-

---

v. Sociedad General de Autores y Editores de España, C-467/08 (ECJ 2010), Opinion of AG Trjstenjak, ¶ 44. Fair compensation may also be due in other situations not expressly mentioned by the directive, *see, e.g.*, Stefan Bechtold, *Directive 2001/29/EC* in *Concise European Copyright Law* 421, 458 (Thomas Dreier & P. Bernt Hugenholtz eds., 2nd ed. 2016); von Lewinski & Walter, *Information Society Directive*, *supra* at 1027–1028, 1061. Such an obligation can arise from the three-step-test under art 5(5) of the Copyright Directive, *see* Stavroula Karapapa, *Private Copying* 127 (2012), or possibly under article 17 of the Charter of Fundamental Rights of the European Union art. 17(2), 2012 O.J. (C326) 391–407 [hereinafter: Charter of Fundamental Rights], *see Luksan v. Petrus van der Let*, C-277/10 (ECJ 2012), Opinion of AG Trstenjak, ¶ 127–134. The ECJ has furthermore emphasized that member states must observe consistency when transposing exceptions and limitations, *see Hewlett-Packard*, C-572/13 at ¶ 38–39, 52, 63. *See also* Copyright Directive recital 32.

1276 *See, e.g., Stichting Brein v. Wullems*, C-527/15, ¶ 62 (ECJ 2017); *Copydan Båndkopi*, C-463/12 at ¶ 87; *ACI Adam BV v. Stichting de Thuiskopie*, C-435/12, ¶ 22–23, 30 (ECJ 2014); *Infopaq Int'l A/S v. Danske Dagblades Forening*, C-5/08, ¶ 56–57 (ECJ 2009); *Commission* v. *Portuguese Republic,* C-53/05, ¶ 22 (ECJ 2006). *See also Verwertungsgesellschaft Wort v. Kyocera*, Joined Cases C-457/11 to C-460/11 (ECJ 2013), Opinion of AG Sharpston, ¶ 67–68.

1277 *See* for an overview of the relevant decisions Christophe Geiger et al., *Limitations and Exceptions as Key Elements of the Legal Framework for Copyright in the European Union – Opinion of the European Copyright Society on the Judgment of the CJEU in Case C-201/13 Deckmyn*, 46 IIC 93, 96–98 (2015). This will especially be appropriate (or even imperative) in cases where the court is required to strike a balance between the rights of the copyright holder and fundamental rights like the freedom of expression or the public interest, *see id.* at 98–99; Matthias Leistner, *Europe's Copyright Decade: Recent Case Law Of The European Court Of Justice And Policy Perspectives*, 51 Common Market L. Rev. 559, 585 (2014); Christophe Geiger & Franciska Schönherr, *Article 5: Exceptions and Limitations* in *EU copyright law* 434, 450–454 (Irinia A. Stamatoudi & Paul Torremans eds., 2014). *Geiger & Schönherr* refer to the unclear meaning of Charter of Fundamental Rights art. 17(2) which states that intellectual property "shall be protected".

1278 *See* for an introduction to U.S. copyright law section I.4. above.

1279 This applies, for instance, to interactive services which are not covered by the statutory license, *see* 17 U.S.C. § 114(d)(2)(A)(i), (3)(C). *See also* Brabec, *Performance Right*, *supra* at 35. Certain limitations on such consensual licenses exist, *see* II Goldstein on Copyright, *supra* at § 7.8.6.3.

1280 However, as statutory licenses are exceptions to the rules, courts have construed them narrowly, *see, e.g., WPIX, Inc. v. ivi, Inc.*, 691 F.3d 275 at 281–282 (2nd Cir. 2012); *Fame Publishing Co., Inc., v. Alabama Custom Tape, Inc.*, 507 F. 2d 667 at 670 (5th Cir. 1975); U.S. Copyright Office, *Jointly Owned Works* at 20.

1281 *See, e.g.,* 17 U.S.C. § 115 (compulsory license for making and distributing phonorecords).

view of the respective regimes in order to contrast these systems to the licensing of musical performance rights through CMOs. Special focus will be put on the rate-setting standards.

a) Overview

Private Copying Exception. The so-called "private copying exception" contained in the Copyright Directive addresses private and non-commercial acts of reproduction on any medium[1282] carried out but natural persons.[1283] This provision does not only refer to musical works or fixations of musical performances, but also to other work categories.[1284] Moreover, there exists an additional, not expressly mentioned requirement that relates to the lawful nature of the source used for copying.[1285]

Broadcasting and Communication to the Public. The Rental & Lending Rights Directive obliges the member states ("shall") to provide for a right to remuneration for the benefit of performers and phonogram producers.[1286] This right applies to phonograms published for commercial purposes, or reproductions of such phonograms which are used for broadcasting by wireless means or for any communication to the public.[1287] Conversely, an exclusive performance right of performers is granted for live performances.[1288]

1282 Conversely, Copyright Directive art. 5(2)(a) refers only to reproductions on paper.

1283 *Id.* at art. 5(2)(b). *See* for a detailed account on all of the requirements Karapapa, *Private Copying*, *supra*.

1284 As recital 38 of the Copyright Directive might suggest, *see* von Lewinski & Walter, *Information Society Directive*, *supra* at 1031. The provision is much more relevant than the comparable provisions in the AHRA, *see* 17 U.S.C. §§ 1001–1010.

1285 *Hewlett-Packard*, C-572/13 at ¶ 59; *ACI Adam*, C-435/12 at ¶ 31, 35, 37–38, 41. *See* for the preceding discussion, *e.g.*, Carine Bernault & Audrey Lebois, *Peer-to-peer File Sharing and Literary and Artistic Property* 30 (2005), *available at* http://privatkopie.net/files/Feasibility-Study-p2p-acs_Nantes.pdf (last visited May 23, 2017); Christophe Geiger, *Legal or Illegal? That Is the Question! Private Copying and Downloading on the Internet*, 39 IIC 597 (2008); Giuseppe Mazziotti, *EU Digital Copyright Law and the End-User* 147–149 (2008); Joost Poort & João Pedro Quintais, *The Levy Runs Dry: A Legal and Economic Analysis of EU Private Copying Levies*, 3 JIPITEC 205, 214–215 (2013); António Vitorino, *Recommendations Resulting from The Mediation On Private Copying and Reprography Levies* 19–20 (2013), http://ec.europa.eu/internal_market/copyright/docs/levy_reform/130131_levies-vitorino-recommendations_en.pdf (last visited May 23, 2017)

1286 Rental & Lending Rights Directive art. 8(2).

1287 *See* on the meaning of the term "wireless" Sylvie Nérisson, *The Rental and Lending Rights Directive* in *EU copyright law* 149, 187 (Irinia A. Stamatoudi & Paul Torremans eds., 2014). The directive furthermore provides for an unwaivable right to equitable remuneration in cases where these persons have transferred their rental rights for a phonogram or an original copy of a film to a producer, *see* Rental & Lending Rights Directive art. 5(1), (2). Subsection 3 clarifies that the management of this right may be entrusted to CMO. Subsection 4 provides for a legal basis for mandatory collective management.

1288 Rental & Lending Rights Directive art. 8(1); Nérisson, *Rental and Lending Rights Directive*, *supra*, at 186–187; Silke von Lewinski, *Rental and Lending Rights Directive* in *European Copyright Law* 249, 321 (Michel M. Walter & Silke von Lewinski eds., 2010).

The most commercially significant music-related statutory licenses in the United States are contained in the sections 112, 114, and 115 of the U.S. Copyright Act.[1289] While the relevant parts of section § 114 refer to the statutory license for the public performance of a sound recording by means of digital audio transmission, § 112 and § 115 refer to ephemeral recordings and mechanicals rights.

Section 114. Apart from entirely exempting certain (re-)transmissions from the scope the exclusive rights in recordings,[1290] section 114 contains a statutory license for the public performance of sound recordings by means of a "subscription digital audio transmission", an "eligible nonsubscription transmission", or a transmission made by a "preexisting satellite digital audio radio service", in case no other exceptions apply.[1291] A basic condition for the digital performances covered by this section is that the transmission is not part of an interactive service.[1292] Detailed rules for determining the royalty rates are furthermore laid down.[1293]

Section 112. Section 112 was primarily conceived to permit ephemeral reproductions[1294] of sound recordings which are necessary for certain lawful uses, especially licensed or exempted broadcasts and other transmissions.[1295] The statutory license contained in this section applies to transmitting organizations and allows them to make phonorecords of sound recordings, especially, if they are entitled to perform these sound recordings in connection with section 114.[1296]

Section 115. Like section 112, the statutory license of section 115 refers to the reproduction right, however, in relation to phonorecords of nondramatic

1289 Paul Fakler, *Music Copyright Royalty Rate-Setting Litigation: Practice Before the Copyright Royalty Board and How It Differs from ASCAP and BMI Rate Court Litigation*, The Licensing Journal June/July 2013, at 3. It has been noted that users often prefer to negotiate directly with right holders rather than relying on the statutory license under section 115; however, the rates set by the CRB significantly influence the voluntarily negotiated agreements, *see* United States Copyright Royalty Board, Library of Congress, *In the Matter Mechanical and Digital Phonorecord Delivery Rate Determination Proceeding: Final Determination of Rates and Terms*, Docket No. 2006-3, at 13. S*ee also* Lemley, *Contracting Around Liability Rules*, *supra* at 478–479.

1290 17 U.S.C. § 114(d)(1) (*e.g.*, nonsubscription broadcast transmission).

1291 *Id.* at § 114(d)(2). The definitions of the terms used in this section can be found in § 114(j).

1292 *Id.* at § 114(d)(2)(A)(i). Further detailed specifications are made in sections § 114(d)(2)(A)(ii)-(iii) and § 114(d)(2)(B)-(C). *See also Arista Records, LLV v. Launch Media, Inc.*, 578 F. 3d 148 at 163–164 (2nd Cir. 2009) (holding that LAUNCHcast, a music service that includes songs based on the consumer's preferences, did not constitute an interactive service).

1293 *Id.* at § 114(f).

1294 Examples of ephemeral copies are, for instance, server and buffer copies, *see* Fakler, *Rate-Setting Litigation*, *supra* at 3.

1295 II Goldstein on Copyright, *supra* at § 7.2.2.2.

1296 Specifically, a transmitting organization may be entitled under the exception under 17. U.S.C. § 114(d)(1)(C)(iv) or a statutory license in accordance with § 114(f), *see* 17 U.S.C. § 112(e).

musical works.[1297] Moreover, the latter entails acts of distribution, also including rental, lease or lending and means of a digital transmission that constitutes a digital phonorecord delivery.[1298] In order to be eligible for this license, the phonorecords of nondramatic musical works that are to be reproduced or distributed must have been distributed to the public under the authority of the copyright owner.[1299] Furthermore, the license only covers distributions to the public for private use; special restrictions apply to phonorecords duplicating sound recordings,[1300] the latter generally falling out of section 115's scope.[1301]

As SoundExchange is the collective designated by the CRB,[1302] the organization manages the collection and distribution of the royalties flowing from the statutory licenses contained in sections 112 and 114 of the U.S. Copyright Act.[1303] The management of amounts due under section 115 is either handled directly or, in many cases, assisted by the HFA[1304] or other organizations like Music Reports.[1305][1306]

b) Rate-Setting Standards

The two most important standards provided for by EU law for the rate-setting under statutory licenses are the "fair compensation" standard and the "equitable remuneration" standard. The first relates to the private copying exception; the second to the performers' remuneration right under the Rental & Lending Rights Directive's article 8(2). The court emphasized already at the outset that both notions must be regarded as an autonomous concepts of EU

1297 *Id.* at § 115(a)(1).

1298 17 U.S.C. § 115(a), (c)(3)(A), (c)(4). *See* for the definitions § 17 U.S.C. § 101 and § 115(d). The license also permits users to make a musical arrangements of the work "to the extent necessary to conform it to the style or manner of interpretation of the performance involved, but the arrangement shall not change the basic melody or fundamental character of the work, and shall not be subject to protection as a derivative work under this title, except with the express consent of the copyright owner", *see* section 115(a)(2).

1299 *Id.* at § 115(a)(1).

1300 *Id. See also* § 115(c)(3)(G).

1301 II Goldstein on Copyright, *supra* at § 7.2.1.1.a. (noting that a producer may produce an independent sound recording closely imitating the original).

1302 37 C.F.R. §380.7.

1303 U.S. Copyright Office, *Music Marketplace*, *supra* at 47.

1304 However, the HFA currently publishes the following note on its website: "HFA is not authorized by its affiliated publishers to accept Notices of Intention to Obtain a Compulsory License for Making and Distributing Phonorecords (NOIs) pursuant to Section 115 of the Copyright Act on their behalf. All NOIs must be sent directly to the publisher", *see* HFA, *Become a HFA Licensee*, https://www.harryfox.com/license_music/become_hfa_licensee.html (last visited April 26, 2017).

1305 *See* for the organization's website https://www.musicreports.com/.

1306 U.S. Copyright Office, *Music Marketplace*, *supra* at 21.

law, which must be interpreted independently from national law, thereby taking into account the context and the objective of the relevant legislation.[1307]

The concept of fairness implies, one the one hand, fairness toward (categories of) right holders, so that the amounts paid to them must not drop below a certain level that would be virtually unacceptable and prejudice their interests. On the other hand, it implies fairness toward users, so that the obligation to make remuneration payments does not exceed a certain level above which the fee appears to be unreasonable; and that only such uses are subject to payments which are authorized by the statutory license. "Fairness", for the present purpose, is, therefore, a two-sided concept. To this effect, the Copyright Directive states that "[a] fair balance of rights and interests between the different categories of rightholders, as well as between the different categories of rightholders and users of protected subject-matter must be safeguarded."[1308] The ECJ has frequently confirmed that this balance must be taken into account when interpreting the notion of fair compensation.[1309] Furthermore, the assessment can be influenced by the fundamental right to property which is contained in article 17 of the Charter of Fundamental Rights.[1310]

One might wonder why the Copyright Directive refers to (fair) "compensation", instead of employing the term (equitable) "remuneration" which had already been preexistent in EU law at the time of the directive's adoption. The answer lies in a compromise between the different legal traditions of the member states: Whereas Continental European countries had enacted statutory remuneration schemes long before the Copyright Directive entered into force, the situation was different in the UK and Ireland.[1311] The notions of fair compensation and remuneration are thus not identical. Remuneration refers to the theories of natural justice which award authors a general right to remuneration for every act of usage of their works.[1312] Compensation, in turn, refers to

---

1307 *Vereniging van Educatieve en Wetenschappelijke Auteurs v. Belgische Staat*, C-271/10, ¶ 25 (ECJ 2011); *Padawan*, C-467/08 at ¶ 32–33, 37; *SENA*, C-245/00 at ¶ 22–24. *See also Hewlett-Packard*, C-572/13 at ¶ 35; *Verwertungsgesellschaft Wort v. Kyocera*, joined Cases C-457/11 to C-460/11, ¶ 75 (ECJ 2013); *Padawan*, C-467/08, Opinion of AG Trjstenjak at ¶ 68.

1308 Copyright Directive recital 31. Note that a fair balance should not only be reached between right holders and users but also between different categories of right holders. Furthermore, it should be noted that recital 31 does not only refer to the concept of fair compensation, but to a fair balance between (certain categories of) right holders and users in general.

1309 *See, e.g., Padawan*, C-467/08 at ¶ 43; *Stichting de Thuiskopie*, C-462/09 at ¶ 25; *Hewlett-Packard*, C-572/13 at ¶ 86.

1310 Geiger & Schönherr, *Exceptions and Limitations*, *supra* at 472–473.

1311 Jörg Reinbothe, *Die EG-Richtlinie zum Urheberrecht in der Informationsgesellschaft*, 50 GRUR Int 733, 738 (2001); von Lewinski & Walter, *Information Society Directive*, *supra* at 1028. *See also Padawan*, C-467/08, Opinion of AG Trjstenjak at ¶ 43, 70–71.

1312 Bechtold, *Directive 2001/29/EC*, *supra* at 459; Geiger & Schönherr, *Exceptions and Limitations*, *supra* at 470–471.

the harm caused to right holders for which a payment may be due.[1313] This is reinforced by recital 35 which states that when

> […] determining the form, detailed arrangements and possible level of such fair compensation, account should be taken of the particular circumstances of each case. When evaluating these circumstances, a valuable criterion would be the possible harm to the rightholders resulting from the act in question.[1314]

Hence, the two terms are conceptually distinct.[1315] Remuneration may be even due in cases where right holders are not (actually or potentially) harmed.[1316] In the context of the foregoing, it is not surprising that the ECJ contrued "harm" to be the central element of fair compensation. Mainly building on recital 35, the court has frequently emphasized that "fair compensation must be regarded as recompense for the harm suffered by the author" by the reproduction of the protected work "without his authorization"; therefore, the notion must "necessarily be calculated on the basis of the criterion of the harm caused to authors of protected works by the introduction of the private copying exception."[1317] The details of this rate-setting standard are controversially discussed in the legal literature.[1318]

The concept of equitable remuneration is largely used in the Rental & Lending Rights Directive. It is noteworthy, however, that the directive distinguishes different nuances of the concept of remuneration including i) "equitable re-

---

1313 Bechtold, *Directive 2001/29/EC*, *supra* at 459; Geiger & Schönherr, *Exceptions and Limitations*, *supra* at 470–471.; Bernt Hugenholtz et al., *The Future of Levies in a Digital Environment* 36 (2003), *available at* http://www.ivir.nl/publicaties/download/332 (last visited May 23, 2017).

1314 Copyright Directive recital 35.

1315 Karapapa, *Private Copying*, *supra* at 125. *See also ACI Adam v. Stichting de Thuiskopie*, C-435/12 (ECJ 2014), Opinion of AG Cruz Villalón, ¶ 41.

1316 Hugenholtz et al., *The Future of Levies*, *supra* at 36.

1317 *Padawan*, C-467/08 at ¶ 40–42. *See also Hewlett-Packard*, C-572/13 at ¶ 36; *Copydan Båndkopi*, C-463/12 at ¶ 21; *ACI Adam*, C-435/12 at ¶ 50; *VG Wort*, joined Cases C-457/11 to C-460/11 at ¶ 31; *Amazon.com v. Austro-Mechana*, C-521/11 at ¶ 47; *Stichting de Thuiskopie*, C-462/09 at ¶ 24, 75.

1318 *See, e.g.*, Hugenholtz et al., *The Future of Levies*, *supra* at 37; Alexander Peukert, *„Copydan/Nokia" und die Zukunft des gesetzlichen Vergütungsanspruchs für die digitale Privatkopie*, 117 GRUR 452, 454–455 (2015); Joost Poort, *Copyright Levies* in *Handbook on the digital creative economy* 235, 240 (Christian Handke & Ruth Towse eds., 2013); Poort & Quintais, *Levy Runs Dry*, *supra* at 214; Reinbothe, *EG-Richtlinie*, *supra* at 738; Jan Nicolaus Ullrich, *Clash of Copyrights – Optionale Schranke und zwingender finanzieller Ausgleich im Fall der Privatkopie nach Art. 5 Abs. 2 lit. b) Richtlinie 2001/29/EG und Dreistufentest*, 58 GRUR Int 283, 291 (2009); Vitorino, *Recommendations*, *supra* at 6–8. *See also* Commission of the European Communities, *Background Document "Fair Compensation for Acts of Private Copying"* 19 (2008), http://ec.europa.eu/internal_market/copyright/docs/levy_reform/background_en.pdf (last visited May 23, 2017). A seminal work in this connection is S.J. Liebowitz, *Copying and Indirect Appropriability: Photocopying of Journals*, 93 J. of Political Economy 945 (1985).

muneration",[1319] ii) "single equitable remuneration",[1320] and iii) "remuneration"[1321] without further specification, whereby it seems that the first is the basic standard.

Since the concept is not defined in the Rental & Lending Right Directive, member states are in principle free to lay down the exact criteria for its determination.[1322] However, such implementation must respect the limits imposed by EU law (flowing from the autonomous interpretation), thereby striking a fair balance between artists and producers on the one hand and between right holders and users (in this case: broadcasting organizations) on the other hand.[1323] For this purpose, equitable remuneration must reflect in particular the value of a certain use in trade.[1324] In order to establish a fair balance between authors or performers and producers, recital 13 specifies that equitable remuneration may be paid upfront on the basis of ongoing payments. Such agreement should take into account the importance of the contribution to the phonogram or film of the authors and performers.[1325] With regard to cross-border cases, the ECJ held that as far as the Satellite & Cable Directive is concerned, remuneration can be due in two member states at the same time.[1326] Therefore, a broadcasting company may not unilaterally deduct the fees paid in a member state from the amounts paid in the state of establishment insofar as the uses possess economic value in both states.[1327]

1319 Rental & Lending Rights Directive art. 3(6), 5.

1320 *Id.* at art. 8(2).

1321 *Id.* at art. 6.

1322 *SENA*, C-245/00 at ¶ 34; *Lagardère Active Broadcast v. Société pour la perception de la rémunération équitable*, C-192/04, ¶ 48 (ECJ 2005).

1323 *SENA*, C-245/00 at ¶ 34–36; *Lagardère Active Broadcast*, C-192/04 at ¶ 49.

1324 *VEWA*, C-271/10 at ¶ 32; *SENA*, C-245/00 at ¶ 37; *Lagardère Active Broadcast*, C-192/04 at ¶ 50.

1325 Judica Krikke, *Directive 2006/115/EC of the European Parliament and of the Council* in *Concise European Copyright Law* 275, 291 (Thomas Dreier & P. Bernt Hugenholtz eds., 2nd ed. 2016).

1326 *Lagardère Active Broadcast*, C-192/04 ¶ 44. The factual background of the case was the following: A broadcasting company established in France relied on a terrestrial transmitter located in Germany in order to cover the entire territory of its home country; the program was only received in a small part of Germany and there was no commercial exploitation in that state, *see id.* at ¶ 12–13. Against this background, the broadcast was not considered as a "communication to public by satellite" within the meaning of article 1(2)(a) of the Satellite and Cable Directive, thereby rendering inapplicable article 1(2)(b) which precludes the application of the laws of more than one member state, *see id.* at ¶ 43. Hence, the application of article 1(2)(b) was a preliminary question which did not affect the interpretation of the concept of equitable remuneration as such. However, a different ruling on this point might have excluded the possibility of payments in both states within the scope of the mentioned directive.

1327 *Lagardère Active Broadcast*, C-192/04 ¶ 54–55. It is noteworthy that the *Amazon* case was decided differently because it was based on different circumstances. There, the court held that fair compensation, by virtue of a mandatory reimbursement option for users, can effectively only be due once in the member states where the final user resides (*Amazon.com v.*

The inclusion of the word "single" to the concept of equitable remuneration must not be understood as meaning that payments should only be made once for the entire term of protection. Rather, it means that the users should make a payment encompassing all groups of right holderss which is subsequently distributed.[1328] Therefore, it would probably be less misleading to speak of *uniform* rather than *single* equitable remuneration. The term "equitable" indicates that users should pay on an ongoing basis if they exploit the phonograms on an ongoing basis.[1329]

As mentioned before, equitable remuneration and fair compensation are two conceptually distinct terms. Therefore, one would expect the court to give this difference effect in its case law. By contrast, however, the court strongly approximates these two concepts, even though it is aware of the different context of the concept of fair compensation. To this effect, the ECJ held that the concept of "remuneration" is "also designed to establish recompense for authors, arising as it does in a comparable situation in which the fact that the works are being used in the context of public lending without the authorisation of the authors result in harm to the latter", thereby explicitly referring to *Padawan.*[1330] Accordingly, "remuneration" constitutes "consideration for the harm caused to authors by reason of the use of their works without their authorization."[1331] Therefore, the ECJ uses essentially the same criteria to assess the concepts of remuneration and fair compensation, basing both on the notion of harm which the court equates to the extent of use made possible by the limitations to copyright.[1332]

Unlike EU law, U.S. law specifies an authority to determine and adjust the rates which are due under the statutory licenses. This authority is the CRB which proceeds according to chapter 8 of the copyright act.[1333] Determinations are usually made every five years,[1334] and an appeal to the Court of Appeals for the District of Columbia is possible.[1335] Even though the tasks of the CRB and the ASCAP and BMI rate courts are comparable, there are several im-

Austro-Mechana, C-521/11 at ¶ 64–65). This ruling was based on the principle that there is no harm caused simply because the levied goods are shipped from one state to another (*see id.* at ¶ 62). Conversely, the decisive element in the *Lagardère* case (economic value) was found in two member states.

1328 von Lewinski, *Rental and Lending Rights Directive*, *supra* at 324–325.

1329 *Id.* at 324.

1330 *VEWA*, C-271/10 at ¶ 28–29. *See also Luksan v. Petrus van der Let*, C-277/10, ¶ 103 (ECJ 2012).

1331 *VEWA*, C-271/10 at ¶ 37.

1332 Leistner, *Copyright Decade*, *supra* at 588 n. 160. *See also VG Wort*, Joined Cases C-457/11 to C-460/11 at ¶ 49; *VEWA*, C-271/10 at ¶ 37–39; *Padawan*, C-467/08 at ¶ 40.

1333 17 U.S.C. §§ 801–805. The CRB also sets rates in respect of section §§ 116, 118, 119 and 1004, *see id.* at § 801(b)(1).

1334 *Id.* at § 804(b).

1335 *Id.* at § 803(d)(1).

portant differences between the two types of proceedings. The most important differences relate to the composition of the rate-setting body, the procedural and evidentiary rules as well as the methodologies and standards used for the actual setting of the respective rates.[1336]

A general standard for rate-setting is provided by the U.S. Copyright Act in that it directs the CRB to set "reasonable rates and terms of royalty payments".[1337] This standard – which sounds similar to the rate court practice – is further specified in order to give the judges more guidance for their decisions. The guidelines governing the rate-setting in respect of section 114 are divided into two categories: First, "preexisting satellite digital audio radio services" and "preexisting subscription services"[1338] and second, other services not covered by the former terms. The distinction between the two sets of standards is the result of the historical development of the statutory licenses, as Congress grandfathered the then existing services along with the enactment of the DMCA in 1998.[1339] The general standard which refers to the mentioned preexisting services and furthermore applies to section 115 provides that the following objectives should be achieved in setting the rates:

> To maximize the availability of creative works to the public.
>
> (B) To afford the copyright owner a fair return for his or her creative work and the copyright user a fair income under existing economic conditions.
>
> (C) To reflect the relative roles of the copyright owner and the copyright user in the product made available to the public with respect to relative creative contribution, technological contribution, capital investment, cost, risk, and contribution to the opening of new markets for creative expression and media for their communication.
>
> (D) To minimize any disruptive impact on the structure of the industries involved and on generally prevailing industry practices.[1340]

The "more recent" standard, applying to section 114's "eligible nonsubscription transmission services" and "new subscription services" as well as employed by section 112, directs the judges to "establish rates that most clearly represent the fees that would have been negotiated in the marketplace between a willing buyer and a willing seller".[1341] In addition, the CRB's decision shall be based on information presented by the parties, including

---

1336 Fakler, *Rate-Setting Litigation*, *supra* at 4–7.

1337 17 U.S.C. § 112(e)(3), (4); § 114(f)(1)(A), (B), (2)(A), B); § 115(c)(3)(C), (D); § 801(b)(1). The act furthermore mandates that the rates distinguish between different acts of uses or types of licensees which are specified in the respective context, *see id.* at § 112(e); § 114(f)(1)(A), (2)(A), (B); § 115(c)(3)(C).

1338 *Id.* at § 114(j)(10), (11)

1339 U.S. Copyright Office, *Music Marketplace*, *supra* at 49; II Goldstein on Copyright, *supra* at § 7.8.6.2.

1340 17 U.S.C. § 801(b)(1).

1341 *Id.* at § 112(e)(4); § 114(f)(2)(B).

(A) whether use of the service may substitute for or may promote the sales of phonorecords or otherwise interferes with or enhances the copyright owner's traditional streams of revenue; and

(B) the relative roles of the copyright owner and the transmitting organization in the copyrighted work and the service made available to the public with respect to relative creative contribution, technological contribution, capital investment, cost, and risk.[1342]

Rates are however not necessarily set by the CRB but can also result from negotiations between right holders and users.[1343] First of all, a rate-setting proceeding entails a voluntary negotiation period of three months.[1344] Moreover, it is expressly stipulated that agreements voluntarily negotiated "at any time" shall be given effect "in lieu of any decision by the Librarian of Congress or determination by the Copyright Royalty Judges".[1345] Indeed, it was the intention of Congress when enacting the foregoing provisions to enable the parties to negotiate voluntary agreements when possible.[1346] For this reason, antitrust exemptions were included to allow the participants to designate a common agent for the collective negotiation of royalty rates.[1347] Participants do have, however, the option to object to the adoption of a negotiated agreement as a basis for the rate-setting decision.[1348] Comparable voluntary agreements may generally be considered in the rate-setting process in addition to the basic factors set forth by the statute;[1349] conversely, the rates set for the public performance of sound recordings must never be taken into account when construing a rate for the use of musical compositions.[1350] Even though this was presumably not intended by this provision,[1351] the license fees payable for the

---

1342 *Id. See* for a discussion of the applicable standards Robert J. Williams, *Public Performance Royalty-Rate Disparity: Should Congress Pamper Pandora's Pandering?*, 48 New Eng. L. Rev. 371, 389–395 (2014).

1343 Yet, the CRB's rulings heavily influence such negotiations, often marking the ceiling of what right holders may charge, *see* U.S. Copyright Office, *Music Marketplace*, *supra* at 29.

1344 17 U.S.C. § 803(b)(3). *See also id.* at § 805.

1345 *Id.* at § 112(e)(5), § 114(f)(3). *See also id.* at § 115(c)(3)(E); § 801(b)(7). *See also id.* at § 114(f)(5) for a special rule on webcasters.

1346 U.S. Copyright Office, *Music Marketplace*, *supra* at 50.

1347 *Id.*; 17 U.S.C. §§ 112(e)(2), 114(e)(1), 115(c)(3)(B).

1348 17 U.S.C. §801(b)(7).

1349 *Id.* at §§ 112(e)(4)(B), 114(f)(1)(B), (2)(B)(ii), 115(c)(3)(D). *See also* Fakler, *Rate-Setting Litigation*, *supra* at 6–7 (noting that the rate courts have put more emphasis on the copyright owners' market power in the negotiation of benchmark agreements than the CRB). *See however* Lunney, *The United States Experience*, *supra* at 346 (stating that "[T]he CRJs generally focus on the same types of considerations in setting the statutory license fees for the sound recording performance right that we see in the judicial rate setting of the musical work performance right").

1350 17 U.S.C. § 114(i). *See* on this provision Joseph Pomianowski, *Toward An Efficient Licensing And Rate-Setting Regime: Reconstructing § 114(i) of the Copyright Act*, 125 Yale L. J. 1531, 1536 (2015–2016).

1351 The second sentence of the foregoing clause reads: "It is the intent of Congress that royalties payable to copyright owners of musical works for the public performance of their works performance of musical compositions and sound recordings differ significantly with the latter greatly outweighing the former in respect of certain uses.[1352]

3.2.6. Comments on the Relationship between CMOs and Users

a) General Remarks

The vast majority of litigation before courts and a good portion of the ASCAP and BMI Consent Decrees are dedicated the CMOs' relations to users. In plain contrast, the CMD is confined to two sparse user-related articles which do nothing more than set forth general principles. The ECJ has, however, developed case law, mainly with regard to the CMOs' fee policies. In this connection, the ECJ has applied article 102 in relation to exploitative and not exclusionary practices.[1353] Whereas the former aims at the simple exploitation of "consumers" in the relevant market, the latter aims at preventing or hindering competition from other competitors; excessive pricing – *e.g.*, in relation to licensing fees – is an example of exploitative practices.[1354] In contrast, U.S. antitrust doctrine does not recognize excessive pricing by itself as an antitrust violation, as high prices are seen as a stimulus to competition rather than an obstacle.[1355] Yet, the rate court proceedings offer a mechanism to thoroughly address the CMOs' pricing policies.

---

shall not be diminished in any respect as a result of the rights granted by section 106(6)", *see* 17 U.S.C. § 114(i).

1352 *In Re Pandora*, 6 F. Supp. 3d 317 at 332–33 (also noting that the rate disparity does not exist for most of ASCAP's revenue because the public performance right in sound recording is much narrower than the analogous right in musical compositions). *See also id.* at 366–367 (stating that publishers withdrew their new media rights to gain higher license fees in direct negotiations); *BMI v. Pandora 2015*, 140 F. Supp. 3d 267 at 275–276.

1353 Drexl, *Collecting Societies*, *supra* at 24 (also stating that this is also valid for the ECJ's decision in *BRT v. SABAM*).

1354 Capito, *Article 82*, *supra* at 167.

1355 *Berkey Photo, Inc. v. Eastman Kodak Comp.*, 603 F. 2d 263 at 297 (2nd Cir. 1979) ("A pristine monopolist, we have held, may charge as high a rate as the market will bear"); *Verizon Communications Inc. v. Law Offices of Curtis V. Trinko, LLP*, 540 U.S. 398 at 407 (2004). ("The mere possession of monopoly power, and the concomitant charging of monopoly prices, is not only not unlawful; it is an important element of the free-market system. The opportunity to charge monopoly prices – at least for a short period – is what attracts "business acumen" in the first place; it induces risk taking that produces innovation and economic growth. To safeguard the incentive to innovate, the possession of monopoly power will not be found unlawful unless it is accompanied by an element of anticompetitive *conduct*.") *See also* III Areeda & Hovenkamp, *Antitrust Principles*, *supra* at ¶ 720; de la Mano et al., *Article 102*, *supra* at 512–513; Drexl, *Competition and Development*, *supra* at 111. Thus, courts have focused on exclusionary conduct when applying U.S. antitrust to CMOs, *see, e.g., Meredith*, 1 F. Supp. 3d 180 at 223; *Radio Music License Comm.*, 29 F. Supp. 3d 487 at 500. However, AG *Wahl* highlights that the Commission has generally been "extremely reluctant" to apply article 102(a) TFEU to dominant undertakings and their pricing policies, *see Autortiesību un komunicēšanās konsultāciju aģentūra / Latvijas Autoru apvienība*, C-177/16, Opinion of AG Wahl at ¶ 3.

b) Obligation to License

Under both U.S. and EU law, a CMO must in principle license their repertoire to interested users. However, this obligation, unfortunately, is less pronounced under article 16(2) of the Collective Management Directive than in the Consent Decrees. Yet, CMOs are under the general duty to treat users according to objective and non-discriminatory criteria. Moreover, there is nothing in the directive that prevents member states from providing for an express obligation to contract in their national regimes.[1356] Yet, litigation history shows that CMOs are usually not reluctant to grant users access to their repertoire (at least in its entirety); the crucial question is rather at what price.[1357] The different types of licenses specified by the Consent Decrees essentially amount to different calculation methods. Different from the United States, EU law does not specify certain license types that CMOs must make available to users. However, the case law and the CMD afford courts and other national authorities sufficient leeway to adapt the licenses by CMOs to the individual case. An obligation to license may, however, have important implications when negotiating license fees, as this obligation can work as a counterweight to the market power of CMOs due to their inability to refuse a license request.[1358] In this sense, collective licensing through CMOs mirrors statutory licensing. The solution by the Consent Decrees, where users may perform ASCAP or BMI's repertoires without any licensing agreement appears to tip the scales, especially toward users.[1359] The question in this connection is whether this is adequate or whether a more balanced solution should be employed. As nothing in the competition case law or in the CMD expressly puts such an obligation of European CMOs, one must look at the member states' national regulation.[1360] EU jurisdictions employ diverging negotiation mechanisms which often involve collective bargaining.[1361]

c) The 100 percent Licensing Issue

The issue of 100 percent or "full-work" licensing appears to be a problem rather specific to the United States, as it flows from the treatment of multiple

1356 Guibault & van Gompel, *Collective Management*, *supra* at 155.

1357 Drexl, *Competition and Development*, *supra* at 262.

1358 *Id.* at 262–263.

1359 U.S. Copyright Office, *Music Marketplace*, *supra* at 94, 157–158.

1360 One could ask, however, whether such an obligation under national law would be compatible with article 16(3) of the CMD, as the article clearly reserves the right for CMOs to assess a license request and to reject it on objective grounds. Article 17 on the obligation of users also points to that direction. In light of recital 9, however, it appears to be permissible.

1361 A special case in this connection is Extended Collective Licensing (ECL), originating in the Nordic countries, which extends the effects of a license agreement to right holders not represented by the negotiating parties. *See* for a discussion Tarja Koskinen-Olsson & Vigdís Sigurdardóttir, *Collective Management in the Nordic Countries* in *Collective Management of Copyright and Related Rights* 243 (Daniel Gervais ed., 3rd ed. 2016).

co-owners of a joint work. Neither the competition case law nor the CMD requires CMOs to offer 100 percent licenses. Whether one of multiple copyright owners may license the work without the consent of the others in the first place is essentially a question of national law, as there is no general concept of joint ownership in European copyright law.[1362] Apart from the joint ownership issue, the Collective Management Directive effectively precludes full-work licenses – in the sense that licensees may use all works in the repertoire "without risk of infringement liability"[1363] – because it expressly gives right holders the right to withdraw certain categories of rights. Thus, a CMO does not have the authority to grant full access to all performance or communication rights of the works in its repertoire if a right holder decides to license her rights directly or entrust another CMO with this task. In contrast, the rate courts have refused to permit ASCAP and BMI to apply corresponding policies. In this light, partial withdrawals and 100 percent licensing are intertwined as far as they relate to the fragmentation of repertoires and rights therein. At first glance, 100 percent licensing puts users at ease, since only a single license is required for the use of a CMO's repertoire, even though a certain share of rights in the covered works is owned by right holders who not members of this organization.[1364] The (immense) administrative burden to coordinate the relations between the co-owners is in turn put on the right holders and CMOs.[1365] However, this proposition rests on the assumption that such coordination is carried out successfully.[1366] In the EU, the problem is mitigated already by the fact that there is often only one CMO per country for the licensing of a particular set of rights.

d) Defining and Applying Rate-Setting Standards

In view of the case law and the legislation discussed above, it is possible to define very general principles of rate-setting common to the U.S. and the EU: Fees charged by CMOs should not be arbitrary but bear a certain relation to the value of the rights that a user obtains; users should not pay twice for the same content; users should not have to pay for unprotected content; a calcula-

1362 This highlighted by the Term Directive which contains, as amended, a rule on the term of copyright protection for musical works with lyrics and cinematographic/audiovisual works which applies "whether or not" the collaborating persons "are designated as co-authors", *see* Term Directive Art 1(7), 2(2). *See also id.* at art. 2(1) stating that member states are free to designate, besides the principle director, further co-authors of a cinematographic and audiovisual work. *See* however Software Directive art. 2(3) ("In respect of a computer program created by a group of natural persons jointly, the exclusive rights shall be owned jointly"). *See also* von Lewinski & Walter, *Status of Harmonization*, *supra* at 1469–1470.

1363 DOJ, *Antitrust Division's Review*, *supra* at 8.

1364 In this light it is conspicuous that the DOJ advices users to continue to obtain licenses from multiple CMOs, *see id.* at 21–22.

1365 *Id.* at 18–22 (suggesting solutions).

1366 *See* for this and many related problems U.S. Copyright Office, *Jointly Owned Works*, *supra* at 18–24.

tion method should be used if the gains (in accuracy) of this method are not outweighed by the costs of its implementation. Many of these principles reflect common sense rather than a legal or economic analysis. Even more difficult is the question of how to define the rate-setting standards in a general fashion and apply them in the individual case. Moreover, the relationship between exclusive rights and rate-setting standards might seem a paradox at first. On the one hand, exclusive rights imply a commitment to negotiations between right holders and licensees; hence, a market-driven approach. On the other hand, rate-setting standards do not always order to refer to a competitive market environment, but also to take broader policy goals into account. This applies to rights to remuneration, but also to licensing via CMOs, where exclusive rights are licensed. The reason for this might be that a functional market in such situations does not, or cannot exist, especially in cases where it is practically not possible to individually negotiate or enforce rights; rights to remuneration and collective management can serve as an answer to this problem. Furthermore, it is a valid policy decision to replace exclusive rights with rights to remuneration, not only because one prefers a liability rule over a property rule but in order to influence the royalty flow by defining rate-setting standards.

Both in the United States and the EU, the question of what constitutes a "proper/correct" rate has received a number of answers; in fact, there is no uniform answer. Certain standards will favor right holders in creating larger license fees while others will trigger reduced fees for the financial benefit of users. As copyright law works with rewards and incentives for the dissemination of creative production, the financial aspect expressed in the license rate will have a significant impact on these factors.[1367] Thus, at this preliminary stage, the question of rate-setting is less a mathematical or general economic issue, but rather a question of what copyright law aims to achieve, also in interaction with competition law. Thus, at the very definition of rate-setting standards, the crucial question boils down to copyright theory, more precisely the aim of the different provisions which confer rights upon authors.[1368] If the copyright law of a jurisdiction aims at granting authors a special reward, this reward might be higher than what could be obtained in a competitive market for the use of the rights. Hence, this decision can very well be a different one when assessing ordinary product markets. Therefore, a special consideration or "treatment" of CMOs in this context is certainly in order. Competition law should not be applied in a way that disregards the aims of copyright law.

Once these aims are identified, it is necessary to consider how to define rate-setting standards in order to best achieve these aims. As far as the rate court proceedings are concerned, U.S. law provides for a market-oriented standard

1367 *Cf.* in this connection *MOBITV 2010*, 712 F. Supp. 2d 206 at 209.

1368 *See, e.g.*, Lunney, *The United States Experience*, *supra* at 363; Williams, *Royalty-Rate Disparity*, *supra* at 392 (arguing that the § 801 standards better reflects the aims of U.S. copyright law than the "willing buyer, willing seller" standard).

– that is, at least, the courts' understanding of the term "reasonable fee". While a similar standard applies to section 112 and to certain "newer" services under section 114, a standard that takes broader policy goals into consideration applies to section 115 and certain older services under section 114 of the U.S. Copyright Act. These standards, more than the market-driven standards, seem to be comparable to the ECJ's decisions on license fees and the rules of the CMD, as it is consistently highlighted that right holders should receive appropriate remuneration for the use of their works. Additionally, the ECJ has emphasized that one must consider the economic value of the rights and the actual use as well as the services provided by CMOs. This, in fact, may be closer to market-driven standards than it seems at first glance if one assumes that a willing buyer and seller acting reasonably would take these factors into account when negotiating the license fee. Hence, it is an essential aspect of the assessment of a license fee whether it corresponds to the value of the rights obtained. The valuation of copyrights thus necessary has however proven problematic in both the U.S. and the EU.[1369]

While the ECJ and the Collective Management Directive have only given general standards, and the final determination will have to be made primarily on the national level, the rate courts have been entrusted with this task in the U.S. It is at this point, the application of rate-setting standards, where a myriad of problems begin. In evaluating whether a license fee is acceptable, one has essentially relied on methods of comparison. While the rate courts refer to historic license fees, the ECJ – with the aim of the Internal Market in mind – compared the fees in different member states in its *Tournier* ruling.[1370] This approach can be taken in respect of both calculation methods and the level of license fees; however, it seems that it is more important for the level of license fees. For instance, it will be comparatively easy to assess a license fee based solely on the gross revenue of a user who only occasionally uses music in its services: Most likely, one would conclude that such method is problematic because it charges for something that is not (entirely) derived from the licensed content; thus, one could order the CMO to adapt the method. In turn, defining exact rates as such is much harder. In any event, the comparison approach has multiple flaws that need not be recounted here in detail.[1371] The main problem – leaving aside that the courts tasked with rate-setting might lack resources

1369 In this connection, *Lunney* highlights that that "even a monopolist will price its goods so that some consumers value them more than the price. Otherwise, the monopolist will not sell any of its goods", *see* Lunney, *The United States Experience*, *supra* at 338 n. 115.

1370 U.S. courts may however take fees charged by other CMOs in the country into account or use them as benchmarks, *see, e.g., ASCAP (Application RealNetworks and Yahoo, Inc.)*, 627 F. 3d 64 at 83 ("Because these two companies operate in the market in such similar manners, BMI's agreements are instructive").

1371 *See, e.g.,* Cirace, *Economic Analysis*, *supra* at 298, 304–305; Lang, *Antitrust Law*, *supra* at 52; Lunney, *The United States Experience*, *supra* at *339. See also* Mestmäcker, *Comparative Observations*, *supra* at 234.

and expertise – is that there is often no competitive market which a case at issue could be compared to.[1372] The very reason for the establishment of judicial rate-setting is often the absence of a competitive market due to the CMOs' monopoly power.[1373] From this perspective, the ECJ's market comparison concept is flawed at the outset: If CMOs possess legal monopolies in the other member states, one must consider whether the license fees charged correspond to rights valued according to market principles. Admittedly, however, such comparison might give a first indication.[1374] One might question whether antitrust courts should act as price regulators in the first place.[1375] *Cirace* has pointed out that rate-setting is a political decision, hence a legislative rather than a judicial task;[1376] however, no matter who sets the price, it is hardly conceivable how a price thus set would yield an efficient result.[1377] In spite of this insurmountable problem, at some point, a decision must be made which will necessarily involve some form of comparison. Perhaps the best solution is providing for an arbitration system which enables (collective) bargaining[1378] with CMOs, a specialized rate-setting authority acting in case the parties cannot reach an agreement. Legislation should provide for a corresponding statutory framework, but too detailed rules might render the process inflexible. In this connection, one could conceive a variety of combined solutions: The act could, for instance, specify a set of calculation methods, whereas a specialized court sets the corresponding rates in the individual case.

It should not be forgotten that the allocation of revenues from users to right holders via rate-setting processes involves important discrimination issues.

1372 *ASCAP (Application of Capital Cities/ABC, Inc.)*, 831 F. Supp. 137 at 144; Korman, *U.S. Position*, *supra* at 176; Poort & Quintais, *Levy Runs Dry*, *supra* at 214. Also under the default EU excessive price doctrine, it must be established what the competitive price in a competitive market might have been and whether the difference to the price actually charged is excessive, *see* de la Mano et al., *Article 102*, *supra* at 520.

1373 *See, e.g., United States v. BMI*, 426 F. 3d 91 at 96; Lunney, *The United States Experience*, *supra* at 339.

1374 Allendesalazar & Vallina, *The Usual Suspects*, *supra* at 384 (advocating an analysis combining the economic value approach with the comparison of the fees in different member states). *See also Autortiesību un komunicēšanās konsultāciju aģentūra / Latvijas Autoru apvienība*, C-177/16, Opinion of AG Wahl at ¶ 81.

1375 III Areeda & Hovenkamp, *Antitrust Principles*, *supra* at ¶ 720b; Crane, *Rate-Setting Courts*, *supra* at 326; Einhorn, *Partial Withdrawal*, *supra* at 200–201; I Hovenkamp et al., *IP and Antitrust*, *supra* at § 22.8; Turk, *Hard Day's Night*, *supra* at 534; U.S. Copyright Office, *Music Marketplace*, *supra* at 90–105; Wünschmann, *Kollektive Verwertung*, *supra* at 163.

1376 Cirace, *Economic Analysis*, *supra* at 299–300, 306 n. 174. *See also Moor-Law*, 527 F. Supp. 758 at 772; Lunney, *The United States Experience*, *supra* at 339.

1377 Cirace, *Economic Analysis*, *supra* at 299–300, 306 n. 174.

1378 Collective bargaining on the side of the users is also practiced in the U.S.: The RMLC, for instance, negotiates with CMOs on behalf of radio stations, *see Radio Music License Comm.*, 29 F. Supp. 3d 487 at 491; the TVMLC carries out the same task on behalf of commercial television stations, *see* Television Music Licensing Committee, *About US*, https://tvmlc.com/about/ (last visited April 26, 2017). *See also Meredith*, 87 F. Supp. 3d 650 at 655.

One does not only have to determine how much users should pay in total but also how these amounts are to be distributed among right holders.[1379] Such allocation should be made, again having the aims of copyright law in mind: Are these aims best served by favoring authors, performers, or derivative right holders and intermediaries? In this connection, the U.S. experience shows that different rate-setting standards for different groups of right holders can lead to significant differences in the royalty return. This phenomenon – which is frequently called the "rate disparity" – refers to that the holders of sound recording rights (in European terminology: related rights) receive much higher fees than the holders of performance rights.[1380] A related problem concerns the situation where the very same rights held by the very same groups of right holders are subject to different standards. This situation occurs where standards distinguish between different types of uses and hence center around the discrimination of different groups of users. Again, the United States offers a good example. As explained above, different standards apply to different groups of users under section 114, a fact that is often criticized.[1381] It seems that the (admittedly very broad) standards provided for by EU law do not trigger by themselves comparable problems of discrimination: The ECJ's case law has been, for the time being, consistent as to the royalty standards applied to different groups of right holders and users. Likewise, such a distinction is not inherent to the notions of fair compensation and equitable remuneration.[1382] Non-discriminatory standards at this kind are preferable as long as they enable courts to adapt them to the individual case and help achieve the aims of copyright law. It is important to emphasize that uniform standards do not (and should not) necessarily mean that equal rates should be paid by all users; in fact, differences are desirable where justified.[1383] One could also ask whether differences between the rate-setting standards for exclusive rights and rights to remunera-

---

1379 It is often the case that not all right holders (*e.g.*, songwriters and performers) are represented by the same CMO; hence, the question how a CMO should distribute revenues among its members is of a different nature, *see* section 3.1.6. above.

1380 Brabec, *Performance Right*, *supra* at 25–26; Turk, *Hard Day's Night*, *supra* at 494–495; U.S. Copyright Office, *Music Marketplace, supra* at 159; Williams, *Royalty-Rate Disparity*, *supra* at 389–391. One major factor is § 114(i) of the U.S. Copyright Act, *see* Pomianowski, *Rate-Setting Regime*, *supra* at 1532.

1381 DiCola, *Copyright Equality*, *supra* (discussing both economic and constitutional problems); Loren, *Dual Narratives*, *supra* (discussing the protection of incumbent industries). *See also* Williams, *Royalty-Rate Disparity*, *supra* at 395–397 (stating that technology neutral standards are in order).

1382 The CMD conceptually leans toward convergence not in terms of standards but in terms of management, as it provides for a definition of "rights revenue" which applies to both exclusive rights and right to remuneration, *see* CMD art 3(h).

1383 DiCola, *Copyright Equality*, *supra* at 1843 ("Regulatory parity is a distinct issue from the level of royalties paid"). *See also* Crane, *Rate-Setting Courts*, *supra* at 315–316 (stating that the comparing benchmark approaches lead to an – not necessarily desirable – equality situation).

tion in musical works and sound recordinds are well founded.[1384] This also relates to the rate-setting procedures and bodies.[1385]

In this connection, it should be noted that the rates charged by CMOs can be influenced by both specialized and general authorities. For instance, especially in the EU, the Commission can act as price regulator (based on article 102(a) TFEU). Accordingly, CMOs do not only have to observe the copyright-specific standards set forth by the directives (*e.g.*, art. 16(2) of the CMD) but also the general standards provided for by competition law. One could wonder whether or to what extent the different standards influence one another. In *Biedrība*, the AG rejected the position of the Dutch government which proposed taking the copyright-standards of the directives into account for the purposes of the antitrust analysis. According to his opinion, the antitrust rules and the copyright-related directives "pursue different objectives and respond to a different logic".[1386] While the background of the provisions is certainly different, the lines blur if one takes a closer look. On the one hand, as stated above, CMOs usually possess a dominant position, so that they fall within the scope of article 102. On the other hand, both set of rules can be understood as price regulation tools. While in most sectors specific price regulation (apart from the antitrust framework) does not exist, the legislator decided to specifically address the fees for copyright licenses in several directives. The question is now whether there can be (or should be) a rate which fulfills the requirements of, for instance, the CMD's article 16 by providing for appropriate remuneration but at the same time conflicts with the TFEU's article 102. Answering the question in the positive appears to threaten the coherence of the regulatory system.[1387] It is hard to allege that a CMO demands appropriate remuneration and, by doing so, abuses its dominant position. Besides, as collective management is often a practical necessity, it does not seem reasonable to strictly separate the standards. Accordingly, the fact that a CMO is capable of demonstrating that its rates fulfill the standards of the copyright-related directives should be a very strong indication that it complies with the antitrust rules. At any rate, the two set of rules are not as different as one might think. For instance, article 16(2) of the CMD provides that tariffs should be "reasonable to [...] the economic value of the use of the rights in trade". This is similar to the judgements of the

1384 As long as EU law distinguishes standards referring to "economic value in trade" and "fair compensation", one must take this difference into account, *see* Quintais, *Proposal for a Directive*, *supra* at 11–12. *See also* Guibault, *Collective Management Directive*, *supra* at 750.

1385 Gervais, *The Landscape*, *supra* at 610–613; U.S. Copyright Office, *Music Marketplace, supra* at 81–84. 155–157 (stating that the duties of the rate courts should be transferred to the CRB). *See also* Fakler, *Rate-Setting Litigation*, *supra* at 5–6.

1386 *Autortiesību un komunicēšanās konsultāciju aģentūra / Latvijas Autoru apvienība*, C-177/16, Opinion of AG Wahl at ¶ 77. The ECJ did not expressly rule on this point in its decision.

1387 However, it should be noted that the EU competition rules pertain to EU primary law, whereas the copyright-related directives are part of EU secondary law, *see* section I.4.1.

ECJ.[1388] In the same vein, the AG acknowledged that CMOs can justify higher fees compared to other member states by showing that their licensees derive, relative to the other member states, increased benefits from the licensed content.[1389]

e) Approaches to Blanket Licensing

Historically, collective management of copyrights has – primarily from a user's perspective – inherently been linked to the practice of blanket licensing. In fact, the blanket license can be described as the main feature of the traditional CMO model: Where, for instance, right holders set the license fees for their works individually, one speaks of centralized management rather than collective management.[1390]

When analyzing the courts' approaches to blanket licensing, it is necessary to develop an understanding of what a blanket license actually means. In its landmark decision in *CBS*, the Supreme Court assessed a license which i) covered the entire repertoire of the CMO and ii) the fee for which did not directly depend on the amount or type of music used,[1391] so that no record keeping was necessary. While the first element has consistently been upheld – both in the U.S. and the EU –, U.S. courts have been inclined to adapt the fee calculation, most notably through the AFBL. A fee for a blanket license requiring some form of recording keeping may be somewhat in tension with the older U.S. case law and a literal reading of the Consent Decrees,[1392] but it seems that U.S. courts have gradually evolved the concept further rather than radically abandoning its traditional understanding. This evolution leads to a broader understanding of the concept of blanket license with an emphasis on the scope of the license rather than its particular way of calculation.[1393] In the seminal

---

1388 *See e.g., Autortiesību un komunicēšanās konsultāciju aģentūra / Latvijas Autoru apvienība*, C-177/16 at ¶ 35 (citing prior case law).

1389 *Autortiesību un komunicēšanās konsultāciju aģentūra / Latvijas Autoru apvienība*, C-177/16, Opinion of AG Wahl at ¶ 129.

1390 Ficsor, *Collective Management*, *supra* at 22–23 (on "centralized" management). *See also* section I.3. above.

1391 *BMI v. CBS*, 441 U.S. 1 at 5. Yet, a flat fee does not mean that the parties did not take into account the amount of previous and expected use, *see ASCAP (Application of Capital Cities/ ABC, Inc.)*, 831 F. Supp. 137 at 162.

1392 *ASCAP (Application RealNetworks and Yahoo, Inc.)*, 627 F. 3d 64 at 84; *ASCAP (Application of Muzak)*, 309 F. Supp. 2d 566 at 579. *See* for a definition of "blanket license" ASCAP Consent Decree § II(E).

1393 In *MobiTV*, the court was asked to rule on a TTTA license and called this license a "blanket public performance license", *see MOBITV*, 681 F.3d 76 at 78. In *AEI* the court focused more on the fact that licensees had requested access to all the works in BMI's repertoire, *see BMI (Application of AEI Music Network)*, 275 F. 3d 168 at 177 ("Here, in contrast [to *Shenandoah*], Applications have requested a license to all of the compositions in BMI's repertory and not to a subset thereof"). *See also ASCAP (Application of Capital Cities/ABC, Inc.)*, 831 F. Supp. 137 at 162, 164 ("As indicated, the approach adopted by the Court takes the fees

European *Tournier* case, the ECJ largely focused on the scope of the blanket license and quite briefly reiterated its general test with regard to a "blanket or flat-rate royalty".[1394] Hence, the ECJ neither categorically obliged CMOs to introduce one, nor did it prohibit them from offering a blanket license with a fee calculation involving recording keeping; it essentially did not deal with this matter in *Tournier*.[1395]

In essence, from the antitrust standpoint, the legality of a blanket license rests on rebutting the fundamental accusations of tying (users have to license the entire repertoire and not subsets) and price fixing.[1396] However, both elements are not only relevant for blanket licenses. In fact, every license issued by a CMO can be viewed from the price fixing perspective; this basically includes the licenses provided for by the Consent Decrees: Also in regard of the PPL – which requires record keeping on the side of the users – right holders would "fix" the price per this particular method of calculation. The same principle, as observed by the Second Circuit, applies to a CMO offering licenses that cover limited parts of its repertoire,[1397] except where price competition is possible, especially by letting right holders freely determine (or negotiate) the fee for the works owned by them and which are licensable through the CMO.[1398] Likewise, every license offered by a CMO aggregating the rights of multiple right holders can be seen from the tying perspective. Both aspects should be considered when carrying out the antitrust analysis.

Traditionally, however, the "classic" blanket license has been at the center of the disputes between users and right holders. This is not surprising as this license type possesses the potential for both great efficiency gains and serious antitrust concerns. U.S. and European courts have dealt with licenses of this type, and courts in both jurisdictions came to the same results insofar as they upheld the license. These courts and authorities concurred that blanket licensing was permissible due to efficiency gains (blanket license is a "new product"[1399]).

paid by each network in 1985 and adjusts it to account for changes in applicants' gross revenues and use of ASCAP music").

1394 *Tournier*, 395/87 at ¶ 45. These statements concerned TFEU art. 102.

1395 In *Kanal 5* the ECJ assessed a calculation method which was based on the user's reports and hence require record keeping, *see Kanal 5*, C-52/07 at ¶ 33–34; *Kanal 5*, C-52/07, Opinion of AG Trstenjak at ¶ 9. The scope of the license was of no special interest.

1396 The scope of the license and the fees can naturally be considered under TFEU art. 102 and § 2 of the Sherman Act as well, which has proven especially important in the EU. Often, however, it seems that there is not much difference between the results of the analysis under the provisions on unlawful combinations except in case of evidential issues.

1397 *CBS v. ASCAP*, 620 F. 2d 930 at 936 n. 7.

1398 *Prof. Lunney* considers the CCC-model as a viable alternative to the traditional model of collective management because it offers an annual blanket license (fee set by the CCC) and a per-copy license (fee set by right holder), *see* Lunney, *The United States Experience*, *supra* at 348, 365–366.

1399 The "new product" approach was followed by the Commission in its *IFPI Simulcasting* decision, for instance, *see* Drexl, *Competition and Development*, *supra* at 214.

Neverthess, the reasons for upholding the license differ significantly. In this connection, blanket licensing is an excellent example how the United States and the European Union can actively share experiences in order to approach the issues under their antitrust laws. This is reflected by the *Tournier* case, where the AG relied on the rationales of U.S. law for his analysis of the blanket license;[1400] arguably, his findings influenced the final judgment of the court.[1401]

As reflected by the case law referred to above, blanket licenses have not been prohibited as such; it was necessary to conduct a more thorough analysis. In the United States, substantial weight is given to the question of whether users could realistically obtain licenses from the right holders directly and, by logical connection, whether the rights grant from right holder to the CMO is of an exclusive nature. Indeed, the violation of antitrust laws is far less obvious if users can actually choose between the blanket and individual licenses and provided that all interested right holders have access to the pooled license.[1402] In stark contrast, direct licensing has not been a decisive factor in the EU. The ECJ did not positively confirm the blanket license, but upheld the license as long as there was no better alternative;[1403] such alternative would have to entirely safeguard the right holders' interest without an increase in management costs.[1404] While acknowledging the blanket license's efficiency gains and the protection of right holders, there is no allusion whatsoever to the users' ability to negotiate direct licenses. It should be observed, however, that blanket licenses combined with an exclusive rights grant do raise antitrust issues, also under article 101.[1405] What is conspicuous in comparison to the U.S. practice is that blanket licenses are considered to be permissible *even though* no options of direct licensing exist.[1406] In fact, European antitrust analysis on the justification of the traditional CMO model often times rests on the premise that direct licensing is generally not possible.

From this perspective, under U.S. law, the relation between right holders and CMOs is strongly connected with their relation to users: If a CMO refuses to give its members the right to issue direct licenses, this will raise the antitrust-based question whether the organization puts unreasonable restraints on its members while at the same time, the practice of blanket licensing will be

1400 *Tournier,* 395/87, Opinion of AG Jacobs at ¶ 49.

1401 Also the Commission looked at the U.S. experiences with CMOs in the course of the preparatory works for the CMD, *see* Impact Assessment 2012 at 143–146 (Annex M).

1402 I Hovenkamp et al., *IP and Antitrust, supra* at § 22.3a1, 22.4a2 (on tying and foreclosure).

1403 In this regard, the Supreme Court employed a similar, but more subtle rationale.

1404 *Tournier*, 395/87 at ¶ 33. Before *Tournier*, it had been noticed that "[i]n Europe, the legitimacy of blanket licensing has never been seriously questioned", *see* Mestmäcker, *Comparative Observations*, *supra* at 229.

1405 Wünschmann, *Kollektive Verwertung*, *supra* at 91.

1406 One of the rare examples where the Commission dealt with this matter is the *MTV/VPL* case, *see* Porter, *Role of Collecting Societies*, *supra* at 675. U.S. courts have frequently found no restraint of trade if direct licensing is possible.

under strict antitrust scrutiny, assessing whether the CMO deprived users of options other than the blanket license. Already before the ruling of the Supreme Court, it had been found that blanket licensing did not violate the Sherman Act because the option of direct licensing existed.[1407] The connection between the right holder and user relations of CMOs can also be observed in the EU, however, from a reverse perspective: The ECJ permitted blanket licenses, as long as there was no other way to entirely safeguard the right holders' interests without increasing the management costs. Thus, allowing the users to negotiate with right holders directly was of no particular concern.

Efficiency might influence the analysis as regards both tying (scope) and price fixing (rate-setting). Efficiency caused the Supreme Court to classify the blanket licenses as a new product;[1408] if this product is different from a mere aggregation of individual licenses, tying will generally be ruled out.[1409] One could also justify the license on a different level: A basic rationale behind the tying argument from the users' perspective might be that without tying, a cheaper license could be obtained. This argument is, however, not well founded, as the "take less – pay less approach", though appealing at first sight, does not always work for performance rights in musical works. Besides the obvious administration and monitoring cost argument which could contradict a lower license fee, one could wonder whether the value derived from the songs (hypothetically) individually licensed exceeds the fee for the blanket license in the first place. For a network, for instance, which "needs one piece of music during a certain program, the value of the license depends upon the music's contribution to network revenues, not on the number of songs played."[1410] As regards price fixing, the Supreme Court rejected the per se approach because the license had in fact a redeeming value and hence was no "naked" restraint. Lower courts used the option of direct licensing to conclude that a blanket license, under these circumstances, did not constitute a restraint of trade. Under EU law, the dogmatic grounds for upholding the blanket license are less clear in the ECJ's analysis. One can assume, however, that a blanket license – in the EU typically without the option of directly negotiating with right holders – requires justification under both articles 101 and 102 TFEU. Such justification can be built on efficiency gains and the protection of the right holders' interest.

One can extensively debate whether, to what extent, and under what circumstances blanket licenses possess a degree of redeeming value justifying permission under antitrust doctrines. The fact is, however, that also recent court

1407 *K-91*, 372 F. 2d 1 at 4 (also highlighting the rate-setting mechanism under the ASCAP Consent Decree).

1408 *BMI v. CBS*, 441 U.S. 1 at 21–23.

1409 I Hovenkamp et al., *IP and Antitrust*, *supra* at § 22.3b2, 22.5.

1410 IX Areeda & Hovenkamp, *Antitrust Principles 2006*, *supra* at ¶ 1717f3. *See also* I Hovenkamp et al., *IP and Antitrust*, *supra* at § 22.3a1.

decisions have not displayed doubts that the advantages of this type of license subsist.[1411] Indeed, it is hard to say that blanket licenses do not have any redeeming value as a general rule; but assuming, even in absence of the entirety of transaction costs savings, the blanket license was a CMO's vehicle to reap license fees higher than market prices, one could reasonably question whether such a cartel of thousands of members would succeed if the members can negotiate individually.[1412] Given the option of direct negotiations, there will be no imposition of anticompetitive output reduction.[1413] Besides, efficiency might not be the only consideration in this context. Although the efficiency gains of blanket licenses are acknowledged by the ECJ, the court appears to accept losses in efficiency if these are necessary for the protection of right holders. In this light, the question is not so much whether one could streamline the licensing process further but, again, whether such means are compatible with this aim. Last, blanket licensing is very different from paradigmatic cases of price fixing and bid-rigging, as it is it openly done[1414] and leads to offering of a product which requires the participation of a large group of right holders;[1415] hence, a new product which individual right holders cannot create.

There remains the question why CMOs should be permitted to issue licenses eliminating price competition amongst the works so licensed. Obviously, a reason might be that other methods of administrating the works covered by the repertoire would lead to an increase in management costs. But let's assume for the sake of argument that alternatives to blanket licenses exist, causing roughly equal or, as the case might be, proportional costs; and let's put aside to what extent one weighs the interests of right holders vis-à-vis the users.[1416] Alternative models comprise a fee calculation linked to the CMOs' internal distribution policies (which are often based on music use)[1417] or a system where every individual right holder sets the price of his or her works in the repertoire, as done by the CCC already mentioned before.[1418] Even proponents of the traditional blanket license should admit that these alternative models do have advantages; highlighting the benefits of the blanket license

---

1411 *See, e.g.*, *Meredith*, 1 F. Supp. 3d 180 at 204–205. The Supreme Court noted, beside the efficiency argument, that compulsory licenses – which continue to be widely used – indicate that bundling constructions can be beneficial, *see BMI v. CBS*, 441 U.S. 1 at 16.

1412 XIII Areeda & Hovenkamp, *Antitrust Principles 2006*, *supra* at ¶ 2104b1 (stating that absent transaction costs savings, a price higher than the market price would not work if right holders can issue direct licenses).

1413 XI Areeda & Hovenkamp, *Antitrust Principles 2006*, *supra* at ¶ 1907c.

1414 Sector specific regulation requiring transparency might also help increase the trust in CMOs.

1415 XI Areeda & Hovenkamp, *Antitrust Principles 2006*, *supra* at ¶ 1907c.

1416 The interest of right holders in not setting the fees themselves might, for instance, simply be that they are not trained to do so; and that they want a CMO to assist them rather than a publisher which is more likely to pursue its own interests.

1417 *BMI v. CBS*, 441 U.S. 1 at 33 (J.P. Stevens, dissenting).

1418 As mentioned before, this model is favored by *Prof. Lunney*, *see* Lunney, *The United States Experience*, *supra* at 365–366 (stating that the Consent Decrees should be amended).

does not mean that there are no other workable models. In turn, however, advantages of other price setting mechanisms do not necessarily render the blanket's benefits obsolete. The question at issue is how antitrust law should deal with a fee-setting model that has, for the most part at least, both beneficial and anti-competitive characteristics. As the court in *Moor-Law*, citing the Third Circuit, observed:

> [T]he test is not whether the defendant deployed the least restrictive alternative. Rather the issue is whether the restriction actually implemented is 'fairly necessary' in the circumstances of the particular case, or whether the restriction 'exceeds the outer limits of restraint reasonably necessary to protect the defendant.'[1419]

It is certainly true that there are licensing models that are less problematic from an antitrust point of view, but this does not automatically render blanket licenses unlawful.[1420] In fact, the problem is not that a CMO offers a blanket license; the problem is that are no further licensing options which allow price competition within the repertoire and between which users could choose. Hence, the actual question is not whether blanket licenses should be prohibited, but whether CMOs should be required to offer further licensing options.

The point here is not categorically ruling out the application of antitrust law to blanket licenses; the point is which instrument the law should use to address the related concerns. It may very well be that blanket license is not an ideal licensing solution, at least in some environments; however, it is questionable whether antitrust law is the right tool to address this issue. Antitrust law is designed as an ex post mechanism condemning unacceptable practices. While ex ante instruments like consent decrees or commitment decisions can be relied upon in principle, the U.S. experience has shown that not all CMOs face equal restrictions; there is, as a matter of principle, no reason why ASCAP should be required to offer a "price competition license" while SESAC is not. It seems that the best way to address this issue is through sector-specific legislation. Such legislation is better suited to reconcile the notorious differences between the antitrust and copyright perspectives regarding collective management. Such legislation should non-discriminatorily require CMOs to offer licensing options other than blanket licenses if this is in line with efficiency consideration[1421] as well as the aims of copyright law.

In summary, it can be stated that blanket licenses are not and should not be prohibited as such by antitrust law. Adaptions to the fee calculation can be

1419 *See also Moor-Law*, 527 F. Supp. 758 at 769 (citing *American Motor Inns, Inc. v. Holiday Inns, Inc.*, 521 F.2d 1230, 1248–1249 (3rd Cir. 1975)). This seems to be similar to the ECJ's approach to the CMOs.

1420 *See also Buffalo Broadcasting*, 744 F. 2d 917 at 933 (stating that antitrust law does not necessarily prohibit practices which are undesirable from an economic point of view); I Hovenkamp et al., *IP and Antitrust*, *supra* at § 22.4a3.

1421 *See* for an economic analysis of CMOs in the online environment Lichtenegger, *Verwertungsgesellschaften*, *supra* at 246–270.

made to fit the needs of the individual case; a flexible concept of blanket licenses as regards fee calculation seems to adequately serve this purpose.[1422] Sector-specific legislation should, however, require CMOs to offer additional license types if warranted by economic analysis and copyright theory.

Whether a blanket license without the option of direct licenses should be permitted is a different issue; the availability of direct negotiations definitely contributes to their validity. This question concerns the European regulation. While the bargaining power argument – i.e. the protection of right holders – is respectable, one could ask whether large users do not already have to option to force right holders to withdraw works from CMO and license them directly; or to issue a non-commercial licenses under article 5(3) of the Collective Management Directive.

f) Of Users, Discotheques, and Streaming Services

CMOs – as undertakings possessing an extremely high degree of market power – are usually prohibited from discriminating against users. The concept of "users" generally includes anyone who publicly communicates (parts of) the repertoire to the public, but not consumers.[1423] While this is not expressly stated in the ASCAP Consent Decrees, it appears that the decree primarily has commercial users in mind.[1424] However, just like in relation to right holders, CMOs may also very well be required to distinguish between different users, or more precisely, categories of users: A television network, for instance, is hardly comparable to a restaurant or a streaming service.[1425] The Consent Decrees expressly acknowledge different groups of users. Also in Europe, competition law obliges CMOs to consider whether users are similarly situated[1426] and the CMD stipulates that licensing terms be based on "objective and non-discriminatory criteria".[1427] A side issue of the *Kanal 5* case was whether a CMO could apply a different calculation method for publicly financed TV stations than for private channels. Essentially, this is a matter of discrimination between users by applying different prices and was hence considered under

---

1422 In *Kanal 5*, the ECJ did not specifically mention the protection of the right holders' interest when it analyzed calculation methods, *see Kanal 5,* C-52/07 at ¶ 41.

1423 *See* CMD art. 3(k) ("'user' means any person or entity that is carrying out acts subject to the authorisation of rightholders, remuneration of rightholders or payment of compensation to rightholders and is not acting in the capacity of a consumer"). *See also* van Gompel, *Directive, supra* at 569.

1424 ASCAP Consent Decree § II(G) reads: "'Music user' means any person that (1) owns or operates an establishment or enterprise where copyrighted musical compositions are performed publicly, or (2) is otherwise directly engaged in giving public performances of copyrighted musical compositions". The BMI Consent Decree does not contain a definition.

1425 The nature of the licensee's service especially influences pricing schemes, *see* IX Areeda & Hovenkamp, *Antitrust Principles 2006, supra* at ¶ 1717f3.

1426 Allendesalazar & Vallina, *The Usual Suspects, supra* at 384–386.

1427 CMD art. 16.

article 102(c) TFEU.[1428] The underlying questions were matters of fact; the national court was thus competent to determine whether STIM, in fact, charged dissimilar royalties and whether private TV stations were in a competitive relationship with a public channel on the consumer market.[1429] The ECJ ruled that, if a dissimilar treatment and a competitive relationship could be found, STIM would "likely" abuse its dominant position.[1430] The practice might, however, be objectively justified (*e.g.*, by the task or method of the financing of public services undertakings).[1431] The differences between different users – translating into types of uses – has been acknowledged for statutory licenses as well.[1432]

From a regulatory perspective, it is worth considering whether new distinctions within the established categories of users should be acknowledged if these users possess very different market strength and economic power. Moreover, one should reflect on the position of "new" categories of users that do not technically obtain licenses from CMOs but still benefit from their repertoire.[1433]

3.3. CMOs and Other CMOs

The relationships between CMOs are subject to EU competition law just like the CMOs' relations with right holders and users; however, there is a distinct perspective taken in this. It is not so much the question of whether there are substantial differences in the bargaining power of one of the CMOs involved, which might lead to an abuse of such power, but whether the cooperation between these organizations has detrimental effects. The Commission was especially vigilant when it found indications that CMOs tried to transpose their traditional national monopolies to the Internet environment.[1434] As the

[1428] *Kanal 5,* C-52/07 at ¶ 43. The application of this article to right holders was alleged in *GVL*, but not answered by the court, *see GVL*, case 7/82 at ¶ 58. In *Tournier*, the AG stated that granting some discotheque owners more favorable conditions than others is not a violation of EU competition law if these "provide a genuine and adequate consideration for that special treatment", *see Tournier*, 395/87 at ¶ 56. Royalties charged to other categories of users could be an indication of an excessive price, *see id.* at ¶ 57.

[1429] *Kanal 5,* C-52/07, Opinion of AG Trstenjak at ¶ 111, 114. The AG had some doubts whether STIM's conduct was lawful because the royalties for SVT were calculated in advance as a prediction whereas the royalties for Kanal 5 and TV 4 were calculated retrospectively, *see id.* at ¶ 112.

[1430] *Kanal 5,* C-52/07 at ¶ 48.

[1431] *Kanal 5,* C-52/07, Opinion of AG Trstenjak at ¶ 47–48.

[1432] *See, e.g., Hewlett-Packard,* C-572/13 at ¶ 74–76.

[1433] *Gyertyánfy* considers "the producers of digital storing devices, providers of internet connection and of mobile telecommunication" as users in the economic sense, *see* Peter Gyertyánfy, *Collective Management of Music Rights in Europe After the CISAC Decision*, 41 IIC 59, 76 (2010).

[1434] Kuik & Dawes, *Media, supra* at 1721. *See also* Press Release, European Commission, *Commission opens proceedings into collective licensing of music copyrights for online use* (May

European Internal Market consists of several national markets predominantly managed by national CMOs, U.S. rules and case law do not exist to an extent comparable to that in the EU. Thus, a succinct account of U.S. law at the end of the chapter appears to suffice for the present purposes.

3.3.1. The Relationship Between CMOs as a Form of Cooperation

When one refers to the relationship between different CMOs, one primarily refers to the various forms of cooperation that exist between these organizations. Since article 101 has been applied exclusively in this connection,[1435] the case law deals with agreements between undertakings and (alleged) concerted practices. Typically, a CMO will only enter into an agreement (or engage in concerted practices) with another CMO if it expects benefits for its organization or its members. Therefore, in most cases, agreements in this field can be regarded as establishing a "win-win" situation for both the CMOs involved; moreover, cooperation is conceivable not only bilaterally, but also multi-laterally. This may, however, be contrary to article 101. While these agreements and practices can in principle be related to various issues, the primary field of examination under EU competition law have been so-called "reciprocal representation agreements" (RRAs). In *Tournier*, the ECJ laid down its understanding of RRAs:

> [A] "reciprocal representation contract" [...] must be taken to mean a contract between two national copyright-management societies concerned with musical works whereby the societies give each other the right to grant, within the territory for which they are responsible, the requisite authorizations for any public performance of copyrighted musical works of members of the other society and to subject those authorizations to certain conditions, in conformity with the laws applicable in the territory in question. Those conditions include in particular the payment of royalties, which are collected for the other society by the society which it has empowered to act as its agent. The contract specifies that each society is to apply, with respect to works in the other society's repertoire, the same scales, methods and means of collection and distribution of royalties as those which it applies for works in its own repertoire.[1436]

Thus, a CMO relies on the services of a CMO based in another country, and vice versa, in order to fulfill, also in foreign territories, the mandate which is given to it by the right holders it represents.[1437] Under this traditional system, a CMO offers licenses to all repertoires acquired from other CMOs by way of RRAs – since the network extended to virtually all other national CMOs one could speak of the "world repertoire". The core features are therefore i) a

---

03, 2004), *available at* http://europa.eu/rapid/press-release_IP-04-586_en.htm (last visited May 23, 2017).

1435 Drijber, *Competition law aspects*, *supra* at 71 (referring to the possibility of joint dominance).

1436 *Tournier*, 395/87 at ¶ 17; *Lucazeau,* 110/88 at ¶ 11.

1437 In *CISAC*, the Commission noted that RRAs are not agency agreements, *see CISAC Agreement,* COMP/C2/38.698 at ¶ 138–139. *See also* European Commission Guidelines on Vertical Restraints ¶ 12–21.

contractual agreement between CMOs which contains ii) a representation clause on iii) a reciprocal basis which leads to a one-stop shop for multi-repertoire licenses. Even though the ECJ referred to rights in musical works, the basic definition can be applied to other work categories or rights attached thereto, albeit the content of the agreement will differ.

In principle, there are two ways to organize the cross-border royalty flow resulting from the RRAs. Under so-called "A agreements", CMOs agree to pass on the collected royalties to the organization represented; under so-called "B agreements", the parties decide not to exchange any data and to distribute the collected royalties only to their own members (right holders).[1438] In the first case, right holders are compensated by transfers arising from the royalties collected by the representing CMO in a particular country, less the administrative costs; in the second case, the reduction of transfers and administrative costs constitutes an advantage, but there is, of course, the danger that the compensation does not accurately match the amount right holders would actually be entitled to.[1439]

The Collective Management Directive defines a "representation agreement" as

> any agreement between collective management organisations whereby one collective management organisation mandates another collective management organisation to manage the rights it represents, including an agreement concluded under Articles 29 and 30;[1440]

It is obvious that the directive incorporates the understanding that a representation agreement (RA) is of a contractual nature and specifies the conditions under which a CMO is represented by a sister society. However, a representation agreement does not necessarily comprise a reciprocal element under this definition. Thus, the CMD implements a broad scope and covers various forms of cooperation between CMOs as long as there is an element of representation.[1441] It is noteworthy that under the directive's definition, it is not necessary that CMOs operate in different member states or territories, whereas the ECJ's definition speaks of reciprocal representation "within the territory for which they are responsible". Moreover, it is not necessary that CMOs mandate each other in relation to all rights in its repertoire, although the wording of the directive implies that this will be the standard case ("the rights it repre-

---

1438 Guibault & van Gompel, *Collective Management 2010*, *supra* at 151 n. 64.

1439 Tuma, *Pitfalls and Challenges*, *supra* at 222–223.

1440 CMD art. 3(j).

1441 There is of course no doubt that the principle of reciprocity has played a fundamental role for the network of representation agreements, *see* Roger Wallis et al., *Contested Collective Administration of Intellectual Property Rights in Music – The Challenge to the Principles of Reciprocity and Solidarity*, 14 European J. of Communication 5, 14 (1999). Here, however, reference is to the scope of ECJ judgements and the CMD. In the following, the term representation agreement will be used. *See also* 2 Walter, *Verwertungsgesellschaftenrecht*, *supra* at 230.

sents"). The rules on the MTL agreement (articles 29 and 30 of the directive) suggest so, as they only cover multi-territorial licenses[1442] for online rights, hence, a category of rights. Conversely, it must be emphasized that the assessment under competition law naturally depends on the content of the agreement at issue, and it can be relevant for the purposes of article 101 whether there is a reciprocal element or whether the involved CMOs are established in different member states.

3.3.2. The European Approach to Representation Agreements

It was already in *Basset* that the ECJ mentioned the compatibility of RAs with EU competition law.[1443] Only two years later, in the *Tournier* and *Lucazeau* cases, the court examined agreements of this type in more detail in connection with the refusal to issue cross-border licenses:

> [R]eciprocal representation contracts between copyright-management societies have a twofold purpose: first, they are intended to make all protected musical works, whatever their origin, subject to the same conditions for all users in the same Member State, in accordance with the principle laid down in the international provisions; secondly, they enable copyright-management societies to rely, for the protection of their repertoires in another State, on the organization established by the copyright-management society operating there, without being obliged to add to that organization their own network of contracts with users and their own local monitoring arrangements. It follows from the foregoing considerations that the reciprocal representation contracts in question are contracts for services which are not in themselves restrictive of competition in such a way as to be caught by Article 85(1) of the Treaty [...].[1444]

Thus, the conclusion of representation agreements does not constitute by itself an infringement of article 101(1) TFEU,[1445] and CMOs may in principle rely on their representation by CMOs in other member states. The ECJ acknowledged that such contracts can be necessary under certain conditions and highlighted two points: On the one hand, they create a licensing system where the origin of the work is of no consideration; on the other hand, they solve the problem that CMOs would face if they had to license, monitor, and enforce the represented rights in (many) other member states. Yet, one must be careful when referring to this decision because its scope is limited in two respects. First, it is doubtful whether it can be applied to all types of uses. The complainants in *Tournier* and *Lucazeau* were discotheque owners and the court made its judgment in light of the analog nature of the uses that were made of protected works at that time. It is, therefore, necessary to scrutinize to what extent a

1442 The agreement refers to licenses which cover the territory of one than more member state, *see* CMD art. 3(m).

1443 *Basset,* 402/85 at ¶ 4. The ECJ merely summarized the opinion of the referring court; the question whether representation agreements were contrary to article 101 was not at issue in the case.

1444 *Tournier*, 395/87 at ¶ 19–20; *Lucazeau,* 110/88 at ¶ 13–14.

1445 *Wünschmann* highlights that RRAs can violate article 101 TFEU if they lead to a partitioning of the Internal Market, *see* Wünschmann, *Kollektive Verwertung*, *supra* at 180, 187–189.

particular RA possesses the potential for solving problems arising from licensing, monitoring, and enforcing rights in other member states, especially with a view to other available technological options. The assessment might differ when a CMO is not obliged, as the ECJ assumed, on economically feasible grounds, to rely on the infrastructure of another CMO in the case of certain work categories or types of uses (namely: online uses).[1446] Second, the ECJ delivered its opinion on the basis of the above-cited understanding of "reciprocal representation contract". The most fundamental criterion in this context was that the CMOs involved did not distinguish within the management process between the repertoires that they had directly acquired by contracts with right holders and the works managed on behalf of another CMO. Only in this way, it was possible for the ECJ to derive the first core purpose of representation agreements, namely to reinforce the principle of international copyright law that right holders are entitled to under the laws of a contracting state to the same level of protection as nationals of that state.[1447] For this reason, the ECJ ruled that the works are subject to the same conditions for the users in a member state "whatever their origin".[1448] Conversely, a representation agreement which puts works of foreign authors at a disadvantage will, therefore, be subject to closer scrutiny under article 101.

The Collective Management Directive again incorporates the principles of the case law. While it expressly leaves the rules on competition unaffected,[1449] it contains some general rules on RAs. It stipulates that CMOs must not discriminate against the owners of rights that are managed under such an agreement, especially in relation to tariffs, fees, collection, and distribution of the royalties.[1450] If a CMO wants to apply deductions other than management fees to the rights revenue, an express consent of the mandating CMO is required.[1451] In this connection, it is questionable whether "B agreements" will subsist in the future, as CMOs will have to exchange data and transfer the amounts arising from the royalties for the use of the protected works which are covered by the representation agreement.[1452] One can also infer from recital 30 that the directive envisages "A agreements" as the standard model.[1453] The diligence

1446 The question to what extent local presence is necessary plays a role in the competition law assessment of representation agreements and will be addressed below.

1447 *Tournier*, 395/87 at ¶ 18; *Lucazeau,* 110/88 at ¶ 12.

1448 *Tournier*, 395/87 at ¶ 19; *Lucazeau,* 110/88 at ¶ 13.

1449 CMD recital 11.

1450 *Id.* at art. 14.

1451 *Id.* at art. 15(1). Thus, deductions for social or cultural purposes are not permitted without the consent of the other CMOs, *see* van Gompel, *Directive*, *supra* at 592.

1452 Guibault, *Collective Management Directive*, *supra* at 746; 2 Walter, *Verwertungsgesellschaftenrecht*, *supra* at 260. It has been argued, however, that B agreements might be a good solution from a competition law point of view, *see* Drexl, *Competition and Development*, *supra* at 223–224.

1453 The recital reads: "[N]or should the collective management organisation be allowed to apply deductions to the rights revenue collected on behalf of another collective management organistandard is comparable to the rules set forth in relation to directly represented right holders: CMOs must "regularly, diligently and accurately" make the payments to the represented CMO within a timespan of nine months from the end of the financial year.[1454]

3.3.3. Restrictions Relating to the Representation of Right Holders

In the *CISAC* decision, the Commission dealt with agreements which prohibited the contracting CMOs, without the consent of the other involved CMO from accepting as members right holders who i) already held membership in the other organization or ii) possessed the nationality of the territory in which the other organization operated.[1455] The clause, therefore, limited the freedom of right holders to choose the CMO of their choice.[1456] The Commission found that such a clause limited the competition on two markets: First, on the right holders' market for the provision of management services; second, on the commercial users' market for the offer of licensing options because the agreement contributed to the establishment of national blocks of rights, which inhibited the emergence of substitutable repertoires as a prerequisite for actual competition.[1457] Therefore, the Commission found an infringement of article 101. On appeal, the General Court confirmed this opinion.[1458] It ruled that membership restrictions like those in questions were examples of clauses "explicitly declared incompatible with the common market" and constituted an "obvious restrictions of competition" because they delimited the Internal Market by na-

---

sation, other than deductions in respect of management fees, without the express consent of the other organisation. It is also appropriate to require collective management organisations to distribute and make payments to other organisations on the basis of such representation agreements no later than when they distribute and make payments to their own members and to non-member rightholders whom they represent. Furthermore, the recipient organisation should in turn be required to distribute the amounts due to the rightholders it represents without delay." Thus, the directive obviously assumes that the mandated CMO transfers the collected royalties to the represented CMO for further distribution, so that it is highly questionable whether B agreements are permitted under this regime.

1454 CMD art. 15(2), (3).

1455 *CISAC Agreement*, COMP/C2/38.698 at ¶ 124. The clause was initially also included in the CISAC model contract, but had been removed prior to the decision in 2008. Yet, most CMOs kept including this rule in their representation agreements, *see id.* at ¶ 30–35, 124 n. 94.

1456 *Id.* at ¶ 125.

1457 *Id.* at ¶ 126.

1458 The CISAC decision was addressed to twenty-four European CMOs of which four appealed against the Commission's ruling in respect of the membership restrictions, *see* Kuik & Dawes, *Media, supra* at 1723. The cases were *AEPI Elliniki Etaireia pros Prostasian tis Pnevmatikis Idioktisias AE v. Commission*, T-392/08 (EGC 2013), *Säveltäjäin Tekijänoikeustoimisto Teosto ry v. Commission*, T-401/08 (EGC 2013), *Société des auteurs, compositeurs et éditeurs de musique v. Commission*, T-422/08 (EGC 2013), *Staatlich genehmigte Gesellschaft der Autoren, Komponisten und Musikverleger reg. Gen. mbH v. Commission*, T-432/08 (EGC 2013). Only the second case is available in English.

tional frontiers.[1459] The court furthermore held that is was not necessary to establish that the membership clause was actually applied in practice[1460] and that it was irrelevant whether the infringing conduct had already been brought to an end prior to the proceeding.[1461] In a different case, the Commission opened preliminary investigations regarding anti-competitive practices by SCAPR, EJI, and CREDIDAM.[1462] It was asserted by Rights Agency, a UK company which represented performers vis-à-vis various CMOs, that the two CMOs in question put unjustified administrative burdens on foreign right holders as requirements for membership and that SCAPR included unlawful restrictions in its recommendation on membership policy. The Commission closed the investigation after the alleged discriminatory documents had been (voluntarily) amended by the mentioned actors.[1463]

Especially in its *CISAC* decision, the Commission made clear that discriminatory clauses regarding membership requirements in representation agreements will infringe article 101. In fact, this already follows from the previous case law on the relationship between CMOs and right holders (*GEMA*, *GVL*, *Daft Punk*, *see* section 3.1. above). Indeed, these decisions on article 102 cannot be regarded as tacitly deeming underlying contractual arrangements between CMOs compatible with 101.[1464] To the contrary, the protection of right holders is closely intertwined with the agreements between CMOs. This protection would be incomplete if a CMO was banned from a certain conduct when facing a right holder directly, while at the same time, it would be permitted to conclude agreements to this effect with sister organizations.[1465] However, applying this principle to representation agreements adds a further important element to the obligations faced by CMOs under the competition laws: Since article 101 does not presuppose a dominant position occupied by the involved undertakings,[1466] the ruling would – in principle – still apply in competitive markets with no dominant organizations. Furthermore, the Commission emphasized a consideration that might not have been fully clear from the previ-

---

1459 *Teosto*, T-401/08 at ¶ 61. *See also AEPI*, T-392/08 at ¶ 58; *SACEM* T-422/08 at ¶ 75; *AKM*, T-432/08 at ¶ 61.

1460 *Teosto*, T-401/08 at ¶ 65; *AKM*, T-432/08 at ¶ 65.

1461 *AEPI*, T-392/08 at ¶ 62; *Teosto*, T-401/08 at ¶ 67; *SACEM* T-422/08 at ¶ 79; *AKM*, T-432/08 at ¶ 66.

1462 SCAPR is the international association of national performers' rights organization and thus comparable to CISAC regarding performing rights; EJI and CREDIDAM are CMOs operating in Hungary and Romania, respectively, *see* Press Release, European Commission, *Antitrust: Commission welcomes steps taken by collective rights management bodies in Hungary and Romania to improve competition* (March 11, 2011), *available at* http://europa.eu/rapid/press-release_IP-11-284_en.htm?locale=en (last visited May 23, 2017).

1463 *Id.*

1464 Kuik & Dawes, *Media*, *supra* at 1724.

1465 This is also reflected by the fact that the rules of the CMD on representation agreements focus on right holders.

1466 Morris, *Trading Functions*, *supra* at 569.

ous cases:[1467] A CMO (based on a RA) must not reject a membership request solely on the grounds that a right holder is already a member of another society. Turning to the assessment under article 102, it seems likely that a CMO that refuses to represent a right holder solely on the basis of his or her membership in another CMO would be considered as abusing its dominant position as long as the representation would not lead to a form of "double membership" where a right holder assigns the same rights in the same works for the same territory; such a practice would most likely not be regarded as an infringement of article 101 if incorporated in representation agreements.[1468]

These conclusions can also be derived from the Collective Management Directive, although articles 14 and 15 on representation agreements are, strictly speaking, not applicable to restrictions on membership. If a CMO, based on a representation agreement, refuses a membership application due to the nationality of the right holders or his or her membership in another CMO, it does not discriminate against right holders whose rights it "manages under a representation agreement", as required by article 14. At issue is rather the opposite case because the rejected right holder's rights are precisely not managed under such an agreement. However, it follows from article 5(2) on the rights of right holders to choose without restrictions the CMO which they wish to entrust with the management of their rights that such conduct would violate the CMD in absence of appropriate justification.[1469] These rights guaranteed by the CMD, as well as the obligation to represent right holders, cannot be altered by an agreement concluded by third parties. Consequently, representation agreements leave unaffected the rights provided for in article 5. Right holders are expressly granted the rights to only assign categories of rights or types of works to CMOs; they can rely on this right to individually manage their rights or to simply assign them to another society, provided that its "scope of activities" is tailored accordingly; the concerns as to "double membership" also apply in this connection. The rights are granted to right holders regardless of whether they contract with a CMO possessing a dominant position or not so that ulti-

1467 In *Daft Punk*, the Commission dealt with a situation where right holders were denied the option of individually licensing their rights; entrusting another CMO with some rights was not prohibited by SACEM's statute and therefore not at issue in the case. The *GEMA I* and *GVL* cases dealt with restrictions based on nationality.

1468 Schierholz, *Collective Rights Management*, *supra* at 1160.

1469 For this interpretation, as long as parallel membership and not only nationality per se is concerned, it is necessary to consider the three examples for prohibited grounds for the refusal to offer management services mentioned in article 5(2) – nationality, residence or establishment – as not exhaustive. The CMD hints at this rationale in article 5(6) where it stipulates that a CMO must not restrict the right to withdraw rights or to terminate the mandate. Apparently, the directive was drafted following the circumstances of the *Daft Punk* case; conversely – even though the CMD does not make explicit reference to this point – this does not mean that a CMO may automatically refuse to manage certain categories of rights only because the right holder is already represented by another CMO (in respect of a different category of rights, for instance); the same should apply to withdrawals.

mately, the distinction between dominant and not dominant undertakings loses relevance in this connection.

Finally, it should be observed that the Commission in *CISAC* referred exclusively to "membership restrictions". However, also right holders who are not members of a CMO can have an interest in making use of the offered management services. Especially in light of the Collective Management Directive, the ruling should be understood as not only covering cases revolving around actual membership but all situations in which a CMO denies a right holder access to its services without justification. First, there is no reason why the prohibition of discrimination under article 101 should only be applied in respect of proper membership; second, the directive grants the right in article 5 to "right holders", irrespective of their status as members. In the case of members' rights that refer to the internal functioning of the CMO, article 6(2) provides for a prohibition of discrimination.

3.3.4. Tariffs, Rebates, and Deductions

The Commission mainly dealt with the issue of licensing fees in its *IFPI Simulcasting* decision[1470] and in the *Cannes Extension Agreement* case.[1471] It concluded that certain provisions in agreements in this ambit could run counter the aims or the EU competition rules.

a) The Coordination of Tariff Systems

In *IFPI Simulcasting*, IFPI[1472] asked the Commission to grant an exception[1473] from the competition rules under article 101(3) TFEU for its model contract which related to licensing required for the process of simulcasting.[1474] The agreement aimed at facilitating the grant of multi-territorial licenses by giving each of the CMOs involved the right to issue non-exclusive licenses for simulcasting in respect of the repertoire of the other contracting parties within the other CMOs' territories of operation. The licensing CMO had the responsibility to collect fees and other remuneration as well as to enforce the rights in

1470 *IFPI Simulcasting*, COMP/C2/38.014.

1471 *Cannes Extension Agreement*, COMP/C2/38.681.

1472 IFPI (International Federation of the Phonographic Industry) is an international association of record and music video producers who hold neighboring rights and are at the same time members of national CMOs. IFPI submitted the notification on behalf of these CMO but was not itself a contracting party, *see IFPI Simulcasting*, COMP/C2/38.014 at ¶ 6–7.

1473 Under the current Competition Regulation, there is no process to apply to the Commission for the grant of an exception; however, the Commission can make a declaratory statement if this is required by the public interest, *see* Competition Regulation recital 14.

1474 "Simulcasting" was defined as the "simultaneous transmission by radio and TV stations via the Internet of sound recordings included in their broadcasts of radio and/or TV signals", *see IFPI Simulcasting*, COMP/C2/38.014 at ¶ 2.

case of infringement.[1475] Thereby, the model agreement effectively established a one-stop shop for simulcasting, since users merely had to approach one CMO in order to obtain a license for the entire territories in which the participating CMOs operated.[1476] The fee which had to be paid for such a license was defined as an "aggregate tariff" composed of the relevant individual tariffs applied by each contracting CMO for simulcasting in its own territory.[1477] Although the Commission generally welcomed the initiative to promote MTL, it considered such a tariff structure problematic from a competition law perspective because it limited the CMO that granted the license in its freedom to charge a fee that it deemed appropriate.[1478] This calculation system would lead to a restriction of competition, since, as the individual CMOs faced no restriction in setting up their national tariffs, it would essentially lead to an identical product (the license covering the repertoires in the territories of the contracting parties) at a largely pre-determined price.[1479] The Commission underlined that it was especially restrictive of competition not to distinguish between the parts of the license that were meant to cover the administrative costs on the one hand and the royalty fee on the other hand because this made it impossible for users to assess the efficiency of the CMO in comparison with the other organizations.[1480] As requested by IFPI, the authority went on to consider whether the exception of article 101(3) was applicable. While the Commission acknowledged that the MTL one-stop-shop constituted a new product, the crucial point of the analysis was whether the intended measures regarding the tariff and pricing system were "indispensable" for the advantages which could be attained by the agreement as a whole. The Commission answered this question regarding the uniform tariff for management costs as well as for license fees in the negative; however, the parties agreed to amend the contract by providing for a separate identification of these items in order to enhance transparency vis-à-vis users.[1481] In relation to the pre-determination of tariffs, the Commission acknowledged that it was legitimate for national CMOs to maintain a certain degree of control over the multi-territorial license issued by a contract partner in order to ensure remuneration for their right holders.[1482] As a result of this

1475 *Id.* at ¶ 19–20. Following the country of destination principle, the royalties were due in every country where the simulcasting could be received, *see id.* at ¶ 21–22.

1476 *Id.* at ¶ 17. More specifically, this meant that every broadcasting station whose signals originated in the EEA could request a license from any participating CMO established in the EEA. This important rule was not included in the original model contract; prior to this amendment, a CMO could only grant multi-territorial licenses to broadcasting stations whose signal originated in its own territory of operation, *see id.* at ¶ 27–28.

1477 *Id.* at ¶ 24.

1478 *Id.* at ¶ 62, 67.

1479 *Id.* at ¶ 76.

1480 *Id.* at ¶ 71.

1481 *Id.* at ¶ 100, 103–104, 107. CMD art. 12(1) is based on a similar rationale, *see* van Gompel, *Directive*, *supra* at 587.

1482 *IFPI Simulcasting*, COMP/C2/38.014 at ¶ 110.

consideration and the changes brought to the agreement by the involved CMOs, the Commission granted an exception and declared article 101(1) inapplicable.[1483]

The *IFPI Simulcasting* Agreement was remarkable because it enabled users to obtain multi-territorial licenses while at the same time avoiding repertoire fragmentation.[1484] However, the CMOs involved had to make concessions in order to achieve the exemption from article 101. First of all, the "customer allocation clause" had to be removed, so that users from the entire EEA could obtain a license from any contracting CMO.[1485] Furthermore, they were required to clarify which part of the license fee related to management costs and what part to the royalty payment. The last point was criticized by the legal literature because, on the one hand, it obliged CMOs to disclose to users and competitors their costs structure which constituted legitimate business secrets.[1486] On the other hand, it was argued that even if CMOs were capable of precisely identifying the management costs, this did not necessarily imply that these amounts correspond to adequate pricing policies.[1487] It is was critically highlighted that the measures envisaged by the Commission in this respect essentially would lead to an infringement of article 101 if the involved CMOs had agreed to them autonomously because this would eliminate the "uncertainty of the rivals' conduct" as a prerequisite of competition.[1488] While these arguments certainly shed a different light on the *IFPI* decision, the simulcasting agreements possessed some conspicuous fundamental characteristics: Under this regime, competition between CMOs was significantly limited from the outset. It flows from the construction of the aggregate tariffs that the uncertainty of the rivals' conduct is not comparable to ordinary markets since individual CMOs maintain a certain control over the price charged by the competitor. Moreover, unlike normal competitive relationships, a CMO would still receive its share for the use of its offer (the repertoire), even in situations where a user chose to approach a "rival" society. From this perspective, the aggregate tariff as such contributed significantly to eliminate the uncertainty of the rival's conduct. The question remains, however, whether the disclosure of management costs was the right tool to meet the concerns associated with the aggregate tariff structure. In any event, it is necessary to consider whether there would have been a way to uphold the agreement with its positive effects under article 101 without the modifications ordered by the Commission. It may be necessary to reflect on the ruling with a view to the CMOs' relationships to users and right holders, rather than on the competitive level governed and restricted by representation agreements. As regards users, a major drawback of

1483 *Id.* at ¶ 107, 115.

1484 Hilty & Nérisson, *Digitization*, *supra* at 7.

1485 *Id.* at 7–8.

1486 Mestmäcker, *Collecting Societies*, *supra* at 357–358.

1487 *Id.*

1488 *Id.* at 358.

the disclosure of internal structures lies in the danger that CMO could lose bargaining power when negotiating licensing agreements with this group, which would ultimately lead to a reduction of collected revenues.[1489] As regards right holders, inducing competition on the level of administrative costs cannot be seen as directly translating these costs to the efficiency of the offered management services.[1490] A CMO that implements very simplified monitoring policies will incur lower administration costs to cover its expenses than a CMO which performs extensive checks; however, a simplified monitoring might deprive a right holder of parts of his revenue for the use of its work.[1491] The problem is not easily solved by the freedom of right holders to choose a society per their preference in the high or low level of monitoring and with corresponding management fees because they will typically lack the information to reasonably make such a decision.[1492] In principle, right holders could use their rights in the general assembly of a CMO to influence the management policies.[1493] Yet, this power only belongs to right holders who are members of the CMO in question and does not serve those members who are dissatisfied with the prevailing policy.

When the Commission reviewed the notified agreement, it concluded that the two problematic provisions restricted competition within the meaning of article 101(1) because they were not "objectively necessary" in order to ensure the appropriate remuneration of right holders and thus for the agreement to exist.[1494] It then again carried out the analysis whether mentioned clauses were "indispensable" under article 101(3). It appears likely that the analysis regarding article 101(1) was influenced by the decisions of the ECJ *in BRT v. SABAM* and *Tournier*. Even if the Commission did not expressly apply these decisions, its approach would still be consistent with the judgments of the court because it asked whether a measure taken by CMOs went beyond what was necessary for the protection of right holders ("appropriate level of remuneration").[1495] Thus, also in relation to representation agreements, CMOs must be careful not to exceed the limits of what is necessary for the attainment of that aim for the purposes of article 101(1).

Although the Collective Management Directive does not contain an explicit requirement under articles 14 and 15 of the directive, it is argued that the tariffs must separate the management costs and license fee.[1496]

1489 Riis, *Collecting Societies*, *supra* at 488.

1490 Philippe Gilliéron, *Collecting Societies and the Digital Environment*, 37 IIC 939, 950 (2006).

1491 Ficsor, *Collective Management*, *supra* at 47.

1492 Riis, *Collecting Societies*, *supra* at 488.

1493 CMD art. 8.

1494 *IFPI Simulcasting*, COMP/C2/38.014 at ¶ 70, 72.

1495 It is, however, not entirely clear whether the Commission applied a proportionality test or a proper indispensability test like the ECJ in *BRT v. SABAM*.

1496 Guibault, *Collective Management Directive*, *supra* at 746.

b) Rebates and Deductions from License Fees

The *Cannes Extension Agreement* decision[1497] centered on the question whether it was lawful to restrict the grant of rebates by an agreement between CMOs. The contract was a hybrid insofar as it was concluded between CMOs and major publishers.[1498] Therefore, competition could be affected between CMOs as well as (potentially) between CMOs and right holders (the involved publishers that held the rights they had acquired from the original authors). The agreement specified certain rules on the relationship between these groups for the management and licensing of mechanical rights against the background of so-called Central Licensing Agreements – agreements which, similar the *IFPI Simulcasting* case, set up a one-stop shop to enable users to obtain a multi-repertoire and multi-territorial license.[1499] The contract specified that a CMO was not permitted to grant rebates to record companies without the written consent of the "relevant member" to this measure.[1500] This clause raised the Commission's concerns under article 101 because, within the system of the underlying Central Licensing Agreements, the participating CMOs charged (to a large extent) an equivalent amount of royalty fees to users.[1501] Price competition was therefore strongly limited, and the grant of rebates was considered as the only remaining element thereof.[1502] While the Commission conceded that the agreement did not prohibit the grant of rebates as such, it pointed out that said provision made this process highly impractical because licenses granted to users usually covered the entire repertoire represented by a CMO; due to this fact, a CMO would have had to obtain the consent of all of its members and of those right holders, whose rights it manages under a representation agreement.[1503] In the end, the Commission accepted the commitments proposed by the parties to the agreement so as to rephrase the clause, making a decision of the competent body of the CMO the only requirement for the grant of rebates.[1504]

The ruling of the Commission is consistent with its decision in the *IFPI Simulcasting* case inasmuch as it considered the grant of rebates to be one of the few factors that remained in order to induce competition between CMOs under systems set up by the Central Licensing Agreements.[1505] This means that

1497 The agreement scrutinized by the Commission extended the duration of the underlying Cannes Agreement and added some new clauses, *see Cannes Extension Agreement*, COMP/C2/38.681 at ¶ 7–10.

1498 *Id.* at ¶ 3.

1499 *Id.* at ¶ 3–4.

1500 *Id.* at ¶ 27.

1501 *Id.* at ¶ 29.

1502 *Id.* at ¶ 30.

1503 *Id.* at ¶ 31.

1504 *Id.* at ¶ 44, 48.

1505 *IFPI Simulcasting*, COMP/C2/38.014 at ¶ 68. Naturally, as is the case with commitment decisions under art. 9 of the Competition Regulation, the Commission did not spell out whether every agreement concluded between CMOs providing for a restriction on the ability to grant rebates will have to be carefully scrutinized under the EU competition rules.

3.3.5. Exclusivity Clauses Relating to the Rights Grant

a) General Remarks

Representation agreements providing for exclusivity clauses have raised several concerns under EU competition law. These clauses restrict a CMO in relation to concluding licensing agreements when representing the repertoire for which it has been mandated by another CMO or when being requested to license its own repertoire. More precisely, the representation agreements stipulated that CMOs were only allowed to grant licenses for a certain territory (territorial allocation) or to certain users (customer allocation). While these concepts formally use different approaches, they are two sides of the same coin: Both lead to a separation of the market for license grants, thereby potentially limiting competition to an extent prohibited under the rules of the TFEU.[1506] It is therefore primarily the ability of a CMO under a representation agreement to directly grant licenses to users based in the territory of the other CMO involved for uses within this territory (territorial exclusivity in a "narrow" sense), which is subject to scrutiny under competition law.[1507] The territorial effect of this kind of restriction is comparable to restrictions regarding the representation of right holders but concerns a different market. The exclusivity relating to the grant of licenses affects the market for the licensing options as well as the market for the representation of other CMOs,[1508] whereas restrictions regarding the representation of right holders concern the market for copyright management services.

---

there was an actual infringement of article 101. However, such a conclusion could have been expected in absence of the proposed commitments by the parties, *see Cannes Extension Agreement*, COMP/C2/38.681 at ¶ 33.

1506 Capobianco, *Licensing of Music Rights*, *supra* at 119; Vinje & Niiranen, *Digital Environment*, *supra* at 411.

1507 Schierholz, *Collective Rights Management*, *supra* at 1177 (stating that territorial non-exclusivity does not refer to the ordinary meaning of the expression – the grant of simple licenses – because under national copyright laws in many cases only the holders of exclusive licenses are in a position to sublicense the protected material, a task fundamental for collective management). However, the free movement of services principle (TFEU art. 56(1)) has a broad scope and applies whenever the user and the CMO are established in different member states, but also when a CMO grants a license to a user established in its territory for the use of its repertoire in another member state, *see* Drexl, *Free Movement of Services*, *supra* at 467–468. *Ficsor* argues that the ECJ in *OSA* effectively approved certain exclusivity clauses to the extent they are indispensable, *see* Ficsor, *Key Issues*, *supra* at 249.

1508 *CISAC Agreement*, COMP/C2/38.698 at ¶ 49.

b) Restrictions as to Users (Customer Allocation)

The Commission scrutinized provisions which restricted a CMO's freedom to offer its licensing services to all interested users in the proceedings centering on the *Santiago Agreement*[1509] and the *Barcelona Agreement.*[1510] The *Santiago Agreement*, like the *IFPI Simulcasting Agreement* and the *Cannes Agreement*, intended to reconcile licenses of a both multi-repertoire and multi-territorial scope, even on a worldwide basis.[1511] It applied to performance rights in musical works for online uses[1512] in order to offer a legitimate source for licensees who wished to provide consumers with online services like the downloading and streaming of music.[1513] The Commission drew its attention to the parts of the agreement which stated that only the CMO established in the user's country of operation was permitted to issue such licenses (customer allocation).[1514] It argued that users were limited in their freedom to choose the most efficient CMO for their respective purposes;[1515] in connection with national monopolies occupied by CMOs in Europe, this system would guarantee absolute exclusivity for each CMO in its country of establishment regarding the rights and uses in question.[1516] At the same time, the participating CMOs were restricted in their power to permit uses within their own territory, since only foreign CMOs could grant licenses for this territory to foreign users.[1517] Due to these concerns, the Commission issued a Statement of Objections addressed to the involved CMOs in 2004.[1518] Two of the organizations – BUMA and SABAM – decided not to defend the contested provisions of the agreement and offered commitments stating that they would not sign agreements containing such customer allocation clauses.[1519] However, the agreement was not renewed after its expiry at the end of 2004.[1520]

1509 *Santiago Agreement,* COMP/C2/38126.

1510 *Notification of cooperation agreements (Case COMP/C-2/38.377 — BIEM Barcelona Agreements),* 2002 O.J. (C132) 18.

1511 *Santiago Agreement, COMP/C2/38126* at ¶ 2–3. The agreement had been notified to the Commission in 2001.

1512 *Id.* at ¶ 2.

1513 Press Release European Commission (May 03, 2004), *supra.*

1514 *Santiago Agreement,* COMP/C2/38126 at ¶ 6. *See* for more details Capobianco, *Licensing of Music Rights, supra* at 119.

1515 Press Release European Commission (May 03, 2004), *supra.*

1516 *Santiago Agreement,* COMP/C2/38126 at ¶ 6.

1517 *Id.* at ¶ 7. The Commission furthermore argued that the *Most Favored Nation* clause contained in the *Santiago Agreement* intensified the exclusivity of the involved CMOs and led to the standardization of licensing terms throughout the EEA.

1518 Press Release European Commission (May 03, 2004), *supra.*

1519 *Santiago Agreement,* COMP/C2/38126 at ¶ 8–12.

1520 *CISAC Agreement,* COMP/C2/38.698 at ¶ 31–32 n.83; Drexl, *Competition and Development, supra* at 221, 268.

The *Barcelona Agreement* can be described as the "mirror agreement" of the *Santiago Agreement*[1521] because it essentially incorporated the same basic characteristics (one-stop-shop, customer allocation clause).[1522] It covered mechanical reproductions of musical works by electronic and online means and was notified to the Commission in 2002.[1523] Also, the Barcelona Agreement was not renewed after 2004.[1524]

In comparison with the *IFPI Simulcasting* decision, in particular, these cases make clear that clauses in representation agreements that directly or indirectly lead to a partitioning of the Internal Market by transposing monopolies to the online world[1525] are likely to conflict with article 101. In this context, the removal of the customer allocation clause was the crucial reason why the IFPI Simulcasting Agreement was accepted by the Commission.[1526] Several reasons contradict the compatibility of such clause with the competition rules and the exemption clause in article 101(3). First, it would eliminate competition between CMOs regarding the licensing terms for online use of musical works because users are bound to their national CMO; second, the emergence of a online music market would be delayed; third, it could have negative effects on right holders; finally, it would be especially detrimental to users with subsidiaries in different member states because they would have to acquire separate licenses.[1527] In turn, CMOs argued that a local presence within the territory of the users was necessary for the effective enforcement of the rights entrusted to them.[1528] The *Tournier* case dealt with the same basic issue, even though it concerned the performance rights for analog uses permitted by mono-territorial licenses. Also, in that case, CMOs allegedly coordinated their conduct so that they would not grant licenses to users established in another member state. The ECJ was clear on this point and ruled that such concerted practices (therefore also agreements) were incompatible with EU competition law.[1529] Thus, for the question of whether CMOs may deny users established in another member state access to their licensing services under representation agreements, it is not primarily relevant whether the case centers the online envi-

1521 Kuik & Dawes, *Media*, *supra* at 1722 n. 59.

1522 Vinje & Niiranen, *Digital Environment*, *supra* at 409–410.

1523 *BIEM Barcelona Agreements*, COMP/C-2/38.377.

1524 Drexl, *Competition and Development*, *supra* at 221, 268; Mathias Elspaß & Moira Kettner, *Article 81 EC* in *European Media Law* 123, 149 (Oliver Castendyk et al. eds., 2008).

1525 Press Release European Commission (May 03, 2004), *supra*.

1526 Schierholz, *Collective Rights Management*, *supra* at 1175.

1527 Vinje & Niiranen, *Digital Environment*, *supra* at 411–12 (also stating that article 101(3) does not apply).

1528 Schierholz, *Collective Rights Management*, *supra* at 1175.

1529 *Tournier*, 395/87 at ¶ 26; *Lucazeau,* 110/88 at ¶ 20. The court did however not expressly specify whether or under which circumstances such agreements could be exempted under article 101(3); this was a key question in the Commission's *IFPI Simulcasting*, *Santiago* and *Barcelona Agreement* cases. *See* section 3.2.3. above.

forment of offline uses, *provided that* an actual agreement[1530] or concerted practice to this effect or with this object can be established. *Whether* there exists such a practice and whether article 101(3) is applicable constitute considerations which in turn can be influenced by the technological means available to CMOs.

c) Restrictions as to Other CMOs (Territorial Allocation)

Two contractual arrangements attracted the attention of the Commission in which CMOs directly restricted their operations in relation to each other by partitioning the territorial scope of their activities in exchange for mutual representation. On the one hand, they agreed not to authorize another CMO to grant licenses for uses made within their territory of operation (exclusive mandate); and on the other hand, they agreed not to engage in business within the territory of the partner society (non-intervention clause).

Until 1996, the *CISAC* model contract stated that every authorization granted by one CMO to another by virtue of representation agreements in order to issue licenses to users was exclusive for the territory in which the authorized organization operated.[1531] This clause was subsequently removed from the contract; however, most European members of CISAC kept including it in their bilateral representation agreements.[1532] The Commission argued that competition was restricted at two levels. First, the clause affected the market for the copyright management services that CMOs provided to each other; second, it affected the market for the licensing of protected content.[1533] As a consequence, a single monopolistic CMO was in the position to license the respective repertoires for a given territory, so that it did not have to fear competition from other CMOs and users were forced to approach this particular CMO as the only legitimate licensing source.[1534] Since the clause no longer appeared in the model contract, CISAC was not involved in the subsequent litigation.[1535] Although this part of the decision (article 2 of the Commission's decision) was addressed to seventeen European CMOs, only two of them asked the General Court to annul the ruling in this respect,[1536] presumably because the organiza-

1530 In *Tournier* and *Lucazeau*, the involved CMOs had removed such clauses from their contracts, *see Tournier*, 395/87 at ¶ 20; *Lucazeau*, 110/88 at ¶ 14.

1531 *CISAC Agreement*, COMP/C2/38.698 at ¶ 22–23.

1532 *Id.* at ¶ 28, 144.

1533 *Id.* at ¶ 140–141.

1534 *Id.*

1535 *CISAC,* T-442/08 at ¶ 6.

1536 *Teosto*, T-401/08 at ¶ 55; *KODA v. Commission* T-425/08, ¶ 58 (EGC 2013). The other CMOs did not appeal to this point of the decision, but only to its article 3, *see Stowarzyszenie Autorów ZAiKS v. Commission*, T-398/08, ¶ 52 (EGC 2013); *Artisjus Magyar Szerzői Jogvédő Iroda Egyesület v. Commission*, T-411/08, ¶ 52 (EGC 2013); *Slovenský ochranný Zväz Autorský pre práva k hudobným dielam v. Commission*, T-413/08, ¶ 62 (EGC 2013); *Autortiesību* tions had already admitted that such clauses were contrary to EU competition law prior to the proceeding.[1537] The court held that the Commission was correct in deeming this rule restrictive of competition: It stated that such an arrangement would lead to an exclusion of the grant of direct (cross-border) licenses and that it reserved for the CMOs involved an unjustified monopoly for their country of operation.[1538]

In contrast to the provisions of the exclusive mandate, the non-intervention clause continued to form part of the CISAC model contract at the time of the proceeding.[1539] The clause obliged each contracting CMO to refrain from any intervention within the territory of the partner society when exercising the mandate provided for in the representation contract.[1540] While the Commission initially interpreted the clause as securing the structure of exclusive monopolies and thus required the CMOs involved to remove the provision from their agreements,[1541] the parties argued that it would merely ensure the rational management of copyrights and that the clause did not prevent a CMO from contracting with the users established in the territory of its partner organizations.[1542] Due to the unclear wording of the provision and the fact that some European CMOs had already removed the clause from their representation agreements, the Commission decided not to take action with respect to the non-intervention clause on the two following conditions: First, the clause was construed as meaning that it merely stipulated a prohibition to interfere with the mandating organization's ability to grant licenses; second, the freedom of

un komunicēšanās konsultāciju aģentūra/Latvijas Autoru apvienība v. Commission T-414/08, ¶ 63 (EGC 2013); *Irish Music Rights Org. Ltd v. Commission*, T-415/08, ¶ 63 (EGC 2013); *Eesti Autorite Ühing v. Commission*, T-416/08, ¶ 63 (EGC 2013); *Sociedade Portuguesa de Autores CRL v. Commission*, T-417/08, ¶ 61 (EGC 2013); *Ochranný svaz autorský pro práva k dílům hudebním o.s. v. Commission*, T-418/08, ¶ 63 (EGC 2013); *Lietuvos autorių teisių gynimo asociacijos agentūra v. Commission*, T-419/08, ¶ 63 (EGC 2013); *Združenje skladateljev, avtorjev in založnikov za zaščito avtorskih pravic Slovenije v. Commission*, T-420/08, ¶ 63 (EGC 2013); *Samband tónskálda og eigenda flutningsréttar v. Commission*, T-428/08, ¶ 51 (EGC 2013); *Tono v. Commission*, T-434/08, ¶ 52 (EGC 2013); *Föreningen Svenska Tonsättares Internationella Musikbyrå u.p.a. v. Commission*, T-451/08, ¶ 59 (EGC 2013); *Sociedad General de Autores y Editores de España v. Commission*, T-456/08, ¶ 7 (EGC 2009), *appeal dismissed*, C-112/09 P (ECJ 2010). Further appeals to article 3 of the decision were brought by CMOs not covered by its article 2, *see AEPI*, T-392/08 at ¶ 52; *Gesellschaft für musikalische Aufführungs- und mechanische Vervielfältigungsrechte v. Commission*, T-410/08, ¶ 55 (EGC 2013); *Performing Right Society Ltd v. Commission*, T-421/08, ¶ 66 (EGC 2013); *SACEM* T-422/08 at ¶ 62; *AKM*, T-432/08 at ¶ 55; *Società Italiana degli Autori ed Editori v. Commission*, T-433/08, ¶ 53 (EGC 2013). Finally, CISAC appealed to the decision, *see CISAC*, T–442/08.

1537 *CISAC Agreement*, COMP/C2/38.698 at ¶ 143.

1538 *Teosto*, T-401/08 at ¶ 72–73.

1539 *CISAC Agreement*, COMP/C2/38.698 at ¶ 29.

1540 *Id.* at ¶ 24–25.

1541 *Id.* at ¶ 40, 145.

1542 *Id.* at ¶ 146–147.

the representing CMO to issue licenses for its own repertoire to foreign users was safeguarded.[1543]

The most controversial aspect of the *CISAC* case was that, in connection with the foregoing clauses, the Commission found that the CMOs involved had established a concerted practice which led to a territorial delineation of the authority to grant licenses in respect of the public performance rights for internet, satellite, and cable exploitation of musical works.[1544] It pointed out that it was not the outcome of "normal competitive conditions" that literally all representation agreements limited the scope of the mandate to the territory in which the respective mandated CMO was established, but the result of a coordination of conduct based on the CISAC model contract.[1545] According to the settled case law of the ECJ, parallel behavior leading to competition conditions that do not correspond to normal market conditions constitutes a strong indication of a concerted practice, unless there are other reasons than the existence of such a practice which may explain the assumed parallel conduct.[1546] Therefore, the Commission strived to invoke evidence in support of its finding of concertation while at the same time, refuting other circumstances which could explain the parallel behavior; the most extensive discussion in this connection concerned the question of whether there was a necessity of local presence.[1547] The Commission regarded the evidence as sufficient for proving the existence of a concerted practice and found an infringement of the competition rules committed by the twenty-four CMOs to which it addressed the decision.[1548] All of them – except BUMA and SABAM – as well as CISAC itself appealed against this finding.[1549] The General Court mainly[1550] dealt with

1543 *Id.* at ¶ 152. *See also CISAC,* T-442/08 at ¶ 22.

1544 *CISAC Agreement*, COMP/C2/38.698 at ¶ 153–154.

1545 *Id.* at ¶ 156.

1546 *Imperial Chem. Indus. Ltd. v Commission*, case 48–69, ¶ 66 (ECJ 1972); *Tournier*, 395/87 at ¶ 24; *Lucazeau,* 110/88 at ¶ 18. *See also CISAC Agreement*, COMP/C2/38.698 at ¶ 170; *CISAC,* T-442/08 at ¶ 29.

1547 *CISAC Agreement*, COMP/C2/38.698 at ¶ 171–199.

1548 *Id.* at ¶ 222–223.

1549 *See* for the cases note 1536 above. *See* for an overview of the judgements Press Release, General Court of the European Union, *The General Court partially annuls the Commission decision finding anti-competitive conduct on the part of copyright collecting societies* (April 12, 2013), *available at* http://curia.europa.eu/jcms/upload/docs/application/pdf/2013-04/cp130043en.pdf (last visited May 23, 2017). Since these decisions are in large parts very similar inasmuch the review of article 3 of the Commission's decision is concerned, it suffices to refer exemplarily to *CISAC v. Commission* in order to illustrate the General Court's reasoning. *SGAE v. Commission* and *STIM v. Commission* constitute exceptions: In the first case, the appeal was rejected because it was not brought in time and the organization could not establish a firm basis for justification, *see SGAE*, T-456/08 at ¶ 19–21; in the second case, the court did not accept the arguments regarding the standard of proof provided by STIM (*see* below). In the following, reference is to the abbreviation of the full names of the involved CMOs because the Commission relies on these in its decision. *See* for the full names CISAC, *CISAC Agreement*, COMP/C2/38.698 at ¶ 8.

the evidential value of the material provided by the Commission and held that neither part of this material conclusively substantiated prohibited conduct. On the one hand, the Commission failed to establish direct proof of a concerted practice. The mere fact that the involved CMOs held meetings and discussions in the course of the drafting of the Santiago Agreement, the Sydney Agreement,[1551] and other representation agreements did not constitute sufficient evidence;[1552] moreover, the court held that the Commission mixed up different kinds of infringement, namely the inclusion of exclusive mandates in representation agreements (which was prohibited as such) and the alleged coordinated territorial delineation.[1553] On the other hand, the Commission likewise did not succeed in rendering implausible the explanations provided by the defendants for the parallel conduct, in which grounds for the existence of a concerted practice could not be found. CISAC and its members argued that effective monitoring and collection of royalties required a local presence in the territory of the license grant; moreover, abandoning the current system might lead to a fragmentation of the repertoire offered by CMOs to users.[1554] Therefore, the territorial delineations that led to the local presence were the result of rational decision-making rather than of a concerted practice.[1555] Conversely, the Commission stated that local presence was not necessary and enumerated several reasons to substantiate its opinion; however, the General Court pointed out that the Commission had not explained how this system would exactly work if, in absence of territorial delineation, CMOs were to become competitors given the reduced incentives for cooperation which was necessary for certain monitoring activities and the prosecution of infringements – this dependence was admitted by the Commission itself in its decision.[1556] While the court acknowledged that technological means can serve to perform certain

1550 As a preliminary question, the Commission argued that CISAC was not entitled to bring an appeal because it was not (formally) an addressee of the decision. The court rejected this allegation and held that CISAC was directly and individually affected because it was "intimately linked" to the decision's actual subject matter, *see CISAC,* T-442/08 at ¶ 77–78. *See also* Anna-Zoe Steiner, *Grenzüberschreitende Lizenzierung von Musikwerken in Europa und die kartellrechtliche Beurteilung des Systems der Gegenseitigkeitsverträge*, 62 ÖBl 202, 205 (2013) (stating that the parties did not bring an appeal against the decision of the court).

1551 The Sydney Agreement related to license grants covering satellite footprints, *CISAG,* T-442/08 at ¶ 115.

1552 *Id.* at ¶ 107–108, 114, 119. *See* for the Commission's reasoning, *CISAC Agreement*, COMP/C2/38.698 at ¶ 158. *See also id.* at ¶164–165.

1553 *CISAC,* T-442/08 at ¶ 124–126. The latter kind of infringement was only prohibited inasmuch as concerted practices caused the appearance of this clause in all representation agreements. Furthermore, the court specified that the market for cross-border licenses was still in development, *see id.* at ¶ 127–130.

1554 *Id.* at ¶ 134–135.

1555 *Id.*

1556 *Id.* at ¶ 149–155. *See* for the portions of Commission decision *CISAC Agreement*, COMP/C2/38.698 at ¶ 177–178.

monitoring tasks from a distance, it highlighted that the Commission had not explained how unauthorized uses should be dealt with.[1557] On these grounds, the General Court upheld the appeals and ruled that the Commission had failed to satisfy the required legal standard for the establishment of a concerted practice.[1558] In contrast, the appeal brought by the Swedish CMO STIM took a different turn because the organization asserted the lack of proof regarding the existence of a concerted practice only at the hearings but not in its underlying action.[1559] Therefore, the plea was regarded as inadmissible and the court went on to discuss the further arguments presented by STIM.[1560] However, it concluded that the decision of the Commission did not severely threaten cultural diversity and that territorial limitations were neither objectively necessary to nor inherent to the protection of copyright.[1561] The court consequently dismissed the appeal and confirmed the Commission's decision.

d) Direct Legal Observations of the CISAC Litigation

One quite obvious lesson that can be learned from the *CISAC* litigation is that it can be hard to establish the existence of a concerted practice, especially if there are no documents of substantial evidentiary value available.[1562] The General Court applied a high standard of proof which was based on two main considerations. First, as a fundamental principle, the burden to substantiate an infringement was strictly put on the Commission and any doubt remaining as to the alleged violation regarding the evidentiary material viewed as a whole had to weigh in favor of the defendant.[1563] This principle was especially relevant when the court assessed the legitimate alternative explanations for parallel conduct. Second, the court applied the doctrine established in *PVC II*.[1564]

1557 *CISAC,* T-442/08 at ¶ 156–159. The court also rejected examples given by the Commission related to international cooperation and licensing models ("Nordic and Baltic cooperation model", Simulcasting and Webcasting Agreements, the Santiago Agreement and the CELAS joint venture) in order to show that local presence was not essential to the CMOs' tasks, *see id.* at ¶ 162–178. Furthermore, it did not attribute any evidential value to a document formerly signed by some CMOs which stated that local presence was not necessary, both technically and economically, *see id.* at ¶ 179–181.

1558 *Id.* at ¶ 182–183.

1559 Under the procedural rules, a new plea cannot be introduced in the course of the proceeding unless i) new facts become known in the course of the proceeding or ii) it serves to amplify a plea contained in the original action, *see STIM*, T-451/08 at ¶ 66.

1560 *Id.* at ¶ 62.

1561 *Id.* at ¶ 85, 89–92.

1562 Kuik & Dawes, *Media*, *supra* at 1725. *See* for the evidential issues in the recent SESAC litigation *Meredith*, 1 F. Supp. 3d 180 at 209–214; *Radio Music License Comm.*, 29 F. Supp. 3d 487 at 497.

1563 *CISAC,* T442/08 at ¶ 91–97 (also citing the relevant case law).

1564 *Limburgse Vinyl Maatschappij NV v. Commission*, joined cases T-305/94, T-306/94, T-307/94, T-313/94 to T-316/94, T-318/94, T-325/94, T-328/94, T-329/94 and T-335/94 (EGC 1999), *appeal dismissed in part, judgement annulled in part*, joined cases C-238/99 P, C-244/99 P, C-245/99 P, C-247/99 P, C-250/99 P to C-252/99 P and C-254/99 P (ECJ 2002).

Under this rule, the applicant is required to provide an alternative explanation for the facts found by the Commission and to challenge the existence of those facts if documents show the existence of a concerted practice.[1565] However, the court ruled that the Commission failed to substantiate that the presented material were "documents" within in the meaning of the *PVC II* decision.[1566]

The different variations of the CISAC case (arising from the different scope of the appeals) permit a detailed insight into the competition law framework that representation agreements are subjected to. The outcomes were: i) the restrictions regarding right holders and the exclusive mandate clause were considered to infringe competition law, ii) the Commission failed to prove the existence of a concerted practice with respect to territorial delineation, and iii) where such a concertation was assumed, it was incompatible with article 101. In the two latter cases, both the Commission and the General Court did not presuppose that the conduct was unlawful as such; for this reason, they examined whether the measure could be objectively justified because the possibility was not excluded that this was necessary for the protection of copyrights and cultural diversity or the granting of multi-repertoire licenses.[1567] Moreover, both authorities assessed article 101(3) but ultimately denied to acknowledge a justification based on this provision.[1568] In contrast, the provisions mentioned in i) were regarded as "restrictions by object".[1569] Under this approach, different than "restrictions by effect", it is not necessary to show that a clause has actual effects on the restriction of competition if its objective is to prevent, restrict, or distort competition within the common market.[1570] This finding is in line with the *Tournier* and *Lucazeau* cases, where the ECJ specified that concerted practices leading to a refusal to grant license to users from other member states cannot be compatible with article 101.[1571] For the present purpose, this must also hold true for actual agreements. It follows from these cases that the mentioned restrictions are restrictions by object; the application of this principle comes close to what could be called a per se rule since no further considerations are necessary for a finding of an infringement.

1565 *Id.* at ¶ 727–728.

1566 *CISAC,* T442/08 at ¶ 90, 99, 101, 102, 119.

1567 *STIM*, T-451/08 at ¶ 73–97; *CISAC Agreement*, COMP/C2/38.698 at ¶ 94–95, 213–221.

1568 *STIM*, T-451/08 at ¶ 98–108; *CISAC Agreement*, COMP/C2/38.698 at ¶ 229–255.

1569 *Teosto*, T-401/08 at ¶ 61–66, 74.

1570 *See, e.g., T-Mobile Netherlands BV v. Commission*, C-8/08 ¶ 29 (ECJ 2009); *Nederlandse Federatieve Vereniging voor de Groothandel op Elektrotechnisch Gebied* v. *Commission,* C-105/04 P, ¶ 125 (ECJ 2006); *Aalborg Portland v. Commission A/S*, Joined Cases C-204/00 P, C-205/00 P, C-211/00 P, C-213/00 P, C-217/00 P and C-219/00 P, ¶ 261 (ECJ 2004); *Établissements Consten S.à.R.L. and Grundig-Verkaufs-GmbH*, joined cases 56 and 58–64, Rep. of Cases English 1966, 299 at 342 (ECJ 1966); *Teosto*, T-401/08 at ¶ 63. *See also* Wollmann, *Art 101 AEUV*, *supra* at ¶ 64.

1571 *Tournier*, 395/87 at ¶ 26; *Lucazeau,* 110/88 at ¶ 20. The ECJ also considered concerted practices having as their mere effect the refusal to grant direct licenses as incompatible with EU law.

These restrictions are essentially cases of discrimination against citizens from other member states because they involve an unjustified rejection of membership (right holders) or licensing (users) requests, which is solely based on the nationality of the respective person. Conversely, in connection with the restrictions mentioned in ii) and iii) that were not based on nationality,[1572] the Commission and the General Court had to assess the effects of the measure and whether it could be justified. This included a weighing of the positive and negative implications of the conduct at issue for the purpose of whether the assumed concerted practice could be regarded as restrictive of competition; thus, this analysis was not only relevant in connection with the exemption clause of article 101(3). In any event, the assessment seems to be in line with the general approach to the representation agreements spelled out in *Tournier* and *Lucazeau* and will most likely apply to other provisions that are considered as "restrictions by effect".

Finally, three aspects regarding the scope of the Commission's decision shall be highlighted. First, the decision (regarding the alleged concerted practice) only concerns performance rights for internet, satellite, and cable exploitation of musical works.[1573] Thus, its scope faces a three-fold limitation in respect of the type of rights, the environment of exploitation, and the work category. This limitation is crucial to the understanding of both the Commission's and the General Court's decision. The Commission's arguments were mainly tailored to the implications of technology for collective management in the music sector and the court refuted some of these arguments because it held that the arguments presented did not sufficiently take these implications into consideration. For instance, the General Court rejected the Commission's arguments regarding the NBC Model or CELAS because it had not explained why the monitoring of mechanical rights posed the same problems as the monitoring of performance rights;[1574] furthermore it did not accept the argument that the rights that the decision aimed for could be monitored effectively without a local presence because it did not set forth how to deal with unauthorized uses.[1575] These considerations show that it is crucial to attach, by a thorough legal, economic, and technical analysis, sufficient importance to the distinct impacts inherent to different work categories, types of rights, creative sectors, and exploitation environments. The latter example of the General Court's analysis points to the second aspect of the scope of the CISAC decision. Even though the Commission was somewhat ambiguous, the decision must be read as not only referring to the legal exploitation of copyrighted ma-

1572 Also with the territorial delineations in place, it would have been possible for CMOs to grant direct licenses for their own repertoire, *see, e.g.*, *CISAC,* T442/08 at ¶ 126. Mainly affected by the alleged concerted practice was the market for the representation of CMOs which did not wish or could grant direct licenses on their own, *see STIM*, T-451/08 at ¶ 95.

1573 *CISAC Agreement*, COMP/C2/38.698 at ¶ 153.

1574 *CISAC,* T442/08 at ¶ 165, 175.

1575 *Id.* at ¶ 159.

terial but also to cases of unauthorized uses where it was the task of the respective CMO to enforce the rights it was entrusted with.[1576] Thus, when the necessity of the local presence was discussed, the entirety of the functions of CMO was taken into account. Third, the Commission, following the judgments of the ECJ, did not question the legitimacy of representation agreements as such; neither did it consider territorial delineation by itself to be contrary to the competition rules.[1577] It was only the alleged alignment of all European CMOs leading to an inclusion of such territorial restrictions in all bilateral representation agreements that the Commission objected to.[1578]

3.3.6. The Problem of Union-Wide Licensing and the Solution of the Collective Management Directive

a) The Need for MTL Options and the Traditional European Licensing Structure

While the Commission's and the General Court's rulings[1579] at the first glance seem to merely concern the legal standard of proof required under article 101 for establishing the existence of a concerted practice, these decisions point to the heart of the challenges and problems faced by collective management in Europe. The underlying background is composed of two intertwined questions: i) What is the impact of technological innovation on the collective management and licensing of copyrights? ii) Is the traditional European system of reciprocal representation (still) justified or should policy makers induce a Union-wide competition between CMOs?

There is a wide consensus that users require licensing options which are tailored to emerging technologies, especially in the digital environment. Accordingly, the lack of licensing options with a territorial scope extending beyond the territory of one (member) state has frequently been underscored.[1580] Even though it is beyond doubt that technology had a big impact on the licensing market, it is hard to specify at what exact point the influence of new technologies reached an intensity justifying alterations of the licensing and

1576 *Id.* at ¶ 142–146.

1577 *CISAC Agreement*, COMP/C2/38.698 at ¶ 95, 259; *CISAC,* T442/08 at ¶ 65, 85, 139.

1578 *CISAC Agreement*, COMP/C2/38.698 at ¶ 156.

1579 It is noteworthy that the parts of the decision dealing with the membership restrictions and the exclusive mandate are largely uncontroversial within the literature; the question revolving around the standard of the proof of a concerted practice has by far attracted most attention.

1580 *See, e.g.,* CMD recital 38–39; Recommendation 2005 recital 8; Capobianco, *Licensing of Music Rights*, *supra* at 115–117; Ficsor, *Collective Management*, *supra* at 113; Gilliéron, *Digital Environment*, *supra* at 942; Kohn & Kohn, *Music Licensing*, *supra* at 197–198; Tanya Woods, *Multi-territorial Licensing and the Evolving Role of Collective Management Organizations* in *Collective Management of Copyright and Related Rights* 105, 132–133 (Daniel Gervais ed., 2nd ed. 2010).

representation system in place. The first initiatives were taken in view of direct broadcasting satellites that enabled a transmission to several countries,[1581] and the emergence of digital technology did not leave the *CISAC* decision unaffected. However, the Commission did not specify the threshold, referred to a point in time, as of which it considered the application of traditional provisions in representation agreements to be contrary to the competition rules.[1582] It was probably the availability of technological innovations like satellite and cable transmissions and the Internet which allowed for the transmission of copyrighted material to multiple territories without requiring a physical presence for licensing and monitoring purposes[1583] that caused the Commission to assess the agreements mentioned in this section under competition law doctrines. This question was of practical importance for the *CISAC* litigation because the necessary precondition for the Commission's decisions was to distinguish – via the detour of the existence of a concerted practice – the case of the ECJ's ruling in *Tournier* and *Lucazeau*. To recall the above sections, the court accepted in these cases that representation agreements were legitimate insofar as they relieved CMOs from the obligation to establish their own infrastructure in other countries and that this consideration could serve as an explanation for parallel behavior other than a concerted practice.[1584] The Commission argued that this explanation was not valid in the context of internet, satellite, and cable technology because it considered a remote monitoring beyond national borders as technically feasible.[1585] With a view to the mentioned ECJ rulings, it argued that the traditional justifications only applied to the "offline world", like the factual situation underlying the discotheque cases.[1586] First of all, it is submitted that the *Tournier* and *Lucazeau* cases must be read in the context of the technologies that were available at that time; therefore, the decisions are limited in two respects. On the one hand, the discotheque rulings concern the licensing of CMOs to small and geographically dispersed users when there was no other option than local monitoring; on the other hand, the ECJ deemed the system of reciprocal representation with its territorial restraints the only economically viable solution.[1587] Yet, when assessing whether a local presence is rendered unnecessary by technological progress, it is fair not to focus on some of the functions fulfilled by CMOs but to consider whether they are in a position to completely fulfill their duties by using the available

---

1581 Ficsor, *Collective Management*, *supra* at 111.

1582 *CISAC,* T442/08 at ¶ 84. *See also CISAC Agreement*, COMP/C2/38.698 at ¶ 63 ("until now").

1583 *See, e.g., IFPI Simulcasting*, COMP/C2/38.014 at ¶ 61.

1584 *Tournier*, 395/87 at ¶ 19, 24; *Lucazeau,* 110/88 at ¶ 13, 18.

1585 *CISAC Agreement*, COMP/C2/38.698 at ¶ 54. *See also IFPI Simulcasting*, COMP/C2/38.014 at ¶ 34, 61.

1586 *CISAC Agreement*, COMP/C2/38.698 at ¶ 64. Accordingly, the Commission considered local presence necessary regarding offline application, *see id.* at ¶ 157.

1587 Capobianco, *Licensing of Music Rights*, *supra* at 118.

technical measures. It was precisely this point that the Commission failed to substantiate in the eyes of the General Court because the authority did not explain how the enforcement of copyright against unauthorized uses could be effectively handled.[1588] Thus, it is necessary to establish why the enforcement of the entrusted rights is not an integral part of a CMO's function. Moreover, one should also keep in mind not only the mere capability of carrying out a task, but also potential differences in the quality of the offered services which might be deteriorated by the use of digital technology. In other words, the mere fact that something is possible by relying on recently developed methods does not mean that its quality is the same. This consideration applies to monitoring and enforcement tasks alike; the answer of this question also requires technical expertise and a cost-benefit analysis. In the offline world, for the time being, the ECJ *Tournier* and *Lucazeau* rulings still apply to representation agreements and practices to this effect where there is no doubt that local presence is needed for monitoring and enforcement tasks.[1589]

b) The MTL Regime of the Collective Management Directive

The Collective Management Directive introduces a new system of cooperation between CMOs which establishes a new type of contractual arrangement. It applies to multi-territorial licenses for online rights in musical works[1590] and implements the "European Licensing Passport", option B2 of the Commission's Impact Assessment 2012.[1591] First of all, the directive sets standards for CMOs that want to engage in business with users on the MTL market ("passport entity"). These organizations must possess the necessary infrastructure and the technical capabilities for this task. This includes the ability to electronically process data for the identification of the managed works and rights, the monitoring of their use and the financial streams between the organization, users, and right holders.[1592] The requirements thereby established can be interpreted as the introduction of an authorization system.[1593] The core provisions of this title of the CMD deal with representation agreements for the grant of multi-territorial licenses for online right in musical works. Such agreements must be non-exclusive and the management of the mandated rights must be carried out in a non-discriminatory manner.[1594] Most importantly, a proper obligation to conclude representation agreements is provided for by the directive whenever a CMO approaches another in order to entrust its right to the other organization for the purpose of granting multi-

1588 *CISAC,* T442/08 at ¶ 144–181.

1589 Capobianco, *Licensing of Music Rights*, *supra* at 118.

1590 CMD art. 23.

1591 Impact Assessment 2012 at 42–44.

1592 CMD art. 24.

1593 Drexl et al., *Comments of the MPI*, *supra* at 18, 30–31, 35.

1594 CMD art. 29(1), 30(3).

territorial licenses.[1595] On the one hand, the CMO acting as the prospective manager of the other CMO's repertoire (mandated CMO) must accept this request. The requirements for this obligation to apply are that the mandated CMO already grants or offers granting multi-territorial licenses in the repertoire of one or more other CMOs and that the managed rights belong to the "same category" of online rights as those mentioned in the representation request.[1596] The notion "same category" should be interpreted as referring to the kind of rights or fields of use and not the kind of music.[1597] Thus, mainstream music and niche repertoires belong to the same category of "online rights". In this way, the rationale of recital 2 of the directive – also the smallest and less popular repertoires should have access to the licensing market – is safeguarded.[1598] Needless to say in view of the scope of the directive's title 3, "same category" rights can only arise from musical works. On the other hand, according to the wording of article 30, the CMO which is the addressor of the request (mandating CMO) is not required to engage in multi-territorial licensing itself, even if it possessed the capabilities provided for in article 24. Thus, for the obligation to contract put on mandated CMOs, it is of no consideration whether the mandating CMO is capable of providing multi-territorial licenses unless it already grants or offers to grant such licenses. In the latter case, the obligation does not apply to the mandated CMO. Conversely, a CMO is not obliged to represent another CMO only because it fulfills the requirements set out in article 24 or to implement an MTL system with regard to its own repertoire; moreover, a CMO not fulfilling these requirements is not obliged to turn to a CMO that offers MTL services.[1599] Finally, a CMO is not covered by article 30 if it aggregates rights in the same works in order to jointly license the rights to reproduction and communication to the public.[1600]

Where a CMO neither offers MTL options itself nor through a representation agreement under article 30, right holders can withdraw their online rights in musical works for the purposes of MTL without having to withdraw the rights necessary for mono-territorial licensing.[1601] This also implies that CMOs will have to consider this special category of rights in their decision-making process, provided of course that they do not make use of the new MTL system. As a consequence, every right holder and every CMO has, from a legal point of view, the opportunity to license their rights on a multi-territorial ba-

1595 van Gompel, *Directive*, *supra* at 602.

1596 CMD art. 30(1).

1597 Sousa e Silva, *The Proposed Directive*, *supra* at 19 n. 84.

1598 Graber, *Collective Rights Management*, *supra* at 41–42. *See also* Arezzo, *Lights and Shadows*, *supra* at 542.

1599 CMD recital 44. CMOs can also outsource services, *see id.* at recital 43.

1600 *Id.* at recital 46

1601 *Id.* at art. 31. This – in relation to article 5 actually redundant – article is effective as of April 10, 2017 which can be referred to as a short "grace period" for smaller CMOs, as well as encouraging right holder to join bigger CMOs, *see* Ficsor, *Key Issues*, *supra* at 247.

sis, even if they do not possess the necessary capabilities to do so on their own. The only requirement for the system to function is that there is at least one CMO on the market which manages the same category of rights and offers representation services for the provision of multi-territorial licenses. Problems for the application of article 31 might arise in a situation where it is unclear whether the author or the publisher holds the rights in a particular work.[1602] The CMD does not expressly specify a term of notice for the withdrawals under article 31.[1603]

In order complement the MTL system, further provisions similar to other parts of the directive are included in title III. Among these are rules on transparency and the provision of information,[1604] on invoicing and reporting in relation to users[1605] and on the payments to right holders.[1606] When reading the provisions on users and right holders, it becomes clear that the actual use of the licensed rights is an important concept for the calculation of the license fee and the distribution of revenues.[1607] The revenues arising from multi-territorial licenses granted under title III of the directive are transferred to the mandating CMO for further distribution.[1608] The mandated CMO is entitled to charge a management fee which does not exceed the reasonable costs incurred for its services.[1609] The additional notion of "and a reasonable profit margin" no longer appears in the final version of the CMD.[1610] While this constitutes a relief for mandating CMOs and, most of all, for smaller CMOs due to their lower management fees, this does not especially incentivize such organizations to build up their own presence on the MTL market. However, the inclusion of this term would have most likely rendered the new MTL system more expensive than the traditional system of reciprocal representation.[1611]

c) The MTL Regime of the Collective Management Directive and New Licensing Models

Whether the obligation of article 30 applies to new licensing models depends on their design. For hybrid entities that are owned or controlled by a CMO, the obligation applies if it engages in multi-territorial licensing of copyrights because article 30 is a "relevant provision" in this case.[1612] However, it

1602 Drexl et al., *Comments of the MPI, supra* at 29–30.

1603 van Gompel, *Directive, supra* at 613.

1604 CMD art. 25, 26, 28(2), 29(2),(3), 30(6).

1605 *Id.* at art. 27.

1606 *Id.* at art. 28.

1607 *Id.* at art. 27(2), 28(1).

1608 *Id.* at art. 28(3).

1609 *Id.* at art. 30(5).

1610 Proposal 2012 at art. 29(2).

1611 Drexl et al., *Comments of the MPI, supra* at 29.

1612 CMD art. 2(3). Therefore, it does not matter that article 30 refers to "CMOs".

is a basic requirement that the organization in question already manages or offers to service other CMOs for the purpose of multi-territorial licensing of their repertoire. In this connection, one could wonder whether this condition is fulfilled if hybrid entities license the repertoire of its owner societies. This would be compatible with a very broad reading of the notion of "other collective management organisations" in article 30, at least if there is more than one owner CMO. The crucial question is which repertoire is licensed and by whom it is controlled. If the hybrid exclusively manages a right holders' repertoire or if there is only one owner society, the situation is unproblematic. In the first case, no CMO is involved,[1613] and in the second case the CMO licenses its own repertoire indirectly by installing a subsidiary. These constellations do not fall within the scope of the directive because otherwise, a CMO would be practically constrained from outsourcing services.[1614] In turn, the involvement of more than one owner CMOs is more challenging. There is the danger that the few CMOs who fulfill the passport requirements join together to license their repertoires, thereby excluding smaller CMOs from the multi-territorial licensing market. Recital 46 states that the obligation to represent "should only apply to collective management organisations which aggregate repertoire and should not extend to collective management organisations which provide multi-territorial licences for their own repertoire only." If the hybrid licenses the repertoire of more than one owner societies, it can be said that it thereby aggregates these repertoires. Furthermore, the inherent rationale of the directive is to prevent CMOs that exclusively manage *their own* repertoire on a MTL basis from having to accept the MTL mandates of other CMOs. For this reason, the directive arguably applies to the hybrids that are controlled by more than one CMO and issue multi-territorial licenses to the repertoire of these societies.

Similar concerns arise with regard to licensing hubs (like ARMONIA), for instance.[1615] As long as they accept new members or expressly offer MTL services to CMOs, no specific problems arise as the access to the MTL market for smaller and less popular repertoires is ensured. If these open structures should change in the future, it is appropriate to require the licensing for accepting MTL mandates under the article 30. On the one hand, the offer of MTL services triggers this obligation; on the other hand, the circumvention concerns mentioned before justifies an application of the directive's title III.

1613 *See also* Arezzo, *Lights and Shadows*, *supra* at 555.

1614 *See also* CMD recital 43.

1615 *See* section 1.1.4.c) above.

3.3.7. The U.S. Experience

a) National Cooperation

The relations of U.S. CMOs with sister organizations can be viewed at from perspective of cooperation on the national and international level. As regards the former the situation is clearly not comparable to the prevailing approach of many European countries where CMOs often possess a legal or de facto monopoly. Thus, since U.S. CMOs compete with one another, no system of representation agreements has developed for the territory of the United States.[1616] Such a system would be problematic from the antitrust perspective: Even though the copyright act permits territorial allocation in copyright licensing,[1617] horizontal agreements among right holders providing for territorial restrictions in their ability to license will often times violate the Sherman Act.[1618] Coordinated conduct might also raise antitrust concerns in other contexts.[1619] That being said, it should be noted that U.S. CMOs nevertheless cooperate in various other ways. For instance, ASCAP, BMI, and SOCAN[1620] collaborate to run MusicMark, a tool which assists in the registration of works.[1621] Furthermore, CMOs unite when it comes to lobbying for legislative reforms or policy proposals.[1622] In fact, the DOJ itself suggested that ASCAP and BMI conclude (non-exclusive) representation agreements to facilitate the licensing of jointly owned works under the 100% licensing rule favored by the department's Antitrust Division.[1623]

1616 *See, e.g.,* U.S. Copyright Office, *Jointly Owned Works*, *supra* at 15–16 (noting that ASCAP and BMI ordinarily collect royalties for their own members only), *see also id.* at 21–22.

1617 17 U.S.C. § 101. The relevant portion of this provision reads: "A 'transfer of copyright ownership' is an assignment [….], whether or not it is limited in time or place of effect […]."

1618 II Hovenkamp et al., *IP and Antitrust*, *supra* at § 33.8a.

1619 *See, e.g., Moor-Law*, 527 F. Supp. 758 at 764, 775 (rejecting allegations that ASCAP and BMI violated section 1 and 2 of the Sherman Act by conspiring to stabilize prices in the licensing market).

1620 The Society of Composers, Authors and Music Publishers of Canada (SOCAN) is a Canadian CMO, *see* SOCAN, *About SOCAN*, http://www.socan.ca/about (last visited April 27, 2017).

1621 MusicMark, *Frequently Asked Questions*, http://musicmark.com/documents/MusicMark-FAQs.pdf (last visited April 27, 2017). Coordination is generally immanent when a composition is co-written by songwriters who are members of different CMOs, *see* U.S. Copyright Office, *Jointly Owned Works*, *supra* at 13–14 (stating that ASACP and BMI have allowed for the cross-registration of works since the 1970s).

1622 *See, e.g.,* ASCAP, *ASCAP and BMI Join Forces to Fight the Department of Justice's Interpretation of Their Consent Decrees*, https://www.ascap.com/press/2016/08-04-ascap-bmi-join-forces-to-fight-doj (last visited April 27, 2017); BMI, *Songwriters' Groups Speak Out on Rate Setting: ASCAP, BMI, SESAC and the NSAI File Joint Letter to Congress on Music Licensing Reform*, https://www.bmi.com/news/entry/songwriters_groups_speak_out_on_rate_setting_file_joint_letter_to_congress (last visited April 27, 2017).

1623 DOJ, *Antitrust Division's Review*, *supra* at 20.

b) International Cooperation

The cooperation of U.S. CMOs with their foreign sister societies is built on a diverging historical development. ASCAP's cooperation with foreign societies was formerly regulated by a special consent decree, the "Foreign Decree".[1624] A comparable decree has never been in place for BMI, which faced problems cooperating with foreign CMOs in its earlier years because BMI is a user-owned organization.[1625] For this reason, the relationship between the international cooperation of CMOs and the antitrust laws has not always been easy. In fact, the DOJ caused ASCAP to withdraw from its CISAC membership because it considered the organization to be a cartel, unlawfully denying BMI access to the international music market.[1626] However, when CISAC's statutes were amended and BMI was admitted to the membership, ASCAP returned in the 1960s.[1627] ASCAP, BMI, and SESAC are nowadays members of CISAC[1628] and particular antitrust concerns have not been raised recently. It should, however, be noted that just like in national context, horizontal agreements to divide the market into domestic and international segments will raise such concerns.[1629] The ASCAP Foreign Decree was later vacated with the AFJ2's entry into force[1630] so that no specific consent decree currently regulates ASCAP's or BMI's (or SESAC's) relations with foreign CMOs.

U.S. CMOs also cooperate with foreign CMOs on the bilateral level for managing the collection and distribution of royalties and have concluded representation agreements for this purpose.[1631] The ASCAP Statute expressly

---

1624 *United States* v. *American Society of Composers, Authors and Publishers*, 1950 Trade Cas. (CCH) ¶ 62,594, 1950 U.S. Dist. LEXIS 1899 (S.D.N.Y. 1950).

1625 Korman, *U.S. Position*, *supra* at 168.

1626 *Id.* at 165. *See also* II Goldstein on Copyright, *supra* at § 7.9.

1627 Korman, *U.S. Position*, *supra* at 165.

1628 *See* for a list of members CISAC, *CISAC Membership* (2015), http://www.cisac.org/Our-Members.

1629 II Hovenkamp et al., *IP and Antitrust*, *supra* at § 33.8a. The original ASCAP Foreign Decree provided that ASCAP was not permitted to prevent "any foreign society from making musical performing rights available on a non-exclusive, non-discriminatory basis to any musical performing rights society other than defendant ASCAP" nor to discriminate or retaliate "against any foreign society which grants or negotiates to grant musical performing rights in the United States to any musical performing rights society other than ASCAP", *see* ASCAP Foreign Decree § IV(E)(1), (2).

1630 ASCAP Consent Decree § XV.

1631 *See* ASCAP, *Affiliated Foreign Societies*, https://www.ascap.com/help/international/affiliated-foreign-societies (last visited April 27, 2017); BMI, *International Agreements With Foreign Performing Rights Organizations*, https://www.bmi.com/international/entry/reciprocal_ representation_agreements_foreign_performing_rights_societies (last visited April 27, 2017); SESAC, *SESAC's Agreements With Foreign Performing Rights Organizations*, https://www.sesac.com/WritersPublishers/HowWePay/foreignpros.aspx (last visited April 27, 2017); SoundExchange, *international partners*, https://www.soundexchange.com/about/international-partners/ (last visited April 27, 2017). *See also* HFA, *Foreign Affiliates*, https://secure.harryfox.com/public/ForeignAffiliates.jsp (last visited April 27, 2017). Since, in many cases, a declares it one of the organization's objectives "[t]o enter into agreements with other similar associations in foreign countries, providing for the reciprocal protection of the rights of the members of each Society [...]".[1632] It was reported that ASCAP, BMI, and SESAC received about $ 700 million from foreign societies in 2014.[1633] This number should however not be underestimated, since it is common practice for many publishers to collect their royalties abroad, bypassing the system of RAs, by joining a local CMO or via sub-publishers.[1634] Sub-publishing involves a publisher located in an overseas market (sub-publisher) who represents the publisher who wishes to promote her works and collect revenues in this territory (original publisher).[1635] As songwriters usually do not have comparable options, they generally depend on a functional system of representation agreements to a greater extent than publishers do.[1636]

3.3.8. Comments on the relationship between CMOs and other CMOs

a) Representation Agreements: Rationales and Legal Status

Representation agreements are not prohibited as such in the United States or the EU. On a fundamental level, it can be observed that the Sherman Act's section 2 can in principle be applied to the relationship between CMOs, as it also covers conspiracies to monopolize.[1637] Conversely, only article 101 TFEU has been applied to the relationships between CMOs, as article 102 presupposes unilateral conduct. Different from the EU, U.S. case law on the relationship of CMOs is sparse; this is due to the fact that collective management works on requirements very different from the EU. Most notably, in the U.S. there exists a relatively uniform music market with a national scope, but also in terms of culture and language. There is not (yet) one single market in the EU, but there are 28. Historically, this stems from the diverging national copyright laws and legal systems overall as well as the different languages and cultural traditions in the 28 member states. Against this background, and given the relatively small size of EU countries compared to the U.S., it is not surprising that cooperation agreements were concluded between CMOs located in differ-

single CMO manages the rights in a particular territory, it is not uncommon that foreign CMOs conclude representation agreements with multiple U.S. CMOs, *see* U.S. Copyright Office, *Jointly Owned Works*, *supra* at 18.

1632 ASCAP Statute art. 1(1)(k). *See also* ASCAP Writer Agreement § 11; ASCAP Publisher Agreement § 11; BMI Publisher Agreement § 5(A)(2), 16; BMI Writer Agreement § 6(a)(iii), 8(b).

1633 Brabec, *Performance Right*, *supra* at 20.

1634 *Id.*

1635 Kohn & Kohn, *Music Licensing*, *supra* at 181.

1636 Brabec, *Performance Right*, *supra* at 41–42.

1637 *See, e.g.*, *Moor-Law*, 527 F. Supp. 758 at 775 ("The alleged conspiracy between BMI and ASCAP discussed above as a possible Section One violation in restraint of trade might also constitute a Section Two conspiracy to monopolize").

ent member states. Relatively recently, these representation agreements have been subjected to closer antitrust scrutiny. Regulating representation agreements in this way is in many respects the logical extension of the protection of right holders and users. If individual CMOs can abuse their dominant position in relation to these groups, such agreements constitute "meta-levels" thereto, insofar as they might be the source of prohibited conduct.

In this connection, the core challenge faced by collective management in Europe is the emergence of new technologies. For territorial restrictions, this means that these will conflict with the competition rules if it can be established that the available technologies render a local presence unnecessary for the functions fulfilled by CMOs. The Commission applied this concept to multilateral cooperation in the *CISAC* decision. In this connection, it is sometimes conveyed that CMOs fiercely defend the system of representation agreements at all costs; however, this is not necessarily so. Some CMOs, at least, appear to rely on representation agreements only to the extent that they offer efficient solutions.[1638] Furthermore, the interests of right holders to adhere to a national society might not be purely economic. Right holders might simply prefer to communicate with the CMOs in their own language.[1639] Besides, the major market for an artist's creation might be located in the country of her residence.[1640]

There is no doubt that a system without intermediaries has the potential of efficiency gains; provided, however, that other actors can adequately assume the functions fulfilled by these intermediaries. The assumption that the advantages of representation agreements in the online environment[1641] are less

1638 In its 2014 public comment on the DOJ's review of the ASCAP and BMI Consent Decrees, the British CMO PRS stated: "PRS is, however, not compelled to appoint ASCAP or BMI to license on its behalf and will always choose the most efficient way of representing its members' rights in the US. In the event that the effect of the Consent Decrees leads PRS to consider it more efficient to license its repertoire directly rather than via an intermediary such as ASCAP/BMI, this would not only have an adverse impact on ASCAP/BMI but may also have the effect of increasing transaction costs for users as they would also be required to negotiate a licence with PRS in addition to ASCAP/BMI", *see* PRS, *Antitrust Division Review of American Society of Composers, Authors and Publishers ("ASCAP") and Broadcast Music, Inc. ("BMI") Consent Decrees ("Review")* 2 n. 2 (2014), https://www.justice.gov/sites/default/files/atr/legacy/2014/08/13/307652.pdf (last visited May 23, 2017). In a merger case involving several European CMOs, the Commission noted that at least SUISA and BUMA/STEMRA were considering to actively compete for mandates from publisher which effected withdrawals, *see PRSfM/STIM/GEMA/JV*, COMP/M.6800 at ¶ 201. Moreover, it has been reported that the German CMO VG Media tried to license its repertoire directly in Spain, *see* Drexl, *Free Movement of Services*, *supra* at 473.

1639 Drexl, *Free Movement of Services*, *supra* at 466 (also highlighting reasons why right holders might want to join foreign CMOs, including better services or options of international exploitation). *See also* Drexl, *Competition and Development*, *supra* at 219.

1640 Drexl, *Free Movement of Services*, *supra* at 466.

1641 The difference of online uses vis-à-vis offline line uses was acknowledged by the Commission in *CISAC*, *see CISAC Agreement,* COMP/C2/38.698 at ¶ 54, 153. *See also* Drexl, *Competition and Development*, *supra* at 218–219.

pronounced does not render such agreements an antitrust violation; the General Court's decision has highlighted that the obsolescence of representation agreements is easier alleged than substantiated. The court focused on the effective enforcement and monitoring of exclusive rights; this may, however, not be the only situation in which representation agreement could be of reasonable use. According to the DOJ, ASCAP and BMI may "consider the possibility of entering into reciprocal agreements with each other confirming that each PRO may license on a non-exclusive basis songs jointed owned by members of the other CMO [...]".[1642] Thus, the question whether and in what ambit a cooperation between CMOs is necessary heavily depends on the specific legal background and the perspective one takes – which does not mean that the 100 percent licensing requirement according to the DOJ's reading of the Consent Decrees is the correct interpretation of these decrees.

Many[1643] efforts toward representation agreements center on the question of how to establish a user-friendly one-stop shop for music; and what sacrifices are deemed necessary and appropriate in order to achieve this aim. The saying, "every light has its shadow" is appropriate in this context. For instance, in the United States, CMOs offer licenses for the entire territory of the country. Yet, due to repertoire fragmentation, users must obtain multiple licenses and, additionally, must take into account potential right holder withdrawals. The traditional RRA model, in turn, sacrifices MTL but works as a means against repertoire fragmentation. Free competition between licensing sources can hardly reconcile both aims.[1644] Even in situations where attempts in this direction are made by industry initiatives, such cooperation between CMOs (and, as the case might be, users and right holders) would also be subject to antitrust law, and the European experience with such models (*e.g.*, IPFI Simulcast Agreement) has shown that this might rather hinder than spur the emergence of innovative solutions.[1645] An entire array of further problems concerns the issue of how the interests of right holders and cultural policy should be weighed in the present context. These considerations should be taken into account along with the efficiency of the licensing process. Just like in connection with blanket licenses, it is questionable whether the antitrust law (alone) is the right tool to address this issue. Legislation – and not antitrust authorities – should step in to design rules that determine to what extent representation agreements are desirable or potentially harmful. The regulatory options are numerous and several proposals have been made. These range from centralized licensing platforms[1646] to setting up joint enforcement agencies[1647] or the creation of new

1642 DOJ, *Antitrust Division's Review*, *supra* at 20.

1643 Drexl, *Competition and Development*, *supra* at 222 (noting that the Recommendation 2005 abandoned the efficiency-oriented approach for the benefits of (large) right holders).

1644 *CISAC*, T-442/08 at ¶ 151 (stating that the Commission failed to explain how this should work).

1645 *See also* Drexl, *Competition and Development*, *supra* at 270.

1646 *See, e.g.*, Brian R. Day, *Collective Management of Music Copyright in the Digital Age: The Online Clearinghouse*, 18 Texas Intell. Prop. L. J. 195 (2010); Drexl et al., *Comments of*

CMOs.[1648] The first attempt at a legislative solution at the EU level has been made in the form of title III of the Directive, which is commented on later in this chapter.

b) The Future of Reciprocal Representation

The developments after the Communication 2005 and the *CISAC* decision imply fundamental changes to the system of reciprocal representation in Europe that governed the relations between CMOs for the longest time. However, it is hard to make general statements, as the applicable sources indicate that there exists great uncertainty in this respect and that little information is publicly available.[1649]

It was reported that the system of RRAs was renegotiated in the wake of the *CISAC* decision leading to the introduction of so-called "carve-out" provisions: While in general, the entire repertoire is represented on a reciprocal basis, the mandating CMO reserves the right to withdraw certain rights in its "own" repertoire in order to issue licenses directly on a multi-territorial basis.[1650] Recent information suggests that several European CMOs have started granting multi-territorial licenses in their repertoires, including PRSfM, STIM, SACEM, SGAE and SIAE.[1651] Such multi-territorial licenses can be combined with a mono-territorial license for the world repertoire in the respective CMO's home country.[1652] Hence, the repertoire that CMOs are able to license under RRAs is decreasing and can be referred to as the "residual world repertoire". This residual repertoire available under national blanket licenses is composed of the world repertoire less the repertoire that i) publishers (by way of withdrawal) and ii) other CMOs (by way of carve-out provisions) license directly to commercial users.[1653] It should, however, be remembered that these chang-

the MPI, *supra* at 33–34; Wünschmann, *Kollektive Verwertung*, *supra* at 235–256. *See also* Christoph B. Graber, *Is there potential for collective rights management at the global level? Perspectives of a new global constitutionalism in the creative sector* in *The Evolution and Equilibrium of Copyright in the Digital Age* 241 (Susy Frankel & Daniel Gervais eds., 2014).

1647 *Cf.* Chin, *Copyright Collective Management*, *supra* at 276 n. 32 (referring to "non practising entities" (NPEs) in the patent context). *See also* Wünschmann, *Kollektive Verwertung*, *supra* at 188.

1648 Turk, *Hard Day's Night*, *supra* at 527–530.

1649 Impact Assessment 2012 at 158–160; Hilty & Nérisson, *Collective Copyright Management*, *supra* at 229; Schwemer, *Online Music*, *supra* at 153.

1650 *PRSfM/STIM/GEMA/JV*, COMP/M.6800 at ¶ 24.

1651 *Id.* at ¶ 25, 185 n.119 (also stating that GEMA has not engaged in multi-territorial licensing).

1652 *Id.* at ¶ 25.

1653 *Id.* at ¶ 25 n. 20, 246. This should also apply if a CMO mandates another society concluding an agreement according to the CMD's article 29. Where CMOs manage related rights, RRAs are usually in place, *see* Hilty & Nérisson, *Collective Copyright Management*, *supra* at 228.

es have mainly focused on one, though innovative and continuously growing, branch of the overall copyright licensing market. According to what is known, new licensing models have emerged for i) online uses of ii) musical works on a iii) multi-territorial basis. It is however uncertain whether one can conclude that for other work categories or offline or mono-territorial uses, the traditional system of RRAs is still in place. In this connection, the Commission observes that also option 3 publishers remain members of CMOs as regards to offline rights and mono-territorial licensing.[1654] Thus, it can be expected that the reciprocal system of representation will remain the standard for analog uses but, at least in the short term, also for online uses of non-musical works.[1655] As regards work categories other than music, the OnLine-Arts system[1656] shows that different models have already emerged. Finally, one should not forget about the important field of statutory licenses. For the management of the corresponding royalty flows, one can also expect representation agreements to subsist from the current perspective.[1657]

Considering the German example, it was reported that the world repertoire (foreign works) was generally available through the CMOs' system of RRAs for uses in Germany.[1658] However, there are also exceptions to this rule. For instance, GEMA indicated that it could no longer license the repertoire covered by the D.E.A.L.-initiative on a mono-territorial basis for uses in Germany.[1659] This situation is somewhat chaotic and, therefore, not especially user-friendly.[1660] As stated above, however, one should be careful when making

1654 *Sony/Mubadala Development/EMI Music Publishing,* COMP/M.6459 at ¶ 198–199. *See also id.* at ¶ 129. The Commission considers it likely that the "Zeta Core License" will cover the world repertoire for the respective national territories, *see id.* at ¶ 246. This license is conceived as single multi-territorial and multi-repertoire licenses covering mechanical and performing rights in the repertoires of involved CMOs and right holders for online exploitation, *see id.* at ¶ 19. *See also* CMD art. 31 (stating that right holders can withdraw their online rights for multi-territorial licensing, while maintaining the mandate for mono-territorial licensing).

1655 Guibault, *Collective Management Directive*, *supra* at 745.

1656 OnLineArt is a platform which acts as a licensing one-stop shop for world-wide online uses of works of fine arts, *see* OnLineArt, *A One-stop-shop for rights on works of art*, http://onlineart.info/#aboutus (last visited April 13, 2017). *See also* Impact Assessment 2012 at 12 n. 51. The members of the platform – CMOs from several parts of the world – contribute to a common database and apply a common tariff; however, also individual tariffs are negotiable, *see* OnLineArt, *The Structure*, http://onlineart.info/the-structure/ (last visited April 13, 2017); Hilty & Nérisson, *Collective Copyright Management*, *supra* at 230. *See* for the member societies OnLineArt, *Members*, http://onlineart.info/#testimonials (last visited April 13, 2017).

1657 *Cf.* Drexl, *Free Movement of Services*, *supra* at 474–475. *See* on the collection of foreign levies for audio visual works – for which no U.S. CMOs exists – Adriane Porcin, *Of Guilds and Men: Copyright Workarounds in the Cinematographic Industry*, 35 Hastings Comm. & Ent. L.J. 1 (2012).

1658 Wiebe et al., *Rights Clearance*, *supra* at 38, 64.

1659 Heyde, *Lizenzierung*, *supra* at 141 n. 45. With regard to the PEDL initiative, this was controversially reported in the literature, *see id.* at 142 n. 50. *See also Sony/Mubadala Development/EMI Music Publishing,* COMP/M.6459 at ¶ 152.

1660 Hilty & Nérisson, *Collective Copyright Management*, *supra* at 229.

general statements, as the applicable sources indicate that there exists great uncertainty in this respect and that little information is publicly available.[1661]

c) Feasibility of MTL under the Collective Management Directive

The approach taken by the CMD is a step in the right direction; however, it remains to be seen whether and to what extent a functional and efficient MTL system in the EU will develop. It is indeed questionable whether the rules of the directive provide for sufficient incentive to represent other CMOs in the MTL process, as the organizations capable of accepting MTL mandates might prefer to keep their infrastructure for themselves.[1662] In light of the high costs of setting up and maintaining such infrastructure, this might be a completely reasonable decision. Further flaws of the current rules include the limitation to authors' rights as well as the lack of guidance regarding split copyrights.[1663] From the perspective of cultural diversity, it is crucial to safeguard the access of smaller repertoires to the MTL market; however, doubts exist whether this framework sufficiently takes into consideration the involved interests.[1664] Even though the rules of the Collective Management Directive ensure the access of smaller CMOs to the MTL market – on the condition that there is a service provider – MTL will put such small actors in a difficult position, especially, if more and more right holders opt to entrust large CMOs having a corresponding infrastructure with the management of their rights or withdraw them for the system to issue direct licenses. In this connection, *Ficsor* questions whether a CMO located in another member state will be able to manage the repertoires from other member states with the same "empathy" as local CMOs.[1665]

To sum up, it can be doubted whether the passport construction sets up the requirements for a fully coherent and functional MTL system.[1666] However, this might be the starting point for discussions regarding a more comprehensive legislative solution in the future, and the experiences gained under the CMD's system will certainly be of value in this process.

1661 *Id.*; Impact Assessment 2012 at 158–160; Schwemer, *Online Music*, *supra* at 153.

1662 *See* Arezzo, *Lights and Shadows*, *supra* at 555 (also stating that that hybrid entities will not face an obligation to contract as long as they manage only one repertoire); Pfeifer, *Umsetzung*, *supra* at 467. However, it has been reported that the Irish CMO IMRO has mandated PRSfM and SACEM to manage its repertoire on an MTL basis, *see PRSfM/STIM/GEMA/JV*, COMP/M.6800 at ¶ 164.

1663 Pfeifer, *Umsetzung*, *supra* at 465. *See* on the Proposal 2012 Drexl et al., *Comments of the MPI*, *supra* at 26–29. *See also* Guibault, *Collective Management Directive*, *supra* at 775 (highlighting the improved information obligations in the final version of the CMD).

1664 Arezzo, *Lights and Shadows*, *supra* at 555–556.

1665 Ficsor, *Key Issues*, *supra* at 246.

1666 *See, e.g.*, Drexl, *Free Movement of Services*, *supra* at 486; Guibault & van Gompel, *Collective Management*, *supra* at 171–174; Lichtenegger, *Verwertungsgesellschaften*, *supra* at 170–176; 2 Walter, *Verwertungsgesellschaftenrecht*, *supra* at 219, 275, 285–286.

III. Concluding Remarks and Observations

This final chapter aims at condensing the observations and conclusions drawn in the prior section to give an overall view of the challenges and solutions presented by the U.S. and EU regulation of CMOs. Divergences and similarities shall be put in a broader context for the two jurisdictions.

1. Orientation and Focus of the Regulation of Collective Management of Copyrights in the European Union and the United States

1.1. Structural Differences and Common Problems

An apparent difference between the U.S. and the EU is the structure of the copyright-related markets. Unlike the U.S., the European licensing market is still largely organized along national borders and thus still rather fragmented; a functioning MTL system has yet to be developed. What is more, there is no uniform European copyright law, so the national copyright acts subsist.[1667] It is a core aim of European competition law[1668] and EU policy overall to create and further develop the Internal Market. A good amount of competition cases involving CMOs center on questions which do not need to be answered in the United States, as a national market for copyrights already exists. This, for instance, concerns the non-discrimination principle relating to nationals of other member states and explains why there is practically no case law in the United States on the relationship between different CMOs. From this perspective, collective management is just another field where the EU tries to pursue the overall Internal Market aim. However, as will be seen in subsection 3, the problem is more complex and rooted in the foundations of copyright law as well as in the EU's constitutional order.

Despite the foregoing, regulators in the EU and the United States must address similar problems, *e.g.*, whether right holders should be entitled to par-

---

1667 *See, e.g.,* Ficsor, *Key Issues*, *supra* at 240 (highlighting the fact that the EU is not a federal state as well as the linguistic and cultural differences between the member states). It is noteworthy that important questions relating to the ownership and transfer of copyrights are still governed by national law. This was highlighted in *MyVideo*, where a German court found that online mechanical rights had not been lawfully transferred to CELAS under the rules of the German Copyright Act, *see MyVideo*, Munich District Court (Landgericht München), Case 7 O 4139/08, ZUM 2009, 788 (2009), *aff'd* 29 U 3698/09, ZUM 2010, 709 (Munich Court of Appeals – Oberlandesgericht München 2010). *See* on this case Mazziotti, *New Licensing Models*, *supra* at 782–783.

1668 *See also* Drexl, *Competition and Development*, *supra* at 264 (in the connection of representation agreements).

tially withdraw their rights or how appropriate rates for users should be calculated. Moreover, even though the EU has several national legal orders and cultural backgrounds, also in the United States, functional one-stop-shop solutions for musical rights have not emerged. This is because licensing-related fragmentation is present in both jurisdictions, yet, in different respects: While territorial fragmentation has traditionally been paradigmatic for the EU, repertoire fragmentation has been the main obstacle for a one-stop-shop solution in the United States. Fragmentation in this sense can be explained by the regulatory models employed as well as the historical development of rights management. Moreover, underlying copyright law as a third factor for fragmentation should not be underestimated.

1.2. Balancing the Interests of Users and Right Holders – A Matter of Perspective

Already a preliminary analysis of the Consent Decrees as well as the Collective Management Directive reveals that the United States and the European Union put emphasis on different aspects of the regulation of collective management. The provisions in the Consent Decrees for right holders are sparse compared to those for users,[1669] and case law on the internal operations of CMOs, as well their relation to right holders, is practically inexistent. This is in stark contrast to the CMD which almost completely ignores users and confines itself to very general principles.[1670] This difference of focus is also visible in the decisions of the Supreme Court and the ECJ and[1671] the initiatives taken by the European Commission.[1672] Hence, the U.S. regulation of CMOs can be described user-centric while EU regulation to a much greater extent focuses on the protection of the right holders. This is mirrored by the historical application of antitrust law to CMOs: While the first U.S. starting point predominantly[1673] concerned the question whether CMOs were an unlawful combination, the early *GEMA* decisions highlighted the protection of right

[1669] In the course of the DOJ's review of the Consent Decrees it was often suggested to amend the decrees to give right holders more flexibility, i.e. permit partial withdrawals, *see* section II.3.1.7.d) above.

[1670] *See* on the Proposal 2012 Podszun, *Neuordnung*, *supra* at 99.

[1671] *See* already Mestmäcker, *Comparative Observations*, *supra* at 231 ("The interests of the members of performing rights organisations are not neglected, but their protection appears to be secondary to the public interest in competition [in the United States]"). *See also* Drexl, *Collecting Societies*, *supra* at 24; Drexl, *Competition and Development*, *supra* at 241 ("[…] US law does not seem to take account of the need to protect authors against players in the copyright industry").

[1672] Drexl, *Competition and Development*, *supra* at 222 (noting that the Recommendation 2005 abandoned the efficiency-oriented approach for the benefits of (large) right holders).

[1673] This is not to say that there were no provisions on right holders in the early decrees, *e.g.* prohibiting the exclusive assignment requirement, *see* Lunney, *The United States Experience*, *supra* at 329. However, this provision can not only be seen from the perspective of protecting right holders, *see* immediately.

holders against CMOs. Explanations for the divergences in the U.S. and EU approaches can be found in the underlying conceptions of CMOs, the regulatory models employed, and the governing principles of copyright law.

In any event, the regulation of CMOs should address the issue comprehensively, taking into account all involved interests. The difference in focus in the U.S. and the EU does not, however, necessarily mean that different legal principles apply; or that some interests remain unconsidered. This is because several rules, though enacted from a particular perspective or under specific circumstances, and appearing to be directed toward one particular aim at first glance, might actually serve multiple purposes. Consider, for instance, the obligation to represent right holders. Such obligation certainly protects right holders in that it ensures non-discriminatory access to management services.[1674] At the same time, however, such obligation will ensure that the no interested licensors are excluded from the CMOs' blanket licenses[1675] – hence mitigating antitrust concerns regarding this type license, especially in the U.S. conception of CMOs. A similar observation can be made in connection with the exclusivity of the rights grant. From a U.S. point of view, prohibiting exclusivity serves as an essential justification for blanket licensing under the rule of reason analysis: As long as users can freely choose between individual negotiations and the blanket license, no illegal conduct will be found; non-exclusivity therefore protects users but can also be seen as enhancing the right holders' freedom to negotiate better deals for themselves. From a European perspective, permitting exclusive rights grants might just as well protect right holders in that they cannot be "forced" by large music users to individually contract with them at unfavorable terms.[1676] Another matter of perspective in the present context are partial withdrawals. Again, partial withdrawals strengthen the right holders' freedom to license their rights themselves – and this also seems to be the position of the Collective Management Directive. On the flipside, partial withdrawals inevitably risk repertoire fragmentation, making the licensing process more complex and putting users at a disadvantage. Moreover, restricting partial withdrawals can be seen as promoting the solidarity principle inherent in the traditional understanding of CMOs in that large right holders cannot "cherry-pick" by keeping the most profitable rights for themselves, to the benefit of smaller right holders. In this light – and given the U.S. conceptions of CMOs (*see* subsection 2), it is surprising that U.S. courts have ruled out the option of partial withdrawals, thereby (most likely, unintentionally) promoting the solidarity function of CMOs. Restricting partial withdrawals can also be seen as means to protect right holders against unreasonable claims of music users;[1677] moreover, they will have a direct impact on representation agreements

1674 van Gompel, *Directive*, *supra* at 573.

1675 I Hovenkamp et al., *IP and Antitrust*, *supra* at § 22.4a1.

1676 *See, e.g.*, Drexl, *Competition and Development*, *supra* at 174.

1677 *Id.* at 242.

concluded with other CMOs. The seminal blanket license fits in this multi-sided picture. In being justified by efficiency gains, one can assume that the cost-saving of the aggregation of rights will result in either lower user fees or higher royalty paychecks.[1678] The issue of management costs is a difficult point, however. In fact, every increase and decrease of administrative costs can either be connected to decreases in the right holders' revenue or assumed to be passed on users. Which one of these consequences occurs will be heavily influenced by the regulatory regimes applying to the fee structure (rather than the internal distribution policies) of CMOs. At first glance, it seems that both groups should benefit from costs saving, but it is up to rate regulation to decide on that point. The only thing that is certain is that any efficiency gains should not be consumed by the intermediary.

The foregoing merely reflects what is actually common knowledge: CMOs are active in (what can nowadays be called) a three-sided market[1679] in which an adjustment in one particular relation affects the other relations entertained by CMOs. It is of utmost importance that these interrelations be considered when designing a regulatory framework for CMOs.

1.3. The Tale of the Author

Having established that EU law, on a fundamental level, puts its main focus on right holders, the question arises of how far this protection goes. This concerns both the relation to users as well as to other right holders. Clearly, there should be limits to the protection of right holders. As stated before, right holders are not only the artists and authors who actually create content for the society's overall benefit, that is, the original works. The tendency toward the emergence of very large right holders can be observed at least since the 1990s.[1680] It is especially questionable whether large right holders like major publishers (which own derivative rights) require the same amount of protection as smaller right holders – it appears, for instance, that their bargaining position vis-à-vis users is sufficient in order to defend their interests against users. Their strong position might also secure them an influential position in the internal structure of a CMO.[1681] Moreover, acknowledging that right holders

1678 *Cirace* argues in light of the *CBS* case that blanket licenses can be justified by their function of protecting right holders rather than by transaction cost savings, *see* Cirace, *Economic Analysis*, *supra* at 292–293, 297. *See* in this connection *Witmark & Sons*, 80 F. Supp. 843 at 850 (highlighting the option that costs can be passed on the users).

1679 *CISAC Agreement*, COMP/C2/38.698 at ¶ 148–57. *See also IFPI Simulcasting*, COMP/C2/38.014 at ¶ 45–48; *Cannes Extension Agreement*, COMP/C2/38.681 at ¶ 19–20; Recommendation 2005 at point 5(d).

1680 Chin, *Copyright Collective Management*, *supra* at 278; Porter, *Role of Collecting Societies*, *supra* at 672.

1681 Chin, *Copyright Collective Management*, *supra* at 277–278. *See also* Mestmäcker & Schweitzer, *Wettbewerbsrecht*, *supra* at 879.

should be protected against large users, one could also ask whether users should likewise be protected against large right holders.[1682] This seems to be more in line with the U.S. approach which conceives CMOs first and foremost as potential price fixing cartels. This is not to say that the special case of large right holders has not been addressed in the EU.[1683]

Everyone agrees that CMOs – since they have great market power by aggregating and pooling rights – should be regulated. In many important respects, publishers are very similar to CMOs, even though they technically do not pool rights held by different persons, but their own (derivative) rights acquired by assignment or other legal constructions. Still, some of them build up large repertoires. Moreover, publishers act as intermediaries just like CMOs, in this case primarily in a two-sided market between authors and users.[1684] In a certain way, publishers also carry out collective management tasks, the collective element being that a wide variety of works created by other persons is managed.[1685] From this perspective – despite the unquestionably important functions carried out by publishers – there is a strong case for the regulation not only of CMOs but also for large right holders like major publishers, even more so if CMOs and publishers cooperate in licensing constructs like CELAS. If a competition law-based solution (*see* subsection 3) is chosen, one might consider whether the (rather strict) market definition applied to CMOs is also applicable in the present context. At any rate, the problem should be seen both in connection with the implications for users and other right holders.[1686] Finally, it is worthwhile that this question can be seen in connection with the more general debate revolving around copyright reform, especially whether modern copyright law focuses too much on the intermediaries and not the authors.[1687]

1682 *See, e.g.,* Tuma, *Pitfalls and Challenges*, *supra* at 225–226.

1683 In the *MTV/VPL* case, the Commission alleged that the combination of large rights holders in a CMO could violate art 101 TFEU, *see* section II.2.3.3. above. *See* on this case Porter, *Role of Collecting Societies*, *supra* at 676. In this connection, it is noteworthy that the ECJ stated (against the background of statutory licensing) that remuneration for right holders should not lead to "overcompensation" to the detriment of users, *see Hewlett-Packard*, C-572/13 at ¶ 85–86.

1684 Drexl, *Competition and Development*, *supra* at 78, 81–82; Kuik & Dawes, *Media*, *supra* at 1760. *See also* Brabec, *Performance Right*, *supra* at 41; Mestmäcker & Schweitzer, *Wettbewerbsrecht*, *supra* at 872–873; 2 Nimmer on Copyright, *supra* at § 8.19[A] n. 11.

1685 Arezzo, *Lights and Shadows*, *supra* at 545. *See also* Mendis, *Directive 2014/26/EU*, *supra* at 309–310.

1686 Drijber, *Competition law aspects*, *supra* at 75–76.

1687 *See, e.g.,* Adolf Dietz, *Schutz der Kreativen (der Urheber und ausübenden Künstler) durch das Urheberrecht oder Die fünf Säulen des modernen kontinentaleuropäischen Urheberrechts*, 64 GRUR Int 309 (2015); Ginsburg, *The Author's Place*, *supra*; Jessica Litman, *Real Copyright Reform*, 96 Iowa L. Rev. 1 (2010); Van Houweling, *Author Autonomy*, *supra*. However, as *Kretschmer* highlights, publishers add substantial value through their activities, *see* Kretschmer, *The Failure of Property Rules*, *supra* at 128.

1.4. The Reduced Principle of Equal Treatment

The preceding subsection highlights that not all right holders should be treated equally – in relation to the CMOs, other right holders, and users – where this is justified by objective differences. The same applies to users. The Consent Decrees, the Collective Management Directive, and courts on both sides of the Atlantic acknowledge this rationale. In fact, the general principle of equal treatment is frequently restricted by an actual duty to discriminate; in some instances, at least, such duties appear to be the rule rather than the exception. To the extent that one distinguishes between users and right holder groups, this actually reflects a general principle of antitrust law that judgments must be made for the individual case.[1688] To the extent that one takes into consideration the aims of copyright law, however, the analysis includes an additional layer of complexity. The principle of equal treatment is also "reduced" in the present sense for statutory licenses.[1689]

2. The Diverging Image of CMOs: Legitimate Functions and Limited Justifications

2.1. Skepticism to the Traditional CMO Model from a Competition Law Perspective

CMOs fulfill similar functions in Europe and the U.S. However, the question is to what extent and under what conditions the law acknowledges these functions. Historically, the U.S. and the EU have taken different approaches to CMOs. In the U.S., the very existence of CMOs was targeted in the 1930s. These organizations have since been regarded first and foremost as potentially detrimental to users and have often been labeled as "necessary evil",[1690] i.e. something that is accepted only to the extent that their efficiency benefits – both in relation to right holders and users – outweighs their negative aspects. Conversely, the starting point of EU regulation appears to be not only the protection of right holders vis-à-vis CMOs themselves but also in relation to users. Perhaps one could say that CMOs are regarded in Europe as something necessary that can also be harmful.[1691] However, such conceptions are not carved in stone: The initiatives taken by the Commission between 2004 and 2014 feature

1688 *See, e.g., Kanal 5*, C-52/07, Opinion of AG Trstenjak at ¶ 52.

1689 *See, e.g., Hewlett-Packard*, C-572/13 at ¶ 41, 49 (on right holder categories and types of uses); II Goldstein on Copyright, *supra* at § 7.8.6.2. (on special safeguards for artists under § 114(g)(2)).

1690 *See, e.g.*, Chin, *Copyright Collective Management*, *supra* at 274; Korman, *U.S. Position*, *supra* at 160; Lunney, *The United States Experience*, *supra* at 320. *See also* Drexl, *Competition and Development*, *supra* at 211–212; Pitt, *Direct Licensing*, *supra* at 53.

1691 *Prof. Gervais* observes that CMOs are often perceived as a "preferred mode of management of copyright, not as a last resort", *see* Gervais, *The Landscape*, *supra* at 595.

U.S. conceptions rather than the traditional European understanding. Conversely, it appears from the case law that the ECJ has remained consistent in balancing the involved interests and, most importantly, acknowledging the important function of CMOs to represent the right holders' legitimate interest.

Even though this antitrust-based skepticism is also common among legal scholars,[1692] a study reported that copyright specialists tend to argue that CMOs should be exempted or at least receive special treatment under competition law.[1693] Describing the application practice in a general fashion especially in the EU, however, has proven difficult and depends on the specific area studied or the perspective taken. While in connection with license fees, the EU approach has been described as a "harsh" treatment of CMOs,[1694] others have seen a "lenient" approach overall.[1695] While the continuing non-application of article 101 is certainly favorable, the market definition (*see* section II.2. above) rather points in the opposite direction. As a general trend, skepticism toward CMOs is higher in the online than the offline environment.[1696]

2.2. Cultural Functions and the Solidarity Principle

The basic functions of CMOs – such as licensing rights, collecting and distributing revenues, monitoring, and enforcement – are acknowledged in the U.S. and the EU as well as the fact that such organizations require a certain size to carry out these tasks.[1697] Cultural functions are, however, a different matter. The word cultural in the present context does not only refer to the CMOs' internal distribution policies that a certain amount of the revenues is not directly allocated to right holders, but used for other purposes like scholarships, for instance.[1698] It also entails the difficult question of the CMOs' role in the promotion of cultural diversity, i.e. niche repertoires or less popular works.[1699]

1692 *See, e.g.,* Chin, *Copyright Collective Management, supra* at 283–284.

1693 Drexl, *Competition and Development, supra* at 273.

1694 Anderman & Schmidt, *EU Competition Law, supra* at 156–159.

1695 Vinje & Niiranen, *Digital Environment, supra* at 399, 403. *See also* Drexl, *Collecting Societies, supra* at 24.

1696 This is especially reflected by the Commission's *Daft Punk* decision, *see* Kuik & Dawes, *Media, supra* at 1748–1749; Lichtenegger, *Verwertungsgesellschaften, supra* at 482–483; Vinje & Niiranen, *Digital Environment, supra* at 406–407.

1697 *BMI v. CBS*, 441 U.S. 1 at 18–19 n. 32; *BRT*, 127-73 at ¶ 10.

1698 *See* in general Gervais, *Theory and Practice, supra* at 7, 17–20; Gervais, *The Landscape, supra* at 593 (highlighting that CMOs provide also services besides their administrative tasks); Lichtenegger, *Verwertungsgesellschaften, supra* at 49–58 (also referring to social services and pension funds). *See also* Dietz, *Legal Regulation, supra* at 912–913 (referring to national regulation in Europe); Kohn & Kohn, *Music Licensing, supra* at 197 (arguing that cultural funding is a governmental task rather than one of CMOs).

1699 One could call this function an *indirect* promotion of cultural activities, *see* Lichtenegger, *Verwertungsgesellschaften, supra* at 63. *See also* John Street et al., *Regulating for creativity and cultural diversity: the case of collective management organisations and the music in-*

As already observed, when a user obtains a blanket license she buys access to works she might not actually want to perform (*e.g.*, because the works are not popular with the targeted audience). Hence, a CMO could essentially be regarded as cross-subsidizing less popular works – the extent of the subsidization depending of course on the distribution policies.[1700] Again, the matter is essentially one of perspective: Policymakers must decide on whether the promotion of cultural diversity in this way justifies the inherent antitrust concerns associated with this model; this weighing should be considered additionally to the question whether access to subsets of the repertoire is feasible or more expensive than the blanket license. In the EU, the CMOs' role in the protection of cultural diversity is readily acknowledged. The CMD makes clear that this rationale is heavily influenced by article 167 TFEU, which confirms that the EU is composed of member states with diverging cultural backgrounds.[1701] This point is problematic in the U.S. In the *Paramount* decision centering the licensing of films, the Supreme Court condemned licensing models which forced users to license "inferior" works because it considered the reward granted by copyright law to be necessarily linked to the quality of the works.[1702] Yet, it is hard to determine the quality of a work or to distinguish "inferior" from "superior" works.[1703] A mere market-based approach does not necessarily reflect the value of a work from the copyright law's perspective; furthermore, works which are not considered of special value today might be regarded as extremely important in the future.[1704] This is essentially a question of what copyright law aims to achieve and what means should be employed for this purpose. Hence, the legislature is better suited to deal with this issue than the courts or competition agencies.[1705] In the context of CMOs – a context different from the *Paramount* case – it might be necessary to separate the basic question of the CMOs' cultural function and the inclusion of less popular works in a license

dustry, Int. J. of Cultural Policy (2016) (focusing on the practices and priorities of different CMOs).

1700 One could also argue that under a use based distribution system, a blanket license might actually harm right holders of less popular works, *see BMI v. CBS*, 441 U.S. 1 at 32–33 (J.P. Stevens, dissenting). On the other hand, one could ask whether such works would be licensed at all, even at a smaller price. In any event, an opportunity for smaller right holders could be direct licensing via internet platforms like YouTube, *see* Chin, *Copyright Collective Management*, *supra* at 277. *See also* Pitt, *Direct Licensing*, *supra* at 161.

1701 CMD recital 3; Ficsor, *Key Issues*, *supra* at 219–226. *See* already Mestmäcker, *Collecting Societies*, *supra* at 344–346 (also emphasizing the different situation in the United States). The European Parliament commissioned an entire study on the cultural diversity issue, *see* Hellenic Foundation for European and Foreign Policy, *Cultural Diversity*, *supra*.

1702 *Paramount Pictures*, 334 U.S. 131 at 158. *See also Moor-Law*, 527 F. Supp. 758 at 766.

1703 It is worthwhile that U.S. copyright law generally does not judge the artistic merits of the work in order to determine whether it deserves copyright protection, *see, e.g.*, *Bleistein v. Donaldson Lithographing Co.*, 188 U.S. 239 at 251 (1903).

1704 *Cf.* Drexl, *Collecting Societies*, *supra* at 19 (referring to the pre-selection by intermediaries).

1705 Lunney, *The United States Experience*, *supra* at 339 (in the context of rate-setting).

from the question how the royalties are distributed. Also in Europe, the usage of works (and therefore, their popularity) is used in the distribution process.[1706]

A further non-economic aspect of CMOs could be paraphrased as the solidarity function which is inherent to the traditional model of collective management.[1707] This function acknowledges that right holders occupy a special role in relation to one another as well as the CMOs that they are affiliated with. Right holders are not simply "clients" of the organization, but actual affiliates subjected to the internal rules.[1708] This does not, however, mean that competition law is inapplicable.[1709] Likewise, solidarity implies respecting the interests of other affiliates despite the diverging self-interests. The solidarity principle must naturally be seen in this context. For instance, a distribution system that favors often-used works – as just mentioned before – may be in tension with this principle.[1710] However, that is not necessarily so: Solidarity could also be understood as respecting the rights and achievements of a more successful member.

The necessary restrictions put on right holders in the wake of the solidarity principle raises serious antitrust issues – and can be seen in connection with the promotion of niche repertoires – because the freedom of right holders is often limited so as to affect competition among the works covered by the repertoire.[1711] A prime example of the right holders' diverging interests is the par-

---

1706 CMD recital 26 (stating that CMOs require accurate data on, *inter alia*, the use of works, in order to accurately distribute the revenues). *See, e.g.,* Handig, *VerwertungsgesellschaftenG*, *supra* at 167.

1707 *See, e.g.,* Ficsor, *Collective* Management, supra at 20, 23; Wallis et al., *Contested Collective Administration, supra*. CMD art. 3(a) stresses that CMOs act for the "collective benefit" of right holders.

1708 Allendesalazar & Vallina, *The Usual Suspects*, *supra* at 374; Stamatoudi, *Love-Hate Relationship*, *supra* at 291–292. Furthermore, right holders can act both as suppliers as well as competitors in relation to CMOs, *see Radio Music License Comm.*, 29 F. Supp. 3d 487 at 501. In *GVL*, the Commission considered right holders as "trading partners" within the meaning of TFEU art. 102(c), *see GVL*, IV/29.839 at ¶ 49–50; however, the ECJ did not deal with this question, *see GVL*, 7/82 at ¶ 58.

1709 *See, e.g., Alden-Rochelle*, 80 F. Supp. 888 at 894; *Witmark & Sons*, 80 F. Supp. 843 at 850; Sladiĉ, *Collective Management*, *supra* at 43. *See also* Riccio & Codiglione, *Monopolistic Positions*, *supra* at 299–300.

1710 *See also Sladiĉ*, *Collective Management*, *supra* at 43 (stating that the solidarity principle is the "direct opposite of the competition by merits").

1711 In this light, the above cited "first principle" of collective management is – paradoxically – in tension with the traditional solidarity function of CMOs: The question is whether those right holders, for whom individual management is *possible* and *practical* may be given incentives (or be forced) to remain within the CMO for the benefit of smaller right holders. In the realm of mandatory collective management the EU legislator strengthens the solidarity; this is not to say, however, that solidarity is the only (or even prevailing) reason for the introduction of mandatory collective management schemes. Conversely, one could also ask if the voluntary accession of right holders to CMOs who can practically manage their rights violates competition law, *see* Lichtenegger, *Verwertungsgesellschaften*, *supra* at 439–441. *See* in this connection CMD recital 19 ("[B]alance between the freedom of rightholders to tial withdrawal issue which plainly contradicts the solidarity principle since certain right holders exit from the collective management system to collect higher royalties for themselves ("cherry-picking").[1712] While this might actually be desirable from an antitrust perspective, it can have strong implications for the management system overall. CMOs are generally said to be in need of the revenues generated by their large and successful members in order to cover the fixed management costs.[1713] As mentioned before, both the Supreme Court and the ECJ acknowledge that CMOs must have a necessary size to fulfill their functions. The question is then how to weigh the interests of the involved right holders whose freedoms will be restricted[1714] and the public interest in the functioning of the collective management system overall. In this connection, it becomes apparent that the solidarity principle is strongly connected to the promotion of cultural diversity, as niche repertoires will usually be less profitable, and smaller right holders will find it hard to manage their rights on their own.[1715] This weighing process is, again, essentially a policy decision and hence a task for the legislator rather than for competition agencies. The Collective Management Directive ensures right holders a great amount of freedom, thereby limiting the solidarity principle of CMOs.[1716] In turn, the U.S. rate courts prevented the withdrawals of major right holders. In doing so, the courts promoted the solidarity principle; this might, however, have been an "unintentional" consequence, as it seems that courts had primarily the position of the users in mind when interpreting the Consent Decrees.

By employing a fair distribution system which focuses on the use of works, the system achieves both protection of the smaller right holders (by providing a management infrastructure which could not be financed without the bigger members) as well as fairness regarding the larger members in receiving a higher proportion of the revenues. In this light, solidarity is also an expression of promoting cultural diversity.

---

dispose of their works and other subject-matter and the ability of the organisation to manage the rights effectively [...]"); 2 Walter, *Verwertungsgesellschaftenrecht*, *supra* at 123, 136. *See also* Mendis, *Directive 2014/26/EU*, *supra* at 311 (highlighting the importance of blanket licenses for less famous works).

1712 Ficsor, *Collective Management*, *supra at* 23 (referring to the "agency-type regime").

1713 U.S. Copyright Office, *Music Marketplace*, *supra* at 97. This might also affect the legality of CMOs, *see* section II.2.3.3. above and section 1.3. *See also* Allendesalazar & Vallina, *The Usual Suspects*, *supra* at 394–395.

1714 *See, e.g.*, Ficsor, *Collective Management*, *supra at* 23, 97–98, 150–151 (referring to mandatory collective management, withdrawals, and royalty distribution). In *GEMA III* the Commission approved restrictions put on members in order to safeguard the proper functioning of CMOs, *see GEMA III*, IV/29-971 at ¶ 37.

1715 Arezzo, *Lights and Shadows*, *supra* at 556.

1716 It has also been said that the directive's requirement that a society represented under a representation agreement must expressly consent to any deductions made by the partner society will induce the withdrawals of larger right holders, *see* Graber, *Collective Rights Management*, *supra* at 42.

3. Regulatory Models: Competition, Monopolies and Minimum Standards Against the Background of Copyright Law

The foregoing considerations have highlighted some problems and conflicts which need to be addressed by regulation. The question remains, however, how such regulation should be designed and to what degree it should be applied.

3.1. The Competition-Monopolism Dichotomy

The seminal dispute in the discussion whether and by what means CMOs should be regulated centers on the question of to what extent CMOs should operate in a competitive environment; or, whether CMOs achieve their objectives best when they possess a de facto or de jure monopoly.[1717] This section will certainly not resolve this dispute but it aims at placing the two positions in perspective of the experiences and differences observed in the U.S. and the EU.

Competition can be seen as a necessary incentive for CMOs to induce efficiency in the course of the management process. This argument refers to the "general" advantages of competition in the form of higher quality and lower prices of the offered services in which the Commission is the driving force.[1718] The absence of competition was considered as hampering the emergence of new and innovative markets, namely in the online environment, and tempting CMOs to abuse their monopolist strength to the detriment of both right holders and users.[1719] To this effect, the Commission argued that more competition would serve in the right holders' interest especially through lower administration costs and consequently lower administration fees.[1720] Moreover, this would

---

1717 *See* for a succinct summary of many arguments and counter arguments *OSA,* C-351/12, Opinion of AG Sharpston at ¶ 74–75. *See also* Wenqi Liu, *Models for Collective Management of Copyright from an International Perspective: Potential Changes for Enhancing Performance*, 18 J. Intellec. Prop. Rights 46 (2012).

1718 *See, e.g.,* AFJ2 Memo at 42; Alain Andries & Bruno Julien-Malvy, *The CISAC decision: creating competition between collecting societies for music rights*, 2008 Competition Policy Newsletter 53, 55, *available at* http://ec.europa.eu/competition/publications/cpn/cpn2008_3.pdf (last visited May 23, 2017); Katz, *Potential Demise, supra* at 590; Riis, *Collecting Societies, supra at* 486–487 (however observing that DG MARKT focused on the rights clearance and creative content aspect); U.S. Copyright Office, *Jointly Owned Works, supra* at 25–26.

1719 Vinje & Niiranen, *Digital Environment, supra* at 418–419. *See also* Kohn & Kohn, *Music Licensing, supra* at 199 (stating that the reduction of administrative expenses does not necessarily translate into lower fees for users).

1720 *CISAC Agreement*, COMP/C2/38.698 at ¶ 132–135. *See also* Chin, *Copyright Collective Management, supra* at 280–281; Einhorn, *Partial Withdrawal, supra* at 299 (arguing that partial withdrawals should be permitted); Katz, *Potential Demise, supra* at 554–559 (challenging the assumption that the traditional advantages attributed to CMOs can only be achieved by these organizations); Merges, *Continuing Vitality, supra* at 26–27 (also mentioning incentives to adapt to new circumstances).

also lie in the CMOs' interest because they could increase their turnover by attracting more mandates from right holders.[1721] In *Tournier*, also the ECJ acknowledged the positive aspects of competition, insofar as the court pointed out that SACEM's high royalty fees and administration costs could possibly be the consequence of the lack of competitive pressure.[1722] Indeed, competition is in principle better suited to determine prices than rate-setting mechanisms under antitrust doctrines.[1723] It was also argued that cultural diversity was not threatened by increased competition.[1724] In this connection, the General Court held that a system of territorial restrictions in representation agreements was not necessary for the protection of less popular repertoires from a competition law perspective.[1725] Furthermore, as envisaged by the Commission, actual competition would possibly lead to the emergence of two to three major European CMOs which would be necessary to possess sufficient power to compete with big CMOs from the United States, China, and India.[1726] However, the Commission also favored the IFPI Simulcast Agreement as a "prototype" for competition on the level of administration fees with the remarkable advantage of reconciling multi-repertoire and multi-territorial licenses.[1727]

However, arguments against competition have been advanced too. First of all, it has been noted that competition can have ambiguous results: On the one hand, the traditional system of representation agreements leaves little room for price competition; on the other hand, national one-stop-shops to the world repertoire for which this system is a prerequisite contribute to the exploitation of economies of scale.[1728] Thus, with the inherent advantages of competition come inherent disadvantages in the specific field of collective management. Institutionally, in the EU, the European Parliament was one of driving forces which was skeptical about competition.[1729] It stressed that a competitive system must not lead to a decrease of the revenues paid to right holders.[1730] Moreover, it is not sure that CMOs facing competition will generate efficiency gains.[1731] Com-

1721 *CISAC Agreement*, COMP/C2/38.698 at ¶ 136. *See also* Press Release European Commission (May 03, 2004), *supra*.

1722 *Tournier*, 395/87 at ¶ 42; *Lucazeau,* 110/88 at ¶ 29.

1723 Mestmäcker & Schweitzer, *Wettbewerbsrecht*, *supra* at 887–888. *See also* Drexl, *Free Movement of Services*, *supra* at 478–479; Lunney, *The United States Experience*, *supra* at 347; Wünschmann, *Kollektive Verwertung*, *supra* at 188–189.

1724 *CISAC Agreement*, COMP/C2/38.698 at ¶ 93–99; Andries & Julien-Malvy, *The CISAC Decision*, *supra* at 55–56.

1725 *STIM*, T-451/08 at ¶ 73–85.

1726 Gyertyánfy, *Collective Management*, *supra* at 79.

1727 Riis, *Collecting Societies*, *supra* at 487–488; Hilty & Nérisson, *Digitization*, *supra* at 7.

1728 Riis, *Collecting Societies*, *supra* at 487.

1729 *See, e.g.,* Resolution 2007.

1730 *Id.* at point 4.

1731 Tuma, *Pitfalls and Challenges*, *supra* at 228. *See also Autortiesību un komunicēšanās konsultāciju aģentūra / Latvijas Autoru apvienība*, C-177/16, Opinion of AG Wahl at ¶ 4–5 (arguing that some markets are not run efficiently when open to competition); Einhorn, petition could also weaken their bargaining power vis-à-vis users with detrimental effects upon the collected royalties.[1732] Several CMOs in the field lead to a multiplication of administrative costs[1733] and competition will only be beneficial to the extent that efficiency gains can cover these expenses. Additional costs arise from evidentiary issues that the CMOs enforcing copyrights are actually entitled to do so.[1734] Furthermore, the European Parliament expressed its wish to maintain the system of reciprocal representation as a means against repertoire fragmentation, i.e. to obtain licenses to the world repertoire.[1735] The cultural diversity issue has also been raised in this connection. CMOs in competition with other organizations might be unable to cross-subsidize weaker members and provide funds for social and cultural purposes.[1736] It can be assumed that CMOs will compete for works in order to offer an attractive repertoire to users.[1737] This implies advertising and marketing expenses which cannot be used for the CMO's management activities.[1738] Since it is likely that CMOs would be reluctant to represent smaller and less popular repertoires focusing primarily on the commercially most attractive right holders, this might also lead to the cross-subsidization of right holders and repertoires which are already commercially successful in order to obtain the mandates for their representation.[1739] At the same time, less successful authors could face troubles in directly contracting CMOs or new licensing models.[1740] Another related consequence is that competitive pressure might result in the disappearance of smaller CMOs or those which today represent such niche-repertoires,[1741] unless they manage to successfully specialize in specific work sectors neglected by bigger organizations.[1742]

What can be inferred from the above-outlined discussion is that the arguments often extend beyond strictly legal considerations. Collective management and its regulation and organization involve economic, social, cultural, and to a certain extent, ideological convictions and interests; therefore, it is neces-

Music Performing Rights, *supra* at 365 (stating that the extent of competition between ASCAP and BMI is uncertain). This is also acknowledged by competition-friendly authors, *see, e.g.*, Chin, *Copyright Collective Management*, *supra* at 279.

1732 Besen et al., *Copyright Collectives*, *supra* at 398–399, 402–403.

1733 Korman, *U.S. Position*, *supra* at 173–174. This also relates to representation agreements with foreign CMOs, *see* U.S. Copyright Office, *Jointly Owned Works*, *supra* at 18.

1734 Ficsor, *Key Issues*, *supra* at 242.

1735 Resolution 2007 points N, O.

1736 Handke, *Collective Administration*, *supra* at 194–195.

1737 Reiko Aoki & Aaron Schiff, *Promoting access to intellectual property: patent pools, copyright collectives and clearing houses*, 38 R&D Management 189, 200 (2008).

1738 KEA, *Collective Management*, *supra* at 19.

1739 Handke, *Collective Administration*, *supra* at 195.

1740 Porcin, *The Quest*, *supra* at 62 (arguing that this might only be possible by transferring their rights to other organizations).

1741 Ficsor, *Key Issues*, *supra* at 241–242; Gyertyánfy, *Collective Management*, *supra* at 83–84.

1742 Riccio & Codiglione, *Monopolistic Positions*, *supra* at 300.

sary not only to consider the competition law perspective but the entirety of the involved interests as well as the characteristics of copyright law. It is undisputed that competitive and monopolistic licensing markets both offer different advantages and drawbacks. While competition between CMOs (and right holders) can lead to efficiency gains, monopolies can offer bigger repertoires, for instance. The trade-off here is between repertoire fragmentation and territorial fragmentation. It seems that the European developments – centering on right withdrawals and competition between repertoires – have so far not fully achieved overcoming both variants of the fragmentation problem[1743] unless a one-stop shop for rights clearance emerges in the future. There might be a different solution than the completely free competition, however. The negative effects of the competitive model can be mitigated by corresponding legislation which forces CMOs to represent niche repertoires and allows them to include these repertoires in a blanket license.[1744] Yet, larger (possibly pan-European) CMOs would still have to build up a management infrastructure also in the smaller member states where niche repertoire is most likely to be popular. This appears to be a rather burdensome task, and it is at least doubtful whether there would be enough incentive to do so. If this argument also extends to the online rights, depends on whether not only the monitoring but only the enforcement functions can be carried out in this environment. While these arguments primarily relate to the right holders' perspective, the situation is more complex in relation to the users' perspective.[1745] As discussed above, management services are more easily substitutable than creative works. It is unclear to which extent these functions can be separated or which should prevail over the other.

The competition-monopoly dichotomy is often discussed on a very fundamental level. However, the real task might not be to decide whether copyright licensing categorically works better under competitive or monopolistic conditions. Rather, it seems that these concepts need to be adapted to the reality of the respective copyright systems. The European market is not comparable to the U.S. market in several important respects. Competition between CMOs might simply work better in a big and rather uniform market with a uniform language and a federal copyright system.[1746] It is highly doubtful whether one can force the emergence of such a market for copyrights by regulating its management;[1747] and under the constitutional order of the EU, quite frankly, it is

[1743] This is an immediate problem for users, *see* Guibault & van Gompel, *Collective Management*, *supra* at 166. *See also* Kohn & Kohn, *Music Licensing*, *supra* at 198.

[1744] *Drexl* – in connection with the concept of "creative competition" – makes a case for a "system of collecting administration based on a principle of open and non-discriminatory access of all works", *see* Drexl, *Collecting Societies*, *supra* at 20, 22. *Gervais* calls, also in relation to users, CMOs a business model of "yes", *see* Gervais, *The Landscape*, *supra* at 597, 615.

[1745] Drexl, *Free Movement of Services*, *supra* at 466–467.

[1746] Ficsor, *Key Issues*, *supra* at 236. *See also* Porcin, *The Quest*, *supra* at 63–64.

[1747] *See*, to this effect Tuma, *Pitfalls and Challenges*, *supra* at 227.

doubtful whether this is actually desirable.[1748] For this task, it is necessary to employ a broader perspective than an antitrust analysis.[1749] In this sense, "one size does not fit all" in connection with the collective management of copyrights. Thus, neither competition nor monopolies should be categorically rejected; it depends on the environment they are applied to. This is not to say that experiences from U.S. law should not be taken into consideration in the EU; in fact, the U.S. approach has had an undeniable influence on the European developments.[1750]

Clearly, in light of the U.S. experience with ASCAP, an organization which engaged in obviously abusive conduct in the earlier days of collective management in the United States, it is apparent that the competition by BMI was seen as a highly beneficial development; however, this is an entirely different story for EU countries where rigid supervision has been in place long before the EU discovered CMOs as a field for regulation.[1751] In this connection, it is worthwhile that SoundExchange is currently the only U.S. CMO designated by the CRB[1752] and it does not seem to operate in a market similar to ASCAP and BMI from a competition perspective.

3.2. Creating Requirements for Competition

Relying on market forces in order to control the activities of CMOs is, in principle, a valid regulatory strategy, just as sector-specific legislation. Neither

1748 Nevertheless, it has been noted that the Commission – which has traditionally pursued a policy of preservation of the cultural heritage and diversity in Europe – focused, roughly as of 2010, on the economic perspective of the cultural industries in order to foster competitiveness and growth, *see* Lichtenegger, *Verwertungsgesellschaften, supra* at 33 (calling this development a "functional change" of the European cultural sector).

1749 *See, e.g.,* in connection with the freedom to provide services *OSA,* C-351/12, Opinion of AG Sharpston at ¶ 76 ("[…] a proper evaluation of those arguments would involve adjudicating between competing allegations of fact, a matter outwith the Court's competence in the context of these proceedings (it is, perhaps, rather a matter for the legislature)". *See also* Mestmäcker & Schweitzer, *Wettbewerbsrecht, supra* at 886 (stating that there is no obligation to create an Internal Market that does not exist for economic reasons). The cultural diversity issue is often equated with the protection of less successful right holders, *see, e.g.,* Chin, *Copyright Collective Management, supra* at 282. While this might make sense from an internal perspective, in the EU, cultural diversity also entails acknowledging the cultural heritage of the member states.

1750 *Tournier,* 395/87, Opinion of AG Jacobs at ¶ 48; Impact Assessment 2012 at 143–146; Ficsor, *Key Issues, supra* at 240; Porter, *Role of Collecting Societies, supra* at 676 (citing the Commission's Statement of Objections in the *MTV/VPL* case). *See also* Gyertyánfy, *Collective Management, supra* at 70–71, 85.

1751 In this connection, is has been argued that it was precisely the lack of regulation of CMOs that caused the emergence of BMI, hence triggering competition, *see* Besen et al., Copyright Collectives, *supra* at 401. *See also* Drexl, *Collecting Societies, supra* at 8. *See also* Riesenhuber, *Rechtewahrnehmung, supra* at 217 (stating that the German legislator presupposed the joining-together of right holders in CMOs).

1752 Lunney, *The United States Experience, supra* at 347. *See also* section II.1.2.4. above.

of these two models is inherently wrong but might need to be applied in different contexts, or in combination with one another. In some instances, a certain degree of regulation can be necessary in order to create the preconditions for a functional competitive environment. In fact, the ASCAP and BMI Consent Decrees constitute a good example how antitrust law is used as a regulative tool to provide for a system in which CMOs can compete. Very generally speaking, the U.S. system combines ex-ante (proactive, prescriptive) regulation by defining commitments with ordinary antitrust enforcement as a rate-setting process ex-post (retroactive, proscriptive) in the sense that it applies, if CMOs and users cannot agree on a license fee. However, this regulation is not uniform; the Consent Decrees apply only to ASCAP and BMI. It has been argued that this puts SESAC – and potentially other emerging CMOs or large right holders which compete with BMI and ASCAP – at an advantage.[1753] These arguments seem plausible. Even though rate court decisions may have effects on SESAC too, SESAC is able to selectively accept right holders as its members, for instance. Private antitrust enforcement can certainly be a helpful tool in the present context, as demonstrated by the recent SESAC litigation. However, it is doubtful whether it can provide for an equal and coherent level playing field – otherwise, one could declare obsolete the Consent Decrees as such. Only uniform rules on transparency can ensure that right holders can compare the services offered by different CMOs. If one accepts that non-regulated actors enjoy advantages, these advantages do not derive market-based rewards. Hence, it is necessary to create equal conditions and equal opportunities for all CMOs (and potentially, other licensing sources) in the market.[1754] In the EU, the good governance minimum standards provided for by the CMD are certainly to be welcomed. However, also in this connection, one could ask – besides the probable subsistence of divergences in national laws – whether there are loopholes in the regulation. References can be made, for instance, to SESAC. As a for-profit entity,[1755] it depends on whether the organization is owned or controlled by its "members" in order to qualify as a CMO under the CMD; if the latter is not the case, SESAC would avoid the requirements which other (but similar) organizations have to comply with. Similar concerns arise in connection with new licensing models like hybrid entities whose status under EU law has not

1753 *Radio Music License Comm.*, 29 F. Supp. 3d 487 at 502; U.S. Copyright Office, *Jointly Owned Works*, *supra* at 25; U.S. Copyright Office, *Music Marketplace*, *supra* at 95–96. *See also* Einhorn, *Music Performing Rights*, *supra* at 365 (alleging that BMI was able to raise its market share significantly because its rival ASCAP was subject to regulation).

1754 This does not necessarily mean that smaller organizations entering the market should face the same full set of obligations as large incumbent CMOs. In fact, EU law already treats businesses according to the size, *see, e.g.*, Directive 2013/34/EU of the European Parliament and of the Council of 26 June 2013 on the annual financial statements, consolidated financial statements and related reports of certain types of undertakings, amending Directive 2006/43/EC of the European Parliament and of the Council and repealing Council Directives 78/660/EEC and 83/349/EEC art. 3, 2013 O.J. (L182) 19–76.

1755 U.S. Copyright Office, *Music Marketplace*, *supra* at 20.

fully been clarified.[1756] Yet, to the extent they provide similar services and fulfill similar functions compared to CMOs, it does not seem reasonable to exempt them from the regulatory framework.

Competition and regulation are thus no mutually exclusive concepts. This should be acknowledged especially if free competition (within the boundaries of antitrust law) is preferred over monopolism as a regulative model. But also in the latter system, antitrust law can occupy an important role. As highlighted by the MPI, antitrust law can work as a "second layer of regulation".[1757] Conversely, antitrust law alone is not the right tool to regulate the collective management of copyrights.[1758] Too many considerations from outside the antitrust realm influence the analysis. Hence, sector-specific legislation should be applied along with antitrust law; whether sector-specific legislation favors competition or monopolies is a different question.

Last, it should not be forgotten that not only licensors but also licensees compete with one another. Diverging rate-setting standards for music users[1759] might hinder them when competing for consumers. Hence, regulation of collective management must also take into account the implications for other related markets.

3.3. Collective Management as a Reflection of Underlying Copyright Systems

As *Prof. Lunney* underscores, collective rights management should not only be discussed in light of the different management models but also with a view to the "relative normative desirability of the particular legal right at issue."[1760] This requires the assessment of policy decisions, for instance, whether a certain (performance) right should be acknowledged,[1761] whether the pro-

1756 *See, e.g.,* Lichtenegger, *Verwertungsgesellschaften, supra* at 166–167; Pfeifer, *Umsetzung, supra* at 456–457.

1757 Drexl, *Competition and Development, supra* at 34. *See also id.* at 270–271 (highlighting the importance of cooperation between sector-specific regulators and competition law enforcers); *Autortiesību un komunicēšanās konsultāciju aģentūra / Latvijas Autoru apvienība*, C-177/16, Opinion of AG Wahl at ¶ 48 ("I am convinced that unfair prices under Article 102 TFEU can only exist in regulated markets"); Mestmäcker, *Collecting Societies, supra* at 351–352 (referring to the different fields of law relevant to collective management of copyrights).

1758 Gervais, *The Landscape, supra* at 603–605; Sousa e Silva, *The Proposed Directive, supra* at 24–25. *See also Autortiesību un komunicēšanās konsultāciju aģentūra / Latvijas Autoru apvienība*, C-177/16, Opinion of AG Wahl at ¶ 49 (favoring sectoral authorities over competition authorities to oversee license fees); Jay M. Fujitani, *Controlling the Market Power Of Performing Rights Societies: An Administrative Substitute for Antitrust Regulation*, 72 Cal. L. Rev. 103 (1984).

1759 Loren, *Dual Narratives, supra* (on the question whether U.S. copyright law favors incumbent businesses).

1760 Lunney, *The United States Experience, supra* at 363.

1761 *See, e.g.,* DiCola, *Copyright Equality, supra* at 1895.

liferation of acknowledged rights leads to a fragmentation which hampers the rights clearance process,[1762] or whether certain exclusive rights should be replaced by rights to remuneration.[1763] As far as MTL is concerned, private international law also influences the licensing process significantly.[1764] Each of these questions logically influences the rights management system: If a particular right is not acknowledged, there is no need to set up a collective licensing structure; if rights are converged, the need for several specialized rights managing entities becomes less apparent; and statutory licenses imply different preconditions for the licensing process (especially in license fee negotiations) than for exclusive rights. Last, licensing is less complicated if rights must only be cleared in one country and not in all territories where, for instance, a broadcast can be received. In the EU, the analysis is complicated by the fact that copyright law is only partially harmonized; very fundamental questions (*e.g.*, copyright ownership or the transfer of rights) remain largely unregulated.[1765] Creating a functional Internal Market for copyright-related goods and services is hard without a structural solution in the form of comprehensive EU copyright legislation.[1766] It seems that a thorough discussion has been lacking in the EU, which puts the copyright *acquis* in perspective with its management.

An even more basic – and problematic – issue in this connection remains what could be called the philosophical foundations, or, as one might say, the justification for copyright protection in the first place. In the United States, "[t]he immediate effect of [...] copyright law is to secure a fair return for an 'author's' creative labor. But the ultimate aim is, by this incentive, to stimulate artistic creativity for the general public good."[1767] Hence, copyright's monopoly is not supposed to convey a "special private benefit".[1768] If copyright protection is granted first and foremost to incentivize creative production (and dissemination), then it seems logical that also copyright management should

1762 Gervais, *Theory and Practice*, *supra* at 12–15.

1763 This issue is part of a larger discussion centering on the question whether IP law should rely on property rules (with strong exclusive rights) or liability rules. *See, e.g.*, Lemley, *Contracting Around Liability Rules*, *supra*; Mark A. Lemley & Philip J. Weiser, *Should Property or Liability rules Govern Information?*, 85 Texas L. Rev. 783 (2007); Merges, *Contracting into Liability Rules*, *supra*.

1764 Axhamn & Guibault, *Extended Collective Licensing*, *supra* at 61–67 (discussing the "country of transmission" rule); Tuma, *Pitfalls and Challenges*, *supra* at 228 (favoring the so-called "emission theory" to enable EU-wide licensing); Vinje & Niiranen, *Digital Environment*, *supra* at 412–413 (rejecting the "country of destination" principle). *See also* Satellite & Cable Directive art. 1(2)(b).

1765 Drexl et al., *Comments of the MPI*, *supra* at 10–11, 18.

1766 *See, e.g.*, Mireille van Eechoud et al., *Harmonizing European Copyright Law: The Challenges of Better Lawmaking* 316–317 (2009); Towse & Handke, *Current Policy*, *supra* at 15.

1767 *Twentieth Century Music Corp. v. Aiken*, 422 U.S. 151 at 156 (1975). *See also* U.S. Const. art. I, § 8, cl. 8.

1768 *Sony Corp. of Am. v. Universal City Studios*, 464 U.S. 417 at 429 (1984). *See also Paramount Pictures*, 334 U.S. 131 at 158.

serve this purpose. Accordingly, CMOs should not serve right holders to reap unjustified additional benefits. The elusive "ideological resistance to collective models in the United States"[1769] might come to mind in this context. In EU law, it is hard to establish a common philosophical concept of copyright law.[1770] The directives enacted so far are based on Internal Market clauses of the TFEU, and the member states with their different legal and ideological traditions retain considerable freedom in respect of copyright legislation.[1771] Yet, if it is determined that the reward for copyright owners is a governing rationale, also this should be considered when regulating collective management. This is perhaps most clearly visible in connection with setting the rate for license fees, as regulators must directly decide on the allocation of financial resources to right holders or users. Hence, different conceptions of IP law can have important reflections on the collective management of copyrights.[1772] It is a direct consequence of the foregoing that regulatory decisions in relation to collective rights management may be fair and sound in one copyright jurisdiction, but undesirable in another.[1773] *Kretschmer* notes that many CMOs "appear to lean toward a 'reward' rationale of copyright [...], rather than a notion of market-efficient administration of exclusive, transferable rights."[1774] This is completely fine if the reward (constituting an increase relative to market-efficient rules) is what copyright law aims to achieve. This is not to say that antitrust principles are not relevant in the CMO-context; however, they should be applied – especially in the European case – with due account to the rationales of copyright law.

1769 Gervais, *The Landscape*, *supra* at 592.

1770 *See, e.g.*, Lichtenegger, *Verwertungsgesellschaften*, *supra* at 52–53.

1771 Ramalho, *Competence in Copyright, supra* at 197–198.

1772 *See* in connection with the different status of publishers Heyde, *Lizenzierung*, *supra* at 210–212. *See also* Dietz, *Legal Regulation*, *supra* at 901–904; Dietz, *A Missed Opportunity*, *supra* at 14.

1773 It seems that the different conceptions of U.S. and EU law are also reflected by the Supreme Court and the ECJ's rulings on CMOs: While the former puts emphasis on efficiency and the concerns of users, the ECJ has focused on the protection of right holders.

1774 Kretschmer, *The Failure of Property Rules*, *supra* at 134–135 (also highlighting that internal distribution policies play an important role in rewarding creators).

IV. Summary of the Most Important Results

- Collective management of copyrights emerged primarily as an answer to practical problems in the management of exclusive rights, both in the United States and European countries. Yet, while the U.S. CMOs engaged in the field of music have traditionally competed with each other, European CMOs have often enjoyed a de facto or de jure monopoly in their countries. Furthermore, the regulatory approach varies: While many EU member states have enacted sector-specific legislation and supervision over CMOs, and the recently adopted Collective Management Directive follows this path on the EU level, U.S. regulation of CMOs, first and foremost, has been based on antitrust law and consent decrees. This is not to say, however, that the European competition law has not been applied to CMOs; in fact, it has served as the primary regulatory tool on the EU level until the introduction of the Collective Management Directive. In this connection, it can be observed both in the U.S. and the EU that the collaboration between antitrust enforcement agencies and authorities specialized in copyright-related matters is not always easy and should be improved.
- Collective copyright management is a special field of antitrust law, both in the EU and the U.S., as a multitude of different considerations influences the analysis. This relates especially to the relevant market that CMOs are active in. CMOs will usually possess a dominant position in the works they represent if the market definition is confined to the repertoire of a single CMO. However, European authorities have been hesitant to qualify CMOs as unlawful cartels; the most coherent way to explain this application practice is that they can usually benefit from article 101(3) TFEU. In the U.S., in contrast, section 1 of the Sherman Act has been applied to CMOs without any apprehensions. In this connection, the antitrust analysis will be stricter if CMOs require right holders to consent to an exclusive rights grant.
- EU law focuses on the protection of right holders to a much greater extent than U.S. law. Yet, exclusive rights grants are generally permitted only in the EU; however, as this practice raises antitrust issues, it should be critically assessed. Moreover, right holders enjoy greater flexibility as regards rights withdrawals. In both jurisdictions, CMOs (at least those covered by the Consent Decrees) are under the obligation to represent right holders.
- U.S. regulation of CMOs focuses on the protection of users to a greater extent than corresponding European regulation. However, the definition and application of rate-setting standards pose problems in both jurisdictions. These tasks must be carried out with due account of the aims of copyright law and is not solely a question of competition law. Collective bargaining agreements under the supervision of a specialized authority appear to be a viable solution to this problem; said authority should set the rates in case the negotiations fail.

- Blanket licenses are not prohibited as such in both the U.S. and the EU; in many instances, their inherent benefits subsist in spite of the development of new technologies. Where technological development renders blanket licenses less beneficial, one should consider whether consumer preference justifies the existence of this type of license.
- A proper construction of the Consent Decrees and the Collective Management Directive reveals that CMOs are in principle under no duty to issue 100 percent licenses.
- While the CMOs regulated by consent decrees are under an express obligation to license, the Collective Management Directive does not contain a comparable rule. The introduction of such obligation should, however, be considered also on the EU level.
- Statutory licensing poses problems similar to voluntary collective management and licensing; this is clearly visible as regards the rate-setting standards and the corresponding procedure but also in respect of the distribution of the amounts among right holders. Yet, both in the EU and the U.S., there exist considerable differences in the legal approaches toward these related concepts. Converging these fields where appropriate would reinforce the coherence of the copyright system.
- The European (Commission's) approach to representation agreements has been largely unsuccessful. Yet, the CMD contains an important step towards the development of a European MTL market. The expansion and adjustment of these provisions should be considered in order to address remaining concerns.
- Regulating collective management of copyrights is essentially a task of weighing the different involved interests, as an adjustment in relation to one group of stakeholders (*e.g.*, right holders) may have a great impact on another group (*e.g.*, users). In this connection, it is clearly visible that the principle of non-discrimination is restricted in many respects. In some instances, CMOs are required to distinguish between different groups of right holders; the same applies to users.
- A more comprehensive regulatory approach to intermediaries, rather than just CMOs, should be considered, accounting for the emergence of new licensing models as well as large publishers. This framework should be flexible enough to allow for the development of models that are alternative to traditional collective management, keeping in mind that effective collective management as an "essential facility" for right holders requires catalogs of a sufficient size to function. In this connection, it is necessary to weigh the interests of economically powerful right holders against the interests of less powerful right holders.
- In principle, de facto or de jure monopolies are, just like competition, a valid approach to collective copyright management. However, the U.S. experience shows that competition can have, to some extent at least, beneficial effects. Yet, European law-makers and competent authorities should keep in

mind that the European licensing market is in many respects not comparable to the licensing market in the United States, for legal, historical, and cultural reasons; furthermore, the constitutional background differs significantly. Nevertheless, experiences made in the U.S. should be taken into account (and vice versa) when made under comparable circumstances. Last, the U.S. should consider the introduction of sector-specific minimum standards, in order to provide a level playing field for competition. For this purpose, the Collective Management Directive can serve as a point of reference.

- The regulation of the collective management of copyrights – be it through antitrust law or sector-specific legislation – cannot be separated from the characteristics and aims of substantive copyright law; these characteristics and aims differ in the U.S. and the EU, but also in the EU member states. In this light, CMOs rightfully possess a special position in the application of antitrust law; this does not necessarily mean that these organizations should be treated more favorably than other entities. The interplay between the aims of antitrust and copyright law can best be taken into consideration by legislative action; supervision by a specialized authority should be established.

References

1. Books and Journal Articles[1775]

Rafael Allendesalazar & Roberto Vallina, *Collecting Societies: The Usual Suspects* in *European Competition Law Annual 2005: The Interaction between Competition Law and Intellectual Property Law* 371 (Claus Dieter Ehlermann & Isabela Atanasiu eds., 2007). [short form citation: Allendesalazar & Vallina, *The Usual Suspects*]

Steven Anderman & Hedvig Schmidt, *EU Competition Law and Intellectual Property Rights* (2nd ed. 2011). [short form citation: Anderman & Schmidt, *EU Competition Law*]

Alain Andries & Bruno Julien-Malvy, *The CISAC decision: creating competition between collecting societies for music rights*, 2008 Competition Policy Newsletter 53, *available at* http://ec.europa.eu/competition/publications/cpn/cpn 2008_3.pdf (last visited May 23, 2017). [short form citation: Andries & Julien-Malvy, *The CISAC Decision*]

Reiko Aoki & Aaron Schiff, *Promoting access to intellectual property: patent pools, copyright collectives and clearing houses*, 38 R&D Management 189 (2008).

Clemens Appl, *Technische Standardisierung und Geistiges Eigentum* (2012).

Clemens Appl, *Es kann nur eine geben! – Monopol und Wettbewerb von Verwertungsgesellschaften*, 16 ipComptence 28 (2016). [short form citation: Appl, *Monopol und Wettbewerb*]

Phillip E. Areeda & Herbert Hovenkamp, *Antitrust Law: An Analysis of Antitrust Principles and Their Application* (3rd ed. 2006, updated 04/2016). [short form citation: Areeda & Hovenkamp, *Antitrust Principles 2006*]

Phillip E. Areeda & Herbert Hovenkamp, *Antitrust Law: An Analysis of Antitrust Principles and Their Application* (4th ed. 2013, updated 04/2016). [short form citation: Areeda & Hovenkamp, *Antitrust Principles*]

Emanuela Arezzo, *Competition and Intellectual Property Protection in the Market for the Provision of Multi-Territorial Licensing of Online Rights in Musical Works – Lights and Shadows of the New European Directive 2014/26/EU*, 46 IIC 534 (2015). [short form citation: Arezzo, *Lights and Shadows*]

Johan Axhamn & Lucie Guibault, *Cross-border extended collective licensing: a solution to online dissemination of Europe's cultural heritage?* (2011), *available at* https://www.ivir.nl/publicaties/download/292 (last visited May 23, 2017). [short form citation: Axhamn & Guibault, *Extended Collective Licensing*]

Stefan Bechtold, *Directive 2001/29/EC* in *Concise European Copyright Law* 421, (Thomas Dreier & P. Bernt Hugenholtz eds., 2nd ed. 2016). [short form citation: Bechtold, *Directive 2001/29/EC*]

Rainer Bechtold et al., *EU Kartellrecht* (2014). [short form citation: Bechtold et al., *EU Kartellrecht*]

[1775] According to the first author's last name.

Reinhold Beiser & Nikolaus Zorn, *Art 118 AEUV* in *Kommentar zu EUV und AEUV* (Heinz Mayer & Karl Stöger eds., updated 05/2010 at rdb.at). [short form citation: Beiser & Zorn, *Art 118 AEUV*]

Carine Bernault & Audrey Lebois, *Peer-to-peer File Sharing and Literary and Artistic Property* (2005), *available at* http://privatkopie.net/files/Feasibility-Study-p2p-acs_Nantes.pdf (last visited May 23, 2017).

Stanley M. Besen et al., *An Economic Analysis Of Copyright Collectives*, 78 Va. L. Rev. 383 (1992). [short form citation: Besen et al., *Copyright Collectives*]

Marcel Bisges, *Ökonomische Analyse des Urheberrechts*, 58 ZUM 930 (2014).

Hermann-Josef Blanke, *Art. 167 AEUV* in *EUV/AEUV* (Christian Calliess & Matthias Ruffert eds., 5th ed. 2016).

BOP Consulting et al., *Collecting Societies Codes of Conduct* (2012), *available at* http://www.ipo.gov.uk/ipresearch-collecting-071212.pdf (last visited May 23, 2017).

Todd Brabec, *The Performance Right – A World in Transition*, 42 Wm. Mitchell L. Rev. 16 (2016). [short form citation: Brabec, *Performance Right*]

Jan Busche, *Art. 102 AEUV* in 3 *Kölner Kommentar zum Kartellrecht* (Jan Busche & Andreas Röhling eds., 2016). [short form citation: Busche, *Art. 102 AEUV*]

Christian Calliess & Stefan Korte, *Dienstleistungsrecht in der EU* (2011).

Ralf Capito, *Article 82 EC* in *European Media Law* 151 (Oliver Castendyk et al., eds. 2008). [short form citation: Capito, *Article 82*]

Antonio Capobianco, *Licensing of Music Rights: Media Convergence, Technological Developments and EC Competition Law*, 26 E.I.P.R. 113 (2004). [short form citation: Capobianco, *Licensing of Music Rights*]

Yee Wah Chin, *Copyright collective management in the twenty-first century from a competition law Perspective* in *The Evolution and Equilibrium of Copyright in the Digital Age* 269 (Susy Frankel & Daniel Gervais, eds., 2014). [short form citation: Chin, *Copyright Collective Management*]

Ed Christman, *Department of Justice Appeals Consent Decree Ruling, BMI Hits Back*, Billboard May 18, 2017, *available at* http://www.billboard.com/articles/business/7800937/department-justice-appeals-consent-decree-bmi-comment (last visited Oct. 11, 2017).

John Cirace, *CBS v. ASCAP: An Economic Analysis of a Political Problem*, 47 Fordham L. Rev. 277 (1978). [short form citation: Cirace, *Economic Analysis*]

Jeff Clark-Meads, *MTV Europe, VPL Resolve Years-Ling Licensing Dispute*, Billboard, May 16, 1998, at 1.

Kevin Coates et al., *Intellectual Property* in *The EU Law of Competition* 1443 (Jonathan Faull & Ali Nikpay eds., 3rd ed. 2014).

Daniel A. Crane, *Bargaining In The Shadow Of Rate-Setting Courts*, 76 Antitrust L. J. 307 (2009). [short form citation: Crane, *Rate-Setting Courts*]

Gerhard Dannemann, *Comparative Law: Study of Similarities or Differences?* in *The Oxford Handbook of Comparative Law* 383 (Mathias Reimann & Reinhard Zimmermann eds. 2006).

Brian R. Day, *Collective Management of Music Copyright in the Digital Age: The Online Clearinghouse*, 18 Texas Intell. Prop. L. J. 195 (2010).

Miguel de la Mano et al., *Article 102* in *The EU Law of Competition* 329 (Jonathan Faull & Ali Nikpay eds., 3rd ed. 2014). [short form citation: de la Mano et al., *Article 102*]

Bennie L. De Whitt, *The American Society of Composers, Authors and Publishers 1914–1938* (1977).

Peter DiCola, *Copyright Equality: Free Speech, Efficiency, and Regulatory Parity in Distribution*, 93 B.U.L. Rev. 1837 (2013). [short form citation: DiCola, *Copyright Equality*]

Adolf Dietz, *Legal Regulation of Collective Management of Copyright (Collecting Societies Law) in Western and Eastern Europe*, 49 J. Copyright Soc'y 897 (2001–2002). [short form citation: Dietz, *Legal Regulation*]

Adolf Dietz, *Marketing and Enforcing Intellectual Property in Europe European Parliament Versus Commission: How to Deal with Collecting Societies?*, 35 IIC 809 (2004).

Adolf Dietz, *The European Commission's Proposal for a Directive on Collecting Societies and Cultural Diversity – a Missed Opportunity*, IJMBR, April 2014, at 7. [short form citation: Dietz, *A Missed Opportunity*]

Adolf Dietz, *Schutz der Kreativen (der Urheber und ausübenden Künstler) durch das Urheberrecht oder Die fünf Säulen des modernen kontinentaleuropäischen Urheberrechts*, 64 GRUR Int 309 (2015).

Josef Drexl, *Auf dem Weg zu einer neuen europäischen Marktordnung der kollektiven Wahrnehmung von Online Rechten der Musik? – Kritische Würdigung der Kommissionsempfehlung vom 18. Oktober 2005* in *Wahrnehmungsrecht in Polen, Deutschland und Europa* 193 (Karl Riesenhuber ed., 2006).

Josef Drexl, *Collecting Societies and Competition Law* (2007), http://www.ip.mpg.de/shared/data/pdf/drexl_-_crmos_and_competition.pdf (last visited April 16, 2015). [short form citation: Drexl, *Collecting Societies*]

Josef Drexl, *Collective Management of Copyrights and the EU Principle of Free Movement of Services after the OSA Judgment – In Favour of a More Balance Approach* in *Varieties of European Economic Law and Regulation* 459 (Kai Purnhagen & Peter Rott eds., 2014). [short form citation: Drexl, *Free Movement of Services*]

Josef Drexl et al., *Comments of the Max Planck Institute for Intellectual Property and Competition Law on the Proposal for A Directive of The European Parliament and of The Council on Collective Management Of Copyright and Related Rights and Multi-Territorial Licensing of Rights in Musical Works for Online Uses in The Internal Market Com (2012) 372* (Max Planck Institute for Intellectual Property and Competition Law Research Paper No. 13-04, 2013), *available at* https://papers.ssrn.com/sol3/papers.cfm?abstract_id=2208971 (last visited May 23, 2017). [short form citation: Drexl et al., *Comments of the MPI*]

Josef Drexl, Max Planck Institute for Intellectual Property and Competition Law, Munich, *Copyright, Competition and Development* (2013), *available at* http://www.ip.mpg.de/fileadmin/ipmpg/content/forschung_aktuell/02_copyright_competition/ report_copyright-competition-development_december-2013. pdf (last visited May 23, 2017). [short form citation: Drexl, *Competition and Development*]

Berend-Jan Drijber, *European competition law aspects of copyright collecting societies* in *Collective Administration of Copyrights in Europe* 67 (Herman Cohen Jehoram et al. eds., 1995). [short form citation: Drijber, *Competition law aspects*]

Daniel P. Ducore, *Settlement of Competition Conduct Violations At The United States Antitrust Agencies And At The European Commission – Some Observations* in *Annual Proceedings of the Fordham Corporate Law Institute* 227 (Barry E. Hawk ed., 2006).

Niamh Dunne, *Commitment Decisions in EU Competition Law*, 10 J. Comp. L. & Eco. 399 (2014). [short form citation: Dunne, *Commitment Decisions*]

Michael A. Einhorn, *Intellectual Property and Antitrust: Music Performing Rights in Broadcasting*, 24 Colum.-VLA J. L. & Arts 349 (2001). [short form citation: Einhorn, *Music Performing Rights*]

Michael A. Einhorn, *The ASCAP And BMI Consent Decrees: Is Partial Withdrawal Wise?*, 62 J. Copyright Soc'y 199 (2014). [short form citation: Einhorn, *Partial Withdrawal*]

Mathias Elspaß & Moira Kettner, *Article 81 EC* in *European Media Law* 123 (Oliver Castendyk et al. eds., 2008).

Volker Emmerich & Daniel Zimmer, *Artikel 101 Abs. 1 AEUV* in 1 *Wettbewerbsrecht* (Ulrich Immenga & Ernst-Joachim Mestmäcker eds., 5. ed 2012).

Michael Enzinger, *Art 49 AEUV* in *Kommentar zu EUV und AEUV* (Heinz Mayer & Karl Stöger eds., updated 01/2016 at rdb.at).

Richard A. Epstein, *Antitrust Consent Decrees in Theory and Practice* (2007).

Paul Fakler, *Music Copyright Royalty Rate-Setting Litigation: Practice Before the Copyright Royalty Board and How It Differs from ASCAP and BMI Rate Court Litigation*, The Licensing Journal June/July 2013. [short form citation: Fakler, *Rate-Setting Litigation*]

Johnathan Faull et al., *Article 101* in *The EU Law of Competition* 183 (Jonathan Faull & Ali Nikpay eds., 3rd ed. 2014).

Mihály Ficsor, *Collective Management of Copyright and Related Rights* (WIPO Pub. No. 855, 2002), *available at* ftp://ftp.wipo.int/pub/library/ebooks/wipo publications/wipo_pub_855e.pdf (last visited May 23, 2017). [short form citation: Ficsor, *Collective Management*]

Mihály Ficsor, *Collective Rights Management from the Viewpoint of International Treaties, with Special Attention to the EU 'Acquis'* in *Collective Management of Copyright and Related Rights* 31 (Daniel Gervais ed., 3rd ed. 2016). [short form citation: Ficsor, *International Treaties*]

Mihály Ficsor, *Collective Management and Multi-territorial Licensing: Key Issues of the Transposition of Directive 2014/26/EU* in *New Developments in EU and International Copyright Law* 211 (Irini A. Stamatoudi ed., 2016). [short form citation: Ficsor, *Key Issues*]

Harry First, *Online Music Joint Ventures: Taken for a Song* (NYU Law School, Public Law and Legal Theory Research Paper No. 78, 2004), *available at* https://papers.ssrn.com/sol3/papers.cfm?abstract_id=508685 (last visited May 23, 2017).

Walter Frenz, *Handbuch Europarecht* (2d ed. 2012).

Jay M. Fujitani, *Controlling the Market Power Of Performing Rights Societies: An Administrative Substitute for Antitrust Regulation*, 72 Cal. L. Rev. 103 (1984).

Jens Thomas Füller, *Art. 101 AEUV* in 3 *Kölner Kommentar zum Kartellrecht* (Jan Busche & Andreas Röhling eds., 2016). [short form citation: Füller, *Art. 101 AEUV*]

Jens Gaster, *Artikel 101 AEUV* in *Europäisches Wettbewerbsrecht* (Helmut Schröter et al. eds., 2nd ed. 2014). [short form citation: Gaster, *Artikel 101 AEUV*]

Andrew I. Gavil et al., *Antitrust Law in Perspective: Cases, Concepts and Problems in Competition Policy* (2nd ed. 2008). [short form citation: Gavil et al., *Antitrust Law*]

Christophe Geiger, *Legal or Illegal? That Is the Question! Private Copying and Downloading on the Internet*, 39 IIC 597 (2008).

Christophe Geiger & Franciska Schönherr, *Article 5: Exceptions and Limitations* in *EU copyright law* 434 (Irinia A. Stamatoudi & Paul Torremans eds., 2014). [short form citation: Geiger & Schönherr, *Exceptions and Limitations*]

Christophe Geiger et al., *Limitations and Exceptions as Key Elements of the Legal Framework for Copyright in the European Union – Opinion of the European Copyright Society on the Judgment of the CJEU in Case C-201/13 Deckmyn*, 46 IIC 93 (2015).

Thomas Gergen, *Die Verwertungsgesellschaft VG Wort – Genese und neue Herausforderungen*, 1 J. European History L. 14 (2010).

Stefan Gering, *Vereinbarungen betreffend gewerbliche Schutzrechte und F&E in Europäisches Kartellrecht* 234 (Thorsten Mäger ed., 2nd ed. 2011).

Tilo Gerlach, *Vor §§ 1 ff UrhWG* in *Praxiskommentar zum Urheberrecht: UrhR* (Artur-Axel Wandtke & Winfried Bullinger eds., 4th ed. 2014).

Daniel Gervais & Alana Maurushat, *Fragmented Copyright, Fragmented Management: Proposals to Defrag Copyright Management*, 2 Can. J. of L. & Tech. 15 (2003). [short form citation: Gervais & Maurushat, *Fragmented Copyright*]

Daniel Gervais, *Keynote: The Landscape of Collective Management Systems* 34 Colum. J. of L. & Arts 591 (2011). [short form citation: Gervais, *The Landscape*]

Daniel Gervais, *Collective Management of Copyright: Theory and Practice in the Digital Age* in *Collective Management of Copyright and Related Rights* 1 (Daniel Gervais ed., 3rd ed. 2016). [short form citation: Gervais, *Theory and Practice*]

Roya Ghafele & Benjamin Gibert, *Counting the Costs of Collective Rights Management of Music Copyright in Europe* (MPRA Paper No. 34646, 2011), *available at* https://mpra.ub.uni-muenchen.de/34646/1/MPRA_paper_34646.pdf (last visited May 23, 2017).

Rebecca Giblin & Jane C. Ginsburg, *We (Still) Need to Talk About Aereo: New Controversies and Unresolved Questions After the Supreme Court's Decision*, 38 Colum. J. K. & Arts 109 (2015).

Philippe Gilliéron, *Collecting Societies and the Digital Environment*, 37 IIC 939 (2006). [Gilliéron, *Digital Environment*]

Douglas H. Ginsburg & Joshua D. Wright, *Antitrust Settlements: The Culture of Consent* (George Mason University Law and Economics Research Paper Series 13–18, 2013), *available at* https://papers.ssrn.com/sol3/papers.cfm?abstract_id=2225894 (last visited May 23, 2017). [short form citation: Ginsburg & Wright, *Culture of Consent*]

Jane C. Ginsburg, *The Author's Place in the Future of Copyright*, 153 Proc. of the Am. Philos. Soc. 147 (2009). [short form citation: Ginsburg, *The Author's Place*]

H. Patrick Glenn, *The aims of comparative law* in *Elgar Encyclopedia of Comparative law* 65 (Jan M. Smits ed., 2nd ed. 2012).

Paul Goldstein, *Goldstein on Copyright* (3rd ed. 2014, updated 06/2016). [short form citation: Goldstein on Copyright]

Christoph B. Graber, *Collective Rights Management, Competition Policy and Cultural Diversity: EU Lawmaking at a Crossroads,* 4 W.I.P.O.J. 35 (2012). [short form citation: Graber, *Collective Rights Management*]

Christoph B. Graber, *Is there potential for collective rights management at the global level? Perspectives of a new global constitutionalism in the creative sector* in *The Evolution and Equilibrium of Copyright in the Digital Age* 241 (Susy Frankel & Daniel Gervais eds., 2014).

Lucie Guibault, *Collective Rights Management Directive* in *EU copyright law* 696 (Irinia A. Stamatoudi & Paul Torremans eds., 2014). [short form citation: Guibault, *Collective Management Directive*]

Lucie Guibault & Stef van Gompel, Collective Management in the European Union in *Collective Management of Copyright and Related Rights* 135 (Daniel Gervais ed., 2nd ed. 2010). [short form citation: Guibault & van Gompel, *Collective Management 2010*]

Lucie Guibault & Stef van Gompel, Collective Management in the European Union in in *Collective Management of Copyright and Related Rights* 139 (Daniel Gervais ed., 3rd ed. 2016). [short form citation: Guibault & van Gompel, *Collective Management*]

Peter Gyertyánfy, *Collective Management of Music Rights in Europe After the CISAC Decision*, 41 IIC 59 (2010). [short form citation: Gyertyánfy, *Collective Management*]

Christian Handig, *Das neue VerwertungsgesellschaftenG 2016 Eine kurze Übersicht über die wesentlichen Änderungen*, 65 ÖBl 164 (2016). [short form citation: Handig, *VerwertungsgesellschaftenG*]

Christian Handke & Ruth Towse, *Economics of Copyright Collecting Societies*, 38 Intern. Rev. of Int. Property & Competition L. 937 (2007).

Christian Handke, *Collective administration* in *Handbook on the economics of copyright* 179 (Richard Watt ed. 2014). [short form citation: Handke, *Collective Administration*]

Gerd Hansen & Albrecht Schmidt-Bischoffshausen, *Ökonomische Funktionen von Verwertungsgesellschaften – Kollektive Wahrnehmung im Lichte von Transaktionskosten- und Informationsökonomik*, 56 GRUR Int 461 (2007).

Robert Heine, *Wahrnehmung von Online-Musikrechten durch Verwertungsgesellschaften im Binnenmarkt* (2008).

Robert Heine & Sonja Eisenberg, *Verwertungsgesellschaften im Binnenmarkt – Die Kollektive Wahrnehmung von Urheberrechten nach der Dienstleistungsrichtlinie*, 58 GRUR Int. 277 (2009). [short form citation: Heine & Eisenberg, *Verwertungsgesellschaften*]

Hellenic Foundation for European and Foreign Policy, *Collecting Societies And Cultural Diversity In The Music Sector* (2009), *available at* http://www.europarl.europa.eu/RegData/etudes/etudes/join/2009/419110/IPOL-CULT_ET(2009)419110_EN.pdf (last visited May 23, 2017). [short form citation: Hellenic Foundation for European and Foreign Policy, *Cultural Diversity*]

C. Scott Hemphill, *Competition and the Collective Management of Copyright* 34 Colum. J. of L. & Arts 645 (2011).

Daniela Hengst, *Art. 101 AEUV* in 2 *Kartellrecht* (Hermann-Josef Bunte ed., 12th ed. 2014). [short form citation: Hengst, *Art. 101 AEUV*]

Johann Heyde, *Die grenzüberschreitende Lizenzierung von Online-Musikrechten in Europa* (2011). [short form citation: Heyde, *Lizenzierung*]

Reto M. Hilty & Sylvie Nérisson, *Collective Copyright Management and Digitization: The European Experience* (Max Planck Institute for Intellectual Property & Competition Law Research Paper No. 13-09, 2013), *available at* http://papers.ssrn.com/sol3/papers.cfm?abstract_id=2247870 (last visited May 23, 2017). [short form citation: Hilty & Nérisson, *Digitization*]

Reto M. Hilty & Sylvie Nérisson, *Collective copyright management* in *Handbook on the Digital Creative Economy* 222 (Ruth Towse & Christian Handke eds., 2013). [Hilty & Nérisson, *Collective Copyright Management*]

Tobias Holzmüller, *Umsetzung der EU-Richtlinie für Verwertungsgesellschaften in deutsches Recht*, 58 ZUM 468 (2014). [short form citation: Holzmüller, *Umsetzung*]

Herbert Hovenkamp et al., *IP and Antitrust An Analysis of Antitrust Principles Applied to Intellectual Property Law* (2nd ed. 2010, 2015 Supplement). [short form citation: Hovenkamp et al., *IP and Antitrust*]

Bernt Hugenholtz et al., *The Future of Levies in a Digital Environment* (2003), *available at* http://www.ivir.nl/publicaties/download/332 (last visited May 23, 2017). [short form citation: Hugenholtz et al., *The Future of Levies*]

P. Bernt Hugenholtz, *The Story of the Tape Recorder and the History of Copyright Levies* in *Copyright and the Challenge of the New* 179 (Brad Sherman & Leanne Wiseman eds., 2012).

Anita Huss-Eckerhult, *Collective Management Organisations (CMOs) at the Intersection Between EU Competition Law and the Freedom to Provide Services*, 7 Int. In-House Counsel J. 1 (2014). [short form citation: Huss-Eckerhult, *Collective Management Organisations*]

Stefan Kadelbach, *EUV Artikel 5* in *Europäisches Unionsrecht* (Hans von der Groeben et al. eds., 7th ed. 2015).

Stavroula Karapapa, *Private Copying* (2012). [short form citation: Karapapa, *Private Copying*]

Michael Karbaum et al., *Rechtsbeziehungen der GEMA zu ausländischen Verwertungsgesellschaften* in *Recht und Praxis der GEMA* 792 (Reinhold Kreile et al. eds, 2nd ed. 2008).

Ariel Katz, *The Potential Demise Of Another Natural Monopoly: Rethinking The Collective Administration Of Performing Rights*, 1 JCLE 541 (2005). [short form citation: Katz, *Potential Demise*]

Ariel Katz, *Commentary: Is Collective Administration of Copyrights Justified by the Economic Literature?* in *Competition Policy and Intellectual Property* 449 (Marcel Boyer et al. eds., 2009).

Ariel Katz, *Copyright Collectives: Good Solution, But For Which Problem?* (2009), *available at* https://papers.ssrn.com/sol3/papers.cfm?abstract_id=1416798 (last visited May 23, 2017).

KEA European Affairs, *The Collective Management of Rights in Europe: The Quest for Efficiency* (2006), *available at* http://www.europarl.europa.eu/meet

docs/2004_2009/documents/dv/study-collective-management-rights-/study-collective-management-rights-en.pdf (last visited May 23, 2017). [short form citation: KEA, *Collective Management*]

KEA European Affairs, *Music licensing and transaction costs in Europe* (2012), *available at* http://www.keanet.eu/docs/music%20licensing%20and%20transaction%20costs%20-%20full.pdf (last visited May 23, 2017). [short form citation: KEA, *Music Licensing*]

Christian Kersting & Daisy Karoline Walzel, *Art. 101 AEUV* in 3 *Kölner Kommentar zum Kartellrecht* (Jan Busche & Andreas Röhling eds., 2016).

Bruce H. Kobayashi, *Opening Pandoras Black Box: A Coasian 1937 View of Performance Rights Organizations in 2014*, 22 Geo. Mason L. Rev. 925 (2014).

Al Kohn & Bob Kohn, *Kohn On Music Licensing* (4th ed. 2010). [short form citation: Kohn & Kohn, *Music Licensing*].

Bernard Korman, *U.S. Position On Collective Administration Of Copyright And Antitrust-Law*, 43 J. Copyright Soc'y 158 (1995–1996). [short form citation: Korman, *U.S. Position*]

Tarja Koskinen-Olsson & Vigdís Sigurdardóttir, *Collective Management in the Nordic Countries* in *Collective Management of Copyright and Related Rights* 243 (Daniel Gervais ed., 3rd ed. 2016).

Reinhold Kreile, *Die Zusammenarbeit der Verwertungsgesellschaften* in *Recht und Praxis der GEMA* 783 (Reinhold Kreile et al. eds., 2nd ed. 2008).

Martin Kretschmer, *Intellectual Property in Music: A Historical Analysis of Rhetorical and Institutional Practices,* 6 Studies in Cults., Orgs. and Socs. 197 (2000).

Martin Kretschmer, *The Failure of Property Rules in Collective Administration: Rethinking Copyright Societies as Regulatory Instruments*, 24 E. I. P. R. 126 (2002). [short form citation: Kretschmer, *The Failure of Property Rules*]

Judica Krikke, *Directive 2006/115/EC of the European Parliament and of the Council* in *Concise European Copyright Law* 275 (Thomas Dreier & P. Bernt Hugenholtz eds., 2nd ed. 2016).

Guido Kucsko, *Einleitung* in *urheber.recht* (Guido Kucsko ed., 2008).

Krzysztof Kuik & Anthony Dawes, *Media* in *The EU Law of Competition* 1709 (Jonathan Faull & Ali Nikpay eds., 3rd ed. 2014). [short form citation: Kuik & Dawes, *Media*]

Mary La France, *From Whether to How: The Challenge of Implementing a Full Public Performance Right in Sound Recordings*, 2 Harv. J. Sports & Entertainment L. 221 (2011).

John Temple Lang, *Media, Multimedia and European Community Antitrust Law*, *available at* http://ec.europa.eu/competition/speeches/text/sp1997_070_en.pdf (last visited April 19, 2017). [short form citation: Lang, *Antitrust Law*]

Matthias Leistner, *Europe's Copyright Decade: Recent Case Law Of The European Court Of Justice And Policy Perspectives*, 51 Common Market L. Rev. 559 (2014). [short form citation: Leistner, *Copyright Decade*]

Mark A. Lemley & Philip J. Weiser, *Should Property or Liability rules Govern Information?*, 85 Texas L. Rev. 783 (2007).

Mark A. Lemley, *Contracting Around Liability Rules*, 100 Cal. L. Rev. 463 (2012). [short form citation: Lemley, *Contracting Around Liability Rules*]

Peter Lerche, *Verwertungsgesellschaften als Unternehmen "sui generis"* in *Recht und Praxis der GEMA* 25 (Reinhold Kreile et al. eds., 2nd ed. 2008).

Peter Lewisch, *Art 102 AEUV* in *Kommentar zu EUV und AEUV* (Heinz Mayer & Karl Stöger eds., updated 08/2013 at rdb.at). [short form citation: Lewisch, *Art 102 AEUV*]

Moritz Lichtenegger, *Verwertungsgesellschaften, Kartellverbot und Neue Medien* (2014). [short form citation: Lichtenegger, *Vewertungsgesellschaften*]

S.J. Liebowitz, *Copying and Indirect Appropriability: Photocopying of Journals*, 93 J. of Political Economy 945 (1985).

Jessica Litman, *Real Copyright Reform*, 96 Iowa L. Rev. 1 (2010).

Wenqi Liu, *Models for Collective Management of Copyright from an International Perspective: Potential Changes for Enhancing Performance*, 18 J. Intellec. Prop. Rights 46 (2012).

Ulrich Loewenheim, *Einleitung* in *Urheberrecht* (Ulrich Loewenheim et al. eds., 5th ed. 2017).

Lydia Pallas Loren, *The Dual Narratives In The Landscape Of Music Copyright*, 52 Hous. L. Rev. 537 (2014). [Loren, *Dual Narratives*]

Glynn Lunney, *Copyright Collectives and Collecting Societies: The United States Experience* in *Collective Management of Copyright and Related Rights* 319 (Daniel Gervais ed., 3rd ed. 2016). [short form citation: Lunney, *The United States Experience*]

Thorsten Mäger, *Einführung und Grundlagen* in *Europäisches Kartellrecht* 39 (Thorsten Mäger ed., 2nd ed. 2011).

Farell Malone & J. Gregory Sidak, *Should Antitrust Consent Decrees Regulate Post-Merger Pricing*, 3 Comp. L. & Econ. 471 (2007).

Giovanna Massarotto, *The Deterrent and Enunciating Effects Of Consent Decrees*, 11 Comp. L. & Econ. 493 (2015). [short form citation: Massarotto, *Deterrent and Enunciating Effects*]

Giuseppe Mazziotti, *EU Digital Copyright Law and the End-User* (2008).

Giuseppe Mazziotti, *New Licensing Models for Online Music Services in the European Union: From Collective to Customized Management*, 34 Colum. J. of Law & the Arts 757 (2011). [short form citation: Mazziotti, *New Licensing Models*]

Gary McIntyre, *The Performance Right Act: Radio Broadcasting Faces Major Challenge in Long Battle Against Music Licensing*, 17 J. Radio & Audio Media 135 (2010). [short form citation: McIntyre, *Performance Right Act*]

Ferdinand Melchiar, *§ 45* in *Handbuch des Urheberrechts* (Ulrich Loewenheim ed., 2nd ed. 2010). [short form citation: Melchiar, *§ 45*]

Dinusha Mendis, *Directive 2014/26/EU on Collective Management of Copyright and Related Rights and Multi-Territorial Licensing of Rights in Musical Works for Online Use in the Internal Market* in *EU Regulation of E-Commerce* 290 (Arno R. Lodder & Andrew D. Murray eds., 2017). [short form citation: Mendis, *Directive 2014/26/EU*]

Peter S. Menell, *In Search of Copyright's Lost Ark: Interpreting The Right to Distribute in The Internet Age*, 59 J. Cop. Soc. USA 1 (2011).

Robert P. Merges, *Contracting into Liability Rules: Intellectual Property Rights and Collective Rights Organizations*, 84 Cal. L. Rev. 1293 (1996). [short form citation: Merges, *Contracting into Liability Rules*]

Robert P. Merges, *The Continuing Vitality of Music Performance Rights Organizations* (UC Berkeley Public Law Research Paper No. 1266870, 2008), *avail-*

able at https://papers.ssrn.com/sol3/papers.cfm?abstract_id=1266870 (last visited May 23, 2017). [Merges, *Continuing Vitality*]
Robert P. Merges et al., *Intellectual Property in The New Technological Age* (5th ed. 2010). [short form citation: Merges, *Intellectual Property*].
Ernst-Joachim Mestmäcker, *Sind urheberrechtliche Verwertungsgesellschaften Kartelle?* in *Ernst-Joachim Mestmäcker – Beiträge zum Urheberrecht* 1 (Karl Riesenhuber ed., 2006). [short form citation: Mestmäcker, *Verwertungsgesellschaften*]
Ernst-Joachim Mestmäcker, *Performing Rights Organizations in the Common Market: Comparative Observations* in *Ernst-Joachim Mestmäcker – Beiträge zum Urheberrecht* 227 (Karl Riesenhuber ed., 2006). [short form citation: Mestmäcker, *Comparative Observations*]
Ernst Joachim Mestmäcker, *Collecting Societies* in *European Competition Law Annual 2005: The Interaction between Competition Law and Intellectual Property Law* 343 (Claus Dieter Ehlermann & Isabela Atanasiu eds., 2007). [short form citation: Mestmäcker, *Collecting Societies*]
Ernst-Joachim Mestmäcker & Heike Schweitzer, *Europäisches Wettbewerbsrecht* (2014). [short form citation: Mestmäcker & Schweitzer, *Wettbewerbsrecht*]
Axel Metzger & Tobias Heinemann, *The Right of the Author to Grant Licenses for Non-Commerical Use*, 6 JIPITEC 11 (2015). [short form citation: Metzger & Heinemann, *Non-Commerical Use*]
P. Sean Morris, *The Reform of Article 82 and the Operation of Competition Principles upon the Normal Trading Functions of Copyright Collecting Societies*, 4 J. IP L. & Practice 566 (2009). [short form citation: Morris, *Trading Functions*]
Massimo Motta & Alexandre de Streel, *Excessive Pricing in Competition Law: Never Say Never?* in *The Pros and Cons of High Prices* 14 (Konkurrensverket, Swedish Competition Authority ed., 2007), *available at* http://www.kkv.se/globalassets/english/research/the-pros-and-cons-of-high-prices-14mb.pdf (last visited May 23, 2017).
Sylvie Nérisson, *The Rental and Lending Rights Directive* in *EU copyright law* 149 (Irinia A. Stamatoudi & Paul Torremans, eds., 2014). [short form citation: Nérisson, *Rental and Lending Rights Directive*]
Matthias Niedobitek, *Art. 167 AEUV* in *EUV/AEUV* (Rudolf Streinz ed., 2nd ed. 2012).
2 Melville B. Nimmer & David Nimmer, *Nimmer on Copyright* (Matthew Bender, Rev. ed. 2015). [short form citation: 2 Nimmer on Copyright]
Ann O'Brien, *Antitrust Division U.S. Department of Justice, Cartel Settlements in the U.S. and EU: Similarities, Differences & Remaining Questions* (2008), *available at* https://www.justice.gov/atr/file/519681/download (last visited May 23, 2017).
Maria A. Pallante, *Comments on ASCAP's Birthday: ASCAP at 100*, 61 J. Copyright Soc'y 545 (2014). [short form citation: Pallante, *Comments*]
Ana María Pérez Gómez Tétrel, *Efficient allocation of risk as an economic function of Collecting Societies* (2007), *available at* http://www.serci.org/2007/perezgomez.pdf (last visited May 23, 2017).
Alexander Peukert, *„Copydan/Nokia" und die Zukunft des gesetzlichen Vergütungsanspruchs für die digitale Privatkopie*, 117 GRUR 452 (2015).
Karl-Nikolaus Pfeifer, *Individualität im Zivilrecht* (2001).

Karl-Nikolaus Pfeifer, *Umsetzung der EU-Richtlinie für Verwertungsgesellschaften in deutsches Recht*, 58 ZUM 453 (2014). [short form citation: Pfeifer, *Umsetzung*]

Gerhard Pfennig, *Umsetzung der EU-Richtlinie für Verwertungsgesellschaften in deutsches Recht,* 58 ZUM 484 (2014).

Nathalie Piaskowski, *Collective Management in France* in *Collective Management of Copyright and Related Rights* 169 (Daniel Gervais ed., 2nd ed. 2010). [short form citation: Piaskowski, *Collective Management in France*]

Ivan L. Pitt, *Direct Licensing and the Music Industry* (2015). [short form citation: Pitt, *Direct Licensing*]

Ruprecht Podszun, *Verwertungsgesellschaften vor der Neuordnung: Der Vorschlag der Kommission zu einer Richtlinie über die kollektive Wahrnehmung von Urheberrechten und verwandten Schutzrechten*, 2013 GPR 97. [short form citation: Podszun, *Neuordnung*]

Joseph Pomianowski, *Toward An Efficient Licensing And Rate-Setting Regime: Reconstructing § 114(i) of the Copyright Act*, 125 Yale L. J. 1531 (2015–2016). [short form citation: Pomianowski, *Rate-Setting Regime*]

Joost Poort, *Copyright Levies* in *Handbook on the digital creative economy* 235 (Christian Handke & Ruth Towse eds., 2013).

Joost Poort & João Pedro Quintais, *The Levy Runs Dry: A Legal and Economic Analysis of EU Private Copying Levies*, 3 JIPITEC 205 (2013). [short form citation: Poort & Quintais, *Levy Runs Dry*]

Adriane Porcin, *The Quest for Pan-European Copyright Licensing Solutions: A Series of Unfortunate Events*, 2009 Concurrences 57. [short form citation: Porcin, *The Quest*]

Adriane Porcin, *Of Guilds and Men: Copyright Workarounds in the Cinematographic Industry*, 35 Hastings Comm. & Ent. L.J. 1 (2012).

Hamish Porter, *European Union Competition Policy: Should the Role of Collecting Societies Be Legitimsed*, 12 E.I.P.R. 672 (1996). [short form citation: Porter, *Role of Collecting Societies*]

João Pedro Quintais, *On Peers and Copyright: Why the EU Should Consider Collective Management of P2P* (2012). [short form citation: Quintais, *On Peers and Copyright*]

João Pedro Quintais, *Proposal for a Directive on Collective Rights Management and (Some) Multi-Territorial Licensing* (Amsterdam Law School Legal Studies Research Paper No. 2013-69, 2013), *available at* http://papers.ssrn.com/sol3/papers.cfm?abstract_id=2351186 (last visited May 23, 2017). [short form citation: Quintais, *Proposal for a Directive*]

Ana Ramalho, *Conceptualising the European Union's Competence in Copyright – What Can the EU Do?*, 45 IIC 178 (2014). [short form citation: Ramalho, *Competence in Copyright*]

Jörg Reinbothe, *Die EG-Richtlinie zum Urheberrecht in der Informationsgesellschaft*, 50 GRUR Int 733 (2001). [short form citation: Reinbothe, *EG-Richtlinie*]

Jörg Reinbothe, *Collective Rights Management in Germany* in *Collective Management of Copyright and Related Rights* 205 (Daniel Gervais ed., 3rd ed. 2016). [short form citation: Reinbothe, *Management in Germany*]

Jörg Reinbothe, *Vor §§ 1ff WahrnG* in *Urheberrecht* (Ulrich Loewenheim et al. eds., 5th ed. 2017). [short form citation: Reinbothe, *Vor §§ 1ff WahrnG*]

Maria Riccio & Giorgio Giannone Codiglione, *Copyright Collecting Societies, Monopolistic Positions and Competition in the EU Single Market*, 7 Masaryk U. J. L. & Tech. 287 (2013). [short form citation: Riccio & Codiglione, *Monopolistic Positions*]

Karl Riesenhuber, *Wachsende Bedeutung zentralisierter Rechtewahrnehmung und die Rolle der Verwertungsgesellschaften*, 60 ZUM 216 (2016). [short form citation: Riesenhuber, *Rechtewahrnehmung*]

Karl Riesenhuber & Alexander v. Vogel, *Europäisches Wahrnehmungsrecht Zur Mitteilung der Kommission über die Wahrnehmung von Urheberrechten und verwandten Schutzrechten im Binnenmarkt*, 15 EuZW 519 (2004).

Thomas Riis, *Collecting Societies, Competition and the Services Directive*, 6 J. Intellectual Property L. & Pract. 482 (2011). [short form citation: Riis, *Collecting Societies*]

Mark Rose, *Authors and Owners: The Invention of Copyright* (1993).

Matthias Ruffert, *Art. 1 AEUV* in *EUV/AEUV* (Christian Calliess & Matthias Ruffert eds., 5th ed. 2016).

Matthias Ruffert, *Art. 288 AEUV* in *EUV/AEUV* (Christian Calliess & Matthias Ruffert eds., 5th ed. 2016).

Anke Schierholz, *Collective Rights Management in Europe – Practice and Legal Framework* in *European Copyright Law* 1145 (Michel M. Walter & Silke von Lewinski eds., 2010). [short form citation: Schierholz, *Collective Rights Management*]

Manuela Maria Schmidt, *Die kollektive Verwertung der Online-Musikrechte im Europäischen Binnenmarkt*, 49 ZUM 783 (2005).

Manuela Maria Schmidt et al., *Geschichte der musikalischen Verwertungsgesellschaften* in *Recht und Praxis der GEMA* 5 (Reinhold Kreile et al. eds., 2nd ed. 2008). [short form citation: Schmidt et al., *Verwertungsgesellschaften*]

Werner Schroeder, *Art. 288 AEUV* in *EUV/AEUV* (Rudolf Streinz ed., 2nd ed. 2012).

Helmut Schröter, *Vorbemerkungen zu den Artikeln 101 bis 105 AEUV* in *Europäisches Wettbewerbsrecht* (Helmut Schröter et al. eds., 2nd ed. 2014) [short form citation: Schröter, *Vorbemerkungen*]

Gernot Schulze, *§ 1 UrhG* in *Urheberrechtsgesetz: UrhG* (Thomas Dreier & Gernot Schulze, 5th ed. 2015). [short form citation: Schulze, *§ 1 UrhG*]

Christoph Schütt, *Fortschritt bei der europaweiten Lizenzierung von Online-Musikrechten*, MMR May 2008, at XVIII.

Jürgen Schwarze, *Die Verwaltung von Urheberrechten im Lichte des europäischen Wettbewerbsrechts* in *Recht und Praxis der GEMA* 47 (Reinhold Kreile et al. eds., 2nd ed. 2008)

Heike Schweitzer, *Commitment Decisions in the EU and in the Member States: Functions and risks of a new instrument of competition law enforcement within a federal enforcement regime* (2012), *available at* https://papers.ssrn.com/sol3/papers.cfm?abstract_id=2101630 (last visited May 23, 2017).

Sebastian Felix Schwemer, *The licensing of online music streaming services in Europe* in *Handbook on the Economics of Copyright* 141 (Richard Watt ed. 2014). [short form citation: Schwemer, *Online Music*]

Fedor Seifert et al., *Die Lizensierung* in *Recht und Praxis der GEMA* 749 (Reinhold Kreile et al. eds., 2nd ed. 2008).

Dorothea Senn, *Competition Law Aspects of Digital and Collective Rights Management* in *Digital Rights Management: The End of Collecting Societies?* (Christoph Beat Graber et al. eds., 2005). [short form citation: Senn, *Competition Law Aspects*]

Molly Shaffer Van Houweling, *Author Autonomy and Atomism in Copyright Law*, 96 Va. L. Rev. 549 (2010). [short form citation: Van Houweling, *Author Autonomy*]

Klodi Shanto & Blerton Sinani, *Methods and Functions of Comparative Law*, 2 Acta Universitatis Danubius. Juridica 25 (2013).

Jorg Sladiĉ, *Introduction to Copyright and Collective Management in Competition Law*, 5 LeXonomica 37 (2013). [short form citation: Sladiĉ, *Collective Management*]

Arthur Snow & Richard Watt, *Risk Sharing and the Distribution of Copyright Collective Income, available at* http://serci.org/2003/snowwatt.pdf (last visited April 14, 2017).

Nuno Sousa e Silva, *The proposed Directive on multi-territorial licensing for online music – Is competition a good idea?* (2013), *available at* http://papers.ssrn.com/sol3/papers.cfm?abstract_id=2375886 (last visited May 23, 2017). [short form citation: Sousa e Silva, *The Proposed Directive*]

Robert Staats, *Umsetzung der EU-Richtlinie für Verwertungsgesellschaften in deutsches Recht*, 58 ZUM 470 (2014). [short form citation. Staats, *Umsetzung*]

Irini A. Stamatoudi, *The European Court's Love-Hate Relationship with Collecting Societies*, 6 E.I.P.R. 289 (1997). [short form citation: Stamatoudi, *Love-Hate Relationship*]

Anna-Zoe Steiner, *Grenzüberschreitende Lizenzierung von Musikwerken in Europa und die kartellrechtliche Beurteilung des Systems der Gegenseitigkeitsverträge*, 62 ÖBl 202 (2013).

John Street et al., *Regulating for creativity and cultural diversity: the case of collective management organisations and the music industry*, Int. J. of Cultural Policy (2016).

Jules Stuyck, *Do We Need 'Consumer Protection' for Small Businesses at EU Level?* in *Varieties of European Economic Law and Regulation* 359 (Kai Purnhagen & Peter Rott eds., 2014).

Paul L.C. Torremans & Irini A. Stamatoudi, *Collecting Societies: sorry, the Community is no longer interested!* 22 E.L. Rev. 352 (1997).

Ruth Towse & Christian Handke, *Regulating Copyright Collecting Societies: Current Policy in Europe* (2007), http://www.serci.org/2007/towsehandke.pdf (last visited May 23, 2017). [short form citation: Towse & Handke, *Current Policy*]

Ruth Towse et al., *The Economics Of Copyright Law: A Stocktake of the Literature*, 5 Review of Economic Research on Copyright Issues 1 (2008).

Ruth Towse, *Economics of Copyright Collecting Societies and Digital Rights: Is There a Case for a Centralised Digital Copyright Exchange?*, 9 Rev. of Econ. Research on Copyright Issues 3 (2012).

Georg Tuder, *§ 8* in *VZKG* (Arthur Weilinger ed., 2016).

Pavel Tuma, *Pitfalls and Challenges of the EC Directive of Collective Management of Copyright and Related Rights*, 2006 E.I.P.R. 220. [short form citation: Tuma, *Pitfalls and Challenges*]

Brontë Lawson Turk, *"It's Been a Hard Day's Night" for Songwriters: Why the ASCAP and BMI Consent Decrees Must Undergo Reform*, 26 Fordham Intell.

Prop. Media & Ent. L. J. 493 (2016). [short form citation: Turk, *Hard Day's Night*]

Jan Nicolaus Ullrich, *Clash of Copyrights – Optionale Schranke und zwingender finanzieller Ausgleich im Fall der Privatkopie nach Art. 5 Abs. 2 lit. b) Richtlinie 2001/29/EG und Dreistufentest*, 58 GRUR Int 283 (2009).

Mireille van Eechoud et al., *Harmonizing European Copyright Law: The Challenges of Better Lawmaking* (2009).

Stef van Gompel, *Directive 2014/26/EU* in *Concise European Copyright Law* 541 (Thomas Dreier & P. Bernt Hugenholtz eds., 2nd ed., 2016). [short form citation: van Gompel, *Directive*]

Peter Vcelouch, *Art 288 AEUV* in *Kommentar zu EUV und AEUV* (Heinz Mayer & Karl Stöger eds., updated 12/2010 at rdb.at).

Thomas Vinje & Ossi Niiranen, *The Application of Competition Law to Collecting Societies in a Borderless Digital Environment in Competition Law Annual 2005: The Interaction between Competition Law and Intellectual Property Law* 399 (Claus-Dieter Ehlermann & Isabela Atanasiu eds. 2007). [short form citation: Vinje & Niiranen, *Digital Environment*]

António Vitorino, *Recommendations Resulting from The Mediation On Private Copying and Reprography Levies* (2013), http://ec.europa.eu/internal_market/copyright/docs/levy_reform/130131_levies-vitorino-recommendations_en.pdf (last visited May 23, 2017). [short form citation: Vitorino, *Recommendations*]

Martin Vogel, *Wahrnehmungsrecht und Verwertungsgesellschaften in der Bundesrepublik Deutschland – Eine Bestandsaufnahme im Hinblick auf die Harmonisierung des Urheberrechts in der Europäischen Gemeinschaft,* 95 GRUR 512 (1993).

Silke von Lewinski, *Introduction* in *European Copyright Law* 3 (Michel M. Walter & Silke von Lewinski eds., 2010).

Silke von Lewinski, *Rental and Lending Rights Directive* in *European Copyright Law* 249 (Michel M. Walter & Silke von Lewinski eds., 2010). [short form citation: von Lewinski, *Rental and Lending Rights Directive*]

Silke von Lewinski & Michel M. Walter, *Information Society Directive* in *European Copyright Law* 921 (Michel M Walter & Silke von Lewinski eds., 2010). [short form citation: von Lewinski & Walter, *Information Society Directive*]

Silke von Lewinski & Michel M. Walter, *Status of Harmonization and Outlook* in *European Copyright Law* 1463 (Michel M Walter & Silke von Lewinski eds., 2010). [short form citation: von Lewinski & Walter, *Status of Harmonization*]

Roger Wallis et al., *Contested Collective Administration of Intellectual Property Rights in Music – The Challenge to the Principles of Reciprocity and Solidarity*, 14 European J. of Communication 5 (1999). [short form citation: Wallis et al., *Contested Collective Administration*]

Michel M. Walter, *Österreichisches Urheberrecht* (2008).

Michel Walter, *Urheber- und Verwertungsgesellschaftenrecht '15* (2015). [short form citation: Walter, *Verwertungsgesellschaftenrecht*]

F. Joseph Warin et al., *To Plead or Not to Plead? Reviewing a Decade of Criminal Antitrust Trials*, July 2006 theantitrustsource, *available at* http://www.americanbar.org/content/dam/aba/publishing/antitrust_source/Jul06_FullSource7_21.authcheckdam.pdf (last visited May 23, 2017).

Richard Watt, *Copyright collectives: some basic economic theory* in *Handbook on the economics of copyright* 167–178 (Richard Watt ed. 2014).

Wolfgang Weiß, *Art. 102 AEUV* in *EUV/AEUV* (Christian Calliess & Matthias Ruffert eds., 5th ed. 2016).

Richard Whish, *Competition Law* (7th ed. 2012).

Christian Wichard, *Art. 118 AEUV* in *EUV/AEUV* (Christian Calliess & Matthias Ruffert eds., 5th ed. 2016).

Andreas Wiebe et al., *Rights Clearance for Online Music* (2014). [short form citation: Wiebe et al., *Rights Clearance*]

Robert J. Williams, *Public Performance Royalty-Rate Disparity: Should Congress Pamper Pandora's Pandering?*, 48 New Eng. L. Rev. 371 (2014). [short form citation: Williams, *Royalty-Rate Disparity*]

Wouter P.J. Wils, *Settlements of EU Antitrust Investigations: Commitment Decisions under Article 9 of Regulation No 1/2003* 4-6, 23 (2006), *available at* https://papers.ssrn.com/sol3/Papers.cfm?abstract_id=900801 (last visited May 23, 2017).

Wouter P.J. Wils, *The Use of Settlements in Public Antitrust Enforcement: Objectives and Principles* (2008), *available at* https://papers.ssrn.com/sol3/papers.cfm?abstract_id=1135627 (last visited May 23, 2017).

Hanno Wollmann, *Art 101 AEUV* in *Kommentar zu EUV und AEUV* (Heinz Mayer & Karl Stöger eds., updated 12/2011 at rdb.at). [short form citation: Wollmann, *Art 101 AEUV*]

David Wood, *Collective Management and EU Competition Law* (2001), *available at* http://ec.europa.eu/competition/speeches/text/sp2001_025_en.pdf (last visited May 23, 2017). [short form citation: Wood, *Collective Management*]

Tanya Woods, *Multi-territorial Licensing and the Evolving Role of Collective Management Organizations* in *Collective Management of Copyright and Related Rights* 105 (Daniel Gervais ed., 2nd ed. 2010).

World Intellectual Property Organization & International Federation of Reproduction Rights Organisations, *Collective Management in Reprography* 5 (WIPO Pub. No. 924, 2005), *available at* http://www.wipo.int/edocs/pubdocs/en/copyright/924/wipo_pub_924.pdf (last visited May 23, 2017).

Christoph Wünschmann, *Die kollektive Verwertung von Urheber- und Leistungsschutzrechten nach europäischem Wettbewerbsrecht* (2000). [short form citation: Wünschmann, *Kollektive Verwertung*]

Christopher S. Yoo, Copyright and Public Good Economics: A Misunderstood Relation, 155 U. Pa. L. Rev. 635 (2007).

Zijian Zhang, *Rationale of Collective Management Organizations: An Economic Perspective*, 10 Masaryk U. J. L. & Tech. 73 (2016).

2. European Commission Official Documents

Commission of the European Communities, *Green Paper of 27 July 1995 on Copyright and Related Rights in the Information Society* 26–28 COM(1995) 382 final, *available at* http://eur-lex.europa.eu/legal-content/EN/TXT/PDF/?uri=CELEX:51995DC0382&from=EN (last visited May 23, 2017).

Commission of the European Communities, *Commission Notice on the definition of relevant market for the purposes of Community competition law*, 1997 O.J. (C372) 5–13. [short form citation: European Commission Guidelines on the Definition of Relevant Market]

Commission of the European Communities, *Communication from the Commission to the Council, the European Parliament and the European Economic and Social Committee The Management of Copyright and Related Rights in the Internal Market* COM(2004) 261 final, *available at* http://eur-lex.europa.eu/legal-content/EN/TXT/PDF/?uri=CELEX:52004DC0261&from=ENpoint (last visited May 23, 2017). [short form citation: Communication 2004]

Commission of the European Communities, *Communication from the Commission — Notice — Guidelines on the application of Article 81(3) of the Treaty*, 2004 O.J. (C101) 97–118.

Commission Recommendation of 18 May 2005 on collective cross border management of copyright and related rights for legitimate online music services, 2005 O.J. (L276) 54–57. [short form citation: Recommendation 2005]

Commission of the European Communities, *Commission Staff Working Document Study on a Community Initiative on the Cross-border Collective Management of Copyright* (2005), *available at* http://ec.europa.eu/internal_market/copyright/docs/management/study-collectivemgmt_en.pdf (last visited May 23, 2017). [short form citation: Study 2005]

Commission of the European Communities, *Staff Working Document Impact Assessment Reforming Cross-Border Collective Management of Copyright and Related Rights for Legitimate Online Music Services* SEC(2005) 1254, *available at* http://ec.europa.eu/internal_market/copyright/docs/management/sec_2005_1254_en.pdf (last visited May 23, 2017). [short form citation: Impact Assessment 2005]

Commission of the European Communities, *Handbook on Implementation of the Services Directive* 42 (2007), *available at* http://bookshop.europa.eu/en/handbook-on-implementation-of-the-services-directive-pbKM7807096/ (last visited May 23, 2017).

Commission of the European Communities, *Communication from the Commission to the European Parliament, the Council, the European Economic and Social Committee and the Committee of the Regions on Creative Content Online in the Single Market* COM(2007) 836 final (2008), *available at* europa.eu/LexUriServ/LexUriServ.do?uri=COM:2007:0836:FIN:EN:PDF (last visited May 23, 2017).

Commission of the European Communities, *Background Document "Fair Compensation for Acts of Private Copying"* (2008), http://ec.europa.eu/internal_ market/copyright/docs/levy_reform/background_en.pdf (last visited May 23, 2017).

European Commission, *Commission Notice Guidelines on Vertical Restraints*, 2010 O.J. (C130) 1–46. [short form Citation: European Commission Guidelines on Vertical Restraints]

European Commission, *Communication from the Commission – Guidelines on the applicability of Article 101 of the Treaty on the Functioning of the European Union to horizontal co-operation agreements,* 2011 O.J. (C11) 1–72. [short form citation: European Commission Guidelines on Horizontal Co-Operation]

European Commission, *Communication from the Commission to the Parliament, the Council, the European Economic and Social Committee and the Committee of the Regions A Single Market for Intellectual Property Rights Boosting Creativity and Innovation to Provide Economic Growth, High Quality Jobs and First Class Products and Services in Europe* (2011), *available at* http://ec.

europa.eu/internal_market/copyright/docs/ipr_strategy/COM_2011_287_en.pdf (last visited May 23, 2017).

European Commission, *Proposal for a Directive of The European Parliament and of The Council on collective management of copyright and related rights and multi-territorial licensing of rights in musical works for online uses in the internal market* (COM(2012) 372 final), *available at* http://ec.europa.eu/internal_market/copyright/docs/management/com-2012-3722_en.pdf (last visited May 23, 2017). [short form citation: Proposal 2012].

European Commission, *Commission Staff Working Document Impact Assessment Accompanying The Document Proposal for a Directive of The European Parliament and of The Council on Collective Management of Copyright and Related Rights and Multi-Territorial Licensing of Rights in Musical Works for Online Uses in the Internal Market* (2012), *available at* http://eur-lex.europa.eu/legal-content/EN/TXT/?uri=CELEX:52012SC0204 (last visited May 23, 2017). [short form citation: Impact Assessment 2012]

European Commission, Communication from the Commission, *Guidelines on the application of Article 101 of the Treaty on the Functioning of the European Union to technology transfer agreements*, 2014 O.J. (C89) 3–50. [short form citation: European Commission Guidelines on TT-Agreements]

3. European Parliament Official Documents

Raina A. Mercedes Echerer, Committee on Legal Affairs and the Internal Market, European Parliament, *Report on a Community Framework for Collecting Societies for Authors Rights* (2002/2274(INI)) (2003), *available at* http://www.europarl.europa.eu/sides/getDoc.do?pubRef=-//EP//NONSGML+REPORT+A5-2003-0478+0+DOC+PDF+V0//EN (last visited May 23, 2017). [short form citation: Echerer, *Report*]

European Parliament resolution of 13 March 2007 on the Commission Recommendation of 18 October 2005 on collective cross-border management of copyright and related rights for legitimate online music services (2005/737/EC), doc. no. P6_TA(2007)0064, *available at* http://www.europarl.europa.eu/sides/getDoc.do?pubRef=-//EP//TEXT+TA+P6-TA-2007-0064+0+DOC+XML+V0//EN (last visited May 23, 2017). [short form citation: Resolution 2007]

European Parliament resolution of 25 September 2008 on collective cross-border management of copyright and related rights for legitimate online music services, doc. no. P6_TA(2008)0462, *available at* http://www.europarl.europa.eu/sides/getDoc.do?pubRef=-//EP//TEXT+TA+P6-TA-2008-0462+0+DOC+XML+V0//EN (last visited May 23, 2017). [short form citation: Resolution 2008]

European Parliament, *Sources and Scope of European Union Law* (2017), http://www.europarl.europa.eu/ftu/pdf/en/FTU_1.2.1.pdf (last visited May 23, 2017).

Marielle Gallo, Committee on Legal Affairs, European Parliament, *Report on the Proposal for a Directive of the European Parliament and of the Council on Collective Management of Copyright and Related Rights and Multi-Territorial Licensing of Rights in Musical Works for Online Uses in the Internal Market* Proposed Amendment, 2012/0180(COD) (2013), *available at* http://www.

europarl.europa.eu/sides/getDoc.do?pubRef=-//EP//TEXT+REPORT+A7-2013-0281+0+DOC+XML+V0//EN (last visited May 23, 2017). [short form citation: Gallo, *Report*]

Minutes of the Sitting of Thursday 23 October 1997, 1997 O.J. (C339) 86–404.

4. United States Copyright Royalty Board Official Documents

United States Copyright Royalty Board, Library of Congress, *In the Matter Mechanical and Digital Phonorecord Delivery Rate Determination Proceeding: Final Determination of Rates and Terms*, Docket No. 2006-3.

5. United States Copyright Office Official Documents

United States Copyright Office, *Views of the United States Copyright Office Concerning PRO Licensing of Jointly Owned Works* (2016), *available at* https://www.copyright.gov/policy/pro-licensing.pdf (last visited May 23, 2017). [short form citation: U.S. Copyright Office, *Jointly Owned Works*]

United States Copyright Office, *The Making Available Right In The United States* (2016), *available at* https://www.copyright.gov/docs/making_available/making-available-right.pdf (last visited May 23, 2017). [short form citation: U.S. Copyright Office, *Making Available Right*]

United States Copyright Office, *Copyright And The Music Marketplace* (2nd ed. 2016), *available at* https://www.copyright.gov/policy/musiclicensingstudy/copyright-and-the-music-marketplace.pdf (last visited May 23, 2017). [short form citation: U.S. Copyright Office, *Music Marketplace*]

6. United States Department of Justice Official Documents

Department of Justice, *Memorandum of the United States in Support of the Joint Motion to Enter Second Amended Final Judgment, United States v. ASCAP, No. 41–1395 (S.D.N.Y. 2000)*, *available at* https://www.justice.gov/atr/case-document/file/485996/download (last visited May 23, 2017). [short form citation: AJF2 Memo]

Department of Justice, *Statement of the Department of Justice on the Closing of the Antitrust Division's Review of the ASCAP and BMI Consent Decrees* (2016), *available at* https://www.justice.gov/atr/file/882101/download (last visited May 23, 2017). [short form citation: DOJ, *Antitrust Division's Review*]

7. ASCAP Offical Documents

Articles of Association of the American Society of Composers, Authors and Publishers (2002), *available at* https://www.ascap.com/~/media/files/pdf/members/

governing-documents/articles-of-association.pdf (last visited May 23, 2017). [short form citation: ASCAP Statute]

American Society of Composers, Authors and Publishers, *Public Comments of the American Society of Composers, Authors and Publishers Regarding Review of the ASCAP and BMI Consent Decrees* (2014), *available at* https://www.justice.gov/sites/default/files/atr/legacy/2014/08/14/307803.pdf (last visited May 23, 2017). [short form citation: ASCAP, *Public Comments 2014*]

Compendium of ASCAP Rules and Regulations, and Policies Supplemental to the Articles of Association (2014), *available at* https://www.ascap.com/-/media/files/pdf/members/governing-documents/compendium-of-ascap-rules-regulations.pdf (last visited May 23, 2017). [short form citation: Compendium of ASCAP Rules]

American Society of Composers, Authors and Publishers, *ASCAP's Survey and Distribution System: Rules and Policies* (2015), *available at* https://www.ascap.com/-/media/files/pdf/members/payment/drd.pdf (last visited May 23, 2017). [short form citation: ASCAP Distribution Rules]

American Society of Composers, Authors and Publishers, *ASCAP Writer Agreements*, *available at* https://www.ascap.com/-/media/files/pdf/join/ascap-writer-agreement.pdf (last visited April 19, 2017). [short form citation: ASCAP Writer Agreement]

American Society of Composers, Authors and Publishers, *ASCAP Publisher Agreements*, *available at* https://www.ascap.com/-/media/files/pdf/join/ascap-publisher-agreement.pdf (last visited April 19, 2017). [short form citation: ASCAP Publisher Agreement]

8. BMI Official Documents

Broadcast Music, Inc., *Public Comments of Broadcast Music, Inc.* (2014), *available at* https://www.justice.gov/sites/default/files/atr/legacy/2014/08/13/307859.pdf (last visited May 23, 2017). [short form citation: BMI, *Public Comments 2014*).

Broadcast Music, Inc., *BMI Standard Writer Agreement*, *available at* https://www.bmi.com/forms/affiliation/bmi_writer_agreement_W800.pdf (last visited April 19, 2017). [short form citation: BMI Writer Agreement]

Broadcast Music, Inc., *BMI Standard Publisher Agreement*, *available at* https://www.bmi.com/forms/affiliation/bmi_publisher_kit.pdf (last visited April 19, 2017). [short form citation: BMI Publisher Agreement]

9. PRS Official Documents

PRS, *Antitrust Division Review of American Society of Composers, Authors and Publishers ("ASCAP") and Broadcast Music, Inc. ("BMI") Consent Decrees ("Review")* (2014), https://www.justice.gov/sites/default/files/atr/legacy/2014/08/13/307652.pdf (last visited May 23, 2017).

10. Press Releases

Press Release, European Commission, *Commission opens proceedings into collective licensing of music copyrights for online use* (May 03, 2004), *available at* http://europa.eu/rapid/press-release_IP-04-586_en.htm (last visited May 23, 2017). [short form citation: Press Release European Commission (May 03, 2004)]

Press Release, *European Commission, Antitrust: Commission welcomes steps taken by collective rights management bodies in Hungary and Romania to improve competition* (March 11, 2011), *available at* http://europa.eu/rapid/press-release_IP-11-284_en.htm?locale=en (last visited May 23, 2017).

Press Release, General Court of the European Union, *The General Court partially annuls the Commission decision finding anti-competitive conduct on the part of copyright collecting societies* (April 12, 2013), *available at* http://curia.europa.eu/jcms/upload/docs/application/pdf/2013-04/cp130043en.pdf (last visited May 23, 2017).

11. Further Electronic Sources and Webpages

Alliance of Artists and Recording Companies, *AARC Summary & Methodology*, https://aarcroyalties.files.wordpress.com/2013/01/aarc-summary-and-methodology.pdf (last visited April 18, 2017).

ARMONIA, *Armonia in Numbers*, http://armoniaonline.com/ (last visited April 16, 2017).

ASCAP, *Message from ASCAP President Paul Williams on Strategy to Fight DOJ Consent Decree Interpretation*, http://www.ascap.com/playback/2016/07/action/doj-strategy.aspx (last visited April 17, 2017).

ASCAP, *Affiliated Foreign Societies*, https://www.ascap.com/help/international/affiliated-foreign-societies (last visited April 27, 2017).

BMI, *BMI & ASCAP Join Forces to Fight the Department of Justice's Interpretation of Their Consent Decrees*, http://www.bmi.com/news/entry/bmi_ascap_join_forces_to_fight_the_department_of_justices_interpretation_of (last visited April 17, 2017).

BMI, *Songwriters' Groups Speak Out on Rate Setting: ASCAP, BMI, SESAC and the NSAI File Joint Letter to Congress on Music Licensing Reform*, https://www.bmi.com/news/entry/songwriters_groups_speak_out_on_rate_setting_file_joint_letter_to_congress (last visited April 27, 2017).

BMI, *BMI Royalty Policy Manual*, http://www.bmi.com/creators/ royalty_print (last visited April 20, 2017). [short form citation: BMI, *Royalty Policy Manual*]

BMI, *Licensing FAQ*, http://www.bmi.com/licensing (last visited April 20, 2017).

BMI, *International Agreements With Foreign Performing Rights Organizations*, https://www.bmi.com/international/entry/reciprocal_representation_agreements_foreign_performing_rights_societies (last visited April 27, 2017).

CISAC, *CISAC Membership* (2015), http://www.cisac.org/Our-Members.

Department of Justice, *Consent Decree Review – ASCAP and BMI 2014*, https://www.justice.gov/atr/ascap-bmi-decree-review (last visited April 17, 2017).

European Commission, *Departments and executive agencies*, http://ec.europa.eu/about/ds_en.htm (last visited April 16, 2017).

European Commission, *Management of Copyright and Related Rights*, http://ec.europa.eu/internal_market/copyright/management/index_en.htm (last visited April 16, 2017).

European Commission, *DG Connect*, http://ec.europa.eu/dgs/connect/ (last visited April 16, 2017).

GEMA, *Subsidiary Companies*, https://www.gema.de/en/about-gema/organisation/subsidiary-companies/ (last visited April 16, 2017).

HFA, *Become a HFA Licensee*, https://www.harryfox.com/license_music/become_hfa_licensee.html (last visited April 26, 2017).

HFA, *Foreign Affiliates*, https://secure.harryfox.com/public/ForeignAffiliates.jsp (last visited April 27, 2017).

IMPEL, http://www.prsformusic.com/impel/pages/default.aspx (last visited April 16, 2017).

MERLIN, *What we do*, http://www.merlinnetwork.org/what-we-do (last visited April 16, 2017).

MusicMark, *Frequently Asked Questions*, http://musicmark.com/documents/MusicMark-FAQs.pdf (last visited April 27, 2017).

OnLineArt, *A One-stop-shop for rights on works of art*, http://onlineart.info/#aboutus (last visited April 13, 2017).

OnLineArt, *Members*, http://onlineart.info/#testimonials (last visited April 13, 2017).

OnLineArt, *The Structure*, http://onlineart.info/the-structure/ (last visited April 13, 2017).

PRS for Music, *Sony/ATV, PRS for Music and GEMA launch joint venture*, http://www.prsformusic.com/aboutus/press/latestpressreleases/pages/sony-atv-prs-for-music-gema-launch-joint-venture.aspx (last visited April 16, 2017).

Radio Music License Committee, *SESAC*, http://www.radiomlc.org/pages/6282116.php (last visited April 17, 2017).

Radio Music License Committee, *Settlement Agreement*, http://imgsrv.radiomlc.org/image/rmlc/UserFiles/File/Final%20SESAC%20RMLC%20Settlement%20Agreement.pdf (last visited April 17, 2017).

Radio Music License Committee, *Our Mission*, http://www.radiomlc.org/ (last visited April 23, 2017).

SACEM, *SACEM Universal Music Publishing International and SoundCloud Strike New European Deal*, https://societe.sacem.fr/en/press-resources/per-publication/Press-releases/a-new-deal-license-sacem-universal-music-publishing-international-and-soundcloud-strike-new-european-deal (last visited April 16, 2017).

SESAC, *How To Affiliate With SESAC*, https://www.sesac.com/writerspublishers/affiliate.aspx (last visited April 19, 2017).

SESAC, *SESAC's Agreements With Foreign Performing Rights Organizations*, https://www.sesac.com/WritersPublishers/HowWePay/foreignpros.aspx (last visited April 27, 2017).

SOCAN, *About SOCAN*, http://www.socan.ca/about (last visited April 27, 2017).

SOLAR, *SOLAR MUSIC*, http://www.solar-music.com/ (last visited April 17, 2017).

SoundExchange, *licensing 101*, https://www.soundexchange.com/service-provider/licensing-101/ (last visited April 18, 2017).

SoundExchange, *international partners*, https://www.soundexchange.com/about/international-partners/ (last visited April 27, 2017).

Television Music Licensing Committee, *About US*, https://tvmlc.com/about/ (last visited April 26, 2017).

12. Table of Cases

12.1. European Union

Aalborg Portland v. Commission A/S, Joined Cases C-204/00 P, C-205/00 P, C-211/00 P, C-213/00 P, C-217/00 P and C-219/00 P (ECJ 2004).

ACI Adam BV v. Stichting de Thuiskopie, C-435/12 (ECJ 2014). [short form citation: *ACI Adam*, C-435/12]

ACI Adam v. Stichting de Thuiskopie, C-435/12 (ECJ 2014), Opinion of AG Cruz Villalón.

AEPI Elliniki Etaireia pros Prostasian tis Pnevmatikis Idioktisias AE v. Commission, T-392/08 (EGC 2013). [short form citation: *AEPI*, T-392/08]

Amazon.com Int'l Sales, Inc. v. Austro-Mechana Gesellschaft zur Wahrnehmung mechanisch-musikalischer Urheberrechte Gesellschaft mbH, C-521/11 (ECJ 2013). [short form citation: *Amazon.com v. Austro-Mechana*, C-521/11]

Artisjus Magyar Szerzői Jogvédő Iroda Egyesület v. Commission, T-411/08 (EGC 2013).

Autortiesību un komunicēšanās konsultāciju aģentūra/Latvijas Autoru apvienība v. Commission, T-414/08 (EGC 2013).

Autortiesību un komunicēšanās konsultāciju aģentūra / Latvijas Autoru apvienība v. Konkurences padome, C-177/16 (ECJ 2017). [short form citation: *Autortiesību un komunicēšanās konsultāciju aģentūra / Latvijas Autoru apvienība*, C-177/16]

Autortiesību un komunicēšanās konsultāciju aģentūra – Latvijas Autoru apvienība v. Konkurences padome, C-177/16 (ECJ 2017), Opinion of AG Wahl. [short form citation: *Autortiesību un komunicēšanās konsultāciju aģentūra / Latvijas Autoru apvienība*, C-177/16, Opinion of AG Wahl]

Bayer AG v. Commission, T-41/96 (EGC 2000), *appeal dismissed*, joined cases C-2/02 P and C-3/01 P (ECJ 2004).

Belgische Radio en Televisie v. Société Belge des Auteurs, Compositeurs et Éditeurs, case 127-73 (ECJ 1974), [short form citation: *BRT*, 127-73]

Belgische Radio en Televisie v. Société Belge des Auteurs, Compositeurs et Éditeurs, case 127-73 (ECJ 1974), Opinion of AG Mayras.

Belgium v. Jean Claude Becu, C-22/98 (ECJ 1999).

B.N.O. Walrave v. Association Union Cycliste Internationale, case 36/74 (ECJ 1974).

Cannes Extension Agreement, Commission Decision of 04.10.2006, COMP/C2/38.681, *available at* http://ec.europa.eu/competition/antitrust/cases/dec_docs/

38681/38681_216_1.pdf (last visited May 22, 2017). [short form citation: *Cannes Extension Agreement*, COMP/C2/38.681]

CISAC Agreement, Commission Decision of 16.07.2008, COMP/C2/38.698, *available at* http://ec.europa.eu/competition/antitrust/cases/dec_docs/38698/38698_4567_1.pdf (last visited May 22, 2017). [short form citation: *CISAC Agreement,* COMP/C2/38.698]

Coditel v. Ciné Vog Films, case 62/79 (ECJ 1980). [short form citation: *Coditel*, 62/79]

Commission v. Council of the European Union, C-94/03 (ECJ 2006).

Commission v. Portuguese Republic, C-53/05 (ECJ 2006).

Compagnie Maritime Belge Transports v. Commission, joined cases C-395/96 P and C-396/96 P (ECJ 2000). [short form citation: *Compagnie Maritime*, C-395/96 P and C-396/96 P]

Confederación Española de Empresarios de Estaciones de Servicio v. Compañía Española de Petróleos SA, C-217/05 (ECJ 2006).

Copydan Båndkopi v. Nokia Danmark A/S, C-463/12 (ECJ 2015). [short form citation: *Copydan Båndkopi*, C-463/12]

Daft Punk, Commission Decision of 06.08.2002, COMP/C2/37.219, *available at* http://ec.europa.eu/competition/antitrust/cases/dec_docs/37219/37219_11_3.pdf (last visited May 22, 2017). [short form citation: *Daft Punk*, COMP/C2/37.219]

Deutsche Grammophon GmbH v. Metro-SB-Grossmärkte GmbH, case 78/70 (ECJ 1971). [short form citation: *Deutsche Grammophon*, 78/70]

Eesti Autorite Ühing v. Commission, T-416/08 (EGC 2013).

EMI Electrola GmbH v. Patricia Im- und Export Verwaltungsgesellschaft mbH, case 341/87 (ECJ 1989). [short form citation: *EMI Electrola*, 341/87]

Établissements Consten S.à.R.L. and Grundig-Verkaufs-GmbH, joined cases 56 and 58–64, Rep. of Cases English 1966, 299 (ECJ 1966).

Football Association Premier League, Ltd v. QC Leisure, joined cases C-403/08 and C-429/08 (ECJ 2011). [short form citation: *Football Association Premier League,* C-403/08 and C-429/08]

Föreningen Svenska Tonsättares Internationella Musikbyrå u.p.a. v. Commission, T-451/08 (EGC 2013). [short form citation: *STIM*, T-451/08]

GEMA I, Commission Decision of 02.06.1971, case IV/26 760, 1971 O.J. (L134) 15–29. [short form citation: GEMA I, IV/26 760]

GEMA II, Commission Decision of 06.07.1972, case IV/26.760, 1972 O.J. (L166) 22–23. [short form citation: *GEMA II*, IV/26.760]

GEMA III, Commission Decision of 04.12.1981, case IV/29-971, 1982 O.J. (L84) 12–20. [short form citation: *GEMA III*, IV/29-971]

Gesellschaft für musikalische Aufführungs- und mechanische Vervielfältigungsrechte v. Commission, T-410/08 (EGC 2013).

Greenwich Film Production v. Societé Des Auteurs, Compositeurs Et Èditeurs De Musique (SACEM), case 22/79 (ECJ 1979). [short form citation: *Greenwich Film Production*, 22/79]

Greenwich Film Production v. Societé Des Auteurs, Compositeurs Et Èditeurs De Musique (SACEM), case 22/79 (ECJ 1979), Opinion of AG Warner. [short form citation: *Greenwich Film Production*, 22/79, Opinion of AG Warner]

GVL, Commission Decision of 29.10.1981, Case IV/29.839, 1981 O.J. (L370) 49–59. [short form citation: *GVL*, IV/29.839]

Gesellschaft zur Verwertung von Leistungsschutzrechten mbH v. Commission, case 7/82 (ECJ 1983). [short form citation: *GVL*, 7/82]

Gesellschaft zur Verwertung von Leistungsschutzrechten mbH v. Commission, case 7/82 (ECJ 1983), Opinion of AG Reischl.

Gesellschaft zur Verwertung von Leistungsschutzrechten mbH v. Commission, case 7/82 (ECJ 1983), Further Opinion of AG Reischl. [short form citation: *GVL v. Commission*, 7/82 (ECJ 1983), Further Opinion of AG Reischl]

G. Basset v. Societé Des Auteurs, Compositeurs Et Èditeurs De Musique, case 402/85 (ECJ 1987). [short form citation: *Basset*, 402/85]

G. Basset v. Societé Des Auteurs, Compositeurs Et Èditeurs De Musique, case 402/85 (ECJ 1987), Opinion of AG Lenz. [short form citation: *Basset*, 402/85, Opinion of AG Lenz]

Heintz van Landewyck SARL v. Commission, joined cases 209 to 215 and 218/78 (ECJ 1980).

Hewlett-Packard Belgium SPRL v. Reprobel SCRL, C-572/13 (ECJ 2015). [short form citation: *Hewlett-Packard*, C-572/13]

H. van der Woude v. Stichting Beatrixoord, C-222/98 (ECJ 2000).

IFPI Simulcasting, Commission Decision of 08.10.2002, Case COMP/C2/38.014, 2003 O.J. (L107) 58–84. [short form citation: *IFPI Simulcasting*, COMP/C2/38.014]

Imperial Chem. Indus. Ltd. v Commission, case 48–69 (ECJ 1972).

Infopaq Int'l A/S v. Danske Dagblades Forening, C-5/08 (ECJ 2009).

International Confederation of Societies of Authors and Composers v. Commission, Case T-442/08 (EGC 2013). [short form citation: *CISAC*, T-442/08]

Irish Music Rights Org. v. Commission, T-415/08 (EGC 2013).

Kanal 5 Ltd v. STIM, C-52/07 (ECJ 2008). [short form citation: *Kanal 5*, C-52/07]

Kanal 5 Ltd v. STIM, C-52/07 (ECJ 2008), Opinion of AG Trstenjak. [short form citation: *Kanal 5*, C-52/07, Opinion of AG Trstenjak]

Kattner Stahlbau GmbH v. Maschinenbau- und Metall- Berufsgenossenschaft, C-350/07 (ECJ 2009).

KODA v. Commission T-425/08 (EGC 2013).

K. Höfner v. Macrotron GmbH, C-41/90 (ECJ 1991).

Lagardère Active Broadcast v. Société pour la perception de la rémunération équitable, C-192/04 (ECJ 2005). [short form citation: *Lagardère Active Broadcast*, C-192/04]

Lietuvos autorių teisių gynimo asociacijos agentūra v. Commission, T-419/08 (EGC 2013).

Limburgse Vinyl Maatschappij NV v. Commission, joined cases T-305/94, T-306/94, T-307/94, T-313/94 to T-316/94, T-318/94, T-325/94, T-328/94, T-329/94 and T-335/94 (EGC 1999), *appeal dismissed in part, judgement annulled in part*, joined cases C-238/99 P, C-244/99 P, C-245/99 P, C-247/99 P, C-250/99 P to C-252/99 P and C-254/99 P (ECJ 2002).

Lucazeau v. SACEM, joined cases 110/88, 241/88 and 242/88 (ECJ 1989). [short form citation: *Lucazeau*, 110/88]

Luksan v. Petrus van der Let, C-277/10 (ECJ 2012).

Luksan v. Petrus van der Let, C-277/10 (ECJ 2012), Opinion of AG Trstenjak.

Marty v. Lauder, case 37/79 (ECJ 1980).

Ministère public v. Jean-Louis Tournier, case 395/87 (ECJ 1989). [short form citation: *Tournier*, 395/87]

Ministère public v. Jean-Louis Tournier, case 395/87 (ECJ 1989), Opinion of AG Jacobs. [short form citation: *Tournier*, 395/87, Opinion of AG Jacobs]

Musik-Vertrieb Membran GmbH v. GEMA, joined cases 55/80 and 57/80 (ECJ 1981). [short form citation: *Membran*, 55/80 and 57/80]

Nederlandsche Banden-Industie Michelin v. Commission, case 322/81 (ECJ 1983).

Nederlandse Federatieve Vereniging voor de Groothandel op Elektrotechnisch Gebied v. *Commission*, C-105/04 P (ECJ 2006).

Notice published pursuant to Article 27(4) of Council Regulation (EC) No 1/2003 in Cases COMP/C2/39152 — BUMA and COMP/C2/39151 SABAM (Santiago Agreement — COMP/C2/38126), 2005 O.J. (C200) 11–12. [short form citation: *Santiago Agreement*, COMP/C2/38126]

Notification of cooperation agreements (Case COMP/C-2/38.377 — BIEM Barcelona Agreements), 2002 O.J. (C132) 18. [short form citation: *BIEM Barcelona Agreements*, COMP/C-2/38.377]

Ochranný svaz autorský pro práva k dílům hudebním o.s. v. Commission, T-418/08 (EGC 2013).

Ochranný svaz autorský pro práva k dílům hudebním o.s. v. Léčebné lázně Mariánské Lázně, C-351/12 (ECJ 2014). [short form citation: *OSA*, C-351/12]

Ochranný svaz autorský pro práva k dílům hudebním o.s. v. Léčebné lázně Mariánské Lázně a.s., C-351/12 (ECJ 2014), Opinion of AG Sharpston. [short form citation: *OSA*, C-351/12, Opinion of AG Sharpston]

Padawan SL v. Sociedad General de Autores y Editores de España, C-467/08 (ECJ 2010). [short form citation: *Padawan*, C-467/08]

Padawan SL v. Sociedad General de Autores y Editores de España, C-467/08 (ECJ 2010), Opinion of AG Trjstenjak. [short form citation: *Padawan*, C-467/08, Opinion of AG Trjstenjak]

Performing Right Society Ltd v. Commission, T-421/08 (EGC 2013).

Phil Collins v. Imtrat Handelsgesellschaft mbH, joined cases C-92/92 and C-326/92 (ECJ 1993). [short form citation: *Phil Collins*, C-92/92 and C-326/92]

PRSfM/STIM/GEMA/JV, Commission Decision of 16.06.2015, case COMP/M.6800, *available at* http://ec.europa.eu/competition/mergers/cases/decisions/m6800_20150616_20600_4523168_EN.pdf (last visited May 22, 2017). [short form citation: *PRSfM/STIM/GEMA/JV*, COMP/M.6800]

Radio Telefis Eireann v. Commission, joined cases C-241/91 P and C-242/91 P (ECJ 1995).

Raiffeisen Zentralbank Österreich AG v. Commission, joined cases T-259/02 to T-264/02 and T-271/02 (EGC 2006), *appeal dismissed*, joined cases C-125/07 P, C-133/07 P, C-135/07 P and C-137/07 P (ECJ 2009).

RAI/UNITEL, Commission Decision of 26 May 1978, Case 78/516/EEC, 1978 O.J. (L157) 39–41.

Reha Training Gesellschaft für Sport- und Unfallrehabilitation mbH v. Gesellschaft für musikalische Aufführungs- und mechanische Vervielfältigungsrechte eV, C-117/15 (ECJ 2016).

Samband tónskálda og eigenda flutningsréttar v. Commission, T-428/08 (EGC 2013).

Säveltäjäin Tekijänoikeustoimisto Teosto ry v. Commission, T-401/08 (EGC 2013). [short form citation: *Teosto*, T-401/08]

Sirena S.R.L. v. EDA S.R.L., case 40/70 (ECJ 1971).

Slovenský ochranný Zväz Autorský pre práva k hudobným dielam v. Commission, T-413/08 (EGC 2013).

Sociedad General de Autores y Editores de España v. Commission, T-456/08 (EGC 2009), *appeal dismissed*, C-112/09 P (ECJ 2010). [short form citation: *SGAE*, T-456/08]

Sociedade Portuguesa de Autores CRL v. Commission, T-417/08 (EGC 2013).

Società Italiana degli Autori ed Editori v. Commission, T-433/08 (EGC 2013).

Société des auteurs, compositeurs et éditeurs de musique v. Commission, T-422/08 (EGC 2013). [short form citation: *SACEM*, T-422/08]

Société Technique Minière v. Maschinenbau Ulm GmbH, case 56/65, Rep. of Cases English 1966, 235 (ECJ 1966).

Sony/BMG, Commission Decision of 03.10.2007, case COMP/M.3333, *available at* http://ec.europa.eu/competition/mergers/cases/decisions/m3333_20071003_590_en.pdf (last visited May 22, 2017).

Sony/Mubadala Development/EMI Music Publishing, Commission Decision of 19.04.2012, case COMP/M.6459, *available at* http://ec.europa.eu/competition/mergers/cases/decisions/m6459_4326_2.pdf (last visited May 22, 2017). [short form citation: *Sony/Mubadala Development/EMI Music Publishing*, COMP/M.6459]

Soulier v. Premier Ministre, C-301/15 (ECJ 2016). [short form citation: *Soulier*, C-301/15]

Soulier v. Premier Ministre, C-301/15 (ECJ 2016), Opinion of AG Wathelet.

Staatlich genehmigte Gesellschaft der Autoren, Komponisten und Musikverleger reg. Gen. mbH v. Commission, T-432/08 (EGC 2013) [short form citation: *AKM*, T-432/08]

Staatlich genehmigte Gesellschaft der Autoren, Komponisten und Musikverleger registrierte Genossenschaft mbH v. Zürs.net Betriebs GmbH, C-138/16 (ECJ 2017).

Stichting Brein v. Wullems, C-527/15 (ECJ 2017).

Stichting de Thuiskopie v. Opus Supplies Deutschland GmbH, C-462/09 (ECJ 2011). [short form citation: *Stichting de Thuiskopie*, C-462/09]

Stichting ter Exploitatie van Naburige Rechten v. Nederlandse Omroep Stichtig, C-245/00 (ECJ 2003). [short form citation: *SENA*, C-245/00]

Stowarzyszenie Autorów ZAiKS v. Commission, T-398/08 (EGC 2013).

Tono v. Commission, T-434/08 (EGC 2013).

T-Mobile Netherlands BV v. Commission, C-8/08 (ECJ 2009).

United Brands Co. v. Commission, case 27/76 (ECJ 1978). [short form citation: *United Brands*, 27/76]

Universal/BMG Music Publishing, Commission Decision of 22 May 2007, case COMP/M.4404, *available at* http://ec.europa.eu/competition/mergers/cases/decisions/m4404_20070522_20600_en.pdf (last visited May 22, 2017).

Universal Music Group/EMI Music, Commission Decision of 21.09.2012, case COMP/M.6458, *available at* http://ec.europa.eu/competition/mergers/cases/

decisions/m6458_20120921_20600_3188150_EN.pdf (last visited May 22, 2017).

Vereniging van Educatieve en Wetenschappelijke Auteurs v. Belgische Staat, C-271/10 (ECJ 2011). [short form citation: *VEWA*, C-271/10]

Verwertungsgesellschaft Wort v. Kyocera, joined Cases C-457/11 to C-460/11 (ECJ 2013). [short form citation: *VG Workt v. Kyocera*, joined Cases C-457/11 to C-460/11]

Verwertungsgesellschaft Wort v. Kyocera, joined Cases C-457/11 to C-460/11 (ECJ 2013), Opinion of AG Sharpston.

Združenje skladateljev, avtorjev in založnikov za zaščito avtorskih pravic Slovenije v. Commission, T-420/08 (EGC 2013).

12.2. United States

Affiliated Music Enterprises, Inc. v. Sesac, Inc., 160 F. Supp. 865 (S.D.N.Y.1958), *aff'd*, 268 F.2d 13 (2d Cir. 1959).

Agee v. Paramount Commc'ns, Inc., 59 F.3d 317 (2d Cir. 1995).

Alden-Rochelle, Inc. v. American Society of Composers, Authors and Publishers, 80 F. Supp. 888 at 894–95 (S.D.N.Y. 1948). [short form citation: *Alden-Rochelle*, 80 F. Supp. 888]

Am. Broad. Cos. v. Aereo, Inc., 573 U.S. ___ (2014).

American Motor Inns, Inc. v. Holiday Inns, Inc., 521 F.2d 1230 (3rd Cir. 1975).

American Society of Composers, Authors and Publishers v. Showtime/Movie Channel, Inc., 912 F. 2d 563 (2nd Cir. 1990). [short form citation: *Showtime/Movie Channel*, 912 F. 2d 563]

American Society of Composers, Authors and Publishers v. MOBITV, Inc., 681 F.3d 76 (2nd Cir. 2012). [short form citation: *MOBITV*, 681 F.3d 76]

Arista Records, LLV v. Launch Media, Inc., 578 F. 3d 148 (2nd Cir. 2009).

Arizona v. Maricopa Cnty. Medical Soc'y, 457 U.S. 332 (1982).

Aspen Skiing Co. v. Aspen Highlands Skiing Corp., 472 U.S. 585 (1985).

Berkey Photo, Inc. v. Eastman Kodak Comp., 603 F. 2d 263 (2nd Cir. 1979).

Bleistein v. Donaldson Lithographing Co., 188 U.S. 239 (1903).

Board of Trade of Chicago v. United States, 246 U.S. 231 (1918).

Broadcast Music, Inc. v. Taylor, 10 Misc. 2d 9, 55 N.Y.S. 2d 94 (N.Y. Sup. Ct. 1945).

Broadcast Music, Inc. v. Columbia Broadcasting System, Inc., 441 U.S. 1 (1979). [short form citation: *BMI v. CBS*, 441 U.S. 1]

Broadcast Music, Inc. v. Moor-Law, Inc., 527 F. Supp. 758 (D. Del. 1981), *aff'd without opinion*, 691 F. 2d 490 (3rd Cir. 1982). [short form citation: *Moor-Law*, 527 F. Supp. 758]

Broadcast Music, Inc. v. Hearst/ABV Viacom Ent. Services, 746 F. Supp. 320 (S.D.N.Y. 1990). [short form citation: *Hearst/ABV Viacom*, 746 F. Supp. 320]

Broadcast Music, Inc. v. DMX, Inc., 726 F. Supp. 2d 355 (S.D.N.Y. 2010), *aff'd*, 683 F. 3d 32 (2nd Cir. 2012). [short form citation: *BMI v. DMX 2010*, 726 F. Supp. 2d 355]

Broadcast Music, Inc. v. DMX Inc., 683 F. 3d 32 (2nd Cir. 2012). [short form citation: *BMI v. DMX Inc.*, 683 F. 3d 32]

Broadcast Music, Inc. v. Pandora Media, Inc., Nos. 13-cv-4037, 64-cv-3787, 2013 U.S. Dist. LEXIS 178414 (S.D.N.Y. Dec. 19, 2013). [short form citation: *BMI v. Pandora 2013*, U.S. Dist. LEXIS 178414]

Broadcast Music, Inc. V. Pandora Media, Inc., 140 F. Supp. 3d 267 (S.D.N.Y. 2015). [short form citation: *BMI v. Pandora 2015*, 140 F. Supp. 3d 267]

Buffalo Broadcasting Co. v. American Society of Composers, Authors and Publishers, 744 F. 2d 917 (2nd Cir., 1984). [short form citation: *Buffalo Broadcasting*, 744 F. 2d 917]

Columbia Broadcasting System, Inc. v. American Society of Composers, Authors and Publishers, 562 F. 2d 130 (2nd Cir. 1977).

Columbia Broadcasting System, Inc. v. American Society of Composers, Authors and Publishers, 620 F. 2d 930 (2nd Cir. 1980). [short form citation: *CBS v. ASCAP*, 620 F. 2d 930]

Copperweld Corp. v. Independence Tube Corp., 467 U.S. 752 (1984). [short form citation: *Copperweld Corp.*, 467 U.S. 752]

Eastman Kodak Co. v. Image Tech. Serv., 504 U.S. 451 (1992). [short form citation: *Eastman Kodak*, 504 U.S. 451]

Fame Publishing Co., Inc., v. Alabama Custom Tape, Inc., 507 F. 2d 667 at 670 (5th Cir. 1975).

Firefighters v. City of Cleveland, 478 U.S. 501 (1986).

Goldstein v. California, 412 U.S. 546 (1973).

Herbert v. Shanley Co., 242 U.S. 591 (1917).

In Re Application of MOBITV, 712 F. Supp. 2d 206 (S.D.N.Y. 2010), *aff'd*, 681 F. 3d 76 (2nd Cir. 2012). [short form citation: *MOBITV 2010*, 712 F. Supp. 2d 206]

In Re Pandora Media, Inc., Nos.12-cv-8035, 41-cv1395, 2013 U.S. Dist. LEXIS 133133, (S.D.N.Y. Sept. 17, 2013). [short form citation: *In Re Pandora Media, Inc.*, 2013 U.S. Dist. LEXIS 133133]

In Re Pandora, 6 F. Supp. 3d 317 (S.D.N.Y. 2014), *aff'd* 785 F.3d 73 (2d Cir. 2015). [short form citation: *In Re Pandora*, 6 F. Supp. 3d 317]

Kubik v. American Composer Alliance, Inc., 54 N.Y.S.2d 764 (N.Y. Sup. Ct. 1945).

K-91, Inc. v. Gershwin Publishing Corp., 372 F. 2d 1 (9th Cir. 1967). [short form citation: *K-91*, 372 F. 2d 1]

L. Spier Inc., v. Bourne Comp., 953 F.2d 774 (2nd Cir. 1992).

Mercoid Corp. v. Mid-Continent Investment Co., 320 U.S. 661 (1944).

Meredith Corp. v. SESAC LLC, 1 F. Supp. 3d 180 (S.D.N.Y. 2014). [short form citation: *Meredith*, 1 F. Supp. 3d 180]

Meredith Corp. v. SESAC, LLC, 87 F. Supp. 3d 650 (S.D.N.Y. 2015). [short form citation: *Meredith*, 87 F. Supp. 3d 650]

Monsanto Co. v. Spray-Rite Serv. Corp., 465 U.S. 752 (1984).

Motion Picture Patents Co. v. Universal Film Co., 243 U.S. 502 (1917).

M. Witmark & Sons v. L. Bamberger & Co, 291 F. 776 (D.N.J. 1923).

M. Witmark & Sons v. Jensen, 80 F. Supp. 843 (D. Minn. 1948). [short form citation: *Witmark & Sons*, 80 F. Supp. 843]

Nat'l Soc'y of Prof'l Engineers v. United States, 436 U.S. 679 (1978). [short form citation: *Nat'l Soc'y of Prof'l Engineers*, 436 U.S. 679]

Nat'l Cable Television Ass'n v. Broadcast Music., Inc., 772 F. Supp. 614 (D.D.C. 1991). [short form citation: *Nat'l Cable Television Ass'n,* 772 F. Supp. 614]

Northern Pacific Railway Co. v. United States, 356 U.S. 1 at 5–6 (1958).
Pandora Media, Inc. v. American Society of Composers, Authors and Publishers, 785 F. 3d 73 (2nd Cir. 2015). [short form citation: *Pandora v. ASCAP 2015*, 785 F. 3d 73]
Radio Music License Comm., Inc. v. SESAC, Inc., 29 F. Supp. 3d 487 (E.D. Pa. 2014). [short form citation: *Radio Music License Comm.*, 29 F. Supp. 3d 487]
Sam Fox Publ'g Co., Inc. v. United States, 366 U.S. 683 (1961). [short form citation: *Sam Fox Publ'g*, 366 U.S. 683]
Schumann v. Albuquerque Corp., 664 F. Supp. 473 (D.N.M. 1987).
Sony Corp. of Am. v. Universal City Studios, 464 U.S. 417 (1984).
Standard Oil Co. of New Jersey v. United States, 221 U.S. 1 (1911). [short form citation: *Standard Oil*, 221 U.S. 1]
State Oil Company v. Kahn, 522 U.S. 3 (1997).
Tampa Elec. Co. v. Nashiville Coal Co., 365 U.S. 320 (1961).
Twentieth Century Music Corp. v. Aiken, 422 U.S. 151 (1975).
United States v. American Society of Composers, Authors and Publishers, 1941 Trade Cas. (CCH), ¶ 56,104, 1941 U.S. Dist Lexis 3944 (S.D.N.Y. 1941).
United States v. *American Society of Composers, Authors and Publishers*, 1950 Trade Cas. (CCH) ¶ 62,594, 1950 U.S. Dist. LEXIS 1899 (S.D.N.Y. 1950). [short form citation: ASCAP Foreign Decree]
United States v. American Society of Composers, Authors and Publishers, 1950–1951 Trade Cas. (CCH) ¶ 62,595, 1950 U.S. Dist. LEXIS 4341 (S.D.N.Y. 1950) [short form citation: ASCAP 1950 Decree]
United States v. American Society of Composers, Authors and Publishers (Application of Shenandoah Valley Broadcasting, Inc.), 331 F. 2d 117 (2nd Cir. 1964). [short form citation: *ASCAP (Application of Shenandoah)*, 331 F. 2d 117]
United States v. American Society of Composers, Authors and Publishers (Application of Turner Broadcasting System, Inc.), 782 F. Supp. 778 (S.D.N.Y. 1991), *aff'd per curiam*, 956 F. 2d 21 (2nd Cir. 1992). [short form citation: *ASCAP (Application of Turner Broadcasting System)*, 782 F. Supp. 778]
United States v. American Society of Composers, Authors and Publishers (Application of Capital Cities/ABC, Inc.), 831 F. Supp. 137 (S.D.N.Y. 1993). [short form citation: *ASCAP (Application of Capital Cities/ABC, Inc.)*, 831 F. Supp. 137]
United States v. American Society of Composers, Authors and Publishers, 832 F. Supp. 82 (S.D.N.Y. 1993), *aff'd* 32 F. 3d 727 (2nd Cir. 1994).
United States v. American Society of Composers, Authors and Publishers (Application of Salem Media of California, Inc.), 981 F. Supp. 199 (S.D.N.Y. 1994). [short form citation: *ASCAP (Application of Salem Media of California)*, 981 F. Supp. 199]
United States v. American Society of Composers, Authors and Publishers (In re Capital Cities/ABC, Inc.), 157 F.R.D. 173 (S.D.N.Y. 1994). [short form citation: *ASCAP (In re Capital Cities/ABC)*, 157 F.R.D. 173]
United States v. American Society of Composers, Authors and Publishers, 129 F. Supp. 2d 327 (S.D.N.Y. 2001). [short form citation: *United States v. ASCAP*, 129 F. Supp. 2d 327]

United States v. American Society of Composers, Authors and Publishers, 2001–2002 Trade Cas. (CCH) ¶ 73,474, 2001 U.S. Dist. LEXIS 23707 (S.D.N.Y. 2001). [short form citation: ASCAP Consent Decree]

United States v. American Society of Composers, Authors and Publishers (Application of Muzak, LLC), 309 F. Supp. 2d 566 (S.D.N.Y. 2004). [short form citation: *ASCAP (Application of Muzak)*, 309 F. Supp. 2d 566]

United States v. American Society of Composers, Authors and Publishers (Application of AOL, RealNetworks and Yahoo, Inc.), 559 F. Supp. 2d 332 (S.D.N.Y. 2008), *aff'd in part, vacated and remanded in part*, 627 F. 3d 64 (2nd Cir. 2010). [*ASCAP (Application of AOL)*, 559 F. Supp. 2d 332]

United States v. American Society of Composers, Authors and Publishers (Application RealNetworks and Yahoo, Inc.), 627 F. 3d 64 (2nd Cir. 2010). [*ASCAP (Application RealNetworks and Yahoo, Inc.)*, 627 F. 3d 64]

United States v. Broadcast Music, Inc., 1996-1 Trade Cas. (CCH) ¶ 71,378, 1994 U.S. Dist. LEXIS 21476 (S.D.N.Y. 1994). [short form citation: BMI Consent Decree].

United States v. Broadcast Music, Inc. (Application of AEI Music Network, Inc.), 275 F. 3d 168 (2nd Cir. 2001). [short form citation: *BMI (Application of AEI Music Network)*, 275 F. 3d 168]

United States v. Broadcast Music, Inc. (Application of Music Choice, Inc.), 316 F. 3d 189 (2nd Cir. 2003). [short form citation: *BMI (Application of Music Choice, Inc.)*, 316 F. 3d 189]

United States v. Broadcast Music., Inc., 426 F. 3d 91 (2nd Cir. 2005). [short form citation: *United States v. BMI*, 426 F. 3d 91]

United States v. Broadcast Music, Inc., No. 64 Civ. 3787 (LLS) (S.D.N.Y. Sept. 16, 2016).

United States v. E.I. du Pont de Nemours & Co., 351 U.S. 377 (1956). [short form citation: *Du Pont de Nemours*, 351 U.S. 377]

United States v. Gillette Co., 406 F. Supp. 713 (D. Mass. 1975).

United States v. Griffith, 334 U.S. 100 (1948). [short form citation: *Griffith*, 334 U.S. 100]

United States v. Grinnell Corp., 384 U.S. 563 (1966). [short form citation: *Grinnell*, 384 U.S. 563]

United States v. Microsoft Corp., 56 F. 3d 1448 (D.C. Cir. 1995).

United States v. Paramount Pictures, 334 U.S. 131 (1948). [short form citation: *Paramount Pictures*, 334 U.S. 131]

United States Postal Serv. v. Flamingo Indus. (USA) Ltd., 540 U.S. 736 (2004).

United States v. Socony-Vacuum Oil Co., 310 U.S. 150 at 223 (1940).

Verizon Communications Inc. v. Law Offices of Curtis V. Trinko, LLP, 540 U.S. 398 (2004).

WPIX, Inc. v. ivi, Inc., 691 F.3d 275 at (2nd Cir. 2012).

12.3. National Courts

Der Tor und der Tod, German Imperial Court (Reichsgericht), 12.05.1926, Case I 287/25, Rgz 113, 413.

Fernsehwiedergabe von Sprachwerken, German Supreme Court, 18 December 1962, Case I ZR 54/61, 65 GRUR 213 (1963).

MyVideo, Munich District Court (Landgericht München), Case 7 O 4139/08, ZUM 2009, 788 (2009), *aff'd* 29 U 3698/09, ZUM 2010, 709 (Munich Court of Appeals – Oberlandesgericht München 2010).

Verlegeranteil, German Supreme Court, 21 April 2016, Case I ZR 198/13, 19 MMR 471 (2016).

Zusammenfassung der wesentlichen Aussagen

Einleitung

Verwertungsgesellschaften (VerwG) spielen als Intermediäre zwischen Rechteinhabern und Rechtenutzern eine wichtige Rolle in der Lizenzierung von Urheber- und verwandten Schutzrechten. Abseits der Auswirkungen neuer Technologien ist insbesondere die Verschränkung von kartell- und urheberrechtlichen Fragestellungen wohl hauptverantwortlich dafür, dass in jüngerer Zeit großes Interesse an diesen Gesellschaften zu beobachten ist. VerwG waren vielfach Gegenstand gerichtlicher Entscheidungen sowie eines umfangreichen Gesetzgebungsaktes auf Unionsebene, nämlich der „Verwertungsgesellschaften-Richtlinie" (RL 2014/26/EU, im Folgenden: VerwG-RL), welche bis 2016 in nationales Recht umzusetzen war. Aber auch in den Vereinigten Staaten sind die Tätigkeiten von VerwG von großer Aktualität, was sich an der Entstehung neuer Arten der Musiknutzung wie Streamingdiensten und ihrem Ringen um akzeptable Lizenzgebühren sowie an der 2016 abgeschlossenen Überprüfung der Regulierung von VerwG durch das Department of Justice (DOJ) zeigt. Gerade die jüngeren Aktivitäten der Europäischen Kommission sowie die VerwG-RL laden daher dazu ein, durch einen Vergleich mit den Vereinigten Staaten über die bisherige Rechtspraxis und Rechtsetzung zu reflektieren und über die weitere Entwicklung nachzudenken. Die Vereinigten Staaten wurden auch deshalb für den Vergleich ausgewählt, da sich die US-amerikanische Regulierung von jener in der EU in vielerlei Hinsicht unterscheidet und unterschiedliche Antworten auf ähnliche Problemstellungen gegeben werden. Die vorliegende Arbeit stellt dementsprechend die rechtlichen Rahmenbedingungen der kollektiven Rechtewahrnehmung in den Vereinigten Staaten und der Europäischen Union rechtsvergleichend dar.

Diese Zusammenfassung versucht, einige wichtige Gedanken und Thesen der Arbeit prägnant zusammenzufassen. Aus Platzgründen werden daher viele Details, Rechtsfragen und Begründungen nicht angesprochen. In dieser Hinsicht darf auf den Haupttext verwiesen werden, in dem die Fragestellung umfassend bearbeitet wurde.

Regulierungssysteme

VerwG sind zunächst – genauso wie andere Organisationen – dem Kartellrecht unterworfen. Dieses bildet die hauptsächliche Regulierungsquelle von VerwG in den Vereinigten Staaten. Zu nennen ist der weitbekannte Sherman Act sowie die kartellrechtlichen „Consent Decrees", welche den „Verpflichtungszusagen" nach Art 9 „Wettbewerbsverordnung" (VO (EG) 1/2003) ähneln. Die Consent Decrees betreffen zwar nur die größten VerwG, nämlich die

ASCAP und BMI. Zu bemerken ist allerdings, dass das amerikanische System der privaten Kartellrechtsdurchsetzung zu einer Regulierung anderer VerwG beigetragen hat. Auch in der EU waren und sind die VerwG Gegenstand kartellrechtlicher Verfahren. Darüber hinaus wurde jedoch klar, dass im Hinblick auf die starken Unterschiede der nationalen Regulierung in den Mitgliedstaaten – in denen VerwG häufig eine rechtliche oder faktische Monopolstellung zukommt – spezialgesetzliche Regelungen notwendig waren. Diese Diskussion mündete 2014 in der Annahme der VerwG-RL. Die „Dienstleistungsrichtlinie“ (RL 2006/123/EG) ist demgegenüber nach der wohl zutreffenden Meinung des EuGH (Rs OSA, C-351/12) in wichtigen Teilen nicht auf VerwG anwendbar. Im selben Urteil kam das Gericht zum Ergebnis, dass nationale Monopole für VerwG grds nicht gegen das Unionsrecht verstoßen.

Anwendbarkeit der kartellrechtlichen Regelungen

Trotz der VerwG-RL bleibt das Kartellrecht für VerwG grds relevant, obwohl diese freilich in großem Maße die Entscheidungen der Kommission und des EuGH kodifiziert hat. Von VerwG zu beachten sind (neben Fragen der Fusionskontrolle, die in der vorliegenden Arbeit nicht angesprochen werden) einerseits das klassische Kartellverbot (§ 1 Sherman Act, Art 101 AEUV) sowie das Verbot des missbräuchlichen Ausnutzens einer marktbeherrschenden Stellung (§ 2 Sherman Act, Art 102 AEUV). In den USA kamen nie ernsthafte Zweifel auf, dass diese beide „Säulen“ des Kartellrechts auf VerwG anwendbar sind. So beabsichtigte das DOJ, welches mit der Durchsetzung des Sherman Acts betraut ist, ursprünglich die Auflösung der ASCAP als illegaler Zusammenschluss mehrerer Rechteinhaber zu Zwecken der Preisabsprache; dieser Ansatz wurde aber schnell zu Gunsten der bereits erwähnten Consent Decrees aufgegeben. Daneben wird in der Rechtsanwendungspraxis – meist parallel zum Kartellverbot – § 2 des Sherman Acts auf VerwG angewandt. Gleichzeitig bestätigt der EuGH in stRsp, dass VerwG „Unternehmen“ iSd Art 101 und 102 sind und somit dem Kartellrecht unterliegen; mehrfach zurückgewiesen wurde die Behauptung, VerwG könnten sich auf Art 106 AEUV – welcher Unternehmen privilegiert, die mit Dienstleistungen von allgemeinem wirtschaftlichen Interesse betraut sind – berufen und so den kartellrechtlichen Verpflichtungen entgehen. Im Unterschied zur US-amerikanischen Praxis gibt es hingegen weder von Kommission noch EuGH eine eindeutige Stellungnahme zur Frage, ob die Verbindung einer Vielzahl an Rechteinhabern im Rahmen einer VerwG ein verbotenes Kartell darstellt. Dennoch ist davon auszugehen, dass Artikel 101 auf diese Konstruktionen Anwendung findet, wobei natürlich eine Freistellung nach Abs 3 möglich ist. Ein weiteres interessantes Detail ist tlw zu beobachtende (und durchaus kritisch zu würdigende) Tendenz, den relevanten Markt anhand jener Werke abzugrenzen, die dem Repertoire einer einzigen Verwertungsgesellschaft zugehören.

Verwertungsgesellschaften und Rechteinhaber

Die Notwendigkeit, Rechteinhaber zu schützen, ergibt sich aus der traditionell starken Position der VerwG, die – wie die Erfahrung zeigt – trotz ihrer Ausrichtung als „Interessenvertretungen" von Urhebern ihre Stellung ausnutzen können. Der vom EuGH entwickelte Grundsatz besagt, dass VerwG nur solche Einschränkungen der Verfügungsfreiheit der Rechteinhaber über ihre Rechte vornehmen dürfen, welche zur Erfüllung ihrer Aufgaben objektiv nötig sind. Bereits in den bekannten GEMA-Entscheidungen der Kommission (71/224/EWG und 72/268/EWG) wurden zudem Praktiken gerügt, die zu einer Diskriminierung von Rechteinhabern auf Grund der Staatsangehörigkeit oder zu einer übermäßigen Bindung an die Gesellschaft führten. Die VerwG-RL übernimmt diese Grundsätze und schreibt zahlreiche weitere Rechte fest, etwa auch die Möglichkeit, Kategorien von Rechten an Werken, die zum Repertoire einer VerwG gehören, herauszunehmen und diese anderweitig zu lizenzieren. Außerdem wird ein diskriminierungsfreier Zugang zu den Wahrnehmungsdienstleistungen der VerwG sichergestellt. Zu erwähnen sind auch die zahlreichen Bestimmungen, die sich auf die innere Organisation von VerwG beziehen. Die Consent Decrees enthalten demgegenüber zwar einige Bestimmungen, die dem Schutz der Rechteinhaber dienen; diese sind im Vergleich jedoch weit weniger umfangreich. Offenbar herrscht die Auffassung vor, dass der Wettbewerb zwischen den VerwG ausreichend sei, um den Rechteinhabern eine akzeptable Position zu vermitteln. Zu nennen ist jedoch einerseits der Wahrnehmungszwang, der in beiden Consent Decrees festgeschrieben ist. Andererseits ist für die Decrees das Verbot einer exklusive Rechteübertragung zwischen Rechteinhabern und VerwG von zentraler Bedeutung. Nicht völlig geklärt ist, ob die Praxis der exklusiven Übertragung von Lizenzzuständigkeiten mit dem Unionsrecht vereinbar ist. Artikel 5 Abs 3 der VerwG-RL hält fest, dass Rechteinhaber jederzeit nicht-kommerzielle Lizenzen vergeben dürfen; daraus wird sich *e contrario* die grundsätzliche Zulässigkeit von exklusiven Mandaten für andere Lizenzen ergeben.

Verwertungsgesellschaften und Rechtenutzer

Den Kern der Ordnungsfragen im Verhältnis zwischen VerwG und Lizenznehmern bilden der Umfang der Lizenz einerseits sowie die Höhe der Lizenzgebühren andererseits. Klassischerweise erhält der Nutzer eine Globallizenz (Blanket License) zum gesamten Repertoire der Gesellschaft gegen eine einheitliche Lizenzgebühr, womit über den Umweg der Gegenseitigkeitsverträge das „Weltrepertoire" abgedeckt ist. Sowohl in der EU als auch den USA behaupteten Nutzer, dass diese Art der Lizenz gegen das Kartellrecht verstoße, da sie (auch) zur Zahlung einer Gebühr für solche Werke verpflichten würde, die für Nutzer von keinem Interesse seien. Die Globallizenz wurde jedoch sowohl vom Supreme Court als auch vom EuGH als grundsätzlich rechtmäßig qualifiziert. Ein wichtiges Argument war die Generierung von Effizienzvorteilen, da eine Lizenzierung von Sub- oder gar individualisierten Repertoires als überaus aufwendig erschien. Im Lichte von technologischen Entwicklungen ist es Gegenstand kontroverser Diskussionen, ob diese Grundsätze heute noch zutreffen; im Allgemeinen ist jedoch davon auszugehen, dass die Globallizenz noch immer wichtige Vorteile bietet. Im Hinblick auf die Lizenzgebühren ist zunächst auf einen wesentlichen Unterschied zwischen dem Kartellrecht der EU und den USA hinzuweisen: Während letztere Rechtsordnung das „Excessive Pricing“ im Regelfall nicht als rechtswidrig ansieht, qualifiziert Art 102 lit a AEUV „unangemessene Einkaufs- oder Verkaufspreise“ ausdrücklich als Kartellverstoß. In diesem Sinn war der EuGH bereits mehrfach mit der Gebührengestaltung der VerwG befasst und bevorzugte einen Lizenzvergleich mit anderen Mitgliedstaaten. Auch in den USA findet trotz der erwähnten Unterschiede eine durchaus effektive Regulierung der Lizenzgebühren statt. Dies geschieht durch die Einführung von sog. „Rate Courts“ durch die Consent Decrees. Diese legen auf Antrag Lizenzgebühren fest, falls die Lizenzverhandlungen zwischen VerwG und Nutzer zu keinem positiven Ergebnis kommen. Die VerwG-RL beschränkt sich auf zwei sehr allgemeine Artikel im Hinblick auf die Beziehungen der VerwG zu ihren Lizenznehmern. Im Gegensatz dazu enthalten die Consent Decrees detaillierte Bestimmungen, die etwa gewisse Lizenztypen (etwa die „Through-To-The-Audience License“) festlegen, die (bestimmten) Nutzern auf jeden Fall gewährt werden müssen. Im Lichte der starken Stellung der VerwG ist es bemerkenswert, dass die VerwG-RL keinen echten Lizenzierungs- bzw Kontrahierungszwang enthält, während die Consent Decrees einen solchen explizit vorsehen. Im Bereich der gesetzlichen Lizenzen bzw. der Vergütungsansprüche existieren sowohl in den USA als auch in der EU eigene Vorgaben zur Festsetzung von Gebühren, welche mit der kartellrechtlichen Praxis nicht durchgehend übereinstimmen.

Verwertungsgesellschaften und andere Verwertungsgesellschaften

Vor dem Hintergrund der europäischen Marktsituation als Union mehrerer Nationalstaaten, in denen sämtliche Handelshindernisse immer noch nicht beseitigt sind, überrascht es nicht, dass die Beziehungen von VerwG untereinander besonders die europäischen Behörden beschäftigt hat. Es geht hier um das natürliche Spannungsverhältnis der (traditionellen) nationalen Monopole mit den Zielen des Binnenmarktes. In der Rs Tournier (C-395/87) nahm der EuGH zu Gegenseitigkeitsverträgen Stellung und beurteilte diese als grundsätzlich mit dem Kartellverbot vereinbar. Die Kommission zeigt sich in ihren späteren Untersuchungen zum System der Gegenseitigkeitsverträge jedoch misstrauisch, was in der CISAC-Entscheidung (COMP/C2/38.698) aus dem Jahr 2008 mündete, in denen 24 europäischen VerwG (darunter die deutsche GEMA sowie die österreichische AKM) die Bildung eines Kartells zur Abschottung nationaler Märkte vorgeworfen wurde. Während das EuG in der Folge bestätigte, dass Gegenseitigkeitsverträge nicht zur Aufteilung der Rechtewahrnehmung nach der Staatsangehörigkeit der Rechteinhaber bzw Nutzer führen dürften, verwarf das Gericht jene Teile der Entscheidung, welche die auf das Gebiet einzelner Mitgliedstaaten ausgerichtete Lizenzierungspraxis auf eine verbotene Absprache der VerwG zurückführten. Das EuG fand keine ausreichenden Beweise für ein solches Verhalten, auch, da die Kommission nicht klar darlegen konnte, wie die Rechtedurchsetzung ohne räumliche Präsenz der VerwG in einem Mitgliedstaat effektiv vorgenommen werden könnte. Die VerwG-RL setzt die Existenz von „Repräsentationsvereinbarungen" voraus und bezieht sich ausdrücklich auf diese. Besonders hervorzuheben ist das neue System der Vergabe von Mehrgebietslizenzen für Online-Rechte an Musikwerken, welche auf dem „European Licensing Passport" Modell basiert. Da die VerwG in den USA untereinander üblicherweise keine ihren europäischen Schwesterngesellschaften entsprechenden Gegenseitigkeitsverträge abschließen, existieren keine vergleichbaren Regelungen bzw Rechtsprechung.

Schlussfolgerungen und abschließende Bemerkungen

Während der Schutz der Nutzer in den USA Ausgangspunkt der Regulierung der VerwG war und immer noch im Fokus steht, bildet den Schwerpunkt der Regulierung in der EU der Schutz der Rechteinhaber; dieser Weg wird von der VerwG-RL fortgeführt. Beachtet werden sollte aber, dass die einzelnen betroffenen Interessen stark verwoben sind, wie etwa am Beispiel der teilweisen Rechteherausnahme oder exklusiven Rechteübertragung deutlich wird. Der US-amerikanische Musikmarkt ist (sprachlich und kulturell) homogener als sein europäisches Gegenstück. Auch die Frage nach den kulturellen Funktionen bzw dem traditionellen Solidaritätsmodell der VerwG wird in den beiden Rechtsordnungen unterschiedlich bewertet. Schließlich ist auf die tendenziell andere Zielsetzung des Urheberrechts der USA, der EU – welches nur teilweise harmonisiert ist – und ihrer Mitgliedstaaten hinzuweisen, welche nicht völlig von der Rechtewahrnehmung getrennt werden kann. Diese Unterschiede sind bei der Übertragung des US-amerikanischen Modells auf die EU zu beachten. Abgewogen werden müssen die unbestreitbaren Vorteile des Wettbewerbs mit den Gefahren, die ein solches System mit sich bringt; weder ein wettbewerbsorientierter Zugang noch ein System nationaler Monopole ist jedoch per se auszuschließen. Diese Frage ist wegen der Vielzahl an betroffenen Interessen eine Aufgabe, die dem Gesetzgeber – und nicht den Wettbewerbsbehörden – vorbehalten sein sollte. Dabei ist zu überlegen, wie in einem (potentiellen) auf Wettbewerb ausgerichteten System in der EU der Zugang zu Nischenrepertoires und die Vergütung der Rechteinhaber in kleineren Mitgliedstaaten erfolgen sollte. Ein umfassender Zugang sollte auch bei der laufenden Kontrolle (etwa der Lizenzgebühren) der VerwG verfolgt werden, bei der kohärente Lösungen wünschenswert wären; dies betrifft auch den Bereich der gesetzlichen Lizenzen bzw der Vergütungsrechte, bei denen sich in ähnlicher Art das Problem der Preisfestsetzung stellt. Angedacht werden sollte darüber hinaus eine Regulierung von Verlagen, die – ähnlich den VerwG – große Repertoires an Werken kontrollieren und lizenzieren.

Index

Bisher erschienene Bände der Reihe:

Band 1: *Mrázek*, Forschung und Entwicklung im Bilanz- und Steuerrecht
Band 2: *Kazemzadeh*, Der Kapitalmarktswap
Band 3: *Hirschböck*, Software in der Bilanz
Band 4: *Konwitschka*, Kapitalerhöhung durch Verrechnung von Gesellschafterforderungen
Band 5: *van Husen*, Genußrechte – Genußscheine – Partizipationskapital
Band 6: *Wiedenbauer*, Urheberrechtsschutz von Multimediaprodukten
Band 7: *van Husen*, Wem gehört das Genossenschaftsvermögen?
Band 8: *Kandera*, Arbeitszeitflexibilisierung
Band 9: *Steindl*, US-Board und Aufsichtsrat
Band 10: *Lang*, Patente, Patentanmeldungen und Erfindungen als Kreditsicherungsmittel
Band 11: *Flammer*, Biotechnologische Erfindungen im Patentrecht
Band 12: *Ceipek*, KFZ-Vertrieb in der EU
Band 13: *Winkler*, Kaufmann quo vadis?
Band 14: *Hanslik*, Grundrechtliche Anforderungen an eine Familienbesteuerung
Band 15: *Twardosz*, Die Umsatzsteuer beim Eigenverbrauch
Band 16: *Loibl-van Husen*, Die Beschäftigungsbewilligung
Band 17: *Pülzl*, Belastungen im Einkommenssteuerrecht
Band 18: *Premm*, Aufwendungen für das Ingangsetzen und Erweitern eines Betriebes
Band 19: *Keppelmüller*, Exportforderungen in der Insolvenz des Abnehmers
Band 20: *Fussenegger*, Nachfrageinteressen und Wettbewerbsrecht
Band 21: *Berkovec*, Die Bilanzierung von Dauerschuldverhältnissen
Band 22: *Kautz*, Die Vorgesellschaft im Körperschaftssteuerrecht
Band 23: *Bauer*, Die Stille Gesellschaft als Finanzierungsinstrument
Band 24: *Gelter*, Neue Rechnungslegungsnormen im Handelsrecht
Band 25: *Wieser*, Die Kapitalflussrechnung in Theorie und Praxis der neueren Rechts- und Betriebswirtschaftslehre
Band 26: *Kittel*, Die Haftung des Aufsichtsrats der Aktiengesellschaft
Band 27: *Prax*, Österreichisches und Italienisches Kollisionsrecht im Lichte der Europäischen Versicherungsrichtlinien
Band 28: *Buzanich*, Einbringung eines freiberuflichen Teilbetriebes
Band 29: *Baumgartner*, Unternehmensschließung oder -fortführung
Band 30: *Seitz*, www und Internet im Bereich der AG-Hauptversammlung
Band 31: *Hofmann*, Due Diligence – Möglichkeiten und Grenzen des Managements
Band 32: *Gratzl*, Grundrechte als Grenzen der Marktfreiheiten
Band 33: *Bachmayer*, Zur Zulässigkeit des Filmzitats im österreichischen Urheberrecht
Band 34: *Genschorek*, Appropriation Art: Die Aneignungskunst im US-amerikanischen und österreichischen Recht
Band 35: *Miernicki*, Collective Management of Copyrights between Competition, Regulation, and Monopolism